INSIDE New York 2006

* the ultimate guidebook

INSIDE
New York

2960 Broadway MC 5727 • New York, NY 10027
Phone: 212-854-2804 • Fax: 212-663-9398 • Web: www.inside-ny.com

Publisher	David Seidman
Editor-in-Chief, Assistant Publisher	Daniel Bessner
Graphic Designer	Emily Lo
Copy Editor and Fact Checker	Marc Williams
Cover Design	Emily Lo, David Seidman

Editorial Staff

Arts and Shopping Editor	Amy Stokes
Leisure and Resources Editor	Garho Kametani
Dining Editor	Marc Williams
Nightlife Editor	Daniel Billings
Neighborhoods Editor	Rachel Bessner
LGBT Editor	Michael Blank
Music Editor	Brandon Melendez

Sales Representatives

Benjamin Gene	Samuel Neuhut
Eric Dwoskin	Lauren Zuffante

Writers

Deborah Bessner	Christopher Pietronigro
Christopher Cerrone	Josie Rice
Brendan Charney	Alissa Seidman
Catrina Cunningham	Dmitry Shevelenko
Nicole Decker	Kenneth Stokes
David Hudson	Carlos Joseph Salinas
Ava Liberman	

Photographers

Daniel Bessner	Michael Pymm
David Brumberg	Ilana Rosman
Shoshana Greenberg	David Seidman
Bill Langer	Benjamin Wasserman
Freda Laulicht	Tamara Wiesen
Emily Lo	Karolina Wojtasik

Special thanks to: Kate Baxter, Anthony Ives, Susan Chang-Kim, Rebecca Rodriguez, Dean Christopher Pratt, Bernadette Maxwell, Russell Malbrough, Catrina Cunningham, the Center for Career Education staff, Nanette Smith, the Office of the Mayor of the City of New York, Judy Bergtraum, Iris Weinshall, Jodi and Jonathan Roberson, Steven Seidman, Glen and Jody Bessner, Mark and Stephanie Stokes, Man-wai, Suette and Abraham Lo, Marcia, Dan and Harel Williams, Alpha Epsilon Pi, Matthew Guldin, Mae Guldin, Seymour and Sheila Bessner, the Rockaway Group, Gabriel Yarmush, Adam Kaufman, Alissa Seidman, the Seidman Family, the Roberson Family, the Belza Family, the Shapiro Family, the Gold Family, the Tenen Family, the Wise family, the A. Team, Tamara Wiesen, Jeanette Tse, Elizabeth Wild, Joshua Hundert, the Merovingian, Sam Boyce, Pat Martinez, Ezra Samet, Georgia Schoonmaker, Gillian DiPietro, Tia Lucas, Joshua Mohrer, Lauren Zuffante, CCIT, Security and Facilities, the Columbia Bartending Agency, CUTTA, Campus Pages, List College, our advertisers, and the stellar staff of INY2006.

Printed by: JT Morris, Inc. *Note:* If you would like your company's address included next to the printer copyright information, please include it.

For sales or advertising Information, please call (212) 854-2804, email publisher@inside-ny.com, or visit http://www.inside-ny.com. Please contact BookWorld Companies at 1-800-444-2524, or Ingram Book Company, if your bookstore would like to carry *Inside New York.*

This is a publication of the Student Enterprises Division of the Columbia University Center for Career Education

city living 5

TOC table of contents

neighborhoods 33

shopping 75

TOC

arts 117

dining 163

nightlife 219

leisure 259

resources 281

maps 293 . index 304 . advertisers 318

City Living

cityliving

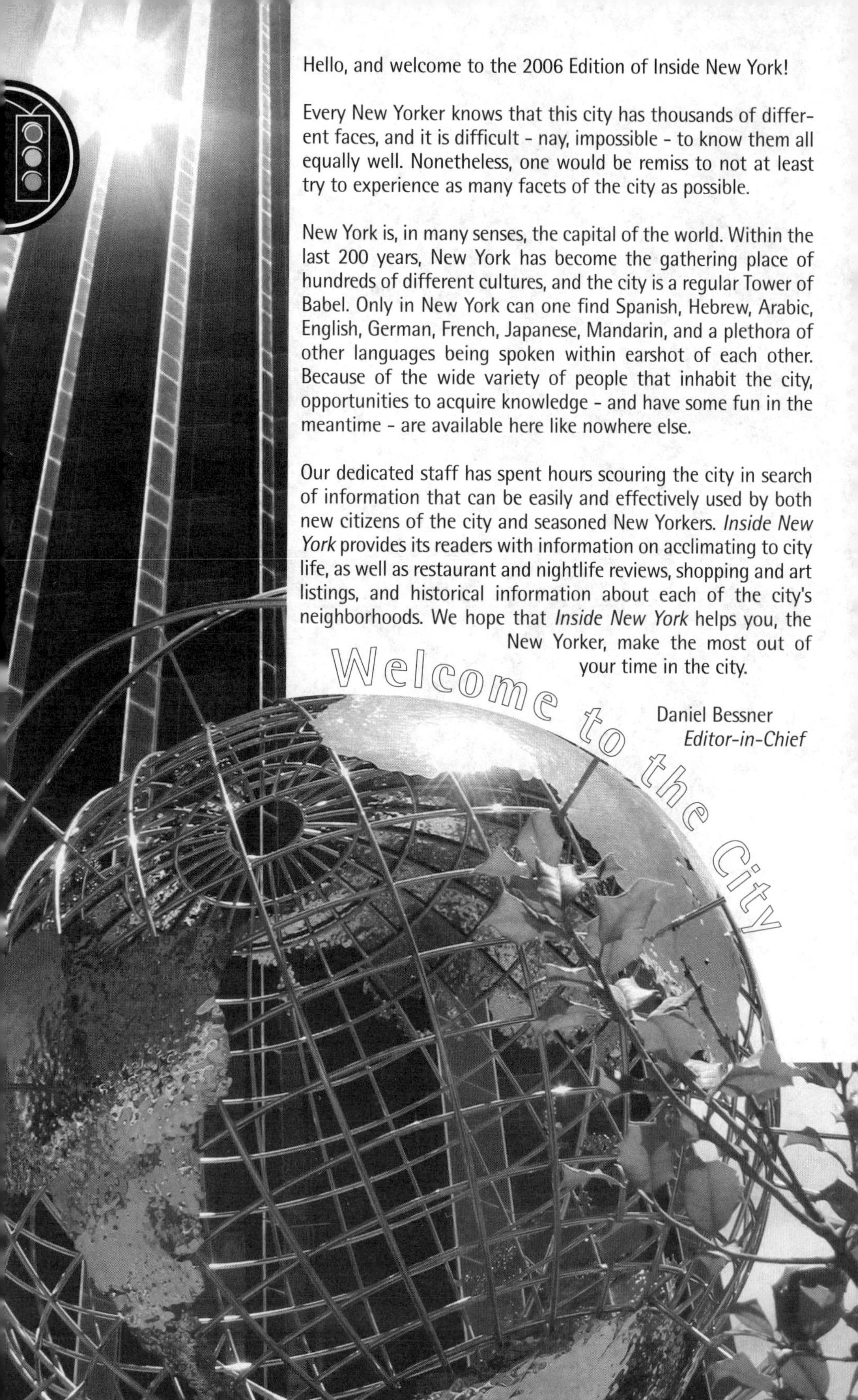

Hello, and welcome to the 2006 Edition of Inside New York!

Every New Yorker knows that this city has thousands of different faces, and it is difficult - nay, impossible - to know them all equally well. Nonetheless, one would be remiss to not at least try to experience as many facets of the city as possible.

New York is, in many senses, the capital of the world. Within the last 200 years, New York has become the gathering place of hundreds of different cultures, and the city is a regular Tower of Babel. Only in New York can one find Spanish, Hebrew, Arabic, English, German, French, Japanese, Mandarin, and a plethora of other languages being spoken within earshot of each other. Because of the wide variety of people that inhabit the city, opportunities to acquire knowledge - and have some fun in the meantime - are available here like nowhere else.

Our dedicated staff has spent hours scouring the city in search of information that can be easily and effectively used by both new citizens of the city and seasoned New Yorkers. *Inside New York* provides its readers with information on acclimating to city life, as well as restaurant and nightlife reviews, shopping and art listings, and historical information about each of the city's neighborhoods. We hope that *Inside New York* helps you, the New Yorker, make the most out of your time in the city.

Daniel Bessner
Editor-in-Chief

transportation

[Subways & Buses]

New York's subway system celebrated its 101st birthday in 2005. Although old, the city's subways comprise one of the most comprehensive transportation systems in the world. They are also some of the busiest; millions of people use subways each and every day. For two dollars, you can go almost anywhere in the five boroughs. Most people would agree that New York's transportation system is improving all the time. Despite recent budget cuts, most subway booths have remained open, and the MTA (Metropolitan Transportation Authority) has made a concerted effort to maintain a clean and effective transportation system.

Overall, the MTA manages to keep our public transportation runing efficiently. New Yorkers will complain about anything and everything, and the subway takes a frequent beating. Regardless, more people are riding subways than ever before. Subway trains are the veins that run through the body of the city, and New York grinds to a halt without them. Nonetheless, suways can be confusing. If you're ever lost, make your way to one of the city's three hearts - Penn Station, Times Square, or Grand Central Terminal - and ask an MTA worker for help.

On the negative side, having a century-old system translates into ongoing repairs, delays, and track changes (mostly done on weekends, check out www.mta.info/nyct/subway to find out what's going on or call (718) 330-1234, the MTA information line). Service alterations confuse even seasoned New Yorkers. Most of the time, commuters are informed of track or schedule changes through white posters plastered throughout subway stations. If you see a white poster at your station, make sure to read it. The sights and sounds of the subways make for a unique New York experience. The grit, aroma, screeches and howls of the trains are juxtaposed with the sounds of street musicians and performers on the platforms, station walls covered with original mosaic tile art, and historic architectural details. The odd collection of commuters, tourists and the occasional vagrant add to the rhythm of the subways. It will soon have you bringing a book and adopting the patented "don't bother me" New York attitude.

Directions

In the city, it is important to always know where you are going. Before setting out on a quest to a new area of New York, make sure to consult a subway or bus map. Always be aware that "uptown" means Bronx- or Queens-bound, whereas "downtown" means Brooklyn-bound. If you accidentally pay your fare and get onto a train going in the wrong direction, try finding an underground passageway leading to the opposite track. The station that allows for the most transfers is the Times Square-42nd St. Station. If you cannot find a station that allows for free transfers, suck up the $2 and exit the station, cross the street, and start over. You can always ask a subway attendant for help. A good tip to remember is that stations that have express-train stops usually allow for free transfers.

Note that a local train makes all stops on its line, while an express train will only stop at major thoroughfares, which are marked by a big white bubble on a subway map. During rush hours, express trains are often very crowded and are sometimes not much faster than locals. If you have a gold MetroCard, you will be able to transfer from the subway to a bus for free. A single ride MetroCard does not allow subway to bus transferring.

Buses

Buses are definitely slower than the subway, but allow for passengers to see much more of the city than they would if they were stashed underground. Most buses stop every few blocks along major streets or avenues. Stops are typically marked by a pole topped with a blue circle bus icon and the names of the buses that stop there. In addition, most stops have a glass-sheltered area. Be forewarned: posted schedules are not always accurate. Sometimes, most frequently during off hours, buses will not run for a long period of time, and then several will come clumped together.

All buses flash their numbers on the screen above the front windshield. They always begin with a letter, then a number. M is for Manhattan, Q for Queens, B for Brooklyn, and Bx is for the Bronx. Most buses run continuously from 7am to 10pm. After that, service is less frequent. It is not unheard of to wait up to an hour for a bus in the wee hours of the morning. Many bus lines run north or south along avenues; if the avenue you are on does not have bus service, walk one block west or east depending on the direction that you are going and catch a bus on this adjacent avenue. There are also cross-town buses that cross through Central Park and operate on other major thoroughfares throughout the city (there is usually a cross-town bus every eight blocks or so). To switch bus lines, ask the driver for a transfer if you've paid in coins. If you've paid by MetroCard, the transfer is saved on your card for two hours.

The seats nearest the driver are reserved for the handicapped, so try not to sit there unless the bus is full and when no elderly, pregnant, or otherwise child-encumbered people are standing. Try to use the back door when exiting to help minimize the time spent at stops. Finally, be courteous

Public Transportation Etiquette

Subways and buses have their own laws:

✔ Know where you are going. There's no chump like the cheesy newcomer who keeps whipping out their map and asking people where the Met is. Thieves know whom to roll, and that would be you if you do this. So always look like you know where you are going, even if you don't.

✔ Always look at the seat before you sit down. You really don't know where that paper, cup, or fluid came from.

✔ Stand up if you see a pregnant lady standing. If you see a lady struggling to take her baby carriage on or off a train, or up or down those stairs, help her.

✔ If a subway car is blowing their horn as they barrel down your track, that means it is - for reasons never explained - not stopping for you.

✔ Always check the train number in the window or on the side of the car to make sure it is the right one. Trains are often out of service or are running on different tracks due to construction and repair work. Again, you will never get an explanation.

✔ Always pay attention to those signs posted next to the subway booth, which tell of delays and late-night construction. It will make your life miserable if you're out partying till 3am, then forced to wait two hours for a train with the mind-numbing sound of jackhammers.

✔ Whip out that MetroCard before you get to the turnstile. Halting and fumbling around your bag for your card makes everyone around you immensely teed off, and you'll get jostled and possibly cursed at too.

✔ When you get into a station, if it's crowded and not too late, head towards one of the two far corners of the track, away from the turnstiles - there are less people there, and you are more likely to get a seat.

✔ Count on delays. With the system in constant repair these days, anticipate your journey taking an extra 15 minutes. You just can't count on a steady train like you used to.

and always let passengers off before you board.

Express buses are the buses of choice for most New Yorkers who live further away from the city – they can decrease a typical commute from an hour and a half to forty-five minutes. Most run between boroughs, and they are subsequently notated by an upper case "X" in the route number. For more information, refer to www.mta.info.

Unwritten Rules

The subway lines aren't easy to decipher because of New York's plethora of trains. There are more trains than colors, which makes distinguishing between the lines slightly more complicated than other cities. Learning the numbers, letters, and other intricacies of subway lines is a difficult but important task. For example, the 7 is a crosstown train that can be faster than the S shuttle during rush hour. Take time to decipher the system, and you will learn the tricks known only to native New Yorkers. A good way to become accustomed to the subway and the city is to spend a day each month exploring a new line. This teaches you the system, and is also a great way to experience new parts of the city. Get out at a random stop, walk around, and take in New York. If you have just secured a new job, time your commute, find an alternate route, and then tack on fifteen minutes for leeway. At night some subway entrances close; you can tell by the lights above the ground on the station entrance. Red means closed and green or white means open. Also, many staircases that look like they lead to subways are exit-only, again denoted by the color of the orb atop the banister pole.

Bus routes can be just as confusing, as many will travel up or down avenues to cross town at various streets. If you plan to use buses, always have a map at the ready. Grand Central Terminal and Times Square both have large information booths with detailed maps for subways and buses, and you can always get a general service map from any fare booth operator or bus driver.

Fares

The fare for a subway or local bus ride is $2. The fare for an express bus ride is $4-$5. If you qualify for a Reduced Fare (65 and older or disabled), you can travel for half price with an application. Children 44 inches tall and under ride for free. Students at New York City public schools have a special "Student MetroCard," which allows them to travel for a discounted rate. Until recently, the coin token was the currency of the MTA, but the invention of the MetroCard has revolutionized the New York City subway system, and tokens are no longer used. Regardless, you are able to pay for the bus in coins; exact change is required, sans pennies and half dollars.

There are two types of cards: Pay-Per-Ride and Unlimited Ride. Unlimited Ride cards are useful for those who plan to make several trips in a day or who commute using public transportation. Here are the types of Unlimited Ride MetroCard available:

- A one-day Fun Pass costs $7 and allows you to ride the subway as many times as you like for one entire day (until 3 am)
- Unlimited 7- and 30-day MetroCards are also available for $24 (reduced fare $12) and $76 (reduced fare $38), respectively, and they allow unlimited usage for that time period until midnight of the last day.
- Beware of the time delay on an unlimited MetroCard: when a card is swiped, it cannot be swiped again for 18 minutes, so you can't get your friends in for free right after you.

It is possible to buy your MetroCard from a machine with cash, or you can use a credit card or debit card. Bulk buying pays off: you can add any amount between $4 and $80 to a MetroCard. Any amount of $10 or more on a Pay-Per-Ride card gives you a 20% bonus. It is also possible to buy MetroCards and Fun Passes at many newsstands and bookstores throughout the city that display the MetroCard symbol.

Transfers

The universal MetroCard that connects New York's transit system allows for free transfers. Most subway stations that service more than one line (for example, Times Square and Grand Central Terminal) allow free transfers between the different lines. Nonetheless, it is useful to know exactly which stations allow for free transfers. For example, Penn Station is actually two separate stations and does not allow for free transfers. Transfer points are marked by an empty white bubble on the subway map; just follow the underground signs to transfer to the correct track. Also, after you use a MetroCard on a subway, you have two hours to use a free transfer for a bus. The same is true from bus to subway and bus to bus; when transferring from bus to bus, you will receive a transfer only if you are using two different lines. So, when you are headed out

New York Transit Museum

Housed in a historic 1936 IND subway station in Brooklyn Heights, and easily accessible by subway, the New York Transit Museum is the largest museum in the United States devoted to urban public transportation history, and one of the premier institutions of its kind in the world. The Museum explores the development of the greater New York metropolitan region through the presentation of exhibitions, tours, educational programs and workshops dealing with the cultural, social and technological history of public transportation. Go to www.mta.info for details of current exhibits and programs, or to shop the Museum's online store.

New York Transit Museum
Corner of Boerum Place
and Schermerhorn Street
Brooklyn Heights
718-694-1868

Gallery Annex & Store
Grand Central Terminal
Shuttle Passage, Main
Concourse
212-878-1016

For more information, visit http://www.mta.info/mta/museum/

for a quick errand, take the subway one way and the bus the other – in this situation, the trip becomes half price.

Passengers with Disabilities

NYC subway riders with disabilities have unique challenges. Unlike the Washington, D.C. Metro, only the key stations in New York's system feature the escalators and elevators that make a subway trip comfortable for those on crutches or in a wheelchair. On its website, the MTA does point out wheelchair-accessible transfer points for subways. Taxi cabs, while expensive, are used by many disabled. Another choice is the bus, as all NYC buses are wheelchair accessible, equipped with a working lift that will hoist a wheelchair up via the back door. Hailing the attention of the bus driver to lower the bus and ramp is usually the hard part. There are city buses for the disabled: Access-a-Ride and other charter buses are available for those who qualify. Call (718)-596-8273 or see www.mta.info/mta/ada/ for further information.

Subway Safety

There are a few unwritten rules about subway safety. If you are traveling alone, watch your back at night, no matter the neighborhood. Always be aware if there is an open MetroCard booth in the subway station you plan on using. If you still feel unsafe taking the subway late at night, there are other, more expensive options - notably cabs - available. Since 9/11, New York's police force has grown, making the subways and neighborhoods of the city noticeably safer. While Metro Police do patrol the subway, you can't always count on them being around if you get in a pinch. If you must take the train late at night, wait in the after-hours waiting area. Avoid walking through long underground tunnels at major train stations after dark. Keep your wallet deep inside your bag and never in a back pocket. Hold your bags close, and if you put them down, keep one strap in your grip at all times. If you get a seat, put your bag on your lap and hold it tightly. Be aware of others in the station, and if someone makes you nervous, just leave. Always act as if you know your surroundings, even if you do not. Don't allow yourself to be seen as an easy mark. Never show weakness. Instead, exude that New York attitude, even if you haven't quite earned it yet.

[Trains]

Long Island Rail Road

The LIRR, or Long Island Railroad, is based out of Penn Station and feeds almost all of Long Island with regular service. Main LIRR stations include Jamaica Station in Queens, and Mineola Station in Nassau. Be sure to buy tickets either at the ticket window or from the automated machines, as a surcharge of over three dollars is added for onboard purchases. Nonetheless, don't worry if the machine at your LIRR station is broken. If this is the case, then the onboard surcharge is waved. Also be aware that the LIRR considers a train to be "on time" if it is running within five minutes of its stated travel time. Therefore, always be sure to arrive at least five minutes before your train is scheduled to depart. Long Island affords a Manhattanite many wonderful beaches and lovely destinations. Fares vary depending on the distance that is traveled by a passenger.

Penn Station at 34th St. (at Seventh Ave.), www.mta.info/lirr/index.html, (718) 217-LIRR, (516) 822-LIRR or (631) 231-LIRR, Lost Articles (212) 643-5228, A C E 1 2 3 *to 34th St.-Penn Station.*

New Jersey Transit

New Jersey Transit is another extensive rail network that delivers hundreds of thousands of commuters a day into New York from the 'burbs. The line is based out of Penn Station and departs from the same area as Amtrak. Like the LIRR, trains and their track numbers are listed on the huge board that hovers over the middle of the station, and finding the right train can be confusing. The trick here is to listen to the announcements closely, as they usually don't announce a train's track until minutes before it is set to depart. When purchasing a ticket for a New Jersey Transit train, always be sure to avoid the long lines that build up around tellers. Most New Jersey Transit stations have machines where one can purchase a ticket with a credit or debit card, alleviating what would otherwise be a long stay in a queue.

Penn Station at 34th St. (bet. 7th and 8th Aves.), (973) 762-5100, Lost Articles (212) 630-7389, A C E 1 2 3 *to 34th St.-Penn Station.*

New Jersey Transit also feeds into SEPTA (South Eastern Pennsylvania Transportation Authority), which is the rail system for Pennsylvania, and the cheapest way to get to Philadelphia. Once you master these rail systems, you will uncover dozens of destinations you can access easily and cheaply.

SEPTA Information (215) 580-7800.

PATH

The PATH (Port Authority Trans-Hudson) trains are a fast and cheap way to commute to and from New Jersey's major cities. The largest portal for PATH trains is now at the Manhattan Mall Station, located at 33rd St. and Sixth Ave., next to Macy's and a block east of Penn Station. The trains also stop at the intersection of 23rd St. and Sixth Ave., 14th St. and Sixth Ave., 9th St. and Sixth Ave., and Christopher and Hudson Sts. The standard fare is $1.50, but you can save some bucks by purchasing Quick-cards, which offer reduced fares for buying in bulk.

Manhattan Mall Station at 33rd St. and Sixth Ave., www.panynj.gov/path/index.html, (800) 234-7284, Lost Articles (201) 216-6078, B D F N R V *to 34th St.-Herald Square.*

Metro North

Metro North is the most expansive commuter line of northern New York State, with train connections to Westchester, upstate New York, and even Connecticut. These trains are relatively cheap (most destinations cost between $6 and $8 if you leave from NYC), and one can rely on a fairly quiet and comfortable ride. If you live uptown, the 125th St. Station is a convenient way of hopping on Metro North's lines that run up the East Side without having to travel all the way down to Grand Central Terminal.

Grand Central Terminal at 42nd Street (at Park Ave.), 125th St. (at Park Ave.), www.mta.info/mnr/index.html (212) 532-4900 or (800) METRO-INFO, Lost Articles (212) 340-2555, 4 5 6 7 S *to 42nd St.-Grand Central or* 4 5 6 *to 125th St.*

Non-NYC Buses

Many bus lines operate out of the Port Authority Bus Terminal, which is easily accessible from the Times Square station. Most of these bus lines offer cheap fairs to Pennsylvania, New Jersey, or Connecticut. Some reliable bus lines include Carl Bieber, Greyhound, and Peter Pan.

Port Authority Bus terminal at Eighth and Ninth Aves. and 40th to 42nd Sts. Take the A C E *to 42nd St./Port*

Authority, or N R W 1 2 3 S to 42nd Street/Times Square.

[Taxis]

Yellow Cabs

At major transit points, such as Grand Central and Penn Stations, you must join a line like an orderly person to catch a cab. Otherwise, you're on your own. Only cabs with the number lit on the top of their roof are available. If you're serious about getting a cab, go to the center of the block to hail one, because other people may try to jump into your cab even if they've arrived later.

Rates, which were recently raised, include $2.50 just to turn the meter on, then 40¢ for each additional fifth of a mile or 120 seconds of stop time. There is an additional $1 charge between 4 pm and 8 pm on weekdays, as well as a 50¢ charge between 8 pm and 6 am every day of the week. Legally, the driver can take up to four passengers, although if you charm him or her you can negotiate up to five. There are the occasional female cab drivers, but the overwhelming majority of drivers are men. Under the Taxi and Limousine Commission guidelines, if you receive bad service, you can take the medallion number of the car (located on the partition and printed on your receipt) and call (212) NYC-TAXI.

Drivers on duty are not allowed to refuse a ride to any destination; nonetheless, always wait before you are firmly seated in the cab before you tell the driver where you are going, as some will refuse to ferry you if they do not feel it is worth it to them. You are also entitled to a smoke and incense-free environment, a quiet ride (sans music and cell phone conversations), and air conditioning if you ask for it. Tipping 10-15% is customary.

Gypsy Cabs

These cabs proliferate in the outer boroughs and Upper Manhattan. Note that they are illegal and unlicensed, and are often not as comfortable as yellow taxis. They do, however, take you to areas that yellow cabs won't. A recent development in the gypsy cab community has been the addition of credit card machines to many cabs. The number of gypsy cabs has fluctuated recently because there have been a few limousine driver murders and robberies in the past five years. Be sure to always agree on a price before you get into one of these; the cost is relatively negotiable, especially to and from airports.

Ferries

The Staten Island Ferry is free and leaves from the tip of Battery Park. The ferry connects lower Manhattan with the only borough that doesn't have a subway connection (although they do have their own individual subway line). The ferry and the concession stands are old, but the experience is classic New York. You'll have some gorgeous views of Ellis Island, the Statue of Liberty, and Manhattan, so think about taking a camera on nice days. Those who suffer from seasickness should approach with caution; the ride is not the smoothest.

South Ferry, www.siferry.com, (718) 815-BOAT, 4 5 to Bowling Green, R W to Whitehall St., 1 to South Ferry.

Cars

While cruising down Broadway in a convertible can be a thrill, owning a car in the city is generally a bad idea. Your insurance rates will skyrocket, and, if you live in an area that has a high rate of car break-ins, you'll need to buy a spot

at a garage that runs upward of $300 per month. Free parking is also incredibly difficult to find on most days. Check with your local precinct or go online to www.nyc.gov/html/nypd/home.html, and check out "Comp-stat" crime rates in your area. Finding gas stations in New York can be inconvenient, and it can take up to an hour to get on a bridge out of the city. Repairing your car will cost more here too. For car washes and repair shops, look on Twelfth Avenue or on 21st St. in Astoria, Queens.

Even with the most highly developed mass transportation system in the world, New York's traffic is infamous. The heavily abused older roads of New York are deteriorating. If commuting from New Jersey, Westchester, and Long Island, it is best to use the commuter rails, which during the day are definitely faster than driving to and from the city. Since September 2001, many of the East and Hudson River crossings have new limitations on carpools, not to mention police officers at all bridge entrances. Once again, Long Island residents have been hurt by a toll hike; crossing the East River costs $4 each way, except on the Queensborough and Downtown (Brooklyn, Manhattan, and Williamsburg) Bridges, which are free but have significant traffic during rush hours. Tolls for entering Manhattan from New Jersey run between $5 and $6. The Marine Parkway-Gil Hodges Memorial Bridge, which connects Queens to Brooklyn, costs $2.25. If you plan to commute to Manhattan by car, invest in an E-ZPass, the electronic toll collection system that bills your credit card. Having E-ZPass cuts an East River toll down to $3.50 and a Hudson River two-way toll to $4. *E-ZPass Information (888) AUTO-TOLL.*

Once you get your car into Manhattan, you will notice that street parking is rare. If you are lucky enough to find a street space, always check for meters and signs about parking limitations. Cars are a luxury in Manhattan, but trust us, use mass transit. Not only will you save money and time, but you won't have to worry about coming back to an empty parking space. If you do decide to purchase a car, make sure to purchase a Club in order to protect your vehicle from being stolen.

Renting a Car

Smart New Yorkers rent a car when they want to escape from the city. Try Zipcars (www.zipcar.com) if you need a car for a few hours on a regular basis. Otherwise, New York Rent-a-Car (www.nyrac.com) has better rates on average than Hertz or the other national chains. Aamcar is another New York local chain (www.aamcar.com). If you are moving, there are the usual U-Haul-type companies, but be forewarned: on all car rentals in New York, not only do they usually favor an in-state driver's license, but they'll ask you for about $500 in cash or a credit card (not a debit card) with that amount reserved on it. Some car rental services refuse to rent to people under 21 and those that do often charge young adults much more than their normal prices. If you need to move, it is often cheaper (in terms of up-front costs) to get a "man with a van." These men advertise all over the city, usually on signposts or at bus stops. Most aren't registered, so use your best judgment when trying to save a few bucks.

For information on long-distance buses and trains or travel to and from airports, please see Resources section.

skyscrapers:

Eight Miles High, Not Falling Fast

What a sight these towers of Manhattan are glittering with millions of goldenspecs, soaring endlessly, as if they were going to touch the sky!
- Langston Hughes

New York City is the City of Skyscrapers. Ask the average American what mental image he or she conjures at the mention of New York and you will more often than not hear the name of one of the litany of skyscrapers that pepper the city. From the Empire State Building to the Chrysler Building, New York City is known for those tall monoliths that both impress and dwarf tourists and locals alike.

How and why were these epic structures created? Skyscraping development began in the late 19th century with the rise of modern industrial monopolies. As cities began to dominate the economic landscape of America, companies relocated to where the business action was taking place. Specifically, ambitious 19th century industrialists wanted to be as close as possible to the city's stock exchange. By the mid-19th century, technology had developed to the point where it was capable of making accurate predictions about the holding capacities of tall buildings. Nonetheless, perhaps the most important factor that led to the development of such gigantic skyscrapers was the aspiration of corporations to outdo one another with displays of their economic and industrial might. Such bravado is prevalent today, as every few years there is a new "World's Tallest Building" ready to pry change from tourist's pockets.

While it is true that the first skyscraper was built in Chicago, New York City was an ideal place for the skyscraper to reach its technological and aesthetic apex. New York has an ineffable magnificence and ostentation that simply cannot be matched anywhere else. Although there were practical considerations for the rise of skyscrapers – for example, many plots of land were too small for construction of wide buildings – they soon became a manifestation of the grandiosity of New York. The more skyscrapers the city built, the more eminent it became.

Although every American knows about the Empire State Building, New York City has over 50 skyscrapers – from 1 Astor Place to the W.R. Grace Building, that should be appreciated by all those whose lives have led them to reside in this most glorious of cities.

finding an

apartment

Before you jump into the hunt, there's one thing you should know: no matter what you do, you will probably end up shelling out several thousand dollars to a broker before you land that "ideal" apartment. Finding an apartment is a dramatic rite of passage, like your first kiss or getting your driver's license. Do not expect the first apartment you see to be the apartment of your dreams (although it may feel like it). Always make sure to look at least five apartments before you make a final decision.

[Inside New York's Top 15 Tips for] [Apartment Hunting]

1) Though apartments in NYC are some of the most expensive per square foot in the world, many buildings are dying for tenants, and rents are slightly negotiable. Many landlords are offering one month free in order to get you to sign. Buildings with "Apartments for Rent" signs are usually a good bet.

2) Do make sure you have a realistic view of your credit history. You will probably have to pay the broker about $50 to run a credit check on you. Don't fill out that paperwork on a fabulous apartment if you know you've had a string of late marks on your credit report. Every little mark counts against you. Landlords have dozens of sterling applicants, so why should they take you?

3) Landlords expect you to make approximately 28 times your monthly rent, unless you are in an apartment share-situation. If you need a guarantor, they need to make approximately 50 times your monthly rent. You will need to prove your income in most cases, so bring pay stubs. Also ask your employer to write a letter stating how much you make and that your future employment prospects are outstanding.

4) Be prepared to plunk down cash or a check on the spot after looking at an apartment. Five minutes can make or break whether or not you get that deal.

5) Try and visit the neighborhood at night before you look at the apartment to get a realistic assessment of how safe you feel there. If you're serious about safety, go to the Compstat page of the NYPD's webpage (www.nyc.gov/html/nypd/home.html) and look up crime statistics, or visit the local precinct to get the real deal.

6) Do research about the neighborhoods you are interested in. Don't waste your or your broker's time looking at places where you would hate to live. Be realistic about what you can afford, too. Go to broker websites or look in the Village Voice or the Times Real Estate Section on Sunday to see what apartments in certain neighborhoods are going for.

7) Be clear what you can and can't live with. Keep in mind, the pickier you are, the more you are going to pay.

8) Draw up a budget, considering your expenses and anticipated salary. A third to 40% of your paycheck will be swallowed up by city, state, and federal taxes. Factor in $50 a month for utilities, about $50 for cable, $50 for phone, $250-$400 for groceries, $70 in subway cards, and however much you spend on entertainment, beauty, dating, and eating out. Remember, high rents mean less money spent on leisure activities. Low rents mean you can party like a rock star and not scrimp every penny. Ideally, try not to spend more than a third of your take-home on rent.

9) If you decide to get roommates, check out their references carefully. There can be some messy situations if things don't work out, such as losing deposits, being stiffed on rent and utility bills, and the hassle of finding someone new. There are many roommate finder services in New York, such as www.roommateaccess.com or www.roommate.com. Look in the classified section of the *Village Voice* or *New York Times.* If you have roommates, try and have them put their expenses under their own names, such as their phone jack. You don't want to be left with the bill.

10) When choosing brokers, be sure that they are accredited and have lots of listings in the neighborhoods in which you are interested. Don't forget to check out their fees first. How much will they charge for you to submit an application and get a credit check? The standard broker fee is 12-15% of the yearly rent, and that is up front, before you pay your deposit and last month's rent.

11) Budget how much it will cost to move into your apartment, as well as the money it will take to get your utilities up and running. Moving in New York can cost up to $3,500, even if you rent the van yourself. If you go to a neighborhood around NYU, Columbia, or the New School, you will see posters tacked onto poles advertising "Man with a Van." These men may be cheap, but they aren't registered anywhere so use your judgment when trying to save a few bucks.
(See Moving and Storage in Resources Section.)

12) Subletting an apartment is a way to get furnished quarters for under market value or escape the city without losing too much money. A great place to look for and post sublets is www.sublet.com. Not only do they have the most listings but they have helpful links on their site that direct you to information about renter's insurance, moving companies, and real estate contracts. Be prepared to be flexible and yield to the dates set by the owner of the apartment. Also, owners can keep your security deposit for even the smallest spot on their rug or tiniest whiff of cigarette smoke, so be careful and play by their rules.

13) There are many no-fee buildings in New York City, such as Windsor Court (31st St. bet. Third and Lexington Aves.). These apartments have in-house brokers, and you must be prepared to sign a contract the day you walk in; otherwise, that apartment will undoubtedly be gone. They are like dorms for twenty-somethings but are actually quite luxurious. Also look on www.thesquare. com for no-broker apartment listings.

14) Check out the outer boroughs, specifically Brooklyn and Queens, for much better deals than in Manhattan. Here you will find much larger spaces in beautiful brownstones for much less money than you would spend in Manhattan. Carroll Gardens in particular has beautiful spaces with lovely planted gardens. Forest Hills, Park Slope, Williamsburg, Brooklyn Heights, Astoria, and Long Island City are all booming, and there are great shops, restaurants, and nightspots in all of these areas. *(For more information check out the Neighborhoods Section.)*

15) Consider getting an apartment with a convertible dining or living room. Temporary walls are not too expensive to put up and can make that space a livable bedroom.

job hunting

Searching for a job in NYC is more challenging than ever. If you don't have one when you arrive, there are several options available. You should consider temping or contracting out. New York doesn't suddenly become cheap if you don't have a job. Life is very expensive here, so always have a backup plan if you find yourself without any source of income. If you think your college degree makes you too good for answering phones, think again. Even Jennifer Lopez worked in a law office before becoming a Fly Girl, and Madonna worked in Dunkin' Donuts while living in the East Village.

[Job Hunting Strategies]

1) Subscribe to the *Village Voice* Classifieds or another notification service. For a fixed fee, they will email you new job listings as they get posted, giving you an advantage. Check the *New York Times* and every other classified section online, and have them email you notifications for free. Many websites have recently added a classifieds section, including The Daily News (http://www. nydailynews.abracat.com)
(both have classified sections on their websites), and Craig's List (www.newyork.craigs list.org).

2) Post your resume all over Web bulletin boards. Most people say this is a waste of time, but what do you have to lose? Nothing! Popular websites include www.monster.com, www.job-hunt.com, www.flipdog.com, and www.hotjobs.com. Many universities allow alumni to post their resume on a university owned website in attempt to create an 'old boys' network for their college. Some universities have 'clubs' (such as the hoity-toity Harvard Club) where alumni can go to hang out, drink, and network.

3) Visit headhunters. Visit a lot of them. It is their job to look for you, and find you they will. This will involve a lot of legwork, but may pay off big time.

4) Know your job market, and what is and isn't realistic. It's not that you can't make it big here, but it's harder when you have so much competition. Initially aiming too high might be a waste of your time. Then again, waking up every day and enjoying your job is a pleasure like none-other, so don't aim too low. Be aware of who and what your qualifications are before applying for a job.

5) Network like crazy. Almost every profession has a professional association, so go to every cocktail, luncheon, and lecture they offer. This is a great way to get your name into the circles you may want to eventually work in.

6) Brush up on your computer skills. Have somebody teach you Quark, PowerPoint, or whatever software you might be called upon to use. Microsoft Word and Excel are overwhelmingly popular programs, so be familiar with these. The New York Public Library offers free classes on oft-used computer programs. Always make sure to include technical knowledge on your resume.

7) Call all your friends and have them call friends. Most jobs are found by word-of-mouth, and take advantage of whatever leads you have. Don't be embarrassed to ask for a favor – that's how the world works.

8) Spiff up your image. New Yorkers have a certain look, and you may have a better chance at getting a job if you don't show up for an interview in khakis and penny loafers. Make yourself presentable: get an expensive haircut and a nice suit. As an up-and-coming young professional remarked, "dark colors rule the city." Act as if you deserve the job you're interviewing for.

10) Go to as many parties as you can. This is a hard job, but someone has to do it. The more you mingle, the greater chance you have of meeting the employer of your dreams and getting a great job. Always bring your business cards. VistaPrint prints free ones (www.vistaprint.com).

11) Consider an internship. This is for those who can afford to do unpaid labor for a while or have a night job. The experience can really be worth it, and many interns get hired.

12) If you are bi- or tri-lingual, consider translating. Check out all the translation agencies in the yellow pages. Many universities run their own translating agencies (for example, the Columbia University Tutoring and Translating Agency, (212) 854-4888).

13) If you attended an Ivy League school or other top college check out TheSquare. TheSquare, Inc. is the online network for alumni and students of top universities including Columbia and 24 others. Join for free at www.thesquare.com and sign up for JobAlert emails to be notified of new postings (you can upgrade to an Executive membership to hear about jobs three days before anyone else). Look for their happy hours, mixers, and other networking events. They are a great way to meet friends, both old and new, and make new contacts to help you with your job search.

14) There is nothing more important than confidence. If you do not think that you should get or deserve to get the job, then neither will your potential employers. Maintain eye contact, do not look down and decide before hand what you want them to know, and make sure you tell them.

BEWARE: Top New York Job Scams

✗ **Envelope stuffing.** When an advertisement says you can work from home doing tasks such as stuffing envelopes, beware. Most of these have you paying a fee to do supposed work from home, and usually these aren't valid business opportunities.

✗ **Promises of fortune.** If it sounds too good to be true, it is.

✗ **Lose weight! Make money!** These are the top two cons of all time, and the combination of the two is major trouble. Nobody is going to pay you to lose weight, unless you're the Princess of York.

✗ **Nanny.** Like the book *Nanny Diaries* explains, babysitting kids for the Park Avenue crowd is no bargain, and you will usually be working for slave wages for long hours.

✗ **Clinical Trials.** Do you really want to sign your life over for the sake of medicine? Think about needles, hospital stays, and the negative effects of radiation.

✗ **Artistic modeling.** Many of these opportunities are ploys by major perverts to take nude photographs of young men and women, either for private viewing or for publication.

✗ **Travel companion.** When an older, single man offers free travel to young women and men, you know there's a catch.

✗ **Personal helper.** There are many people in NYC who need nursing care, and sometimes this is put under the guise of a "helper." Be clear what your duties would and wouldn't be.

✗ **Freelance writer/producer.** Beware of guidebooks, television production companies, or sundry publications that promise riches down the line when they "make it big." You will need a contract stipulating how much and when you would get paid.

✗ **Join in on this exciting start-up opportunity!** Never invest or put up capital in an upstart business unless it is your own company.

dogs

Many New Yorkers are in need of a friend, and many find this friend by purchasing a dog. A dog can be a great addition to your apartment if you are willing to accept all responsibility for the animal and its actions. Before purchasing a dog, always make sure your landlord allows pets in their buildings. Be aware that dogs can be difficult to care for; if you've ever seen an otherwise elegant gentleman scooping up the indelicacies of his fluffy Shitzu, you know that owning a dog requires a certain type of love that not all people have. Although the task of owning a dog in a city defined by small, enclosed spaces may seem daunting, according to a veteran dog-walker, "You can house a Great Dane in a studio if you give it enough love." Nevertheless, most New Yorkers opt for small ankle-biters like Bichons and Poodles, though there is the occasional Labrador Retriever or German Shepherd on the sidewalk.

If you do decide to purchase a canine, there are certain rules you must adhere to. It is important to walk your dog at least three times a day, but don't expect to let your loyal friend roam free down Broadway. Unleashed dogs may be subject to $100 fines. It's an unwritten rule that many police officers and park attendants allow dogs to frolic leashless in most city parks before 8:30am and after 9pm.

Having a dog in Manhattan requires a significant time commitment. If you're like many New Yorkers and see your home only in the dark, you'll have to hire a dog-walker. Services start at around $14 per dog for a half-hour jaunt. If you give your dogs names like Buffy, Mimi, or Uncle Joe, you may feel they require doggy daycare, which costs around $60 a day. If you don't have the means, at least take your pooch to a "Dog Run" in a public park. You can locate the nearest Dog Run by visiting the NYC Parks Department's website (http://www.nycgovparks.org/sub_your_park/interactive_maps/park_map.php) and search all Park facilities. Here, it's not just rump-sniffing and roughhousing – your dog has the opportunity to develop important social skills with his or her friends who share the sidewalks. Do you really want your dog to grow up socially awkward? He or she needs to be exposed to others like it. When on a Dog Run, it is imperative that you remember a pooper-scooper because failing to clean up after your pup carries a steep fine.

Having a dog in NY is expensive, but most canine owners find it worth the cost. Owning a dog is rumored to increase your chances of meeting attractive strangers, so be sure to frequent the parks as much as possible. If that doesn't work out, you'll still have a devoted lap-warmer and playmate who, if well trained, will obey your every command.

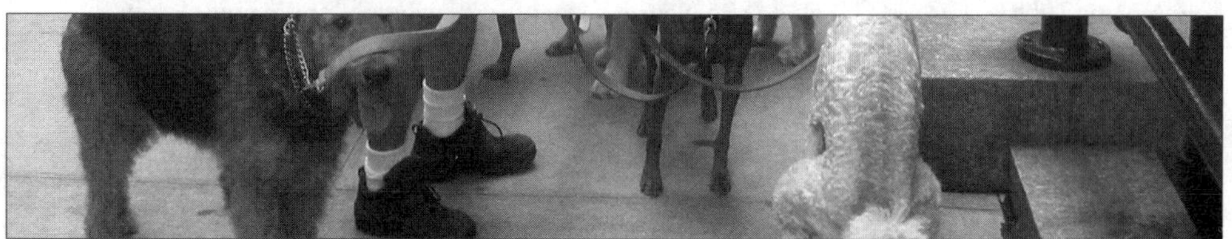

dating

New York is known for its neurotic, single people. Both *Seinfeld* and *Friends* made millions by portraying the crazy lives of New York singles. Many restaurants and clubs are filled to the brim with these types of people, eating alone, talking on their cell phones, writing haikus, and looking for someone to love. In the city, age makes a difference, and many people have a difficult time finding someone they like who is their own age. Wacky body image ideals can also be a blow to many city-dwellers egos. Due to these reasons and more, many New Yorkers end up going online or relying on their friends to introduce them to people, although some join clubs in an attempt to meet that special someone. Also helpful in the search for love are online dating services, www.match.com or www.jdate.com. Now more than ever before singles are listing themselves online. The stigma once associated with online dating has mostly disappeared, adding a whole new dimension to the enjoyable game of love.

When dating, always remember to play it safe. Dating in New York may be more challenging than anywhere else. It is so difficult, in fact, that *Sex and the City* dealt primarily with this problem. Here, trusting everybody you meet can be quite dangerous. Meet your date in a public place with lots of people and only invite someone up to your apartment if you fully trust them. Bringing a cell phone along on a date is always a good idea in case of an emergency. For both men and women, if you have a roommate, make sure that they are okay with you bringing people home casually or romantically. Always check the protocol, as an upset roommate makes for a difficult life.

Good Restaurants to Bring a Date:

Duvet:

This fun and festive bed-oriented restaurant is the perfect place for a date. The loud and casual atmosphere shows your date that you're a fun person who can appreciate a good time. A bit expensive, but an unforgettable experience.

Café Lalo:

Featured in the Tom Hanks-Meg Ryan hit, *You've Got Mail*, the ambience never fails to please. They also serve delicious food to precede your tasty dessert. The cakes and brownies are best served warm, topped with ice cream. Although they don't accept credit cards, you will not break the bank here.

Café des Artistes:

The laid back atmosphere of this French establishment plus the fantastic desserts make Café des Artistes a perfect candidate for the "I-like-you-let's-be-together" third or fourth date. Can be a bit pricey, so make sure they are worth the money. Try the cheese plate: it's heaven.

History

In the era when homos, commies, and the A-bomb made nightmares for decent folk, times got tough for the sexually subversive. Thanks to Senator Joe McCarthy's crazed warnings of the "pervert peril" and homosexual communists, Eisenhower banned gay federal employees and began FBI files on queers. Not surprisingly, in New York City the following years brought police crackdowns on gay bathhouses and bars making queer life quite miserable. By the summer of 1969, however, gays and lesbians decided to take a stand when the issue came to a head at the Stonewall Inn on Christopher Street.

Part of a series of raids on gay establishments, the Stonewall bust marked the beginning of the gay rights movement. Rioting broke out when the police loaded up paddy wagons with drag queens and other gay men. An irate gathering crowd attacked the cops first with fists and beer bottles and then creatively moved on to trashcans and parking meters. Many were sick of being persecuted by homophobic and bigoted police officers. Someone finally decided to conclude the evening by incinerating the bar. The police and the city were shocked. The *New York Daily News* ran a saucy story titled "Homo Nest Raided, Queen Bees Are Stinging Mad," which astutely declaimed that "the police are sure of one thing. They haven't heard the last from the girls of Christopher Street." Indeed, in addition to the riots themselves, which went on in some form for three days, the Stonewall incident birthed a powerful and proud gay rights movement. One fun flyer that kept up the heat in the following months read, "Do you think homosexuals are revolting? You bet your sweet ass we are!" Viva la resistance. Viva la revolution.

Annual Happenings

Many gays still feel discrimination and alienation, and certain activities, such as the St. Patrick's Day Parade, remain closed to them. In a response to demonstrate solidarity, every year in June there is Pridefest, a collection of events that celebrate LGBT life. The main event is the Lesbian, Gay, Bisexual, and Transgender Pride March that runs from 59th St. and Fifth Ave. down to Christopher and Greenwich Sts. There's a rally in Bryant Park, a "Dykes on Bikes" motorcade, a fair, and performance stage at the march's end, and an afternoon through nighttime dance on the piers that is partially illuminated by the specially lit lavender and white Empire State Building. Details for Pridefest change from year to year, so visit their website at www.nycpride.org for current information.

The summer and fall are filled with additional fun happenings. In early June, check out the New Film Festival, or as it is also known, the New York Lesbian and Gay Film Festival. For details, call (212) 571-2170 or visit the website at www.newfestival. org. On July 14, dress up in drag and promenade down Gansevoort St. for the Bastille Day celebration. In November go see the MIX: New York Lesbian and Gay Experimental Film/Video Festival with details found at www.mix nyc.org.

Resources

Plug yourself into the most diverse gay and lesbian community in America. The following publications will keep you up to date with local and city-wide gay events, usually in enough time for you to plan the perfect date:

The New York Blade,
(212) 268-2701
A relatively popular addition to the growing number of gay and lesbian New York publications, this free weekly can be found throughout the city.

MetroSource, *(212) 691-5127.*
A comprehensive listing of community businesses, this quarterly also features articles on various gay-related topics.

Time Out New York, (212) *539-4444.*
An essential guide to everything that's happening in the city, it's a must for everyone and includes a special gay and lesbian section in every edition.
The following organizations can provide help and counter discrimination and homophobia:

The Gay + Lesbian Switchboard,
(212) 989-0999.
If you have a question about almost anything gay-related, or don't know where to turn for help, it can provide answers.

Lesbian + Gay Community Services Center, *208 West 13th St., www.gay-center.org, (212) 620-7310.*
Founded in 1984, the center sponsors many activities, including lectures and dances. It houses an extensive gay historical archive.

Gay + Lesbian Alliance Against Defamation, *150 West 26th St., Suite 505, www.glaad.org*
GLAAD is a media advocacy organization established to ensure fair and accurate reportage of issues and events concerning the homosexual community.

Michael Callen-Audre Lorde Community Health Center at www.callen-lorde.org, **NYC Gay and Lesbian Antiviolence Project** at www.avp.org
Gay AA at http://www.royy.com.

Religion

Gays and lesbians and organized religion are far from mutually exclusive. The many gay and gay-friendly congregations that march every year in the Gay Pride Parade signal not only their existence, but the need that many gays and lesbians have for a spiritual community. The following is a modest sampling of these organizations. Contact the Lesbian and Gay Community Center (see Resources) for additional information and a comprehensive list.

Metropolitan Community Church,
(212) 629-7440.
Founded in the early 1970s by Troy Perry, the MC is an amalgamation of the Catholic, Anglican and Lutheran Churches.

Congregation Beth Simchat Torah,
(212) 929-9498.
This lesbian and gay synagogue lies in the heart of the West Village.

Dignity, New York, *(212) 627-6488.*
The largest Catholic gay organization is vocal in its opposition to the faith's traditional position on gays and lesbians. Its Episcopalian counterpart is called Integrity, *(212) 691-7181.*

West Park Presbyterian Church,
(212) 362-4890.
The day after the official Presbyterian Council struck down amendments that would have sanctified same-sex relationships, this progressive church defiantly flew the rainbow flag.

Saint Paul's, *(212) 265-3495.*
This Roman Catholic Parish is always in hot water with the Archdiocese for sponsoring a very active gay and lesbian congregation.

LGBT Events

After seeing *RENT* on Broadway, many queers wonder why some of the characters are so anxious to leave New York and make it to Santa Fe. In reality, the city is one of the greatest places in the world to be gay. From gay softball and hockey leagues for the locals, to annual events like the Pride March and the Village Halloween Parade, there is no shortage of activities for the LGBT community in New York City. For a more formal introduction, be sure to visit the recently renovated LGBT Community Center, located in the West Village for more than twenty years.

There are special events at all times of the year to satisfy every taste. Come to the city in June, and you'll be able to participate in NYC's annual LGBT Pride Week, culminating in the Pride March and a dance on the Hudson River. In October, try the Village Halloween Parade. While not exclusively an LGBT community event, the Halloween Parade is always a fun time and you're sure to meet some interesting characters. In December, New York joins the international community in observing World AIDS Day with a large-scale glitzy gala at Carnegie Hall followed by a candlelight vigil in City Hall Park. April sees the annual MIX NYC, a festival for hundreds of gay and lesbian experimental filmmakers who screen their work at several locations all over Manhattan. The largest AIDS fundraiser in the world takes place annually in May. AIDS Walk New York is a 10k walk that passes by many of the city's most famous landmarks and brings 40,000 people out to support Gay Men's Health Crisis, the world's most comprehensive provider of AIDS services for men, women and children.

You should also try out college campuses for listings of LGBT community events throughout the year. Barnard, Columbia, NYU, and other city colleges and universities usually join together in December for a first Friday dance. Additionally, various organizations exist on campus for all sorts of interests. There are social groups, a gay business oriented group, Queer activism, support groups, free health clinics, and much more. Many campus organizations also sponsor events for the LGBT community like Columbia's Queer Author lecture series or NYU's Diva and Masquerade Balls.

In addition to all these various happenings, there are always more featured in the plethora of newspapers and periodicals available on the streets of the city. Papers like the *Village Voice* or *Time Out NY* have weekly listings of LGBT events in New York, as well as bar and lounge reviews, gallery openings, theater performances, etc. There is always someplace to go and something to do for everyone in New York City: art galleries, sporting events, parades, marches, dances, dinner, and drinks. Take advantage of the many opportunities this place offers to the LGBT community, and appreciate the unique atmosphere and the beautiful people of New York. Being gay is now part of the mainstream in the city, and opportunities are opening up every day. Don't miss out!

politics

New York's politics are both entertaining and complex, and if you pay attention to local happenings and vote you can make a difference. Most New Yorkers don't vote. With elections coming under heavy scrutiny since the 2000 Presidential campaign and the city's archaic voting machines came under fire, the Election Board has had its hands full. Other organizations, such as the school board, are very active as well. Talk radio, the local papers, and NY1's debates are good ways to keep track of who is doing what to whom.

New York City is unique in that it contains five counties. Most American cities are within counties and not the other way around. Each borough is a specific county: Manhattan is New York County; Brooklyn is Kings County; Queens is Queens County; Staten Island is Richmond County; and the Bronx is Bronx County. In order to persuade Brooklyn to become incorporated into New York City, the position of borough president was created in hopes of preserving borough pride. The borough president acts as an advocate, spokesperson and cheerleader for his or her own borough. Extensive and well-funded offices allow borough presidents to hold investigations, put together committees, and issue reports and recommendations to the City Council. It is also the job of the borough president to appoint members of the Community Boards that are located within their borough. For more information, visit www.nyc.gov.

The bureaucratic structure of New York is organized around the New York City Council and Community Boards, whose main office is located in that "Bullpen" at City Hall. The Council votes on everything regulated by the city government, including zoning, sanitation, quality-of-life issues, recycling, and taxes. Traditionally, the council (and the city itself) is a Democratic one, although recently Republican Mayors Rudolph Giuliani and Michael Bloomberg have enjoyed the support of most New York citizens. Representation in the Council is roughly proportional to a district or borough's population and is based on a census conducted by the government. In the 2000 census, Brooklyn had the largest population at roughly 2.5 million people, followed by Queens at 2.2 million, Manhattan at 1.5 million, the Bronx at 1.3 million, and Staten Island at roughly 443,000 people.

Besides the City Council, New Yorkers' lives are affected by their local Community Board. Community Boards are decision making councils who deal with local issues and concerns. Almost every neighborhood has its own community board. The purpose of local Community Boards is to improve the quality of life of their constituents; they determine local budgets and deal with zoning issues. Community Board meetings can range from real snoozers to royal battles: one time, a Community Board meeting in the East Village resulted in squatters hurling cat feces at board members who were unsympathetic to their plight. New York is truly a city of free expression.

Political History

New York City has been a political entity since it began to take shape in 1626. In the 19th century, an average person's political involvement began with the political club. NYC Democratic political clubs are a holdover from Tammany Hall, New York's legendary Democratic political machine that controlled city government from the mid 19th through the early 20th centuries. Tammany relied on waves of new immigrants for the majority of its support. As time went on and Tammany began to be exposed for its illegal political tactics, immigrants left the organization and began to become involved with the labor movement. Tammany soldiered on until 1933, when Mayor Fiorello LaGuardia won a three-way race as a fusion candidate who opposed the Tammany machine. After his three terms, the institution was powerless and disappeared from American politics.

Getting Involved

Although not as important as they once were, political clubs still exist today. Each club covers sets of election districts based on groupings of several city blocks. Particularly thriving are the five clubs on the Upper West Side, a traditionally intellectual, liberal area. The one Republican and four Democratic clubs keep West Siders some the most politically active citizens in the city. To find the name and number of a political club near you, call either the Democratic County Committee at (212) 687-6540, or the Republican County Committee, located in Staten Island, at (718) 351-4800.

Students may register to vote in New York after they have been in the city for 30 days. After you register, you may be called for jury duty. While school is in session, you can postpone jury duty by responding to summonses with a letter explaining your status. Students who change housing each year need to update their address to vote. For information on absentee ballots, call the NYS Board of Elections at (800) 367-8683.

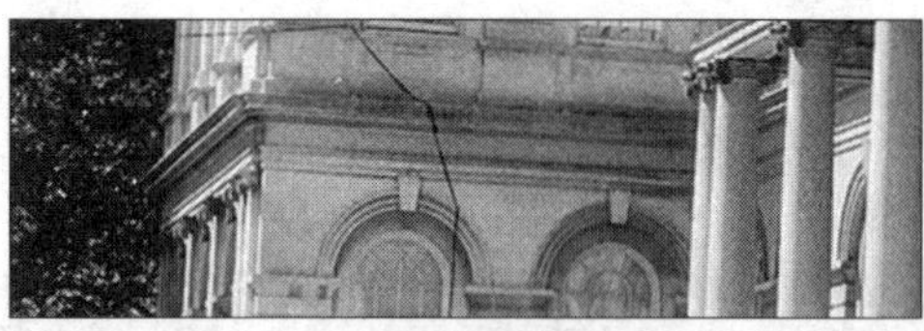

Spotlight on:

New York City Mayor Michael Bloomberg

1. When and why did you first come to New York City?

After graduating from Harvard Business School, I was hired by Salomon Brothers to work on Wall Street in the summer of 1966.

2. Why did you decide to run for Mayor?

I wanted to give back to the City that I love. I have always tried to help through philanthropy, but that only goes so far. The best way to help New York City and New Yorkers is through public service, and that's why I ran for Mayor.

3. How has the city changed since you've been Mayor?

Almost four years ago, when I was inaugurated as Mayor, smoke was still rising from the World Trade Center site. New Yorkers throughout the city were asking the same questions: Will we be able to come back? Can we recover? Where once there was doubt, New Yorkers believe again.

We are safer today than we have ever been in modern memory; we have taken our City from fiscal crisis to fiscal stability; we are building affordable housing; we are creating new jobs. We've redoubled our commitment to fighting crime and to ending homelessness. We are improving and reforming our school system.

There is a spirit, a confidence, an expectation for the future that is new and exciting. The state of our City is strong - and we are going to make it even stronger for the future.

4. What's your favorite thing to do in New York?

One of the great things about New York is its diversity – it's what keeps the City vibrant, young and strong. There is no better way to appreciate the mix of cultures and languages than to march in the City's many parades - from the Columbus and Saint Patrick's Day Parades to the Puerto Rican and West Indian Day Parades. I try to attend as many festivals and parades as I can across the five boroughs, and it's one of my favorite things to do as Mayor and as a New Yorker.

5. What is it about New York City that makes you proud to represent it as its Mayor?

This is the greatest city in the world. While New York is known for its unparalleled diversity, it also has a singular character unlike anywhere else. New Yorkers are intelligent, resilient and strong. As Mayor, I've got the greatest job in the world. It is an honor and a privilege to represent this city. If you do this job right, you can change what happens here in the city, and you can even change the world.

6. Do you have any advice for new New Yorkers?

You are in a city of infinite possibilities. The great thing about New York is that whatever you want to do, all the opportunities are right here, at your fingertips. Try to take advantage of everything the City has to offer. Go to restaurants, museums, Broadway shows or baseball games. If you work hard enough, you can do just about anything in the greatest city in the world.

inside

NYC Politics

There are many issues that regularly splash onto local headlines. New York's Rockefeller drug prohibition laws have been recently reformed, although activists say more work must be done to eliminate mandatory minimum sentencing laws that many say contribute to New York State's "Prison Industrial Complex". The theory states that political power is drained from the city by conservative upstate districts where prison populations add to population counts, but inmates are not allowed to vote. One of the more emotional recent issues concerns the destiny of the former site of the World Trade Center. Neighborhood groups, business associations, corporate interests and government agencies all weigh in.

Not surprisingly, most of the day-to-day political battles concern local self-interest. Those lucky enough to afford a view of Central Park fight for its preservation; Harlem residents bond together to hold the lid on gentrification; residents in high-rent areas ask for more police protection, while marginalized minorities and residents in low-income areas complain about police intimidation. Furthermore, ethnic identity still plays a large part in political affiliation.

New York is full of startling contrast; some of the most striking divisions arise out of income inequality. Walking next to some of the most expensive real estate in the world, you encounter many who advocate for or seek donations for the impoverished. Controversy is often spurred by efforts to move out of the public eye the homeless and others who make a living on the street. Former Mayor Giuliani is famous for his success cleaning up the area around 42nd Street (once known for its prostitutes, now for its Disney marquees).

The state of New York City's public schools is a continuing battle. Managing a unified school system in a city this large and diverse is no easy task. Many inner city schools are criticized for being subpar, and local parents fight hard for limited city funds needed for reform.

New York offers a home to all political affiliations. As a result, agreement does not come easy. But then again, that's what makes the city so much fun.

Housing

If an apartment is rent stabilized, the following conditions must be met. Rent must be lower than $2000, and the apartment building must have been built before 1974. It must also contain six or more units and must not be owned by a hospital, university, or other institution. To research an apartment's rent regulation status, call the DHCR's information line at (866) ASK-DHCR or visit www.dhcr.state.ny.us/index.html. See if a landlord is raising the rent above the legal limit, though DHCR won't reveal an apartment's rental history unless you live in that apartment.

Neighbors

With regard to irritating, noisy neighbors, the City Council doesn't enforce noise pollution laws enough to help punish offenders. First, try contacting your local community affairs office. Police will then serve the offending neighbor with a summons. Alternatively, get your noisy neighbor to agree to an impartial mediation with the Community Disputes Resolution Program office. Once resolutions are signed by both parties, peace and quiet can be had by all. How to get your pay phone quarters back:

Payphones

Most pay phones are run by companies. If a pay phone steals your quarter, call the State Public Service Commission comment line at (800) 335-2120.

Driver's Licenses

Converting an out-of-state driver's license to a New York license is not a big deal. If your license has been expired for less than a year and was active for more than six months, the defunct piece of plastic can be the ticket to getting a New York license. See Resources for DMV listings.

Libraries

New York's libraries are a great way to save money on books, videos, and DVDs. The movies tend to run towards the musical, the depressing, the documentary, and the kiddie, but if you look hard enough you'll find what you're looking for. The biggest library branch is the one next to the NYPL main building on 42nd St. and Fifth Ave., on 40th St. and Fifth Ave. They have hundreds of selections, although the long lines, long wait for certain books, and often grouchy service can dampen the mood.

DSL

High speed Internet is also expensive, although there is now more competition among DSL providers than there is among cable providers. Many telephone companies offer DSL service, as does Time Warner. Expect to pay $40-60 a month for the

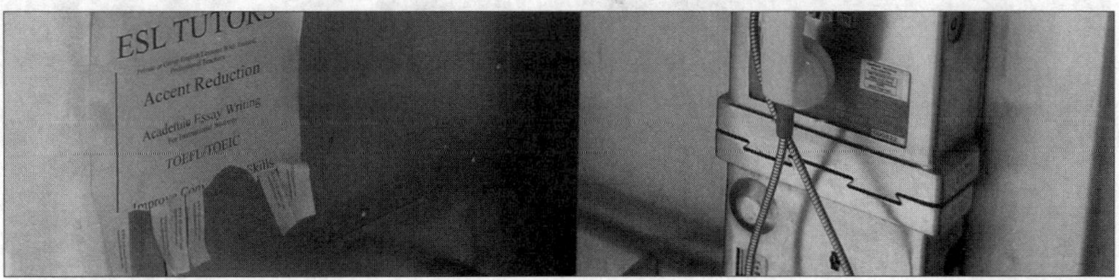

fastest service. You usually get a discount if you are already a customer of the DSL service provider. One main advantage to DSL is that you can store, file, and archive your emails easily. Another advantage of DSL is that it frees up phonelines that were previously being used by your modem. If you are a high-volume Internet user or work from home, DSL is the way to go.

Groceries

If you live in the boondocks of New York, ordering groceries online might actually save you money and time, although they usually only offer the basics (two kinds of Pop Tarts instead of ten). Netgrocer.com is a popular city grocer. Think of it as an Internet version of Sam's Club or Costco. Otherwise, you can try the cheaper supermarkets like C-Town or Met. Their produce is terrible, but if you stock up on their specials, particularly with canned products, you can save a bundle. We know, New Yorkers always have empty fridges, but then again New Yorkers always have empty wallets too. One of the many paradoxes of city living is that if you'd like to go out more, cook more.

Phone Service

Verizon is the top provider in New York, but expect to pay about $50 a month for basic service. You can try MCI, AT&T and other competitors who are newer to the market, but you will find that they run about the same price, and some don't even have basic options like voicemail. To save money on phone service, there are some great options in New York. For long distance, buy calling cards at your local bodega. You just dial an access number, punch in the number printed on the card, and you get up to 100 times the minutes than you could for the same cost. This is the way to go for international calls. Ditch your phone company's calling card, they are a rip-off. You can also buy calling cards with 800 numbers if you know you will be traveling.

Hopstop.com

New and old New Yorkers alike know that it can sometimes be very difficult to determine which subways allow weary travelers to reach their destinations quickest. Luckily, the internet revolution has resulted in the development of a website that tells New Yorkers the quickest way to reach their destination. The website - www.hopstop.com - is a must-see for every New Yorker. The site is intuitively designed and easy to use. Be sure to check it out next time you're wondering how to get to Washington Square Park or Rockaway Beach, Queens.

Wireless Hot-Spots

The Internet can be an expensive or unrealistic proposition for many young New Yorkers. Many of New York's youth are unable to pay their utility bills, let alone splurge on the internet. Also, many downtown apartments don't have internet

Address Locator

In order to find the cross street of an address, follow these simple steps:

NORTH-SOUTH AVENUES

1. Cancel the last digit of the house number
2. Divide the remaining number by two
3. Add or deduct the key number (list follows)

*On street or address numbers with an asterisk, omit step 2.

For example, take 1100 Broadway:
1. Cancel the last digit so you are left with 110
2. Divide 110 by two, leaving you with 55
3. Subtract 31, the key number for Broadway addresses over 1000.

Thus, 1100 Broadway is at 24th St.

Avenues A, B, C, D	Add 3
First Avenue	Add 3
Second Avenue	Add 3
Third Avenue	Add 10
Fourth Avenue	Add 8
Fifth Avenue	
1-200	Add 13
201-400	Add 16
401-600	Add 18
601-775	Add 20
*776-1286	Subtract 18
Sixth Avenue	Subtract 12
Seventh Avenue	
1-1800	Add 12
1800 + above	Add 20
Eighth Avenue	Add 9
Ninth Avenue	Add 13
Tenth Avenue	Add 13
Eleventh Avenue	Add 15
Amsterdam Avenue	Add 59
Broadway	
1-754 =	All below 8th St.
754-858	Subtract 29
859-958	Subtract 25
1000 + above	Subtract 31
***Central Park West**	Add 60
Columbus Avenue	Add 59
Lexington Avenue	Add 22
Madison Avenue	Add 27
Park Avenue	Add 34
Riverside Drive	
*1-567	Add 73
*567 + above	Add 78
West End Avenue	Add 59

EAST-WEST STREETS

Addresses for any east-west street begin at the avenue listed below:

East Side:

Number	Avenue
1	Fifth Avenue
101	Park Avenue
201	Third Avenue
301	Second Avenue
401	First Avenue
501	York or Avenue A
601	Avenue B

West Side:

Number	Avenue
1	Fifth Avenue
101	Sixth Avenue
201	Seventh Avenue
301	Eighth Avenue
401	Ninth Avenue
501	Tenth Avenue
601	Eleventh Avenue

If you get lost or confused, don't be afraid or embarrassed to ask for directions or call 311, New York City's new non-emergency information hotline. Everyone gets lost at least once; its a rite of passage for even the most hard-core New Yorkers.

access. What is a tech-savvy, poor or incapable citizen to do?

The answer is easy: go to an Internet Cafe! Within the last five years internet cafes have sprung up all over the city, from the Bowery to Broadway. Many copy stores, such as Kinko's or Village Copier, now allow their patrons to access the internet while they wait for their copies. There are even downtown establishments which provide coffee and cake for their cyber savvy patrons. Besides being a great way to check your e-mail, research Arrested Development, or post messages on a Nirvana message board, Internet Cafes are also great places to meet new and exciting people. History has never allowed for a better or more elegant pick-up line than, "Can I plug you in?"

Some good places to check out are: Internet Cafe on E. 83rd, Village Copier on 13th St. and Sixth Ave., and XS New York, which is right off Times Square.

Recent Subway Changes

The subway system has recently undergone some changes on a couple of their lines. The D replaces the W, the W now runs between Whitehall St. and Astoria. The B replaces the Q in Brooklyn. The N goes over Manhattan Bridge and runs express on Broadway. Furthermore, the 9 train has gone the way of both disco and the dodo bird and has been eliminated.

Neighborhoods

neighborhoods

Financial District

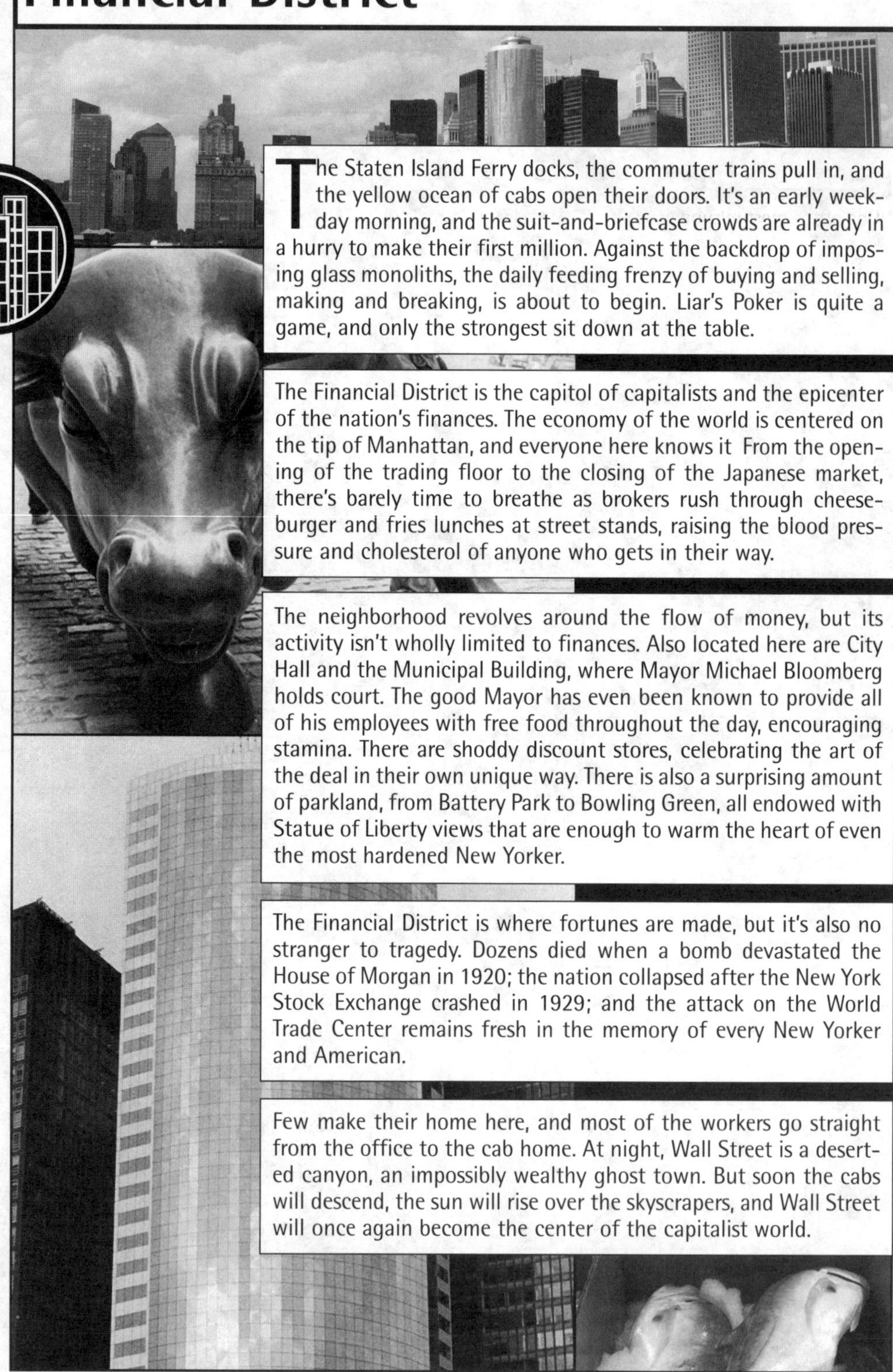

The Staten Island Ferry docks, the commuter trains pull in, and the yellow ocean of cabs open their doors. It's an early weekday morning, and the suit-and-briefcase crowds are already in a hurry to make their first million. Against the backdrop of imposing glass monoliths, the daily feeding frenzy of buying and selling, making and breaking, is about to begin. Liar's Poker is quite a game, and only the strongest sit down at the table.

The Financial District is the capitol of capitalists and the epicenter of the nation's finances. The economy of the world is centered on the tip of Manhattan, and everyone here knows it From the opening of the trading floor to the closing of the Japanese market, there's barely time to breathe as brokers rush through cheeseburger and fries lunches at street stands, raising the blood pressure and cholesterol of anyone who gets in their way.

The neighborhood revolves around the flow of money, but its activity isn't wholly limited to finances. Also located here are City Hall and the Municipal Building, where Mayor Michael Bloomberg holds court. The good Mayor has even been known to provide all of his employees with free food throughout the day, encouraging stamina. There are shoddy discount stores, celebrating the art of the deal in their own unique way. There is also a surprising amount of parkland, from Battery Park to Bowling Green, all endowed with Statue of Liberty views that are enough to warm the heart of even the most hardened New Yorker.

The Financial District is where fortunes are made, but it's also no stranger to tragedy. Dozens died when a bomb devastated the House of Morgan in 1920; the nation collapsed after the New York Stock Exchange crashed in 1929; and the attack on the World Trade Center remains fresh in the memory of every New Yorker and American.

Few make their home here, and most of the workers go straight from the office to the cab home. At night, Wall Street is a deserted canyon, an impossibly wealthy ghost town. But soon the cabs will descend, the sun will rise over the skyscrapers, and Wall Street will once again become the center of the capitalist world.

history

One of the most misunderstood real estate scams in history occurred here in 1626. Legend has it that, for the equivalent of $24, Pieter Minuit, the Director General of New Netherlands, bought the island of Manhatta – now Manhattan –from its inhabitants. He encountered little trouble, since to the Native American sellers, private and transferable property was a totally foreign concept. Unfortunately for Minuit, the natives who sold him the land couldn't actually lay claim to that which they sold, and so the first real-estate scam in American history was completed.

But this swindle came years after an even more brazen land grab. In 1609, the Dutch East India Company hired Henry Hudson to find a passage to India and China. During one of his explorations, he found both the harbor and river that currently bears his name. When news of the high-quality harbor reached home, the Netherlands immediately laid claim to it and the rest of the island of Manhattan.

New Amsterdam, as it was called, became New York when the army of the English Duke of York drove away the Dutch in 1664, after which the city became prosperous on equal parts trade and piracy. When Washington was defeated at the 1776 Battle of Long Island, in what is now Brooklyn Heights, a seven-year military occupation ensued. Manhattan didn't see American rule until 1783.

Because of its easy access to both the Atlantic and the mainland, Manhattan's harbor flourished, and the island quickly became the biggest center of commerce in America. Shipping gave way to finance as the neighborhood's driving industry and marinas ceded ground to larger and larger buildings, culminating in the cathedrals of commerce that define the city's skyline.

[local *gems*]

Most Non-Luger Luger's

MarkJoseph Steakhouse is one of the top steakhouses in New York City, often being compared to Brooklyn's Peter Luger's. Although the rest of the Financial District may become a ghost town at night, head to MarkJoseph for some of the city's best steak.
261 Water St. (off Peck Slip), (212) 277-0020, 2 3 to Wall St.

Most Capitalist Place in the World

The world's largest security exchange and the site of some of the greatest financial disasters in world history, the New York Stock Exchange is a great place to watch the rat race in progress. Watch all the activity, but remember, this is a place of business.
20 Broad St. (bet. Exchange and Wall Sts.), (212) 656-5168, N R to Rector St. or 2 3 4 5 to Wall St.

Most Convenient Cruise

Every half hour, the doors to the Staten Island Ferry open, and commuters and tourists alike crowd on for the gorgeous – and free – half-hour ride across the harbor. The views of the Statue of Liberty are better than you'll get on Liberty Island itself.
(718) 815-BOAT. 1 to South Ferry, 4 5 to Bowling Green, R W to Whitehall St.

Oldest Church

Trinity Church is one of the oldest churches in the city, and is the burial ground of such New York notables as Alexander Hamilton. At 306 years old, the Church isn't getting any younger, although it can be seen in the recent movie *National Treasure* as the hiding place of the national treasure.
79-89 Broadway (at Wall St.), 212-602-0872, 2 3 to Wall St.

Greasiest E-mail

Alongside the plastic chairs at the grotty downstairs Burger King at Broadway near John is a wall of shiny computers. Twenty minutes of surfing are yours with any Value Combo. Need more time? You'd better be hungry...
182 Broadway. (212) 385-0575. R W to Cortlandt St.

TriBeCa

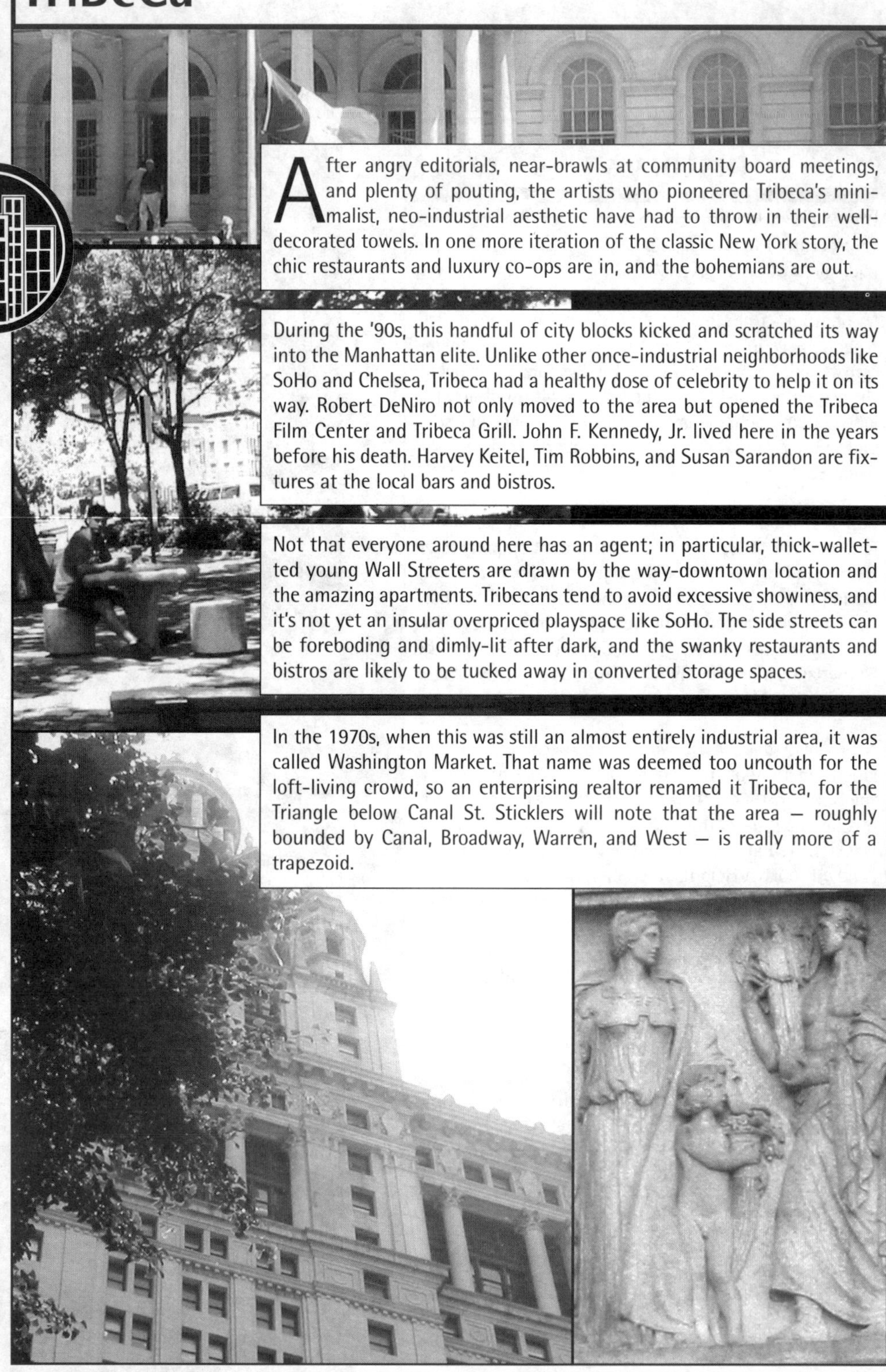

After angry editorials, near-brawls at community board meetings, and plenty of pouting, the artists who pioneered Tribeca's minimalist, neo-industrial aesthetic have had to throw in their well-decorated towels. In one more iteration of the classic New York story, the chic restaurants and luxury co-ops are in, and the bohemians are out.

During the '90s, this handful of city blocks kicked and scratched its way into the Manhattan elite. Unlike other once-industrial neighborhoods like SoHo and Chelsea, Tribeca had a healthy dose of celebrity to help it on its way. Robert DeNiro not only moved to the area but opened the Tribeca Film Center and Tribeca Grill. John F. Kennedy, Jr. lived here in the years before his death. Harvey Keitel, Tim Robbins, and Susan Sarandon are fixtures at the local bars and bistros.

Not that everyone around here has an agent; in particular, thick-walletted young Wall Streeters are drawn by the way-downtown location and the amazing apartments. Tribecans tend to avoid excessive showiness, and it's not yet an insular overpriced playspace like SoHo. The side streets can be foreboding and dimly-lit after dark, and the swanky restaurants and bistros are likely to be tucked away in converted storage spaces.

In the 1970s, when this was still an almost entirely industrial area, it was called Washington Market. That name was deemed too uncouth for the loft-living crowd, so an enterprising realtor renamed it Tribeca, for the Triangle below Canal St. Sticklers will note that the area – roughly bounded by Canal, Broadway, Warren, and West – is really more of a trapezoid.

history

Twenty years before the last bucketful of sludge was drained from the swamp now known as Gramercy Park, Tribeca's parks were already stepping grounds for genteel young ladies wielding parasols.

Beginning modestly in 1813 with Bear Market, which dealt in fruit and produce, by the mid-19th century Tribeca was a major point of transfer for the increased shipping and commerce moving through lower Manhattan. Its cast-iron facades and spacious five and six-story buildings were factories and storage facilities, and Tribeca joined SoHo in becoming an extensive light manufacturing zone. By 1939, Bear Market and the surrounding area were renamed Washington Market; the market itself sustained a greater volume of business than all other city markets combined. It remained a vital part of the city's produce market until most companies left the area in the early '60s and were quickly replaced by the real-estate developers.

The Washington Market Urban Renewal Project was launched almost immediately and office buildings, institutions like the Borough of Manhattan Community College, and public parks sprang up in the neighborhood. In the '70s alone, the area's population jumped from 243 to more than 5,000. Development continued into the '90s: construction of Stuyvesant High School, the city's most competitive public high school, was completed in 1993 at a cost of over $150 million. Illegal lofts were quickly converted into luxury residences as had been done a decade or two earlier in SoHo, with the important distinction that these lofts were open to non-artists as well as those of the creative class.

[local *gems*]

Coolest Local Music

The Knitting Factory has long been one of New York City's cool music haven, and the tradition continues there today. One can kick back with a drink or two (although they do I.D.) and listen to eclectic music from the likes of artists such as Ashlee Simpson and Dead Meadow. Bring your hipster gear or feel out of place.
81 Franklin St., (212) 219-3006. ① to Franklin St.

Cheapest Pakistani Food

Come to the Pakistani Tea House to enjoy some of New York's best – and cheapest – Pakistani food. Everything from the Nan Bread to the Chicken Makhani is delightful. There are also vegetarian options, for those who are concerned with such matters.
176 Church St. (bet. Duane and Reade Sts.), (212) 240-9800. ①②③ to Chambers St.

Best Celebrity Sighting

Come to Tribeca's Greenwich Street in hopes of seeing some of New York's more famous faces, including Robert DeNiro, Christopher Walken, Mick Jagger, and Sarah Jessica Parker. Admission is free, so bring a friend!
1 Greenwich St. (bet. Duane and Reade Sts.). ① to Franklin St.

Best Tribeca Breakfast

Low-for-these-parts prices and the cute setting keep all-American Kitchenette hopping, and the breakfasts are large and luscious. For lunch, try the Soup Pot across the street, owned and operated by the same team.
80 W. Broadway (at Warren St.), (212) 267-6740. ①②③ to Chambers St.

Best Place to Gawk

Designed by Frank Gehry, tribeca ISSEYMIYAKE – yes, that's how the staff insists you spell the name of experimental Japanese fashion designer Issey Miyake's boutique – looks like the world's most exclusive robot clothing store. There are odd, android-like mannequins, anime murals, and a giant titanium tornado in the middle, and that's just the beginning. Also awesome is Miyake's A-POC line; it stands for A Piece of Cloth, with dotted lines along which you can cut out your clothes.
119 Hudson St. (at N. Moore St.), (212) 226-0100. ① to Franklin St.

Chinatown

Shining fish eyes. Porcelain tea kettles. Wizened ginseng roots. Glinting jewel-studded watches. Tiger-penis aphrodisiacs. Chinatown is a teeming bazaar, where someone in the know can buy just about anything.

The streets are mostly tiny, and the thick, sweaty crowds are a claustrophobe's nightmare. But within this riot of gold and scarlet there are discoveries at every step: melting red-bean pastries, miniature jade dragons, or the drugstore on Grand Street where deer antlers are still weighed out in brass handscales.

Chinatown seems caught in perpetual chaos, with too many people doing too much in too small a space—and, indeed, the neighborhood is bursting out of its seams. Having successfully reduced Little Italy to a tiny shadow, Chinatown is now gunning for the Lower East Side and even SoHo. It's also broadening its ethnic makeup, and many of the shops and restaurants now have Thai, Cambodian, Vietnamese, or Korean owners.

The hard sells of the sidewalk knockoff hawkers and the streams of baseball-capped suburbanites ogling roasting ducks in shop windows can make Chinatown feel fake, a manufactured piece of tourist exotica. Though many recent immigrants have favored other, less chaotic Chinatowns, like Flushing in Queens or Sunset Park in Brooklyn, Manhattan's Chinatown remains a living, bustling ethnic community with a residential population in the hundreds of thousands. Walk a few blocks away from the main drags, and you'll find a different Chinatown, with the video rental stores, dentists, and unassuming tea shops that the neighborhood uses to breathe.

history

Volumes have been written on the history of this complex neighborhood. Chinatown sprang up in the mid-to-late 19th century, with the first wave of immigration to this country. Prior to the Chinese immigration, the area now regarded as Chinatown was part of the notorious Five Points district, which consisted of mainly Irish and some Jewish immigrants. Residents at the time characterized the neighborhood as a lawless place, notorious for its vice, violence and prostitution.

The first recorded Chinese resident was a merchant from Kwantung who moved into 8 Mott Street in 1858. By the 1870s, there were almost 2000 Chinese living within the boundaries of Canal, Worth, Mulberry, and the Bowery—the area which became Chinatown proper.

Migration was not easy for the Chinese. Isolationist leaders had not allowed them to leave their homeland, and immigrants were greeted with fear and even hatred when they arrived in the United States.

New York's Chinatown grew slowly, as immigration laws kept men from sending for their families. Immigrants were restricted to a few types of businesses, and many opened hand laundries; soon, there were restaurants and shops to attract visitors. The population grew after the Exclusion Act was repealed in 1943, reaching 20,000 by 1965. As restrictions and prejudices began to wane in the late '60s, Chinatown expanded into parts of the Lower East Side and Little Italy, becoming the largest Chinese community in the Western world.

[local *gems*]

Most Democratic Wall

Even more Democratic than Prague's altar to John Lennon, Chinatown's Wall of Democracy is a mind-boggling collage of posters, news articles, and hand lettered statements on current events in China. Come, and maybe learn and little.
Bayard St. (bet. Mulberry and Mott Sts.). J M N R W Z 6 *to Canal St.*

Dirtiest Name (with best food)

Although the term 69 may conjure some racy images, the food at Chinatown's 69 is some of the best and cheapest in the city. The beef and pork are both tender and delicious, and the wonton soup is to die for. In fact, its so cheap you can bring a whole group of people to experience some of Chinatown's best food.
69 Bayard St. (bet. Mott and Elizabeth Stss), (212) 227-1173. J M N R W Z 6 *to Canal St.*

Most Inscrutable Clairvoyants

On weekends, the fortune-tellers in Columbus Park set up shop under red banners advertising "fortune." Their cards and long reeds promise to uncover buried truths; you imagine them revealing the trail of your future life. This is a dream that's bound to be broken: "fortune" is the only word of English that many speak.
Bet. Mulberry and Baxter Sts., south of Bayard St.

Most Miles Per Dollar

The legendary Chinatown bus services can get you from Canal Street to Boston for an incredible ten dollars. They also go to D.C., Philadelphia, Baltimore, and several other East Coast cities. Yeah, the seats can be cramped and uncomfortable; given, the driver will rarely speak English; true, Boston/New York buses sometimes use routes creative enough to include Providence; sure, there are documented ties to organized crime. None of this seems to matter when your ticket costs less than an airport sandwich.
See www.staticleap.com/chinatownbus for a list of companies.

Little Italy

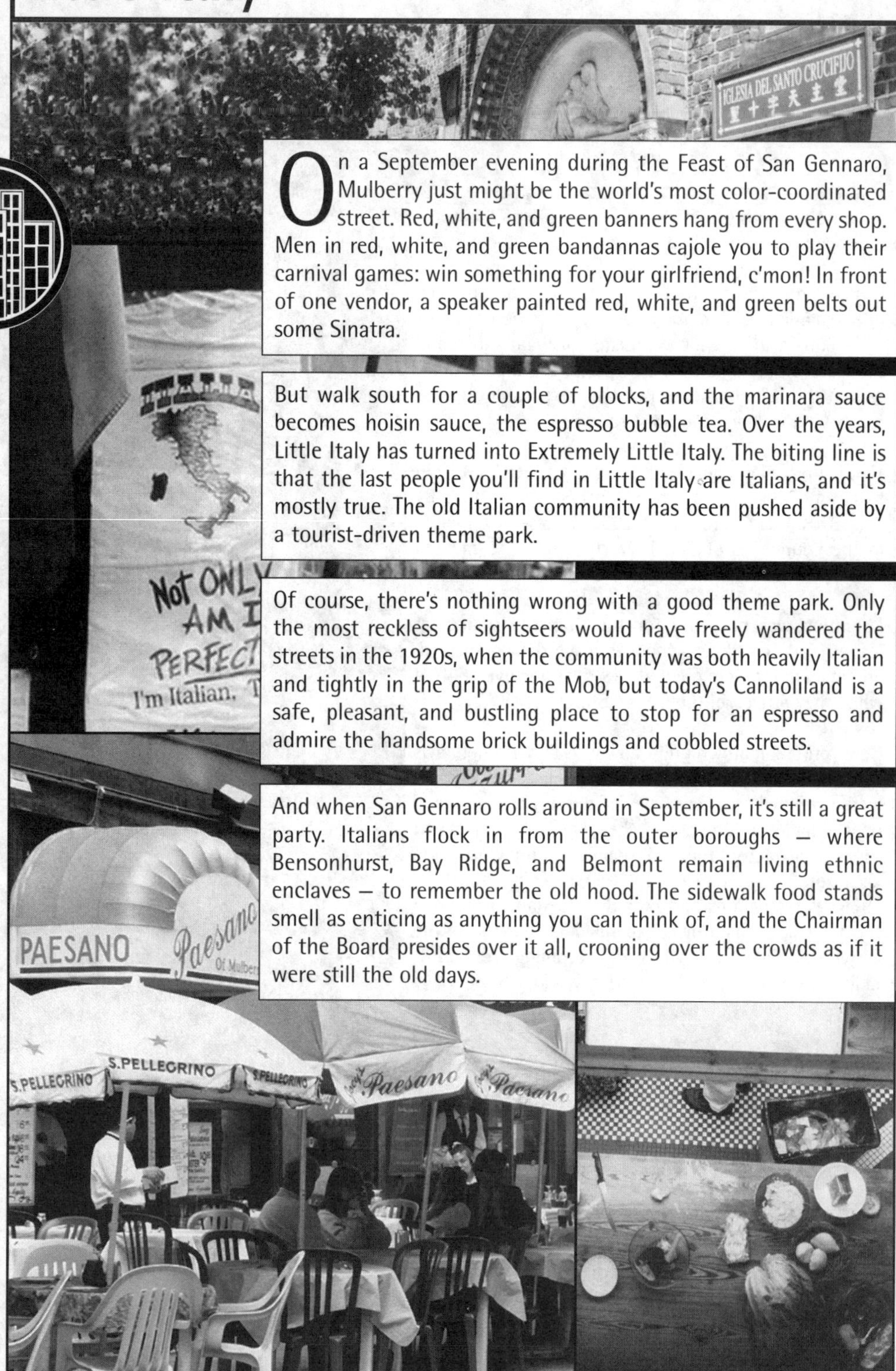

On a September evening during the Feast of San Gennaro, Mulberry just might be the world's most color-coordinated street. Red, white, and green banners hang from every shop. Men in red, white, and green bandannas cajole you to play their carnival games: win something for your girlfriend, c'mon! In front of one vendor, a speaker painted red, white, and green belts out some Sinatra.

But walk south for a couple of blocks, and the marinara sauce becomes hoisin sauce, the espresso bubble tea. Over the years, Little Italy has turned into Extremely Little Italy. The biting line is that the last people you'll find in Little Italy are Italians, and it's mostly true. The old Italian community has been pushed aside by a tourist-driven theme park.

Of course, there's nothing wrong with a good theme park. Only the most reckless of sightseers would have freely wandered the streets in the 1920s, when the community was both heavily Italian and tightly in the grip of the Mob, but today's Cannoliland is a safe, pleasant, and bustling place to stop for an espresso and admire the handsome brick buildings and cobbled streets.

And when San Gennaro rolls around in September, it's still a great party. Italians flock in from the outer boroughs – where Bensonhurst, Bay Ridge, and Belmont remain living ethnic enclaves – to remember the old hood. The sidewalk food stands smell as enticing as anything you can think of, and the Chairman of the Board presides over it all, crooning over the crowds as if it were still the old days.

history

Beginning with the explorer Giovanni da Verrazzano's 1524 arrival in Manhattan's bay, Italians have been an important part of New York City's history. Immigrants from Northern Italy arrived in the early 17th century, but their numbers were dwarfed by larger waves of Southern Italian and Sicilian immigrants, who came to New York in the late 19th century.

From 1880 to 1900, the number of Italians in New York rose from 12,000 to almost 220,000 and doubled to 545,000 by 1910. Most of the Italian immigrants settled in lower Manhattan, an area packed with poor immigrant families living in crowded, unsanitary tenements in neighborhoods dotted with religious institutions. Immigrants tended to cluster according to their relations in the Old World, with Genoans, Calabrians, and Sicilians living on the east side, and Piedmontese, Tuscans, and Neopolitans to the west. This was the era chronicled by Francis Ford Coppola in *The Godfather, Part II*, where Sicilian Vito Corleone establishes himself as the benefactor of his community.

By the mid-20th century, most Italians — like the fictional Corleone — had moved out of the old neighborhood to greener places, like Staten Island, Brooklyn, Long Island, and New Jersey.

[local *gems*]

Most Italian in Little Italy

Before leaving Little Italy, make sure to stop by La Mela Ristorante, a (very) authentic Italian eatery. The portions are huge and the food – especially the marinara sauce – is delicious. The atmosphere is pure old New York, so be ready to have your world rocked by those who, if they wanted to, could snap you like a pretzel, capiche?
167 Mulberry St. (bet. Grand and Broom Sts.), (212) 431-9493. 6 to Spring St.

French Where There Shouldn't Be French

Although never Continental enemies, a little bit of France has invaded Little Italy. Café Gitane is French through and through, from the aloof waitstaff to the menu offerings. The café offers the perfect ambiance for flipping through fashion magazines, drinking coffee, and watching people.
242 Mott St. (bet. Prince and Houston Sts.), (212) 334-9552. N R to Prince St.

Nicest Place to Get Booked

The old Police Headquarters, with its ornate copper dome and shining chandeliers, must have been a gorgeous place to reflect on your dismal future in jail. Too bad it's now a luxury co-op building.
240 Centre St. (bet. Grand and Broome Sts.). N R to Prince St.

Most "Noo Yawk" Church

The Holy Crucifix Church is stately and sedate stone Roman Catholic church. It's in the heart of Little Italy — smack up against an irreverent art gallery. It offers Sunday mass in English, Chinese, and Spanish – but not Italian. Even the Church knows when to give in to the forces of the city.
378 Broome St. (bet. Mott and Mulberry Sts.). 6 to Spring St.

Lower East Side

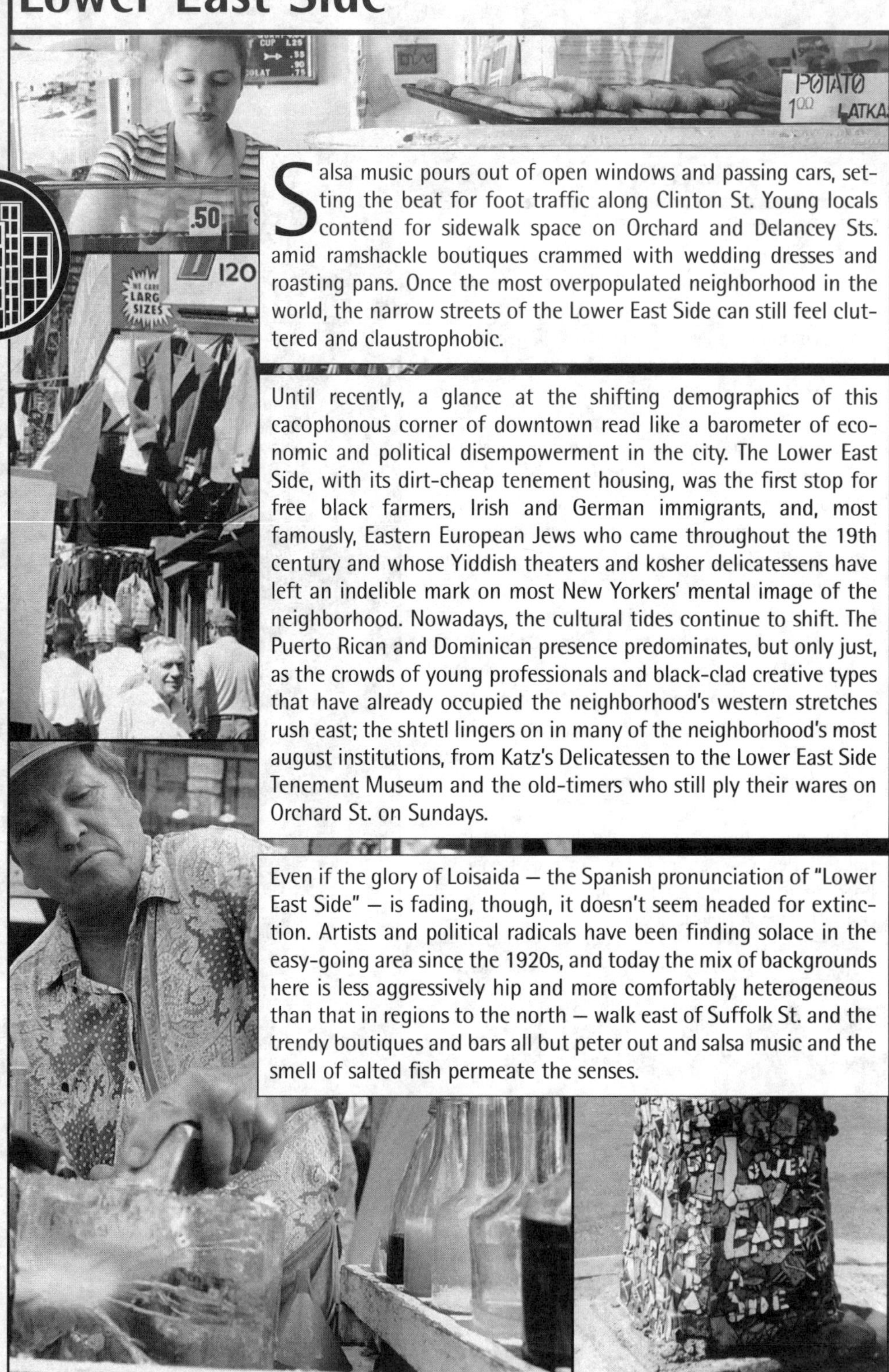

Salsa music pours out of open windows and passing cars, setting the beat for foot traffic along Clinton St. Young locals contend for sidewalk space on Orchard and Delancey Sts. amid ramshackle boutiques crammed with wedding dresses and roasting pans. Once the most overpopulated neighborhood in the world, the narrow streets of the Lower East Side can still feel cluttered and claustrophobic.

Until recently, a glance at the shifting demographics of this cacophonous corner of downtown read like a barometer of economic and political disempowerment in the city. The Lower East Side, with its dirt-cheap tenement housing, was the first stop for free black farmers, Irish and German immigrants, and, most famously, Eastern European Jews who came throughout the 19th century and whose Yiddish theaters and kosher delicatessens have left an indelible mark on most New Yorkers' mental image of the neighborhood. Nowadays, the cultural tides continue to shift. The Puerto Rican and Dominican presence predominates, but only just, as the crowds of young professionals and black-clad creative types that have already occupied the neighborhood's western stretches rush east; the shtetl lingers on in many of the neighborhood's most august institutions, from Katz's Delicatessen to the Lower East Side Tenement Museum and the old-timers who still ply their wares on Orchard St. on Sundays.

Even if the glory of Loisaida — the Spanish pronunciation of "Lower East Side" — is fading, though, it doesn't seem headed for extinction. Artists and political radicals have been finding solace in the easy-going area since the 1920s, and today the mix of backgrounds here is less aggressively hip and more comfortably heterogeneous than that in regions to the north — walk east of Suffolk St. and the trendy boutiques and bars all but peter out and salsa music and the smell of salted fish permeate the senses.

history

For immigrants traveling from the provincial areas of Europe, the tenements that dominated the landscapes of the Lower East Side must have been a chilling sight. Infamous for providing the worst housing conditions in the city, these five-story firetraps absorbed most of the first major wave of immigrants who passed through Ellis Island and could not afford anything better. During the last two decades of the 19th century, the largely Irish population was joined by Italians and Eastern European Jews who crowded in by the thousands. The area became saturated: by 1920, the Jewish population alone peaked at over 400,000. New laws and housing plans failed to alleviate the situation. The first city housing project, built in 1936 as a last-ditch effort to provide housing for immigrants, portended the limited success of projects in general.

But great spirit arose out of poverty, and the neighborhood soon became as well known for its wealth of intellectual and artistic life as for its overcrowding. During the early part of this century, Yiddish theater flourished along Second Ave., area newspapers grew into forums for intellectual debate, and performers like George Gershwin, Irving Berlin, and the Marx Brothers cut their teeth.

The '50s and '60s saw revolutionaries, writers, and musicians populating the northern boundaries, an area that later expanded and became known as the East Village. The Lower East Side fell into decline as rents once again decreased and crime, drugs, and dilapidated housing became prominent neighborhood features. In the '80s, the area stabilized somewhat after an influx of Latinos arrived, who dubbed the area "Loisaida."

[local *gems*]

Best Pastrami in the City (and Perhaps the World)

Katz's Delicatessen is known primarily for one thing, and that is it's pastrami. Hailed by average Joe's and gourmands alike, the Pastrami offered at Katz's is both thickly cut and incredibly tasty. For the movie lover in us all, one can come and reenact the famous "o" scene from *When Harry Met Sally.*
205 E. Houston St., (212) 254-2246. F V *to Lower East Side-Second Ave.*

Most Vinegary Clerks

The staff at the around-since-forever Guss's Pickles smell pretty pickled themselves, but don't let that stop you from ordering yourself a cheap, satisfying, and mouth-puckeringly sour pickle on a stick. It's an open storefront, with no doors or walls and a row of huge barrels containing a panoply of pickles.
85-87 Orchard St. (at Broome St.), (917) 701-4000. F J M Z *to Delancey St.*

Most Mayer For Your Buck

The 20s gangster theme starts as you enter the door to the Lansky Lounge and are greeted by zoot-suited bouncer who could knock an average Gus out with his right-hand and steal the man's dame with his left. Named after Jewish gangster Mayer Lansky, the Lounge offers gigantic martini's and good food, all in honor of Meyer, Bugsy, and the rest of Murder, Inc.
104 Norfolk St (bet. Delancey and Rivington Sts.), (212) 677-9489. F J M Z *to Delancey St.*

Cheapest Action Movie

On the ground floor of Alchemy 106 is a pleasant, hip Internet café, where the WiFi comes strong and clear and any of their wide selection of coffees gets you half an hour at a terminal. Walk upstairs and you're in a violent underworld, where twitching men hooked up to X-Boxes and plasma TVs blast each other to bits to loud house music.
106 Delancey St. (bet. Essex and Ludlow Sts.), (212) 358-8574. F J M Z *to Delancey St.*

SoHo

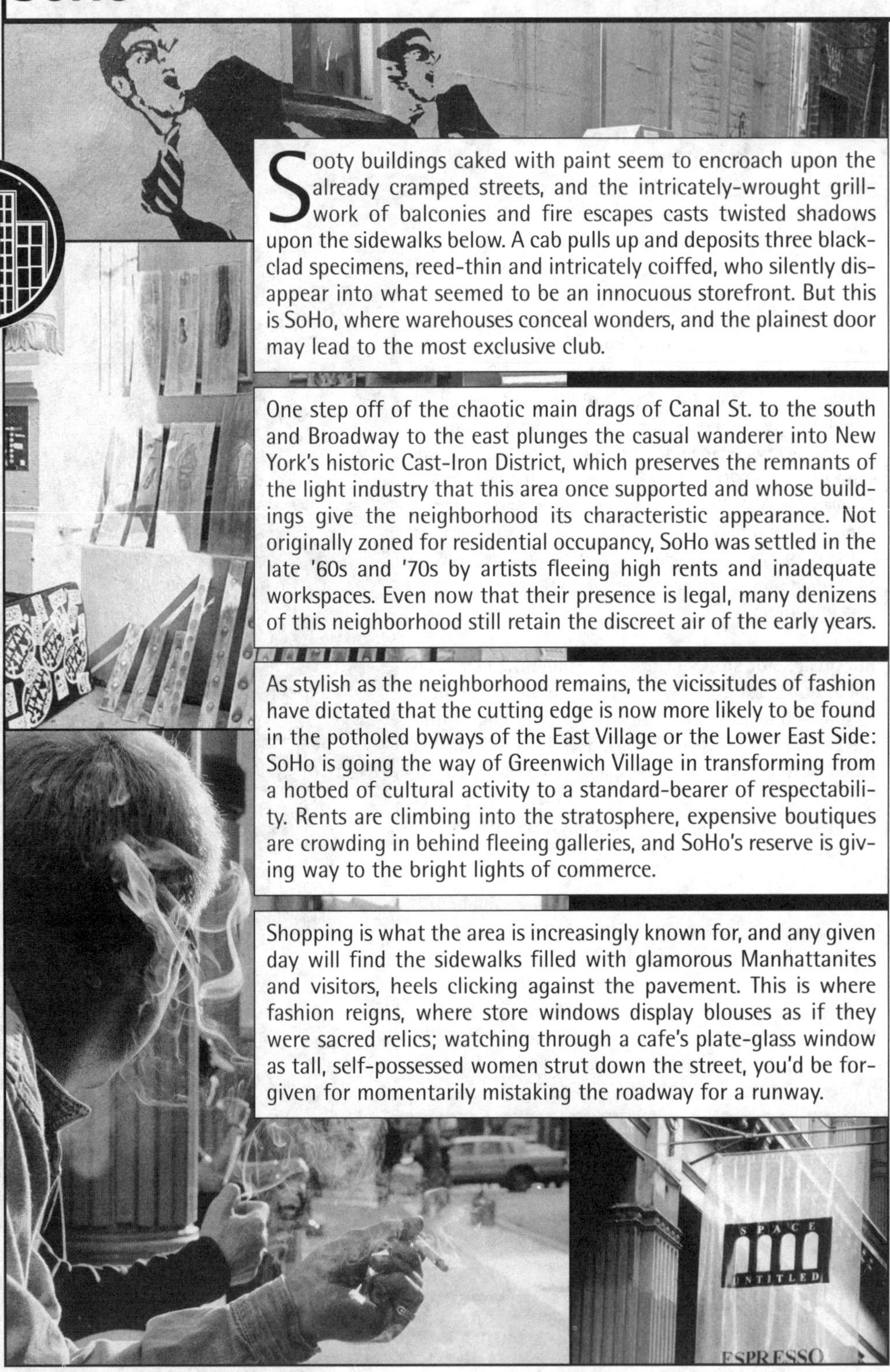

Sooty buildings caked with paint seem to encroach upon the already cramped streets, and the intricately-wrought grillwork of balconies and fire escapes casts twisted shadows upon the sidewalks below. A cab pulls up and deposits three black-clad specimens, reed-thin and intricately coiffed, who silently disappear into what seemed to be an innocuous storefront. But this is SoHo, where warehouses conceal wonders, and the plainest door may lead to the most exclusive club.

One step off of the chaotic main drags of Canal St. to the south and Broadway to the east plunges the casual wanderer into New York's historic Cast-Iron District, which preserves the remnants of the light industry that this area once supported and whose buildings give the neighborhood its characteristic appearance. Not originally zoned for residential occupancy, SoHo was settled in the late '60s and '70s by artists fleeing high rents and inadequate workspaces. Even now that their presence is legal, many denizens of this neighborhood still retain the discreet air of the early years.

As stylish as the neighborhood remains, the vicissitudes of fashion have dictated that the cutting edge is now more likely to be found in the potholed byways of the East Village or the Lower East Side: SoHo is going the way of Greenwich Village in transforming from a hotbed of cultural activity to a standard-bearer of respectability. Rents are climbing into the stratosphere, expensive boutiques are crowding in behind fleeing galleries, and SoHo's reserve is giving way to the bright lights of commerce.

Shopping is what the area is increasingly known for, and any given day will find the sidewalks filled with glamorous Manhattanites and visitors, heels clicking against the pavement. This is where fashion reigns, where store windows display blouses as if they were sacred relics; watching through a cafe's plate-glass window as tall, self-possessed women strut down the street, you'd be forgiven for momentarily mistaking the roadway for a runway.

history

SoHo first drew widespread attention after Mayor John V. Lindsay succeeded in striking down the most outrageous of Robert Moses' notorious urban renewal projects – a proposal to link the East River bridges and the Holland Tunnel by carving an east-west expressway through Broome St. Voters, academics, and politicians all eventually agreed that tax revenue from the garment industries on Broome was essential, and the Renaissance-style buildings of what many began to call SoHo were sturdy, handsome, and ultimately habitable.

SoHo's low rents and spacious lofts initially attracted artists searching for ample work spaces, and they began discreetly moving into the area. Although residing in a light manufacturing zone was illegal, landlords turned a blind eye. But as more and more "illegal" lofts materialized, legalization became inevitable. In the area with the greatest number of resident artists, laws slowly changed to accommodate more and more of them legally. At first, only those working in the visual fine arts were eligible; in 1968, eligibility was extended to those in the performing and creative arts. Finally, in 1971, a series of legal solutions resulted in SoHo's designation as the first mixed-use zone for artist housing.

Concurrently, an Artist Certification Committee was formed to ensure that SoHo housing went only to artists; thus, the reflexive element of the law began to reinforce SoHo's privileged status. Overseen by the Department of Cultural Affairs, this 20-person committee demanded hard proof that prospective residents were artists, often examining slides or other work samples. The committee still operates today, though it has no enforcement power and both residents and landlords now routinely ignore the old artists-only policies.

[local *gems*]

Most Bang For Your Puck

Erected in 1886, the Puck Building – so named because it was the original printing plant for America's first humor magazine, *Puck* – is a beautifully expansive building whose bottom floors host balls and galas and whose top floors are home to apartments and offices.
295 Lafayette St. (at. Houston St.), 274-8900. B D F V to Broadway-Lafayette St.

Best SoHo Sushi

Blue Ribbon Sushi is famous for it's ... well ... sushi! Most who come here leave satisfied, and those who don't need to have their palettes. Try their famous Green Tea Crème Brulee. If you come on a hot night, there's a fairly good chance you'll meet a celebrity - so bring a pen and paper.
119 Sullivan St. (bet. Prince and Spring Sts.) (212) 343-0404. C E to Spring St.

Most Thrilling Bathrooms

The main attraction at stylish Bar 89 is the fabulous unisex bathroom. Latch the glass doors ever-so-precisely, and they become opaque; fumble, and you'll be exposing everyone in the room to things better kept private.
89 Mercer St. (bet. Spring and Broome Sts.), (212) 274-0989. N R to Prince St.

Most Breathing Room

No doubt the ten-dollar sandwiches finance the rent at high-ceilinged Space Untitled, but dorm-room dwellers can take advantage of this capacious cafe and gallery for the price of a cup of coffee.
133 Greene St. (bet. Houston and Prince Sts.), (212) 260-8962. R W to Prince St.

Least Pretentious Boutiques

Many of the coolest accessories can be found street shopping at the tables along Broadway. Among the people selling "I love New York more than you do" tees and bootleg CDs are quite a few aspiring young designers selling their stuff.

East Village

It's noon in the city, but while the rest of the island heads out for lunch, the East Village is just waking up. Security gates roll up to reveal the cheap restaurants and second-hand stores for which the area has long been known, and sleepy-eyed punks and hipsters emerge from crumbling tenements. Life for the majority of these denizens of downtown is nocturnal, driven by a circadian rhythm that demands a glimpse of sunrise before a night's revels end in exhausted sleep.

Much of the current popular mythology of the East Village centers around its beatnik past and their cast of characters, including Charles Bukowski, Allen Ginsberg, and Amiri Baraka. These revolutionaries who advanced the bohemian lifestyle and radical politics that solidified the neighborhood's reputation. The recreational hard drug use of literary luminaries like William S. Burroughs also set the stage for the East Village's darker side, and when the economic plunge of the '70s sent downtown into darkness, the drug traffic exploded.

Today, panhandlers are as likely to be teenagers with multiple piercings as they are to be middle-aged men who populate most city streets; these ruffians take up their positions along St. Mark's Place across from used CD stores, comic book stores, and vintage clothing shops, most of which don't close much before midnight. Music clubs like CBGBs and the Mercury Lounge showcase local hopefuls nightly, and political plays are performed at La MaMa or P.S. 122; afterwards, crowds sweep out onto Ave. A to hit the multitude of bars which line this main drag and stagger into all-night eateries like the Yaffa Café.

The East Village of today is a largely romanticized place. The simple, hedonistic bohemian culture that it evokes was long ago evicted by rents that have restricted tenants to the fairly wealthy, and the East Village now peddles its outlaw image to outsiders: that scowling kid flipping through the record bins on St. Mark's or slouching by the Astor Pl. cube is more likely to be from Long Island than Ave. B. But in today's wealthy Manhattan, this is a given anywhere downtown – and, starving artists or not, the East Village remains one of the best places anywhere to stay up way, way too late.

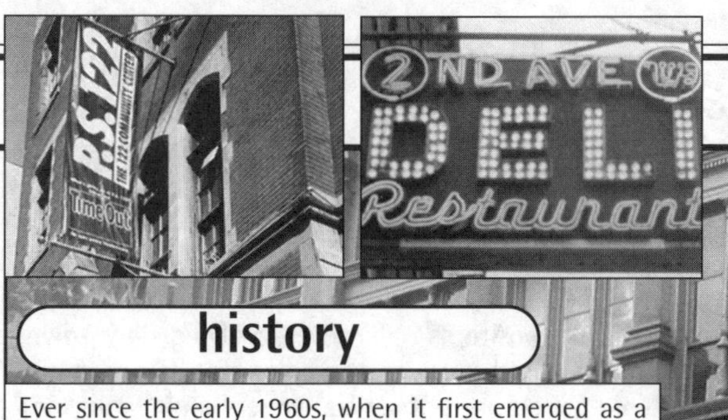

history

Ever since the early 1960s, when it first emerged as a distinct neighborhood, the East Village has been known as a clearinghouse of revolution and decay. Jump-started into life by intellectuals, artists, musicians, and writers frustrated with rising rents that were taming the West Village in the late '60s, the area supported a level of political and artistic radicalism for which its western neighbor was always a bit too genteel. These pioneers set up coffee shops and poetry houses and opened various bookshops, saloons, bars, and jazz clubs like Slug's and the Five Spot. Most recently, the area has absorbed large numbers of Latinos and Ukrainians.

Drugs and their associated evils were largely responsible for the neighborhood crisis of the '70s; residents repeatedly demanded police protection from the dealers and government funding for their dilapidated tenements. But such aid was not sufficient, and locals banded together to reclaim vacant lots and abandoned buildings from urban decay. A large community of squatters took hold of such spaces, and in the '80s they fought both neighborhood bullies and the wave of gentrification that continues today.

The conflict came to a head in 1989 as police attempted to impose a curfew at Tompkins Square Park, the cultural and geographical hub of the East Village and one of the city's prime targets for redevelopment. The resulting riot, one of worst in recent memory, was solidly won by the cops, who arrested the rioters and closed the park. Despite continuing marches and violent protests, it wasn't reopened until 1992, and the rupture between the law and the community remains an open wound.

[local *gems*]

Most Brilliant College Students

A free college tuition is one of the benefits of being accepted into prestigious Cooper Union, along with being located in one of the most entertaining spots in the city. Every U.S. President (except for Dubya) has spoken at the school's Great Hall, and the building further houses the Houghton Art Gallery.
51 Astor Pl., (212) 323-4120. 6 *to Astor Pl.*

Forget Freedom Fries

Head down to Pommes Frites for some of the best French Fries this side of the Somme. Choose from tons of sides, including vinegar, mayonnaise, and plain ole' Ketchup. After enjoying some fries, walk around the area and check out St. Mark's Place for some debaucherous fun.
123 Second Ave., (212) 674-1234. N R *to 8th St.-NYU*

Hello, Ukraine!

Ukraine has recently entered American's consciousness with the corruption and drama that defined the 2004 Ukrainian Presidential Elections. Now, learn more about the land of L'viv and Donetsk at Manhattan's Ukrainian Museum. The two floor museum has rotating exhibits, so call ahead to be sure you are interested in whatever is currently being showcased.
103 Second Ave. (bet. 12th and 13th Sts.), (212) 228-0110. F L V *to 14th St.*

Most Intimate Green Spaces

Amid Alphabet City's gentrifying grit are a surprising number of community gardens, little oases with often-gorgeous details. Look for the lovely retreat on 6th St. and Ave. B, where poetry readings and performances are often held, or the tower with found objects and other bric-a-brac.
At 4th St. and Ave. B

Most Old-School Soda

An egg cream, the quintessential turn-of-the-century New York drink, contains no eggs or cream, but rather cold milk, seltzer, and Fox's U-Bet Chocolate Syrup. The countermen at Gem Spa news stand know that the recipe is open to no variation, and their faithful reproductions are yours for two bucks a piece.
131 Second Ave. (at St. Mark's Pl.), (212) 995-1866. 6 *to Astor Pl.*

Greenwich Village

In the awkward juxtapositions of an ever-evolving downtown, Greenwich Village holds court as the elder statesman of hip. Having sheltered generations of artists, writers, and revolutionaries in its crooked byways, the Village is simply content to maintain its reputation, becoming surprisingly serene and preserving its geographic boundaries as no other downtown neighborhood has.

The Village's predictability supplies a large part of its tourist-friendly charm: the central axis of MacDougal and Bleecker Sts. has hosted a cluster of cafes from time immemorial, Washington Square Park is an open playground for residential and visiting masses alike, and the attitude-filled shops that crowd the New York University area foist their schlocky wares upon newcomers 365 days a year, be they tourists or the fresh crop of gawky freshmen who arrive each fall.

Yet just when nostalgic critics begin to arm themselves with accusations of the neighborhood's having sold out, the Village reveals its ability to surprise, both in alleys and in avenues. Amid the bustle of NYU, one of the city's largest and most prestigious universities, the Washington Mews afford weary walkers a welcome respite; the Chess Shop, nestled at the intersection of Thompson and 3rd Sts., benevolently smiles upon enthusiasts of all ages who gather to outstrategize each other, if not to buy; and the abrupt eruption of Greenwich Ave. boasts a multitude of small bars and cafes set back from the broad street and off the beaten path.

In truth, Greenwich Village should not be reprimanded for remaining true to its deepest roots as a genteel enclave of the upper class; its relative reserve presents a nice contrast to the crazy fluctuations of the surrounding areas. The Village isn't a sell-out, but rather one of the city's few neighborhoods to have artfully blended its past with its present, avidly supporting a gay and artistic community while still accommodating the anonymous families who quietly thread their way through the sea of tourists to pick up dinner at Balducci's. As long as there's art, intellect, and radical politics in the Village, it will preserve the vitality that has surprised visitors for the last century.

history

During New York's 19th-century explosion, Greenwich Village thrived. Its residents commissioned famous architects and artists for their buildings, beautiful churches sprang up, and literary salons, art clubs, and private galleries soon clogged lower Broadway.

As the art scene increased in importance early in the 20th century, the Village's distance from the financial constraints of Midtown's Broadway theaters and publishing powerhouses resulted in the development of a phenomenon for which the neighborhood would become famous: the bohemian lifestyle. Experimental theater, galleries specializing in avant-garde art, and irreverent "little magazines," the forerunners of today's zines, exploded onto the scene. Wild parties, candlelit tearooms, novelty nightclubs, and bizarre boutiques soon followed.

Just prior to the Depression, "artistic flats" became the era's local euphemism for what we'd now call gentrification, luxury apartments that displaced many of the long-term residents who had spawned the artistic ferment that first put the neighborhood on the map.

Following the Depression's end, the Beat Generation arrived and the Village saw the first stirrings of gay culture. Once again, writers and artists of all kinds congregated here, fueling the divergent but intimately connected genesis of the hippie movement and the gay revolution. Near Sheridan Square, a 1969 police raid on a local gay bar resulted in the Stonewall Rebellion, a seminal moment in the developing movement for gay and lesbian rights. With the '80s came the AIDS epidemic, which hit the community hard and sparked increased activism that continues today.

[local *gems*]

Most Romanesque Church

King Juan Carlos II of Spain provided funds for the renovation of the Romanesque Judson Memorial Church, whose modern minimalist interior clashes with its elaborately etched exterior. The church is a beautiful example of late 19th century architecture.

55 Washington Sq. South (bet. Thompson and Sullivan Sts.), (212) 477-0351. N R to 8th St.-NYU.

Most Starbucks Within a Block

Everyone knows that this Seattle monolith has overtaken New York City, but never has it been so apparent than on the blocks between St. Marks and Broadway in the Village. There is a Starbucks in a Barnes and Nobles, and a Starbucks on either side of Astor Pl. Come and get your java fix. Then get it again. And again.

N R to 8th St.-NYU, 6 to Astor Pl.

Most Books Per Square Foot

"8 Miles of Books" was the Strand's old boast, but a new floor has recently upgraded it to 16; it's the most dizzying, disorganized sprawl of used and new books you'll ever see. As long as you're not looking for anything specific, this is a penny-pinching bibliophile's paradise.

828 Broadway (bet. 12th and 13th Sts.), (212) 473-1452. L N R W 4 5 6 to 14th St.-Union Sq.

Best Medium Rare

The bistro burger at Corner Bistro is perfectly done, charred outside, moist inside, dressed up with cheese and bacon. The prices are great, the beer's good – and, of course, it takes fierce struggle to get a table. But even the lines here are a Village institution.

331 4th St. (near Horatio St.), (212) 242-9502. A C E L to W. 4th St.

Fanciest Dawn Dinner

Milou Café's menu, from warm red cabbage salad with goat cheese on, is available round the clock – perfect for gourmet vampires.

92 Seventh Ave. South (bet. Bleecker and Grove Sts.), (212) 414-9824. 1 to Christopher St.

Gramercy

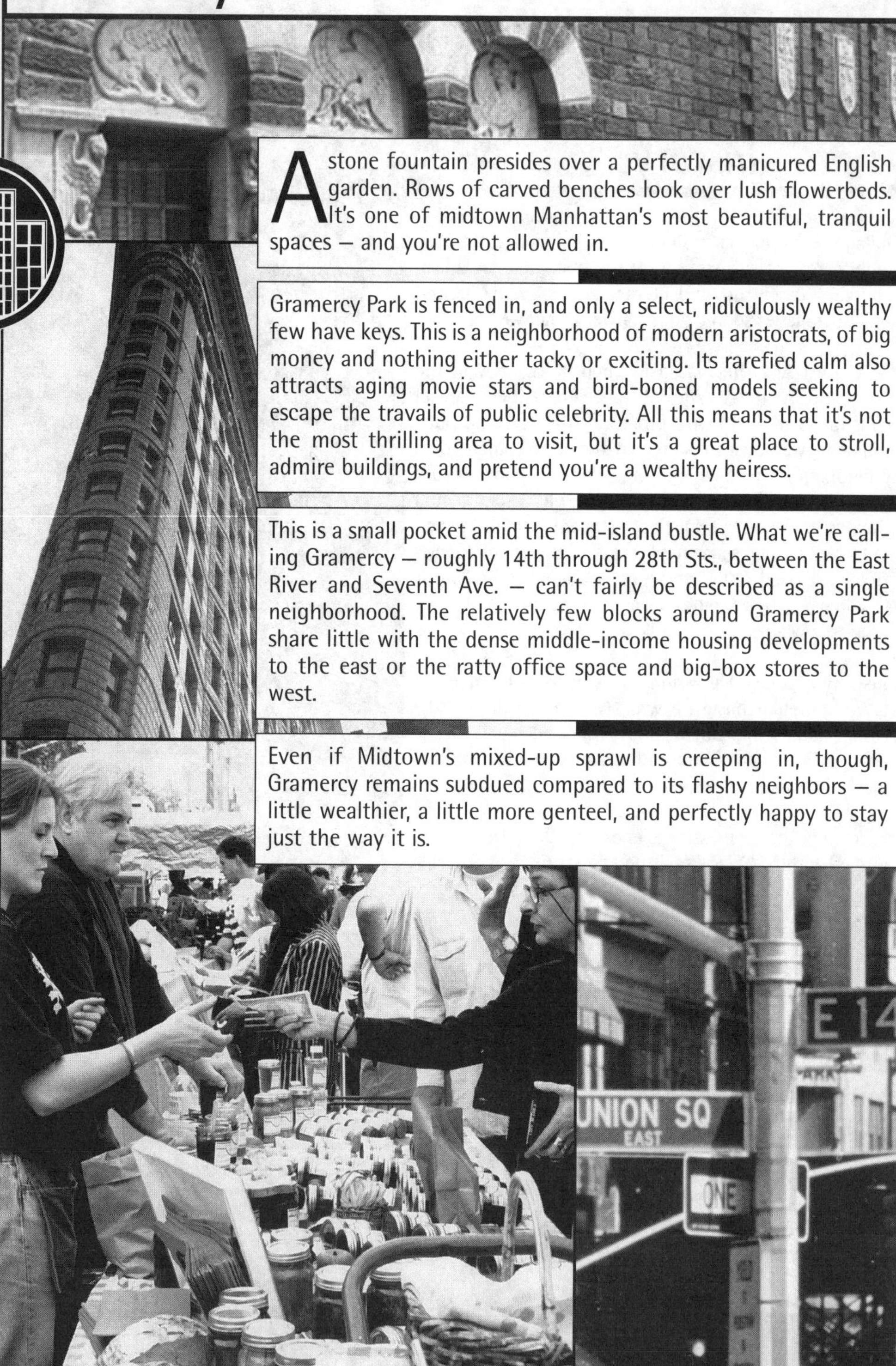

A stone fountain presides over a perfectly manicured English garden. Rows of carved benches look over lush flowerbeds. It's one of midtown Manhattan's most beautiful, tranquil spaces – and you're not allowed in.

Gramercy Park is fenced in, and only a select, ridiculously wealthy few have keys. This is a neighborhood of modern aristocrats, of big money and nothing either tacky or exciting. Its rarefied calm also attracts aging movie stars and bird-boned models seeking to escape the travails of public celebrity. All this means that it's not the most thrilling area to visit, but it's a great place to stroll, admire buildings, and pretend you're a wealthy heiress.

This is a small pocket amid the mid-island bustle. What we're calling Gramercy – roughly 14th through 28th Sts., between the East River and Seventh Ave. – can't fairly be described as a single neighborhood. The relatively few blocks around Gramercy Park share little with the dense middle-income housing developments to the east or the ratty office space and big-box stores to the west.

Even if Midtown's mixed-up sprawl is creeping in, though, Gramercy remains subdued compared to its flashy neighbors – a little wealthier, a little more genteel, and perfectly happy to stay just the way it is.

history

Although originally a swamp, the area surrounding Gramercy Park has long been one of the most fashionable addresses in New York City. Thanks to its intellectual residents at the turn of the century, the historical Gramercy has been called an "American Bloomsbury." Past residents include James Harper, founder of the Harper Collins publishing house, Theodore Roosevelt, Edith Wharton, Eugene O'Neill, and O. Henry, who wrote *The Gift of the Magi* in Pete's Tavern, a local restaurant.

In 1831, Samuel Ruggles, longtime trustee of Columbia College, drained the swamp and laid out 66 English-style lots around a private park – Gramercy Park. In the 1920s, the development of high-rise apartment buildings, the extension of the Third Avenue elevated train, and the onset of the Depression meant that an address around Gramercy Park was no longer as desirable as it once was. The neighborhood's majestic mansions crumbled a bit, and the turn-of-the-century elite shopping mecca dubbed Ladies' Mile became a "temple of love" after an influx of brothels. On the heels of a capital flight came a vibrant population of lefty artists, including Andy Warhol, who installed his legendary Factory here. Gramercy became an enclave for groups of rebels, ranging in identity from communists to junkie divas, and heavy drug traffic and drifters plagued the area.

[local gems]

Name that Does Not Actually Say What It Is

Although Gramercy Tavern may sound like the name of a pub, it is in fact one of the best restaurants in New York City, and has been for years. Serving New American standards, Gramercy Tavern is a great place to check out and be checked out by the many famous faces who may stroll through its doors.

42 E. 20th St., (212) 477-0777. Ⓝ Ⓡ *to 23rd St.*

Highest Pie in the Sky

While 21 stories barely constitutes a skyscraper in modern New York City, this triangular office building that stands at the intersection of Fifth Ave. and Broadway impressed turn-of-the-century tourists. The limestone façade and steel frame of the building is seen by many as representing the dawn of the skyscraper era. The Flatiron Building has also been the star of several movies, the most recent being , where it stood in as the office building of Peter Parker's *Daily Bugle*.

175 Fifth Ave. (bet. 23rd St. and Broadway). Ⓝ Ⓡ *to 23rd St.*

Best Model-Spotting

Is she six feet or taller? Thin enough to look easily breakable? Clad in at least one ridiculous item of clothing? Congratulations – you've found a model. Walk down Park Ave. south from 23rd St. to Union Square during the afternoon and you should spot at least a couple.

⑥ *to 23rd St.*

Most Urban Jungle

At Fifth Ave. at 28th St. is your usual vaguely-ratty office district. At Sixth Ave., it's the Amazon. This is the Flower District, especially concentrated on 28th between Sixth and Seventh, where the dozens of tiny flower shops crowded in beside each other fill the sidewalk with their wares during the day. It's mostly a wholesale operation, and it's at its most beautiful in the early mornings, as decorators and shopowners hoist boxes of roses and violets above their heads as they sashay across the sidewalks.

① *to 28th St.*

Chelsea

Down by the river early on a Chelsea morning, all one hears is the whoosh of cars on the West Side Highway. The brick warehouses and car-repair shops that line the street are shuttered. A couple of taxis cruise without a fare in sight.

Then the old warehouse gates slide open, revealing white wall after gleaming white gallery wall. Chelsea is the most recent of Manhattan's has-been industrial neighborhoods to be transformed by a wave of artists. As SoHo became more and more expensive, studio-dwellers fled to the massive empty warehouses near the piers of this former shipping district. Not long after the artists' arrival came art dealers, gallery openings, and rows of chic restaurants and bars. In little more than a decade, Chelsea changed completely.

This is a pattern that's been repeated in many now-arty neighborhoods, from SoHo to Brooklyn's Williamsburg and DUMBO. But there's a twist in Chelsea's story. During its reconfiguration, it became home to a significant chunk of Manhattan's gay population. It's now home to a big, ostentatious queer scene, and the buff, beautiful Chelsea Boy has become an icon. Chelsea Girls are in rather shorter supply; the Chelsea male gay community has always dwarfed the lesbian one.

As it travels the well-worn path of gentrification, Chelsea is calming down. Families are moving in, as are big chain stores and developments like the huge Chelsea Piers sports complex on 23rd St. at the river *(212) 336-6666,* C E *to 23rd St.*). But this also means that Chelsea's residential blocks are some of the quietest and prettiest south of Central Park. Manhattan's story over the last 20 years has been one of new wealth, and Chelsea has worn its money well.

history

Number one on any self-respecting tour of New York's sordid past must be The Chelsea Hotel. Opened in 1884, on 23rd St. between Seventh and Eighth Aves., it continues to bask in its well-earned rep as an underground mecca for some of the city's more interesting visitors.

Back in 1912, survivors from the Titanic spent a night here, but their brief stay has nothing on some of the hotel's more long-term company. This is where Welsh poet Dylan Thomas spent his days – before he had more than a few too many at Greenwich Village's White Horse Tavern and died of alcohol poisoning. Leonard Cohen, Mark Twain, Tom Wolfe, O. Henry, and Arthur C. Clarke all lived here. It's trashy, Benzedrine-riddled vibe was immortalized by Andy Warhol's film *Chelsea Girls*.

One of the hotel's most notorious moments of celebrity history came when ex-Sex Pistol Sid Vicious and his girlfriend Nancy Spungen forked over the deposit for a room key back in 1978. Vicious was always the most unhinged (and un-talented) of the Sex Pistols. After the Sex Pistols broke up, Vicious found himself at loose ends, with a mounting heroin addiction.

On October 12, 1978, Nancy was found dead in her room at the Chelsea Hotel. She had been stabbed several times in the stomach. There were no witnesses; Vicious looked the likely – and only – suspect, but he never confessed to the murder. Two months later – out on bail for knifing Patti Smith's brother in a bar brawl – he died of a drug overdose.

[local *gems*]

Most Hip Galleries

Chelsea has long been known for being the New York home to many up-and-coming artists. The area includes tons of interesting art shows. Recent exhibitions have included a display of human and bodily oddities, as well as an exhibit about narrative figural art and it's relation to human fear and suffering.
535 W. 20th St. (bet. Tenth and Eleventh Aves.), (212) 929-0500. A C E *to 23rd St.*

Most Peaceful Chelsea Experience

Had enough of all the buff bods strolling around Chelsea? Need some time to read the new Augusten Burroughs book or peruse the latest issue of *Vogue*? If so, then head down to the General Theological Seminary's greenery and read amongst other like-minded individuals.
Ninth Ave. at 20th St. C E *to 23rd St.*

Most Beautiful Post Office

This astonishing example of the McKim, Mead, and White architectural firm still stands strong right near Penn Station. Be sure to admire the strong columns as the passersby whisk around you. The Post Office must hold a place in every American's heart for bearing the famous postal worker's slogan known to every school child.
Eighth Ave. at 30th St. A C E 1 2 3 *to Penn Station-34th St.*

Most Brownie for Your Buck

Taylor's Prepared Food and Bakeshop serves brownies the size of Buicks. For under five dollars, it's a cheap – if not exactly healthy – meal. Big deal, so it's a million calories? You only live once.
228 West 18th St. (bet. Seventh and Eighth Aves.), (212) 378-2895. 1 *to 18th St.*

Most Fabulous Coffee

The Day-Glo colors and paisley patterns at Big Cup Tea and Coffee might recall the '60s, but the very buff, short-coiffed gay male clientele is pure '90s. Nurse an iced tea on one of the comfy couches behind the gigantic windows and write those haikus the world is dying to hear.
228 Eighth Ave. (bet. 21st and 22nd Sts.), (212) 206-0059. C E *to 23rd St.*

Midtown

If New York is a cathedral of consumption, Midtown is the holy of holies.

Like no other place in the world, Midtown offers just about every pleasure that can be bought – and some that can't – from the vulgar to the surreal: the gleaming lights of Broadway, the gaudiness of Times Square, the sterile beauty of Rockefeller Center, and countless hotels, bars, and restaurants that cover the spectrum from glamorous to grungy. Throw in three large concert halls, labyrinthine department stores, three major bus and train terminals, and dozens of corporate headquarters, and you have an idea of what Frank Sinatra was singing about: make it here and you'll make it anywhere, since a cab to "anywhere" is just five bucks.

Midtown isn't a pretty neighborhood. Most of it is devoted to office space, and for block after dirty block, identical hulking towers cast their shadows over streets of sad little shops and lunch counters. In the more traveled areas, particularly Times Square, the grinning, flashing ugliness can be as crushing as it is exciting.

In its humming, grinding heart, Midtown isn't somewhere where you'd want to live, and few people do. To find homes here, you need to head outward, toward the rivers. On the Hudson side, Clinton or Hell's Kitchen – residents use both names interchangeably, though as you might expect realtors prefer the former – is mostly low-rise and relatively working-class, though a wealthier crowd has recently been moving. As the name attests, this was once a boiling, violent center of Irish and Italian gangs. Against the East River, Murray Hill is a markedly more patrician neighborhood, where the Morgans and Havemeyers once supped at each others' brownstones.

But Midtown doesn't care much about those who live along its flanks. It is a destination, not a home, somewhere that only wealth can live comfortably. The postmodern monoliths of Fortune 500 companies, the stately grandeur of Grand Central Station, the glitz of Bergdorf's: somewhere among these icons lies the essence of Midtown. A neighborhood by convenience, the belt that holds the city together, Midtown keeps the wheels of consumption moving as nowhere else in New York does.

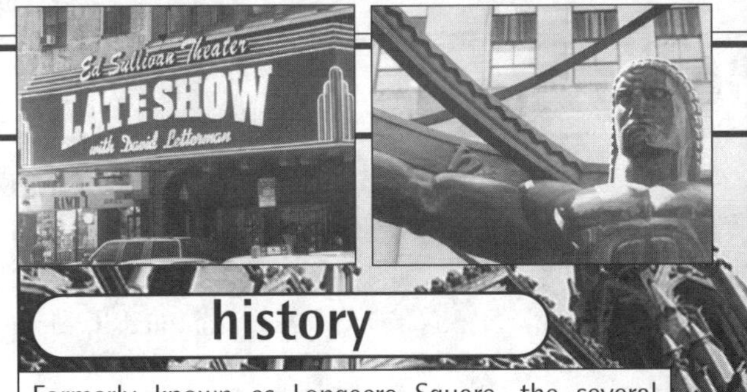

history

Formerly known as Longacre Square, the several blocks which now comprise Times Square have long been held in the American imagination as a hotbed of vice. Turn-of-the-century "silk hat" brothels first brought carriages and cabs into the area for quite a different reason than to visit the Astors, who maintained the neighborhood's exclusivity until the 1890s. A few years later, the *New York Times* erected a new building on 43rd St., and the square was renamed. In commemoration, the *Times* hosted a New Year's Eve gala, complete with the famous ball drop over which Dick Clark now presides.

During the Depression, the theaters that had popped up before World War I became cheap "grinder" houses, establishing the association between Times Square and pornographic film. Unemployed men lining 42nd St. turned to prostitution as a means of income, contributing to the increase in commercialized sex.

World War II disrupted theater production and further developed the area's more sordid entertainment as servicemen on leave made Times Square a mecca for prostitutes and live nude revues. During the following decades, whole blocks near Times Square were lined with naked neon women, until in the early '90s the city and the Disney Corporation scrubbed the area clean, kicking out the sex stores and installing chain stores. This government-sanctioned cleansing has led to comments such as that of columnist and longtime city resident Fran Liebowitz: "I didn't move to New York at the age of 17 because it was clean. I moved here because it was interesting. Now, it's less interesting."

[local *gems*]

Most Public Sweet Nothings

Take a friend to Grand Central Terminal. Go to the main entrance of the Oyster Bar. Nearby, two arches form a four-cornered dome. Stand your accomplice at one of the corners, face to the wall, and walk to the diagonally opposite corner. You'll be able to hear each others' whispers with startling clarity; passersby undoubtably will think you're crazy.

S 4 5 6 7 *to Grand Central.*

Most Typically New York Experience

Although this may seem boring to the hardened tourist, one must be sure to check out Times Square when staying in the city. The area has undergone a drastic transformation within the last ten years alone, and who knows how long this particular incarnation will last. Once an area that brought to mind neon signs with several X's in the titles, Times Square is currently a hub of wholesome family fun, suitable for all ages.

A C E N R W S 1 2 3 7 *to Times Sq-42nd St.*

Most "Sea"-sonably Fun Experience

Marvel at the ingenuity of the masters of warfare at the Intrepid Sea Air Space Museum. The Intrepid was a World War II aircraft carrier, and is now currently parked on the Hudson River, next to the Westside Highway. There are many military heirlooms on display at the museum, and even a stand that lets you purchase your own personal dog-tag.

Pier 86, 46th St. and Twelfth Ave., (212) 245-0072

Most Convenient Concert

It's always a party inside the Times Square subway down near the platform for the Grand Central shuttle: the MTA gives the space over to loud, lively, and talented musicians and performers. The hip-hop dancers are especially worth seeing.

A C E N R W S 1 2 3 7 *to 42nd St.-Times Sq.*

Ritziest Antiques

Christie's, the august British auction house, puts most about-to-be-auctioned items out for free public viewing. Almost as good as a museum, but bite-sized.

20 Rockefeller Plaza (bet. 48th and 49th Sts.), (212) 636-2000. B D F V *to 47th St.*

Upper East Side

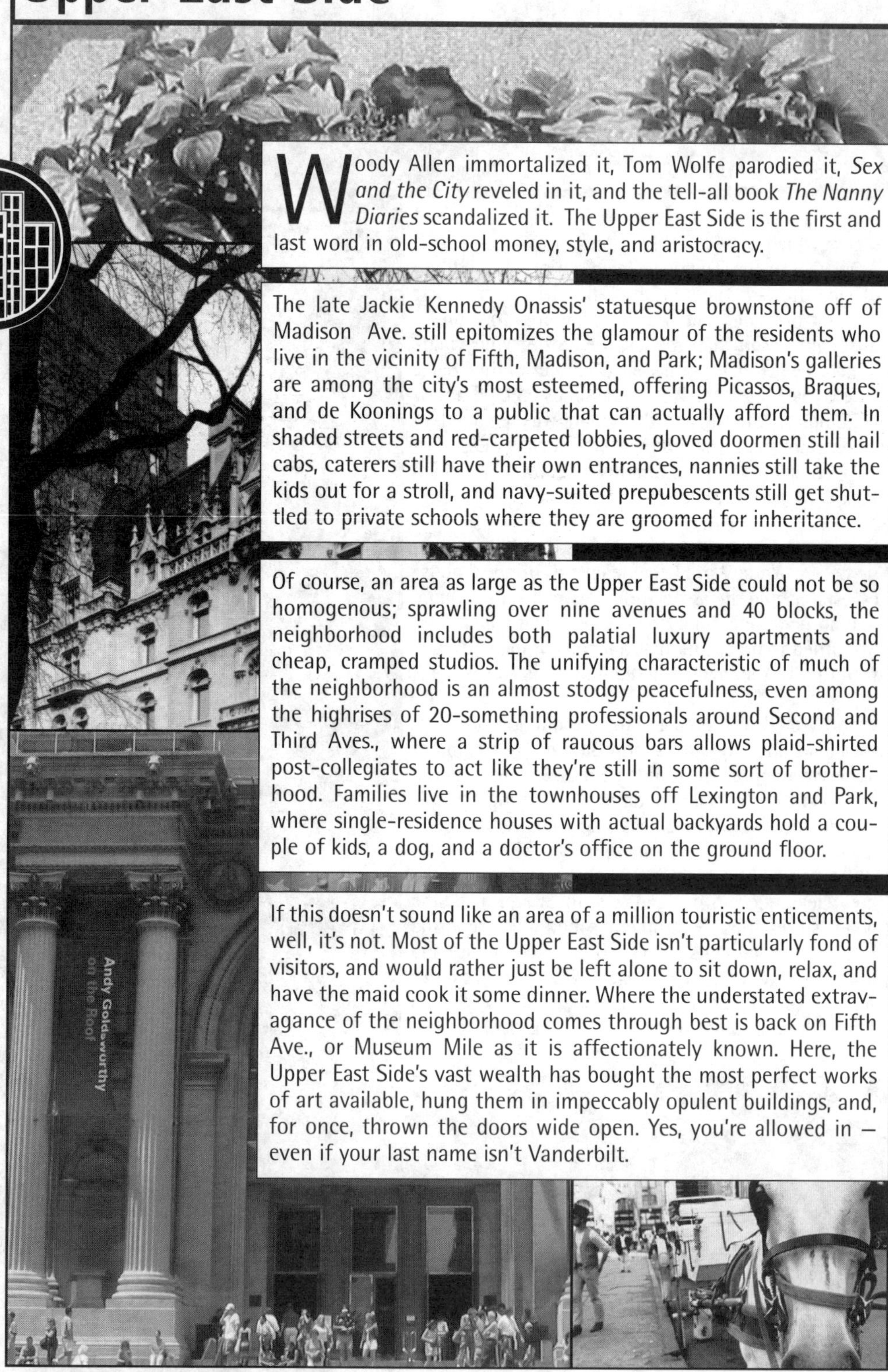

Woody Allen immortalized it, Tom Wolfe parodied it, *Sex and the City* reveled in it, and the tell-all book *The Nanny Diaries* scandalized it. The Upper East Side is the first and last word in old-school money, style, and aristocracy.

The late Jackie Kennedy Onassis' statuesque brownstone off of Madison Ave. still epitomizes the glamour of the residents who live in the vicinity of Fifth, Madison, and Park; Madison's galleries are among the city's most esteemed, offering Picassos, Braques, and de Koonings to a public that can actually afford them. In shaded streets and red-carpeted lobbies, gloved doormen still hail cabs, caterers still have their own entrances, nannies still take the kids out for a stroll, and navy-suited prepubescents still get shuttled to private schools where they are groomed for inheritance.

Of course, an area as large as the Upper East Side could not be so homogenous; sprawling over nine avenues and 40 blocks, the neighborhood includes both palatial luxury apartments and cheap, cramped studios. The unifying characteristic of much of the neighborhood is an almost stodgy peacefulness, even among the highrises of 20-something professionals around Second and Third Aves., where a strip of raucous bars allows plaid-shirted post-collegiates to act like they're still in some sort of brotherhood. Families live in the townhouses off Lexington and Park, where single-residence houses with actual backyards hold a couple of kids, a dog, and a doctor's office on the ground floor.

If this doesn't sound like an area of a million touristic enticements, well, it's not. Most of the Upper East Side isn't particularly fond of visitors, and would rather just be left alone to sit down, relax, and have the maid cook it some dinner. Where the understated extravagance of the neighborhood comes through best is back on Fifth Ave., or Museum Mile as it is affectionately known. Here, the Upper East Side's vast wealth has bought the most perfect works of art available, hung them in impeccably opulent buildings, and, for once, thrown the doors wide open. Yes, you're allowed in — even if your last name isn't Vanderbilt.

history

As with most of upper Manhattan, there wasn't much to see until Central Park opened to the public in the 1860s. Back then, omnibuses and horsecars transported parkgoers uptown, where much of the landscape resembled an affluent countryside.

The eastern section of the region developed quickly as the Second and Third Ave. elevated lines, completed in 1879, eased transportation between the urban center and the outlying regions, attracting Irish and German immigrants who settled in the brownstones and tenements lining the streets of an area that came to be known as Yorkville.

The development that would earn the Upper East Side its elite reputation, however, was construction to the west along what would become the luxurious Fifth, Madison, and Park Aves. From Astor to Tiffany, New York's wealthiest barons erected mansion after mansion facing the new park. Although most were later demolished, the Carnegie and Frick mansions remain as the Cooper-Hewitt Museum and the Frick Collection, respectively.

Park Avenue's reputation as a glamorous address developed after the New York Central Railroad buried its above-ground tracks and elegant apartment buildings lined the newly-cleared blocks. In the 20th century, the Upper East Side cemented its reputation for both ethnic diversity and upscale living. Even the former working-class, immigrant-packed Yorkville area became desirable after the demolition of the Third Ave. elevated line in 1956 and the construction of dozens of high-rise buildings.

[local *gems*]

Most Independent Bookstore

One of four locations scattered throughout the city, the Upper East Side's Shakespeare & Co. bookstore offers a diverse selection of books along with the soul of an independently run business that you won't find at your Barnes and Nobles. Come and enjoy the relaxed atmosphere while perusing some of the naughtier books found in the sex section.
939 Lexington Ave. (bet. 68th and 69th Sts.), (212) 570-0201. 6 *to 68th St.-Hunter Ave.*

Best Expensive Dessert

Famous for both their frozen hot chocolate and Garden of Eden ambiance is Serendipity III. After being featured in the John Cusack vehicle *Serendipity*, the popularity of the already famous dessert haven skyrocketed. Come on any night and watch couples gaze lovingly at each other before scarfing down massive desserts.
225 E. 60th St., (212) 838-3531. F N R W 4 5 6 *to 59th St.-Lexington Ave.*

Cheapest Chic Accessories

So maybe you can't afford to buy a purse on Madison Ave. That shouldn't stop you from accessorizing at Tender Buttons, where the selection numbers in the thousands and the materials range from silver to leather to crystal to good old plastic.
143 E. 62nd St. (bet. Lexington and Third Aves.), (212) 758-7004. F N R W 4 5 6 *to 59th St.*

Most Democratic Admissions

Most of Museum Mile has at least one "pay what you wish" night per week, and if getting in for free is your wish, it's their command. Schedules change, so look at museum web sites for details. At the Met, tickets are always "suggested admission," and it's a suggestion the penniless are free to decline.

Best Park View

During the summer, the roof garden at the Met puts you on top of Central Park's gorgeous green canopy. Sip some wine, listen in on the ritzy pick-up scene, or just bask in the view.
1000 Fifth Ave. (bet. 79th and 84th Sts.), (212) 535-7710. 4 5 6 *to 86th St.*

Upper West Side

On most nights, the Upper West Side's stretch of Broadway buzzes with activity, but its shine is amiable, unlike the garish lights of Midtown some 20 blocks away. The enormous illuminated Revlon Fountain at Lincoln Center reflects the glow of the complex's concrete buildings; taxis noisily make their way up and down the avenues, shuttling the uptown elite to Opening Night at the opera. Collegiate types from nearby Fordham Law School and academic outposts further north barhop along Amsterdam Ave., while those with more refined palates sample tortes and ladyfingers at the dessert cafes tucked away in side-street brownstones.

Nobody has ever mistaken the Upper West Side for the East Village. This is where young professionals get up at dawn to grab their bagel from H&H before catching the subway to work, where parents drop their kids off at the "progressive" private schools on West End Avenue, where writers jog in Central and Riverside Parks before sitting down at their desks. When Upper West Siders say they're going shopping, they're talking about groceries.

But this isn't an old-money neighborhood, a retreat for the secure and stagnant. Residents harbor dreams of fame and success, from investment bankers with freshly-drafted novels to activists certain that better days are to come. The Upper West Side has long been central to liberal, largely Jewish, intellectual life, and the new generation of parents retains a certain sensitivity to community spirit and a soft spot for post-hippie products with earnest labeling and anti-corporate pledges. The difference these days is that the journalists, academics, and activists have been joined by investment bankers and account executives who crave playpens and La-Z-Boys as much as they covet the upper rungs of the corporate ladder.

Urbane, ambitious singles also inhabit the slick apartment complexes of Broadway; their presence supports an active singles scene both in Amsterdam's bars and Barnes & Noble's cafe, both of which feel like a pre-planned mixer on weekend nights. Comfortable, and with an eye to community, the Upper West Side strives for that difficult balance between the mentality of an amiable small city and the sophistication of a massive metropolis.

history

It's hard to imagine now, but the Upper West Side was once viewed as a distant suburb of (what is now) downtown Manhattan. Before the completion of the Ninth Ave. elevated train in 1879, the area known as Bloomingdale was a green, largely undeveloped refuge from the crowded city. The famous West Side apartment complex, once the backdrop for Rosemary's Baby and the site of John Lennon's assassination, was christened The Dakota because residents felt it was so far away from the city's hub that it might as well have been out in the Dakotas.

Before the development of Frederick Law Olmsted's Central Park, from 1858 to 1873, what's now the Upper West Side was comprised of small, distinct villages, all of which operated independently of each other. The completion of the park spurred a wave of building, and, by the turn of the century, cultural institutions such as the American Museum of Natural History resided in the neighborhood. The real boom came after 1904, when the Interborough Rapid Transit subway – the first in the country – opened its first line, from Harlem to City Hall; a few years later, the Upper West Side finally felt like part of the city.

More ethnically diverse than its easterly neighbor, the area between Columbus and Amsterdam Aves. is still home to a Latino community. This part of the neighborhood underwent a cultural facelift of sorts in the 1960s when Lincoln Center was built. While people still debate the aesthetic merits of the Center, many arguing that it's an ugly blot on the landscape, few deny its contribution to the arts. Other architecture projects are in the works..

[local *gems*]

Most Popular Fountain

Be sure to check out Lincoln Center's incredibly famous fountain, which has been featured in such modern day classics as *The Producers* and *Muppets Take Manhattan.* Revel in the beauty that is the Metropolitan Opera House while you are there, and you may even get a glimpse at a celebrity or two walking by to get to their apartment.

1 to 66th St.-Lincoln Center.

Most Calories for Your Buck

Check out the Upper West Side's Krispy Kreme on your way to catch a show at the Metropolitan Opera House. This southern import is so delicious that it is a proven fact that a human being can not consume less than three at one time. Be sure to stop by when the donuts are fresh to get a real culinary experience. This chain epitomizes the notion that cheap is delicious.

1 2 3 to 72nd St.

Most Endearing Alleyway

On 94th St. between Broadway and West End is the gate to Pomander Walk, a private fairy tale of a street lined with miniature Tudor houses with little English gardens in front. A short wait should find you someone to let you through the gate; inside, it feels somewhere between a children's book and a sound stage.

Most Enduring Special

Through boom and bust, the pessimists at Gray's Papaya have kept up their Recession Special, which gives you two franks and a tropical drink for under three bucks.

2090 Broadway (bet. 71st and 72nd Sts.), (212) 799-0243. Open 24 hours. 1 2 3 to 72nd St.

Most Delectable Window Display

Zabar's, at Broadway and 80th St., and Citarella, at Broadway and 75th St., have shelves and shelves of food that you won't find at your neighborhood Safeway. Check out their olives, foreign pastries, cheese, and fish. Great for that Tuscan dinner you always wanted to make.

1 to 79th or 86th Sts.

Morningside Heights

In many ways, Morningside Heights is as removed from the hustle and bustle of Manhattan today as it was at the turn of the century, when the majority of the area was still farmland. Outside the perimeter of most city-dwellers' travels, the Heights is an anomalous territory. Geographically part of Harlem, Morningside is nevertheless mainly characterized by its ubiquitous throngs of college students, professors, and administrators at the several campuses located in the neighborhood, mixing the business of education with the otherwise restful quietude of a largely residential area.

This chunk of western Harlem was christened Morningside Heights with the arrival of Columbia University, St. Luke's-Roosevelt Hospital, and the Cathedral Church of St. John the Divine at the turn of the century; the area later became known as the "academic acropolis," since Barnard College, the Jewish Theological Seminary, Union Theological Seminary, Bank Street College of Education, and the Manhattan School of Music all call Morningside home.

With so many smaller communities within the larger academic one, a congenial air pervades the neighborhood, and even the many panhandlers who congregate around the rich kids from the 'burbs become familiar faces. Although cast-iron gates enclose most campuses, many schools support vigorous community service programs; however, the biggest changes effected by students are inadvertent and perhaps unwanted, as chains like Starbucks and Foot Locker push out the mom-and-pop stores that are so important to Morningside's small-town-in-a-big-city feeling. Columbia's massive expansion plans have made long-time residents irate, with many arguing that new buildings have created an unbecoming architectural schizophrenia, marring the neighborhood's landscape.

For the most part, the academic community has given Morningside its character, especially after Columbia drove out the remnants of Harlem below 110th St. These blocks of Amsterdam and Columbus, packed with bodegas and Spanish-speaking shops and restaurants, offer an alternative to the squeaky-clean offerings around Broadway. But a few blocks uptown, from 110th to 120th Sts. between Morningside and Riverside, bookbag-toting students clutch their coffee and cigarettes while they peruse book stands and dodge cars, oblivious to the distant skyscrapers and the not-so-distant projects that bookend their insular community.

history

The Battle of Harlem Heights took place here, around what's now 119th and Broadway, on September 16, 1776. That day, the Yanks pushed back the Brits, but – in a pattern that has repeated itself in music, art, and men's magazines ever since – soon abandoned the city to the British. The battlefields remained fields until 1818, when the Bloomingdale Asylum took up residence on the future campus of Columbia University and housed its director in Columbia's present-day Maison Française. The Leake and Watts Orphan Asylum took over the site in the 1840s only to follow Bloomingdale up to Westchester County in the 1890s.

Just before the turn of the century the area was still a backwater, but several big ideas were encouraged by the paving of area roads and the promise of subway accessibility. The Anglican Church began construction on the world's largest cathedral, St. John the Divine, and it remains unfinished to this day; its bizarre hybrid of architectural styles reflects the various visions of its several collaborators over a century.

Ulysses S. Grant and his wife were re-buried in Grant's Tomb, constructed in 1897, by which time Columbia was busily moving into its present location. Soon, it was joined by Barnard College and the Jewish and Union Theological Seminaries. Within 20 years, the modern institutions were all in place, and although the neighborhood is no longer an isolated backwater, reminders of its open fields, orphans, and lunatics linger on in its grassy campuses and its student bodies.

[local *gems*]

Most Filmed Campus

Come visit beautiful Columbia University to get a glimpse of the campus that has been featured in dozens of Hollywood flicks over the years. The site of both Peter Venkman's soliloquy at the end of which he decides to become a ghostbuster and Peter Parker's chastisement at the hands of a professor, the university offers a scenic campus that one would be remiss to miss.
1 to 116th St.-Columbia University.

Most Beatnik Bar

The West End is not only the bar where "Columbia had it's first beer," but is also the former hang-out of such Beatnik luminaries as Jack Kerouac, Allan Ginsberg, and Lucien Carr. Although the bar has changed over the past 60 years, the cool-vibe represented by any worthy Beatnik still resonates in it's hollow halls. Recently, the West End has gained national recognition by being named *Playboy's* "College Bar of the Month."
2911 Broadway (bet. 113th and 114th Sts.), (212) 662-8830. 1 to 116th St.-Columbia University.

Best Free Folk Music

Most Friday and Saturday nights, Postcrypt hosts a free folk-music and popcorn night in the basement of Columbia's St. Paul's Chapel. Artists from Ani DiFranco to Suzanne Vega have performed here. Performances start at 9 pm, but show up early: only 35 people are allowed into the small room.
Columbia Campus, near Amsterdam Ave. at 117th St., (212) 854-1953, www.postcrypt.org. 1 to 116th St.-Columbia University.

Most Intellectual Street Shopping

Forget the bookstores. Your wallet will be much happier if you fill your bookshelf from the used book tables on Broadway between 110th and 114th Sts. Sweet deals and great reading can be had here at any time.

Most Overwhelming Slice of Pizza

The jumbo slice at Koronet's is the Godzilla of the pizza world. Happily triple your cholesterol for only $2.75. Open late, so don't be deterred from coming after a night on the town.
2848 Broadway (bet. 110th and 111th Sts.), (212) 222-1566. 1 to 110th St.-Cathedral Parkway.

Harlem

In the collective imagination, Harlem has two identities: its glorious heritage as the intellectual, political, spiritual, and artistic capital of black America, and its tragic recent history as a community besieged by poverty, crime, drugs, racism, and political disempowerment. In truth, Harlem accommodates not only these images, but also many others in between. Today, Harlem absorbs not only the black population for which it is famous, but Cubans and Dominicans as well. Trying to balance the needs of the upwardly mobile with the realities of deeply-rooted poverty, Harlem is undergoing radical — and in some cases painful — economic and cultural transformations.

The largest neighborhood in all of Manhattan, stretching from the Hudson River and West Harlem to Spanish Harlem and the East River, Harlem's diversity is inscribed in its buildings and on its streets. Handsome rowhouses and brownstones, many beautifully restored and pristinely kept, lie next to others that are derelict and abandoned. Twelfth-generation African-Americans mingle with first-generation immigrants in both housing projects and historic, genteel brownstones along Striver's Row, Hamilton Heights, and Sugar Hill. Upscale restaurants, supper clubs, boutiques, and other small businesses are sprouting up amid fast-food joints, flea markets, thrift stores, and bodegas. Lush casitas and public gardens that function as neighborhood gathering places dot a landscape of crumbling tenement buildings.

Fortunately, through the efforts of both the city and native sons and daughters, Harlem is currently experiencing an economic and social resurgence, as successful locals return to rebuild it. Harlem's club scene in particular is experiencing a renaissance the likes of which it hasn't seen since the fifties, and sometimes it seems like a new boutique opens every week.

But regardless of whatever passing entertainment or guidebook attraction Harlem may boast, it is first and foremost a place where people live. In a neighborhood where people are truly neighborly, the words of Langston Hughes reverberate in the hearts of many: "Harlem is a place where I like to eat, sleep, drink, and be in love. I like to work, read, learn, and understand life."

history

In 1925, when Alain Locke edited *The New Negro*, an anthology of poetry and prose by up-and-coming black artists, he wrote, "I believe that the Negro's advantages and opportunities are greater in Harlem than in any other place in the country, and that Harlem will become the intellectual, cultural, and financial center for Negroes of the United States." Some believe that the Harlem Renaissance of the late 1920s proved Locke correct, but Harlem's population in the early part of that decade was by no means entirely black.

Many immigrants from Ireland and Germany initially settled around 125th St.; nonetheless, as more and more blacks moved into the area, whites began to leave. The combined effect of white flight and black migration from southern Manhattan, as well as other parts of the country, helped solidify the African-American presence in Harlem.

This new concentration of blacks spurred the Harlem Renaissance, as many wealthy Harlemites began entertaining and organizing the literary and social clubs that fostered authors and poets like Countee Cullen, Langston Hughes, and Zora Neale Hurston.

The devastation of the Depression sent the area spiraling into decline, and racial tensions erupted in several large-scale riots in 1943, 1964, 1968, and 1977.

Today, many of the most prominent leaders of the black community, like former mayor David Dinkins, still call Harlem home; perhaps for this reason Nelson Mandela has called Harlem "the Black capital of the world."

[local *gems*]

Jazziest Nightclub

The Cotton Club has been a Harlem legend since before you or your parents were born, and it's still swinging. The sight of many early jazz and bebop performances, the lounge was an important center during the Harlem Renaissance of the early 20th century. Show times vary widely, so be sure to call before visiting.
656 W. 125th St. (bet. Broadway and Riverdale Dr.), (212) 663-7980. ❶ *to 125th St.*

Most Elegant Uptown Houses

No visit to Harlem is complete without seeing Striver's Row, two blocks of some of the most beautiful houses in New York City. The first occupants of these houses were millionaires such as William Randolph Hearst. Since around the 1920s, the row has housed prominent doctors, lawyers, and entertainers, the so-called "strivers" of the Harlem community. Truly elegant architecture.
Bet. 138th and 139th Sts. ❷❸ *to 135th St.*

Best Market

La Marqueta – Spanish for "The Market" – is one of New York City's finest marketplaces. La Marqueta offers its customers a large selection of both African and Caribbean foods. Products range from bacalao (Dried salted codfish) to tropical fruits. As one local resident remarked, La Marqueta is "the best place for Spanish products at the best prices."
1607 Park Ave. ❻ *to 116th St.*

Most Meat on One Slice

Some of the best, and certainly the most overstuffed, pizza in the neighborhood is at Slice of Harlem. Brooklynites and Villagers might disagree, but many claim it's the best around.
308 Lenox Ave. (bet. 125th and 126th Sts.), (212) 426-7400. ❶❷❸ *to 125th St.*

Healthiest Harlem Hangout

Strictly Roots is perhaps the only vegetarian restaurant in a neighborhood otherwise deeply dedicated to meat. This Rasta establishment is the place to go if you're in the mood for meatless patties and other vegetarian versions of classic Jamaican foods. For a quick pick-me-up try their fresh-squeezed fruit and vegetable juices, and don't miss their homemade cakes.
2058 Adam Clayton Powell, Jr. Blvd. (at 123rd St.), (212) 864-8699. ❷❸ *to 125th St.*

Washington Heights

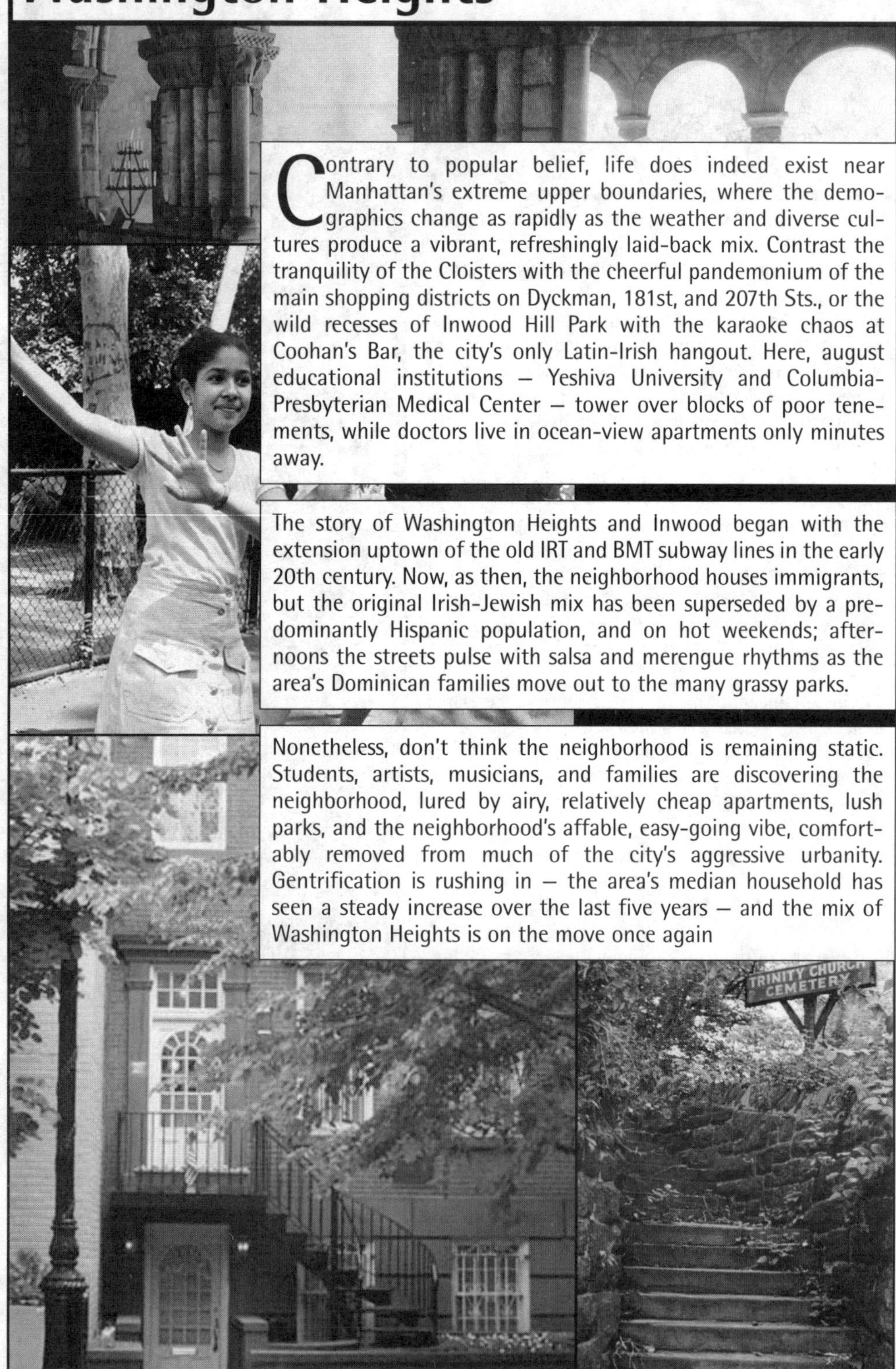

Contrary to popular belief, life does indeed exist near Manhattan's extreme upper boundaries, where the demographics change as rapidly as the weather and diverse cultures produce a vibrant, refreshingly laid-back mix. Contrast the tranquility of the Cloisters with the cheerful pandemonium of the main shopping districts on Dyckman, 181st, and 207th Sts., or the wild recesses of Inwood Hill Park with the karaoke chaos at Coohan's Bar, the city's only Latin-Irish hangout. Here, august educational institutions – Yeshiva University and Columbia-Presbyterian Medical Center – tower over blocks of poor tenements, while doctors live in ocean-view apartments only minutes away.

The story of Washington Heights and Inwood began with the extension uptown of the old IRT and BMT subway lines in the early 20th century. Now, as then, the neighborhood houses immigrants, but the original Irish-Jewish mix has been superseded by a predominantly Hispanic population, and on hot weekends; afternoons the streets pulse with salsa and merengue rhythms as the area's Dominican families move out to the many grassy parks.

Nonetheless, don't think the neighborhood is remaining static. Students, artists, musicians, and families are discovering the neighborhood, lured by airy, relatively cheap apartments, lush parks, and the neighborhood's affable, easy-going vibe, comfortably removed from much of the city's aggressive urbanity. Gentrification is rushing in – the area's median household has seen a steady increase over the last five years – and the mix of Washington Heights is on the move once again

history

After the IRT subway arrived at the beginning of the 20th century, Washington Heights developed rapidly: the Polo Grounds stadium, Presbyterian Hospital, and Yeshiva University all arose in the next decade, and many Greek and Irish immigrants made the area home.

As Jews fled European oppression, many settled in the Heights, and ethnic tensions erupted; right-wing groups and Irish gangs vandalized synagogues and assaulted young Jews during the '30s and '40s, and many immigrants became disenchanted with the neighborhood. By the '60s, the area was largely abandoned by the Irish and Jewish and became home to a predominantly African-American, Puerto Rican, and Cuban population. The 1965 assassination of Malcolm X in the Audubon Ballroom was simultaneously a reminder of earlier conflict and a harbinger of the crime wave that would hit the area in the '80s and '90s – accompanied, not surprisingly, by an upswing in drugs, poverty, and overcrowding.

Dominicans soon came to outnumber other residents during this period; by 1990, there were more Dominicans in Washington Heights than in any other community in the United States. District lines were eventually redrawn to offer residents better government representation, and in 1991 Guillermo Linares became the country's first elected official of Dominican descent. Still, such representation has done little to ease growing tension between residents and police; in the summer of 1992, after a police officer fatally shot a drug dealer, the neighborhood erupted in riots that lasted for several days.

[local *gems*]

Most New York Farm

The Dyckman Farmhouse Museum is a museum housed in a 1784 farm that educates viewers about life in New York back in the 18th century. The museum is an important reminder to all urbanites that the city did not simply spring from the soil fully grown, but is the product of centuries of slow development.
4881 Broadway (at 204th St.), (212) 394-9422. Ⓐ to 207th St.

Oldest City House

For a taste of the American Revolution, one should visit the Morris-Jumel Mansion, where General George Washington housed his Manhattan troops in October and September of 1776. The mansion is also Manhattan's oldest house, built in 1765. A beautiful taste of a long-gone time.
65 Jumel Terrace (at 160th St.), (212) 923-8008. Ⓒ to 163rd St.-Amsterdam Ave.

Most Junk for a Dollar

A subway fare uptown costs more than anything you'll find at Jack's 99¢ World, a well-stocked emporium of snacks and household items. Don't forget about the sales tax!
655 West 181st St. (bet. Broadway and St. Nicholas Ave.), (212) 981-1064. Cash Only. Ⓐ① to 181st St.

Most Delicious Vegetable Cake

The unbelievable carrot cake at Carrot Top Cafe makes it easy to follow mom's advice and eat all the veggies on your plate.
3931 Broadway (bet. 164th and 165th Sts.), (212) 927-4800. MC, V, AmEx. ① to 168th St.

Cheapest Salvadorean Food

Try the pupusas, a kind of quesadilla with pork, at El Ranchito. Their chicken is also tasty and moist, all for less than a $10 meal.
4129 Broadway (at W. 174th St.), (212) 928-0866. Ⓐ to 175th St.

The Bronx

Between the affluence of Riverdale and the poverty of Morrisania, the Sunday pace of Little Italy and the swift deluge of cars across the Major Deegan, the Bronx is a borough defined by contrasts. With acres of parkland, what many outsiders envision as a desert of concrete is in fact New York's second-greenest borough.

The unifying attitude among Bronx residents seems to be a sense of improvement and the promise of a better borough. Adolfo Carrion, Jr., the Bronx Borough President, observes: "I've seen areas go from looking like Berlin after the war to [...] a healthy working community. We're starting to change the fundamental culture of poverty which formerly imbued everything."

The South Bronx represents the closest thing to the glass-and-asphalt jungle which far-off Hollywood portrays. However, recent development has given the area a welcome boost. Omar Morales, a longtime resident of Southern Blvd., motions toward a housing block of new white siding and red shutters and explains: "That section used to be nothing but burned-out buildings."

The Fordham area is geographically and demographically the center which holds the Bronx together: Latino, black, and Afro-Caribbean cultures are integrated here, and merengue mixes with hip-hop to provide the soundtrack for the area's cultural convergence. Sprinkle in a few Fordham students from New England and Long Island and the mix is complete.

Tucked away west of Van Cortlandt Park lies Riverdale, one of New York's richest areas, where opulent mansions line graveled, winding streets. Popular images aside, the Bronx is as filled with different faces as any other borough.

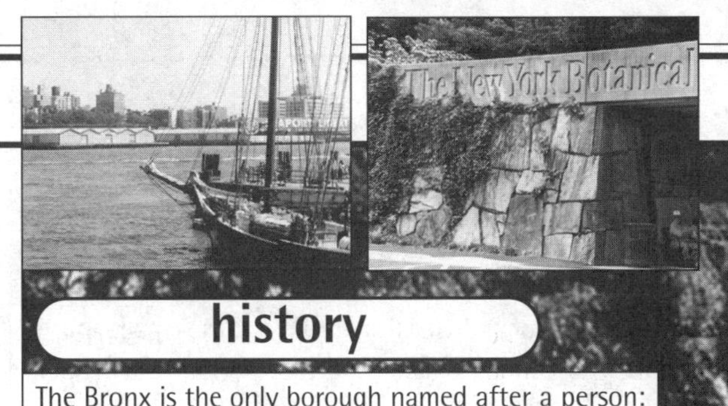

history

The Bronx is the only borough named after a person: its namesake is Jonas Bronck, a Swedish sailor who built a farmhouse when he cleared about 500 acres of land to the east. By 1700, Bronck's farm was destroyed and most of the land was split between four large manors: Pelham, Morrisania, Fordham and Phillipsburg.

The Bronx became famous for its landscaping and recreational attractions. In the late 19th century, the Grand Concourse was built, modeled after tree-lined French boulevards. In 1891, the New York Botanical Gardens opened, followed by the Bronx Zoo. At 2,764 acres, Pelham Bay Park is still the city's largest green area.

The borough was consolidated into New York City in 1898, and immigrants flocked there after 1904, when the first subway connecting the Bronx with Manhattan was completed. Droves of Yugoslavians, Armenians, and Italians arrived, as well as many Jews from Central and Eastern Europe. Business in the borough took off, with the Hub and Fordham Road becoming major shopping centers. Yankee Stadium was opened in 1923 and the Bronx Bombers soon became the world's most famous baseball team.

After World War II, an influx of poor people, displaced by so-called urban renewal in Manhattan, moved to the southern neighborhoods, and poverty grew in the South Bronx, allowing it to fall into a steep decline ever since.

[local *gems*]

Best Bronx Street Festival

Celebrate Bronx Week, a festival every year, is held in the beginning of the summer. Brace yourself for floats, parades, special events, and much neighborhood pride. *See www.streetfairsnyc.com, or www.ilovethebronx.com for details.*

Largest Park in the City

At 2700 acres, Pelham Bay Park is the largest park in New York City. Some features of the park include the Glover Rocks, a plaque commemorating a battle that took place there during the Revolutionary War, and Hunter Island, home to an ancient garden maze that sat next to former owner John Hunter's mansion.
6 to Pelham Bay Park.

Most Cultural Community Center

The cultural community center at Casa del Sol is indigenous to the South Bronx. It hosts the Adverse Possessions Gallery and Theatre as well as special events like the annual Mott Haven Summer Street Festival, and the People's Environmental Bike Tour of the South Bronx. It founded and continues to manage ten community gardens throughout the neighborhood.
672/674 E. 136th St. (bet. Cypress Ave. and Bruckner Blvds.), (718) 292-6443. Hours: M-Su, varied hours, call for information. 6 to Cypress Ave.

Best Bargain Hunting

One of the borough's oldest and most popular shopping strips, the Hub, is the ideal place for bargain hunting. Rumor has it that clothing designers will visit the Hub to discover the newest in urban street style, create clothes accordingly, and then market them to the suburbs.
Third Ave. (at E. 149th St.). 2 5 to Third Ave.-149th St.

Most Irish Bronx Experience

An Beal Bocht Café is Gaelic through and through, right down to its name. They sell groceries and serve up scrumptious Irish food in the daytime, and deliver pints of lager by night. Entertainment includes live Irish folk music and poetry readings which happen almost every night of the week.
445 W. 238th St. (bet. Greystone and Waldo Aves.), (718) 884-7127. Hours: M-Su 10am-4am. 1 to 238th St.

Brooklyn

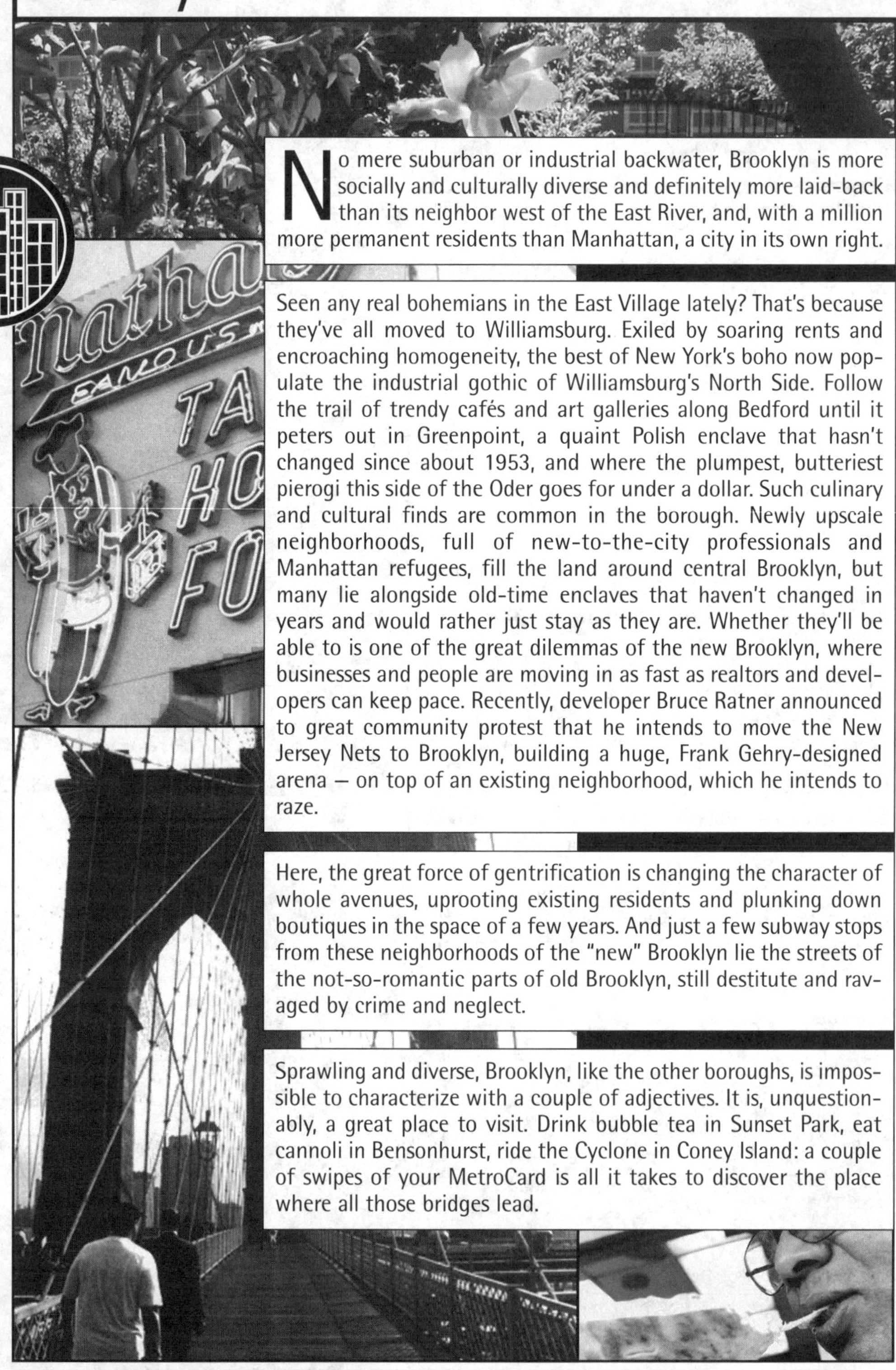

No mere suburban or industrial backwater, Brooklyn is more socially and culturally diverse and definitely more laid-back than its neighbor west of the East River, and, with a million more permanent residents than Manhattan, a city in its own right.

Seen any real bohemians in the East Village lately? That's because they've all moved to Williamsburg. Exiled by soaring rents and encroaching homogeneity, the best of New York's boho now populate the industrial gothic of Williamsburg's North Side. Follow the trail of trendy cafés and art galleries along Bedford until it peters out in Greenpoint, a quaint Polish enclave that hasn't changed since about 1953, and where the plumpest, butteriest pierogi this side of the Oder goes for under a dollar. Such culinary and cultural finds are common in the borough. Newly upscale neighborhoods, full of new-to-the-city professionals and Manhattan refugees, fill the land around central Brooklyn, but many lie alongside old-time enclaves that haven't changed in years and would rather just stay as they are. Whether they'll be able to is one of the great dilemmas of the new Brooklyn, where businesses and people are moving in as fast as realtors and developers can keep pace. Recently, developer Bruce Ratner announced to great community protest that he intends to move the New Jersey Nets to Brooklyn, building a huge, Frank Gehry-designed arena – on top of an existing neighborhood, which he intends to raze.

Here, the great force of gentrification is changing the character of whole avenues, uprooting existing residents and plunking down boutiques in the space of a few years. And just a few subway stops from these neighborhoods of the "new" Brooklyn lie the streets of the not-so-romantic parts of old Brooklyn, still destitute and ravaged by crime and neglect.

Sprawling and diverse, Brooklyn, like the other boroughs, is impossible to characterize with a couple of adjectives. It is, unquestionably, a great place to visit. Drink bubble tea in Sunset Park, eat cannoli in Bensonhurst, ride the Cyclone in Coney Island: a couple of swipes of your MetroCard is all it takes to discover the place where all those bridges lead.

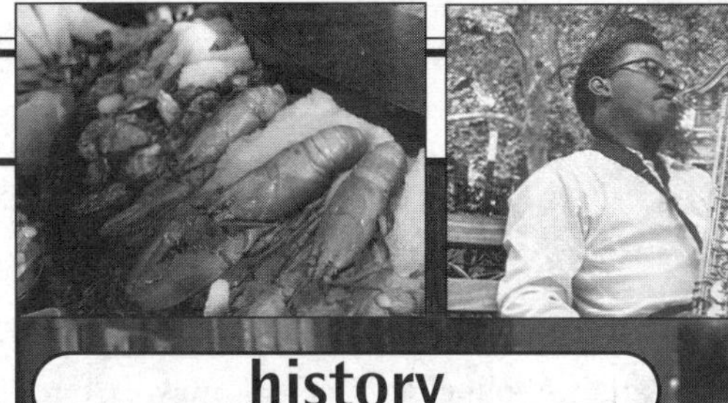

history

Like Manhattan, the borough of Brooklyn was originally settled by Dutch explorers. When the Dutch purchased land from the Canarsie Native Americans and linked together three villages in 1642, the new community called itself "Breuckelen," or "Broken Land."

Brooklyn remained rural until the 1800s, when large numbers of immigrants began to settle in the area. By 1814, Robert Fulton's steamboat service established regular transportation to Manhattan and helped develop stronger commercial links between the two island communities.

In 1833, Brooklyn was asked to join Manhattan in forming a city, but refused and incorporated itself as a separate city the next year. It remained an independent city even after the opening of the Brooklyn Bridge in 1883, an event which altered Brooklyn's social and economic geography more than any other. Brooklyn, then known as the "City of Churches," became a borough of Greater New York in 1898, a decision called "The Great Mistake" by writer Pete Hamill.

Brooklyn remains New York's most populous borough and maintains its own flavor and symbolic autonomy. Brooklyn's sense of self has nonetheless been subject to many vicissitudes, exemplified by the fate of the Dodgers, who won the World Series for the first time ever in 1955 and moved to Los Angeles two years later. Brooklyn is most fondly thought of as a hometown by the millions who have grown up here. No where else in the world will you find a pride quite like that exhibited by Brooklynites.

Least Meaty Meat Market

Catch a glimpse of the wonderous wheatgrass selection: the regular, free, and surprisingly well attended events include not only workshops on everything from forgiveness to colon health, but folk music and singles events. Just don't even think of wearing fur.

782 Union St. (bet. Sixth and Seventh Aves.) (718) 622-0560. (F) to Seventh Ave.

Most Old-School Brooklyn

The boardwalk and beaches of Coney Island are what most picture when thinking about historic Brooklyn, and it is still a fun, cheap getaway.

Coney Island, (D)(F)(W) to Stillwell Ave. *See Leisure Section*

[local *gems*]

Most Diverse Hangout

Riverside Park is a tiny park by the East River, situated in the shadow of the Domino Sugar Refinery. People from every segment of the local population hang out here during the warm part of the year when the park offers respite from the otherwise solidly concrete neighborhood.

Grand St. (at Kent Ave.), (L) to Bedford Ave.

Best Stoop Sales

The North Side section of Bedford Avenue offers an unofficial marketplace for clothes and other personal effects – on most weekends the sidewalks are filled with stoop sales. These provide a great opportunity to talk to strangers and spend money on other people's old photos, records, and clothing.

Bedford Ave. (around N. 7th St.). (L) to Bedford Ave.

Most Beautiful Brooklyn Brownstones

Carroll Gardens, long a staunch Italian neighborhood, was named for its great brownstones with their narrow, gated front yards. Smith St., between the Carroll and Bergen subway stops, is Brooklyn's hottest restaurant and bar strip, with tons of lauded French bistros and New American restaurants.

(F) to Carroll St.

Best Sicilian Slice in the City

L & B Pizzeria is one of those New York Pizzeria's that put the city on the culinary map. Putting the sauce on top of the cheese is not the only thing that makes the pizza unique. It's taste and consistency cannot be beat. Although in the winter, one can order a slice and sit inside, the real scene occurs during the summer time. Come with several friends, order a tray or half-tray and spumoni, and enjoy Brooklyn's local character.

(B) to 25th Ave., (N) to Ave. U

Best Way to Spend a Saturday

Head for one of many neighborhood streets for bargain shopping. All the name brand shoes and sportswear can be found here for considerably less than in the city. Knickerbocker Avenue and Graham Avenue in Bushwick are two good blocks to explore.

(M) to Knickerbocker Ave., (M) to Flushing Ave.

Queens

Subway lines snake above ground, jet engines growl before takeoff, and a mile-wide sea of yellow cabs idles, drivers waiting before they can speed off on the highway. Queens is a latter-day point of entry for people from all over the city and the world. Almost every immigrant comes through here, via LaGuardia or JFK, and in huge numbers, they stay.

Queens, home to over 100 different ethnic groups and over 120 linguistic groups, is one of the most ethnically diverse spots in the world. In neighborhood after neighborhood, new residents form tight communities with fellow travelers. Forest Hills and Kew Gardens have long been predominantly Jewish and Italian, while Woodside, Rockaway Beach, and Long Island City harbor house the Irish. Astoria is a little Greece, while Jamaica, Far Rockaway, and Elmhurst boast the borough's largest black population, and Jackson Heights supports communities of both Latin Americans and South Asians.

Unlike Brooklyn, a bona fide city with a strong sense of civic pride, Queens is a loosely-bound collection of different neighborhoods. Just as letters to Brooklyn must be addressed to Brooklyn, and not simply to New York, a birthday card to your aunt in Belle Harbor will be promptly lost unless "Belle Harbor" appears on the envelope.

Queens was and remains a suburb, without any great civic or municipal ambitions. Its basic demographic group is the family, large or small, and its basic interests are family interests. The eternal popularity of Queens to immigrants comes simply because it's a reasonably cheap and pleasant place to live, work, and play. Queens boasts the comforts of suburbia while retaining an urban consciousness; the pace of life is a little less hectic than that of Manhattan, and that's exactly how most people here want it.

history

When Queens was merged into New York in 1898, much of it was still fenced off into farms, and, in the eastern section of Queens, there was little aspiration to become a city. A non-binding referendum introduced to voters in 1894 found Flushing, Hempstead, and other outlying areas solidly opposed to consolidation. This lack of a distinct borough community was mitigated by the secession of far eastern areas toward Nassau County as well as increasing urbanization, but much of the original identity crisis remains today. By the '20s and '30s, Queens was beginning to develop its current character, with tree-lined rows of modest brick and wood-frame houses.

Queens was already developing when the 1939 World's Fair that solidified its role as New York's primary locale for recreation, arenas, and beautiful parks. Preparation for the Fair converted Flushing Meadows/Corona Park from a dumpsite to the city's second-largest landscaped recreation area. LaGuardia Airport (named after Mayor LaGuardia) and bridges were built, streets were widened and sports stadiums were constructed.

More peaceful than the ghettos of Manhattan, from the 1960s to the present day, Queens has become the borough of choice for the latest influx of immigrants: a place where newcomers can solidly establish themselves at arm's length from big-city pressures. By 1990, first-generation immigrants made up more than a third of the population of Queens, the greatest percentage in the five boroughs. Queens is also the most ethnically diverse borough, housing immigrants from dozens of foreign countries.

Stop into Sac's Pizza Place for some delicious thin crust pizza. Gourmands should also spend time shopping at the handful of ethnic delis that line this street.

7541 Broadway (at Jewel Ave.), (718) 204-5002. E F G R V to Forest Hills-71st Ave., then the Q65A.

Get Some Grub

Get on the Queens-bound R train, and ride it out to Steinway St. Be warned, the subway ride to Queens is notorious for making unexplained changes on weekends. Walk up the street to an inexpensive cafe and gorge on the cheap eats.

[local *gems*]

Best Pub Crawl

Rockaway Beach, the peninsula most people believe belongs to Brooklyn, is one of Queens' most diverse neighborhoods. The biggest presence is Irish, and this is one of the best pub-crawling districts you could hope for; the neighborhood houses at least 11 local bars.

A S *to 116th St.*

Best Outside Shopping

Austin St. has long been Queen's famous outdoor mall, housing a large selection of stores. Located right off of Queens Boulevard, the street starts hopping during the summer months when local youths crowd its pool halls and eateries, ready to enjoy a night out on the town.

E F G R V *to Forest Hills-71st Ave.*

Most Social Action in a Library

The Queens Borough Public Library isn't just for reading anymore; come see the mini-sized art gallery, or participate in a range of community-action programs. Makes you wish your old library was as socially conscious.

89-11 Merrick Blvd. (bet. 89th and 90th Sts.), (718) 990-0767 or (718) 990-0768.
E J Z *to Sutphin Blvd.-Archer Ave.*

Lounge with the Most Offerings

Cavó, a cool, local lounge offers dinner, drinking, and dancing. There are levels and seating arrangements to satisfy your every preference, even a pretty outdoor bar featuring tables with parasols. The food is good and cheap: "2 crepes, 6 bucks" boasts one regular. Expect a busier scene on the weekends, with a music selection encompassing American, Greek, and Arabic favorites.

4218 31st Ave., (718) 721-1001. N *to 31st St.*

Cheap Shopping

A field day for browsers, Butala Emporium, a colorful shop in Jackson Heights, offers everything from Sanskrit comic books to Indian jewelry, all at affordable prices. The varied selection exemplifies the unusual shopping offerings of Little India.

37-46 74th St., (718) 899-5590. 7 *to 74th St.- Broadway.*

Best Queens Pizza

Staten Island

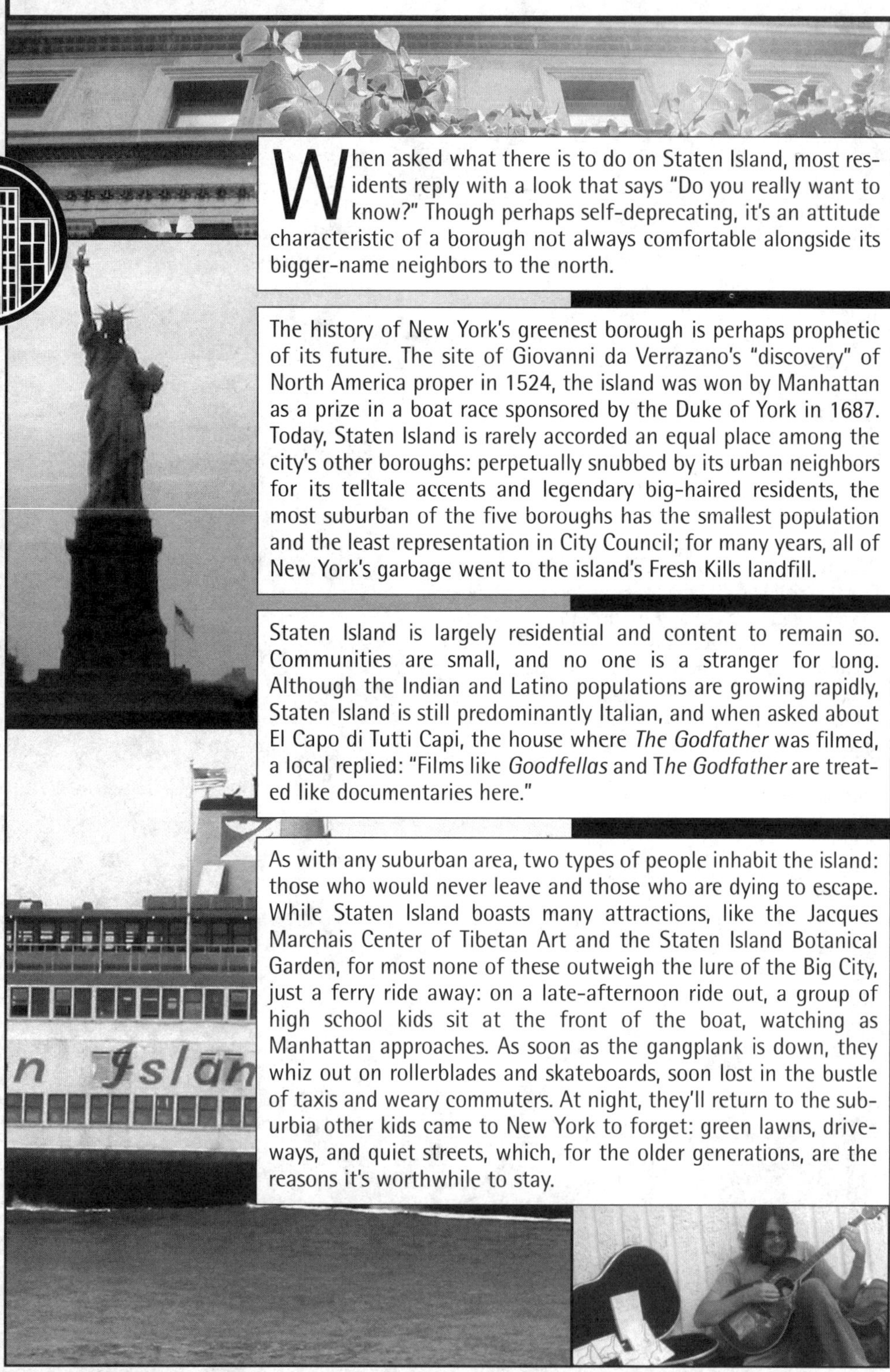

When asked what there is to do on Staten Island, most residents reply with a look that says "Do you really want to know?" Though perhaps self-deprecating, it's an attitude characteristic of a borough not always comfortable alongside its bigger-name neighbors to the north.

The history of New York's greenest borough is perhaps prophetic of its future. The site of Giovanni da Verrazano's "discovery" of North America proper in 1524, the island was won by Manhattan as a prize in a boat race sponsored by the Duke of York in 1687. Today, Staten Island is rarely accorded an equal place among the city's other boroughs: perpetually snubbed by its urban neighbors for its telltale accents and legendary big-haired residents, the most suburban of the five boroughs has the smallest population and the least representation in City Council; for many years, all of New York's garbage went to the island's Fresh Kills landfill.

Staten Island is largely residential and content to remain so. Communities are small, and no one is a stranger for long. Although the Indian and Latino populations are growing rapidly, Staten Island is still predominantly Italian, and when asked about El Capo di Tutti Capi, the house where *The Godfather* was filmed, a local replied: "Films like *Goodfellas* and *The Godfather* are treated like documentaries here."

As with any suburban area, two types of people inhabit the island: those who would never leave and those who are dying to escape. While Staten Island boasts many attractions, like the Jacques Marchais Center of Tibetan Art and the Staten Island Botanical Garden, for most none of these outweigh the lure of the Big City, just a ferry ride away: on a late-afternoon ride out, a group of high school kids sit at the front of the boat, watching as Manhattan approaches. As soon as the gangplank is down, they whiz out on rollerblades and skateboards, soon lost in the bustle of taxis and weary commuters. At night, they'll return to the suburbia other kids came to New York to forget: green lawns, driveways, and quiet streets, which, for the older generations, are the reasons it's worthwhile to stay.

history

Henry Hudson gave Staaten Eylandt its original name in 1609, when he sailed into the bay which now bears his name. In 1639, the Dutch opened Staten Island to colonization, but the area remained difficult to settle due to conflicts with native inhabitants; there were constant skirmishes, and the Dutch and Native Americans attempted to reach a peace agreement five times.

Staten Island became a province of New Jersey after the British took control of New York in 1664. From then on, the island was known as Richmond County, after the Duke of Richmond, son of Charles II.

Largely a secluded place for fishing and farming and reachable only by boat for years, Staten Island remained isolated until 1713, when a public ferry began carrying passengers to New York. Staten Island became officially incorporated into New York City in 1898. Staten Island's independent streak remains today, which may seem surprising since the 1964 construction of the Verrazano-Narrows bridge to Brooklyn. Fed up with garbage dumps filled largely with trash from elsewhere, the citizens of Richmond voted overwhelming in 1993 to secede from the city, though the vote was only symbolic. The Fresh Kills landfill was closed in 2002, but Staten Islanders remain uncertain participants in New York City.

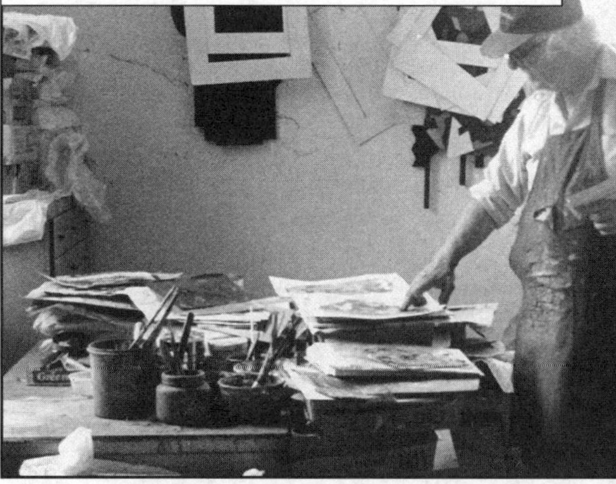

[local *gems*]

Cheapest Animals

An alternative to the always crowded Bronx Zoo, take a stroll through the Staten Island Zoo, Staten Island's smaller and cheaper counterpart. Wednesdays are free.

614 Broadway (bet. Clove Rd., Broadway, and Forest Ave.), (718) 442-3100, Cash Only, Admission: $2-$3, Hours: M-Su 10am-4:45pm.

Most Historic Town

The exhibit at Richmond Town documents local history and includes, among other historic buildings, the oldest surviving elementary school in America. Volunteers dress in 18th-century costume to re-enact everything from candle-making to war declarations.

441 Clarke Ave., (718) 351-1611. S74 from Whitehall Ferry.

Largest Landfill

Take a car to the Staten Island Expressway towards the bridge and get a glimpse of Fresh Kills Landfill, which is rumored to be visible from space.

Best Views from Ashore

Forget the Circle Line; the Staten Island Ferry is now absolutely free and also boasts excellent musicians below deck.

Docks at the foot of Whitehall St., (718) 806-6940. ① to South Ferry, ④⑤ to Bowling Green, or Ⓡ Ⓦ to Whitehall St.

Most Famous Ices

From the traditional lemon to more exotic flavors like honeydew, the ices at Ralph's Ices are the perfect warm weather treat.

501 Port Richmond Ave., (718) 273-3675, www.ralphsices.com. ① to South Ferry, Staten Island Ferry to S44.

New York City's *neighborhoods*

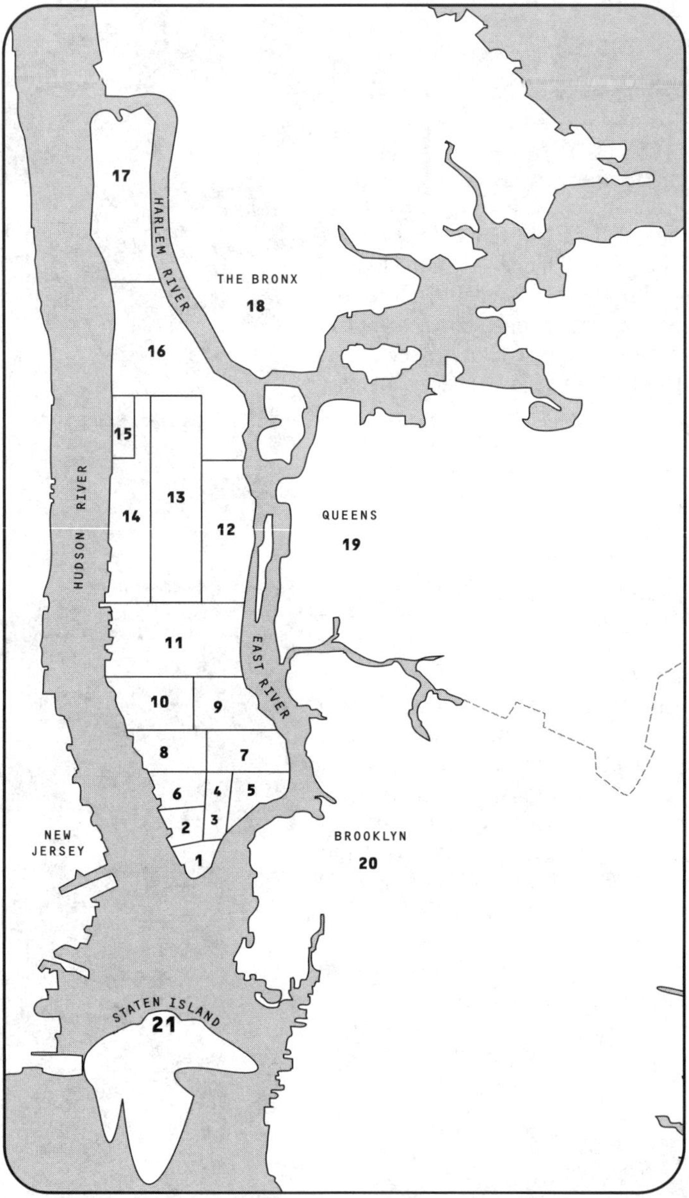

1. Financial District
2. TriBeCa
3. Chinatown
4. Little Italy
5. Lower East Side
6. SoHo
7. East Village
8. Greenwich Village
9. Gramercy
10. Chelsea
11. Midtown
12. Upper East Side
13. Central Park
14. Upper West Side
15. Morningside Heights
16. Harlem
17. Washington Heights
18. Bronx
19. Queens
20. Brooklyn
21. Staten Island

Shopping

shopping

shopping in

nyc

New York is Cloud Nine for shoppers. In this fast-paced fashion metropolis, anything is available, from anywhere, at any price. Despite the growing "mallification" of Manhattan specialty shops and boutiques, they continue to thrive alongside retail flagships. The greatest number of one-of-a-kind stores in the world are concentrated in this city.

As one of the epicenters of the fashion world, New York pleases all tastes and wallet sizes. Shopping in the city is like jumping into a private fantasy world, where you can try on new clothes and personas that will transform you.

Whatever the fetish, it can be indulged here. For gourmands, the food and spice shops are enough to make you salivate. The shoe selection is incredible. Sexy or even Goth-like lingerie? No problem. Film and comic-strip buffs will find stores that cater to their tastes. The world's music is on display here, and there is a book on every imaginable subject. The list of shops is exhaustive, and the entire spectrum can't be covered here, but be assured, New York always has exactly what you're looking for. Now all you have to do is learn how to track it down.

Each neighborhood, with its unique 'flavor,' provides diversity for New York's shoppers. Fifth Avenue has been nicknamed "Millionaire's Row," and the East Side represents the high end of shopping with its elegant windows and its flagship names. SoHo is Manhattan's young and hip end, while the Lower East Side embodies its bargain side. Chelsea displays the island's artsy trends. NoLita (North of Little Italy) is New York's up-and-comer: tiny boutiques have become big business in this cutting-edge shopping neighborhood. New York shopping never stops transforming to please its finicky and discriminating shopaholics. Shopping in New York is a worthwhile activity even when strapped for cash. Manhattan's greatest shopping lure is the notion of 'The Bargain.' After all, Loehmann's started in Brooklyn.

A city without borders, New York has plenty of shopping not confined by four walls. Open-air markets offer classic kitsch, bizarre Americana, and designer duds. Puppets sit next to Persian carpets, designer make-up next to sneakers with wheels, and D-cup bras swing in the breeze next to bamboo shoot planters. Give a market a little time, and it will present you with a find or two.

Vintage shops have been making a comeback in recent years, with many wealthy New Yorkers throwing away classic garments that stand the test of time. Many stores take these throw-offs and offer them to shoppers who are more than willing to mend a loose seam for the chance to wear Dior. Even Hollywood actresses shop at these stores, looking for that distinctive style that will set them apart at the next major event. Vintage shopping isn't always cheap, but it is always an adventure in style.

Like Carrie Bradshaw on *Sex and the City*, Rachel Green on *Friends*, or any of New York's most famous shoppers, you will likely find yourself making the occasional splurge. But when you're surrounded by endless options, moments of weakness are perfectly understandable and should be expected.

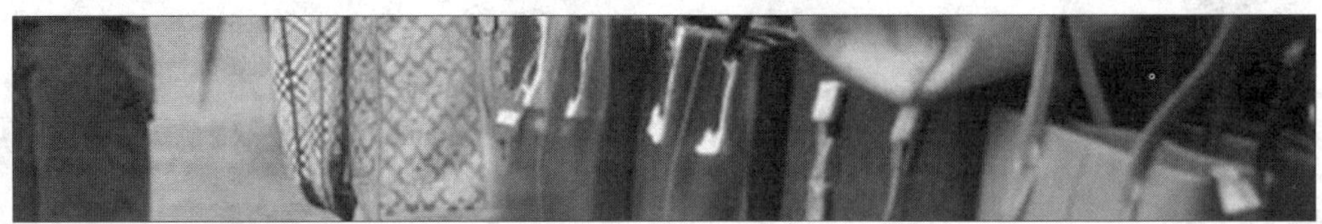

Upscale Vintage

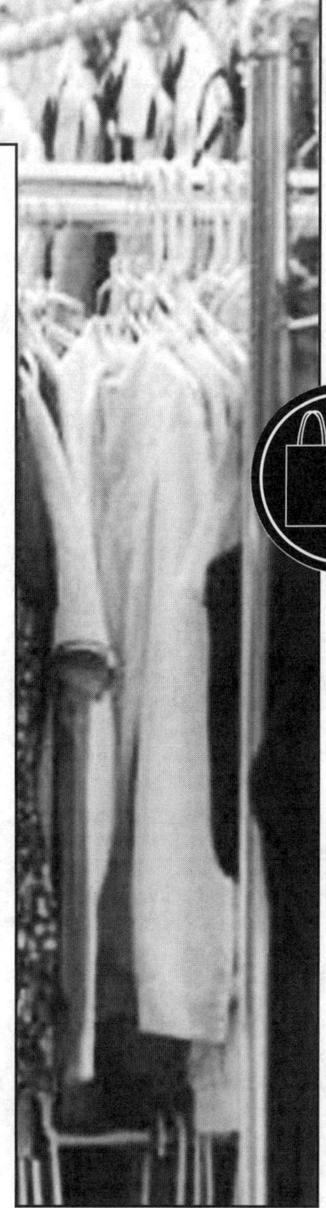

The appeal of vintage clothes shopping is not just about living on a budget or seeking a cool alternative to the numbing normalcy that crowds most closets. While those familiar with the ordeal of shuffling through rack after rack of skuzzy, stained tee-shirts and scratchy polyester sweaters love to brag about the thrill of finding that perfect leather jacket or scoring some under-priced haute label gear, there is an entire world of vintage beyond the swarms of annoying middle-schoolers and greasy hipsters that usually populate New York's used clothing stores.

Actually, to call the numerous upscale retail and consignment shops scattered throughout the city "used clothing stores" is totally misleading: these are couture boutiques on par with anything on Madison Avenue. In fact, because of the one-of-a-kind nature of the relics to be had, their sheer uniqueness and exclusivity cannot be matched even by the better known élite flagships. Though usually on the smaller side in terms of selection, these stores will tend to specialize in a specific era or type of dress, making them designer outposts from decades past. Often, there will be impeccably preserved styles from sometimes defunct but still important fashion houses. It wasn't always Gucci and Prada, or Dolce and Gabbana, there were plenty of names in the business making far more interesting prêt-à-porter that few people just discovering fashion would know anything about. This is what makes upscale vintage shops so exciting: they carry not just the labels that are just as pricy as when they first appeared, but also the more sporty and affordable creations for scooting around the city. You know, for those days when the red carpet is just too much trouble.

Slick day dresses in outrageous prints and all kinds of hip boots, voluptuous, sparkly sweaters, and cool '80s pumps are what you might find lining the walls of these stores. Typically there's little on the shelf for men, with an occasional rack in the back, usually holding mostly shirts with an ominously unisex appeal. But don't let that slow you down guys, grab an adventurous girlfriend and sneak a peek at what you're missing. Even if you know you're not going to get something you like, it's worth it just to see the well rounded collections.

The proprietors of these boutiques, such as Resurrection (*217 Mott St. at Prince St., (212) 625-1374. Hours: M-Sa 11am-7pm, Su 12pm-7pm. MC, V, AmEx, DC. N R to Prince St.*), which carries the most extreme, and exciting, styles; or David Owens (*154 Orchard St. at Stanton St. (212) 677-3301. Hours: M-Su 11am-7pm. MC, V, AmEx. F V to Second Ave.*), who has a great selection of leather and fur jackets alongside fun shoes; even the better known Marmalade and New York Vintage (for information, please see the listings) are experts in the field and cater to a clientele not afraid to make a statement with their apparel.

In fact, the shoppers who frequent these places might call their allegiance to these clothes a lifestyle choice. Apparently, once you've made the plunge into the past, there's no coming back.

Japan in New York

New York is famous for its multiculturalism, its waves of immigrants, and its vibrant ethnic enclaves, all of which give the city its cosmopolitan texture. Yet Japan, despite a ubiquitous presence at every level of New York's cultural life and its status as an epicenter of pop trendiness, lacks the kind of easily identifiable social cluster that other communities have achieved. Unlike the Greeks in Astoria, the Poles in Bay Ridge (and yes, the Chinese in Chinatown), the Japanese have managed to maintain an ethnic identity while integrating themselves into every part of the city. Without adhering to one single neighborhood, Japanese culture makes itself felt throughout New York in any number of ways, from tiny eateries on side streets known only to locals, to the grand Cherry Blossom Festival held every spring at the Brooklyn Botanical Gardens, which thousands attend.

Probably the most important institution of its kind, the Japan Society works hard to make sure this type of cross-cultural contact is not only always available, but also constantly evolving, with its Midtown offices hosting frequent lectures, gallery openings, and small exhibits about all things Japan. The land of the rising sun is also a big exporter of style to New York, and not just in the hordes of Japanese hipsters crowding the streets of the East Village or at the Japanese-run thrift store Tokyo Seven. The best of fashion from Japan struts its most important stuff through designer labels such as Yohji Yamamoto (*103 Grand St. at Mercer. (212) 966-9066. Hours: M-Sa 11am-7pm, Su 12pm-6pm. MC, V, AmEx, D. 1 2 3 to Canal St.*) who maintains a flagship store here in SoHo, or the avant-garde, and oddly French-titled, Comme des Garçons (*520 W. 22nd St. at Tenth Ave. (212) 604-9200. Hours: T-Sa 11am-7pm, Su 12pm-6pm. MC, V, AmEx, DC. C E to 23rd St.*) in Chelsea.

These are still the (literally) cutting edge labels that began making a splash in the '80s, and continue to do so with their confabulous takes on deconstructed (a.k.a. ripped up and inside-out) fashion. There is even a Manhattan chain of salons and spas, called Hoshi Coupe, which is Japanese owned and staffed by Japanese kids staying in the city for a while (all working hard to bring some Tokyo fashion into your life). Emerge ready to take on the world after a reenergizing massage with your new threads and hip 'do.

If clothes and hairstyles aren't your cup of green tea, there is always Manga, the celebrated home-grown graphic art from Japan. Not only has manga inspired numerous American rip-offs, infiltrating Saturday morning cartoons and inspiring Hollywood action flicks, but it still reigns at comic book stores throughout the boroughs, titillating adolescents as well as adults with its sometimes racy take on all topics from total fantasy to current politics. While manga can be found at any decent comic book store, if you search it out alongside some more intellectually nourishing fare, a great place to start looking would be downtown at the Japanese language Zakka Bookstore. The point is, there's no one single destination in New York if you've got a craving for something Japanese that doesn't involve raw fish. So keep your eyes open, Japan has more to offer New York than sushi, and can make for a truly holistic cultural experience.

Columbus Circle

For many people, the reason they moved to New York in the first place was to escape the benighted landscapes of Middle and Suburban America, whose siren song has always been sung by that quintessential eruption of capitalism known as the Mall. Moving to the city is supposed to mean never having to rely again on chain retailers again, to rediscover the joys of selection and diversity that have been suffocated across vast swathes of this great nation. However, even Manhattanites need khakis, groceries, and Coach handbags from time to time. And if they can get them all during the same trip out, well, who's to say there's anything wrong with that? Especially if that trip takes them to the Shops at Columbus Circle, the hotel/residential/restaurant/retail complex in the enormous new Time-Warner Skyscraper at the South-West corner of Central Park, which attempts to mesh the suburban Mall ideal into the definitive urban space.

To be honest, the Shops at Columbus Circle are truly part of a mall in the most traditional sense, however much their proprietors try to tout this project as a prominent, luxury version of what already exists in every city in the continental US. In the end, these are stores, many of whom exist elsewhere in the city, in a place designed to suck shoppers off the bustling streets and trap them in an air-conditioned paradise. But for all this, the owners dressed the place up mighty fine, employing renowned architecture firm Skidmore, Owings, and Merril to come up with the final, dizzyingly high, plans. They outfitted the concourse "rest areas" in opulent Barcelona Chairs and marble floors, perhaps as a way to match the high-status retailers whose glossy exteriors shimmer from one end of the ground floor to the other. You certainly won't find any GAPs here (though you may find a two-floor J. Crew), which is exactly the point: this is a little wedge of Madison Avenue on the bottom edge of the Upper West Side, the standard bearer of the middle class in Manhattan. So what better way to combine a slice of the upper crust in a bourgeois milieu than with a skyscraping mall? It's prestigious but conveniently located and packed with great stores for the harried masses without a lot of free time on their hands. Nevertheless, you're going to need plenty of liquid cash on hand if you want to make the most of this place. Of course, everyone knows about the shiny new Whole Foods emporium in the basement area of the Shops, teeming with delicious, socially and ecologically friendly treats for you and yours. But what about the now infamous Masa on the fourth floor, with its prix-fixe meal rate of $300 per person? This is no regular mall food court – you're not paying that much for a hotdog on a stick or greasy Chinese food.

But the real reason to visit one of Manhattan's only malls isn't about swooning over menus or ogling the jewels in window displays. It's a little reminder of why malls are so successful wherever they pop up, even when that happens to be Broadway and 59th St.: they're really fun. You definitely begin to feel like a giddy preteen when that first blast of recirculated air hits you full in the face, and you know that all the best in brand name shopping is just a few, very well pedicured, footsteps away.

A B C D 1 *to 59th St.-Columbus Circle.*

Spas: Sit Back & Relax

Everyone needs to be spoiled once in while. Whether it's a quick trip to the masseuse, a revitalizing fruit facial, or simply a new 'do, New York's world class salons and spas have what it takes to transform the most jaded New Yorker into a well polished gem. Take a break, relax, and treat yourself to an afternoon of high-class pampering. Your mind and body will thank you for it.

If you're concerned about cost, don't worry. Many of New York's spas offer discounts for first time members. Additionally, a number of the city's most elite salons (Vidal Sassoon, John Frieda, and others) offer special rates and discounts. Make sure to call ahead for dates, times, and restrictions.

Allure Day Spa and Hair Design

Descend the stairs and leave the hectic citylife and your worries behind. Comfort and cleanliness meet the eyes in a room that is aesthetically pleasing and which quickly relaxes the mind. With a wide variety of facials, body treatments (including various wraps and massages), waxing, manicures, and hair styling, there is bound to be something your body will love and you can afford.

139 E. 55th St. (at Lexington Ave.), (212) 644-5500, MC, V, DC. E V 6 to 51st St.-Lexington Ave.

Ajune

A small storefront leads to a quieter and chic-er back where the treatment begins. This beauty mecca treatment is doctor approved by Dr. Mauro C. Romita the Founder and Medical director of Ajune. Once inside you can de-stress yourself with a deep tissue massage, or pamper yourself with a long lasting manicure or pedicure. The facials will be sure to leave your skin smooth, soft, and wrinkle free. This spa is a definite recommendation.

1294 Third Ave. (bet. 74th and 75th Sts.), (212) 628-0044, www.ajune.com, by appointment only. V, MC, Amex, D. 6 to 7th St.

Body Central

"Blissed-out" is the feeling this holistic wellness center grants to its clientele. Between the Feng Shui décor, amazingly friendly staff and personalized treatments, it seems no detail was overlooked in freeing you from the stress of life. Wherever tension may be harbored, there is a remedy to relieve it. Therapeutic ultrasound, moist heat application, aromatherapy and subtle chiropractic adjustments are part of the specialty treatments. Offering pure mental relaxation, with massages, chiropractic therapy, and physical wellness, like pilates, this is the ultimate non-traditional spa indulgence. Body Central offers special student rates, and if you call for a same-day appointment you can also receive a discount.

99 University Pl., Fifth Fl. (bet. 11th and 12th Sts.), (212) 677-5633, www.BodyCentralNYC.com. Hours: M W 12:30pm-9pm, T R 8:30am-9pm, F 8:30am-3pm, Sa 10am-4pm. 1 2 3 to 14th St.

Back to the Basics Massage

Your body (and soul) will thank you for this one. Arguably the best rub in Manhattan, Back to Basics is a completely unpretentious and personal spa. Their staff of well-trained professionals have a unique concern for both their clients emotional and physical wellness. And if getting a massage isn't your thing, visit Back to Basics for a number of their other spa services. Sophia's skin treatments are to die for...

Back to Basics Massage, 315 W. 57th St, Suite 208. M-F 10am-9pm, Sa-Su 10am-6pm. A B C D 1 to 59th St.-Columbus Circle. For more information visit www.backtobasicsmassage.com or call (212) 974-0988.

Faina European Day Spa

Release all of your tension at this beautiful spa. Offering everything from facials to waxing, the Faina European Day Spa provides treatments designed differently for each client, depending on his or her skin type. Big spenders should treat themselves to one of the spa packages, where you can indulge every part of your body. Full body scrubs or polishes cost approximately $65 for 30 minutes of ultimate pleasure and relaxation.

315 W. 57th St. (bet. Eighth and Ninth Aves.), Suite 402, (212) 245-6557, www.fainaeuropeanspa.com. Hours: M-F 10am-8pm, Sa 9am-6pm, Su 10am-6pm. MC, V, AmEx. A B C D 1 to 59th St.-Columbus Circle.

Finesse Day Spa

In it's first year of operation this spa has developed a killer reputation. Already ranked "Best of City Search" and featured twice in Time Out New York, Finesse is known for its creative exfoliating treatments. Try the mango/ginger body scrub and accompanying vicky shower. The spa's uniquely southwestern atmosphere also makes it ideal for both men and women.

Finesse Day Spa, 133 W. 25th St., Second Fl. East. M-Th 10am-8pm, F-Su 10am-10pm. A C E 1 *to 23rd St. For more information visit www.finessedayspa.com or call (212) 352-3434.*

John Frieda

If you want to feel like a princess (or a prince) treat yourself to an afternoon at John Frieda. Their premium location on Fifth Ave. is known for dishing out some of New York's hottest hair cuts. Undoubtedly, your stylist will work to find the best cut and color for you. Prices are generally high, but rightfully so. For significantly discounted rates, students should try to book an appointment during one of John Frieda's weekly training sessions (Wednesday, every other Tuesday).

797 Madison Ave. 4 5 *to 86th St. For more information call 212-879-1000 or visit www.johnfrieda.com.*

Metamorphosis Day Spa

The philosophy of this intimate spa states that Metamorphosis is a, "place where silence and tranquility reign and your health, beauty, and comfort are [their] only concerns." The array of services runs the gamut from typical spa treatments to more innovative goodies, such as the Fruitopia facial treatment, where a pumpkin enzyme peel will invigorate your senses. This spa caters to men as well as women, providing services that include laser hair removal and the "Iron Man Package," consisting of a scalp treatment and a deep tissue massage, among other services. Feel like royalty after pampering your body at Metamorphosis.

127 E. 56th St. (bet. Lexington and Park Aves.), Fifth Fl., (212) 751-6051, www.metspa.com. Hours: M-F 10am-9pm, Sa 10am-5pm. N R W 4 5 6 *to 59th St.-Lexington Ave.*

Oasis Day Spa and Salon

No place can compare to this literal oasis. Upon entering the spa, no matter what service you are receiving you are led into the locker rooms to change into your robe and slippers. Next, head to the relaxation lounge to drink tea or water while reading magazines about the Hamptons. The plethora of services is amazing – the spa also has a full service hair salon. Get a facial while waiting for the deep conditioner to penetrate each strand of hair. The full body treatments are exquisite – try the new Body Coffee Scrub or the Nourishing Seaweed Wrap. Reasonable prices make the Oasis number one.

One Park Ave. (bet. 32nd and 33rd Sts.), (212) 254-7722,

www.nydayspa.com. Hours: M-F 10am-10:15pm, Sa-Su 9am-9:15pm. MC, V, AmEx, D. ❻ *to 33rd St.*

Portofino

For some reason, this local chain of "sun centers" has captured a high profile clientele, rife with supermodels and actors, whose faces proceed to grace the seats of the waiting room. Maybe it's the reasonable package deals, the comfortable rooms, the personal stereo-system, or the gracious staff who keep you from being too embarrassed about your (flawless) fake bake.

104 W. 73rd St. (at Columbus Ave.), (212) 769-0200, Open M-F 9am-8pm, Sa 9am-7pm, Su 10am-6pm. MC, V, AmEx. Ⓑ Ⓒ *to 72nd St.*

Shija Day Spa

Walking over flower petals, you are led to a large room in which there is no end to the pampering when you enter this slice of paradise. This traditional spa goes the extra mile with relaxation-inducing lighting and music in every room. Offering soothing facials, heavenly massages, therapeutic body treatments and lavish manicures and pedicures, you can treat yourself to luxury. Treatments for two, such as the Girlfriend special for buddies, the Mother-Daughter package, and couple's treatment allow you to share your relaxation with someone special. You emerge feeling refreshed and ready to face the hectic-ness of life in New York City.

37 Union Square West, Fourth Fl. (bet. 16th and 17th Sts.), (212) 366-0706, www.shija.com. Hours: M-Su 11am-8pm. ❶❷❸ *to 14th St.*

Shizuka New York

One of New York City's hidden treasures, Shizuka is definitely worth the battle through Bloomingdale's traffic. The East Side spa attains a balance of relaxation and reinvigoration within the hubbub of New York City by providing a perfect blend of peace and energy. From the fresh water sweetened with ripened strawberries offered upon arrival to the combination of steam and cool air within the spa., all five senses achieve satisfaction. The members of the Shizuka team personalize each visit specifically to the needs of the clients by requesting thorough dermatology and inquiring about environmental preference. The knowledge and training of the cosmologists become apparent as they narrate each step of the process with a concise explanation without interrupting the serenity of the atmosphere. With affordable prices for special occasions, Shizuka is the place to turn for complete body enhancement.

133 E. 58th St., Suite 512 (bet. Park and Lexington Aves.), (212) 644-7400, www.shizukany.com. Hours: M-Su 10am-8pm. MC, V, AmEx, D. ❹❺❻ *to 59th St.*

Vidal Sassoon

Walk inside the Crown Building and take the elevator to the second floor to find this elite salon. The stylists can all be trusted to cut your hair classically while finding the most flattering cut for your face shape, a magazine's picture will not be necessary. Vidal Sassoon uses mostly Wella products and spends extra time making sure their costumers are well taken care of and comfortable. All their employees are experienced and professional.

730 Fifth Ave. (bet. 56th and 57th Sts.), (212) 535-9200, www.sassoon.com, by appointment. V, MC, AmEx, D. ❹❺❻ *to 59th St. Additional Manhattan Locations.*

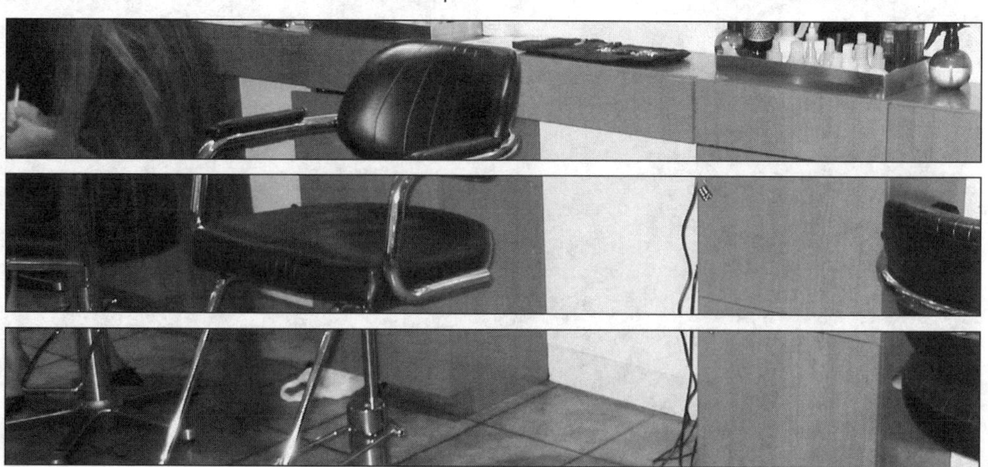

listings

[Accessories]

Agatha

This cute shop sells inexpensive trinkets that everyone will love. Stocked with jewelry and boxes they have a wide collection of faux gold. With all items being under $150 who can go wrong?
159A Columbus Ave., (212) 362-0959, www.agatha.fr, M-Sa 10am-8pm, Su 12pm-6pm, MC, V, AmEx. 1 *to 66th St.-Lincoln Center.*

Alexia Crawford

This jewelry designer made a name for herself when she was featured at Barney's almost ten years ago. Now, she not only has a store of her own, but her accessories are also sold in stores all over the country. Crawford creates affordable jewelry, bags, and scarves that rival the great designers. Despite the low price tag, you won't be able to tell the difference between her pearls and Fortunoff's. The quaint and colorful store deals exclusively in those pieces that you never knew you couldn't live without.
199 Prince St. (bet. MacDougal and Sullivan Sts.), (212) 473-9703, www.shopalexiacrawford.com. Hours: M-R 11 am-7pm, F-Sa 11 am-8pm, Su 12pm- 6pm. MC, V, AmEx, D. C E *to Spring St.*

House of a Million Earrings

Ethnic-inspired clothing, posters, paintings, crafts, and books. Hand-made jewelry, incense, and greeting cards are also for sale at this family-owned business. Great place for gifts.
169-17 Jamaica Ave., Jamaica, Queens (at 169th St.), (718) 297-7950, Hours: M-Su 9am-6pm. MC, V, AmEx, D. E *to Jamaica Ctr./Parsons /Archer.*

Jelly

This Brooklyn shop stocks an impressive variety of eclectic shoes and accessories for both men and women. From ties to jewelry, the store deals in all things vibrant, youthful, and loud. Prices range widely, and although nothing is inexpensive, Jelly seems to supply most goods for less money than its Manhattan counterparts. If you like what you see, check out the clothing at sister store Butter just up the street at 407 Atlantic Avenue.
389 Atlantic Ave. (bet.

Hoyt and Bond Sts.), (718) 858-8214, Hours: T-Sa 12pm-7pm, Su 12pm-6pm. MC, V, AmEx. 2 3 4 5 *to Nevins St.*

Jutta Neumann

Jutta Neumann is famous for his leather sandals, belts, bags, jewelry and accessories. Pretty much if you want to find something in leather, you can find it here. He is best known for his custom made sandals, but a new line of bohemian style bags seems to be a growing trend.
158 Allen St., (212) 982-7048, www.juttameimann newyork.com, T-Sa 12pm-8pm, MC, V, AmEx. F *to Lower East Side-Second Ave.*

Kate Spade

While Kate Spade attracted cult followers with fashionable handbags and luggage, she has expanded her Hamptons-chic line to shoes, journals, papers, hats, and even some clothing. The sale items on the lower level are a good bet. Check out Jack Spade, the male counterpart to this store, around the corner.
454 Broome St. (at Mercer St.), (212) 274-1991, www.katespade.com. Hours: M-Sa 11am-7pm, Su 12pm-6pm. MC, V, AmEx. N R *to Prince St.*

Flight 001

This chain of stores has been popping up all over Manhattan selling items for the modern traveler. While they sell a variety of travel bags and books, customers can also pick up interesting items such as barf bags or an anti-motion sickness bracelet that prevents nausea.
96 Greenwich Ave., (212) 691-1001, M–F 11am-8:30pm, Su 11am–8pm, Su 12pm–6pm, MC, V, AmEx. A C E *to 14th St;* L *to Eighth Ave.,* 1 2 *to 14th St.*

LeSportsac

Grandmothers and college students alike appreciate the simple, colorful designs of LeSportsac bags, purses, makeup cases, and luggage. Well worth their slightly expensive price tags, these high-quality items have been known to last for years. Also available at Macy's, Bloomingdale's, and other department stores.
176 Spring St. (at W. Broadway), (212) 625-2626. www.LeSportsac. com. Hours: M-Sa 11 am-7pm, Su 12pm-6pm. MC, V, AmEx, D. C E *to Spring St.;*
1065 Madison Ave. (at 80th St.), (212) 988-6200. Hours: M-F 10am-7pm, Sa 12pm-6pm, Su 12pm-5pm. MC, V, AmEx, D. 6 *to 77th St.*

Swatch

Everyone's favorite purveyor of wrist eye-candy is a sweet shop for those interested in a fun watch or for people obsessed with the constantly evolving selection of the collect-'em-all series. Of course, there are also more serious styles for those interested in making a statement without going over the top. Prices run from inexpensive to "you-want-how-much-for-that-chunk-of-plastic?".
438 W. Broadway (at Prince St.), (212) 613-0160, www.swatch.com. Hours: M-Sa 10 am-8pm, Su 11am-7pm. MC, V, AmEx. C E *to Spring St. Additional locations at 100 W. 72nd St., 640 Broadway, and 1528 Broadway.*

Verve

While this store specializes in accessories, Verve is also known for their footwear. Bags, hats, scarves, and jewelry are available for a range of prices. While they do carry some designer products, the knockoff bags and hats are the best deal. The friendly salespeople make this a great place to stop for the finishing touches to a great outfit.
353 Bleecker St. (bet. Charles and W. 10th Sts.), (212) 691-6516. Hours: M-Sa, 11am-8pm, Su 12pm-6pm. MC, V, AmEx, D. 1 *to Christopher St.,* A B C D E F V *to W. 4th St. Additional locations at 282 Columbus St. and 105 Christopher St.*

[Art Supplies]

A.I. Friedman

Ask a salesperson at this gigantic Chelsea store to categorize their merchandise, and they will invariably struggle. You can't blame them; the shop's stock ranges from Filofaxes to handbags, office furniture to art supplies, stationary to custom frames, origami to at least thirty variations of tape. The store specializes in both quantity and quality, and all wares tend to be sleek and top-of-the-line. They are particularly proud of their Swedish Bookbinders Design section (priced from $3 to $60), colorfully hand-covered albums, notepads, and cards that can't be found anywhere else in New York.
44 W. 18th St. (at Fifth Ave.), (212) 243-9000, www.aifriedman.com. Hours: M-F 9am-7pm, Sa 10am-7pm, Su 11 am-6pm. MC, V, AmEx. 1 *to 18th St.,* F V *to 14th St.*

B&H Photo-Video-Pro Audio

A zoo of a store that caters to the amateur just as readily as it caters to the professional. B&H covers all of the bases from digital photography to traditional photography and video equipment. Sales clerks are generally in abundance and are more than willing to assist customers. It is no secret that they offer the highest-quality equipment for the best price, so the store is usually packed. Check the website's quick dial phone directory for a listing of department extensions before calling the store.
420 Ninth Ave. (at 34th St.), (212) 444-6615, www.bhphotovideo.com. Hours: M-R 9am-7pm, F 9am-1pm (winter), 9am-2pm (summer), Su 10am-5pm. MC, V, AmEx, D. A C E 1 2 3 *to 34th St.-Penn Station.*

Lee's Art Shop

Paints and brushes are just the beginning at this valuable resource for artists who work in any medium. The shop offers drafting supplies, silk

screens, a good selection of pens and stationery, and a high-quality framing service.
220 W. 57th St. (at Seventh Ave.), (212) 247-0110. Hours: M-F 9am-7:30pm, Sa 9:30am-7pm, Su 11pm-6pm. MC, V, AmEx. A B C D 1 to 59th St.-Columbus Circle, N R W to 57th St.-Seventh Ave.

Ivy League Stationers

This store is literally packed to the gills with art projects waiting to happen. Everything from leather-bound journals to printer cartridges to scratch n' sniff stickers can be found here. Photo developing is significantly less expensive here than at other nearby locations, and the second set is free. They will also gladly give you change for the train or bus without forcing you to make a purchase. Chances are that if you enter the store, something will catch your eye.
2955 Broadway (at 116th St.), (212) 316-9741. Hours: M-F 8am-7pm, Sa 9am-7pm, Su 9am-6pm. MC, V, AmEx, D. 1 to 116th St.-Columbia University. Additional locations in Manhattan.

Pearl Paint

The labyrinthine motherlode of supplies for all media, these four crowded floors offer one-stop shopping for students and pros. Staff members will assist you in investigating nooks and crannies. The crotchety warehouse elevator serves as a reminder of the gritty conditions that once characterized everything below Canal Street.
308 Canal St. (at Broadway), (212) 431-7932, www.pearlpaint.com. Hours: M-F 10am-7pm, Sa 10am-6:30pm, Su 10am-6pm. MC, V, AmEx, D. J M N R W 6 to Canal St.; 207 E. 23rd St., (212) 592-2179. N R to 23rd St.

Sam Flax

Whether in search of canvas or some stylish wrapping paper, shoppers will find it all at this well-staffed store. Check out the sale section in back for some good furniture bargains.
12 W. 20th St. (at Fifth Ave.), (212) 620-3000. Hours: M-F 9am-7pm, Sa 10am-7pm, Su 12pm-5pm. MC, V, AmEx, D. N R W to 23rd St.; Additional Locations at 425 Park Ave. and 900 Third Ave.

[Bookstores]

General

192 Books

Walking into this huge store can seem overwhelming at first. With its high ceilings and reading tables, it feels more like a library than a bookstore. But the collection is extensive, especially for art books. Weekly readings make you feel more at home than in other commercialized bookstores.
192 Tenth Ave., (212) 255-4022, www.192books.com, T–Sa 11am-7pm, Su–M 12pm-6pm, MC, V, AmEx, C E to 23rd St.

Barnes and Noble at 82nd St.

This branch was the first of the megastores in Manhattan, now dwarfed by its downtown colleagues but still a nice oasis from the chaos of Broadway. The selection is remarkable, and *New York* magazine has named the coffee bar on the mezzanine a major West Side singles scene.
2289 Broadway (at 82nd St.), (212) 362-8835, www.barnesandnoble.com, *Hours: Su-R 9am-11pm, F-Sa 9am-12am. MC, V, AmEx. 1 to 79th St.; B C to 81st St. Additional locations in Manhattan.*

Community Book Store and Cafe

This integral part of Park Slope's social life carries a mixture of current best-sellers and classic fiction with a wonderful cafe and garden in the back. The owners also coax well-known authors out for readings.
143 Seventh Ave. (at Garfield Carroll St.), Park Slope, Brooklyn, (718) 783-3075. Hours: M-Sa 10am-9pm, Su 11am-9pm. MC, V, AmEx. B Q to Seventh Ave.

Crawford Doyle

This shop offers good browsing for high-quality fiction. Besides this, Crawford Doyle is an interesting alternative to the mega-bookstores that have begun to take over Manhattan.
1082 Madison Ave. (at 81st St.), (212) 288-6300. Hours: M-Sa 10am-6pm, Su 12pm-5pm. MC, V, AmEx. 6 to 77th St.

Labyrinth Books

Professors and students alike applaud this addition to Morningside Heights' healthy population of bookstores. Relying on a strong selection of academic titles rather than coffee bars and comfy furniture, Labyrinth is a welcome retreat for hard-core bibliophiles.
536 W. 112th St. (at Broadway), (212) 865-1588, www.labyrinth-books.com. Hours: M-F 9am-10pm, Sa 10am-8pm, Su 11am-7pm. MC, V, AmEx, D. 1 to 110th St.-Cathedral Pkwy.

The Last Word

A breath of fresh air in Morningside Heights, this bookstore offers students text books and recreational reading material at discount prices. Ask about the bargain tables which can always be seen in front of the store, and you'll undoubtably be told about how they received this or that great book for a dollar or two. A must-see for any book lover.
1181 Amsterdam Ave., (at 118th St.), (212) 864-0013, Hours: M-Sa 11am-7pm. 1 to 116th St.-Columbia University.

Shakespeare & Co.

One of several locations, this shop offers a diverse selection of books with the soul of an actual bookstore. Staff don't mind if you grab a book, find a corner, and read.
939 Lexington Ave. (at 69th St.), (212) 570-0201, www.shakeandco.com.

Hours: M-F 9am-8pm, Sa 10am-7pm, Su 11am-5pm. MC, V, AmEx, D. 6 *to 68th St.*
Additional locations in Manhattan at 137 E. 23rd St., 71C Broadway, 1 *Whitehall St.*

St. Mark's Bookshop

Why go to a chain when everything you'd ever want can be found in the tall racks of this favorite? The literature, sci-fi, gay lit, and mystery collections are all well stocked. It's just cooler to shop here.
31 Third Ave. (at 9th St.), (212) 260-7853, www.stmarksbookshop.com. Hours: M-Sa 10am-12am, Su 11am-12am. MC, V, AmEx. 6 *to Astor Pl.*

Foreign Language

Kinokuniya Bookstore

This bookstore offers Japanese books (some in English translation) along with a diverse selection of stationery and gifts. It is directly across from the Rockefeller Skating Rink.
10 W. 49th St. (at Fifth Ave.), (212) 765-7766, www.kinokuniya.com/newyork. Hours: M-Su 10am-7:30pm. MC, V, AmEx ($10 minimum). B D F V *to 47-50th Sts.-Rockefeller Ctr.*

K & W Books and Stationary

One of the biggest Chinese bookstores, K & W carries Hello Kitty toys along with a large selection of books in Chinese and in English, on topics like martial arts, bonsai care, and Buddhism.
131 Bowery St., (212) 343-0780, Hours: M-Su 10:30am-7:30pm. MC, V. J M N R W Z 6 *to Canal St.*

Lectorum Book Store

Spanish and Latin American books in Spanish and Portuguese are dispersed among translations of popular titles by the likes of Stephen King and James Clavell. Bibles, dictionaries, and a host of other reference books round out the selection. Check up front for information about lectures and readings.
137 W. 14th St. (at Sixth Ave.), (212) 741-0220, www.lectorum.com/libreria. Hours: M-Sa 9:30am-6:15pm, Su 12pm-6pm. MC, V, AmEx, D. F L V 1 2 3 *to 14th St.*

Libraire de France

One-stop shopping for French émigrés and Francophiles, New York's largest French-language bookstore sells magazines upstairs and a vast assortment of literature, history, and biographies downstairs.
610 Fifth Ave., on the Rockefeller Center Promenade, (bet. 49th and 50th Sts.), (212) 581-8810, Hours: M-Sa 10am-6pm. MC, V, AmEx. B D F V *to 47-50th Sts.-Rockefeller Ctr.*

Macondo

Named after the famous town in *One Hundred Years of Solitude*, at Macondo one can pick up an import from either Spain or South America.. The store caters to native speakers with an excellent selection of literature, plays, and poetry, although prices reflect the import costs.
221 W. 14th St. (at Seventh Ave.), (212) 741-3100. Hours, M-Su 10am 6pm. AmEx. 1 2 3 *to 14th St.*

LGBT-Oriented

Creative Visions

This neighborhood bookstore has a large selection of what you can't find in the LGBT section of Barnes and Noble, and that includes a helpful, friendly staff. Items here range from books by highbrow queer authors to seedy, obscure porn vids. Browse as long as you like among the pleasant book displays, or strike up a nice conversation with someone from the neighborhood.
548 Hudson St. (bet. Charles and Perry Sts.), www.creativevisiobooks.com, (212) 645-7573. Hours: Su-R 1pm-10pm, F-Sa 12pm-11pm, MC, V, AmEx. 1 *to Christopher St.-Sheridian Sq.*

Oscar Wilde Memorial Bookshop

For over twenty-five years, New York City's flagship gay bookstore has been offering books for and by gay men and women, as well as videotapes, music, magnets, T-shirts, and jewelry. Occasional readings by established authors are scheduled.
15 Christopher St. (at Sixth Ave.), (212) 255-8097. Hours: M-Su 11am-7pm. MC, V, AmEx, D. 1 *to Christopher St.*

Specialty

Applause Theatre and Cinema Books

With scripts, books, and screenplays, this store is perfect for the cinephile who has plenty of time to browse through an incredibly large selection.

211 W. 71st St. (at Broadway), (212) 496-7511, www.applausepub.com. Hours: M-Sa 10am-9pm, Su 12pm-6pm. MC, V, AmEx, D. 1 2 3 to 72nd St.

Argosy Bookstore

Rare books, old maps, and lithographs fill this time warp of towering bookshelves and cluttered desks. The only real bargains here are on the outside table.

116 E. 59th St. (at Park Ave.), (212) 753-4455, www.argosybooks.com. Hours: M-F 10am-6pm (Sep.-Apr. also Sa 10am-5pm). MC, V, AmEx. F N R W 4 5 6 to 59th St.-Lexington Ave.

Biography

Muckrakers, voyeurs, and fan club presidents come to this high-ceilinged and brick-walled store for the latest on their respective celebs. It also boasts an impressive gay and lesbian section.

400 Bleecker St. (at W. 11th St.), (212) 807-8655. Hours: Su-R 11am-10pm, F-Sa 11am-11pm. MC, V, AmEx. 1 2 3 to 14th St.-Eighth Ave.

Bookberries

Coffee table books are the specialty of this store – huge volumes loaded with pictures, especially along the lines of travel and food. A children's section is located in the rear.

983 Lexington Ave. (at 71st St.), (212) 794-9400. Hours: M-Sa 10am-6:30pm, Su 10:30am-6pm. MC, V, AmEx. 6 to 68th St.-Hunter College.

Complete Traveler Antiquarian Bookshop

The best store for new, out-of-print, antiquarian books providing information for real trips (though sometimes out-dated), and fuel for the imagination. The prices reflect the quality and selection. The staff is amiable, knowledgeable, and willing to discuss anything from city politics to traveling in sub-Saharan Africa.

199 Madison Ave. (at 35th St.), (212) 685-9007. Hours: M-F 10am-7pm, Sa 10am-6pm (non-summer months also Su 12pm-5pm). MC, V, AmEx, D, DC. B D F N R V W to 34th St.-Herald Sq., 6 to 33rd St.

Drama Bookshop

Drama stocks plays, biographies, acting/directing and writing manuals, and much more.

250 W. 40th St. (bet. Seventh and Eighth Aves.), (212) 944-0595, www.dramabookshop.com. Hours: M-Sa 10am-8pm, Su 12pm-6pm. A C E N R S W 1 2 3 7 to 42nd St.-Times Sq.

East-West Books

As the name suggests, the emphasis here is on introducing Western readers to the literature of the East. The store specializes in religious and philosophical traditions from Mahayana Buddhism to neo-Confucianism. The staff will make special orders to meet your needs.

78 Fifth Ave. (at 13th St.), (212) 243-5994, Hours: M-Sa 10am-7:30pm, Su 11am-6:30pm. MC, V, AmEx. F L V to 14th St.-Sixth Ave., L N R W 4 5 6 to 14th St.-Union Sq.

Forbidden Planet

Comic book fans seeking everything from superheroes to the latest Eightball cruise the racks to weed out the best of the new and used selection. But the big thing here is science fiction with significant dashes of fantasy and horror.

840 Broadway (at 13th St.), (212) 473-1576. Hours: M-Sa 10am-10pm, Su 11am-8pm. MC, V, AmEx, D. L N R W 4 5 6 to 14th St.-Union Sq.

Kitchen Arts and Letters

With a fabulous selection of over 9,000 cookbooks, this store will help anyone discover his or her inner gourmand.

1435 Lexington Ave. (bet. 93rd and 94th St.), (212) 876-5550. Hours: M 1pm-6pm, T-F 10am-6:30pm, Sa 11am-6pm. MC, V. 6 to 96th St.

Midtown Comics

This store is a dream come true for comic fanatics and has everything one would want in a comic book store. From mainstream to alternative, the store has extensive amounts of back issues to browse through. The staff is very knowledgeable and can help you if you cannot find what you are

looking for if you are having trouble.
200 W. 40th St., (212) 302-8192, www.midtowncomics.com, M-Sa 11am-9pm, Su 12pm-7pm, MC, V, AmEx. A C E N R W 1 2 3 7 to Times Sq.-42nd St.

Municipal Art Society Urban Center Books

Books on every architectural topic, from urban design to Freudian interpretations of city planning, line the walls of this cozy nook, complete with a fireplace and library ladders. Enjoy a recent purchase in their outside courtyard.
457 Madison Ave. (at 51st St.), (212) 935-3595. Hours: M-R 10am-7pm, F 10am-6pm, Sa 10am-5:30pm. MC, V. 6 E V to Lexington Ave.-51st St.

Mysterious Bookshop

Serving the city's voracious mystery readers, this store stocks out-of-print books as well as a healthy number of interesting British imports.
129 W. 56th St. (at Sixth Ave.), (212) 765-0900, Hours: M-Sa 11am-7pm. MC, V, AmEx, D. N R W to 57th St.-Seventh Ave., F to 57th St.

Partners & Crime Mystery Bookseller

Serving Village mystery aficionados, P&C carries a lot of out-of-print books. The staff will special-order books not in stock. Call for a schedule of readings.
44 Greenwich Ave. (at Charles St.), (212) 243-0440, www.crimepays.com, Hours: M-R 12pm-8pm, F-Sa 12pm-10pm, Su 12pm-7pm. MC, V, AmEx, D. 1 to Christopher St.

Printed Matter

Squeezed amongst the chichi galleries of the Meatpacking district is this gem of a shop. Hard to find art books, politics-inspired art 'zines, and international art publications from previous decades are all in stock here, making it a great place to dawdle away an hour soaking up some culture.
535 W. 22nd St (at Ninth Ave.), (212) 925-0325, www.printedmatter.org, Hours: T-F 10am-6pm, Sa 11am-7pm. MC, V, AmEx. C E to 23rd St.

Rizzoli

Get lost in this warm store that specializes in beautiful architecture, art, design, and coffee-table books. Literature and nonfiction selection may not be inspiring, but it certainly is adequate.
31 W. 57th St. (bet. Fifth and Sixth Aves.), (212) 759-2424, Hours: M-F 10 am-7:30pm, Sa 10:30am-7pm, Su 11am-7pm. MC, V, AmEx. N R W to 57th St.-Seventh Ave.

St. Mark's Comics

From X-Men to less conventional titles like Sexy Sushi, there's enough here for any comic book connoisseur. Also stocks a large selection of toys, posters and old comics.
11 St. Mark's Pl. (at Second Ave.), (212) 598-9439, Hours: Su-T 10am-11pm, W-Sa 10am-1am, MC, V, AmEx, D. 6 to Astor Pl.

Sufi Books

If there were such a thing as a neighborhood spiritual bookshop, this would be TriBeCa's. This bookstore, with a quiet admosphere and a soft-spoken staff to match contains a wealth of Eastern religion resources and smaller sections on Judaism and Christianity to feed spiritual quests of any ilk. There's also a large space next door for meditation and yoga classes.
227 W. Broadway (bet. Franklin and White Sts.), (212) 334-5212, www.sufibooks.com. Hours: T-Sa 1pm-7:30pm. MC, V, AmEx, D. 1 to Franklin St.

West Side Judaica

This haven of Judaica supplies music, art, and children's educational tools as well as a number of books dealing with Jewish issues. They also are willing to order hard to find books. They close at 3pm on Fridays for Shabbat and don't reopen until Sunday.
2412 Broadway (at 88th St.), (212) 362-7846, Hours: M-R 10:30am-8:45pm, F10:30am-2:30pm, Su 10:30am-5:45pm. MC, V, AmEx, D. 1 to 86th St.

Zakka

Insight into the world of Japanese "manga." Bookstore, boutique, and video palace focusing on rising Japanese pop culture.
147 Grand St., (at Lafayette St.) (212) 431-3961, www.zakkacorp.com Hours: W-M 12pm-7pm, MC, V, AmEx, D. J M N R W Z 6 to Canal St.. University

Bank St. College Bookstore

This store serves the fledgling schoolteachers of the nearby Bank St. College with an extensive selection of children's books and educational theory and planning guides.
610 W. 112th St. (at Broadway), (212) 678-1654, Hours: M-R 11am-7pm, F-Sa 10am-6pm, Su 12pm-6pm. MC, V, AmEx. 1 to 110th St.-Cathedral Pkwy.

Columbia University Bookstore

Not just for students. Despite its abundance of textbooks, this store provides one-stop shopping for all the proper accoutrements of the enthusiastic collegian, from sweatshirts to pennants. It has a sizable selection of new fiction books as well.
Columbia Campus, entrance at 2922 Broadway and 115th St., (212) 854-4131, www.columbia.bkstore.com, Hours: M-Su 9am-9pm; Summer hours M-F 9am-7pm, Sa-Su 11am-6pm. MC, V, AmEx, D. 1 to 116th St.-Columbia University

Ed's Book Exchange

Specializing in buying and selling textbooks, both old and new. Come here to experience the glory that is Union Turnpike: the most dangeous street in America.
Queens, 17627 Union Tpke., (718) 969-7173, Hours: M-R 10am-5:30 pm, F 10am-4pm. MC, V, AmEx, D. F to 169th St.

Fashion Design Books

Located at the heart of

FIT's campus, this unique take on the university bookstore stocks a plethora of fashion mags – from the popular to the obscure – and art and design books. In lieu of office accessories, you'll find art and sewing supplies.
250 W. 27th St., (bet. Seventh and Eighth Aves.), (212) 633-9646, www.fashiondesignbooks.com, Hours: M-R 9am-6:30pm, F 9am-5pm. MC, *V, AmEx, D,* ❶ *to 28th St.*

Manhattan Books
Mainly catering to the textbook needs of students at the nearby college. This can be a good spot to find steals on reference books like dictionaries and style guides. The real attraction is that they'll pay out a small amount of cash for almost any textbook or other academic text, so if something has proven hard to unload, give this place a shot.
150 Chambers St. (at W. Broadway), (212) 385-7395, Hours: M-T 9am-7pm, W-F 9am-6pm. MC, V, AmEx, D. ❶❷❸ *to Chambers St.*

New York University Bookstore
Lines wind around the block at the beginning of each semester at this academic standard. Students get no special discounts.
18 Washington Pl. (at Washington Sq. Park), (212) 998-4667. Hours: M-R 10am-7pm, F-Sa 10am-6pm. MC, V, D. Ⓝ Ⓡ *to 8th St.-NYU.*

Used

Gryphon Bookshop
Crowded shelves of used books climbing almost to the ceiling and piled on the floor. There are books here that can be found nowhere else in Manhattan. You just have to look hard.
2246 Broadway (at 80th St.), (212) 362-0706, Hours: M-Su 10am-12am. MC, V, AmEx, D. ❶ *to 79th St.*

Housing Works Used Book Cafe
Housing works is a minority-controlled organization dedicated to serving those living with and affected by AIDS in New York City. Housing Works operates the Used Books Cafe, located in SoHo, and four thrift stores throughout Manhattan. At the bookstore, an impressive space with soaring ceilings and spiral staircases, one can browse over 45,000 new, used, and rare books, records, and CDs, read at the cafe with a cup of coffee, attend an author reading, a concert (UBC has just launched its Live from Home Acoustic Music Series), or just ogle the hipster clientele. The thrift stores offer excellent bargains on vintage and second-hand men's and women's clothing, shoes, jewelry, books, and furniture.
126 Crosby St. (bet. Houston and Prince Sts.), (212) 334-3324, Hours: M-F 10am-9pm, Sa 12 pm-9pm, Su 12pm-7pm. MC, V, AmEx. ⓃⓇ *to Prince St.,* ❻ *to Bleecker St.*

Murder Ink
This specialty bookstore named after the Lanksy-Siegel crew featuring new and used mystery fiction is every sleuth-wannabe's dream. Their stock includes many classic whodunits as well as novels featuring elements of espionage and suspense. A mecca for the city's true mystery buffs, this shop has frequent book-signings that draw some big names. The staff really knows their stuff.
2486 Broadway (at 92nd St.), (212) 362-8905, www. murderink.com, Hours: M-Sa 10am-9pm, Su 11am-7pm. MC, V, AmEx. ❶❷❸ *to 96th St.*

The Strand Bookstore
Advertising "eight miles of books," The Strand is an awesome sight: two cavernous floors of bookshelves stuffed solid and tables crammed into the space in between. Browse slowly, and with the proper investment of time, and you'll turn up books you never dreamed existed.
828 Broadway (at 12th St.), (212) 473-1452, www.strandbooks.com, Hours: M-Sa 9:30am-10:30pm, Su 11am-10:30 pm. MC, V, AmEx, D. ⓁⓃ ⓇⓌ❹❺❻ *to 14th St.-Union Sq.*
95 Fulton St. (at Water St.), (212) 732-6070, Hours: M-F 9:30am-9pm, Sa-Su 11am-8pm. MC, V, AmEx, D. ⒶⒸⒿⓂⓏ ❶❷❸❹❺ *to Broadway-Nassau St. and Fulton St.*

[Clothing]

Boutiques

99X
This boutique sells some of the hippest threads in the city, with the usual high prices. The look is that oh-so-trendy '60s

Fashion Week

Each September and February, over a hundred fashion designers gather in Bryant Park to present their latest designs. Traditionally, New York City is the first of the four fashion capitals (NYC, London, Milan, and Paris) to host its Fashion Week. Here, the show is arranged by 7th on Sixth, an association that organizes and arranges nearly all American runway shows.

Check out 7th on Sixth's website (www.mercedesbenzfashionweek.com) for details on the various shows. They anticipate over 70 shows for this fall with about 126,000 fashion-conscious folk will turn out for the show. So if you read *Vogue* and *Glamour* over and over again, Fashion Week is your kind of holiday. And don't fret – Heidi and Gisele will all be there to celebrate with you.

mod, featuring a large selection of British imports from labels like Fred Perry, Lonsdale, and Ben Sherman.
84 E. 10th St. (bet. Third and Fourth Aves.), (212) 460-8599, www.99xny.com, Hours: M-Sa 12pm-8pm, Su 12pm-7pm. MC, V, D. N R to 8th St., 6 to Astor Pl.

Addison on Madison

This store will fulfill the needs of a man who likes high quality dress shirts. The collection is classic; the Egyptian-cotton shirts are very soft and can be worn in a professional or casual setting. While they are not cheap, ranging around $75 a shirt, you will find little that is less expensive on the famous Madison Avenue.
29 W. 57th St., Ninth Fl., (212) 308-2660, M-F 10am-6pm, MC, V, AmEx. N R W to Fifth Ave.; F to 57th St.

APC

Clothes so simple and perfect that you wonder simultaneously why they cost so much and how you've lived without them for so long. Classics like jeans and button-down shirts hover around the $100 range, so clasp your credit card tightly. It's hard to resist such flawless incarnations of old standards at any price.
131 Mercer St. (bet. Prince and Spring Sts.), (212) 966-9685, www.apc.fr. Hours: M-Sa 11am-7pm, Su 12pm-6pm. MC, V, AmEx, D. N R to Prince St.

Atrium

Increasingly reminiscent of Diesel. This store carries similar styles, but from diverse brands, so the experience is big and loud, with lots of jeans, good club wear, clothes that run tight and tarty for the ladies, and loose and bold for the men. All this flash doesn't necessarily come cheap, but the good selection of exclusive shoes and hard to find foreign labels makes up for the blaring music and crowded floor.
644 Broadway (at Bleecker St.), (212) 473-3980. www.atriumnyc.com, Hours: M-Sa 10am-9pm, Su 11am-8pm. MC, V, AmEx, D. N R to Prince St., 6 to Bleecker St.

Baldwin Formal Wear

Formal tuxedo purchase or rental is made simple at this upscale and classy shop. With an attentive, friendly staff and an impressive selection of styles, you'll be sure to find the perfect look. Expert fitting and tailoring is available on the premises, so you can walk out ready for any special occasion. If you have a large group, make sure to call and ask about their special deals.
1156 Sixth Ave. (at 45th St.), (212) 245-8190, www.nyc tuxedos.com. Hours: M-F 9am-7pm, Sa 10am-5pm. MC, V, AmEx. B D F V to 42nd St.-Bryant Park.

Big Drop

This new and hip boutique offers woman's clothing, shoes, bags, and jewelry. Always on top of fashion, it is mostly young and beautiful model types that are to be found here, but don't be discouraged if you aren't frequenting the runways. The salespeople are more than glad to help you pick out that perfect outfit and then some. Be sure not to miss the signature cell phone charms.
174 Spring St. (bet. W. Broadway and Thompson St.), (212) 226-9292. Hours: M-Sa 11am-8pm, Su 12pm-8pm. MC, V, AmEx, D. N R to Prince St.

Blue

If Cinderella were set in modern-day downtown New York, then her gown surely would have come from here. This shop offers one-of-a kind fancy dresses that fall somewhere between little girl fairy-tale fantasy and grown up chic. Definitely worth a look if there's an upcoming ball you would like to attend.
137 Ave. A (at 8th St.), (212) 228-7744. Hours: M-Sa 12pm-7pm, Su 12pm-5pm. MC, V, AmEx. N R to 8th St. 6 to Astor Pl., L to First Ave.

Calypso

This store was opened by Christiane Celle and features high-end fashion with her own line and fragrance collection. The stores' signature sorbet colors fill the space and give a hippy yet sophisticated feel. The store also began featuring bedding and home accessories to add to the extensive collection of clothing.
240 Mulberry St., (212) 925-6544, M–Sa 11am–7pm, Su 12pm–6pm, MC, V, AmEx. B D F to Broadway–Lafayette St.; N R to Prince St.; 6 to Bleecker St.

Cantaloup

Downtown comes uptown with this boutique, which features up-and-coming designers from around the world. It is particularly popular for its transition pieces (work to nightlife) and the sexy edge on all of its clothing. Prices range from $110 to $300 for bottoms and $60 to $275 for tops. In-demand bags that are hard to find in America are also a specialty; they proudly stock Ronny Kopo, Luella Bartly, and Kale.
1036 Lexington Ave. (at 74th St.), (212) 249-3566. Hours: M-Sa 11am-7pm, Su 12pm-6pm. MC, V, AmEx, D. 6 to 77th St.

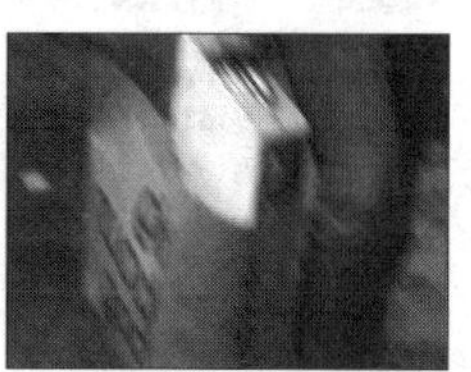

Cronick Valentine

Cronick Valentine's uniqueness comes from its ability to excel at the art of "reusing." At this cute shop, customers can browse the store's patented T-Shirt Graveyard and turn their old tee shirts into everything from new IPOD cases, to tote bags and duvet covers. Where else can one turn that Foreigner t-shirt from the 1984 World Tour into something useful? If you do not have personal clothing to spare, Cronick Valentine also sells pre-made items from vintage tee shirts. The concept of the store is in and of itself interesting, and the execution is impeccable. Perhaps Cronick's provides the perfect reason to finally get rid of your old raggedy tees.
324 E. 9th St., (212) 288-7767, www.cronickvalentine.com, Hours: Su, T-R 12pm-7pm, F-Sa 12pm-9pm. Ⓛ to First Ave.

Conquete

Brash styles from a French design team might be a bit Euro for some guys, but this menswear boutique also offers some great clothes that slide easily into any wardrobe. There is a rainbow of button-down shirts, perfect for other harder-to-match pieces. The good selection of classy bathing suits means no one has an excuse to go without in summertime.
255 W. 23rd St. (bet. Seventh and Eighth Aves.), (646) 638-2646. Hours: M-Sa 10:30am-9pm, Su 12pm-7pm. MC, V, AmEx. ❶ to 23rd St.

Forward

Here's a shop like no other. First of all, every piece is hand-made and one-of-a-kind. Second, the store is owned by the Business Improvement District of the Lower East Side, and its sole purpose is to attract shoppers to the neighborhood. Every six months the BID selects four to six designers who not only sell their pieces at Forward but also collectively run the store. There's an alumni rack where the best of the best are allowed to stock a piece or two after their six months are up. Prices range dramatically from $20 to $700, every dime supporting struggling designers.
72 Orchard St. (bet. Broome and Grand Sts.), (646) 264-3233. Hours: M-Su 12pm-7pm. MC, V, AmEx, D. Ⓕ to Delancey St.

Intermix

Since its opening in 1994, this Flatiron-based boutique has become a mini-fashion empire with satellite stores in Boston, South Beach, and Tokyo. You can find the must-have Mia & Lizzie jewelry featured on *Sex and the City* exclusively at the Madison Ave. store.
1003 Madison Ave. (at 77th St.), (212) 249-7858. Hours: M-Sa 10am-7pm, Su 12pm-6pm. MC, V, AmEx. ❻ to 77th St. Additional location on 125 Fifth Ave. (at 19th St.), 365 Bleecker St., and 1003 Madison Ave.

Jeffrey New York

The astonishingly well selected styles by the leading designers from around the world make Jeffrey the leader of the pack when it comes to posh clothing for men and women. Unfortunately, the prices are as breathtaking as the designs, but it's worth a visit just to see the best of the best and consult with this fashion oracle.
449 W. 14th St. (at Tenth Ave.), (212) 206-1272. Hours: M-W, F 10am-8pm, R 10am-9pm, Sa 10am-7pm, Su 12pm-6pm. MC, V, AmEx. Ⓐ Ⓒ Ⓔ to 14th St.

Marmalade

Hand-picked vintage and vintage-inspired clothing and accessories from the '60s, '70s, and '80s line the walls of this edgy boutique. They are particularly lauded for their extensive shoe collection, and their prices, which generally fall under $100. If you look hard enough you'll even spot the rack or two of men's clothing, which, although sparse, hits the vintage nail right on the head. Be prepared to make a statement with these clothes; despite the sweet store name, this is probably not what your grandmother wore.
172 Ludlow St. (at E. Houston St.), (212) 473-8070. Hours: M-R 12pm-9pm, F-Sa 12pm-10pm, Su 12pm-8:30pm. MC, V, AmEx. Ⓕ Ⓥ to Second Ave.

Mayle

Opened by a model, the store epitomizes the neighborhood. This chic boutique looks like it is filled with incredible vintage finds but is in fact Mayle's signature style. Pieces like the teal hand-knit scarves and classic ivory wool coat are exquisitely crafted and made just in time for your walk down Fifth Avenue.
252 Elizabeth St., (212) 625-0406, M-Sa 12pm-7pm, Su 12pm-6pm, MC, V, AmEx. Ⓑ Ⓓ Ⓕ to Broadway–Lafayette St.; ❻ to Bleecker St.

Olive and Bette's

Selling the latest trends and even creating new ones, this shop has always been at the head of fashion. The store is cramped with a sizeable selection of tank tops and t-shirts. Brands like Diesel, Seven, Juicy and three dot attract a following of native New York women who don't mind dropping a few extra bucks for quality.
252 Columbus Ave. (at

72nd St.), (212) 579-2178, www.oliveandbettes.com. Hours: M-Sa 11am-7pm, Su 12pm-6pm. MC, V, AmEx, D. 1 2 3 to 72nd St. Additional locations at: 1070 Madison Ave., 384 Blee-cker St., 158 Spring St.

Opening Ceremony

Away from the frantic pace of lower Broadway, this independent boutique is full of sleek, hip clothes, which are a bit dressy, but not fussy, giving the store a clubby atmosphere without being snobbish. It's full of people genuinely interested in design; every season they showcase unknown labels from a different country, so there's plenty of stuff on the racks and in the shoeboxes from Hong Kong all the way to Brazil. There are also very well priced in-house geometric sweaters, for those with slimmer means.
35 Howard St. (at Broadway), (212) 219-2688, Hours: M-Sa 11 am-8pm, Su 12pm-7pm. MC, V, AmEx. J M N R W Z 6 to Canal St.

TG-170

The most sophisticated of the small boutiques on the Ludlow strip features simple dresses, skirts, and tops in subtle but fashionably retro designs, as well as Freitag bags and wallets.
170 Ludlow St. (bet. Houston and Stanton Sts.), (212) 995-8660, Hours: Hours: M-Sa 11 am-8pm, Su 12pm-7pm. MC, V, AmEx., F V to Second Ave.

Unis

Best described as a boutique devoted to men who aren't interested in screaming label affiliation from down the street. The subtle, mostly mod, In-store designed clothing combines a reserved palette with relaxed but neat cuts, making clothes that aren't glittery or gutsy, but resemble those pieces you feel like throwing on any day in any mood, like they've been in your wardrobe forever. Not cheap, but not unreasonable for the neighborhood.
226 Elizabeth St. (at Prince St.), (212) 431-5533. Hours: M-Sa 12pm-7pm, Su 12pm-6pm. MC, V, AmEx, D. 6 to Spring St., N R to Prince St.

Department Stores

Active Warehouse

The bi-level shop is stocked with the latest footwear and clothing. Although most of the clothing available is North Face Brand, they also have quite an abundance of basketball jerseys.
514 Broadway, (212) 965-2284, www.activeware housenyc.com, M-Sa 9am-9pm, Su10am-8pm, MC, V, AmEx. 6 to Spring St., N R to Prince St.

Barney's

Power dressers and those looking for something more elegant put dents in their bank accounts at this airy, beautiful legend, which still holds its head high despite its original Chelsea store's closing. Head to the top floor for the lowest prices and most casual wear. Check out Barney's Warehouse Sales in February and September to find good deals on usually pricey items.
660 Madison Ave. (at 61st St.), (212) 826-8900, www.barneys.com, Hours: M-F 10am-8pm, Sa 10 am-7 pm, Su 11am-6pm. MC, V, AmEx, D. N R to Fifth Ave., 4 5 6 to 59th St.-Lexington Ave. and Lexington Ave.-63rd St.

Bergdorf Goodman

Tour the museum-quality merchandise, worthy of its chandelier and marble surroundings in this home of high fashion. To actually purchase something, leave the clientele of wealthy Upper East Siders behind and travel to the

Getting Rid of Old Clothes

Have you shopped so much that your new boots won't fit in your overflowing closet? Are you looking for some funky retro wear? No problem! As the old saying goes, one person's trash is another's treasure. In New York City, it is just as easy to find someone to take your old hand-me-downs as it is to find someone selling brand-new items.

While the city is brimming with thrift shops, only certain ones are regulated so as to keep the prices cheap and affordable. The Goodwill operates several locations throughout the city (visit locator.goodwill.org for a location near you). Usually large and well-stocked, these stores welcome anyone, regardless of their financial situation.

The Salvation Army also maintains a strong presence in Manhattan and the boroughs (visit www.satruck.com/FindStore.asp for a location). Touting itself as "America's thrift store," the Salvation Army stresses that buying from its stores is in and of itself a charitable act.

Keep your eyes open. A church, temple, school, or shelter in your area is likely to be sponsoring a clothing drive at some point. So go ahead and make some room in that closet for a few more items, while helping others in the New York area stay warm in winter and stylin' in summer.

fifth floor where less expensive (though still somewhat pricey) sportswear abounds. All cash and credit card transactions occur in a "back room" whose doors blend with the walls. Window displays here are among Fifth Ave.'s finest and are worth a trip.
754 Fifth Ave. (at 58th St.), (212) 753-7300, Hours: M-F, Sa 10am-7pm, R 10am-8 pm, Su 12am-6pm. MC, V, AmEx, D. N R W to Fifth Ave.-59rd St.

Bloomingdale's

Although the trademark perfume arcade is usually a zoo, the upper floors are open and bright. Helpful salespeople are always eager to match people with outfits bearing three-digit price tags.
1000 Lexington Ave. (at 59th St.), (212) 705-2000, Hours: M-W 10am-10pm, R 10am-8:30pm, F-Sa 10am-10pm, Su 11am-7pm. MC, V, AmEx. N R W 4 5 6 to 59th St.-Lexington Ave. and Lexington Ave.-63rd St.

Henri Bendel

Henri Bendel is one of the plushest shopping experiences around. An elegant staircase winds its way up through the multi-story townhouse, maintaining the splendor of Bendel's original boutiques while incorporating modern accents. Henri Bendel has an amazing make-up selection, and similar types of clothing to Bergdorf Goodman or Saks, but it's even classier.
712 Fifth Ave. (at 56th St.), (212) 247-1100, Hours: M-W, F-Sa 10am-7pm, R 10am-8pm, Su 12pm-6pm. MC, V, AmEx, D. N R to Fifth Ave.-59th St.

Macy's

"The Largest Store in the World" often resembles the chaos of the Thanksgiving Day parade they sponsor, especially after work and around Christmas. Most items are lower priced than other department stores, but the service and bathrooms reflect this reduction.
34th St. (at Broadway), (212) 695-4400, Hours: M-Sa 10am-8:30pm, Su 11am-7pm. MC, V, AmEx. B D F N R V W to 34th St.-Herald Sq. Additional locations in Manhattan and Brooklyn.

Pearl River Mart

Sort of like a Chinese Woolworth's, this two-floored department store stocks all the staples that five-and-dimes used to, with a twist: bamboo mats, bedding supplies, electronics, video rentals, a minigrocery section, and traditional cookware.
477 Broadway (at Grand St.), (212) 431-4770, Hours: M-Su 10am-7pm. MC, V, AmEx, D. J M N R W 6 to Canal St.

Saks Fifth Avenue

This classy store makes for great, if somewhat dizzying, browsing. Window displays make the Fifth Ave. promenade a bit more exciting. Unfortunately, Saks is a bit expensive.
611 Fifth Ave. (bet. 49th and 50th Sts.), (212) 753-4000. Hours: M-W, F-Sa 10am-7pm, R 10am-8pm, Su 12pm-6pm. MC, V, AmEx, D, DC. B D F V to 47th-50th Sts.-Rockefeller Ctr.

Takashimaya

An experience in itself, this Japanese import is synonymous with elegance and ambiance. A Barney's from the East, there's no better place to find a one-of-a-kind gift or splurge item. Its Asian tea and delicacies department is to die for, and the fresh flower department is a favorite of urbanites craving greenery. The midtown oasis leaves shoppers with a lighter spirit, not to mention a lighter wallet.
693 Fifth Ave. (at 54th St.), (212) 350-0100, Hours: M-Sa 10am-7pm, Su 12pm-5pm. MC, V, AmEx, DC. F to 57th St., E V to Fifth Ave.-53rd St.

Discount Shopping

Burlington Coat Factory

Why pay more? With five floors of discount coats, suits, shirts, and casual sportswear, you're sure to find what you need at the right price.
707 Sixth Ave. (at 23rd St.), (212) 229-1300, Hours: M-Sa 9am-9pm, Su 10am-6pm. MC, V, AmEx, D. F V N R W 1 to 23rd St. Additional locations at 1801 South Ave. and 45 Park Pl.

Century 21

Determined shoppers will find designer items for as much as 80 percent off. The other departments attract a slightly less bloodthirsty crowd. Don't go wearing bulky clothing because there are no dressing rooms; it's standard to try things on over what you're wearing. Known for their professional and courteous security staff.
22 Cortlandt St. (bet. Broadway and Church St.), (212) 227-9092, Hours: M-W, F 7:45am-8pm, R 7:45am-8:30pm, Sa 10am-8pm, Su 11am-7pm. MC, V, AmEx. R W to Cortlandt St., A C J M Z 2 3 4 5 to Broadway-Nassau St. and Fulton St.

Conway Stores

Conway is a mandatory stop for bargain hunters everywhere. Shoppers flock here for the incredible prices: expect to get a really big bang for your buck. Words of caution: take heed of the weekend mobs and of items that are listed as slightly irregular (e.g. underwear).
1333 Broadway (at 35th St.), (212) 216-9133, Hours: M-Sa 8am-8pm, Su 10:30am-7pm. MC, V, AmEx, D. B D F N R V W to 34th St.-Herald Sq.

Daffy's

For more reasonable prices than most department stores, this heavily advertised pit stop for savvy shoppers sells clothes, shoes, lingerie, and accessories, usually by lesser known European designers. During clearance sales, some items are slashed to less than $5.
111 Fifth Ave. (at 18th St.), (212) 529-4477, Hours: M-Sa 10am-9pm, Su 12pm-7pm. MC, V, D. L N R W 4 5 6 to 14th St-Union Sq. Additional location on Madison Ave.

Domsey Warehouse

In this 30,000-sq. ft. warehouse, you'll be

and children's wear. You will find Hawaiian shirts, military uniforms, prom dresses, bridal gowns, and cowboy boots all in one place. After many hours of treasure hunting, unique finds will make it all well worth it.
Brooklyn, 431 Kent Ave., (718) 384-6000, Hours: M-F 9am-6pm, Sa 9am-7pm, Su 11am-5:30pm. J M to Hewes Ave.

Filene's Basement
This bargain superstore carries Calvin Klein, Perry Ellis, Kenar, and other designer names. It is worth a look for shoes, lingerie, coats, suits, and evening wear. Check out the occasional clearance sales where many prices are slashed to below $5.
620 Sixth Ave. (bet. 18th and 19th Sts.), (212) 620-3100, www.filenes basement.com, Hours: M-Sa 9:30am-9pm, Su 11am-7 pm. MC, V, AmEx, D. 1 to 18th St.; F L V to 14th St.
Additional location at 2222 Broadway.

Loehmann's
As legendary as Century 21 in designer junkie circles, this five-floor Chelsea outpost rewards the shopper with lots of big-name labels and high stock turnover (which justifies frequent trips.)
101 Seventh Ave. (bet. 16th and 17th Sts.), (212) 352-0856, www.loeh manns.com, Hours: M-Sa 9am-9pm, Su 11am-7pm. MC, V, D. 1 to 18th St.

Strawberry
While Manhattan fashionistas may consider this store passé, there are many bargains to be had at this reasonably-priced staple. While the trendy is mixed with frumpy, shoppers can find stylish looks with small price tags if they look hard enough.
226 W. 125th St., (212) 663-4677. Hours: M-Sa 10am-8 pm, Su 12am-6pm. MC, V, AmEx, D. 2 3 to 125th St.

Syms
Originally a men's suit warehouse, today Syms sells complete lines of men's, women's, and children's designer clothing at heavily discounted prices. With items from over 200 brand labels in stock and a convenient color-coded price tag system to tell you what's in your price range, Syms is a great place for both apparel aficionados who crave the ultimate bargain and novice shoppers who just need a nice, cheap ensemble.
45 Trinity Pl. (at Rector St.), (212) 797-1199, www.syms.com, Hours: M-F 8am-8pm, Sa 10am-6:30pm, Su 12pm-5:30pm. MC, V, AmEx, D. 4 5 to Bowling Green, 1 R W to Rector St.

TJ Maxx
This off-price retail department store offers home furnishings, accessories, and clothing for the whole family. With 40 percent to 60 percent off brands such as Tommy Hilfiger, Ralph Lauren, DKNY, and Jones NY, you will be able to find a good deal if you have the time and the patience to sift through endless racks in search of a good buy.
620 Sixth Ave. (bet. 18th and 19th Sts.), (212) 229-0875, www.tjmaxx.com, Hours: M-Sa 9:30am-9pm, Su 11am-7pm. MC, V, AmEx, D. F L V to 14th St., 1 to 18th St., F V to 14th St.

Flagship Designers

agnès b.
This store offers the finest in smart, up-to-date women's wear with a touch that makes you feel like Ingrid Bergman. A great way to spend a Sunday.
79 Greene St. (bet. Spring and Prince Sts.), (212) 431-4339, www.agnesb. com, Hours: M-Su 11am-7pm, MC, V, AmEx. N R to Prince St

Anna Sui
Rock-n-roll style meets the runway and boutique world in this small designer outpost. Leather pants hang alongside sequined camouflage dresses, and the atmosphere is relaxed enough to allow for trying it all on without feeling conspicuous. It's expensive, but markdowns are often cheap enough for a splurge.
113 Greene St. (bet. Spring and Prince Sts.), (212) 941-8406. M-Sa 11:30am-7pm, Su 12pm-6pm. MC, V, AmEx, DC. N R to Prince St., C E to Spring St.

Bally
One of the best-known leather companies in the world, this Swiss tannery sells a vast selection of high-quality leather shoes, bags, belts, and accessories.
628 Madison Ave. (at 59th St.), (212) 751-9082, Hours: M-W, F 10am-6:30pm, R 10am-7pm, Sa 10am-6pm, Su 12am-5pm. MC, V, AmEx. N R W to Fifth Ave., 4 5 6 to 59th St.-Lexington Ave.

Calvin Klein
Pay tribute to the commercial master who made a young American public hunger for androgyny. Along with its refined, simple men's and women's wear, this flagship megastore boasts roomfuls of classically styled home accessories and a full staff of the predictably trendy, long-limbed sales specimens.
654 Madison Ave. (at E. 60th St.), (212) 292-9000, Hours: M-W, F-Sa 10am-6pm, R 10am-7pm, Su 12 pm-6pm. MC, V, AmEx, D, Diners. N R W to Fifth Ave., 4 5 6 to 59th St.-Lexington Ave.

Chanel
Coco would be proud. Complete with uniformed doormen, this sparkling shrine to simple elegance with a flair sells clothing, jewelry, shoes, accessories, and of course, perfume.
3 W. 57th St. (bet. Fifth and Madison Aves.), (212) 355-5050, Hours: M-W, F 10am-6:30pm, R 10am-7pm, Sa 10am-6pm, Su 12pm-5pm. MC, V, AmEx, DC. E V to Fifth Ave., N R to Fifth Ave., W to Fifth Ave.-59th St.

Comme des Garçons
High-flying artists frequent this airy, high-ceilinged boutique for shimmery garments designed by trail-blazing Japanese designers Rei

Kawakubo and Junya Watanabe. This is statement clothing in all its extraordinary glory. The prices here can flame like rockets, and your credit card might just burn and burn.
520 W. 22nd St. (by Tenth Ave.), (212) 604-0013, Hours: Su 12pm-6pm, Tu-Sa 11am-7pm. MC, V, AmEx. C E to 23rd St.

Dolce & Gabbana
This flagship boutique, worshipped by the wealthy and known to the "in" as D&G, carries the latest sports line from Dolce and Gabbana in all its raw vibrancy. This two-floor unisex store features a variety of styles in colors like fuchsia, lime green, and azure blue. For the tamer soul, there is also conservative wear like black pants and khaki blazers. If you are looking for accessories, they also have their own line of belts, bags, and shoes.
825 Madison Ave., (212) 249-4100, Hours: M-Sa 11am-8pm, Su 12pm-6:30pm. MC, V, AmEx. 6 to 68th St.

Emporio Armani
Cleanly cut casual suits that are a bit more accessible price-wise than Armani's main line. Just about everything looks classy in the renovated Stanford White building.
601 Madison Ave. (at 57th St.), (212) 317-0800, Hours: M-Sa 11am-8pm, Su 12pm-6pm. MC, V, AmEx. 4 5 6 to 59th St., F N R W to Fifth Ave.

Gucci
Tom Ford's looks find their home in this ultra-modern Fifth Avenue showcase. The quality of leather goods is excellent, and the clothes upstairs are sleek. In a store that caters to "the beautiful people," be prepared for some high-end and high-attitude sales help. Walking away with that Gucci bag will make most feel like a million bucks.
685 Fifth Ave. (at 54th St.), (212) 826-2600. www.gucci.com, Hours: M-W, F 10am-6:30pm, R, Sa 10am-7pm, Su 12pm-6pm. MC, V, AmEx, D, Diners. E N R V to Fifth Ave.
840 Madison Ave. (at 70th St.), (212) 717-2619, Hours: M-W, F-Sa 10am-6:30pm, R 10am-7pm, Su 10am-5pm. MC, V, AmEx, D, DC. 6 to 68th St.

J. Lindeberg
Cool Swedish designer threads (with prices to match) are tight and trim, with a little retro flare, like big belt buckles and bell bottoms. Mostly for those not afraid to make a statement, but the clean lines and not too far-out patterns means these clothes stand out without making a ruckus. Better known for their menswear, there is also a selection for women downstairs.
126 Spring St. (at Greene St.), (212) 625-9403, Hours: M-Sa 11am-7pm, Su 12pm-6pm. MC, V, AmEx, D. C E to Spring St.

Miu Miu
Prada's second breakthrough strikes a more contemporary look for a younger crowd.
100 Prince St. (bet. Mercer and Greene Sts.), (212) 334-5156. Hours: M-Sa 11am-7pm, Su 12am-6pm. MC, V, AmEx. N R to Prince St., B D F V to Broadway-Lafayette St.
Additional location at 831 Madison Ave.

Nicole Farhi
An emporium from the Turkish-French designer, whose London base makes itself felt in her well-cut, muted, yet extremely detailed pieces for men, women, and home. Farhi likes solid construction paired with the harder flavors like fringe, ruche, or a bold pattern in a familiar place. This makes for stylish clothes that don't play to trends, but still feel in the moment and are fairly affordable compared with their Madison Avenue counterparts. There's also a respectable restaurant in the downstairs for those who want to make a day of it.
10 E. 60th St. (at Fifth Ave), (212) 223-8811, Hours: M-F 10am-6pm, Sa 11am-6pm, Su 12pm-5pm. MC, V, AmEx, D. N R W to Fifth Ave.-59th St., 4 5 6 to 59th St.

Prada
Chic, classic, and stylish, Prada is still at the top of its fashion game. With an enormous wave in the middle of the store's floor plunging into stadium seating for public events and galas, Prada's interior looks less like a store and more like a performance space. Explore the downstairs hallways and find racks of high-quality clothing, shoes, and accessories among hundreds of television screens interspersed in the racks displaying clips of movies as well as videos of old collections.
575 Broadway (at Prince St.), (212) 334-8888, www.prada.com. Hours: M-Sa 11am-7pm, Su 12pm-6pm. MC, V, AmEx, D. N R to Prince St., B D F V to Broadway-Lafayette St.
Additional locations in Manhattan at 841 Madison Ave., 45 57th St., 724 Fifth Ave.

The Shops at Columbus Circle
New York City's newest mall recently opened to much hoopla.

MALLS

Defined by its elegance, The Shops offers its patrons only the best (for which you'll have to pay the best prices). A great way to spend a day, one can grocery shop, buy a book and DVD and learn how to shave properly, all within 100 feet.
60 Columbus Circle, methods of payment vary with establishment, A B C D 1 to 59th St.

Manhattan Mall
Its dominating presence highlighted in glass and neon incites feelings of either veneration or loathing. Billed as having the "Largest food court in New York City," how could it not incite strong emotions?
33rd St. and Sixth Ave., methods of payment vary with establishment. B D F N R W to 34th St.-Herald Sq.

555 Soul, Inc.
The styles here are nothing if not original. The prices on the hip-hop

clothes are moderate to expensive, but most would say they're worth it.
290 Lafayette St. (at Prince St.), (212) 431-2404, Hours: M-Su 11am-7:30pm. MC, V, AmEx, D. N R to Prince St., B D F V to Broadway-Lafayette St.

Abercrombie & Fitch

Carrying women's, men's, and children's "rugged, authentic" clothing, this

TRENDY BASICS

two-floor flagship A&F offers the same homogenous clothing and accessories that you can find in their other locations and in their notoriously risqué catalog. A&F has become a clothier of choice for young New Yorkers, from streetwise b-boys to preppy coeds.
199 Water St. (South Street Seaport), (212) 809-9000, www.abercrombie.com, Hours: M-Sa 10am- 9pm, Su 11am-8pm, MC, V, AmEx, D. A C to Broadway-Nassau St., J M Z 2 3 4 5 to Fulton St.

American Apparel

The appeal of this store is their wide variety of tees and other cotton basics made here in the USA to ensure fair labor and a living wage, without passing on the expense to the customer. As a rule, every piece seems to come in an assortment of colors that are easy on the eyes and which slip effortlessly into your casual drawer.
198 Houston St. (at Orchard St.), (212) 598-4600, www.americanapparelstore.com. Open M-R 11am-10pm, F-Sa 11am-12am, Su 12pm-9pm, MC, V, AmEx. F V to Second Ave.
Additional locations at 373 Sixth Ave., 712 Broadway, 104 N. 6th St., and 121 Spring St.

Anthropologie

A grown-up version of Urban Outfitters. Created by the same company with a similar blend of house wares and clothing, the bent here is more stylish than trendy. There are lots of classic and basic pieces that are of high quality, but most are prohibitively priced at around $70 and up. The clearance racks generally yield some good finds though, and sometimes paying full price isn't so bad, since the clothes are unlikely to either fall apart or go out of style quickly.
375 W. Broadway (at Spring St.), (212) 343-7070, www.anthropologie.com, Hours: M-Sa 11am-8pm, Su 11am-6pm. MC, V, AmEx, D. C E to Spring St., 6 to Spring St.
Additional location at 85 Fifth Ave.

Barney's Co-Op

This is the house that denim built. Though the shelves abound with designer look-alike clothes from Barney's more trend-oriented store label, the Co-Op is actually humming with folks in search of this moment's hottest jeans assured of finding their style and size on the massive overstuffed back wall.
236 W. 18th St. (bet. Seventh and Eighth Aves.), (212) 826-8900, Hours: M-F 10am-8pm, Sa 11am-7pm, Su 12am-6pm, MC, V, AmEx. 1 to 18th St.

Betsey Johnson

In-your-face girly chic means not being afraid to wear lace alongside faux leather or to pair zebra stripes with pink fishnets. Straightforward, sexy slip dresses are surprisingly affordable on sale. The store itself looks like some funky teenagers took a paintbrush to mom's boudoir.
138 Wooster St. (at Prince St.), (212) 995-5048, www.betseyjohnson.com. Hours: M-Sa 11am-8pm, Su 12pm-7pm. MC, V, AmEx. N R to Prince St.
Additional Locations in 248 Columbus Ave., 251 60th St., and 1060 Madison Ave.

Club Monaco

This Ralph Lauren owned chain offers a sleeker, more urban version of casual staple stores like J. Crew and Banana Republic. Some of the clothes could be mistaken for Helmut Lang or Prada but cost much less – think Eurochic.
2376 Broadway (at 87th St.), (212) 579-2587, www.clubmonaco.com. Hours: M-Sa 10am-9pm, Su 11am-7pm, MC,V, AmEx. 1 to 86th St.
Additional locations in Manhattan.

Diesel

Two stories worth of youth culture in all its incarnations. Pump your system full of caffeine with a visit to the cappuccino bar before ravaging the aisles of shoes, underwear, outerwear, and accessories.
770 Lexington Ave. (at 60th St.), (212) 308-0055, www.diesel.com. Hours: M-Sa 10am-8pm, Su 12pm-6pm. MC, V, AmEx, D, DC. F N R W 4 5 6 to 59th St.-Lexington Ave.
Additional location in Union Sq.

Eastern Mountain Sports

The outdoorsman's Garden of Eden. Wandering

around this store, shoppers can easily envision themselves reaching the highest heights or paddling down rapids. EMS has gear for all ages and ability: from active-wear to boots, to sleeping bags to tents. This veritable smorgasbord of outdoor treats is topped off by a very helpful, knowledgeable, and friendly staff, which can help you in picking socks or fitting you with a backpack.
20 W. 61st St. (at Broadway), (212) 397-4860, Hours: M-F 10am-9pm, Sa 10am-8pm, Su 12pm-6pm, MC, V AmEx. A B C D 1 to 59th St.-Columbus Circle.
Additional location at 591 Broadway.

French Connection
Modish store deftly blending '70s and '80s retro and classic clean lines to produce well-tailored and pricey clothes suitable for work and play. Seasonal sales yield bargains on silk weaves, linen, and slinky, quasi-Parisian dresses.
700 Broadway (at W. 4th St.), (212) 473-4486, www.frenchconnection.com. Hours: M-F 11am-9pm, Sa 10am-9pm, Su 11am-8pm. MC, V, AmEx, D. B D F V to Broadway-Lafayette St.

Gap
For a clean, crisp look, check out this home for basics like khakis, whites, blacks, and cotton t-shirts. This mega-chain takes a utilitarian approach to merchandising: stores are packed with folded sweaters, tees and the ever-present wall of jeans and khakis.
1212 Sixth Ave. (at 48th St.), (212) 730-1087, www.gap.com. Hours: M-F 8am-9pm, Sa 10am-9pm, Su 11am-7pm. MC, V, AmEx, D. 1 to 50th St.
Additional locations in Manhattan.

H & M
Crowded to the point of suffocating, Euro-import H & M draws hordes of fashion-hungry New Yorkers to its Manhattan outlets with its chic clothes at ludicrously cheap prices. Of course, no one ever accused H & M of making their clothes well. But if you want to look like a million bucks and only pay wholesale, follow the Scandinavian lead.
34th St., Herald Sq. (at Sixth Ave.), (646) 473-1164, www.hm.com, Hours: M-Sa 10am-9pm, Su 11am-8pm. B D F N R V W to 34th St.-Herald Sq.
Additional Locations in Manhattan.

Jimmy Jazz
This men's clothing store contains all of the upscale hip-hop gear that one would ever desire. Going beyond the mainstream brands like Phat Farm and Fubu they sell names like Pepe and Mecca that are harder to find in New York City. They also have footwear so one can stock up on Tims or Nike's, embracing their hip-hop roots.
617 181st St., (212) 928-1939, M-F 9am-7:30pm, Sa 9:30am-8pm, Su 11am-6:30pm, MC, V, AmEx. A B C D to 125th St.

Medici
When searching for women's shoes, one lusts after ultra trendy for reasonable prices. This store offers this exact combination with Italian shoes that are geared for the young, professional woman. Well-displayed and with a wide selection you can also afford to buy more than one pair.
420 Columbus Ave., (212) 712-9342, M-Su 10am-8pm, MC, V, AmEx. B C to 81st St., 1 to 79th St.

Old Navy
Those catchy commercials don't lie. Old Navy has a lot to offer for men, women, boys, and girls. Their styles are often simple, yet take their inspiration from the more expensive fashion trends at a fraction of the cost.
300 W. 125th St. (at Manhattan Ave.), (212) 531-1544. Hours: M-Sa 10am-9pm, Su 11am-8pm, MC, V, AmEx, D. A B C D to 125th St.
Additional locations in Manhattan.

Scoop
With many locations around the city, this fashionable boutique has been bringing women and girls the latest in "affordable" designers and popular casual wear. They boast a large collection of clothing from brands like Seven, Juicy Couture, and Marc Jacobs, which always draw the beautiful people, though the staff is courteous to all who enter Scoop's doors.
532 Broadway (at Spring St.), (212) 925-2886, www.scoopnyc.com. Hours: M-Sa 11am-8pm, Su 12pm-7pm. MC, V, AmEx, D. N R to Prince St., 6 to Spring St., B D F V to Broadway-Lafayette St.
Additional locations in Manhattan at 1275 Third Ave., and 873 Washington St.

Stüssy
Skater-surfer gear with a West Coast feel endures. It is worth the price to have a T-shirt that reads "Stüssy" and relive junior high
140 Wooster St. (at Prince St.), (212) 274-8855, www.stussy.com, Hours: M-Th 12pm-7pm, F-Su 11am-7pm, MC, V, AmEx. N R to Prince St.

Urban Outfitters
This hipster playground for the post-mall generation packs its industrial-esque interior with racks of multicolored, funky kid fashion, suitable for day or evening urban outings. Weave through aisles of vintage clothing, sassy sundresses, and trendy house wares while swaying to the smooth rhythms of ambient music.
374 Sixth Ave. (at Waverly Pl.), (212) 677-9350, www.urbanoutfitters.com, Hours: M-Sa 10am-9pm, Su 12pm-8pm, MC, V, AmEx, D. A B C D E F V to W. 4th St.
Additional locations in Manhattan at 526 Sixth Ave., 162 Second Ave., 2081 Broadway, 628 Broadway.

Von's School of Hard Knocks
Over six years ago a

father-and-son sneaker and men's sportswear business spawned the School of Hard Knocks, a men's line with a large hip-hop influence. Everything from jackets and caps to sneakers and knapsacks can be had for relatively low prices. Women's and children's lines are also sold here.
Corona, Queens. 106-11 Northern Blvd. (at 106th St.), (718) 898-1113, www.hardknocksusa.com. Hours: M-Sa 10am-8pm. MC, V, AmEx, D. 7 to 103rd St.-Corona Plaza.

Zara
This well-priced and good-looking Spanish chain is a favorite of the international crowd. Although the carbon-copy designer looks have been called "scandalous" by fashion's inner circle, shoppers find the low prices rather shocking. From one-season staples to everyday standbys, this chain is sure to please.
750 Lexington Ave. (at 59th St.), (212) 754-1120, www.zara.com, Hours: M-Sa 10am-8pm, Su 12pm-7pm. MC, V. F N R W 4 5 6 to 59th St.-Lexington Ave.
Additional locations in Manhattan at 39 34th St., 689 Fifth Ave., 101 Fifth Ave., 580 Broadway.

Alice Underground
Behind the hippie-ish exterior is one of

VINTAGE

Manhattan's biggest and best vintage stores. Skip the bargain bins because there's usually a good reason why the items are being unloaded for so cheap, and shell out a little more for pants and jackets off the racks, where the finds can range from the fabulously unique to solid standards. An excellent selection of winter coats.
481 Broadway (bet. Grand and Broome Sts.), (212) 431-9067. Hours: M-Su 11am-7:30pm. MC, V, AmEx. J M N R Z 6 to Canal St.

Andy's Chee-Pees
Though ironically on the expensive side, Andy's houses a large selection of mostly polyester-influenced vintage men's and women's clothing, plus a more reasonably priced collection of used jeans. Always in stock: your great-grandpa's cabana wear, but he'd roll over in his grave if he saw what they're charging for it.
691 Broadway (bet. 3rd and 4th Sts.), (212) 420-5980. Hours: M-Sa 11am-9pm, Su 12pm-8pm. MC, V, AmEx. N R to 8th St., 6 to Bleecker St., B D F V to Broadway-Lafayette St.

Beacon's Closet
A wide assortment of used clothing fills the racks in this Williamsburg shop, and it doesn't take too much hunting to find something really nice like a suede jacket or a pair of perfectly worn boot-cut Wranglers. The prices tend to be a little expensive for Brooklyn but are still about one-third what you'd pay in Manhattan. Plus, they'll buy your unwanted clothes or take them in a trade.
Williamsburg, Brooklyn. 88 North 11th St. (at Berry St.), (718) 486-0816. Hours: M-F 12am-9pm, Sa-Su 11am-8pm. MC, V, AmEx, D, DC. L to Bedford Ave.

Cheap Jack's Vintage Clothing
Don't be fooled by the name of this groovy vintage store. The place is anything but cheap. Browse through the vast selection of plain and Hawaiian shirts, one-of-a-kind coats, and vintage-style dresses on the first floor. Head downstairs to find jeans. Patience and a keen eye may lead to a heavenly bargain.
841 Broadway (bet. 13th and 14th Sts.), (212) 777-9564, www.cheapjacks.com. Hours: M-Sa 11am-8pm, Su 12pm-7pm. MC, V, AmEx, D. L N R W 4 5 6 to 14th St.-Union Sq.

INA
This Little Italy clothing store features fabulous designer vintage for both men and women. It carries current collections, but the real treasures are their vintage designer items.
21 Prince St. (bet. Mott and Elizabeth Sts.), (212) 334-9048. Hours: Su-R 12pm-7pm, F-Sa 12pm-8pm. MC, V, AmEx. N R to Prince St., 6 to Spring St.
Additional location in Manhattan at 208 E. 73rd St., 101 Thompson St.

Out of the Closet Thrift Shop
Who'd have thought you could find vintage clothing on the Upper East Side? Visit this eclectic second-hand boutique housed in a historic building. Feel better about the prices by reminding yourself that a portion of sales go to AIDS-related charities.
220 E. 81st St. (at Second Ave.), (212) 472-3573. Hours: Tu-Sa 10:30am-5pm. MC, V, AmEx, D. 6 to 77th St.

Rejoice
The name says it all: run by an angelic, blonde brother-sister tag-team, this store is one of the better vintage places on

all of the East side, which also happens to buy/trade/sell music on the side. A small location with judiciously selected items at affordable prices. Full of the basics of any wardrobe: good men's cowboy shirts, worn-in tees, and old school flared jeans, as well as a wide variety of funky shoes, awesome vintage blouses, and sweaters for the ladies (think 1982's *Tootsie*, but with more sex appeal).
182 Orchard St. (at Houston St.), (212) 777-6606. www.rejoice exchange.com. Open M-Sa 12:30pm-6:30pm, Su 12:30pm-6pm. MC, V, AmEx, D. F V to Second Ave.

Screaming Mimi's

You might pass by Screaming Mimi's if not for the window display, which shows off its kooky wares. You'll find some of the most outrageous vintage clothing in the city here, including Elvis suits, pink leisure outfits, leather pants, and neon-colored patched shirts. The excellent condition of the clothing marks up the prices a bit, but the pieces are well worth it if you dare to wear them.
382 Lafayette St. (at E. 4th St.), (212) 677-6464. Hours: M-Sa 12pm-8pm, Su 1pm-7pm. MC, V, AmEx, D, DC. B D F V to Broadway-Lafayette St., 6 to Bleecker St.

Tokyo Seven

Trip down the dank steps into an underground world of designer consignment that you can definitely afford. Men and women pack into this tiny Japanese-run, decidedly un-vintage used clothing store. Every label is here, and there are plenty of shoes and accessories scattered about. The constantly revolving merchandise lets you come back every weekend to find something new that you just have to have.
64 E. 7th St. (at First Ave.), (212) 353-8443. Hours: M-Sat 12pm-8:30pm, Sun 12pm-8pm. MC, V, AmEx. N R to 8th St.-NYU.

What Comes Around Goes Around

This is quite possibly the largest and most famous vintage store in all of New York, so be prepared to spend a lot of time scouring the store in search of that perfect faded baseball jersey. They have the largest selection of vintage jeans and leather and will make special orders so that you get exactly what you're looking for. Though it may be slightly overpriced, it is a worthwhile trip for the serious shopper.
351 W. Broadway (bet. Grand and Broome Sts.), (212) 343-9303. www.nyvintage.com. Hours: M-Sa 11am-8pm, Su 12pm-7pm. MC, V, AmEx. N R to Prince St., C E to Spring St.

[Computing]

J&R Music World

Covering an entire block and soaring into the sky, this store carries everything in video, audio, music, and computers. The sales staff aren't all experts, so ask for a lot of different opinions before you buy anything. Since everything is on display, customers can fiddle to their hearts' content.
23 Park Row (bet. Beekman and Ann Sts.), (212) 238-9000. Hours: M-Sa 9am-7:30pm, Su 10:30am-6:30pm. MC, V, AmEx, D. 2 3 to Park Pl., A C to Broadway-Nassau St., E to Chambers St., J M Z to Fulton St., R W to City Hall.

Tekserve

Tekserve may be the most famous computer store in the world. The specialty here is Apple, and they will gladly fix yours or sell you a new one altogether. Beyond basic sales and repairs, Tekserve also deals in professional-quality audio and visual systems, and they accept Apple Loan, Apple's line of credit. The staff is hip and remarkably friendly.
119 W. 23rd St. (bet. Sixth and Seventh Aves.), (212) 929-3645. Hours: M-F 9am-7pm, Sa 10am-5pm, Su 12pm-5pm. MC, V, AmEx, D. 1 to 23rd St.

[Cosmetics]

Face Stockholm

This Swedish based company excels at the basics. Personal attention is easy to come by in this airy boutique. The $9 nail polish selection makes you wish you had more fingers. A favored stop for fashionistas and actresses, you might even spot a celeb or two.
110 Prince St. (at Greene St.), (212) 334-3900. www.facestockholm.com. Hours: M-W, F-Sa 11am-7pm, R 11am-8pm, Su 12pm-6pm. MC, V, AmEx. N R to Prince St. Additional locations at 1263 Madison Ave. (at 90th St.), (212) 987-1411 and 226 Columbus Ave. (at 70th St.), (212) 769-1420.

Jo Malone

This British-based store specializes in perfume and has recently added a new feature in which customers can customize their own scent. Inside the store there is a machine that divides up ingredients that can be added to each other to make the final perfume. As an added bonus the machine shoots only a little scent into the air so the patron does not feel overwhelmed and can smell all the scents individually.

949 Broadway, (212) 673-2220, www.jomalone.co.uk, Hours: Mon-Sa 10pm-8pm; Su 12pm-6pm, MC, V, AmEx, N R to 23rd St.

Kiehl's

The latest and, as many claim, greatest in all-natural skin care and cosmetics. Also available at Barney's and Saks.

109 Third Ave. (at 13th St.), (212) 677-3171, www.kiehls.com, Hours: M-Sa 10-7, MC, V, AmEx. N R W 4 5 6 to 14th St.-Union Sq.

L'Occitane

This small French company has all of the essentials plus skin care. They have a great selection of their own perfumes and candles.

146 Spring St. (at Wooster St.), (212) 343-0109, www.loccitane.com, Hours: M-Sa 11am-7pm, Su 11pm-7pm. MC, V, AmEx, D. C E to Spring St.

Additional locations at 247 Bleecker St. (at Leroy St.), (212) 367-8428, 101 University Pl. (at 12th St.), (212) 673-8630, Grand Central Terminal, Lexington Passage, (212) 557-6754, and 510 Madison Ave. (at 52nd St.), (212) 826-5020.

M.A.C. Cosmetics

Cosmetophiles are more than willing to pay a high price for the name "M.A.C." and the creamy, metallic signature look. Try the "Diva" lipstick – proceeds go to an AIDS charity. Excellent quality, too. Also at Bloomingdale's, Macy's, and Saks.

113 Spring St. (at Mercer St.), (212) 334-4641, www.maccosmetics.com, Hours: M-W 11am-7pm, R-Sa 11am-9pm, Su 12pm-7pm. MC, V, AmEx, D. N R to Prince St., C E to Spring St.

Additional locations at 139 5th Ave., Second floor (at 21st St.), (212) 505-3563 and 14 Christopher St., (212) 243-4150.

Origins

This cosmetics haven (a subsidiary of Estee Lauder) houses earthy lotions, creams, make-up, and powders, like "clear head shampoo" and "the Zen gardener" infused with essential oils and all natural botanical extracts. The store carries a complete line of devices for destressing, including books on reflexology, massage oils, and other soothing creams. All the beauty products strive to achieve balance and harmony, Origins' two key words. Oprah is said to be a fan.

175 Fifth Ave. (bet. 22nd and 23rd Sts.), (212) 677-9100, www.origins.com, Hours: M-S 10am-8pm, Su 12pm-6pm. MC, V, AmEx, D. N R to 23rd St.

402 W. Broadway (at Spring St.), (212) 219-9764, Hours: M-Sa 10am-9pm, Su 11am-7pm. MC, V, AmEx, D. C E to Spring St.

Additional locations at 2327 Broadway (at 84th St.), (212) 769-0970, and 44 W. 50th St., (212) 698-2323.

Sephora

This French high-scale cosmetics and perfume store is gaining ground in America. The sales people keep a hands-off policy: customers can try anything without asking. Run around and try the latest scents and beauty potions from world-renowned designers. Expect to leave looking as though your face is a two-year-old's coloring book. This store holds an endless list of brand-name products arranged in alphabetical order.

555 Broadway (at Prince St.), (212) 625-1309, www.sephora.com, Hours: M-Sa 10am-9pm, Su 11am-8pm. MC, V, AmEx, D. 6 to Spring St. B D F Q to Broadway-Lafayette St., N R W to Prince St.

Additional locations at 1500 Broadway (at 42nd St.), (212) 944-6789, 2103 Broadway (at 73rd St.), (212) 362-1500, and 130 W. 34th St. (at Seventh Ave.), (212) 629-9135.

Condomania

Prophylactics of all shapes, sizes, and flavors.

[Erotica]

Merely browsing here can often be an amusing experience. Condomania even has the latest technology in condoms, including the "reservoir tip" that could fit a baseball, and looks like a light bulb.

351 Bleecker St. (bet. Christopher and W. 4th Sts.), (212) 691-9442, Hours: Su-R 11am-11pm, F-Sa 11am-12am, MC, V, AmEx. 1 to Christopher St.

The Pink Pussycat

At this Village landmark you can find all manner of erotica, from lingerie and clothing to, well, other things designed to aid your love life. The store isn't known for its service, so come armed with knowledge. A bag bearing its famous name is bound to create the necessary reaction from any lover.

167 W. 4th St. (bet. Sixth and Seventh Aves.), (212) 243-0077, Hours: Su-R 10am-2am, F-Sa 10am-3am. MC, V, AmEx. A B C E F V to W. 4th St., 1 to Christopher St.

DV8

If you're the type of gal made less of sugar than spice, then come to this S&M shop for toys more naughty than nice. The staff is friendly and eager to help anyone from the dilettante to the professional. At the front of the store, find information about classes, workshops, and events in the New York S&M and leather community.

211 W. 20th St. (bet. Seventh and Eighth Aves.), (212) 807-0486, Hours: M-W 12pm-7pm, R-F 12pm-9pm, Sa 12pm-8pm, Su 12pm-6pm, MC, V, AmEx, D. 1 to 23rd St.

The Leather Man

A virtual department store for the gay male lover. Come here for a great selection of leather clothes designed for either public or private wear. The in-store workshop will customize any product to your need, and has same-day tailoring for leather pants. The collection is extensive.
111 Christopher St. (bet. Bleecker and Hudson Sts.), (212) 243-5339, Hours: M-Sa 12pm-10pm, Su 12pm-8pm, MC, V, AmEx. ❶ to Christopher St.

Toys in Babeland

Try this sexual boutique if you want to feel a wholesome vibe while shopping for female erotica. More than just a store, Babeland offers workshops, organizes outings, and hosts speakers in order to promote healthy lesbianism. Check out the books and video collection after ogling classy and kitschy pleasure devices.
94 Rivington St. (bet. Orchard and Essex Sts.), (212) 375-1701, Hours: M-Sa 12pm-10pm, Su 12pm-7pm, MC, V, AmEx. Ⓕ Ⓙ Ⓜ Ⓩ to Delancey St.

London

This fun leather store has the requisite goods combined with an inviting, playful atmosphere. Find clothing, toys, and kitschy doo-dads to give as presents to liberated lovers of any sexual preference.
84 Christopher St. (bet. Bleecker St. and Seventh Ave.), (212) 647-9106, Hours: Su-R 10am-12am, F-Sa 10am-2am, MC, V, AmEx, D. ❶ to Christopher St.

[Eyeglasses]

Alain Mikli

One-of-a-kind and limited edition glasses (eyejewelry some might say) are secreted away in this minimalist boutique from the France-based designer. As a result, these spectacles can be quite expensive, better suited for architects and kooky society matrons than anyone else, although their high quality both in stylishness and material mean the pain of parting with a large sum is more than made up for with the thrill of indisputable chic.
986 Madison Ave. (at 76th St.), (212) 472-6085, Hours: M-Sa 10am-6pm, R to 6:30pm, Su 12pm-5pm, closed Sun. in July and August, MC, V, AmEx. ❻ to 77th St.

Robert Marc

This designer store offers the chicest eyewear around. While the prices are steep for both male and female prescription glasses and sunglasses, the frames are sturdy and stylish. Also check out Robert Marc's one-of-a-kind necklaces that double as glasses holders.
436 W. Broadway (at Prince St.), (212) 343-8300, www.robertmarc.com, Hours: M-F 11am-8pm, Sa 11am-7pm, Su 12pm-6pm. MC, V, AmEx. Ⓒ Ⓔ to Spring St, Ⓝ Ⓡ to Prince St.
Additional locations at 1046 Madison Ave. (at 79th St.), (212) 988-9600 and 190 Columbus Ave. (at 68th St.), (212) 799-4600.

Selima Optique

This eyeglasses store is more of a boutique. While they specialize in hip, funky, and pricey eyewear, they also have a great collection of snazzy hats and creative umbrellas. The staff is more than helpful in decorating you from head to toe in extravagant pieces. They will outfit both men and women in the funkiest glasses and sunglasses.
59 Wooster St. (at Broome St.), (212) 343-9490, www. selimaoptique.com, Hours: M-Sa 11am-8pm, Su 12pm-7pm, MC, V, AmEx, D. Ⓒ Ⓔ to Spring St., Ⓝ Ⓡ to Prince St.
Additional location at 899 Madison Ave. (at 72nd St.), (212) 988-6690.

Sterling Optical

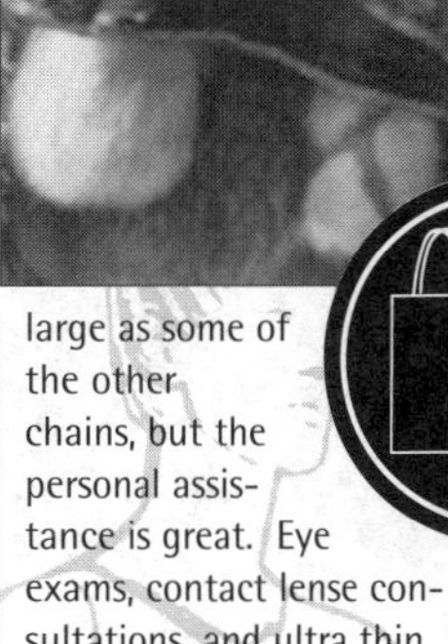

Excellent selection of designer frames. Not as large as some of the other chains, but the personal assistance is great. Eye exams, contact lense consultations, and ultra thin lenses are available. Twenty percent off any complete pair of contacts or glasses with student or faculty ID.
2647 Broadway (bet. 100th and 101st Sts.), (212) 865-3980, www. sterlingoptical.com. ❶ to 103rd St.
Additional locations throughout Manhattan.

[Flea Markets]

Annex Antiques Fair and Flea Market

The "original" and most famous flea market in the city, the Annex gathers over 500 vendors every weekend in a trio of parking lots that stretch along Sixth Ave. While you try to distinguish between trash and treasure, you might stumble upon a celebrity or two – its rumored that Catherine Deneuve is a long-time-fan.
Sixth Ave. from 24th St.

to 27th St., (212) 243-5343, Hours: Sa-Su 6am-5pm. F V *to 23rd St.*

SoHo Antiques Fair and Flea Market

Not as large or as great for people-watching as the Annex, but that's an advantage if you are strapped for time or are not a flea-market veteran with a great attention span. Find everything from clothing to collectibles and furniture.

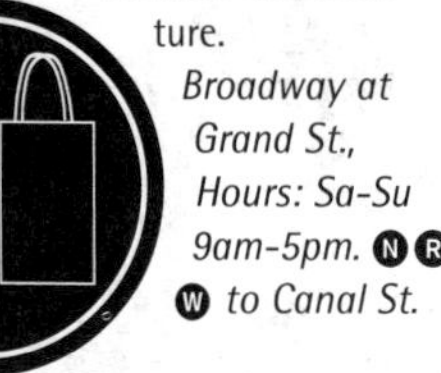

Broadway at Grand St., Hours: Sa-Su 9am-5pm. N R W *to Canal St.*

[Flowers]

Lotus NYC

Located in the heart of Greenwich Village, this small shop is chock full of exotic flowers in a variety of imaginative colors. This florist specializes in weddings and events, although you can also just drop in to pick up a small houseplant or bouquet. The staff is adept at creating imaginative though pricey arrangements.

161 Seventh Ave. (at Perry St.), (212) 463-0555, www.lotus212.com. Hours: M-F 10am-6pm, Sa 11am-5pm. MC, V, AmEx, D. 1 2 3 *to 14th St.*

Prudence Designs

This tiny florist is all about signatures, of which it has many. The color chartreuse, for example, can be found throughout the store, from the business cards to the fresh roses. Dachshunds are another favorite, gracing ornaments, pillows, and handbags. The florists here are known for wrapping bouquets in coconut leaves, starting at $30, and for filling Chinese food take-out containers with arrangements, starting at $50.

228 W. 18th St. (bet. Seventh and Eighth Aves.), (212) 691-1541, Hours: M-F 9am-7pm, Sa 12pm-7pm, MC, V, AmEx, D. 1 *to 18th St.*

Studio Artiflora

This small shop is more about a style than straight forward flowers. Aside from flowers, it is filled with "floral-related objects," which include everything from vases and vessels to fishbowls. The florists here consider themselves to have a "different point of view" when it comes to flowers. They argue that arrangement is just as important to floral success as the flowers themselves. Individual arrangements start at $25 and average $50-$75.

144 W. 19th St. (bet. Sixth and Seventh Aves.), (212) 645-1177, Hours: M-Sa 10am-6pm, MC, V, AmEx, D. 1 *to 18th St.,* N R *to 28th St.*

[Gifts & Miscellaneous]

A Bear's Place

You can release your inner child with tons of stuffed bears that you can play with. Along with the extensive plush animal collection, you can find educational games that are geared toward younger children. Children's luggage is also sold here for the little traveler.

789 Lexington Ave., (212) 826-6465, www.eabearsplace.com, M-F 9am-6:45pm; Sa 9am-6pm, MC, V, AmEx. 4 5 6 *to 59th St.,* N R W *to Lexington Ave.*

American Girl Place

The popular doll collection has opened a new store that not only sells basic dolls, but an abundance of the accessories and outfits for girls as well. Now, young girls and women alike can buy matching outfits for themselves and their dolls as well as get their picture taken in the photo studio, go to the Doll and Hair Salon, or shop at the bookstore.

609 Fifth Ave., (212) 371-2220, www.americangirl.com, Hours: M-W 10am-7pm; R-Sa 9am-9pm; Su 9am-7pm, MC, V, AmEx. B D F V *to 47-50th Sts.-Rockefeller Center.*

Abracadabra Superstore

TV stations, movie studios, and theaters are the biggest patrons of this dark and wild costume and statue shop. Abracadabra will sell you Venetian masks identical to those featured in that notorious orgy scene from *Eyes Wide Shut*. Even if you're not the orgy type, Abracadabra can still give you a stunning Halloween costume. The selection can't be beat.

19 W. 21st St. (bet. Fifth and Sixth Aves.), (212) 627-5194, Hours: M-Sa 11am-7pm, MC, V, AmEx, D. 1 *to 23rd St.,* F V *to 23rd St.*

Aphrodisia

Here, you'll find herbs, spices, and a variety of teas intended to rejuvenate mind, body, and soul.

264 Bleecker St. (bet. Sixth and Seventh Aves.), (212) 989-6440, Hours: M-Sa 11am-7pm, Su 12pm-5pm, MC, V, AmEx, D. A B C D E F V *to W. 4th St.*

Browne & Co. Stationers

One of the last printing shops in New York City. the staff uses letter presses dating back to 1844 to make custom stationary, invitations, etc. All the paper is printed on famous Crane's paper and the quality makes this shop perfect if you need great paper products.

211 Water St., (212) 748-8651, Hours: T-Su 10am-6pm, MC, V, AmEx. 2 3 4 5 J M Z *to Fulton St.,* A C *to Broadway-Nassau St.*

Card-o-Mat

This card-filled cubbyhole can come up with a sentimental rhyme or a witty remark for any occasion. The store also offers small gifts like candles, journals, and picture frames to go with whatever cards you choose.

2884 Broadway (at 112th St.), (212) 663-2085, Hours: M-Sa 10:30am-9pm, Su 11am-7pm, MC, V. 1 *to 110th St.-Cathedral Pkwy.*

Daily 2.3.5

The toys and gifts in this little store run from old board games to the Strawberry Shortcake dolls your sister used to

play with after school – it's the junk you always wondered what had happened to. It's all brand-spanking new, and though the prices seem to have gone up since the early '80s, the decidedly uncampy displays mean you don't feel too silly shelling out.
235 Elizabeth St. (at Prince St.), (212) 334-9728, Hours: M-Sa 12pm-8pm, Su 12pm-7pm, MC, V, AmEx, D. F V *to Lower East Side-Second Ave.*

DDC Lab

That item that you saw when backpacking through Europe that you thought you could never find again...is here. This store features items that you cannot get anywhere else and are also extremely unique. With a coffee bar inside, the clothing has a raw and artsy feel. But don't expect prices to match an artist's budget. Really, though, where else in New York can you find sneakers commemorating Hong Kong's transfer to Chinese rule?
180 Orchard St., (212) 375-1647, M-W 11am-7pm, T-Su 12pm-6pm, MC, V, AmEx. F *to Second Ave.*

Delphinium

This store is not exactly Hallmark, being more oriented towards an LGBT crowd, but the salacious novelties and cards in stock should tickle any friend or family member. Fun pet accessories line the floor, while more adult housewares are sprinkled throughout.
653 Ninth Ave. (at 47th St.), (212) 333-3213, Hours: M-Sa 11am-8pm, Su 12pm-7pm, MC, V, AmEx, D, DC, C E *to 50th St.*

Exit 9

A great gift selection no matter what you're looking for. There are lovely candle holders and picture frames for tame tastes, funky knickknacks and odd books for strange tastes, and a selection of flasks, cigarette cases, and lighters for self-destructive tastes. Never worry about shopping for your friends and family again.
64 Ave. A (bet. 4th and 5th Sts.), (212) 228-0145, Hours: M-F 12pm-8pm, Sa 11am-8pm, Su 12pm-7pm, MC, V, AmEx, D. F V *to Second Ave.,* 6 *to Astor Pl.*

Firefighter's Friend

This independently owned novelty store carries New York firefighter and police t-shirts, caps, patches, and pins. Though the store is small and cramped, they offer a variety of items and sizes. They also ship nationwide. The quality is much higher than anything sold on sidewalks, but so are the prices.
263 Lafayette St. (at Prince St.), (212) 226-3142, www.nyfirestore.com, Hours: M-Sa 10am-6pm, Su 12pm-5pm, MC, V, AmEx, D. N R *to Prince St.,* 6 *to Spring St.*

Jerry Ohlinger's Movie Material Store

Shoeboxes of old publicity shots, movie stills, posters, and playbills crowd this treasure trove of memorabilia for avid film buffs. Color stills go for around $3.50. Don't miss the autographed pics of Orson Welles and Montgomery Clift by the door.
253 W. 35th St. (bet. Seventh and Eighth Aves.), (212) 989-0869. Hours: M-Su 1pm-8pm. MC, V, AmEx, D. A C E 1 2 3 *to 34th St.-Penn Stn.*

Mariposa

New-age music and massive wall displays strive to put this beautiful boutique's butterfly wares into naturalistic context. Lepidopterists can check out the carefully mounted winged specimens in their infinite variety behind clear Plexiglas frames.
South St. Seaport, Pier 17, (212) 233-3221, Hours: M-Su 10am-9pm, MC, V, AmEx. A C J M Z 2 3 4 5 *to Fulton St.*

Maxilla and Mandible

This store is literally filled to the rafters with perfect seashells, fossilized trilobites from exotic locales, authentic antlers and skulls, and insects preserved in amber.
451 Columbus Ave. (at 82nd St.), (212) 724-6173, Hours: M, T-Sa 11am-7pm, Su 1pm-5pm, MC, V, AmEx, D. 1 *to 79th St.,* B C *to 81st St.*

Our Name is Mud

Paint your own pottery at this cool little store. Up front is a gallery with finished "functional" pieces like mugs, vases, planters, frames, and pitchers in bright colors. After a little instruction, you can move to the back, pick your own unfinished piece, and, for $5 per 1/2 hour, paint it yourself. Perfect for private parties, bridal showers, and birthdays. They also offer nine-week hand-building courses for $215. Thursdays and Fridays are adult nights, so no kids are allowed after 6pm. You can bring your own beer and wine and paint till you drop.
59 Greenwich Ave. (at Seventh Ave.) (212) 647-7899, Hours: M-W, Sa 11:30am-8pm, R-F

11:30am-11pm, Su 11:30am-7pm, MC, V, AmEx. 1 2 3 to 14th St. Additional locations in Manhattan.

Possibilities at Columbia

Located blocks away from Columbia University, this card and trinket store is perfect for gifts of all occasions. From greeting cards to mugs, the store is filled with items that contain inspirational quotes. Good for a last minute gift for a friend or professor.
2871 Broadway (at 112th St.), (212) 865-1510, Hours: M-Sa 9am-9pm, Su 10am-8pm, MC, V, AmEx. 1 to 110th St.-Cathedral Parkway.

Pier 17

Three levels of somewhat overpriced tourist shops may not seem like anything special, but at least you can get some great views of the Brooklyn Bridge from the top floor.
South St. (at Fulton St.), Hours: M-Sa 10am-9pm, Su 11am-8pm. A C J M Z 2 3 4 5 to Fulton St.

Studio Museum in Harlem Gift Shop

When you walk into this brightly colored shop you can browse through the large selection of African inspired textiles and jewelry. Specializing in select jewelry collections, the store has high price pieces as well as costume jewelry. The gift shop also stocks children's gifts like storybooks that are specially made for children of color.
144 West 125th St., (212) 864-0014, www.studiomuseumharlem.org, Hours: W-F 10am-6pm, Sa 12pm-6pm, Su 12pm-6pm, MC, V, AmEx. 1 to 125th St.

Totem Design

This store is stocked with furniture, lighting and accessories that are all one of a kind and fits the store's philosophy that "objects evoke meaning". All the pieces are very sleek and created by designers that try to combine art and design in their pieces. The pieces are arranged like an art exhibition and it is fun to walk though and look at individual pieces.
71 Franklin St., (212) 925-5506, Hours: M–Sa 11am–7pm, Su12pm–5pm, MC, V, AmEx. 1 to Franklin St.

[Grocery]

Aji Ichiban

This is a Hong Kong-based store that specializes in exotic candy. Nicknamed the "munchies paradise" they have a variety of foods such as dried tea plum, sesame coconut and mini crabs to snack on. Their best sellers are the yogurt, apple and sesame-flavored marshmallows and sweet yellow dried tomatoes. The best part is they offer free samples so you can figure out what you like best.
37 Mott St., (212) 219-4010, www.ajiichibanusa.com, Hours: M-Su 10am-8:30pm, MC, V, AmEx. 6 J M N R W to Canal St.

A.L. Bazzini

This store carries nuts galore: brazil nuts, pine nuts, peanuts, and more. You can also find dried fruit, gift baskets, and a bunch of other specialties. For cheap fun, stop by for a look around, and treat yourself to an ice cream cone.
339 Greenwich St. (at Jay St.), (212) 334-1280, Hours: M-F 8am-8pm, Sa 8:30am-7:30pm, Su 8am-6:30pm, MC, V, AmEx. 1 to Franklin St.

Alleva Dairy, Inc.

Its fourth-generation owner, Bob Alleva, serves up hot and cold sandwiches for under $5. Mozzarella is made fresh daily at the oldest Italian cheese store in America.
188 Grand St. (at Mulberry St.), (212) 226-7990, 1-800-4-ALLEVA, Hours: M-Sa 8:30am-6pm, Su 8:30am-3pm, MC, V, AmEx. J M N R W Z to Canal St.

Brooklyn Brewery

New York's closest approximation to a hometown beer is brewed here, and on weekends they open the place up. That means free brewery tours, beer tastings, and merchandise for sale. The hats and T-shirts make excellent gifts for any beer lover on your list. They've recently begun using the brewery as a gallery and performance space as well, making a trip to the brewery a perfect day of cheap fun for a variety of different tastes.
Brooklyn. N. 11th St., (bet. Barry and Wyeth Sts.), (718) 486-7422. MC, V, AmEx. L to Bedford Ave.

Chelsea Market

Once a Nabisco biscuit factory, Manhattan's largest wholesale and retail food concourse located in the heart of Chelsea offers a multitude of fresh dining options from fudge to fish and everything in between. The building's brick and terracotta arches and wood-beamed walls provide a haven from the typical urban surroundings while satisfying even the most refined palates.
75 Ninth Ave. (bet. 15th and 16th Sts.), Hours: M-F 9am-10pm, Sa-Su 8am-8pm, A C E L to 14th St.

Citarella

With humble beginnings as a small fish market, this gourmet grocer now boasts a full range of fresh fish, meat, and pastas. Best known for its extensive selection of fresh local and imported seafood, Citarella also carries a sampling of foie gras, caviar, and cheeses for all your dinner party needs - both here and in the Hamptons.
2135 Broadway (at 75th St.), (212) 874-0383,

Hours: M-Sa 7am-9pm, Su 9am-7pm, MC, V, AmEx. ❶❷❸ *to 72nd St. Additional locations in Manhattan at 1313 Third Ave. and 424 Sixth Ave.*

Confucious Plaza Vendors

Be prepared to wait in long lines for up to 20 minutes at this outdoor market where fresh produce is sold in bulk poundage. Nowhere else, though, could you get two pounds of specialty mushrooms for only $1 or three pounds of broccoli for $1.50.
Bowery (at Division St.). Cash Only. Ⓑ Ⓓ *to Grand St.*

Dean & Deluca

One of New York's most revered specialty food stores, Dean & Deluca is the Zabar's of downtown. Stop by for a caffeine break at the stand-up espresso bar, pick up some paté for your next dinner party, and ogle the produce section, full of fruits and vegetables suitable for a still-life. They also offer specialty breads, meats, cheeses, desserts, and quality-packaged foods.
560 Broadway (at Prince St.), (212) 226-6800. Hours: M-Sa 10am-8pm, Su 10am-7pm. MC, V, AmEx, D. Ⓝ Ⓡ *to Prince St.,* ❻ *to Spring St.*

Di Palos' Fine Foods

Di Palos' has everything you need when you're planning an Italian feast. The guys who work here are charming and will help you choose the ingredients: fresh mozzarella, sun-dried tomatoes, sausages, bread, and a lot more for what is sure to be an unforgettable meal.
200 Grand St. (at Mott St.), (212) 226-1033, Hours: M-Sa 9am-6:30pm, Su 9am-4pm, MC, V, AmEx, D. ❻ *to Spring St.*

Dynasty Supermarket

This is one of Chinatown's largest supermarkets, boasting a full herb and medicine counter, an in-house butcher and fishmonger, a beef-jerky bar, and, best of all, weekly sales.
68 Elizabeth St. (at Hester St.), (212) 966-4943, Hours: M-Su 9:30am-8:30pm, MC, V. Ⓝ Ⓡ Ⓦ *to Prince St.,* Ⓑ Ⓓ *to Grand St.*

Economy Candy

Calling itself a "nosher's paradise" on the Lower East Side, this is the best discount store in the city for penny candy, imported chocolates, nuts, sweets, and gourmet savories like mustards, chutney, tea, and spices. Try their dense, chewy, pistachio-laden Turkish delight, the most authentic this side of Byzantium.
108 Rivington St. (bet. Essex and Ludlow Sts.), (212) 254-1531, Hours: Su-F 9am-6pm, Sa 10am-5pm, MC, V, AmEx. Ⓕ Ⓙ Ⓜ Ⓩ *to Delancey St.*

Elk Candy

Resist, if possible, the urge not to eat the cute, stylized candies crafted at this Yorkville landmark, renowned for more than sixty years for its marvelous marzipan.
1628 Second Ave. (bet. 84th and 85th Sts.), (212) 585-2303, Hours: M-Sa 9am-6pm, MC, V, AmEx. ❹❺❻ *to 86th St.*

Fairway

"Like no other market" reads the awning, and this is indeed the most popular, largest, and lowest-priced produce and gourmet market on the West Side. A full deli counter offers prepared hot and cold dishes, the cheese department stocks an array of imports, and the bakery sells over a million bagels every year.
2328 Twelfth Ave. (at 133rd St.), (212) 234-3883, Hours: M-Su 8am-11pm, MC, V, AmEx. ❶ *to 125th. St.*
2127 Broadway (at 74th St.), (212) 595-1888. Hours: M-Su 6am-1am. MC, V, AmEx, D. ❶❷❸ *to 72nd St.*

Gourmet Garage

With its original location a converted garage in SoHo, Gourmet Garage was a pioneer in delivering gourmet goods at wholesale prices to the public. The Upper West Side location offers the same selection of breads, cheeses, organic produce, daily prepared foods, and a whole Kosher Cellar downstairs.
2567 Broadway (at 96th St.), (212) 663-0656, Hours: M-Su 7am-10pm, MC, V, AmEx, D. ❶❷❸ *to 96th St.*
453 Broome St. (at Mercer St.), (212) 941-5850, Hours: M-Su 7am-9pm. Ⓝ Ⓡ *to Prince St.*

Italian Food Center

An extraordinary Italian grocery for everything from sandwiches to the ingredients you'll need to imitate your favorite Italian restaurant's risotto. They offer delivery throughout Manhattan, and they cater and have a mail order catalog service.
186 Grand St. (at Mulberry St.), (212) 925-2954, Hours: M-Sa 8am-7pm, Su 9am-6pm. MC, V, AmEx. ❻ *to Spring St.,* Ⓙ Ⓜ Ⓝ Ⓡ Ⓦ Ⓩ ❻ *to Canal St.*

JASMart

An Osaka outpost way uptown, this small grocery-cum-video store is

JASMart

An Osaka outpost way uptown, this small grocery-cum-video-store is stocked with all your favorite Japanese snack treats you never knew existed. While jalapeño shrimp puffs might not be your flavor, the interesting selection of teas, soup mixes, ice creams, vegetables, and meats from Asia bring in a crowd of expatriates clamoring to rent Japanese soap operas or comfort themselves with a little taste of home.
2847 Broadway (at 110th St.), (212) 866-4780, Hours: M-Sun 10am-10pm, MC, V, AmEx. ❶ *to 110th St.-Cathedral Pkwy.*

Kalyustan's

Chefs and an international crowd frequent this multi-story gourmet ethnic food market that wholesales every kind of Indian spice imaginable and features a vast assortment of Middle Eastern delicacies. The small café upstairs stars falafel that couldn't be more authentic.
123 Lexington Ave., (bet. 28th and 29th Sts.), (212) 685-3451. Hours: M-Sa 10am-8pm, Su 11am-7pm. MC, V, AmEx, D. ❻ *to 28th St.*

La Maison du Chocolat

As one might guess, chocolate is this store's specialty, and it comes in many shapes and sizes, none of which even approach being healthy or veer far from being absolutely divine. The staff is very professional and very friendly.
1018 Madison Ave. (bet. 78th and 79th Sts.), (212) 744-7117, Hours: M-F 10am-7pm, Sa 10am-6pm, MC, V, AmEx, D. ❻ *to 77th St.*
30 Rockefeller Ctr. at 49th St. (bet. Fifth and Sixth Aves.), (212) 265 9404. Hours: M-F 9:30am-7pm, Sa 10am-6pm, MC, V, AmEx, Ⓑ Ⓓ Ⓕ Ⓥ *to 47-50th Sts.-Rockefeller Ctr.*

Myers of Keswick

If you have been craving traditional English scones and jam, then this is the place to get them. The spot serves as an English market and local shop that sells a variety of foods such as Cornish pastries, Shepard and kidney pies. This is a cute store to browse as well, with its shelves stocked with jars of clotted cream, tea and sauces.
634 Hudson St., (212) 691-4194, M-F 10am-7pm, Sa 10am-6pm, Su 12pm-5pm. Ⓐ Ⓒ Ⓔ *to 14th St.;* Ⓛ *to Eighth Ave.*

Milano Market

Located right outside Columbia's campus, this gourmet Italian deli and grocery store is stocked from floor to ceiling. In addition to countless sandwich combinations, the store has a pastry counter full of cakes and cookies, a gourmet cheese counter, a sushi counter, a fresh fruit stand, and every-day grocery items. Most items are slightly more expensive than their grocery store counterparts.
2892 Broadway (at 112th St.), (212) 665-9500, Hours: M-Su 6am-1am, MC, V, AmEx, D. ❶ *to 110th St.-Cathedral Pkwy.*

Mondel Chocolates

Florence Mondel has been catering to Morningside Heights chocoholics for more than 50 years. Her modest store is filled with homemade fudge and marzipan, as well as a dozen different kinds of truffles.
2913 Broadway (at 114th St.), (212) 864-2111, Hours: M-Sa 11am-7pm, V, MC, AmEx. ❶ *to 116th St.-Columbia University.*

M. Rohrs' House of Fine Teas & Coffee

Satiating the caffeine addictions of locals for over 100 years with its wide selection of refined tea leaves and coffee beans, Rohrs' is here to stay. Wooden counters, aged tea canisters, and beveled mirrors retain the shop's original old-world charm, an anomaly among slick coffee bars.
303 E. 85th St. (at Second Ave.), (212) 396-4456, www.rohrs.com, Hours: M-Su 7am-9:30pm, MC, V, AmEx. ❹ ❺ ❻ *to 86th St.*

NY Cake & Baking Distributor

If you have a love of baking then this store can fill all your cake and pastry supply needs. The place is packed with giant bags of pie filling and chocolate as well as a variety of any other kind of bake ware you might desire. The cake pan section is particularly huge and you will never find such an accumulation of spatulas in one place ever again.
56 22nd St., (212) 675-2253, www.nycake.com, M-Sa 10am-6pm, MC, V, AmEx. Ⓝ Ⓡ ❻ *to 23rd St.*

Ten Ren Tea and Ginseng Co.

Masters of the ancient but still sophisticated Chinese ritual of tea preparation, the folks at Ten Ren not only sell teas (ranging from $8 to $125 per lb.) but also provide lessons on the proper brewing and enjoying of the venerated green leaf. Superb black teas, jasmine teas, and ginger are also sold.
75 Mott St. (bet. Canal

Union Square Greenmarket

This oasis amidst Manhattan mayhem attracts chefs from all over NoHo and SoHo for ultra-fresh exotic ingredients like elephant garlic and verbena, as well as locals from the neighborhood who come for the bargains on vegetables. With dozens of vendors selling fresh bunches of all produce imaginable, you may forget that you are in New York.
Broadway at 14th St., (bet. 17th St. and Union Sq.), (212) 477-3220, www.cenyc.org, Hours: M, W, F, Sa 8am-6pm. L J M N R W 6 *to 14th St.-Union Sq.*

Washington Market

An open-air farmer's market resplendent with produce, flowers, baked goods, and other delicious items. Organic items are aplenty, as are the real-life farmers, who haul their wares from New Jersey and upstate New York..
Greenwich St. (at Reade St.), June 1-December 1, Hours: Sa 8am-5pm (rain or shine), Cash Only. A C 1 2 3 *to Chambers St.*

Whole Foods

For gourmet foodies and plebian squares alike, this big market is somewhere between a Dean & Delucca and a Fairway, intersecting at the notion of high quality and freshness. All this comes at a price, but the gleaming stocks of natural and organic produce, flavorful cheeses, and other delectables purveyed by equitably treated employees mean sustainability and community awareness never tasted so good.
10 Columbus Circle (basement of Time-Warner Building), (212) 823-9600, Hours: M-Su 8am-10pm, MC, V, AmEx. A B C D 1 *to 59th St.-Columbus Circle.*

Zabar's

A name with impressive cachet in uptown circles, this longtime Upper West Side institution is the prime source for gourmet meats, cheese, breads, and produce. Upstairs is an equally well-stocked kitchenware department featuring at least 30 kinds of whisks. The store can get shoulder-to-shoulder crowded on the weekends and during the holidays.
2245 Broadway (at 80th St.), (212) 787-2000, Hours: M-F 8am-7pm, Sa 8am-8pm, Su 9am-6pm, MC, V, AmEx. 1 *to 79th St.*

[Housewares]

ABC Carpet and Home

Expect to find ample mother/daughter pairs ooh-ing and aah-ing their way through six floors of housewares, antiques, and knickknacks. Although fairly expensive, the store is worth a visit for its creative window displays and extraordinary finds such as a gilded bird cage ten feet tall. The Parlour Café on the ground floor allows weary shoppers to lounge and lunch on the furniture that they probably can't afford to buy.
888 Broadway (at 19th St.), (212) 473-3000, Hours: M-R 10am-8pm, F-Sa 10-6:30pm, Su 12pm-6pm, MC, V, AmEx. L N R W 4 5 6 *to 14th St.-Union Sq.*

Bed Bath and Beyond

This moderately priced emporium of all things domestic is a good bet for college students in need of supplies like dishes, rugs, and even furniture. The convenience of everything in one store sometimes lets you forget you could get what you're buying elsewhere for cheaper.
620 Sixth Ave. (bet. 18th and 19th Sts.), (212) 255-3550, www.bedbathandbeyond.com, Hours: M-Su 8am-9pm, MC, V, AmEx, D. 1 *to 18th St.,* L *to Sixth Ave.,* F V *to 14th St.*
Additional locations in Manhattan at 410 61st St. and 1932 Broadway.

Broadway Panhandler

Both trendy and reliable, this kitchenware store has everything you need to stock the kitchen of your new Manhattan loft. The prices are reasonable, and the salespeople are more than helpful. Fun tablecloths or dishes are mixed with a collection of classic pots and pans. Stop in for a quick kitchen pick-me-up or a cooking emergency; they are sure to have what you need. From cooking ware to cookbooks this store is a savior.
477 Broome St. (at Wooster St.), (212) 966-3434, www.broadwaypanhandler.com, Hours: M-F 10:30am-7pm, Sa 11am-7pm, Su 10:30am-6pm, MC, V, AmEx, D. C E *to Spring St.,* N R *to Prince St.*

Crate and Barrel

For the last minute housewarming party or largely decorative kitchen paraphernalia, the label delivers the rare combination of style and value. This "upscale IKEA" is ready to equip the urban warrior with the bare necessities, from crème

 Downtown Furniture

New York style without New York prices, Downtown Furniture offers trendy buys to furnish any and every room. With friendly and knowledgeable service, you will find exactly what you are looking for, and if not, something better. Conveniently located, it's your best option to furnish anything from a dorm room to a new apartment.
165 Grand St., (bet. Centre and Baxter Sts.), (212) 966-7201. N R W to Canal St.

brulée dishes to martini glasses.
650 Madison Ave. (at 59th St.), (212) 308-0011, Hours: M-F 10am-8pm, Sa 10am-7pm, Su 12pm-6pm, MC, V, AmEx, D. N R W 4 5 6 to 59th St.-Lexington Ave.

Dom USA

Need some inflatable furniture for your dorm room? Have a fondness for house wares made of neon-colored plastic? You'll find all that and plenty more for the home at this trendy decorator hot spot, as well as sundry other junk, from pens to pillboxes. Most of it is inexpensive and equally suitable for gift-giving or feeding your personal flair for home decorating.
382 W. Broadway (bet. Spring and Broome Sts.), (212) 334-5580, Hours: M-Sa 11am-8pm, Su 11am-7pm, MC, V, AmEx. A C E to Spring St., N R to Prince St.

Fishs Eddy

Mix and match from overstocks of commercial dishes and glasses to set a dinner table that no one else will have. Watch the price tags, though. Don't leave without checking out the bins in the back for $1 saucers and the shelves around the sides for $2 wine glasses.
889 Broadway (at 19th St.), (212) 420-9020, www.fishseddy.com, Hours: M-Sa 10am-9pm, Su 11am-8pm, MC, V, AmEx. L N R 4 5 6 to 14th St.-Union Sq.
Additional locations in Manhattan at 2176 Broadway and 1388 Third Ave.

Industrial Plastics

The bare-bones aesthetic of this store belies its amazing selection of all things plastic: costume jewelry, decorative boxes, giant animals, and glittery adhesive linings for whatever you can imagine. A do-it-yourself paradise for the home-improver, but also a neat place to scoop up some trinkets and toys.
309 Canal St. (at Broadway), (212) 226-2010, Hours: M-F 9am-5:30pm, Sa 9am-4:30pm, MC, V, AmEx. 1 to Canal St.

Just Bulbs

The name really says it all. Find every imaginable light bulb, including those for decoration, gifts, and specific holidays.
936 Broadway (bet. 21st and 22nd Sts.), (212) 228-7820, Hours: M-F 9am-6pm, R 9am-7pm, Sa 10am-6pm, Su 12pm-6pm, MC, V, AmEx, D, DC. N R to 23rd St.

Mxyplyzyk

Long indispensable to interior designers and the young trend crowd, Mxyplyzyk features relentlessly elegant home furnishings that inspire feelings of mushy love. The merchandise is so original and well selected that it is hard to argue even with the lonely row of slippers. Yes, the prices can skew high, but even the $4 cups are, somehow their own works of art.
123/125 Greenwich Ave. (at 13th St.), (212) 989-4300, Hours: M-Sa 11am-7pm, Su 12pm-5pm, MC, V, AmEx. A C E L 1 2 3 to 14th St.

Pottery Barn

A yuppie store that carries everything from beds to plates to sun umbrellas. The perfect place to shop for a new home if you have some money and are into darker colors and sophisticated styles and prices. This store is similar to Crate and Barrel.
1965 Broadway (at 67th St.), (212) 579-8477, www.potterybarn.com, Hours: M-Sa 10am-9pm, Su 11am-7pm. 1 to 66th St.
Additional Locations in Manhattan at 127 59th St. and 600 Broadway.

Saigoniste

This trendy housewares shop is filled with plates, bowls, candles, and chopsticks, all imported from Vietnam. With plush pillows, creative lighting, and soothing candles, this small shop has the appearance of a living room. Their colorful products are original and also affordable.
186 Spring St., (212) 925-4610, www.saigoniste.com, Hours: M-Sa 11am-7pm, Su 12pm-6pm, MC, V, AmEx, D. 6 to Spring St.

S & B Electrical Supply Store

This Brooklyn mainstay has been in business since 1969 and will almost certainly last another 36 years. Run by one of the hardest working men in Brooklyn, the store offers courteous and professional service where one knows that they are not being taken advantage of. A convenient and easy way to fix all of your electrical needs, S & B sells lights, wire and all sorts of needed electrical supplies.
247 Kings Highway (bet. W. 8th and W. 9th Sts.), (718) 266-0432, www.sbelectrical.com, Hours: M-F 8am-5pm, Sa 8am-12pm, closed Sunday, AmEx, MC, V. N to Kings Highway.

Supermud Pottery Studio

Who says arts and crafts are just for kids? Here you can take a class in wheel throwing or just stop in and paint pre-made pottery with your own decorative designs. Perfect for those simply looking to relax and get their hands dirty, as well as those

seeking more thoughtful gifts for friends and family. Relive those ceramic parties you enjoyed as a kid.
2744 Broadway (bet. 105th and 106th Sts.), (212) 865-9190, Hours: T-Su 12pm-6pm, Closed Mondays, AmEx, MC, V, D. (1) to 103rd St.

University Housewares
This is a great neighborhood resource, which in many ways doubles as a hardware store with a touch of class. They maximize their small size with floor-to-ceiling shelves stacked with all the basics, yet high quality goods are the norm, and the friendly staff are happy to help you navigate the sometimes confusing array of mixing bowls and dustbusters.
2901 Broadway (at 113th St.), (212) 882-2798, Hours: M-F 8am-8pm, Sa 9am-7pm, Su 9am-6pm, MC, V, AmEx, D. (1) to 110th St.-Cathedral Pkwy.

Urban Archaeology
The stock is sold both wholesale and retail at this furniture store, which houses a collection of architectural ornaments, artifacts, and lighting fixtures in the kitschy retro vein in what was once a four-story candy factory.
143 Franklin St., (212) 431-4646, Hours: M-F 8am-6pm, Sa 12pm-6pm. (1) to Franklin St.

White Trash
From shiny silver toasters to impressively tacky glassware sets, your own grandmother probably got rid of '50s and '60s junk like this twenty years ago. Nevertheless, it's all hip again and the prices aren't too inflated to not be a reasonable and interesting alternative to outfitting your home in department store standards.
304 E. 5th St. (bet. First and Second Aves.), (212) 598-5956, Hours: M-Sa 2pm-8:30pm, MC, V. (F) to Second Ave., (6) to Astor Pl., (N)(R) to 8th St.

[Music & Movies]

Bleecker Bob's Golden Oldies Record Shop
Packed with a huge vinyl selection, including rare albums, Bob's is a hub for DJs and music collectors alike. Their rock, metal, indie, emo, punk, and hardcore CD selection draws everyone else. Other bonuses include the posters, pieces ("for tobacco only"), and a body piercing/tattoo shop in the back.
118 W. 3rd St. (bet. MacDougal St. and First Ave.), (212) 475-9677, Hours: M-Su 11am-1am, MC, V, AmEx, D. (A)(B)(C)(D)(E)(F)(V)(1) to W. 4th St.

Chelsea Second Hand Guitars
Go in and try one on for size: Strats, Les Pauls, Fenders, etc. You'll find vintage guitars for the finger-pick connoisseur. Become the next Kurt Cobain.
220 W. 23rd St. (bet. Seventh and Eighth Aves.), (212) 675-4993, Hours: M-Sa 12pm-7pm, MC, V, AmEx. (1) to 23rd St., (C)(E) to 23rd St.

Dance Tracks
If you're disappointed in the dance/electronica selection of your neighborhood megastore, look no further. At Dance Tracks, you'll discover a wide selection of euro-dance, club imports, your favorite DJ's remixes, and house music. The knowledgeable staff also gives fine recommendations catering to your particular taste, be it techno or trance.
91 E. 3rd St. (at First Ave.), (212) 260-8729, Hours: M-R 12pm-9pm, F 12pm-10pm, Sa 12pm-8pm, Su 1pm-6:30pm, MC, V, AmEx, D. (F)(V) to Second Ave.

Disc-O-Rama
This small chain was serving downtown New York's audio/visual needs before the words "DVD" and "CD" entered our vocabulary. Though they've updated their inventory since then, offering an extensive collection of current music and video releases, Disc-O-Rama still keeps it old-school with a vinyl depart-

ment and album prices that are always cheaper than a movie ticket. Try finding either of those features in a megastore.
40 Union Sq. E. (bet. 16th and 17th Sts.), (212) 260 8616, ww.discorama. com, Hours: M-F 8:30am-6:45pm, Sa 10am-6pm, Su 11am-5:45pm. MC, V, AmEx. L N R W 4 5 6 *to 14th St.-Union Sq.*

Elmo Lounge

Downstairs from the famous Elmo restaurant is one of the newest live music venues in New York. Decorated like the legendary nightclub, The El Morocco, this place is a good time. With palm motif wallpaper and mirror tiles on the walls one gets transported to Miami in the 1950's but the music is good and everyone seems to be having a good time.
156 Seventh Ave., (212) 337-8000. C E *to 23rd St.*

Fat Beats

Indispensable for hip-hop fans, this well-stocked shop also doesn't do too badly in the acid jazz and reggae departments either. Secondhand bins are an amazing source of classics.
406 Sixth Ave. (bet. 8th and 9th Sts.), (212) 673-3883, Hours: M-Sa 12pm-9pm, Su 12pm-6pm. MC, V, AmEx. A B C D E F V *to West 4th St.*

Generation Records

The best selection of punk, hardcore, and underground music in the city. Cheap movie and music posters, T-shirts, used CDs, and an extensive vinyl stock soothe the emotional scars inflicted by the glaring staff. Come here for CDs you can't find anywhere else.
210 Thompson St. (bet. Bleecker and 3rd Sts.), (212) 254-1100, Hours: M-R 11am-10pm, F-Sa 11am-1am, Su 12pm-10pm, MC, V. A B C D E F V *to W. 4th St.,* 6 *to Bleecker St.*

Kim's Mediapolis

The newest installment of the Kim's stores boasts videos, DVDs, music, and books. There's an enormous collection of Hollywood and indie movies, and rentals are cheaper than bigger video chains. Beware late fees – they can cost you the family farm. It's very hip, and the staff is knowledgeable.
2906 Broadway (bet. 113th and 114th Sts.), (212) 864-5321, Hours: M-Su 9am-12am, MC, V, AmEx. 1 *to 116th St.-Columbia University.*
6 St. Marks Pl. (at Third Ave.), (212) 505-0311, Hours: M-Su 10am-12am. MC, V, AmEx. 6 *to Astor Pl.,* L *to Third Ave.*

Matt Umanov Guitars

Anyone in a band knows this long-time Village institution. This shop offers acoustic and electric instruments at reasonable prices, as well as a knowledgeable staff.
273 Bleecker St. (bet. Sixth and Seventh Aves.), (212) 675-2157, Hours: M-Sa 11am-7pm, Su 12pm-6pm, MC, V, AmEx, 1 *to Christopher St.-Sheridan Sq.*

The Music Factory

The latest in contemporary music, including hip-hop, gospel, jazz, reggae, and soul. Many artists often do in-store signings or performances here to promote their material. Cassettes, vinyl, CDs, and even videotapes are available at very affordable prices at this local DJ hangout.
Jamaica, Queens. 162-01 Jamaica Ave. (at 162nd St.), (718) 291-3135, Hours: M-Sa 10am-8pm, Su 11am-6:30pm. MC, V, AmEx, D. E *to Jamaica Ctr.*

Norman's Sound and Vision

Super-friendly and knowledgeable Norman claims his store has the "best selection of jazz in New York." Also browse the vast assortment of rock, punk, indie, Latin, and world music. Downstairs features used videos, CDs, vinyl, and laserdiscs, plus T-shirts and even leather jackets. The eager and

T-shirts and even leather jackets. The eager and unpretentious staff won't make you feel ashamed for buying the new Britney CD.
67 Cooper Sq. (at 7th St.), (212) 473-6599, Hours: M-Su 10am-11pm, MC, V, AmEx, D, DC. 6 *to Astor Pl.*

Other Music

A well-deserved haven for indie-rock lovers that also offers a full selection of ambient psychedelia and noise. Keep an eye out for special in-store performances that have already featured Yo La Tengo and Howe Head.
15 E. 4th St. (bet. Broadway and Lafayette St.), (212) 477-8150. Hours: M-F 12pm-9pm, Sa 12pm-8pm, Su 12pm-7pm, MC, V, AmEx. B D F V *to Broadway-Lafayette St.,* 6 *to Bleecker St.*

Sam Ash

Ever want to DJ? Sprawling along 48th St., these four music shops fulfill almost every music-making need, selling acoustic instruments, recording equipment, MIDI systems, computers and software, DJ equipment, lighting, sheet music, and other items. The staff knows its stuff, and all locations (except for #163) rent and repair instruments and equipment.
155, 160, 159, and 163 W. 48th St. (bet. Sixth and Seventh Aves.), (212) 719-2299, Hours: M-F 10am-8pm, Sa 10am-7pm, Su 12pm-6pm, MC, V, AmEx, D. N R W *to 49th St.,* B D F V *to 47-50th Sts.-Rockefeller Ctr.,* 1 *to 50th St.*

Secondhand Rose

This store is perfect for movie fanatics who need to decorate the walls of their new apartment. The extensive collection of posters is overwhelming but you can be sure that you can find that Vin Diesal poster you're looking for. The employees are also very informative and can help you if you get lost.
138 Duane St., (212) 393-9002, M-F 10am-6pm; Sa, Su by appointment only, MC, V, AmEx. A C *to Chambers St.,* N R *to City Hall,* 6 *to Brooklyn Bridge.*

Tower Records

New York's first music superstore has been surpassed in size by many others but still has a strong selection, although it can be hard to find major rock titles here, oddly enough. Also check out its counterpart, Tower Video and Books, which has a stellar video selection downstairs and a bookstore upstairs. Interesting note: Nirvana played one of their first (and some may say best) acoustic shows at this Tower Records.
692 Broadway (at 4th St.), (212) 505-1500, Hours: M-Su 9am-12am, MC, V, AmEx. N R W *to 8th St.,* 6 *to Astor Pl.*
Additional locations in Manhattan at 721 Fifth Ave., 20 4th St., 1961 Broadway.

Vinylmania

Specializing in house music and imports, this store lets you listen before you buy.
60 Carmine St. (bet. Seventh Ave. and Bedford St.), (212) 924-7223, Hours: M-W 11am-8pm, R-Sa 11am-9pm, MC, V, AmEx. A B C D E F C *to West 4th St.*

Virgin Megastore

Redefining the idea of the megastore, this flashy three-level entertainment complex boasts movie theaters, over one thousand listening booths, and a wide selection of videos, laser discs, and CD-ROMs.
1540 Broadway (bet. 45th and 46th Sts.), (212) 921-1020, Hours: Su-R 9am-1am, F-Sa 9am-2pm, MC, V, AmEx, D. A C E N R S W 1 2 3 7 *to 42nd St.-Times Sq.*
Additional location in Manhattan at 52 E. 14th St.

[Salons]

Aveda

Haircuts that would normally set you back $65 are free in the training class. Expect to wait a month. No coloring.
233 Spring St. (bet. Varick and Prince Sts.), call for an appointment, (212) 807-1492. C E *to Spring St.*
Additional locations in Manhattan.

Bumble and Bumble

Leave a message explaining what you want done, and they'll get back to you if they think they can use you for the training class.
146 E. 56th St. (bet. Third and Lexington Ave.), Cut: $10, Color: $20, call for an appointment, (212) 521-6500. N R W 4 5 6 *to 59th St.-Lexington Ave.*
Additional location in Manhattan at 415 13th St.

Crisca Hair Salon

Stop in for a moderately priced haircut with no appointment necessary.
21 E. 51st St. (bet. Fifth and Madison Aves.), (212) 759-4743, MC, V. E V *to Fifth Ave.-53rd St.*

Hoshi Coupe III

This Japanese owned and operated salon is great for a dose of Tokyo hipster spunk, with Asian pop music blaring and Vogue Nippon lying around. Along with the fun haircuts, the stylists will throw in a head massage (and that New York rarity, a student discount). One problem for those who might see it as such is that English really is a second language here, potentially jeopardizing those of you with highly specific requests, but probably worth the risk.
2801 Broadway (at 108th St), (212) 663-0460, Hours: M-Sa 10am-6pm, MC, V. 1 *to 110th St.-Cathedral Pkwy.*
Additional locations at 214 E. 9th St. and 259 W. 19th St.

Kropps and Bobbers

While the stylists taking care of your head here may be cooler than you, they'll never let on, making this salon a sure bet for the less adventurous who still want to have an edge. The funky décor is a cross between Peewee's Playhouse and a bombed out cracker factory, which all seems in keeping with the customers' sometimes playfully ironic hairdos.
173 Orchard St. (at Stanton St.), (212) 260-6992, Hours: M-Su 11am-9pm, Cash only. F V *to Second Ave.*

Mudhoney

Small and dark, packed with photos of famous clients, $100 hair sauce bottles rolling off the shelves, patrons and stylists sporting faux-hawks, severe bangs, and plenty of attitude make this the place for the best rock n' roll haircut in New York, period. Not to be confused with Mark Arm's Seattle outfit.
148 Sullivan St. (at Houston St.), (212) 533-1160, Hours: T-F 12pm-8pm, Sa 12pm-6pm, Cash only. 1 *to Houston St.*

Scott J

Columbia students pamper themselves with professional cuts and excellent makeup or waxing at this convenient location. Service can be expensive for a college student, but you get what you pay for (and that is a great haircut).
2929 Broadway (bet. 114th and 115th Sts.), Second Fl., (212) 666-6429, MC, V. 1 *to 116th St.-Columbia University. Additional locations in Manhattan.*

The Service Station

Bodies in need of a tune-up, look toward the twelve-foot Gulf sign. Cuts start at $40. The shop offers an array of body tweakings, including manicures, tanning, and electrolysis.
137 Eighth Ave. (bet. 17th and 18th Sts.), (212) 243-7770. 1 *to 18th St.*

TwoDo Salon and Spa

TwoDo Salon offers upscale hair treatments without the arrogant attitudes. It is small enough to be personal with a friendly staff, but not so tiny that it feels claustrophobic. For a special indulgence, take care of your stressed-out hair by giving it a Kerastase conditioning treatment, which is a TwoDo specialty. Whether your getting highlights or special occasion styles, prices will not break the bank, and you'll look like you spent a fortune when you're done. The TwoDo Spa has the essential services: manicures, pedicures, facials, and waxing.
210 W. 82nd St. (bet. Broadway and Amsterdam Aves.), (212) 787-1277, www.twodo.com, Hours: T-F 9am-9pm, Sa 9am-5pm. 1 *to 79th St.*

Vidal Sassoon

You can't get scheduled till they take a look at your hair. All of the hair stylists here are experienced and professional. Their avant-garde models and extensive lines of hair care products attest to their overall high quality level. Twenty percent off the already cut-rate prices for students.
90 Fifth Ave. (bet. 14th and 15th Sts.), call for appointment, (212) 229-2000. L N R W 4 5 6 *to 14th St.-Union Sq. Additional location at 730 Fifth Ave. (bet 56th and 57th Sts.), (212) 535-9200.*

[Shoes]

Anbar Shoe Steal

The southeastern corner of TriBeCa is a bargain shopper's paradise, and this is by far the best outlet for great shoe deals. Quality, name-brand footwear goes for close-out prices and the selection is remarkably good, especially for those seeking sizes other than a seven or eight. Perfect for finding cheap and stylish accessories to match an end-of-season clothes purchase in an unusual color.
60 Reade St. (at Church St.), (212) 227-0253, Hours: M-F 9am-6:20pm, Sa 11am-5:45pm, MC, V, AmEx, D. A C 1 2 3 *to Chambers St.*

Kenneth Cole - Reaction

Never accused of being right-wing, Kenneth Cole's style is definitely fashion forward. While the pulsating speakers, moderate prices, and clean lines are far from innovations, they are welcome diversions from the $124 jeans at neighboring stores. The long lines at the register prove that some things never go out of style.
130 E. 57th St. (at Lexington Ave.), (212) 688 1670, www.kennethcole.com, Hours: M-Sa 10am-8pm, Su 11am-6pm MC, V, AmEx. N R W 4 5 6 *to 59th St.-Lexington. Ave. Additional locations in Manhattan.*

Manolo Blahnik

In the dream life of shoe-fetishists, Manolo Blahnik's ultra-sexy, elegant stilettos reign supreme. Despite the steep prices, addicts like the *Sex and the City* girls tend to indulge in a "fab" pair on a regular basis. As a tribute to the show, Blahnik designed a Sarah Jessica Parker shoe that is now a popular buy in his midtown shop. These ultra-chic stilettos compare with Jimmy Choo's in beauty, sexiness, and, alas, price.
31 W 54th St., (212) 582-3007, Hours: M-F 10:30am-6pm, Sa 10:30am-5:30pm, MC, V, AmEx. E V *to Fifth Ave.-53rd St.*

Otto Tootsie Plohound

The nonsensical name speaks well for a store full of outrageous shoes from no-name labels, alongside the usual designer suspects. Men and women looking for fun sneakers or hot boots will both be pleased with the selection in this bastion of footwear fetishism.
413 W. Broadway (at Spring St.), (212) 925-8931, Hours: M-F 11:30am-7:30pm, Sa 11pm-8pm, Su 12pm-7pm, MC, V, AmEx. C E *to Spring St. Additional locations at Manhattan at 137 Fifth Ave., 273 Lafayette St., 38 E. 57th St.*

Sacco
Trendy, retro, and classic, this chic shop carries it all. Make this store your first stop for well-made, eclectic women's footwear. Shoes tend to be dressy and relatively expensive, but there are always sale selections. Clearances offer an additional 20 percent off the sale price.
324 Columbus Ave. (at 75th St.), (212) 799-5229, www.saccoshoes.com, Hours: M-F 11am-8pm, Sa 11am-7pm, Su 12pm-7pm, MC, V, AmEx, D. 1 2 3 to 72nd St.
Additional locations in Manhattan at 94 Seventh Ave., 118 E. 59th St., 14 E. 17th St., and 111 Thompson St.

Shoe Biz
A division of Steve Madden, the store has lots of trendy shoes for those who need a lift. Whether stacked or spike heels, platform or wedge, most of the shoes fall somewhere between casual and funky formal. This is a good store for fashion-conscious teens and the young at heart who want to walk tall while spending small.
41 W. 34th St., (212) 736-3283, www.stevemadden.com, Hours: M-Sa 10am-9pm, Su 11am-7pm, MC, V, AmEx, D. B D F N R V W to 34th St.-Herald Sq.

[Sports]

Bicycle Habitat
If the quality of a bike store can be determined by counting the number of customers' bikes that are chained outside, then this is one of the best in the city. Customers here are serious about their bikes, and the same people can be found day after day checking out new models, picking up parts, or just discussing their obsession.
244 Lafayette St. (bet. Prince and Spring Sts.), (212) 431-3315, www.bicyclehabitat.com, Hours: M-R 10am-7pm, F 10am-6:30pm, Sa-Su 10am-6pm, MC, V, AmEx. N R W to Prince St., 6 to Spring St.

Blades, Boards & Skates
The helpful staff would readily join their patrons on Astor Pl. at one of the wheels-only lunch break congregations. Slick new styles of in-line skates, roller skates, and standard skater gear also available at not-so-unconventional prices.
659 Broadway (bet. Bleecker and 3rd Sts.), (212) 477-7350, www.blades.com, Hours: M-S 10am-9pm, Su 11am-7pm, MC, V, AmEx, D. B D F V to Broadway-Lafayette St., 6 to Bleecker St.
Additional locations in Manhattan at 901 Sixth Ave. and 120 W. 72nd St.

Gotham Bikes
A good place to buy or rent a bike without being intimidated by a staff of gearheads trying to push an Italian racing model when you just want to ride through the park.
112 W. Broadway (bet. Duane and Reade Sts.), (212) 732-2453, www.gothambikes.com, Hours: M-W, F-Sa 10am-6:30pm, R 10am-7:30pm, Su 10:30am -5pm, MC, V, AmEx. 1 2 3 to Chambers St.

Paragon Sports
Whether the game is badminton, snowboarding, or basketball, this sports superstore is sure to have the right gear. The shoe department often has better deals than the chains.
867 Broadway (at 18th St.), (212) 255-8036, www.paragonsports.com, Hours: M-Sa 10am-8pm, Su 11:30am-7pm, MC, V, AmEx. 1 to 18th St., L N R W 4 5 6 to Union Sq.-14th St.

Tents & Trails
Manhattan's low-key place for gearheads. If you're sick of battling it out in super-crazy stores, this outdoor clothing and equipment store is the place for you. The prices are the best in town.
21 Park Pl. (at Church St.), (212) 227-1760, Hours: M-W, Sa 9:30am-6pm, R-F 9:30am-7pm, Su 12pm-6:30pm, MC, V, AmEx. 2 3 to Park Pl.

[Stationary]

Il Papiro
This satellite shop sells the paper goods produced at the Il Papiro factory in Florence and sold throughout Italy. Each piece is meticulously hand-marbleized in the tradition of the Mace Ruette, the bookbinder of Louis XIII of France. At $22 a sheet, store patrons are commonly left wondering what exactly can be done with this famous paper. Fear not, the store provides the answer. Namely, a variety of other paper-related wares from feather and inkwell sets to wax seal sets to any size and color of leather book imaginable.
1021 Lexington Ave. (bet. 73rd and 74th Sts.), (212) 288-9330. Hours: M-F 10am-6pm, Sa 10am-5:30pm. MC, V, AmEx. 6 to 77th St.

Kate's Paperie
Sheaves of fanciful wrapping paper and reams of stationery fill every nook of this location, augmented by paper-related merchandise ranging from kites to hatboxes to desks.
561 Broadway (at Prince St.), (212) 941-9816, www.katespaperie.com, Hours: M-F 10am-7:30pm, Sa 10am-7pm, Su 11am-7pm, MC, V, AmEx. N R to Prince St.
Additional Locations in Manhattan at 8 13th St., 1282 Third Ave., and 140 57th St.

Lincoln Stationers
This two-floored mega stationary store has everything you need, from office supplies to fancy wedding stationary. The fancy stationary, pens, and gifts are beautifully displayed on the upper level. In order to get to the abundance of functional office supplies, you must venture down to the basement. With a variety of pens and papers to choose from, the staff is very friendly and willing to help you sort through the sea of planners, address books, cards, and to help you find exactly what you need.
1889 Broadway (at 63rd St.), (212) 459-3500, Hours: M-F 9am-8:30pm, Sa 10am-7pm, Su 11:30am-6:30pm, AmEx, MC, V, D. 1 to 66th St.

Thrift Stores

With New York prices being obscenely high (and still rising), many city dwellers are looking to thrift stores to provide them with most of their clothing and accessories. Thrift stores are secondhand shops that take donations of various items and resell them at very discounted rates. Originally, these stores were designed for those who could not afford retail clothing, and due to the charitable nature of these shops, most of their proceeds are donated to charity. While this concept still holds true, recently wearing hand-me-downs has become a fashion trend due to the fact that many thrift store items are one of a kind.

New York has become riddled with all types of these shops, ranging from smaller boutiques to chains like Goodwill and Salvation Army. Thrift stores like Cancer Care Thrift Store (*1480 Third Ave., (212) 879-9868*) and Memorial Sloan-Kettering Cancer Center Thrift Shop (*1440 Third Ave., (212) 535-1250*) have their proceeds go to cancer research and look more like small boutiques than second-hand shops. Both Cancer Care and Memorial Sloan-Kettering are known for carrying beautiful evening dresses, custom jewelry and, occasionally, designer handbags that range in price from $10 to $350. Another location that donates proceeds to scientific research is the Arthritis Foundation (*121 E. 77th St., (212) 772-8116*). These two stores also supply an abundance of antiques, books and artwork that are in good condition to buy for a home or apartment.

For higher quality thrift stores that have more antiques, two great places to check out are Acquired Taste (*220 E. 10th St., (212) 995-5064*) and Saved (*82 Berry St. (718) 388-5990*). These stores are the vogue for handcraft because most of their items are individually customized. The antique clothing and accessories are all unique and are guaranteed to come straight from the epoch they're associated with. One can find rare items such as a 1920s embroidered kimono or a rhinestone studded velvet evening dress from the 1950s. After several minutes of browsing, it soon becomes difficult to determine what is old and what is new. If you would really like to search for furniture, be sure to stop by A Furniture Find (*2668 Broadway, (212) 877-3450*). Another location to check out is the City Opera Thrift Shop (*222 E. 23rd St., (212) 684-5344*), which offers great clothing at discount rates. Saved becomes even more exceptional in that owner-designers Noel Hennessy and Sean McNanney remake most of the merchandise, and in some instances allow young designers to contribute some of their own pieces to their growing number of items.

If you are looking to buy in bulk for the cheapest prices possible, then try hitting chain stores like Goodwill Industries (*multiple locations, goodwillny.org*) or Salvation Army (*multiple locations, salvationarmy.org*). Do not look forward to finding designer labels at these stores, although you will find massive amounts of Gap and Ann Taylor merchandise lining the racks. Don't forget that you can not only purchase clothing from these stores, but can donate old clothes as well. Thrift stores appreciate all manner of donations, and are more than happy to accept new and used clothing. The way in which you donate goods varies on the thrift store, although some provide a service where they pick up items from donors. Thrift stores are both a great way to find excellent clothing at cheap prices and do your part in making New York City a better place for those less fortunate.

inside look:

Rational Fashion

1) Could you explain your businesses' history?

Rational Fashion started during my junior year of college. Already an experienced eBay seller, I was approached by a close friend with whom I had collaborated on a previous business plan. He had recently purchased a pair of designer jeans on eBay, the world's most prominent online marketplace, at a significant discount. We found a wholesaler located in Washington Heights and bought our first lot of fifty pairs of jeans. The rest is history...
We currently operate our own warehouse in Manhattan's Garment District with a dedicated staff of three. We ship roughly 500 orders per week and are paced to have $1 million in sales during 2005.

2) What made you decide to start Rational Fashion, after the so-called dot.com crash of the late nineties?

I wasn't concerned with the dot-com crash. That was a result of a group of zealous entrepreneurs hashing out ideas and business plans at an unreasonable pace and eager investors throwing tons of money at them. Rational Fashion is neither a content-based website nor a radical concept that will take massive public acceptance. Our profit potential isn't based on unrealistic ad revenue. We're simply a virtual discount clothing store on the corner of www street and .com avenue. We're open 24 hours a day, 7 days a week, and the whole world is just a click away.

3) What is the key to running a successful internet business?

The key to successful internet sales is using as many channels as possible to attract customers. eBay is a great start but it is by no way an absolute solution. As the world's #1 online marketplace, eBay takes a significant cut of sales. Between listing fees, final value fees, and what are known as "bells and whistles" (gallery images, bold face titles, etc, all used to make ones listings stand out) eBay gets roughly 10% of all gross sales. It is therefore important to expand to other channels. Overstock.com and Amazon.com both offer a less expensive auction based marketplace.

Shopping engines are like search engines of e-commerce sites. Merchants such as RationalFashion.com will upload their entire inventory into the system in a process called catalog syndication. This will allow customers to compare products and prices in one location. If a customer clicks through on a certain merchant, that merchant pays a per-click fee to the shopping engine. Froogle.com, Shopzilla.com, and Price grabber.com are examples of these engines.

Another way to attract customers is through paid search. Paid search allow merchants (or anyone for that matter) to bid on certain key words. On google.com for examples, you may sometimes see "sponsored links." Merchants make auction-style bids on their price-per-click and are placed accordingly. Nordstrom.com pays over $1.00 for clicks on keywords such as "Seven Jeans." The competition is fierce and it can get expensive, but the conversions can be worth the cost, as you are attracting the right customer at the right time.

4) Do you find it important to be located in the center of world fashion, New York City?

While I have always been a proponent of virtual-locations, some business needs to be done face-to-face. This is especially true in the garment business. Nothing beats a hand shake.

5) How would you say you take advantage of the city, in both a business and personal sense?

The city is great because you have many worlds all packed into a very small island. It's full of treasures that aren't always entirely obvious which is why it's important to be equipped with a top notch guide to the city!

Arts *arts*

the roots of museum

New Yorkers often take their city's wealth of art for granted – museums and galleries are full of tourists, not natives. New York City and its environs serve not only as a home to collections of ancient treasures donated by magnanimous New Yorkers of yore but also as a laboratory for pioneering artists. The city's galleries, museums, and auction houses cater to visitors of various levels of interest, from the merely curious to the connoisseur. On Museum Mile, you will find many of the city's largest and most popular tourist destinations. In Chelsea, SoHo, and Brooklyn's DUMBO, you'll find galleries showing works of modern/contemporary artists - trailblazers for a new movement in the aftermath of Pop Art.

Museum Mile

Many of New York City's superstar museums are planted along this stretch of Fifth Ave., bordered by the leafy recesses of Central Park. You may be tempted to join the legions of out-of-towners who, armed with maps and water bottles, attempt to conquer The Mile in a single day; resist the urge, as it is an impossible feat. Avoid museum burnout and art-overload by staggering visits and limiting yourself to a few sections of the larger museums at a time. As a New Yorker, you don't have to try to see everything in a single day. Many of the museums along the Mile stay open until 8pm on one weekday night. Most working New Yorkers choose to visit during these times, when the crowds are far less daunting than on the weekends. *See Listings for locations, hours, and directions.*

❶ El Museo del Barrio

The museum was founded in

1969 by a group of Puerto Rican educators, artists, parents, and community activists in East Harlem's Spanish-speaking neighborhood: El Barrio. Today, it is the city's only museum dedicated to representing Puerto Rican, Caribbean, and Latin American art and culture. Its collection spans from traditional secular and religious sculpture and painting to video, photographs, paintings, and works on paper by living Hispanic artists.

❷ Museum of the City of New York

Roll your eyes if you must, but

the city's self-importance is deserved. This treasury of artifacts of New York history holds more than 1.5 million paintings, prints, photographs, costumes, toys, rare books, manuscripts, sculptures, and decorative objects that tell stories from the city's past. The museum's permanent collection contains everything from a late nineteenth-century police paddy wagon to a comprehensive collection of Courier and Ives color lithographs. Rotating exhibitions focus on specific time periods and historical figures from the city's storied past.

❸ The Jewish Museum

The largest Jewish museum this

side of the world, this collection uses art as the primary medium to present the many aspects of Jewish culture and history as it has existed for over four millennia. Designed to be relevant to a broad audience, the museum seeks to both provide a "touchstone of collective memory" and demystify the label "Jewish." In 2002, the museum gained notoriety because of a scandalous exhibit about the Holocaust as pop-art. Be sure to take advantage of the museum's "pay what you wish" on Thursdays.

❹ The Cooper-Hewitt Museum

The Smithsonian's National

Museum of Design champions form and function in one fell swoop by exploring the way that design shapes visual culture and influences quality of life. The historic Carnegie Mansion houses the

Fifth Avenue
Madison Avenue
2 105th St.
1 104th St.
103rd St.
102nd St.
101th St.
100th St.
99th St.
98th St.
97th St.
96th St.
95th St.
94th St.
93rd St.
3 92nd St.
4 91st St.
90th St.
89th St.
5 88th St.
87th St.
6 86th St.
85th St.
84th St.
83rd St.
82nd St.
7 81st St.
80th St.
79th St.
78th St.
77th St.
76th St.
75th St. 8
74th St.
73rd St.
72nd St.
71st St.
9 70th St.

museum's expansive collection, which includes everything from textiles to a recently discovered sketch of a silver candelabra by Michelangelo.

5 The Solomon R. Guggenheim Museum

When architect Frank Lloyd Wright designed the spiral ramps and shell-like exterior to house the Guggenheim's collection over forty years ago, he initiated a fiery debate over the importance of art and architecture. From the outset, the Guggenheim's board of directors believed that visitors would be drawn to the museum building itself, regardless of what artworks were housed inside it. This antipathetic attitude toward art is glaringly apparent throughout the galleries that house the permanent collection. The many works by Van Gogh, Picasso, Braque, Matisse, and Modigliani are relegated to low-ceilinged, sterile warrens that visitors chance upon if they wander off the ramps where the museums' special exhibitions are displayed.

6 The Neue Galerie

German for "New Gallery," this small and intimate collection, which opened in the fall of 2001, is the most recent addition to Museum Mile. The gallery is dedicated entirely to German and Austrian art and boasts works by artists rarely seen in the United States. If you can't find the Shiele or the Klimt you are looking for here, you will probably have to travel to Vienna. Treat yourself to brunch in the charming Café Sabarsky, which offers an extensive menu of German savories and sweets in its Art Nouveau-style salon. *1048 Fifth Ave (at 86th St.), (212) 628-6200. Hours: Sa-M 11am-6pm, F 11am-9pm. Admission: $10 adults, $7 seniors and students. 4 5 6 to 86th St.*

7 The Metropolitan Museum of Art

Even seasoned New York art lovers still get lost in the Met's maze of galleries once in a while. As the largest museum in New York City, the Met boasts an encyclopedic collection of over two million works from all over the globe, from the ancient to the contemporary. Treat yourself to a series of short visits and try to see a new section of the museum each time you come. Don't be discouraged by long lines for special exhibitions; certain spaces within the museum are always empty. You will never have to elbow your way into Astor Court, a quiet garden space in the Asian galleries, which is modeled after a Ming Dynasty scholar's court; you will also find room in the museum's American wing. It is worth winding your way to the single set of elevators that access the Iris and B. Gerald Cantor roof garden, where monumental sculptures by contemporary artists are displayed. Grab a snack and gaze out over the great expanse of Central Park.

8 The Whitney

Begun as one family's private enterprise in the early 1930s, the Whitney Museum of American Art has promoted works by living American artists overlooked by other galleries and museums since its inception. By 1932, the first of the Whitney's Biennial Exhibitions quickly established the museum as the vanguard showcase of contemporary American painting. A cultural incubator for many American movements, including Abstract Expressionism and Pop Art, the museum provided an arena in which artists excluded from the mainstream could be celebrated. Highlights from the museum's extensive permanent collection include several mobiles by Alexander Calder and early works by German-born artist Willem de Kooning, as well as a corner gallery filled with the subtly voyeuristic paintings of Edward Hopper.

9 The Frick

Housed in one huge mansion on Fifth Ave., the Frick was built by railroad tycoon Henry Clay Frick. Inside are over one thousand paintings, sculptures, and works on paper by Old Masters such as Rembrandt, Goya, Titian, and El Greco. The collection is arranged throughout the sixteen rooms of the mansion with little regard for national or chronological categorization, which gives the museum a far more intimate feel than many of its neighbors up the Mile. The interior Garden Court, with its skylight and rose-colored marble fountain, will give you some ideas about how to spend your first million.

Galleries in New York

New York has fostered the cutting edge of the art world for decades. The art world's epicenter has always been the ever-flourishing gallery culture of lower Manhattan. While artists like multimedia pioneer Bill Viola and celestial abstractionist Ross Bleckner enjoy solo exhibits at swank 57th Street galleries like Mary Boone's and Pace Wildenstein, the proverbial struggling artists start from scratch at galleries like Esso in Chelsea, where Parsons, School of Visual Arts, and Pratt grads forge new paths into the sunset of Pop Art. They start at the BoHo paradise Pierogi 2000 in Williamsburg and on the walls and sidewalks of the East Village and SoHo, where street-level graffiti artists turn pocked cement into canvas.

Rising rents have caused many galleries to flee well-established SoHo for the increasingly crowded warehouses of western Chelsea, the Lower East Side, Williamsburg, and even far off in Brooklyn's dreary DUMBO, although a few hangers-on still crowd the legendary cast-iron buildings in SoHo. There are even some hip galleries that began in their founders' smallish apartments as full-scale diorama projects. These spaces now are usually the galleries that continue to provide top-billing to the unknowns and the assuredly will be-knowns.

Don't be intimidated by suspicious plainclothes guards or uppity desk clerks found at some exhibits: just remember that these are probably interns who spend their off-hours windexing the doors with paper towels. If you can't get up the nerve to hob-knob with the posh in first-rate galleries and auction houses, try secondary market galleries. At low-key spots like The Drawing Center on Wooster St., or Exit Art on Broadway, you can see up-and-coming artists share the spotlight in group shows. In fact, these galleries often have works by extremely well-known artists whose other pieces hang in museums around the world. Stroll through the big names and yearn for the millions of dollars it would take to outfit yourself in beautiful art, or marvel at the free admission of these museum-quality shows that not only change more rapidly than anything at the Met, but usually expose you to far more topical art and artists.

Gallery Openings

Few people seem to know that gallery openings are, in fact, quite open to the public. While most of us imagine these events to be too exclusive to include the average pedestrian art lover, the opportunity to rub elbows with well known local artists and downtown celebs is actually easier than you might think. Really, all you need to know is when and where to show up for your free wine and a little bit of culture.

A good place to starts would be www.patrickmcmullan.com/homepage.html, or www.thenewyorkartworld.com/index.html. Don't worry too much about not fitting in or looking appropriately chic A rule of thumb might be to avoid khakis and flip-flops: for all their diversity of fashion, this crowd is still some of Manhattan's most judgmental and it's always preferable to avoid a cool once-over.

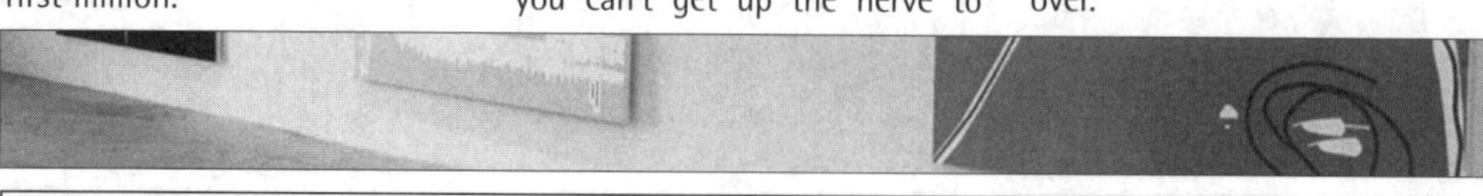

listings

Museum Listings]

A

bigail Adams Smith luseum
hn Quincy Adams' aughter wanted to replicate Mount Vernon here, ut ended up with a carage house. Formerly a otel with offices for tandard Oil, the museum splays Colonial American emorabilia from the 320s-40s in reconstructed rooms, which include a avern, kitchen, bedroom, nd several parlors. There re lectures regularly, ong with live music and n outdoor cafe during ne summer months.
21 E. 61st St. (bet. First nd York Aves.), (212) 38-6878. Hours: T-Su 1am-4pm Admission: $3 or adults, $2 seniors and tudents. N R 4 5 6 to 9th St.-Lexington Ave.

lternative Museum
ounded and operated by rtists, this strikingly ntrospective, nonprofit rganization features a ange of works that compel viewers to examine the elationship between society and art.
2 W 82nd St. (212) 966-444. www.alternative useum.org, Admission: uggested $3, Hours: Tu-a 11am -6pm. N R W to Prince St.

merican Folk Art nstitute
lasses and workshops are ffered in all manner of media. Lectures and other panels are also held here. The American Folk Art Institute is actually located across the street from the Museum of Art and Design.
45 W. 53rd St. (bet. Fifth and Sixth Ave.), (212) 265-1040. Hours: T-Su 10:30-5:30 pm, F 10:30am - 7:30pm, free on Friday from 5:30pm-7:30pm. Admission: $9 adults, $7 students and seniors. E V to 53rd St.-Fifth Ave., F to 47-50 Sts.

American Museum of Moving Image
This museum is devoted to the art, history, technique, and technology of the visual media and its influence on culture and society. Housed in the old Paramount Studios into the heart of Queens' old movie district, the museum is a treasure trove of movie memorabilia from the 1930s and 1940s. Regular film series at the Riklis Theater screen over 500 movies a year, which are free with admission.
Queens. 35th Ave. (at 36th St.), (718) 784-4520. www.ammi.org, Hours: W-F 11am-5pm, S-Su 11am-6pm. Admission: $10 adults, $7.50 students and seniors, $5 children ages 5-18. G R V to Steinway St.

American Museum of Natural History
A taxidermist's paradise and proud owner of a fantastic new wing packed with dinosaurs, the museum also houses a Hall of Human Evolution and Biology, chronicling human development from ape to homo-sapiens. Eat lunch under the whale.
W. 79th St. (at Central Park West), (212) 769-5100. Hours: M-Su 10am-5:45pm. Admission: $13 adults, $10 for seniors and students, $7.50 for children 2-12. B C to 81st St.-Museum of Natural History.

Asia Society and Museum
One of America's preeminent organizations celebrates Asian cultural awareness with notable film series, lectures, and an art collection featuring sculpture, paintings, ceramics, prints, and bronzes from across Asia. Prominent authors and public leaders speak regularly here. Other programs for the public include dance performances, well-attended art exhibits usually gathered from private collections, and receptions involving community and professional organizations.
725 Park Ave. (at 70th St.), (212) 288-6400. Hours: T-Su 11am-6pm, F 11am-9pm, free on Friday from 6pm-9pm. Admission: $10 adults, $7 for seniors, $5 for students. 6 to 68th St.

Asian American Arts Center
As the name suggests, Asian-American artists have top billing at this thriving community arts center, which supports activities ranging from traditional dance performances to *Art Spiral*, the journal on contemporary Asian-American artists. In February, the Asia Folk Arts Festival brings traditional arts produced both in the States and abroad for display.
26 Bowery St. (bet. Bayard and Pell Sts.), (212) 233-2154. www.artspiral.org, Hours: M, T, W, F 12:30pm - 6:30pm, R 12:30pm-7:30pm. Free admission. S to Grand St., W 6 to Canal St.

B

Bronx Museum of the Arts
Representing the urban experience through photography, sculpture, and painting, this community museum pays special attention to the African, Asian, and Latino heritages that define the modern day Bronx. Shows change every three months. Free on Wednesdays.
Bronx. 1040 Grand Concourse (at 165th St.), (718) 681-6000. Hours: W 12pm-9pm; R-Su 12pm-6pm. Admission: $5 adults, $3 students and seniors, children under 12 free. B D to 167th St.-Grand Concourse, 4 to 161st St.

Brooklyn Museum of Art

This is a world-class museum with strong permanent collections and impressive special exhibitions. The American paintings are excellent, the Egyptian Wing is outstanding, and there's a lovely sculpture garden as well. Located next to the Brooklyn Botanical Gardens, the museum is a great place to get away from it all while remaining in the City. For the first Saturday of each month (except September), the museum stays open until 11 pm and includes free entertainment.

Brooklyn. 1200 Eastern Pkwy. (at Washington Ave.), (718) 638-5000. Hours: W-F 10am-5pm, Sa-Su 11am-6pm. Admission: $8 adults, $4 students and seniors. 2 3 *to Eastern Pkwy-Brooklyn.*

C

Casa Italiana of Columbia University

Ubiquitous in the press but nowhere to be found on Columbia University's campus, intellectual Umberto Eco is a scholar in residence at this recently remodeled institution, where lectures and events concerned with Italian culture are hosted regularly in the center's mock High Renaissance auditorium.

1161 Amsterdam Ave. (at 118th St.), (212) 854-2306, www.italianacademy.columbia.edu. 1 *to 116th St.-Columbia University.*

Casa Italiana of NYU

The former home of General Winfield Scott, hero of the Mexican-American War and Chief-of-Staff of the U.S. Army in the 1850s. Call for information about free lectures, films, and art exhibits that focus on Italian culture.

24 W. 12th St. (bet. Fifth and Sixth Aves.), (212) 998-8730. Hours: M-F 9am-5pm. Admission is free. F V L 1 2 3 *to 14th St.*

Chelsea Art Museum

Located in the heart of the Chelsea gallery district, this mid-sized museum combines the ample exhibition space of a larger art institution with the intimate feel and sleek chrome and glass interior more akin to many of the neighboring galleries. The museum, which opened in the fall of 2002, is housed in a three-story brick building that used to be a Christmas ornament factory. The museum's founders use the space to present the works of mid-career artists from the US and Europe. Highlights from the permanent collection include works by surrealist painter and sculptor Jean Arp, Robert Motherwell, Joan Mitchell, and artist/founder Jean Miotte.

556 W. 22nd St. (at Eleventh Ave.), (212) 255-0719, www.chelseaartmuseum.org. Hours: W-Su 12pm-6pm. Admission: $6 for adults, $3 for students and seniors. C E *to 23rd St.*

China Institute

The Institute specializes in both ancient and contemporary art that provides visitors with a new understanding of modern China. From calligraphy to architecture, the museum presents the many different faces of Chinese art. They also have many interesting lectures that encompass the interpretation of art as well as issues concerning contemporary China.

125 E. 65th St., (212) 744-8181. Hours: M-Sa 10am-5pm; T-R 10am-8pm. $5 admission, $3 for students and seniors. F N R W 4 5 6 *to Lexington Ave.-63rd St.*

Children's Museum of Manhattan

Apartment-bred kids get a taste of nature in the Urban Tree House, learn how television works at the Time Warner Media Center, and read about the life and works of Dr. Seuss at this creative and interactive museum for children of all ages. Lots of wild water fun when the weather gets hot.

212 W. 83rd St. (bet. Broadway and Amsterdam Ave.), (212) 721-1234, www.cmom.org. Hours: T-Su 10am-5pm. Admission: $7 for all older than 1, $4 for seniors. B C *to 81st St.,* 1 *to 86th St.*

The Cloisters

This smorgasbord of medieval European glories is also the finest picnic spot in the city. The Met has its famed medieval collection here, including the breathtaking Unicorn tapestries, and medieval-themed readings and concerts keep hobbyists and scholars busy. The Cloisters themselves are a collection of European chapels and buildings in the Gothic and Romantic styles that were purchased, dismantled, and shipped overseas stone by stone by John D. Rockefeller and George Barnard, then reassembled way uptown. It is the only museum in the country dedicated to the art of Medieval Europe.

Fort Tryon Park, (212) 923-3700. Hours: T-Su 9:30am-5pm. Admission: $10 adults, $5 students and seniors. Cash only. A *to 190th St.*

The Cooper-Hewitt Museum

The Smithsonian's National Museum of Design utilizes its 11,000 square feet to present landmark historical pieces as well as pioneering contemporary designs. Attention is paid to both the one-of-a-kind and the mass-produced. The building itself, once the Carnegie Mansion, boasts an eye-catching ceiling and an intricate staircase. Come free between 5pm and 9pm on Tuesdays.

2 E. 91st St. (bet. Madison and Fifth Aves.), (212) 849-8400. Hours: T-R 10am-5pm, F 10am-9pm, Sa 10am-6pm, Su 12pm-6pm. Admission: $10 adults, $7 students and seniors, children under 12 free. 4 5 6 *to 86th St.*

Cooper Union

An all-expense-paid college specializing in art, architecture, and engineering education, Cooper Union's standards are some of the highest in the country. The school houses the Houghton Art Gallery and the Great Hall, the site of an 1860 speech by Abraham Lincoln.

Cooper Sq. (at 7th St.),

(212) 353-4100. Hours: M-F 11am-7pm, Sa 12pm-5pm. Admission free. 6 to Astor Pl., N R to 8th St.-NYU.

Czech Center
Exhibits on Czech culture and contemporary art. One recent show included photographs taken by blind children.
1109 Madison Ave. (at 83rd St.), (212) 288-0830, www.czechcenter.com. Admission: Free. Hours: T-W, F 9am-5pm, R 9am-7pm. 4 5 6 to 86th St.

D

Dahesh Museum
This tiny museum is the only museum in America dedicated to collecting and exhibiting 19th and early 20th century European academic art. Changing exhibitions focus on such aspects of 19th century art as salons, academies and the birth of museums as well as on the lives of individual artists and their patrons.
580 Madison Ave. (bet. 56th and 57th Sts.), (212) 759-0606. Hours: T-Su 11 am-6 pm. Admission: $9 adults, $4 students and seniors. N R W 4 5 6 to 59th St.-Lexington Ave., 1 to Columbus Circle.

Deutsches Haus
Lecture series by scholars and cultural emissaries, readings by visiting German language authors, and a beautiful gallery space and library with an extensive periodical section are all open to the public. The NYU community enjoys a free film series showcasing everything from Weimar cinema to the contemporary work of artists like Wim Wenders. Their ten-week German language programs cost $450.
42 Washington Pl. (bet. University Pl. and Fifth Ave.), (212) 998-8660. MC, V. N R to 8th St.-NYU

The Drawing Center
This nonprofit organization has an extensive collection of works on paper, including lots of drawings by a variety of new and established artists. The operation has been so successful that a second space recently opened across the street. Call for hours.
35 Wooster St. (bet. Grand and Broome Sts.), (212) 219-2166. A C E to Canal St., 1 to Canal St.

Dyckman Farmhouse Museum
A museum of 18th-century farmhouse life, located in one of Manhattan's oldest residences, reminds urbanites that the city did not simply spring from the soil full-grown. Period furnishings and quiet gardens maintain the mood. Benches out front are ideal for catching rays or hanging out with the area's elderly population.
(Currently closed for renovations). 4881 Broadway (at 204th St.), (212) 304-9422. Hours: W-Su 10am-4pm. Admission: Free. A 1 to Inwood- 207th St.

E

Ellis Island Immigration Museum
Twelve million immigrants came to Ellis Island between 1892 and 1954. This museum opened in 1990 as a tribute to the journey those people made. Give yourself about three hours to explore the artifacts. If you don't feel like shelling out the $4 or making the trip, take the virtual tour on the website.
Ellis Island, New York Harbor. www.ellisisland.com. Call (212) 363-3206 for ferry and tour times. www.ellisisland.com, Admission: $7 adults, $5 seniors, $3 students. Take N R W to Whitehall St., 4 5 to Bowling Green, walk through Battery Park to Castle Clinton to pick up tickets.

El Museo del Barrio
Originally a project in an East Harlem classroom, the sole American museum of Puerto Rican arts and culture has graduated to Museum Mile. Nearly 8,000 objects span over 800 years of history. The museum recently added more gallery space and celebrated its 25th anniversary.
1230 Fifth Ave. (at 104th St.), (212) 831-7272, www.elmuseo.org. Hours: W-Su 11am-5pm. Admission: $6 adults, $4 students and seniors, children under 12 free. 6 to 103rd St.

F

Fashion Institute of Technology
Exhibits feature famously fabulous designers, as well as work by talented FIT students.
227 W. 27th St. (at Seventh Ave.), (212) 217-7999. Admission free. 1 to 28th St.

Fire Museum
If a field trip to the fire station is a favorite childhood memory, don't miss this chance to relive it. The collection, housed in a renovated Beaux-Arts style firehouse from 1904, is the country's largest. It is full of all standard firehouse trappings, old engines, pump cars, and plenty of intriguing New York City fire history.
278 Spring St. (bet. Houston and Varick Sts.), (212) 691-1303. Hours: T-S 10am-5pm, Su 10am-4pm. Admission: $5 adults, $2 children. C E to Spring St., 1 to Houston St.

Fraunces Tavern Museum
George Washington gave his farewell address to his troops at this Georgian mansion, which was home to the Departments of Foreign Affairs, Treasury, and War during New York's brief spell as a capital city. Now the museum specializes in American history and culture of the 18th and 19th centuries, with plenty of period rooms in which to play pretend. Below is a dark-paneled restaurant.
54 Pearl St. (at Broad St.), (212) 425-1778. Hours: T-W, F 10am-5pm, R 10am-7pm, Sa 11am-5pm Admission: $3 adults, $2 for students and seniors. R W to Whitehall St., 4 5 to Bowling Green, 2 3 to Wall St.

The Frick Museum
Steel kingpin Henry Clay Frick built this mansion with his fine art collection and a future museum in mind. The museum has

Free Admission Everyday: public art

Often obscured, overlooked, or dismissed with mild bewilderment, pieces of public sculpture pepper the city; with a little research, it's possible to make sense of the more abstract works.

In the mid-'60s, sculptures were chosen to represent the urban redevelopment programs that were reshaping the city. City beautification through sculpture placement was also taking place around the same time downtown, with the Parks department's ambitious program called "Sculpture in Environment." Twenty-nine contemporary sculptures were placed throughout Manhattan, including Astor Place's familiar tilted steel black box, which formally goes by the name "Alamo," but is usually referred to as The Cube. The piece, designed by Bernard Rosenthal in 1967, was one of the first abstract sculptures on city property and has since served as a hangout for skateboarders. It's location in front of Cooper Union at the intersection of the NYU-inhabited Greenwich Village, the Hipster-laden East Village, the oh-so-stylish NoLiTa and the hordes of SoHo shoppers means the Cube is a meeting place par excellence. Ignore the bird droppings, the burnouts, and the graffiti to enjoy the lyrical contrast of modern automation engraved in the sculpture with its more wedding-cake, fin-de-siècle surroundings.

been realized and now offers a rare chance to view masterpieces displayed in a residential setting. Highlights include portraits by El Greco, Rembrandt, and Renoir, with waterscapes by Turner. One of the most soothing spots in the city is the sun-lit, virtually sound-proof indoor courtyard with marble benches and a drizzling fountain. The mail-in procedure for free tickets to Sunday concerts is an ordeal, but no tickets are required to listen in from the courtyard.
1 E. 70th St. (at Fifth Ave.), (212) 288-0700, www.frick.org. Hours: T-R, Sa 10am-6pm, F 10am-9pm, Su 1pm-6pm. Admission: $12, $5 for students, $8 for seniors. 6 *to 68th St.*

G

Goethe Institute
Lovers of German culture visit this multi-story gallery, conveniently located right across the street from the Metropolitan Museum of Art. While the interior is short on feng shui proportionality, the proprietors constantly rotate the exhibitions to ensure that there's never a dull moment.
1014 Fifth Ave. (bet. 82nd and 83rd Sts.), (212) 439-8700. Hours: W-Sa 12pm-7pm. 6 *to 77th St.*

Solomon R. Guggenheim Museum
It's now hard to imagine upper Fifth Ave. without Frank Lloyd Wright's famous spiral of a building, home to one of the most remarkable 20th century art collections in the world. The controversial new addition, a rectangular tower, was opened in 1992 and houses the permanent collection. Special exhibits wind their way down interior ramps. This may not be the best way to view art, but it's surely the most distinctive.
1071 Fifth Ave. (at 88th St.), (212) 423-3500, www.guggenheim.org/new_york_index.html. Hours: F 10am-8pm, Sa-W 10am-5:45pm. Admission: $15 adults, $10 students and seniors, children under 12 free. 4 5 6 *to 86th St.*

H

Hayden Planetarium
What is a black hole? Does Planet X exist? Find out at "The 20 Most Asked Questions About the Universe And the Answers." This is just one of many programs at the astronomy department in the domed building adjacent to the Museum of National History. Weekends find a young crowd at the ever-popular 3-D laser light shows. Pink Floyd is an old standby, while a more recent show featuring Nirvana and friends from Seattle ("Laser Grunge") rocks a little harder. It doesn't get much better than listening to Heart-Shaped Box while lasers fly by on-screen. Call to verify hours and showings.
80th St. (bet. Columbus Ave.and Central Park West), (212) 769-5900. Order tickets by calling (212) 769-5200, www.amnh.org. Hours: October-June, M-Su 10am-5:45pm, F 10am-8:45pm, July-September, Sa-Su 12pm-4:45pm. B

C to 81st St.-Museum of Natural History.

The Hispanic Society of America

Described by a delighted visitor as "one of the city's hidden gems," the museum modestly presents the art, literature, and cultural history of Spain in an opulent Spanish Renaissance style mansion in Washington Heights. Paintings by Goya, Velasquez, Zurbaran, and El Greco abound, and the society's collection of Hispano-Mooresque lusterware vessels is not to be missed. The Society also runs a reference library, which is open to the public.

613 W. 155th St. (at Broadway), (212) 690-0743, www.hispanicsociety.org. Hours: T-Sa 10am-4:30pm, Su 1pm-4pm. Admission and library use free. A C to 155th St., 1 to 157th St.

I

International Center for Photography

Founded in 1974, this museum and education complex recently moved from its original space in a townhouse on Museum Mile to new digs in Midtown. The center explores photography's identity as both an art form and a communication tool with a rotating slate of special exhibits that highlight the work of individual photographers as well as historic movements such as Surrealism and Photo secession. They also offer classes for all levels of instruction.

1133 Sixth Ave. (at 43rd St.), (212) 860-1777. Hours: T-R 10am-5pm, F 10am-8pm, Sa-Su 10am-6pm. Admission: $10 adults, $7 students and seniors. 6 to 96th St.

Intrepid Sea-Air-Space Museum

The former aircraft carrier USS Intrepid, commissioned in 1943, served 31 years in the US Navy. It survived numerous attacks, including seven bombings, five kamikaze assaults and a torpedo. The carrier retired in 1974, it now exhibits naval destroyers, guided-missile submarines, aircrafts, and Felix DeWeldon's original Iwo Jima Memorial Statue.

Pier 86 (at Twelfth Ave. and 46th St.), (212) 245-0072, www.intrepidmuseum.org. M-F 10am-5pm, Sa-Su 10am-6pm. Admission: $16.50 for adults, $12.50 for students, seniors, and veterans, $4.50 for children. A C E to 42nd St-Port Authority, N R S W 1 2 3 7 to 42nd St.-Times Sq.

Islamic Cultural Center and Mosque

The city's central mosque holds prayer and study sessions on Sundays, language and religion courses for women on Saturdays.

97th St. (bet. First and Second Aves.), (212) 722-5234. 6 to 96th St.

The Isamu Noguchi Garden Museum

More than 300 works in granite, steel, and marble, including the famous Akari paper sculptures by Isamu Noguchi, who also designed the twelve galleries and garden. Open April to October.

Queens. 36-01 43rd Ave. (at 36th St.), (718) 204-7088. Hours: M, R-F 10am-5pm, Sa-Su 11am-6pm. Admission $5 adults, $2.50 students and seniors. Cash only. 7 N W to 33rd St. (Queens).

J

Japan Society

An all-purpose center of Japanese art and culture, located, appropriately enough, in Japan House, with exhibitions on the second floor and a stone-lined pool garden on the first floor.

333 E. 47th St. (bet. First and Second Aves.), (212) 832-1155, www.japansociety.org. Hours: T-F 11am-6pm, Sa-Su 11am-5pm. Admission: $12 for adults, $10 students and seniors, F 5 6 7 S to 42nd St.-Grand Central, E V to Lexington Ave.

The Jewish Museum

The country's largest collection of Judaica, housed in an imperious French Renaissance structure, boasts over 14,000 works in the permanent collection. Works detail the Jewish experience throughout history and feature archeological pieces, ceremonial objects, modern masterpieces by Marc Chagall and Frank Stella, and even an interactive computer program based on the Talmud. Admission is free, Thursdays from 5pm-8pm.

1109 Fifth Ave. (at 92nd St.), (212) 423-3200, www.thejewishmuseum.org. Hours: Su-W 11am-5:45pm, R 11am-8pm, F 11am-3pm. Admission: $10 adults, $7.50 students and seniors, children under 12 free. 4 5 6 to 86th St.

K

King Juan Carlos I Center

King Juan Carlos the First himself showed up along with Queen Sophia and Hillary Clinton to inaugurate the new hub of Spanish culture in the city. Housed in architect Stanford White's historic 19th-century, Renaissance-style Judson Hall, the center encourages the study of Spain and the rest of the Spanish-speaking world through lectures, colloquia, and conferences with scholars and dignitaries.

57 Washington Sq. South (Thompson St. and Sixth Ave.), (212) 998-3650. A B C D E F V to W. 4th St.

L

Lower East Side Tenement Museum

Think your apartment or dorm room is cramped? This museum will make whatever space you do have seem more than adequate. Chronicling an era when these streets were the most densely packed in the world, this museum, founded in 1988, is the first attempt the city has made at preserving a tenement. Like most tenements, this building predated existing housing laws; this one dates from 1863. Bedrooms were typically 80 square feet and tenants had no running water, no flush toilets, and no electric lights. Most rooms even lacked windows. Founders Ruth J. Abram and Anita Jacobson strive to recreate the conditions in this progressive

attempt at reclaiming an often overlooked piece of the city's history.
97 Orchard St. (bet. Broome and Delancey Sts.), (212) 431-0233. Call for tour hours. Ad-mission: Price varies depending on the tour. Call ahead for information. B D to Grand St., F to Delancey St., J M Z to Essex St.

M

Jacque Marchais Museum of Tibetan Art

Housed in a two-story stone building resembling a Buddhist mountain temple and set in a terraced garden overlooking New York Bay, the center features a permanent collection of Tibetan and other Buddhist art and ethnography. Notable past visitors include the Dalai Lama, who came in 1991.
Staten Island. 338 Lighthouse Ave., (718) 987-3500. Hours: W-Su 1pm-5pm. Admission: $5 adults, $3 students and seniors, $2 children. 1 to South Ferry, 4 5 to Bowling Green, Staten Island Ferry to S70 bus.

Merchant's House Museum

The museum provides a quaint glimpse into the lives of the merchant family who occupied this late-Federal and Greek Revival house. The slender row house has seven period rooms and a garden filled with heirlooms from the family's 100 years of residence. The house was constructed in 1832 at a time when wealthy merchants, such as the family who once lived in this house, were moving north of Manhattan's Southern tip. A National Historic landmark, the house remains as the only New York City family home that is preserved intact from its 19th century roots. While small, the house contains an intriguing collection of furniture, decorative arts, clothing and personal memorabilia. As the only historic museum in Greenwich Village, the Merchant's House presents a unique glimpse into the city's past in everything from its red brick and marble exterior to the rumored family ghosts still using the 19th-century house.
29 E. 4th St. (at Bowery St.), (212) 777-1089, www.merchantshouse.com Hours: R-M 1pm-5pm. Admission: $6 adults, $4 students and seniors, children under 12 free. N R W to 8th St., 6 to Astor Pl., B D F V to Broadway-Lafayette St.

The Metropolitan Museum of Art

Where to begin? The Met seems to be as big and sprawling as the city itself, and similarly the trick is finding the treasures. Favorites include the spectacular Temple of Dendur, the American Wing Garden Court, the medieval section, and, in the summer, the Roof Garden where an older crowd sips white wine and ponders the sculptures (out loud). Don't try to do too much or to follow a strict plan, since this is the best place to get lost in New York City.
1000 Fifth Ave. (at 82nd St.), (212) 879-5500, www.metmuseum.org. Hours: T-R, S 9:30am-5:30pm, F-Sa 9:30am-9pm. Admission: $12 adults, $7 students and seniors. 4 5 6 to 86th St.

Micro Museum

A funky museum with a small exhibit space and a large community presence, the Micro Museum may be small in size but it is privy to new art movements and permits any local performers to use the free space. Visitors can sit at computer terminals to watch new video works, or examine the installation of jackets festooned with colorful flowers and vines. There are brightly colored solar-powered art exhibits in the windows and the museum holds occasional interactive tours of the talking furniture and athletic equipment that doubles as the owner's personal motivator while in use. The museum plays an integral role in its neighborhood by teaming with local businesses to organize street festivals and performances throughout the summer.
Brooklyn. 123 Smith St. (bet. Dean and Pacific Sts.), (718) 797-3116, www.micromuseum.com. Hours: Sa 12-6pm, professional use daily 9am-10pm. Admission Free, tickets for performances and shows range from $10-$25. F G to Bergen St., M R 1 2 4 5 to Court St. or Borough Hall.

Morris-Jumel Mansion

Down from the remaining farmhouse is the area's extant Georgian mansion where Washington kept his troops during the Revolution. A choice exhibit displays the obit of Vice President Aaron Burr's wife Elise Jumel, whose early life as a "lady of the night" once scandalized New York society.
160th St. (east of St. Nicholas Ave.), (212) 923-8008. Hours: W-Su 10am-4pm. Admission: $3 adults. Cash only. C to 163rd St.-Amsterdam Ave.

The Museum for African Art

Exhibits seeking to facilitate a greater understanding of African art change twice a year at this two-floor showcase, one of two of its kind in the country. Complex exhibits often incorporate elements of folk art, sculpture and more conventional mediums to examine pervasive concepts in the tradition. Past exhibits include "Secrecy: African Art That Conceals and Reveals" and "Face of the Gods: Art and Altars of the Black Atlantic World." Film and video presentations, performance art, and interactive, hands-on workshops take place in the newly opened Educational Department.
Queens. 36-01 43rd Ave., (718) 784-7700, www.africanart.org. Hours: M, R-F 10am-5pm, Sa-Su 11am-6pm. Admission: $6 adults, $3 students and seniors. 7 to 33rd St.

Museum of American Illustration

View the work of key illustrators like Norman Rockwell and N.C. Wyeth at the home of the elite Society of Illustrators, which claims a long history of service to none other than the United States Army. Educational oppor-

tunities include sketch classes and lectures.
128 E. 63rd St. (bet. Park and Lexington Aves.), (212) 851-8948, www.americanillustration.org. Hours: T 10am-8pm, W-F 10am-5pm, Sa 12pm-4pm. Admission dependent on tour. Call ahead for information. N R W 4 5 6 *to 59th St.-to Lexington Ave.*

Museum of Arts and Design

Formerly known as the American Craft Museum, this Midtown institution changed its name in October 2002 to better reflect its focus on both the materials and the processes used by visual artists from around the world. The museum also offers workshops and demonstrations in everything from glassmaking to quilting that correspond to its current special exhibit.
40 W. 53rd St. (bet. Fifth and Sixth Aves.), (212) 956-3535. Hours: T-W, F-Su 10am-6pm, R 10am-8pm. Admission: $9 adults, $6 students and seniors. E V *to Fifth Ave.*

Museum of Chinese in the Americas

No Chinatown experience is complete without a visit to this community-oriented museum, the first ever dedicated to the history of the Chinese in the Americas. The award-winning exhibition, entitled "Where Is Home?," features a moving collection of memorabilia, photographs, and commentary exploring the diverse identities and experiences of Chinese-Americans.
70 Mulberry St., Ste. 209 (at Bayard St.), (212) 619-4785. Hours: T-Su 12-6pm. Admission $3 adults, $1 students and seniors. J M N R W Z 6 *to Canal St.*

The Metropolitan Museum of Art: roof garden

Another island of tranquility populated by outdoor sculpture is actually in both the least and the most likely place imaginable. The roof garden of the Metropolitan Museum offers you a million dollar postcard perfect picture of New York. While it can be tricky to locate (you usually have to ask a guard how to get up, even if you've been before) the lyrically geometric stick figures by Joel Shapiro help to further enliven even more an already dramatic panorama. It's always nice to pretend you can afford this kind of a view.

Museum of Comic & Cartoon Art

In spite of its covert location in a sparsely marked office building and its limited hours, this museum draws legions of comic book fans and seeks to expand in upcoming years. The collection ranges from animation, anime, television cartoons, comic books, comic strips, gag cartoons, illustrations, editorial cartoons, caricature, graphic novels, and computer-generated arts. The exhibitions explore the many ways in which the genre has sparked dialogue about contemporary political and social issues and recorded events throughout history. The museum's motto appears to be "telling stories through pictures," a theme that ranges from Dave Sim's projected 300 issues of Cerebus to Gary Larson's Far Side cartoon.
594 Broadway, (212) 254-3511, www.moccany.org. M, F-Sa 11am-6pm and by appointment. Admission is $3. N R *to Prince St.*

Museum of the Fashion Institute of Technology

With all the aspiring fashion designers running around the halls of FIT, it is only appropriate that their museum would hold the largest collection of inspirational apparel for the students. Holding everything from costumes to textiles it holds items dating back to the 18th century. The museum also holds gorgeous jewelry and an extensive collection of fashion photographs. They hold a yearly Fashion Design Student Show where students can flaunt their own designs and give a glimpse of the future of fashion.
Seventh Ave., (212) 217-7642. Hours: T-F 12pm-8pm; Sa 10am-5pm. Admission: Free. 1 *to 28th St.*

Museum of Jewish Heritage

This somber space at the tip of Manhattan offers the city's most organized collection of artifacts from Jewish life during

the twentieth century as a way of memorializing the Holocaust. Check out their special exhibitions that usually pertain to Jewish culture in America for some interesting historical tidbits.
36 Battery Pl. (at Little West St.), (646) 437-4200. Hours: Su-F 10am-5:45pm, W 10am-8pm, F 10am-5pm. Admission $10, $7 Seniors, $5 Students. 4 5 to Bowling Green, 1 to Rector St.

MoMA

Contemporary paintings and sculptures by such greats as Picasso, van Gogh, and Warhol, as well as new exhibitions focusing on such subjects as MoMA's car collection, contemporary drawing, avant-garde architecture, and the relationship between Matisse and Picasso.
11 W. 53rd St., (212) 708-9400, www.moma.org, Hours: S-R 10:30am-5pm, F 10:30am-8pm, closed Tues. Admission: $12 adults, $8.50 students and seniors, pay-what-you-wish Friday afternoon. E V to Fifth Ave.-53rd St., B D F to 47th-50th Sts.

Museum of Sex (MoSex)

Whether you like to be educated or titillated, the Museum of Sex has something for everyone. The museum explores the evolution and cultural significance of human sexuality through a variety of media ranging from painting and sculpture to performance and video. This broad survey mixes shock and educational value, allowing the visitor to experience everything from erotic bronze-age poetry to the innovative sex furniture of the future. Even if the exhibitions themselves don't entice you, you'll undoubtedly enjoy the guilty pleasure of exploring the "taboo" with complete strangers. Don't forget to make a stop at the gift shop. With items ranging from genitalia-inspired pasta to vibrating lipstick, you're sure to find something that meets your fancy. Must be 18 or older to enter.
233 Fifth Ave. (at 27th St.), (212) 689-6337, www.museumofsex.com. Hours: Su-F 11am-6:30pm, Sa 11am-8pm. Admission: $14.50 adults, $13.50 students, V, MC, AmEx. N R 6 to 28th St.

Museum of Television and Radio

Watch TV all day and still feel cultured. Computer consoles and viewing cubicles access tens of thousands of programs (and you thought cable was overwhelming), though if your tastes are very obscure, you should order ahead of time. A nostalgic display of Kermit the Frog and friends is worth the trip alone.
25 W. 52nd St. (bet. Fifth and Sixth Aves.), (212) 621-6800. Hours: T-Su 12pm-6pm, R 12pm-8pm. Admission: $10 adults, $8 students, seniors, $5 for children under 14. N R W to 49th St., B D F V to 47th-50th Sts.

Museum of the City of New York

In light of its ego, it's fitting that New York was the first city to get its own museum. Exhibits glorify New York's vast history and include photographs, furniture, costumes, and toys. The Sunday concert series and the Big Apple Film make the trip worthwhile.
1220 5th Ave at 103rd St., (212) 534-1672, www.mcny.org. Summer Hours: W-Sa 10am-5pm, Su 12pm-5pm, Admission: $12 families, $7 for adults, $4 for children, 6 to 103rd St.

N

National Academy of Design

Founded in 1825 to promote the art of design in America through painting, sculpture, architecture, and engraving, the academy still strives to meet its same purpose through training young artists and interns (ask Ms. Stokes) and serving as a fraternal organization for other distinguished American artists. Its permanent exhibit features works by some 19th century masters, such as Winslow Homer, John Singer Sargent, and Thomas Eakins as well as some contemporary artists such as Robert Rauschenberg, Isabel Bishop, and Phillip Johnson.
1083 Fifth Ave. (bet. 89th and 90th Sts.), (212) 369-4880, www.nationalacademy.org, Hours: W-R 12pm-5pm, F-Su 11am-6pm. Admission: $10 adults, $5 students and seniors. 4 5 6 to 86th St.

National Museum of the American Indian

The old Customs House at the foot of Broadway houses this satellite branch of the Smithsonian's Museum of the American Indian in Washington. The museum displays a vast permanent collection of various national dress, culture, and art.
1 Bowling Green (at the foot of the Bowery), (212) 514-3700, www.nmai.si.edu. Hours: M-W 10am-5pm, Th. 10am-8pm, F-Su. 10am-5pm. Admission: Free. 4 5 to Bowling Green, 1 to Rector St.

New York Hall of Science

While designed primarily for kids, this playground of hands-on exhibits appeals to the science nut in everyone. The newly expanded exhibition hall boasts a Technology Gallery, with access to the Internet and a wide range of CD-ROMs. Who can resist entering the Realm of the Atom or the World of the Microbes?
Flushing, Queens. 47-01 111th St., Flushing Meadow Park, (718) 699-0005, www.nyhallsci.org. Hours: T-W 9:30am-2pm, R-F 9:30am-5pm, Sa-Su 12pm-5pm. Admission: $9, $6 students and children 5-17, $3 children 2-4; free R 2pm-5pm. 7 to 111th St.

New Museum of Contemporary Art

Established in 1977, this museum considers itself the vanguard for contemporary art in the city. Its Zenith Media Lounge is New York's only museum space dedicated to digital art, sound works, and experimental video. The museum hosts six major

exhibitions a year, as well as five Media Lounge shows. The museum also sponsors public programs designed to broaden public understanding of contemporary visual culture. These programs include talks, performances, and screenings, and are open to the public. The museum is a great place to witness the wonderful and the weird in the world of contemporary art.
583 Broadway (bet. Houston and Prince Sts.), (212) 219-1222, www.newmuseum.org. Hours: T-Su 12pm-6pm, R 12pm-8pm. Admission: $6 adults, $3 students and seniors, 18 and under free. The Media Lounge is always free. 6 to Spring St. or Bleecker St., N R W to Prince St., C E to Spring St., B D F V to Broadway-Lafayette St.

The New York City Transit Museum

While you may consider the turnstiles in subway stations to be antique, the originals are really housed in this authentic 1930s subway station. Vintage subway maps and mosaics comprise the permanent collection, along with exhibitions chronicling the development of rapid transit. Tag along with a school group for a field trip to places like the Metro-North car-repair facility. Be sure to stop by the gift shop to pick up some interesting items.
Brooklyn Heights, Brooklyn. 130 Livingston St. (bet. Boerum Pl. and Schermerhorn Ave.), (718) 694-5100, www.mta.nyc.ny.us/mta/museum. Hours: T-F 10am-4pm, Sa-Su 12pm-5pm. Admission: $5 adults, $3 students, seniors, and children. M R 2 3 4 5 to Borough Hall.

New York Historical Society

An imposing building across from Central Park houses both a library and a museum with a wealth of information and images of New York dating up to the turn-of-the-century. The museum features a permanent installation of 19th century paintings.
2 W. 77th St. (at Central Park West), (212) 873-3400, www.nyhistory.org. Hours: T-Su 10am-6pm. Admission: $5 adults, $3 students and seniors. B C to 81st St.-Museum of Natural History.

New York Unearthed

Archaeology and New York may seem like strange bedfellows, but this relatively small museum does the juxtaposition justice. Artifacts along the lines of cannon balls and bones, as well as excavation finds are on display. The Lower Gallery offers the chance to watch conservationists working busily behind glass. Take the New York Systems elevator down for a simulated dig. And you thought this city was just built on top of a bunch of garbage.
17 State St. (at Water St.), (212) 748-8628. Hours: M-F 10am-5pm. Admission: Free. 4 5 to Bowling Green.

Nicholas Roerich Museum

Discreetly hidden among a row of brownstones, this museum honors Nicholas Roerich, the artist who designed an international peace symbol during World War II.
319 W. 107th St. (bet. Broadway and Riverside Dr.), (212) 864-7752. Hours: T-Su 2pm-5pm. Contribution box. 1 to 110th St.-Cathedral Pkwy.

Picasso statue on NYU's campus

In the court between the towers of the residential complex at New York University Towers, Picasso's 1968 "Bust of Sylvette" is a towering presence between Mercer St. and LaGuardia Place. Critics complain that the piece exemplifies the problems inherent in enlarging a small piece to monumental scale, but that doesn't mitigate local resident's pride in having the 20th-century master's work grace their otherwise empty courtyard. Besides, the Towers are so atrocious and block so much light in the neighborhood, a free masterpiece for the masses is the least they could do for the rest of us. In fact, this is one of several outdoor Picassos in the city.

P

Police Academy Museum

Ever really wanted to see Al Capone's machine gun? Other police memorabilia and crime-related items are also on exhibit.
235 E. 20th St. (bet. Second and Third Aves.), Second Floor, (212) 477-9753. Hours: T-Sa. 10am-5pm. Admission free. 6 to 23rd St.

P.S.1 Contemporary Art Center

If the name didn't give you a clue, P.S.1 is housed in an old school building, three stories high. The gallery has plenty of nooks and crannies, all of which are filled with interesting and enlightening contemporary art exhibits. The gallery's exhibits are temporary – so you can visit P.S.1 again and again. On Summer Saturdays, a fake beach, saunas, good beer, and a DJ make for a party full of hipsters.
Long Island City, Queens. 22-25 Jackson Ave., (718) 784-2084. Hours: R-M 12pm-6pm. Admission: $5 adults, $2 for students and seniors E V *to 23rd St.-Ely Ave.,* 7 *to 45 Rd.-Court House Sq.,* G *to 21st St.*

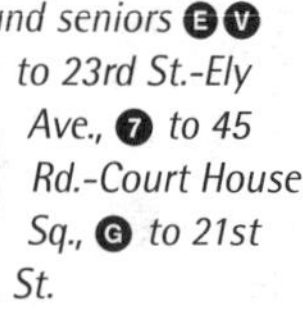

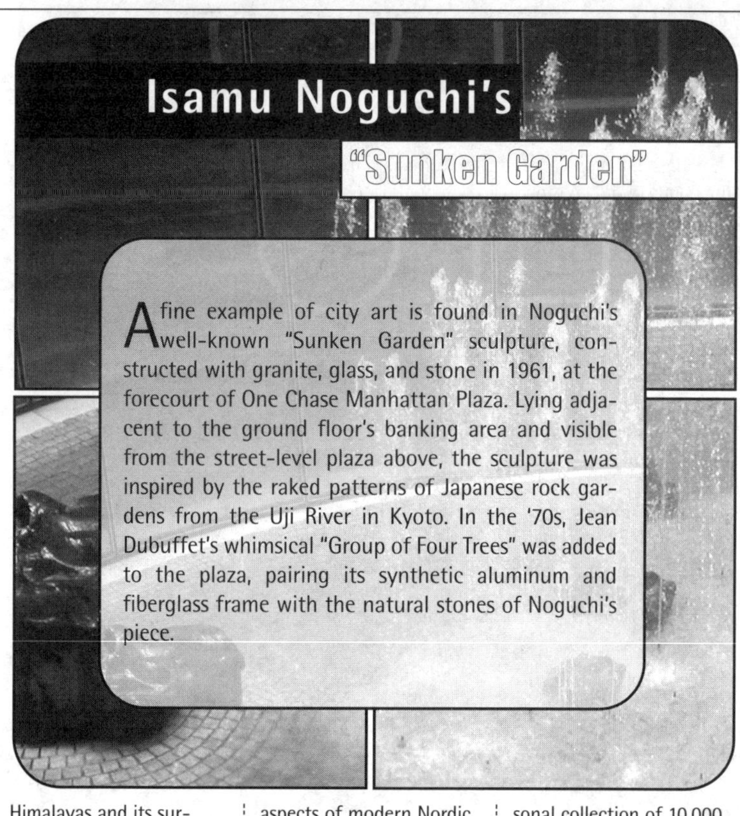

Isamu Noguchi's "Sunken Garden"

A fine example of city art is found in Noguchi's well-known "Sunken Garden" sculpture, constructed with granite, glass, and stone in 1961, at the forecourt of One Chase Manhattan Plaza. Lying adjacent to the ground floor's banking area and visible from the street-level plaza above, the sculpture was inspired by the raked patterns of Japanese rock gardens from the Uji River in Kyoto. In the '70s, Jean Dubuffet's whimsical "Group of Four Trees" was added to the plaza, pairing its synthetic aluminum and fiberglass frame with the natural stones of Noguchi's piece.

Q

Queens Museum of Art

The must-see exhibit of this small museum, which is located right opposite the Unisphere and housed in the original U.N., is the largest scale model of its kind, of New York City.
Flushing, Queens. NYC Building, Flushing Meadows Corona Park, (718) 592-9700. Hours: T-F 10am-5pm, Sa-Su 12pm-5pm. Admission: $5 adults, $2.50 students and seniors. 7 *to Willets Point-Shea Stadium.*

R

Rubin Museum of Art

Recently opened, this museum is the only one in the Western World devoted to the art of the Himalayas and its surrounding area. That vast region produces a wide variety of art that the museum presents in a way that forces the viewer to appreciate it in the context of their own culture. The collection is made up of painting, sculpture, and textiles, dating over two millennia.
150 W. 12th St., (212) 620-5000. Hours: T-Sa 11am-7pm, R-F 11am-9pm, W, Su 11am-5pm, $7 admission, $5 students and seniors. L 1 2 3 *to 14th St.*

S

Scandinavia House: The Nordic Center in America

You don't have to be Swedish to appreciate this clean-lined, modern museum, which represents all aspects of modern Nordic culture through temporary art and design exhibits, including photography, sculpture, and installation. The museum also hosts film screenings, lectures, and language classes. Children will delight in the cozy playroom and learning center, and visitors of all ages will appreciate a bite at the Café Aquavit and a peek at the avant-garde gift shop.
58 Park Ave. (bet. 37th and 38th Sts.), (212) 879-9779. Hours: M-F 12pm-5pm. Admission: Free. 6 *to 33rd St.,* 4 5 6 7 S *to 42nd St.-Grand Central.*

Schomburg Center for Research in Black Culture

The Center was founded in 1925 to showcase scholar and historian Arturo Alfonso Schomburg's personal collection of 10,000 items, documenting the development of Black history worldwide. Priceless volumes, photographs, and newspapers are among the five million articles housed here.
515 Malcolm X Blvd. (at 135th St.), (212) 491-2200. Call for specific hours. Admission free. 2 3 *to 135th St.*

Skyscraper Museum

This extremely tiny museum makes the most of their big surroundings by hosting a series of walking tours and lectures about the world's first "vertical metropolis." The intricate models and architectural drawings on display are not just for nerds and will impress anyone even remotely interested in the subject.
39 Battery Pl. (at Little

West St.), (212) 968-1961, www.skyscraper.org. Hours: W-Su 12pm-6pm. Admission: $5 general, $2.50 for students and seniors. Cash only. 4 5 to Bowling Green, 1 to South Ferry, R to Whitehall St.

South Street Seaport Museum

Here you'll discover detailed exhibits on maritime history in New York's past and present in the museum's gallery or their restored ships. Go for the walking tours of Manhattan's many harbors, or see the gallery's collection of watercolors and model ships. The Melville Library also houses impressive archives on port business.
207 Front St., (212) 748-8600, www.southstseaport.org. Summer hours: M-Su 10am-6pm, winter hours: W-M 10am-5pm. Admission: $8 adults, $6 students. Melville Library by appointment only (212) 748-8648. J M Z 2 3 4 5 to Fulton St., A C to Broadway-Nassau St.

Studio Museum in Harlem

From its origins as a rented loft in 1967, this museum has burgeoned into one of the most innovative in New York, focusing on arts from Africa and Black America. The artists-in-residence program gives emerging artists gallery space and the Cooperative School Program puts professional artists in Harlem schools.
144 W. 125th St. (bet. Lenox and Seventh Aves.), (212) 864-4500. Hours: W-F 12pm-6pm, Sa 10am-6pm, Su 12pm-6pm. Admission: $7 adults, $3 students, children under 12 free. A B C D 1 2 3 4 5 6 to 125th St.

T

Theodore Roosevelt's Birthplace National Historical Site

The 26th president of the United States spent his first 14 years on this site, with a memorial replica of the original house being rebuilt and furnished with musty artifacts. Probably more exciting to the crowds of elementary school field-trippers and senior citizens, peeking at the private curios of a very public family does offer some mild titillation.
28 E. 20th St. (at Broadway), (212) 260-1616. Hours: W-Su 9am-5pm. Admission: $3. Cash only. N R to 23rd St.

U

Ukrainian Museum

This small museum features exhibits of contemporary Ukrainian culture and history. Recent exhibitions have included folk art and Easter Eggs.
203 Second Ave. (bet. 12th and 13th Sts.), (212) 228-0110, www.ukrainianmuseum.org. Hours: W-Su 1pm-5pm. Admission: $1.50. L N R W 4 5 6 to 14th St.-Union Sq.

W

The Whitney Museum of American Art

A motherlode of American avant-garde and post-modern art. Lively, provocative shows are the rule here, including the ever-controversial Biennial, an exhibit of contemporary works held in odd-numbered years that never fails to rile the critics.
945 Madison Ave. (at 75th St.), (212) 570-3676, (877) WHITNEY, www.whitney.org. Hours: W-R, Sa-Su 11am-6pm, F 1pm-9pm. Admission: $12 adults, $9.50 students and seniors, free for children under 12 and NYC Public High School students. 6 to 77th St.

Y

Yeshiva University Museum

The country's oldest Jewish institution of higher learning regularly holds exhibits on both historical and contemporary Jewish themes. The space has recently relocated to downtown.
15 W. 16th St. (bet. Fifth and Sixth Aves.), (212) 294-8330, www.yumuseum.org, Hours: T-R 10:30am-5pm, Su 11am-5pm. Admission: $6 adults, $4 students and seniors. L N R W 4 5 6 to 14th St.-Union Sq.

[Museum Index by Neighborhood]

BRONX
Bronx Museum of Art

BROOKLYN
Alternative Museum
The Brooklyn Museum
D.U.M.B.O. Arts Center
Micro Museum
The New York City Transit Museum

CHELSEA
Chelsea Art Museum
Dia Center for the Arts
Fashion Institute of Technology
Ruben Museum of Art

CHINATOWN
Asian American Arts Center
The Drawing Center

EAST VILLAGE
Merchant's House Museum

FINANCIAL DISTRICT
Faunces Tavern Museum
Museum of Jewish Heritage
National Museum of the American Indian
New York City Urban Experience
New York Unearthed
Skyscraper Museum
South Street Seaport Museum
Ellis Island

GRAMERCY
Cooper Union
Museum of Comic and Cartoon Art
Museum of Sex
Police Academy Museum
Scandinavia House
Theodore Roosevelt Birthplace
Yeshiva University Museum

GREENWICH VILLAGE
Bronfman Jewish Center
Casa Italiana of New York University
Deutsches Haus
Forbes Magazine Galleries
King Juan Carlos I Center
La Maison Française
Morgan Library

HARLEM
African American Wax Museum
Black Fashion Museum
Museum of African American History and Art
Studio Museum in Harlem
Schomberg Center for Research in Black Culture

LITTLE ITALY
Storefront for Art and

[Gallery Listings]

A

Ace Gallery
Once the biggest private gallery in the city, Ace is still one of New York's larger galleries, and it is worth trekking west of SoHo's main streets to visit it. Many of the gallery's smaller rooms that branch off the main hall are larger than an entire Upper East Side gallery. This secondary market gallery focuses on contemporary drawing, painting, and sculpture, and the works are highly priced. Past exhibitions have included work from Frank Gehry, Sol Lewitt, and Robert Rauschenberg. Their current address is *275 Hudson St. (at Dominick St.), but they are moving in the late fall, so call ahead: (212) 255-5599, www.acegallery.net. Hours: T-Sa 10am-6pm.* ❶ *to Canal St.,* Ⓒ Ⓔ *to Spring St.*

Acquavella
Uptown gallery hoppers never overlook this treasure of 19th and 20th century European masters and postwar European and American pieces.
18 E. 79th St. (bet. Madison and Fifth Aves.), (212) 734-6300. Hours: M-F 10am-5pm. Cash only. ❻ *to 77th St.*

Apex Art
Off the beaten path of art

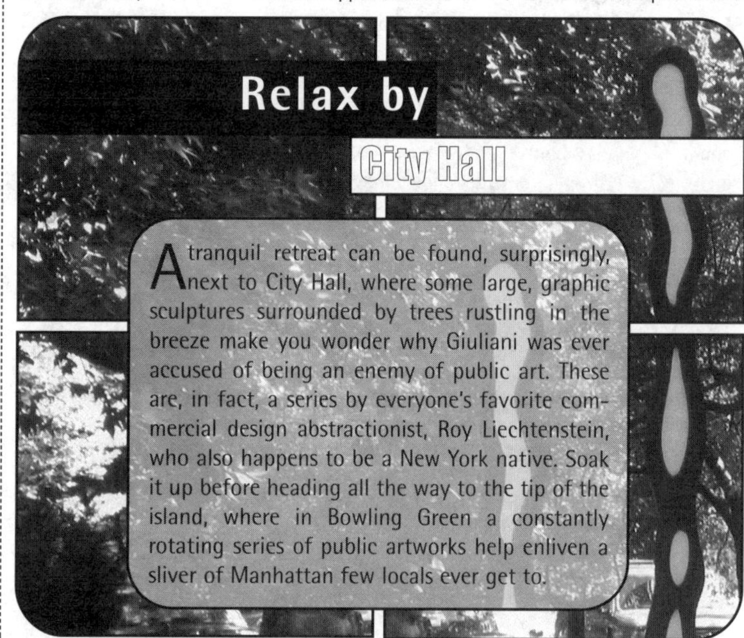

Relax by City Hall

A tranquil retreat can be found, surprisingly, next to City Hall, where some large, graphic sculptures surrounded by trees rustling in the breeze make you wonder why Giuliani was ever accused of being an enemy of public art. These are, in fact, a series by everyone's favorite commercial design abstractionist, Roy Liechtenstein, who also happens to be a New York native. Soak it up before heading all the way to the tip of the island, where in Bowling Green a constantly rotating series of public artworks help enliven a sliver of Manhattan few locals ever get to.

and offering a fresh perspective, this is one of the best places to find innovative work. Appreciating it comes easily also, since the staffers are far less aloof than most of their SoHo counterparts. Shows tend to feature a combination of efforts by a few different artists and include both painting and sculpture.
291 Church St. (bet. Walker and White Sts.), (212) 431-5270, www.apexart.org, T-Sa 11am-6pm. 1 to Franklin St.

Artist's Space
A testing ground where new artists get the chance to cut their teeth, pay their dues, and show their stuff to the gallery world. Shows generally focus on a central theme and contain several new artists with work that fits in. Check out up-and-coming talent in its larval stages.
38 Greene St. (bet. Grand and Broome Sts.), (212) 226-3970, www.artists-space.org, Hours: T-Sa 11am-6pm. J M N R W Z 6 to Canal St.

Austrian Cultural Forum
Located in a slim skyscraper that had even the most staid architecture critics ooh-ing and ahh-ing, the ACF is definately a worthwhile destination on a detour. Although the gallery is small and the musical or lecture events sporadic, everything here is as top notch as the exterior suggests. Oh, and did we mention its free?
11 E. 52nd St. (at Fifth Ave.), (212) 319-5300. Hours: M-Sa 10am-6pm. E V to 53rd St.

B

Barbara Gladstone
This enormous space has tall ceilings and two levels displaying contemporary and modern art in various media, including rotating painting, sculpture, photography, and video installations and photography.
515 W. 24th St. (bet. Tenth and Eleventh Aves.), (212) 206-9300. Hours: M-F 10am-6pm. C E to 23rd St.

Brent Sikkema
The generic gallery setting with white walls and monotonous lighting belies the extremely untraditional artistic works displayed within. Works of contemporary artists, such as Burt Barr, Amy Sillman, and Vik Muniz have cast their creative (and sometimes creepy) shadows upon these walls, and the quirky curation often surprises even the most seasoned New York gallery hound. The crowds may make the space a little stuffy, so visit in the morning or enjoy heavy air as part of the artistic ambiance.
530 W. 22nd St. (bet. Tenth and Eleventh Aves.), 212-929-2262, www.brentsikkema.com. Hours: M-F 11am-6 pm. C E to 23rd St.

Bronwyn Keenan
If you are looking for something new, this gallery is known for finding emerging talent and will always provide viewers with something novel. Having the typical gallery look of high ceilings, white walls and timber floors, the gallery has a cool 1940s cage elevator to shepherd people from floor to floor. Definately check out this gallery if you enjoy photography, as the photographs outnumber the other forms of art.
3 Crosby St., (212) 431-5083, T-Su 10am-6pm. J M N R W Z 6 to Canal St.

Bullet Space
This "Urban Artist Collaborative" in a deteriorating building showcases city artists known for the provocative and politically charged. The stark gallery also has a musical space, community center, and residence for artists. By appointment only.
292 E. 3rd St. (bet. Aves. C and D), (212) 505-8312, www.bulletspace.org. F V to Lower East Side-Second Ave.

C

Cheim & Read
At first this gallery is very hard to find, with its grey brick entrance and sunken in glass doors. The gallery is known for selling works by many high profile pop artists, such as Diane Arbus and Robert Mapplethorpe Goldin. Showcasing painting, drawing, sculpture and photography, the gallery exhibits both amateur and more experienced artists. This is a very good gallery to see old and new talent.
547 W. 25th St., (212) 242-7727. T-Sa 10am-6pm. C E to 23rd St.

Christie's
Scope out the goods at the free public viewing five days before auction at this New York branch of the London legend. 19th and 20th century European art, traditionally favored here, are still strong suits.
20 Rockefeller Plaza, (212) 636-2000, www.christies.org. Hours: M-F 10am-5pm. B D F V to 47-50th Sts.-Rockefeller Ctr.

D

Danese
Artists here take some risks, but some more established work also keeps it safe. Eager students typically tend to frequent the wine bar, so a little look-see at openings could be rewarding.
41 E. 57th St. (bet. Madison and Park Aves.), (212) 223-2227, www.danese.com. Hours: M-R 10am-6pm, F 10am-4pm. F to 63rd St., F N R W 4 5 6 to 59th St.

Daniel Reich Gallery
Capitalizing on his current status as the darling of the big ticket armory show, Reich's gallery is one of the hottest around, displaying an exciting array of mostly graphic paintings and drawings.
537A W. 23rd St. (at Tenth Ave.), (212) 924-4949. Hours: T-Sa 11am-6pm. C E to 23rd St.

David Zwirner
First opened in 1993, the gallery focuses on the works of emerging artists in the United States and foreign countries. The completely white space concentrates on the larger pieces of work with hanging lights to accent the paintings well. Along with contemporary artists the gallery will occasionally exhibit paintings by mas-

ters such as Max Ernst, Rene Magritte, and Pablo Picasso and have many catalogues to brows through to learn about artists that one might not be familiar with.
525 W. 19th St. (bet. Tenth and Eleventh Aves.), (212) 727-2070, www.davidzwirner.com. Hours: T-Sa 10am-6pm, C E to 23rd St., 1 to 18th St.

DCA Gallery
By combining seven galleries from Denmark with the support of the Danish Ministry of Culture, this gallery specializing in contemporary Danish Art was established. Showcasing only Danish artists allows those who may not otherwise be seen to be seen by the international community.
525 W. 22nd St., (212) 255-5511, www.dcgallery.com. T-Sa 10am-6pm. C E to 23rd St.

Dia Center for the Arts
Dia opened its main exhibition facility in a four-story renovated warehouse in 1987, dedicating it to large-scale, long-term exhibitions offering artists the opportunity to develop new work or a focused presentation of work on a full floor of the building.
548 W. 22nd St. Fourth Fl., (212) 989-5566, www.diacenter.org. Hours: W-Su 12pm-6pm. Admission: $4 adults, $2 students and seniors. C E to 23rd St.

Deitch Projects
No stranger to the art world, this gallery has featured the works of George Condo, Keith Haring, and Yoko Ono, to name a few. Look for the installation pieces and the precise attention paid to balancing the quirky exhibits with the more serious and mysterious ones.
76 Grand St. (bet. Wooster and Greene Sts.), (212) 343-7300. Hours: M-F 12pm-6pm. N R to Canal St., C E to Spring St.

Doyle New York
Founded in 1963, this auctioneer and appraiser is a relative newcomer to the auction business. The firm specializes in fine art, jewelry, furniture, and design elements at a price range that is far lower than items handled by Christie's, Sotheby's, or Phillips auction houses. Over the years, the auction house has handled the estates of Louis Armstrong, James Cagney, and Marion Anderson. It recently auctioned off treasures from the renowned New York restaurant The Russian Tea Room.
175 E. 87th St., (bet. Lexington and Third Aves.), (212) 427-2730, www.doylenewyork.com. Check website for details. 4 5 6 to 86th St.

D.U.M.B.O. Art Center
D.U.M.B.O., or Down Under the Manhattan Bridge Overpass, is an attractive area for artists who want an alternative to the exorbitant rents of Manhattan studios. Located on the Brooklyn waterfront, the gallery's surrounding neighborhood is home to 1000 artists who gain free membership to the Dumbo Art Center (DAC), and the exhibitions focus on artists whose studios are in the area. The center collaborates with other arts organizations to organize festivals and promote experimentation within the D.U.M.B.O community. The October "Art Under the Bridge Festival" encourages local galleries and studios to open their doors to the public.
Brooklyn. 30 Washington St. (bet. Plymouth and Water Sts.), (718) 694-0831. www.dumboarts-center.org. Hours: R-M 12pm-6pm. A C to High St.

E

Esso
If there is a mien that suggests I-just-became-legal-at-a-drinking-establishment, then the artistic counterpart that suggests I-just-finished-art-school reigns at this funky downtown space, where pop art is reworked for a generation that grew up on the Smurfs and Atari.
531 W. 25th St. (bet. Seventh and Eighth Aves.), (212) 560-9728. Hours: T-F 11am-6pm. 1 to 28th St.

Exit Art
A huge upstairs loft space, complete with a cafe made for lingering when gallery hopping becomes tiresome, as well as a shop filled with art trinkets. Never stodgy, themed group shows are favored. Past innovations include having the artists move their studios into the gallery and an exhibit of art/paraphernalia from social protest movements. Openings here should not be missed.
548 Broadway (bet. Prince and Spring Sts.), (212) 966-7745, www.exitart.org. Hours: M-F 10am-6pm. Suggested contribution of $2. 4 5 6 to Spring St.

F

Feigen Contemporary
This newly opened gallery is one of many that crops up on the streets of Chelsea hoping their artists (and their rental space) will have some longevity. Past exhibits include digitally tweaked color photo prints of stark interiors and human and bodily oddities.
535 W. 20th St. (bet. Tenth and Eleventh Aves.), (212) 929-0500. Hours: T-Sa 11am-6pm. C E to 23rd St.

Forbes Magazine Galleries
What good is it to merely read *Forbes Magazine* if you can't fantasize about what to buy once you make the famous "Forbes 500" list? Check out the galleries of "Wall Street's Bible" and ogle the luxe collection of Fabergé eggs, jewelry, toy boats, lead soldiers, and fine art. The collection is fit for a czar, although entry is free. Free guided tours are available with a reservation made one month in advance for a group of 10 or more.
62 Fifth Ave. (at 12th St.), (212) 206-5548. Hours: T-W, F-Sa 10am-4pm. Admission: free. F N R W 4 5 6 to Lexington Avenue-53rd St.

Fredericks Freiser Gallery
Located in an 1860's brownstone, this gallery was one of the first to establish itself in Chelsea. Representing a small

group of US and foreign artists, the gallery focuses on cutting edge art, such as paintings by Thomas Trosch and strives to expose their works to New York City culture.
504 W. 22nd St., (bet. Tenth and Eleventh Aves.), (212) 633-6555, www.fredericksfreiser-gallery.com. C E *to 23rd St.*

G

Gagosian

A vast gallery filled by established artists who are often eager to take advantage of the space. As such, large paintings, three-dimensional pieces, and sculpture come into play, and the results can be more absorbing than a similar show executed in a smaller area. Even when the physical potential isn't utilized, the art is usually worth checking out.
980 Madison Ave., Sixth Floor (at 76th St.), (212) 744-2313, www.gagosian.com. Hours: T-Sa 10am-6pm. 6 *to 77th St.*

Galerie St. Etienne

Austrian and German art from the early twentieth century has enjoyed something of a renaissance in the New York cultural consciousness. Take a trip to this gallery, which specializes in both, as it is especially relevant right now.
24 W. 57th St., Ste 802 (at Fifth Ave.), (212) 245-6734, www.gseart.com. Hours: T-F 11am-5pm. E V *to 53rd St.*

Gavin Brown's Enterprise

Join Chelsea's trendiest crowds at this ultra-hip, if somewhat pretentious, gallery. Nestled in a chic new spot among old warehouses, Gavin Brown and his "family" of artists have received great press coverage. Stop in at the adjoining bar, complete with disco-light floor, after the gallery closes.
436 W. 15th St. (bet. Ninth and Tenth Aves.), (212) 431-1512. Hours: T-Sa 10am-6pm. A C E L *to 14th St.*

Greene Naftali Gallery

The space is bathed in natural light. Works are contemporary and tend to be experimental. Genres range from sculpture and painting to multimedia exhibits.
526 W. 26th St., Eighth Fl. (bet. Tenth and

Graffiti as art

Although usually associated with the blight of New York during the '70s and '80s, graffiti has certainly evolved in the civic consciousness of younger generations more used to its ubiquitous urban presence than their parents. Now graffiti is no longer a direct barometer of social decay, as the high-rent, graffiti-scrawled East Village can attest, but is assessed by the jaded eyes of passersby like any other public art: if you're going to put it out there, it better be good. But labeling graffiti as real art is still going out on a limb, as the NYPD undoubtedly believes. Nonetheless, New Yorkers love flirting with the taboo, and there is definitely something risky about celebrating what began as petty public vandalism. It's a classic example of a unique, city-based art form (like Jazz and Hip-Hop before) being appropriated, or at least explored, by society at large. It is a subculture spawning a new trend in the pop world, with even suburban kids adhering to this once urban code and inventing their own tags and pieces to scribble. As anyone serious about it will tell you, graffiti can also be about community improvement, about testing graphic boundaries in a very positive, and public, way. By covering the symptoms of depressed areas and simultaneously uncovering their beauty through an indigenous art form, graffiti addresses public concerns. Everyone knows how Keith Haring got his start marking up the subways of New York with his idiosyncratic babies before making it big in the art world.

Eleventh Aves.), (212) 463-7770, www.greenenaftaligallery.com. Hours: T-Sa 10am-6pm. C E *to 23rd St.*

Grey Art Gallery

Both foreign and domestic contemporary artists display their work at this offbeat gallery on New York University's main campus.
100 Washington Sq. East (at Waverly Pl.), (212) 998-6780, www.nyu.edu/greyart. Hours: T, R-F 11am-6pm, W 11am-8pm, Sa 11am-5pm. Suggested contribution $2. N R *to 8th St.-NYU.*

J

Jack Tilton

The artists shown here are respected, but not necessarily for producing expected conventional pieces. Often, the stuff on display requires a second look to see what's really going on. On closer examination, a recent collection of Fred Tomaselli's paintings focusing on birds, leaves, and butterflies proved to be elaborate mosaics using pills instead of tiles.
8 E. 76th St., (212) 737-2221, www.jacktiltongallery.com. Hours: T-Sa 10am-6pm. 6 *to 77th St.*

Jessica Fredericks Gallery

Housed in a brownstone-like building, this space consists of one main viewing room showcasing established and emerging artists.
504 W. 22nd St. (bet. Tenth and Eleventh Aves.), (212) 633-6555. Summer hours: T-F 12pm-5pm, winter hours: T-Sa 11am-6pm. C E *to 23rd St.*

John Connelly Presents

This innovative gallery started from humble beginnings in John Connelly's own apartment when he invited several artist friends to transform the entire home into a life-size, avant-garde diorama. Follow-up shows have been in the same vein.
526 W. 26th St., Ste. 1003 (at Tenth Ave.), (212) 337-9563, www.johnconnellypresents.com/. Hours: T-Sa 11am-6pm. C E *to 23rd St.*

K

Knoedler Gallery

Not to be missed by art historians or art historians in-the-making: the oldest New York-based art gallery, established in 1846, exhibits such modern greats as Nancy Graves, Robert Motherwell, Frank Stella, and Robert Rauschenberg.
19 E. 70th St. (bet. Madison and Fifth Aves.), (212) 794-0550, www.knoedlergallery.com. Hours: M-F 9:30am-5pm. 6 *to 68th St.-Hunter College.*

L

Leo Castelli

Don't want to take a risk? The next best thing to playing it safe at a big museum is found here. The art is by people who have made a name for themselves, either in the art world or culture at-large. Back in 1958, Castelli hand-picked Jasper Johns for a one-man show, thus launching pop art and minimalism. They even show some Picassos here.
18 E. 77th., (212) 249-4470, www.castelligallery.com. Hours: M-F 10am-5pm. 6 *to 77th St.*

M

Marlborough

A good place to see works by relatively well known contemporary and modern artists, this is just one of multiple Marlborough Gallery spaces worldwide. Although their focus is on selling big-ticket pieces from the estates of well-known artists such as Jackson Pollock and Franz Kline, the atmosphere in the gallery is laid back and comfortable.
40 W. 57th St. (bet. Fifth and Sixth Aves.), (212) 541-4900, www.marlboroughgallery.com. Hours: M-F 10am-5:30pm. A B C D 1 *to 59th St.-Columbus Circle.*

Matthew Marks

Marks fills his two downtown spaces, both outposts of his extinct Madison Ave. gallery, with contemporary big names, including Nan Goldin, Brice Marden, and Willem de Kooning.
523 W. 24th St. (bet. Tenth and Eleventh Aves.), (212) 243-0200, www.matthewmarks.com. Call for Hours. C E *to 23rd St.*

Mary Boone Gallery

This longtime SoHo staple recently headed for greener pastures up north, and it now carries an elegant address on Fifth Avenue. Many artists, among them Ross Bleckner, who had a solo show at the Guggenheim a couple of years back, came along for the ride.
745 Fifth Ave., Fourth Fl. (at 57th St.), (212) 752-2929, www.maryboonegallery.com. Hours: T-Sa 10am-6pm. N R W *to Fifth Ave.-59th St.*

Miriam and Ira D. Wallach Art Gallery

Columbia University's resident gallery presents traveling exhibitions throughout the year, curated by professors and students who ensure an academic tilt to the line-up. Lectures and receptions are often sponsored in conjunction with exhibits.
Columbia University, Schermerhorn Hall, Eighth Floor (116th St. and Broadway), (212) 854-7288. Hours: W-Sa 1pm-5pm. 1 *to 116th St.-Columbia University.*

Momenta Art

The neighborhood's most grown-up gallery, still floating beyond the orbit of the conventional. The focus is on group shows featuring works by many artists reflecting a central, provocative theme, and the execution ranges from competent to brilliant. Well worth the trip for anyone looking for something beyond the SoHo scene.
Brooklyn. 72 Berry St. (bet. 9th and 10th Sts.), (718) 218-8058, www.momenta art.org. Hours: M-F 12pm-6pm. L *to Bedford Ave.*

N

New World Art Center

This "New Renaissance" gallery has an ambitious agenda, as it seeks to unite fine, graphic, liter-

ary, film, video, photographic, designing, and performing artists under one roof. The splintered focus keeps exhibitions turnover high and banishes stagnation.
250 Lafayette St. (bet. Prince and Spring Sts.), (212) 966-4363. Hours: M-Su 11am-6pm. MC, V, AmEx, D. C E to Spring St., 6 to Spring St., N R to Prince St., B D F V to Broadway-Lafayette St.

O

O.K. Harris

The goal of O.K. Harris is to show the most significant art of our time. With a variety of contemporary painting, sculpture and photography, they pull together a very interesting selection of artists worth seeing. The gallery also offers lectures to various student and fine arts organizations in order to educate people on the importance of modern art.
383 W. Broadway, (212) 431-3600, www.okharris.com. T-Sa 10am-6pm. C E at Spring St.

P

Pace Wildenstein Gallery, Midtown

An old hand at this art thing, this multilevel space hosts solo exhibitions of big-name artists like Alexander Calder and Chuck Close.
32 E. 57th St. (at Madison Ave.), (212) 421-3292, www.pacewildenstein.com Hours: T-Sa 9:30am-6pm. N R W to 59th St.

Pace Wilderstein Gallery, Chelsea

A Manhattan art world standard with several outlets throughout the city, the Chelsea branch is a testament to the quality that sustains its popularity. Housed in a large and accessible street level space, the Chelsea space presents solo shows by some living, established NYC artists (increasingly becoming a rare breed in the art world).
534 W. 25th St.. (bet. Houston and Prince Sts.), (212) 929-7000. Hours: T-Sa 10am-6pm. N R to Prince St.

Participant, Inc.

The gigantic lines ever-present outside this shoebox sized gallery attest to its increasing popularity with more than just an in-the-know art crowd. The space is devoted to live performances that blur the line between audience and performer (à la the gallery's name), sometimes with a comic intent. Just don't forget to sign the ominous legal release wavers before entering.
95 Rivington St. (at Essex St.), (212) 254-4334. Hours: W-Su 12pm-7pm. F V to Second Ave.

Pat Hearn

Formerly part of the East Village and SoHo scenes, Hearn's Chelsea gallery presents offbeat work by emerging to mid-career Contemporary American and European artists. A veteran of the art scene, she has propelled numerous artists' careers, among them George Condo and Philip Taaff.
530 W. 22nd St. (bet. Tenth and Eleventh Aves.), (212) 727-7366. Hours: T-Sa 12pm-6pm. C E to 23rd St.

Paula Cooper Gallery

You'll have to squint to read the lettering at this gallery's entrance on the south side of the street. Woodwork in the two rooms resembles a cross between a barn and a church. Tall ceilings in the back room allow for massive installments. Natural light filters through fogged windows.
534 W. 21st St. (bet. Tenth and Eleventh Aves.), (212) 255-1105. Summer hours: T-F 10am-5pm, winter hours: M-F 10am-6pm. C E to 23rd St.

Peter Blum

Generally on the beaten path in terms of content, with frequent swerves into the odd and obscure. In addition to paintings and sculptures by known artists, architectural sketches and non-Western archeological artifacts have been known to make an appearance in this large, rectangular room.
99 Wooster St., (212) 343-0441, www.peterblumgallery.com. Hours: T-F 10am-6pm, Sa 11am-6pm. C E to Spring St.

Phillips de Pury & Luxembourg

This London-based auction house and gallery has been in business since 1796 and is the only auctioneer to have ever held a sale inside Buckingham Palace. Today, Phillips has branches in Geneva, Zurich, Paris, London, and Berlin. Its New York headquarters specializes in the sale of modern and contemporary American art, furniture, and photography. Phillips' sale room, with 50-foot ceilings and panoramic windows overlooking the Hudson River and lower Manhattan, is open for public viewing a few days before each auction. For those looking to do more than just browse, ancillary services include private treaty sales, trust and estate services, evaluations, and appraisals.
450 W. 15th St. (bet. Ninth and Tenth Aves.), (212) 940-1200, www.phillips-dpt.com. Hours: M-F 10am-5pm. A C E L to 14th St.

Phyllis Kind

Since the work of established white male artists still constitutes the majority of what makes it into serious galleries, this deceptively large space often contains shows that challenge this order. Artists like Betty Saar regularly produce some of the most thought-provoking installations you're likely to see.
136 Greene St., (212) 925-1200. Hours: T-Sa 10am-6pm. B D F V to Broadway-Lafayette St., N R to Prince St.

Pierogi 2000

The name reflects the way the traditional Polish flavor of the community melds with the influx of forward-focused artists. Like most Williamsburg galleries, the art here is as far outside of the mainstream as the location. The gallery serves as everything from an outlet for resurrections of art treasures unseen for years to a center for lots of the neighborhood's resident artists, many of whom can be found hanging out on its stoop.
Brooklyn. 177 N. 9th St., (bet. Bedford and Driggs Aves.), (718) 599-2144.

Hours: F-M 12pm-6pm. Ⓛ *to Bedford Ave.*

PostMasters Gallery

Works that challenge much of what's taken for granted in the art world regularly show up here. Shows have included artists working together as a team to produce installations of seemingly ordinary scenes from everyday life, as well as works that directly question the idea of art-as-business.
459 W. 19th St. (at Tenth Ave.), (212) 727-3323. Hours: T-Sa 11am-6pm. ① *to 18th St.*

PPOW Gallery

Started in the '80s in the East Village by two women, this gallery moved here after it had built a solid reputation as a space that embraced anti-establishment artists. The two rooms generally each contain work by a different artist. Female artists' works are well represented here, as are others offering perspectives that don't fit into the old standards, like those of the late well-known AIDS-chronicler David Wojnarowicz, whose estate is owned by the gallery.
555 W. 25th, (212) 941-8643, www.ppowgallery.com. Hours: T-Sa 11am-6pm. Ⓒ Ⓔ *to 23rd St.*

R

Rivington Arms

Fashionistas and Brooklyn hipsters intersect at this gallery run by the children of New York society mavens and downtown royalty. With the intent of making the Lower East Side into the new Chelsea, evolution has become a byword for the diverse installation pieces at this small but creative gallery full of gala guys and gals.
102 Rivington St. (at Essex St.), (646) 654-3213, www.rivingtonarms.com. Hours: W-F 11am-6pm, Sa-Su 12pm-6pm. Ⓕ Ⓥ *to Second Ave.*

Ronald Feldman Fine Arts

Artists with sufficient talent execute ideas that could easily fall on either side of the thin line dividing success and failure. A Roxy Paine show consisted of 2,200 hand-made mushrooms, each unique, displayed so that they appeared to be sprouting from the floor. It was wacky indeed, and it garnered rave reviews.
31 Mercer St. (bet. Grand and Canal Sts.), (212) 226-3232. Summer hours: M-R 10am-6pm, F 10am-3pm, winter hours: T-Sa 10am-6pm. Ⓙ Ⓜ Ⓝ Ⓡ Ⓦ Ⓩ ⑥ *to Canal St.*

S

Skarstedt Fine Art

Located amongst the flurry of Madison Avenue galleries, Skarstedt distinguishes itself with historical exhibitions of Contemporary American and European artists. The gallery fosters a critique of popular culture through its original presentation of postmodern artworks by big-name artists such as Jeff Koons and Cindy Sherman. Its mission to explore identity, originality, authorship, and media is more akin to a downtown gallery, but such ambitions make Skarstedt unique among its Upper East Side peers.
1018 Madison Ave. (bet. 78th and 79th Sts.), (212) 737-2060, www.skarstedt.com. Summer hours: T-F 10am-5pm, winter hours: T-Sa 10am-6pm. ⑥ *to 77th St.*

SoHo Photo Gallery

One of the most well-established photography galleries in town, with shows highlighting many different styles. They offer a lot of educational classes to the public on the history and work of various photographers and others to improve artistic skills. Call for schedule and information.
15 White St. (bet. Sixth Ave. and W. Broadway), (212) 226-8571, www.sohophoto.com. Hours: R 6pm-8pm, F-Su 1pm-6pm. ① *to Franklin St.*

Sotheby's

Don your most expensive suit or pretend you're an heir(ess) when you attend a viewing at Manhattan's leading auction house. Collectibles sold here range from jewels and vintage wine to decorative and fine arts. Admission is free, but the glossy catalog will set you back about 25 bucks.
1334 York Ave. (at 72nd St.), (212) 606-7000. Hours: M-F 9am-5pm. ⑥ *to 68th St.,* Ⓕ *to 63rd St.-Lexington Ave.*

Staley-Wise

Love photography? Sorting through the different styles that get thrown together, all involving a camera and film as media, can be daunting. This is the place for those who love glamorous photography, featuring works ranging from old *Life* magazine-style celebrity photos to work by today's most prominent fashion photographers.
560 Broadway (at Prince St.), (212) 966-6223. Hours: M-F 11am-5pm. Ⓝ Ⓡ *to Prince St.*

Swann Auction Galleries

Founded some sixty years ago as an auction house for rare and antique books, Swann maintains an exclusive atmosphere with a collection of rare and expensive works. As a self-proclaimed world leader in the art market, Swann Galleries is also open to the public and provides a unique venue to view photographs, autographs, and vintage posters. The best way to experience this gallery is by attending one of the public auctions. The bidders and their reactions can be as engaging as the works of art involved, and the amounts of money tossed about are often enough to strike even the most avid collectors.
104 E. 25th St., (212) 254-4710, www.swanngalleries.com. Hours: R 10am-3pm, F-W 10am-2pm. Open for approximately 40 auctions yearly. Ⓝ Ⓡ Ⓦ ⑥ *to 23rd St.*

T

Tepper Galleries

Like uptown auctioneer Doyle New York, Tepper handles large estate sales with a focus on American, European, and Asian antiques. The biweekly auctions are free and open to the public, as are the auction previews held from 9am to 7pm the preceding day.

Unlike Sotheby's, Christie's, or Phillips de Pury & Luxembourg, which all charge upwards of $25 per catalogue, Tepper catalogues are free for the taking. *110 E. 25th (bet. Park and Lexington Aves.), (212) 677-5300, www.tepper-galleries.com. Bi-weekly auctions Saturdays at 10am, previews on Fridays preceding the sale day 9am-7pm. N R 6 to 23rd St.*

Triple Candie

A 4,700-square foot exhibition space in the heart of Harlem, Triple Candie opened in 2001 with an exhibit entitled "Rumors of War," and its promotion of politically active art proceeds unrestrained. Created as a venue for contemporary arts and ideas, its goal is to celebrate freedom of ideas and to promote local artists in a public and progressive environment. To that end, exuberant and exciting works are arranged in the warehouse-like space to provide an audience with the most intimate connection of the artist's vision, and public or private parties bring the fun back to the often-stuffy world of art exhibition. *461 W. 126th St. (at Amsterdam Ave.), (212) 865-0783, www.triple-candie.org. Hours: R-Su 12pm-5 pm. A B C D to 125th St., 1 to 125th St.*

W

White Box

The intense shows occurring in the cramped space of this politically conscious gallery pack 'em in on opening nights. Here, satire, often in the form of live performances, goes hand in hand here with good art, turning the walls into the stage set for whatever is taking place. Stop by on an off hour to watch rehearsals for the main event. *525 W. 26th St. (at Tenth Ave.), (212) 714-2347, www.whiteboxny.org. Hours: T-Sa 10am-6pm. C E to 23rd St.*

William Secord Gallery

This gallery is known for its carefully curated and meticulously selected dog art. Canine addicts not satiated by this gallery alone need not fear. The Dog Museum, once directed by Secord as well, thrives in St. Louis. *52 E. 76th St., Third Fl. (bet. Park and Madison Aves.), (212) 249-0075, www.dogpainting.com. Hours: M-Sa 10am-5pm. Closed Saturday in July and August. 6 to 77th St.*

[Gallery Index by Neighborhood]

BROOKLYN
Pierogi 2000
Momenta Art

CHELSEA
Barbara Gladstone Gallery
Brent Sikkema
Chiem and Reid
Daniel Reich Gallery
David Zwerner
DCA Gallery
Frederick Freiser Gallery
Gagosian
Gavin Brown's Enterprise
Greene Naftali Gallery
Jessica Fredricks Gallery
John Connelly Presents
Mary Boone
Matthew Marks
Metro Pictures
Paula Cooper Gallery
Pat Hearn
Phillips de Pury & Luxembourg
303 Gallery
White Box

EAST VILLAGE
Bullet Space
Participant, Inc.
Rivington Arms

GRAMERCY
Swann Galleries
Tepper Auction House
Thread Waxing Space

GREENWICH VILLAGE
Grey Art Gallery

HARLEM
Triple Candie Gallery

MIDTOWN
Austrian Cultural Forum
Christie's
Danese
Galerie St. Etienne
Marlborough
Mary Boone Gallery
PaceWildenstein Gallery

SoHo
Ace Gallery
Alternative Gardens
Artist's Space
Basilo
Bronwyn Keenan
Exit Art
Gagosian
Jack Tilton
Jim Deitsch Projects
Leo Castelli
New World Art Center
O.K. Harris
Peter Blum
Phyllis Kind
PostMasters
PPOW
Ronald Feldman
SoHo Photo Gallery
Stanley Wise
Wooster Gardens

TRIBECA
Apex Art

UPPER EAST SIDE
Acquavella
Gagosian
Knoedler Gallery
Leo Castelli
Skarsted Fine Art
Sotheby's
William Secord Gallery

Classes and Workshops Listings

From brushing up on your high school French to writing workshops for aspiring novelists to lessons in the art of the tea ceremony, the opportunities for hands-on culture abound. With institutions and societies dedicated to national cultures and alternative lifestyles, New York City is a giant marketplace for the exchange of skills, stories, and information. Below is just a sampling of the many institutions devoted to promoting different aspects of all this city has to offer.

A

Alliance Française

Brush up on the language of love at Tuesday's $8 ($6 for students) screenings of French flicks. Dance classes and more than 200 language courses are also available. Members enjoy free films, food and wine tastings, travel seminars, art excursions, discounts on French performances around the city, and use of the multimedia library.
111 E. 59th St. (bet. Lexington and Park Aves.), (212) 355-6100, www.fiaf.org. Hours: M-R 9:30am-7:30pm, F 9:30am-6pm, Sa 9am-2pm. F N R W 4 5 6 *to Lexington Ave-59th St.*

The American Academy of Arts and Letters

Recent initiates Oliver Sacks and Elie Wiesel attest to the prestige of this exclusive society created to honor American artists, writers, and composers for their accomplishments. Check out samples of honorees' works inside the gallery. For a good look at the neighboring Trinity Church Cemetery, stop by the South Gallery.
633 W. 155th St. (bet. Broadway and Riverside Dr.), (212) 368-5900, artsand letters.org. Call for appointment. Admission free. 1 *to 157th St.*

American Ballet Theatre

Drop-in classes run to the tune of $12 a pop ($110 buys ten classes) for aspiring prima donnas at one of the country's premier studios. Alaine Haubert and Diana Cartier teach regularly, though guest instructors from the ABT Artistic Staff occasionally fill in. Advanced dancers should stop by at 10am during the week, while the 6pm weekday classes will best serve intermediates.
890 Broadway, Third Fl. (bet. 19th and 20th St.), (212) 477-3030, www.abt.org. Cash Only. L N R W 4 5 6 *to 14th St.-Union Sq.*

The American Numismatic Society

If you had one of those penny books as a kid, this is your chance to see what you may have had if you'd only stuck with it. Numismatics, the study of coins and medals, has been practiced in these hallowed halls since 1858, and their library maintains over 70,000 volumes. Some of the Society's other pursuits include a fellowship program for grad students and museum professionals, publishing monographs and journals, and running an annual conference on coinage in America.
96 Fulton St. (at William St.), (212) 234-3130. Hours: T-F 9am-5pm. Admission free. A C J M Z 2 3 4 5 *to Fulton.-Broadway-Nassau*

Americas Society

Inter-American policy issues come up for debate at the conferences and study groups organized by the Society's Western Hemisphere Department. The Cultural Affairs department offers an extensive arts library, lectures in conjunction with special exhibits, and concerts with receptions for the wine-sipping crowd.
680 Park Ave. (at 68th St.), (212) 628-3200, www.counciloftheamericas.org. Hours: T, R-Sa 12-6, W-Su 12pm-6pm. Cash Only. 6 *to 68th St.-Hunter College*

Angel Orensanz Foundation

Situated in an old, not quite refurbished synagogue, this new performance space plays host to many musical and performing arts events, occasionally even a fashion show. A group of local artists' work is also on display around the building, whose rickety stairways, peeling paint, and anachronistic neon blue backlighting lend a creepy elegance to the often informal gatherings here.
172 Norfolk St. (bet. Houston and Stanton St.) (212) 529-7194, www.orensanz.org. Cash only. F V *to Second Ave.*

The Asian American Writers' Workshop

Unlike its counterparts, the weekly sessions held by Other Countries are free except for a $2 fee for the space. Anyone is welcome to attend and should bring copies of their work to read at the session. This year, the AAWW offers six-week long workshops which cost about $125, and feature topics such as poetry writing, fiction-in-progress, how to get published, and screenwriting as well as discussion groups and book clubs.
16 W. 32nd St., Tenth Fl. (bet. Broadway and Fifth Ave.), (212) 494-0061, www.aaww.com. Hours: M-F 12pm-7pm. B D F N R V W *to 34th St.-Herald Sq.*

B

Ballet Academy East

Itching to test those dancing shoes? Drop in here, and, for $11, you can sample one of the jazz, ballet, or tap classes.
1651 Third Ave. (bet. 92nd and 93rd Sts.), (212) 369-2723, www.balletacademy east.org. Hours: M-F 9am-9pm, Sa 9am-3pm. 6 *to 96th St.*

Bronfman Jewish Center

In a townhouse built for Lockwood de Forest, a wealthy exporter, the center presents free lectures focusing on Jewish religious concerns and Israeli

politics for an almost exclusively NYU audience. De Forest founded workshops in India to revive the art of woodworking, so the center is replete with the fruits of his labor-original, intricately-carved teak wood imported from India.
7 E. 10th St. (bet. University Pl. and Fifth Ave.), (212) 998-4114. Hours: M-R 8am-9pm, F 8am-3am. L N R W 4 5 6 to 14th St.-Union Sq.

C

China Institute in America

America's oldest bicultural organization focusing on China promotes awareness of Chinese culture, history, language, and arts through semester-long classes in Mandarin, Cantonese, Tai Chi, calligraphy, cooking, and painting. Seminars, lecture series, and film screenings with Chinese and Chinese-American themes are also regularly scheduled.
125 E. 65th St. (bet. Lexington and Park Aves.), (212) 744-8181, www.ecnext.com. Hours: M, W, F 10am-5pm, T, R 10am-8pm. Admission: $5, 6 to 68th St.-Hunter College

G

Gotham Writer's Workshop

Workshops in fiction writing, poetry, screenwriting, and a number of other genres are offered at seven different locations in Manhattan. They even have online classes for your convenience – check out www.write.org for pertinent info. Classes meet once a week for three hours and cost about $400 for a ten-week semester. The teachers are widely published writers.
1841 Broadway, Ste. 809 (bet. 60th and 61st Sts.), (212) 974-8377, www.writingclasses.com. Hours: M-F 9am-5pm, A B C D 1 to 59th St.-Columbus Circle.

L

La Maison Française

The epicenter of French life at NYU. Call for information about free lectures, usually in French, along with conferences and exhibitions, which are presented in the center's historic 19th century carriage house.
16 Washington Pl. (bet. University Pl. and Fifth Ave.), (212) 998-8750. Hours: M-F 10am-6pm. N R to 8th St.-NYU

M

Martha Graham Center of Contemporary Dance

Home of the Martha Graham Dance Ensemble, this contemporary dance school trains young dancers in her technique, which is an artistic vision rather than simply a dance system.
316 E. 63rd St. (bet. First and Second Aves.), Lower Level, (212) 521-3611, www.marthagraham dance.org. Call for schedule. F N R W 4 5 6 to 59th St.-Lexington Ave.-59th St.

N

New York Society Library

George Washington, James Fenimore Cooper, Henry Thoreau, and Herman Melville all frequented the oldest circulating library in New York, founded in 1754. Nowadays you'll have to fork over $135 ($90 for students) for the privilege of perusing literature in the luxurious reading rooms. Nonmembers are accommodated in the ground floor's reference room.
53 E. 79th St. (bet. Madison and Park Aves.), (212) 288-6900. M, W, F 9am-5pm, T, R 9am-7pm, Sa 9am-5pm, Su 1-5pm. Cash only. 6 to 77th St.

New York Zendo Shobo-ji

New Yorkers looking to escape urban chaos seek out this serene temple, complete with rock gardens, instructions on correct breathing, meditation, posture, etiquette, and Oriental floor cushions. Hardcore enthusiasts can partake of a purer experience on one of the weekend retreats held at an affiliated monastery in the Catskills.
223 E. 67th St. (bet. Second and Third Aves.), (212) 861-3333. $15 per session, $50 membership for one month. Cash only. 6 to 68th St.-Hunter College.

92nd Street Y

One of New York's most valuable cultural resources serves as an umbrella organization for a multitude of classes, workshops, and speaking and reading series, as well as important dance artists. The reading series is by far the city's most star-studded, drawing nationally and internationally renowned poets and authors. Tickets run around $5-$7 for students.
1395 Lexington Ave. (at 92nd St.), (212) 415-5500, www.92y.org. Hours: M-F 9am-7pm. 4 5 6 to 86th St.

P

Poets House

This free reading room and resource center houses the largest collection of poetry books in the country. Call for information about programs.
72 Spring St. (bet. Crosby and Lafayette Sts.), (212) 431-7920. Hours: T-F 11am-7pm, Sa 11am-4pm. 6 to Spring St.

S

The Spanish Institute

Exhibitions acquaint visitors with various forms of Spanish culture. Semester-long language classes are offered, and they include the perks of access to both the reference collection and reading room with current publications.
684 Park Ave. (bet. 68th and 69th Sts.), (212) 628-0423. Call for schedule. $60 per membership, 6 to 68th St.-Hunter College.

U

Urasenke Chanoyu Center

The Kyoto-based organization dedicates itself to the chado, or The Way of Tea, a strictly scripted ceremony infused with serenity, order, and calm. The New York chapter is one of five U.S. branches of the Urasenke organization, and it offers monthly traditional Japanese tea ceremonies that are open to the public. Call aheadfor dates and times, as they usually change every season.
153 E. 69th St. (bet. Lexington and Third Aves.), (212) 988-6161, www.urasenke.or.jp. 6 to 66th St.-Hunter College.

Southfirst Gallery

The Southfirst art gallery is located in the currently booming and hip Williamsburg section of Brooklyn. It is situated on 60 N. 6th St., in a grey building that from the outside appears to be the quintessential small contemporary urban space. The owners, Maika Pollack and Florian Altenberg, purchased a residential home with the intention of living there. Unfortunately, one of the zoning conditions of the building they purchased was that it had to have some sort of commercial usage. Maika, an Art History major, was friends with many local artists and decided that their 'commerce' would be an informal gallery featuring the works of their friends. They had no aspirations to achieve commercial success, but after the gallery was reviewed in *Time Out New York* shortly after opening, a buzz began to spread throughout the five boroughs. Once they received such critical acclaim, both Maika and Florian began to take the business side of their gallery more seriously. Their goal – which was achieved – was to add a professional credibility to the gallery while maintaining a grass-roots sensibility. They outgrew their space and in November of 2002 moved to their current location in Williamsburg. Now, the Hudson River and lower Manhattan skyline can be seen from the entrance. The sleek, simple industrial lines of the building offer an interesting contrast to the often high-concept and spacey modern art on display. The atmosphere is friendly, inviting all to come in and chat during the open hours, 1pm-6pm Fri-Sat and by appointment. The owners seek to create a space where students, art lovers, buyers, and walkers-by can all merge and appreciate art together. Maika delights in conversing about the art and relaying her passion for it to others, so be sure to ask if you have any questions about displayed works. The gallery is part of the Williamsburg Gallery Association, a collective that offers help and support to the many small galleries in the area. Most of the artists on display at Southfirst are young MFA's, just starting out their artistic careers. The gallery provides a jumping point for the artists of the future. Maika and Florian take great pride in offering a vital home for up-and-coming young artists. While most of Southfirst's showings feature new artists, the gallery has also had an Alice Neil drawing on display. Generally, Southfield can be relied on for having extremely diverse exhibits. The gallery averages around 6 shows a year, doing both individual and group showings. The Southfirst-Gallery is a trendy up-and -coming space visitors can rely on for shows that offer plenty of character, community, and great art.

Address: 60 N. 6th St,
Brooklyn sNY 11211
Phone: 718 559 4884
www.southfirst.org
info@southfirst.org
(L) to Bedford Avenue.

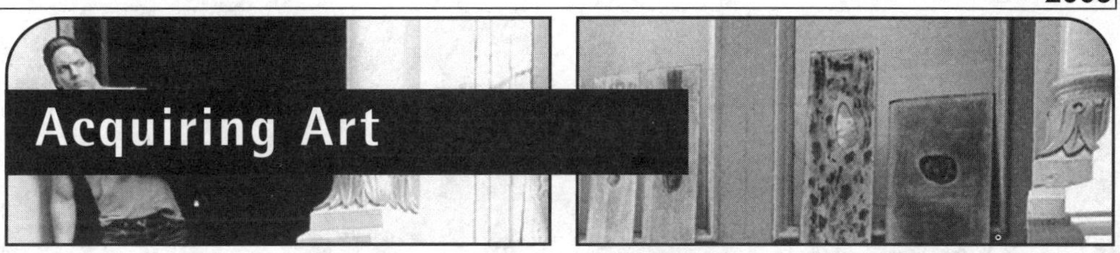

Acquiring Art

New York provides a great outlet for buying art. The multitude of sources available makes it easy to purchase art despite having little disposable income. When searching for cheaper art, it is important to be aware about art fairs and galleries where one can generally find good, cheap art. Below are some suggestions for places to search when looking to purchase art on a budget.

The most reasonably priced art will be contemporary, and one will find that investing in emerging artists does not necessarily have to be expensive. The largest selection of contemporary art can be found at art fairs that have original pieces from the Van Goghs and Cezannes of the future. Emerging artists are generally concerned with getting their art onto the market, and many price their works decently low. Three major art fairs that occur annually in New York city are the AAF Contemporary Art Fair (*Oct. at Pier Twelfth Ave. and 52nd St.; (212) 225-2003; aafnyc.com*); the Scope Art Fair (*March at the Hotel Gansevoort, 18 Ninth Ave. at 13th St.; (212) 268-1522; scopeart. com*), and the Frere Independent Art Fair (*149 W. 24th St., (212) 604-0519; frereindependent.com*). The AAF Fair has historically provided thousands of pieces at affordable prices. The vibe of the fair is Upper East Side casual, and the AAF offers free lectures for first time buyers and collectors. The Scope Art Fair is designed for a younger and trendier crowd than the AAF and features up-and-coming artists and galleries. The most experimental fair of the three is the Frere Independent, which is geared toward an edgier crowd. The Art Expo New York (*March; Jacob Javits Convention Center; 655 W. 34th St.; brought to you by the International Arts and Framing Group; (888) 608-5300 for specific dates*) is a wonderful find for those seeking emerging talent in a variety of the arts. You will find artists, architects and even interior designers showcasing their works to a large audience of seasoned art dealers and art lovers alike.

For more expensive pieces you can travel to the New York Ceramics Fair (*Jan. hosted by Caskey & Lees; (310) 455-2886 for more information*), where one can find an abundance of ceramics and glass created by well-known artists and sold by well-known galleries and dealers. Ranging from early classical to contemporary designs, the fair provides a rare collection that is targeted for those in the know. The Outsider Arts Fair (*Jan.; Puck Building; 295 Lafayette St.; (212) 777-5218 for more information*) showcases many new artists as well as a few already established contemporary ones. Do not expect to find a fantastic deal, although the fair is a great place to check out new artistic discoveries recently made by top galleries. The Armory Show - The International Fair of New Art (*March; Pier 90 and 92, Twelfth Ave. E 50th and 52nd Sts.; (212) 645-6440 for more information*) is a great spot to see international art that one might never find in the US again. Some of the pieces are exquisite and the fair has been known to display works that may be controversial in many US galleries. Thousands of galleries come from around the globe to New York to show their work at this fair. Prices tend to be high, but it is a great place to go and browse.

Another way to acquire art is to go right to the source and venture out on open studio tours or visit artists' workplaces to view (and purchase) their art. Many established artists have exclusive agreements to sell their works through specific galleries so it is better and their prices tend to be higher. There are some tours that will allow artists the freedom to haggle with customers themselves and this is when you can get great deals. DUMBO Art Theater Under the Bridge (*Oct.; (718) 694-0831 dumboartscenter.org/festival*) is held every October and provides New York art enthusiasts with dance parties and parades at and around the warehouse location. Another great tour is TOAST: Tribeca Open Artist Studio Tour (*Apr.; (212) 479-7323, toastartwalk.com*), the two-time-a-year studio tour at the Woolworth building that is conducted by the Lower Manhattan Community Council (*212) 219-9401; www.lmcc.net*), which offers both guided and self-guided tours of studios in the neighborhood.

performing arts in nyc

Roaring New York

The city's professional theater was launched in 1750 with an imported production of *Richard III*, the first in a succession of exchanges between the British and American stages that has proved extremely fruitful for both New York and London theater.

The New York theater scene as we know it today really got its start around the turn of the century. The city's elite frequented productions by stage luminaries such as Lunt and Fontanne, the Barrymores, and the Booths. Meanwhile, the "common folk" packed the city's vaudeville, variety, and minstrel theaters located along the Bowery. Vaudeville often fed Broadway during the teens and '20s; before launching their movie careers, performers such as the Marx Brothers graced Broadway stages with their vaudeville circuit reviews.

Edna St. Vincent Millay and her literary friends helped to launch the Provincetown Playhouse and similar avant-garde theaters in Greenwich Village. The Group Theater featured the works of playwrights such as Eugene O'Neill and Clifford Odets. O'Neill called the city home during the pre-World War I period, and his Pulitzer Prize-winning drama *Anna Christie* (a ribald story of the Lower East Side nightlife scene) was set in the Golden Swan, a saloon frequented by the playwright himself.

Broadway's heyday was in the late 1920s, when hundreds of shows opened each year. In a time of such bounty, there were certainly a few bad apples. Critics of the time, such as Robert Benchley,

Dorothy Parker, and Alexander Wollcott, were never out of work. Several New York writers, playwrights, actors and critics lunched together regularly at midtown's Algonquin Hotel. These vicious and fecund roundtables are the stuff of legend; they served as an artistic think-tank in a time of tremendous theatrical activity. George S. Kaufman, along with his myriad writing partners such as Moss Hart and Marc Connolly, was very active during this period and penned scores of incredible comedies inspired by the exploits of the Algonquin intellectuals.

The World War II and post-war periods were also quite fruitful for New York drama, as two brilliant young playwrights came to make their mark on American theater. Tennessee Williams set new standards with works such as *A Streetcar Named Desire*, *The Glass Menagerie*, *Cat on a Hot Tin Roof*, and *Camino Real*. Brooklyn-based Arthur Miller gave us American classics *Death of a Salesman*, *The Crucible*, and *A View from the Bridge*.

Papp and Circumstance

Impresario Joseph Papp founded the Public Theater, producing works such as *Hair* and *A Chorus Line*. In addition, Papp founded the New York institution Shakespeare in the Park. Papp's goal for the Public to produce all of Shakespeare's plays was met posthumously in 1997, when *Henry VIII* played in open-air in Central Park's Delacorte Theater. Off-Broadway and Off-Off-Broadway theaters boomed with the works of innovative new groups and artists such as the Open Theater and the Wooster

Group. In the late '70s and early '80s, playwrights such as August Wilson and Wendy Wasserstein brought minority voices to Broadway. The mid-'80s witnessed the introduction of a genre of AIDS-related plays such as *The Normal Heart* by Larry Kramer and Tony Kushner's *Angels in America.*

The '80s also ushered in the era of the über-musical: theatrical monsters of varying quality that crushed all in their path. These musicals - *Cats, The Phantom of the Opera,* and *Les Miserables* - are characterized by extremely high production values and attract large audiences with the promise of spectacle and bombast.

This is a song for Broadway...

Large musicals still dominate Broadway, but they have taken on a different quality from the brassy productions of the '80s. Disney's Tony Award-winning *The Lion King* was hailed by critics and audiences alike. *Rent*, a '90s version of Puccini's opera *La Bohéme*, traveled uptown to Broadway from downtown's esteemed New York Theater Workshop.

Confronted by the staggering drop-off in tourism in the wake of the terrorist attacks of September 11, many of New York City's arts institutions find themselves in dire financial straits. The effects have been particularly noticeable for Broadway and off-Broadway theaters. Despite strong reviews, many shows are forced to close prematurely as a result of diminished ticket sales. The theaters are now relying on selling last-minute tickets at discounted rates in order to fill the seats. One of the positive results of these tough financial times is an increase in cultural attendance by New York residents. As the number of out-of-town tourists dwindles, museums and theaters hope to encourage the city's culture vultures to be tourists a little closer to home.

Broadway

At the heart of New York's tourist industry is the legendary 42nd St., whose glittering lights and Broadway theaters draw visitors from all over the world. Despite the enormous amount of revenue generated by successful shows and high-ticket prices, launching a production is among the most expensive and risky of all business propositions. As a result of the prohibitive fiscal pressures faced by all new productions, a thriving community has started to develop away from Midtown's main drag in some of the downtown theaters, many of which were originally used by famous companies at the turn of the century. *See below for more information on Off-Off Broadway shows.*

Off-Off Broadway

It's pretty clear what someone's talking about if they mention a Broadway show, but what exactly does the phrase "Off-Off" signify? Here's a simple guide:

Broadway means the district of theaters clustered around Times Square, usually between 41st and 53rd Sts. Tickets easily cost as much as $75 a pop for an average seat, $40 if you don't mind the last row. Lately shows like *Rent*, *Cabaret* and *The Lion King* have been drawing huge crowds and enlivening the strip.

Off-Broadway originally meant theaters in Greenwich Village, the majority of which have a seating capacity of 500 or less. Lately, however, this term has come to refer to smaller theaters anywhere in the city. Off-Broadway shows tend to have greater literary and social importance, a wider variety in production quality, and cheaper ticket prices (max $40).

Off-Off Broadway is a term used to refer to productions featuring actors who are non-equity, working in theaters of less than 100 seats. Here you can find exciting, daring performances at shoestring prices. Conversely, of course, there are the occasional shows too avant-garde to stomach. Conservative theatergoers should perhaps avoid Off-Off-Broadway. For adventurous risk-takers, though, Off-Off Broadway theater will likely provide abundant rewards.

Broadway Bargains

How to Find Cheap Tickets on Broadway (Without Really Trying)

Prices for Broadway and Off-Broadway shows are high enough to put a damper on anyone's New York adventures. Fortunately, there are a variety of ways to get your hands on some cheap tickets. If you are willing to make a few sacrifices, like waiting in lines or standing for the first half of the performance, attending New York's best performances can be affordable.

General rush tickets and student-rush tickets, which require a student ID for purchase, are usually sold by the theater a few hours before curtain and cost about $20. Be prepared to wait in line for both rush tickets and the other more risky option of standby tickets, which are released directly before curtain at sold-out shows. Lottery tickets are another discount option; everyone puts his or her name in a drawing, and the ticket purchaser is chosen at random. Some venues accept only cash for rush and standing-room-only tickets, so check the theater's policy before you wait in line. Many performance companies offer special student discounts independent of the larger wholesale options, so it can never hurt to call and inquire ahead of time about a particular company's student-rush policy.

Off-Off Broadway

Off-off Broadway shows are always another affordable option. While reading reviews before you purchase your tickets is the safest route to enjoying the performance, the monetary stakes are low enough to encourage risk-taking. These smaller shows, whose ticket prices generally range from $5 to $25, are unique pieces performed in an intimate setting.

TKTS

Run by the Theatre Development Fund, it has proven one of the most well-known ways to obtain cheap tickets. TKTS sells tickets for Broadway, Off-Broadway, Dance, and Music events. Tickets are 50% or 75% of the original price plus a $3 service charge. Boards outside of the TKTS stands list all available shows, and changes in availability can occur on an hourly basis in response to box office demand. TKTS sells only same-day tickets and is known to release a bunch of tickets a half-hour before the show. While buying tickets here can often be risky, especially when facing unpredictable lines, some of the best Broadway shows will give TKTS permission to sell leftover tickets directly before the show starts. TKTS accepts only cash and traveler's checks. There are two TKTS locations, and since both sell from the same pool of tickets, neither has a better selection.

TKTS Times Square Theatre Center is located in Duffy Square (at Broadway and 47th St.), (212) 221-0013. Hours: 3pm-8pm for M-Sa evening performances, W and Sa matinees 10am-2pm, all Su performances 11am-7pm. Cash and traveler's checks only. A C E N R S W 1 2 3 7 *to Times Sq.-42nd St.*

TKTS Lower Manhattan Theatre Centre (at South Street Seaport, the corner of Front and John Sts., the rear of the Resnick/Prudential Building at 199 Water St.), (212) 221-0013. Hours: M-Sa 11am-6pm for all evening performances, Su 11am-3:30pm for evening performances. Cash and traveler's checks only, A C J M Z 2 3 4 5 *to Fulton St.-Broadway/Nassau. *At this TKTS location only, matinee tickets must be purchased the day before.*

Theater Development Fund

If you work in the theater industry or if you are an educator in New York, The Theater Development Fund offers discounted theater tickets to many Broadway and Off-Broadway shows. The program was designed to help students, teachers, union members, retired people, the clergy, and members of the armed forces, among others, afford the theater. You pay an annual fee of $15 to be added to their mailing list, which alerts you to upcoming bargains. You can buy up to 9 tickets for each show you attend at only $14-$16 per ticket. (212) 221-0885. Apply online at www.tdf.org.

Hit Show Club

The club distributes discount coupons (usually for 25-50% off), which can be redeemed at the theater box office days or even hours before the performance begins. You can pick up coupons in person at the Ninth Avenue

office or call to have your name added to their mailing list.
630 Ninth Ave. (bet. 44th and 45th Sts.), 8th Fl., (212) 581-4211. A C E to 42nd St.-Port Authority, N R S W 1 2 3 7 to 42nd St.-Times Sq.

Audience Extras

This promotion service offers members free tickets (for a $3.50 reservation service charge per ticket) to over 1,000 different entertainment events each year, including dance performances, concerts, movie premieres, and sporting events. The promotion service distributes free tickets to members when a show is in previews, expects a reviewer of celebrity to attend, or wants to seat a full house for a myriad of other reasons. They do not focus specifically on Broadway shows, but their extremely low prices and the variety of their selections make the $85 membership fee and subsequent $85 annual dues worthwhile. All members are allowed one or two tickets per performance depending on availability, or with an additional donation to The Memorial Foundation for the Arts of at least $35, members can get up to four tickets. A portion of the reservation service charge goes to the Memorial Foundation to aid non-profit theaters.
Call (212) 647-0685 for a sample of available performances, (212) 989-9550 for membership information and reservations.

Usher

If you are willing to volunteer some of your time in return for watching a show for free, ushering is an amazing option. Policies vary from theater to theater and even from show to show, but generally all you have to do to get in for free is arrive well before the show starts, hand paying customers a program, and escort them to their seats. Some theaters already have long lists of available ushers (and your name will go to the bottom of the list), but you still may be needed as a last-minute fill-in. To get on the list, simply make a quick phone call to your theater of choice. The best time to call is on weekdays from 10am to 4pm.

Go With A Group

If you tend to go to the theater with a group of friends or relatives anyway, invite a few extra people along and sign up for a group discount. Discounts of 10-20% are usually available for groups of 20 or more. You can order tickets by calling the box office directly or by calling (800) 833-3121.

Scalpers

This is probably the most risky way to obtain tickets, so if you choose this route, keep in mind that it is illegal; neither the police nor the theater will be sympathetic if you are duped by a scalper. It is also important to note that you will often be ripped off when purchasing tickets from a scalper. Be aware that some scalpers also peddle fake tickets, and then split before you are refused entry to the performance.

Two-for-Ones

Many universities are part of a theater promotion program that offers students coupons known as "twofers": Two tickets to big-budget productions for the price of one. Visit your school's Student Activities office for information about the program.

Shakespeare in the Park

Productions are generally good, though the star-studded casts can be underwhelming and overblown, but what better way to spend a balmy summer evening than sitting under the night sky in this intimate theater-in-the-round and watching some of the finest dramas of the Western world?

Tickets are free, but regular working folks will have to take a personal day to line up at sunrise and obtain seats to the more popular shows. Weekends can also be sacrificed to the cause. Remember that the bigger the stars, the longer the queue. Tickets are distributed the day of the performance beginning at 1pm at the Delacorte and Public Theaters. Show up an hour or two early for the less-hyped productions and many, many hours early for productions like *A Midsummer's Night Dream* in which Patrick Stewart (of *Star Trek: the Next Generation*) starred a few years ago. The tradeoff for the long wait in the hot sun is that you get to experience some of the best Shakespeare performances in the world, completely free.

June-September, Delacorte Theater, Central Park (at W. 79th St.), (212) 539-8500. B C to 81st St.

LINCOLN CENTER

As you sit in the sun, surrounded by stately marble buildings, listening to the carefree banter of street vendors and passersby, you watch an elderly man flitting around from person to person, talking intently. Socrates in the Athenian agora? Not quite. He's an opera patron at Lincoln Center's central plaza, asking people for their opinion of the latest Metropolitan Opera premiere. You could be forgiven for mistaking this for the ancient home of Western intellect and culture.

Lincoln Center is the internationally acclaimed center of New York's performing arts world. If you enjoy music, dance, theater, or film - whether as a serious connoisseur or casual audience member - you cannot visit or live in New York without going to a production at Lincoln Center.

The Lincoln Center complex is so vast that most New Yorkers are unaware of the full extent of its offerings. That's hardly cause for blame; with eleven organizations residing and performing in nine main buildings and several adjoining halls, Lincoln Center is the largest performing arts complex in the world. Also connected to the Lincoln Center plaza are the campuses of Fordham Law and Business schools.

In 1955, a committee conceived the Lincoln Center project in order to revitalize the Upper West Side. They hoped that the complex would signal that both New York and the American artists it showcased had come of age as major players on the international performing arts stage. The best-known resident companies are the Metropolitan Opera, New York City Ballet, New York City Opera, and the New York Philharmonic. Their seasons are heavily subscribed, they have flagship buildings, and they command huge budgets. Lower-profile but still prestigious are the Chamber Music Society, Lincoln Center Theater, the Lincoln Center Jazz Orchestra, and the Film Society of Lincoln Center, which hosts the New York Film Festival. Additionally, Julliard, the School of American Ballet, and the New York Public Library Performing Arts branch are all housed in the complex, and these institutions represent the educational goals of Lincoln Center's founders. The final component of the complex is actually a group. Lincoln Center Presents, a programming series that presents annual events such as the Lincoln Center Festival and Midsummer Night Swing each summer, the American Song-book, and the Live From Lincoln Center series, have offerings that will appeal to all with an open mind.

At the moment, plans are under way for a renovation of the whole complex. The extent is as yet unclear, but there will be major changes to both the architecture and in the affiliated companies. The New York Philharmonic, citing the inferior acoustics of its current home in the Avery Fischer Hall at Lincoln Center, plans to move back to its original home at Carnegie Hall in 2006 and discussions about their replacement are already underway.

Regardless of these changes, Lincoln Center will remain a preeminent destination for performing arts audiences of varied tastes and interests.

film

Flip through the phonebook and you'll easily see that New York has movie theaters aplenty, both mainstream and independent. What isn't as apparent is how moviegoers manage to find engaging, high-quality films, when the selection at any given time can seem so overwhelming. This is where film festivals serve their purpose. Since they consist of either contest entries from people dedicated to filmmaking or hand-picked slates of essential viewing, festivals are easy-to-digest assortments of interesting fare.

New York City plays host to many big-name events: the most star-studded are the New York Film Festival in the fall, the New Directors/New Films Festival hosted by MoMA in the winter; and the new TriBeCa Film Festival in the spring. These are rife with expensive galas and hyped feature films that will soon be distributed nationally, with a variety of smaller pictures vying for attention on the side. There isn't a specific theme or philosophy guiding the choices, other than the shared goal of bringing new, worthy films into the spotlight. The centerpiece films sell out quickly, so movie buffs should be aware of when ticket sales begin, or they will either be shut out or at the mercy of scalpers. Savvy festival attendees sign up for the official newsletters, which have updates about new selections as well as contests and discount offers.

Of course, not everyone agrees on what constitutes a "worthy" film. Alternative festivals that have sprung up in response to the bigger affairs compete to be the most cutting-edge and non-commercial. The largest and most organized of this category are the staunchly anti-mainstream t (*March, Anthology Film Archives, 32 Second Ave., $8.50*) and the Arlene's Grocery Picture Show (*April, Arlene Grocery, 95 Stanton St., $5*), hosted by the popular Lower East Side music venue, which touts itself as the place to take a film that no one else will show. Festival favorites are awarded canned food as prizes. The crowds at these are much rowdier and grungier than audiences at the mainstream festivals, and the after-parties feature more kegs than champagne. There is a heavy emphasis on shorter films with paltry budgets, and the events rarely sell out. Still, it's fun to see what's out there: from a wildly foul trailer park love story that casts homeless people as the stars, to a touching portrait of an aging bodybuilder and his family, to collages of bizarre 1970s children's shows — it's all been done.

Between these two poles of the festival spectrum are dozens of events with a narrower focus. The Human Rights Watch International Film Festival (*June, Walter Reade Theatre at Lincoln Center, $9.50*) shows hard-hitting documentaries that shed light on living conditions in places around the world such as Colombia or Pinochet's Chile. There are also festivals sponsored by other countries, including the Israel Film Festival (*June, Clearview Cinemas at 59th St. bet. Second and Third Aves., $10*), the New York Iranian Film Festival (*June, Anthology Film Archives, 32 Second Ave., $7*), and the French Short Film Festival (*June, Two Boots Pioneer Theater, 155 E. 3rd St.*), all of which aim to expose American audiences

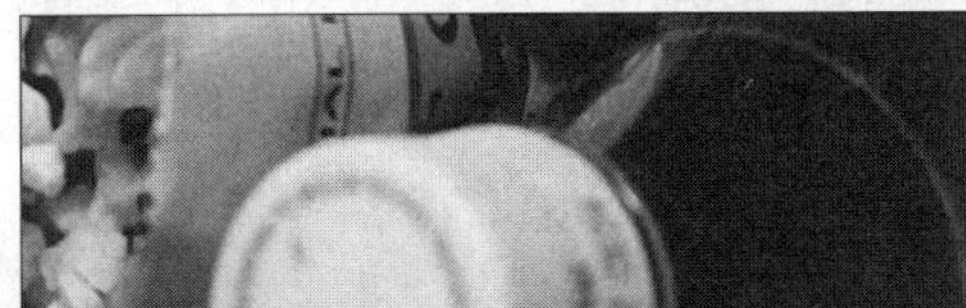

history of film in NYC

1900–1940

At the turn of the century, budding filmmakers shot footage of the city's vaudeville and theatrical shows and other sites. Even footage of buildings under construction was popular with audiences. After perpetual sunshine had drawn the studios to California, agents and executives still scanned New York stages for talent, realizing, in the late 1920s, that many of the stunningly beautiful silent-screen stars had squeaky speaking voices and needed to be replaced by Broadway actors.

In the early 1930s, stage diction was the rage and actors imitated the accent of the English upper-class. Straight-talking Humphrey Bogart, however, had his big break on Broadway in *The Petrified Forest*. Barbara Stanwyck and Joan Crawford both started out as Broadway "hoofers."

1940–1990

In the 1940s, neo-realism, film noir, and avant-garde filmmaking deepened the power and complexity of image on film. NYC, with its combination of grit and glamour, was the perfect setting for noir classics like Billy Wilder's *The Lost Weekend*. In the 1950s when Hollywood was focusing on teenyboppers and Technicolor, New York television and filmecs found increasing meaning in realism. *On The Waterfront* was a revolutionary combination of acting and on-location shooting whose stark simplicity stood out from the over-elaborate productions of the dying studio system.

Realism in Film Depiction

Realism merged with pageantry in the 1972 production of *The Godfather*, which marked the beginning of a decade of great American films, most of them reflections on the American Dream - New York style. Directors like Coppola, Pacino, and Scorcese united to present the world with defining images of New Yorkers - images which still form an international perception of this city and its people. With hindsight, it now seems clear that in 1986, when Spike Lee scraped together funding for his second feature-length film, *Do the Right Thing*, he was setting the stage for a surge of independent films which would revolutionize the business.

Independent Films

Independent films continue to provide a much needed alternative to blockbusters, while also allowing the art and business of filmmaking to be passed on to the next generation. On any given day in NYC, there are any number of films in production. Theatres like the Angelika, Lincoln Plaza, and The Film Forum offer the world's best cinema-and countless organizations like The Independent Feature Project are nurturing and networking with the filmmakers of tomorrow.

to films that present different cultural perspectives. These film festivals are a great opportunity to catch filmmakers on the rise, before they have been corrupted by Hollywood. The Asian American International Film Festival (*June, Asia Society, 725 Park Ave., $9.50*), the New York International Latino Festival (*July*), and the New York Gay and Lesbian Film Festival (*June, Tischman Auditorium, New School, 66 W. 12th St.*) bring together films from filmmakers who share similar backgrounds and concerns. Though all have some predictable offerings with stale messages, they also have films that startle and impress with the twists they put on stereotypes and ideas often taken for granted. Most of the festivals mentioned show primarily new work, but there are also numerous series devoted to classic cinema, notably at the American Museum of the Moving Image and in the Golden Age of Cinema Festival (*May through July at NYU's Cantor Film Center, 36 E. 8th St.*), as well as many one-time events celebrating a filmmaker, era, or concept, curated by the local independent cinemas.

Summer, in particular, is a great time to catch area festivals. Theaters also take their projectors outside for evening showings so audiences can cuddle up with the sounds of crickets and cars on the highway augmenting the soundtrack. Some of the best of these festivals are the Bryant Park Film Festival (*dusk, Mondays in Jun. through Aug., Sixth Ave. at 42nd St.*), the Rooftop Films Series in Brooklyn (*Fridays in Jun. through Sept., Peter's Car Corp., 265 McKibbin St.*), and Riverflicks (*dusk, W-F in July/August, Hudson River Park, Pier 54 & Pier 25*).

listings

[Theater Listings]

A

Actor's Playhouse
Gay-and-lesbian-themed shows command the stage at this off-Broadway space. Though the seats may be dingy and worn and the floor may retain a stickiness from soda spilled long ago, it is still the best queer theater in town.
100 Seventh Ave. (bet. Christopher and Bleecker Sts.), (212) 463-0060. MC, V, AmEx, D. 1 to Christopher St.

The Afrikan Poetry Theater, Inc.
Fledgling poets, playwrights, directors, and actors perform here regularly. For those in need of more structured training, various dance, drum, and Shakespeare classes are available.
Jamaica, Queens. 176-03 Jamaica Ave. (at 176th St.), (718) 523-3312. Cash only. F to Jamaica-179th St.

Apollo Theater
Featuring such performers as Josephine Baker, the Supremes, and Bill Cosby since it started integrating black audiences and performers in 1935, this multi-use theater is in full swing thanks to a revival effort in the '80s. The televised "Amateur Night" rages on Wednesdays, and comedians and children's flicks also find space here. The stage even hosted James Brown's post-prison comeback concert.
253 W. 125th St. (bet. Adam Clayton Powell Jr. and Frederick Douglass Blvds.), (212) 531-5300, www.apollotheater.com. A B C D to 125th St.

Astor Place Theater
The theater has currently housed the famous Blue Man Group for many years, allowing people to come and see three bald and blue figures perform music and art before their eyes. Although the performance is engaging, the theater is also a good reason to visit this venue. Originally built in 1831 in a series of connected buildings, it was designated as a historic landmark in 1963. The building is designed in a Greek style that incorporates marble columns and once served as a residence to the Vanderbilt's.
434 Lafayette St., (212) 254-4370. 6 to Astor Pl., N R to 8th St.-NYU.

Atlantic Theater
Theater buffs have long insisted that the stage is hallowed ground, but in this case the metaphor rings true. The Atlantic Theater Company, founded in 1985 by David Mamet and William H. Macy, moved into this renovated church in 1991. For a break from tacky musicals, the company proclaims the Atlantic as a place "where great stories are told."
336 W. 20th St. (bet Eighth and Ninth Aves.), (212) 691-5919. C E to 23rd St.

B

Blue Man Group
See Astor Place Theater

Bouwerie Lane Theater
Founded in 1973 by Eve Adamson, this European-style, one-stage theater is one of the few dedicated to producing classics.
330 Bowery (at Bond St.), (212) 677-0060. 6 to Bleecker St., B D F V to Lafayette St.

Bowery Poetry Club
This is the latest project of Bob Holman, poetry popularizer extraordinaire. He helped engineer the rejuvenation of the Nuyorican Poets Café in the late '80s, and he also guides the People's Poetry Gathering and teaches at Bard College in upstate New York. Here, in a cozy cafe and bar with an art gallery on one side and a stage in the back, poets and performers of all kinds come for readings, plays, and concerts. The small seating area for the stage is somewhat uncomfortable (with hard seats), but if you go on a good night, you'll forget all about where you're sitting as you listen. Acts range from nervous college students reading overly intellectual rambles to acts by Andy Warhol's buddy Taylor Mead, with interesting off-off-Broadway shows and world music in between. Be sure to check out the poetry chapbooks and CDs for sale; they give a small taste of the ever-growing scene this venue fosters.
308 Bowery (at 1st St.), (212) 614-0505, www.bowerypoetry.com. Cash only. F V to Second Ave.

C

Castillo Theater
For the last decade, this space has served as a "cultural laboratory" for Artistic Director Fred Newman to practice Developmental Theater, a genre which is predicated on a number of post-modern philosophies, but boils down to the idea of psychotherapy for performer and audience members alike. The focus is on Black, Latino, gay, and international avant-garde theater. This means you can expect anything.
543 W. 42nd St. (bet. Tenth and Eleventh Aves.), (212) 941-5800 (corporate office). www.castillo.org. MC, V, AmEx, D. A C E to 42nd St-Port Authority.

Centerfold Coffeehouse at Church of St. Paul and St. Andrew
Poetry readings are free but hit or miss, so prepare to indulge some neophyte

bards. Evening jams with folk and jazz bands provide dependable, cheap weekend entertainment.
263 W. 86th St. (bet. Broadway and West End Ave.), (212) 362-3328. 1 to 86th St.

Center for the Arts
(College of Staten Island)
Many island residents ignore CSI's performance space, favoring Manhattan for theatrical pursuits. This is a true shame considering the 450 seat theater, 9,000 seat concert hall, and art gallery housed within the center. Past well-known acts such as Shawn Colvin and Tito Puente have graced the concert stage.
Staten Island. 2800 Victory Blvd., (718) 982-2787. R W to Whitehall St., 4 5 to Bowling Green, 1 to South Ferry, take Staten Island Ferry, then take S61, S62.

Chashama
Times Square and 42nd St. are all about bright marquees and monster budgets, right? Nope, as this pair of theaters has proven itself to those who leave Broadway hits wanting something more. Increasingly, small independent drama companies – people who actually see their work as art – are setting up shop alongside the big-time ventures and offering fare that is still far from the typical musical or staid play. In 1995, a group of actors took over this space and turned it into a collective for developing artists and their works-in-progress. Visual artists get to use the storefront windows for zany installations, and theater companies on shoestring budgets can use the stages to perform for larger audiences than they would get in one of the East Village or Chelsea hole-in-the-wall theaters. Potential viewers who are on a shoestring budget are in luck too because the shows are very inexpensive (and oftentimes free).
201 and 217 E. 42nd St. (bet. Second and Third Aves.), (212) 391-8151, www. chashama.org. www.TheaterMania.com and www.SmartTix.com. S 4 5 6 7 to 42nd St.-Grand Central.

Cherry Lane Theater
Founded in the '20s by a literary circle headed by the poet Edna St. Vincent Millay, Cherry Lane's productions are lead by the best of the century's avant-garde and adventurous new pieces.
38 Commerce St. (bet. Seventh Ave. and Barrow St.), (212) 989-2020. A B C D E F V to W. 4th St. 1 to Christopher St.

Colden Center For the Performing Arts at Queens College
Classical, pop, jazz, theater, opera, and children's events weekly. Call the box office for more precise information.
Queens. 65-30 Kissena Blvd., (718) 544-2996. 7 to Main St.

Collective Unconscious
Every possible configuration of campy art and anti-art event takes place at this downtown performance space. The hip, tongue-in-cheek crowd doesn't take anything very seriously, especially not the art world. Look oiut though, they're in the process of raising money to move into new digs.
145 Ludlow St. (bet. Stanton and Rivington Sts.), (212) 254-5277. Call for schedule and show times. Cash only. F J M Z to Delancey St.

F

The Flea Theater
The home of the Bat Theater Company, you'll be pleased to find both experimental productions of classics and recent, more avant-garde plays. Plays usually run for a week or two, so catch them while you can. You'll also find poetry readings at the theater.
41 White St. (bet. Broadway and Church St.), (212) 226-2407. 1 to Franklin St., J M N R W Z 6 to Canal St..

45 Bleecker
Here, as with many venues, the mainstream is upstairs, and the offbeat, untested performances are underground. The relationship between the two stages within the 45 Bleecker theater is more self-conscious than in many places but has fostered a very fruitful relationship. In the primary space are relatively long-running off-Broadway shows written and produced by people with a good track record which usually garner good publicity. The resident company, the Culture Project, focuses on adaptations and plays examining important individuals' lives. The lower level black box is a bit claustrophobic and plagued with poles that obstruct some views of the stage. There, new playwrights and unknown companies get a chance at spillover from above, when people can't get tickets to the other show or are merely curious about the other shows going on downstairs. The main stage benefits by fostering creativity in-house, and audiences in turn get two distinct experiences, if not for the price of one, at least in one place.
45 Bleecker St., (Lafayette St.), 212) 253-7017, www.45bleecker.com. 6 to Bleecker St.

G

Galapagos Art Space
With real estate becoming increasingly expensive in this city, even in Williamsburg and the DUMBO area, it makes sense for starving artists of all kinds, to get together to buy a performance space. That's what has happened here, in this almost impossible to categorize venue of many slashes: bar/theater/cinema/gallery/concert venue. Only its cavernous size reveals that it was once a mayonnaise factory, and it now creates emulsions of a different kind, as resident artists collaborate on their various projects. The directors take no grants, so the whole experiment relies on putting together high-quality, innovative programming that will draw and impress audiences. Numerous festivals run here, creative non-profits of all kinds rent it out for their own shows, and DJs are glued to their turntables until well into the wee hours, keeping people in the mood for

cutting-edge art.
Williamsburg, Brooklyn. 70 N. 6th St., (718) 384-4586, www.galapagosartspace.com. Cash only. L to Bedford Ave.

H

HERE Arts Center

Stop by HERE for a daily dose of multi-disciplinary fine art and performance arts from a wide variety of young and up-and-coming artists. With multiple galleries, subsidized stages and event spaces, this is three floors of fun with a community unlike any other; there's something for everyone.
145 Sixth Ave. (bet. Spring and Broome Sts.), (212) 647-0202, www.here.org. C E to Spring St.

I

The Irish Repertory Theatre

Intimate performance space for Irish and Irish-American plays.
132 W. 22nd St. (bet. Sixth and Seventh Aves.), (212) 727-2737. F V 1 to 23rd St.

J

Joyce Theater

The unlikely successor to a former porno palace, this hotbed of talent inherited a large stage and virtually clear sightlines, which create an ideal setting for performances by top touring companies from around the world. Bookings range from weekly engagements to a month-in-residence with the Feld Ballet and Margie Gillis. The Joyce often subsidizes in-theater production costs. "All Together Different" is a program that promotes the seven most promising up-and-coming companies.
175 Eighth Ave. (at 19th St.), (212) 242-0800. Tickets: $18-$27. 1 to 18th St.

Joyce SoHo

All professional and aspiring dancers are familiar with this branch of the Joyce, the venue of choice for seeing all genres in a setting that's not stiflingly formal. Performances are on Friday and Saturday nights with tickets available 30 minutes before curtain.
155 Mercer St. (bet. Houston and Prince Sts.), (212) 334-7479. Cash only. N R to Prince St., B D F V to Broadway-Lafayette St.

K

The Kraine Theater

One of New York's most eclectic venues, the Horse Trade Theater group manages this "best of the blackbox." With titles such as *Vampire Geishas* of Brooklyn, the theater may be off-Broadway but the productions are seldom poor. Upstairs, the Horse Trade's Red Room houses late night performances.
85 E. 4th St. (at Second Ave.), (212) 460-0982. B D F V to Broadway-Lafayette St., 6 to Bleecker St.

L

La MaMa Experimental Theater

Four small theaters offer new and experimental dance and theater, as well as off-beat performances. The avant-garde nature of the place means shows are hit or miss, but cheap tickets make it worthwhile to test the odds.
74A E. 4th St. (bet. Second Ave. and Bowery St.), (212) 475-7710, www.lamama.org. F V to Second Ave., 6 to Astor Pl.

Lucille Lortel Theater

Cramped between the music-pumping, glitter merchandise shops of Christopher St. is this supremely immodest performance space, which claims to be New York's foremost off-Broadway theater. A recent success for the theater has been the acclaimed *Mrs. Klein*, chronicling the life and times of famed psychoanalyst Melanie Klein.
121 Christopher St. (bet. Hudson and Bleecker Sts.), (212) 924-2817, www.lortel.org. 1 to Christopher St.

M

Manhattan Theater Club

Terence McNally, A.R. Gurney, and Richard Greenberg are just a few of the playwrights whose work has been featured at MTC, one of the oldest subscription-based theater companies in the city. The company presents a broad range of work, mixing audience-pleasers and more challenging pieces on its two stages. MTC received a great deal of media attention in 1998 as the site of McNally's controversial Corpus Christi.
131 W. 55th St. (bet. Sixth and Seventh Aves.), (212) 399-3000, www.mtcnyc.org. N R W to 57th St.-Seventh Ave.

Mint Theater

Broadway and off-Broadway are both awash in revivals these days, as if there weren't thousands of starving playwrights struggling to get their work produced. Surprising considering that many audiences stumble out of a revival

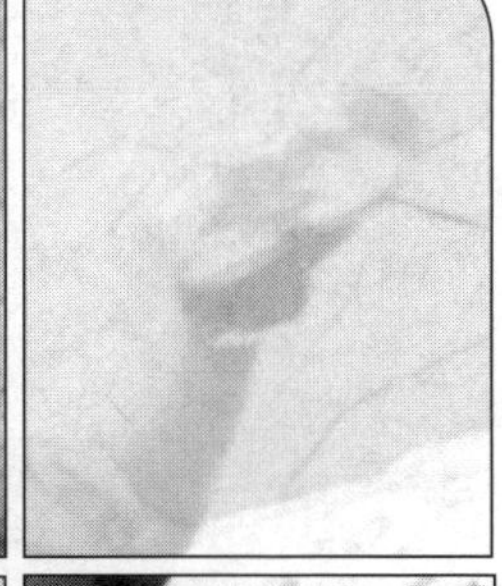

wondering just why it was revived. Not so with this theater, which does revivals of signature works by obscure writers, as well as obscure works by famous writers. The small theater feels intimate rather than cramped because it invites the audience to have an intense experience as part of the well-crafted action. Despite its convenient location, shows that go up here feel different, like throwbacks to a time when the quality work on stage was contemporary rather than recycled.
311 W. 43rd St., Fifth Floor (bet. Eighth and Ninth Aves.), (212) 315-9434, www.mint theater.org. MC, V, AmEx. A C E N R S W 1 2 3 7 *to 42nd St.-Port Authority.*

N

National Black Theatre

Family values are the focus at this company, founded in 1968 by Broadway star Barbara Ann Teer. Performances take place year-round, and acting workshops are also available.
2031-33 Fifth Ave. (bet. 125th and 126th Sts.), (212) 722-3800. 2 3 *to 125th St.*

New York Theater Workshop

This downtown theater staple caters to a hip crowd and often presents work from the farther corners of the mainstream. It's the original home of Broadway sensation *Rent*, as well as the rock musical *Bright Lights, Big City*, and *The Most Fabulous Story Ever Told*. The annual "Just Add Water" festival presents work in development for future seasons. Rush tickets are available for most performances.
79 E. 4th St. (at Second Ave.), (212) 780-9037, www.nytw.org. D. F V *to Second Ave.*

Nuyorican Poet's Cafe

Founded in 1975 as a performance space for the Spanish-speaking voices of the New York literary scene, it remains one of the most significant outlets for outsider art. In addition to poetry slams and other readings, which helped create the resurgence of poetry as an aspect of cafe culture throughout the country, a night's program often includes theater, a video presentation, or a jam session. The Nuyorican Poets have garnered enough respect for their work to sustain several published anthologies and to tour the globe performing. Don't pass up the chance to see them at home.
236 E. 3rd St. (bet. Aves. B and C), (212) 505-8183, www.nuyorican.org. Cash only. F V *to Second Ave.*

O

The Ohio Theater

Anything goes here, since the stage is rented out to various freelance performance groups.
66 Wooster St. (bet. Spring and Broome Sts.), (212) 966-4844. N R *to Prince St.,* C E 6 *to Spring St.*

P

Performance Space 122

This small performance space in a converted church serves as a showplace for cutting-edge dance, theater, and performance art. Artists range from obscure-but-talented newcomers to established members of the downtown scene. Runs tend to be short and very popular, so try to get tickets in advance.
150 First Ave. (at 9th St.), (212) 228-2328, www.ps122.org. F V *to Second Ave.*

Pearl Theater

This classic repertoire/resident company sticks to a strict pre-WWI itinerary, with conventional productions of Shakespeare, Moliere, Sophocles and others of their ilk, as well as revived relics. Shows generally run seven weeks. Heterogenous crowd with plenty of local traffic.
80 St. Mark's Pl. (bet. First and Second Aves.), (212) 598-9802, www.pearlthe atre.org. N R *to 8th St.,* 6 *to Astor Pl.*

Playwrights Horizons

Long the anchor of Theater Row, this theater company has been premiering innovative and new American plays for the past 25 years. The work of Christopher Durang and Wendy Wasserstein was first presented here, as was Stephen Sondheim and James Lapine's Pulitzer Prize-winning musical *Sunday In The Park With George*. The upstairs Studio Theater presents work by up-and-coming writers.
416 W. 42nd St. (bet. Ninth and Tenth Aves.), (212) 279-4200, www.playwrightshori zons.org. A C E N R S W 1 2 3 7 *to 42nd St.*

R

Rattlestick Theater

A vehicle for its artistic director, this tiny production company doesn't shy away from risks, an attribute that can cut both ways.
224 Waverly Pl. (bet. Perry and 11th Sts.), (212) 627-2556, www.rattlestick.org. A C E L 1 2 3 *to 14th St.*

Repertorio Español

Though just a drop in the sea of New York's overwhelmingly English-language performing arts centers, this venerable institution is a dignified and hard working force to be reckoned with. Since 1968, these dancers, actors, and directors have aimed to broaden discourse in the performing arts with productions in their cozy yet elegant theater. The ensemble stages classic Spanish-language drama as well as adaptations of novels by the likes of Gabriel Garcia Marquez and Mario Vargas Llosa. Not only that, the company actively fosters young playwrights and commissions new works, in addition to hosting top-notch Spanish dance productions. Even non-Spanish speakers can enjoy the offerings: headsets that provide simultaneous translation are available.
Gramercy Arts Theater, 138 E. 27th St., (212) 889-2850, www.repertorio.org. 6 *to 23rd St.*

S

Second Stage

Dedicated to reinventing

plays that "didn't get a fair shot the first time around," this unassuming theater of second chances has produced the works of Stephen Sondheim, Edward Albee, August Wilson, Athol Fugard, Mary Zimmerman, and Wallace Shawn, to name a few.
307 W. 43rd St. (at Eighth Ave.), (212) 246-4422, www.secondstagetheater.com. A C E N R S W 1 2 3 7 *to 42nd St.-Times Sq.*

Signature Theatre Company
Under the leadership of visionary artistic director James Houghton, the Signature has carved out a unique mission: highlighting the work of one major playwright each season. Past seasons have included retrospectives and world premieres from Arthur Miller, John Guare, Adrienne Kennedy, and Sam Shepard.
555 W. 42nd St. (bet. Tenth and Eleventh Aves.), (212) 244-7529. A C E N R S W 1 2 3 7 *to 42nd St.-Times Sq.*

SoHo Repertory
Home for anything new and compelling, from freshly adapted literary works to personal dramas. Well known for excellent casting choices, the theater generally offers several overlapping runs from which to choose.
46 Walker St., (bet. Broadway and Church Sts.), (212) 334-0962.

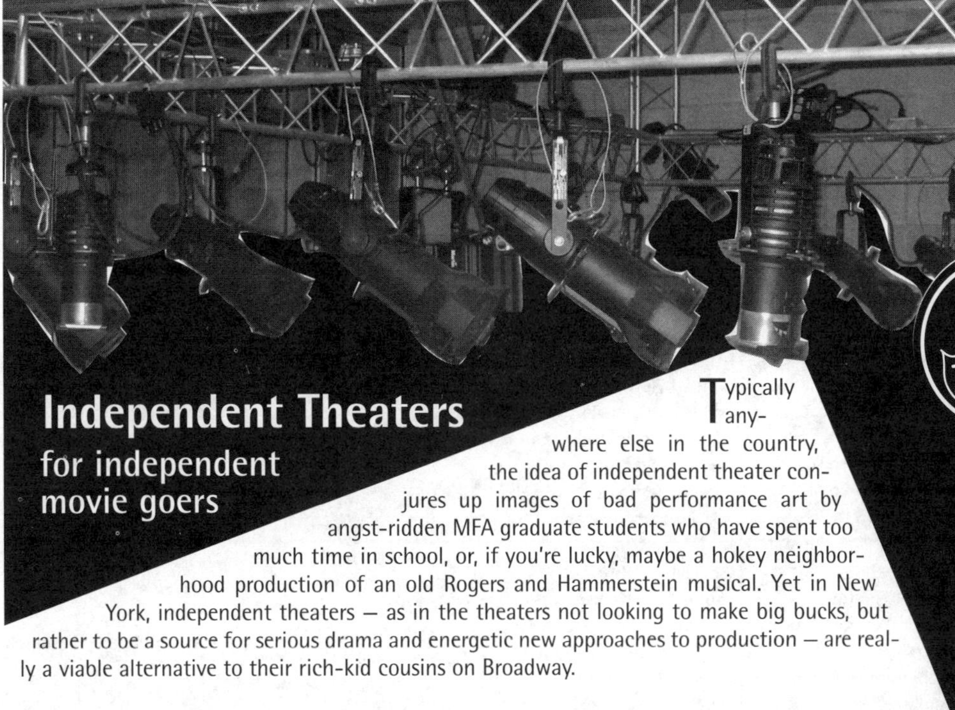

Independent Theaters
for independent movie goers

Typically anywhere else in the country, the idea of independent theater conjures up images of bad performance art by angst-ridden MFA graduate students who have spent too much time in school, or, if you're lucky, maybe a hokey neighborhood production of an old Rogers and Hammerstein musical. Yet in New York, independent theaters — as in the theaters not looking to make big bucks, but rather to be a source for serious drama and energetic new approaches to production — are really a viable alternative to their rich-kid cousins on Broadway.

Indeed, a lot of famous actors, directors, and writers got their starts on independent stages, and these theater companies continue to be hotbeds of raw talent unlikely to transition to the plasticy pasteboard chime of Times Square. To say that these shows are more intellectually stimulating isn't always accurate, but they are certainly more sophisticated in what is put on stage for precariously cobbled-together budgets: it's easy to wow when you have blockbuster grade millions being spent, but what's more amazing is awing an audience on a shoestring budget. And the results can be fantastic, such as La MaMa's recent staging of seven different Greek plays each with an avant-garde performance that was a blazing, acrobatic deviation from anything seen before, or the contemplative, opera-inflected sexual-aesthetic musings of Valhalla at New York Theater Workshop, and the even smaller, dramatic-comedic fare at HERE Arts Center.

These shows don't have to be perilously Off-Off-Off Broadway (it does exist) for you to be getting the genuine article. In fact, the whole concept behind independent theater is that it is accessible, just in, you know, a better, smarter, more fun, and cheaper way than those sometimes disappointing Broadway spectacles. So why on earth wouldn't you seek these shows out? Isn't this "culture" the whole reason people claim they move to New York anyway?

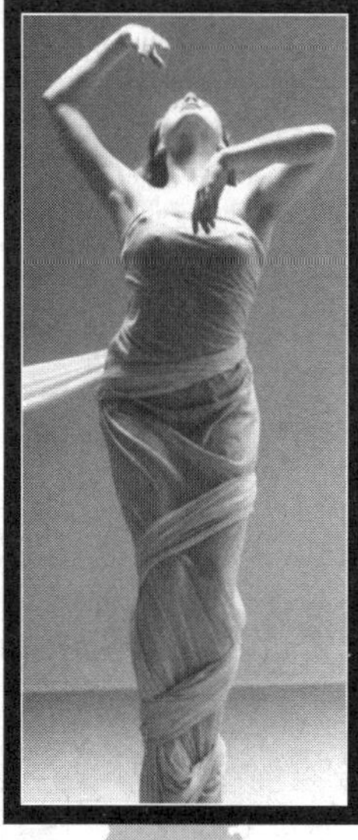

www.sohorep.org. Cash Only. J M Z R W *to Canal St.,* 1 *to Franklin St.*

St. Clement's Church

A working theater for 35 years, this charming little church has hosted some of the best off-Broadway theater in the city. Episcopal services are still held here Sundays and Wednesday nights. Conveniently located on Restaurant Row and around the corner from the greatest concentration of ethnic restaurants in the city.
423 W. 46th St. (bet. Ninth and Tenth Aves.), (212) 246-7277, www.stclementscnyc.org. A C E N R S W 1 2 3 7 *to 42nd St.*

St. Mark's Church in the Bowery

A quiet and beautiful cultural oasis in the bustling East Village, this century-old church is home to three excellent arts "projects," including Danspace, Poetry Project, and the Ontological Theater. Most notable is the Poetry Project, one of the only programs of its kind, which offers special literary events and workshops for budding poets, as well as a forum for both well-known and up and coming poets to read their work.
131 E. 10th St. (at Second Ave.), (212) 674-8194. Cash only. 6 *to Astor Pl.*

T

Thalia Spanish Theater

One of New York's hottest stages for established and new Hispanic playwrights, actors, and directors. Three productions yearly, as well as three ongoing showcases in music, dance, and special events.
Sunnyside, Queens. 41-17 Greenpoint Ave. (bet. 41st and 42nd Sts.), (718) 729-3880. Cash only. 7 *to 40th St.-Lowery St.*

Theatre for a New Audience

Some of the most innovative, provocative, thoughtful, and coherent productions of Shakespeare and other classics.
154 Christopher St., Suite 3D, (bet. Greenwich and Washington Sts.), venue changes regularly, (212) 229-2819, www.tfana.org. 1 *to Christopher St.*

Theater for the New City

Not to be confused with Theatre for a New Audience, this scrappy East Village outpost of bizarre performance art and radical philosophy holds its own across the street from P.S. 122. In the lobby are ancient, overstuffed sofas where grungy, dazed-looking Bohemians lounge, reading from pamphlets and manifestoes among the books for sale. Flyers and postcards advertising upcoming performances and goings-on elsewhere paper every possible space. Performances in the boxy, high-ceilinged theater range from puppet shows to wildly experimental acts to acrobatics. This is definitely not the place you want to go for a nice, calm evening of theater, especially if you've never been to an off-off Broadway show. But if you enjoy a message with your entertainment, or can handle the extra-wacky and low-budget, drop by. After this, nothing will seem strange.
155 First Ave. (at 10th St.), (212) 254-1109, www.theaterforthenewcity.net. Cash only. F V *to Second Ave.*

TriBeCa Performing Arts Center

Inconspicuously housed in the main building of the Boro of Manhattan Community College, this large venue is easy to miss. That would be a shame since the programming is excellent, offering multicultural music, dance, theater from around the world, and urban youth-themed performances consistent with the diverse student population. The college connection means cheap student-rate tickets.
199 Chambers St. (at Greenwich St.), (212) 346-8510, www.tribecapac.org. 1 2 3 *to Chambers St.*

U

Upright Citizens Brigade Theatre

Because they not only teach classes but also offer nightly improv and sketch comedy with affordable tickets, there's always something happening at this relatively small club, associated with the similarly titled, though now defunct, TV series.
307 W. 26th St. (bet. Eighth and Ninth Aves.), (212) 366-9176. www.uprightcitizens.org. Cash only. C E *to 23rd St.*

V

Variety Arts Theater

The place to go for campy theater and a distorted dose of pop culture. Recent productions have included a new work by writer/drag queen Charles Busch and a musical based on the life of Patsy Cline. Proof that theater doesn't have to be dull, stodgy, or squeaky-clean.
110 Third Ave. (bet. 13th and 14th Sts.), ticket line (212) 239-6200. L N R W 4 5 6 *to 14th St.-Union Sq.*

W

Williamsburg Art Nexus

This gallery, theater, and rehearsal space in-one is located in Brooklyn's trendiest neighborhood. WAX cultivates a supportive environment for con-

temporary artists in all media and strives to spread art love. WAX features a one-room gallery space and a white-walled black-box theater available for rent to local artists and performers.
Brooklyn. 205 N. 7th St. (bet. Driggs and Roobling Sts.), (718) 599-7997, www.wax205.com. L *to Bedford Ave.*

[Music Halls]

A

Amato Opera House
Head downtown to see the divas of tomorrow paying their dues in an intimate setting. An alternative for opera lovers who lack the funds for nosebleed seats at the Met. One of Amato's goals is to foster opera appreciation by making it more accessible, so many performances are English translations of Italian operas.
319 Bowery St. (bet. E. 2nd and Bleecker Sts.), (212) 228-8200. Cash only. B D F V *to Lafayette St.*

Avery Fisher Hall
Over a hundred virtuosos led by Kurt Masur play Western classics, with an emphasis on European standards and American innovations. Home to the New York Philharmonic.
10 Lincoln Center Plaza (bet. 64th and 65th Sts.), (212) 875-5030, www.lincolncenter.org. 1 *to 66th St.*

B

Barge Music
Excellent chamber music on the moonlit water. Bring a date and get all mushy on this converted coffee barge.
Brooklyn. Fulton Ferry Landing, (718) 624-4924. Cash only. A C *to High St.*

Black Spectrum Theater Company, Inc.
Offering three to five large-scale productions a year, with directors favoring socially conscious works by both emerging and established writers, makes this theater a must-see. Kids and teens get in on the action with their own productions.
Jamaica, Queens.119 Merrick Blvd. (at 177th St. and Baisley Blvd.), (718) 723-1800, www.blackspectrum.com. Cash only. E *to Parsons Blvd.*

Boy's Choir of Harlem
Founded in 1968, this legendary choir has evolved from a small church group to an internationally-acclaimed phenomenon, singing classical, contemporary, spiritual, and jazz music at their year-round world-wide performances.
2005 Madison Ave. (bet. 127th and 128th Sts.), (212) 289-1815. Cash only. 4 5 6 *to 125th St.*

The Brooklyn Academy of Music
Although the Brooklyn Philharmonic has distinguished itself with its range and repertoire, running the gamut from European classics to selections from African-American traditions, its pet projects are clearly those rooted in the avant garde, which are best realized in BAM's provocative yearly New Wave festival that pushes the boundaries of classical music.
Brooklyn. 30 Lafayette Ave. (at Hanson Pl.), (718) 636-4111 (tickets), (718) 636-4100, www.bam.org (Brooklyn Philharmonic). MC, V. B 2 3 4 5 *to Atlantic Ave.*

C

Carnegie Hall
A century has passed since Tchaikovsky conducted at its inauguration, but this stage keeps abreast of musical trends in their many variations. The Beastie Boys and the Tibetan Freedom Fighters have appeared on the same stage as classical giants like Emanuel Ax. Jazz performers are also frequent guests.
881 Seventh Ave. (at 57th St.), (212) 903-9600, www.carnegiehall.org. A B C D 1 *to 59th St.-Columbus Circle.*

E

Elmo Lounge
Downstairs from the famous Elmo restaurant is one of the newest live music venues in New York. Decorated like the legendary nightclub, The El Morocco, this place provides listeners with a good time. With palm motif wallpaper and mirror tiles on the walls, one gets transported to Miami in the 1950s - but the music is good and forces everyone to groove to the beat.
156 Seventh Ave., (212) 337-8000, C E *to 23rd St.*

J

The Julliard School
Few would deny that Julliard students are the best of the best, the cream of the musical crop, so to speak. Prodigies from all over the world converge at Lincoln Center to study with illustrious faculty and soak up the influence of the inspiring professional talent on display there. Practice in performance is almost as important as practice in technique, and the school's location provides students with the perfect opportunity to get plenty of experience. Naturally, the performers need an audience, and New Yorkers are an appropriately attentive, discriminating bunch. Modern dance and music of every kind are on the bill most nights, and recitals are often free. Who knows? Maybe the striking virtuoso cellist you watch now is the Yo-Yo Ma of the future.
60 Lincoln Center Plaza, (at Broadway and 66th St.), (212) 799-5000, www.juilliard.edu. 1 *to 66th St.-Lincoln Center.*

M

Manhattan School of Music
Prodigies at one of the country's most prestigious conservatories perform, usually for free. Call ahead for scheduled performances and times.
120 Claremont Ave. (at 122nd St.), (212) 749-2802, www.msmnyc.org. Cash Only. 1 *to 125th St.*

Merkin Concert Hall
This modest performance space and new music venue is home to the

Festival Chamber Music Society, which strives to provide quality music in a "warm, beginner-friendly environment." Each performance begins with a short lecture about the piece and ends with a champagne reception where audience members can meet the artists.
129 W. 67th St. (bet. Broadway and Amsterdam Ave.), (212) 501-3330. Cash only. 1 to 66th St.-Lincoln Center.

Metropolitan Opera
When the Carnegies were the nouveau riche, Old Money's monopoly on the city's theater boxes frustrated the family so much that they went and built their own opera house. Though the original Met was further downtown, its current location retains a historic stodginess. A safely classical though consistently outstanding repertory.
Lincoln Center (at Broadway and 66th St.), (212) 362-6000. 1 to 66th St.-Lincoln Center.

Miller Theater
With some of the lowest ticket prices in the city and steep discounts for students, this theater generally draws a young and casual audience from the surrounding neighborhood. The programming is centered on cutting-edge classical music and the heart of the offerings is the Composer Portrait Series, which showcases the works of a single composer. The theater also runs a series of 4pm-6pm early music concerts in sacred spaces on or around the Columbia University campus. See listing for St. Paul's Chapel.
Broadway and 116th St. (at Columbia University), (212) 854-7799, www.millertheater. com. 1 to 116th St.-Columbia University.

Music Before 1800
In Morningside Heights' Corpus Christ Church on certain Sunday afternoons, it's easy to slip back a few centuries. In the church's austere nave, the group Music Before 1800 resurrects songs that used to echo in the churches and courts of Medieval and Renaissance Europe. They play authentic instruments and host visiting groups that specialize in music from specific eras or regions. Often the audience is mostly filled with the senior citizens and students from nearby institutions such as Columbia University and the Manhattan School of Music. Dedicated connoisseurs of Medieval and Renaissance music can buy season passes and get a much-needed vacation from the modern world, courtesy of these skillful troubadours.
529 W. 121st St. (bet. Broadway and Amsterdam Ave.), (212) 666-0675, www.mb1800.org. 1 to 125th St.

N

New York City Opera
Renews and redefines the soul of opera through stellar, innovative performances of both forgotten and familiar classics. NYCO is world-renowned for its risk-taking World Premiere Festival, which introduces opera-goers to works they couldn't see anywhere else. The New York State Theater is smaller and less overwhelming than the Met's theater, and the ticket prices are more affordable.
New York State Theater at Lincoln Center (at Broadway and 66th St.), (212) 870-3570. 1 to 66th St.-Lincoln Center.

New York Philharmonic
Over a hundred virtuosos led by Kurt Masur play Western classics, with an emphasis on European standards and American innovations.
See Avery Fisher Hall.

S

St. Paul's Chapel
The Music at St. Paul's Program at St. Paul's chapel, located on the Columbia University cam-

pus, is co-sponsored by Miller Theater (see listing) and showcases sacred music outside the context of worship service, as well as secular chamber music appropriate to the sacred setting. The concerts, which include chamber works, organ pieces, and non-instrumental vocal recitals generally take place on Tuesday evenings and are free and open to the public.
1116 Amsterdam Ave. (at 117th St., Columbia University), (212) 854-6625. Cash only. 1 to 116th St.-Columbia University.

[Dance Theaters]

A

Alvin Ailey American Dance Theater
"The dance came from the people. It should be given back to the people," this theater's namesake once said. Alvin Ailey developed the repertoire here with unique pieces often set to music by jazz greats such as Duke Ellington and Wynton Marsalis.
211 W. 61st St. (bet. Tenth and Eleventh Aves.), (212) 246-3027. www.alvinailey.org. A B C D 1 to 57th St.-Seventh Ave.

American Ballet Theater
This dance giant, once led by legends like Lucia Chase, Oliver Smith, and Mikhail Baryshnikov, and now headed by former Principal Dancer Kevin McKenzie, continues to stage staggering performances at its home at Lincoln Center. Classical ballet had its first renaissance here, and new works have been commissioned specifically for the ballet by key composers such as Balanchine, Antony Tudor, and Agnes de Mille. Call for schedules.
Metropolitan Opera House, Lincoln Center (at Columbus Ave. and 64th St.), (212) 362-6000. 1 to 66th St.-Lincoln Center.

B

Ballet Academy East
Itching to test those dancing shoes? Drop in here and for $12 you can sample one of the jazz, ballet, or tap classes.
1651 Third Ave. (bet. 92nd and 93rd Sts.), (212) 410-9140, www.balletacademyeast.com. 6 to 96th St.

D

Dance Theater of Harlem
This world-renowned, neo-classical company, founded in 1969 as a school and now one of the country's most competitive dabbles in a bit of everything: jazz, tap dance, modern ballet, and sub-genres. Students of all ages and all levels perform in a monthly open house, usually with accompanying performances by guest artists.
466 W. 152nd St. (bet. St. Nicholas and Amsterdam Aves.), (212) 690-2800, www.dancetheaterofharlem.com. B C D to 155th St.

Dance Theater Workshop
There must be some kind of modern dance magic in the Chelsea air. Just down the street from the venerable Joyce Theater, this space, also dedicated to modern dance, opened in the fall of 2002, but has already garnered a great deal of praise. Its impressively modern Artist Resource Media Lab and spacious Bessie Schoenberg Theater allow dancers and choreographers to make the most of new technology. Plus, its rehearsal studios face the street with walls made of glass, so passersby can watch classes for free. Some of the companies that perform are B-list, and not quite up to the Joyce, but as a newcomer it has the freedom to experiment and does so with aplomb, helping New York keep its place on the cutting edge of the dance world.
219 W. 19th St. (bet. Seventh and Eighth Aves.), (212) 924-0077, www.dtw.org. MC, V, AmEx. 1 to 18th St.

N

New York City Ballet
Co-founded in part by George Balanchine after WWII, this top-notch company produces a particularly breathtaking Nutcracker with champagne galore and lots of three-year-olds made up like dolls. In residence at the $30 million New York State Theater, the ballet has the largest repertory of any company.
New York State Theater at 20 Lincoln Center Plaza (63rd St. and Columbus Ave.), (212) 870-5570, www.nycballet.com. 1 to 66th St.-Lincoln Center.

New York Theatre Ballet
Few of the uninitiated in the world of dance know of this chamber ballet company, which is often eclipsed by the fame of larger ballet companies in the city such as the New York City Ballet and the American Ballet Theater. George Balanchine's choreography, which spawned the latter companies, has been the touchstone for American ballet for over fifty years. But this ensemble stubbornly sticks to its non-Balanchine roots, and adhere to the styles of Enricho Cecchetti and Antony Tudor, who are far less well known here. The NYTB performs works that are generally unfamiliar to American audiences. The dancers' technique isn't on par with that of the bigger companies, and the company's small budget prevents them from using the larger stages in the city. Nevertheless, the repertory is refreshingly different, especially when you can't stomach another Balanchine piece. The company's school, Ballet School New York, offers classes for all levels.
30 E. 31st St. (at Madison Ave.), (212) 679-0401, www.nytb.org. Cash only. 6 to 33rd St., N R to 28th St.

[Film]

A

Angelika Film Center
This independent film multiplex offers cappuccino and gelato from the well-stocked cafe, and there is always the possibility of running into

celebrities like Bono or Brad Pitt.
18 W. Houston St. (at Mercer St.), (212) 995-2570, www.angelikafilmcenter.org. B D F V *to Broadway Lafayette St.,* N R *to Prince St.,* 6 *to Bleecker St.*

Anthology Film Archives

Examining film as an art form on par with that of the hallowed halls of the Met, this gallery organizes viewings, reviews, opening parties, and curated exhibitions of their rotating collection. This new approach appeals not just to film buffs already in-the-know, but those of us looking for something more than the current blockbuster can offer.
32 Second Ave. (at 2nd St.), (212) 505-5181. www.anthologyfilm archives.org. Hours vary. Cash only. F V *to Second Ave.*

B

BAM Rose Cinemas

The cinema located in the Brooklyn Academy of Music's (BAM) building is extraordinary and benefits from being located in a growing urban arts center. The four screen theater opened in 1998. The theater is unique because one screen is devoted to BAMcinematek classic movies. Definately worth the money, as one can watch both old and new movies while supporting a non-profit institution that helps to expose young children to the arts.
30 Lafayette Ave. at Flatbush Ave., Brooklyn, (212) 236-5849, M N R W *to Pacific St.,* 1 2 4 5 *to Atlantic Ave.*

C

Cinema Village

This single movie screen may have a reputation for hosting questionable flicks of the porn persuasion, but it actually accommodates a far wider array of independent films with themes ranging from gay and lesbian to kung fu action and African Diaspora.
22 E. 12th St. (bet. University Pl. and Fifth Ave.), (212) 924-3363, www.cinemavillage.com. Cash only. L N R W 4 5 6 *to 14th St.-Union Sq.*

Clearview's Waverly Twin

Your basic two-theater movie house, which vacillates between mainstream and art films. This can lead to interesting juxtapositions, such as *Godzilla* and *The Ice Storm.*
323 Sixth Ave. (at 3rd St.), (212) 929-8037. A B C D E F V 1 *to W. 4th St.-Christopher St.*

City Cinemas Village East

By all indications this seems to be just another many-screened showplace for big-budget Hollywood productions, but within the nondescript exterior lies the preserved interior of the old Yiddish Theater complete with original adornments and multi-tiered theater-style seating. So for a real treat, buy a ticket for whatever is showing in Theater Number One and get there early to check out this historical landmark.
189 Second Ave. (at 12th St.), (212) 529-6799. L N R W 4 5 6 *to 14th St.-Union Sq.*

F

Film Forum

Two programs run in this classic setting. Program One has first-run independent and foreign feature films as well as some excellent documentaries. Program Two, however, screens revivals including reissues of individual classics as well as film series featuring everything from the complete works of great, if sometimes obscure, directors to genre films.
209 W. Houston St. (at Sixth Ave.), (212) 727-8110. Cash only. 1 *to Houston St.*

K

Kim's Video and Audio

Less pedantic than their East Village counterparts, the staff here still knows what's up and has no qualms about either helping you sift though a bunch of out-there directors or matching your trivia on obscure Weimar-era actresses. Foreign film selection here also beats the East Village locations.
144 Bleecker St., (at Thompson St.), (212) 260-1010. 6 *to Bleecker St.*

Kim's Video

The most interesting and comprehensive selection of videos in town including everything from the typical new releases to the most esoteric arthouse, foreign, and genre flicks. Be forewarned: most everything is arranged by director or some odd category, so come well-informed with something in mind or deal with the staff, who are knowledgeable but a little overeager to prove it.
85 Ave. A (bet. 5th and 6th Sts.), (212) 529-3410. F V *to Second Ave.*

L

Landmark Sunshine Cinema

Originally an old vaudeville house, this space was redesigned into a new movie theater that is both comfortable and pleasant. Three screens and stadium style seating give the viewer the variety of movies and comfort they need to enjoy a show, even if there is a six-foot giant in front of you. The theater is very clean, and an excellent espresso bar serves coffee and locally baked cookies and pastries.
Houston St. (bet. First & Second Ave.) (212) 236-5849. F V *to Second Ave.*

Lincoln Plaza Cinemas

Down the street but still in the shadow of its titan neighbor Sony, this smallish theater doesn't want to do the big-budget Hollywood schtick anyway, preferring foreign and independent film festival standouts (and a few surprises.)
1886 Broadway (bet. 62nd and 63rd Sts.), (212) 757-2280, www.lincolnplazacinema.com. 1 *to 66th St.-Lincoln Center.*

M

The Movie Place

Avoid the weekend hordes at Blockbuster and that migraine-inducing light too. There is a comparable selection here, and more importantly,

they deliver to your doorstep. The staff loves movies, which is more than you can say for a movie chain.
237 W. 105th St. (at Broadway), (212) 864-4620, www.nymovieplace.com. 1 to 103rd St.

N

NYU Cantor Film Center
By the students, for the students, and offered at the oh-so student-friendly rate of two dollars a pop.
36 E. 8th St. (at University Pl.), (212) 998-4100. Cash only. N R to 8th St., 6 to Astor Pl.

P

The Paris
Highbrow European first runs and revivals show at this tony midtown movie house behind the Plaza Hotel. Very civilized.
4 W. 58th St. (at Fifth Ave.), (212) 688-3800. N R to Fifth Ave-59th St.

S

The Screening Room
The place to catch independent and foreign film hits after they leave the Angelika/Film Forum, or classics like *Breakfast at Tiffany's* that are shown every Sunday. The non-traditional seating makes it feel as comfy as a Blockbuster night, without the Bud Light and the remote. Diners at the restaurant next door get seated first for shows, so with a dinner-and-a-movie date, you can score a loveseat.
54 Varick St. (at Laight St.), (212) 334-2100. 1 to Canal St.

Sony Theaters Lincoln Square
Perhaps the city's glitziest theater where sweeping murals depicting stars of the '30s and '40s and higher-than-average ticket prices try to suggest a larger-than-life cinematic experience. The big-budget box-office hits are as predictable as ever.
1992 Broadway (at 68th St.), (212) 336-5000. 1 to 66th St.-Lincoln Center.

Sunshine Cinemas
The old-time movie-house marquee exterior belies the thoroughly modern cinemas inside this Lower East Side landmark, which specializes in avant-garde, art-house, independent and revival films. If that's not your cup of tea, then maybe the flavor-it-yourself popcorn bar will entice you inside (ranch and jalapeño!).
143 E. Houston St. (bet. First and Second Aves.), (212) 330-8182. F to Second Ave.

W

Walter Reade Theater/Film Society of Lincoln Center
Since 1985, the luxurious Walter Reade Theater has been the home of New York's elite film club, which screens everything from Jim Carrey to Godard, with an emphasis on the latter end of the spectrum. New Directors/New Films, in conjunction with the MoMA, has premiered work by such directors as Pedro Almodovar and Peter Greenaway, while film festivals sport titles like Rendezvous With French Cinema Today. Overall, rich in retro and avant-garde classics, just avoid the post-film talk if you fear pretension.
165 W. 65th St. (bet. Broadway and Amsterdam Ave.), (212) 875-5600. Cash only at box office. 1 to 66th St.-Lincoln Center.

[Miscellaneous]

D

Don't Tell Mama
Wrest control of the microphone away from fellow exhibitionists at this extrovert's paradise where patrons are invited to sing along with the waitstaff, the pianist, and the mixed clientele.
343 W. 46th St. (bet. Eighth and Ninth Aves.), (212) 757-0788, www.donttellmama.com. Hours: M-Su 4pm-4am. 1 to 50th St.

J

Jamaica Arts Center
A neo-Italian Renaissance structure built in 1898 houses a non-profit community cultural center dedicated to making all genres of the performing arts accessible to the Jamaica community.
Jamaica, Queens. 161-04 Jamaica Ave. (at 161st St.), (718) 658-7400. Cash only. E J Z to Jamaica Center.

L

Langston Hughes Community Library and Cultural Center
There are year-round readings and performances, as well as a wealth of reference materials in the on-site library. It would be a shame not to take advantage of what this amazing library has to offer.
Corona, Queens. 100-01 Northern Blvd. (at 100nd St.), (718) 651-1100. 7 to 103rd St.-Corona Plaza.

N

The National Arts Club
Unlike many groups dedicated to advancing the role of art in America, this one is by invitation only. Unless you have great connections or your name has enough cache to put you on a level with Martin Scorsese or Ethan Hawke, who are both members, you're probably out of luck. However, until you make it to that point, you can still get into the beautiful Tilden Mansion, the national landmark that houses this 110-year old club. During regular hours, four galleries with small, carefully chosen exhibits are open for viewing. The dress code is strictly enforced, so plan ahead. Step inside to shmooze with some of New York's finest.
15 Gramercy Park South (at 20th St. bet. Lexington and Park Aves.), (212) 475-3424, www.nationalartsclub.org. Cash only. 6 to 23rd St.

S

Symphony Space
Playing host to an incredible range of talent, this brand-new and spacious theater consistently offers up unique programs, which often incorporate music, film, theater, and dance within a single unifying theme. Student memberships are available for a nominal fee.
2537 Broadway (at 95th St.), (212) 864-1414. 1 2 3 to 96th St.

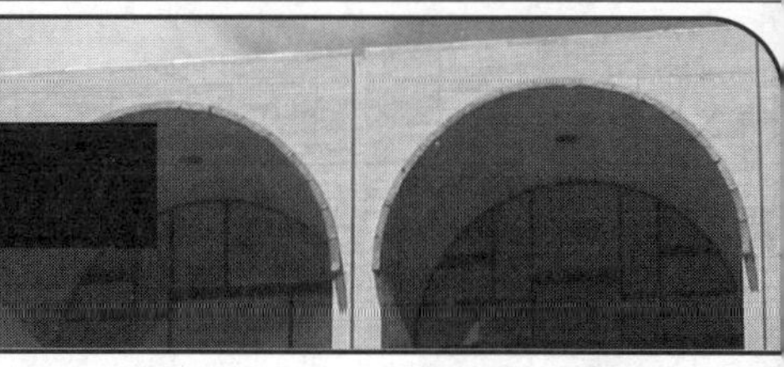

Opera in NYC

Where is one to look for compelling music-drama? Fear not, my fellow urbanites, for your little hometown happens to boast some of the finest expression of arguably man's most consummate art form: opera, music-drama's great granddaddy. Sure, it's hard to bust rhymes over Isolde's *Liebestod*, but if the conditions are right, a night at the opera can prove a truly exhilarating, even cathartic experience.

Manhattan's Upper West Side is home to two of the nation's - and one of the world's - most important opera houses, both nestled tightly in the city's performing-arts mecca, Lincoln Center (66th St. and Broadway). The Metropolitan Opera (www.metopera.org, (212) 362-6000) has set the standard for international operatic performance since the genre's Golden Age in the early decades of last century. Maintaining a season repertory of twenty-five to thirty operas, the Met showcases the world's greatest singers in some of the most visually lush, if conservative, productions around, accompanied by what is widely considered the country's top professional orchestra. Newcomers would be well advised to look to Puccini's *Tosca* and *La Boheme* as points of departure; Julie Taymor's (director and designer of Broadway's *The Lion King*) puppet-laden, visually stunning *Die Zauberflöte (The Magic Flute)* is sure to grab opera-newbies with its populist appeal.

Just a hop, skip, and jump from the reigning world champ of opera houses is New York City Opera (*www.nycopera.com, (212) 870-5570*), the second of Lincoln Center's daunting duo. The house excels at a very different task, programming rare and gutsy (and often American) repertoire in modern productions. In addition to the staple Turandots and Carmens, NYCO presents this season two new American operas, adaptations of Antoine de Saint-Exupéry's *The Little Prince* and Aristophanes' *Lysistrata*; 1965's suspenseful, macabre *The Mines of Sulphur* in its first major New York City staging; Gilbert and Sullivan's *Patience*; and even Frank Loesser's very non-operatic, supremely musical-theater *The Most Happy Fella.*

Both the Metropolitan Opera and NYCO are equipped with English titles systems, making utter bewilderment that much more difficult. Also, both institutions do their part in making performances more financially feasible for struggling students. The Met offers student discounted tickets at $25 (weekdays) and $35 (F-Sa) for seats that usually go for upwards of $150; NYCO sells tickets half-price to students a week prior to the performance, and reserves a limited number of $16 tickets to be sold the day of the opera.

Don't be fooled, however: opera in New York is not confined to 66th St. A whole host of smaller companies exist throughout the boroughs, offering both traditional and contemporary approaches to the art form in more intimate settings than either of the city's big houses. For more traditional fare, try DiCapo Opera Theater (*184 E.76 St., (212) 288-438; www.dicapo.com*), Regina Opera Company (*Brooklyn, (718) 232-3555; www.reginaopera.org*), and Amato Opera Company (*319 Bowery, (212) 228-8200; www.amato.org*), located right next to the legendary punk-rock haven CBGB. The Bronx Opera Company (*718) 365-4209, www.bronxopera.org*) gives performances of one repertoire staple and one rarely performed work at Lehman College's Lovinger Theatre in the Bronx, as well as at several varying locales around New York. For the more adventurous, Brooklyn Academy of Music (*30 Lafayette Ave., Brooklyn, (718) 636-4100, www.bam.org*) offers modern and experimental opera, as does the Upper West Side's Symphony Space (*96th St. and Broadway, (212) 864-1414*), which recently produced a new jazz opera dedicated to Gertrude Stein, and performed highlights from four Chinese operas in the Beijing and Shoaxing styles. The Opera Orchestra of New York (*212) 799-1982, www.oony.org*) conducts concert performances of several operas at Carnegie Hall each season, and boasts some of the finest singers on the international circuit.

For the less conventional opera-going experience, try Met in the Parks, the Metropolitan Opera's summer series of free outdoor concerts performed in some of the city's greener locales. And for a truly unique experience, spend a night at Café Taci (*10 Waverly Pl., (212) 678-5345*), where you can enjoy a plate of spaghetti with a side of wailing soprano. This little novelty has lost something in the move to its chicer downtown location (it was until this year an Upper West Side establishment), but there's still something indefinably charming about this live-opera-performing restaurant.

Dining
dining

dining in

No matter what type of lifestyle you choose to pursue in New York, dining here will be an important part of your experience. Dining in this city simply has no comparison. It's like buying an infinitely condensed greatest-hits album of world cuisine, wrapped in a soft corn taco and served on a rainbow tray with silverware and chopsticks. This variety and quantity of options makes New York City dining impossible to define. Where else can you truly enjoy New York strip steak or a bowl of Manhattan clam chowder?

There is no better way to grasp this city's diversity than to try and decide where to go for a meal. In terms of both quantity and quality, New York's ten thousand restaurants offer a sampling of culture and cuisine unparalleled in the rest of the world.

Because some of the best food in New York is also some of the cheapest, dining here is an exploration rather than an expense. Indeed, there are dining rooms in this city that consistently re-define opulence for the world, but aside from those few exclusive establishments trying to out-do one another, the vast majority of culinary gems you will encounter here are moderately priced.

As a newcomer to a city of such size and diversity, choosing which restaurant to eat at first might be the biggest challenge of your New York experience. One way to navigate New York's teeming restaurant culture is to visit some of the city's many famous locales. New York is a city of neighborhoods. If you're looking for Cantonese cuisine that rivals China's, look to New York's Chinatown for the best dim sum, healing soups, fruit puddings, and shakes the city has to offer. Although you can grab a quick dinner of fried rice and spring rolls on any Manhattan block, you can find some of the Western Hemisphere's most authentic Chinese dining in the heart of this district. Likewise, if you're looking for pizza that meets the Authentic Neapolitan Pizza Association's guidelines for the perfect crust, your best bet is to head a couple of blocks north from Chinatown into Little Italy for a quick brick-oven slice. If you're feeling saucy, walk over the Brooklyn Bridge and grab a slice from Grimaldi's or one of Brooklyn's many other excellent pizza places.

To succeed in the restaurant business in this city takes more than luck – it takes confidence, daring, and above all, style. Even a restaurant that seems to do everything perfectly can become a flash in the pan, disappearing after a year or two. New York competition is tougher than anywhere else, and the restaurant industry here is one of the toughest markets imaginable. It is by the slimmest chance that a restaurant succeeds. With that in mind, we owe it to this city and its surviving restaurants to go out and taste as much as we can.

New York isn't called the "Big Apple" for nothing. One bite of NYC will turn the most pious man a heathen. New York City is a dining heaven. Nevertheless, in a place of such prodigious size, it is very important to choose wisely when dining. This guide will give you the most tender section of the beef. When all is said and done, it should be clear why the finest filet mignon and the tastiest red snapper are both preceded by the succinct yet incredibly meaningful adjective – New York.

Looking the Part: Inside Dining Etiquette

With such a wide array of dining options in the city, the dos and don'ts of dining are no less varied. Elaine and George from *Seinfeld* found out the hard way in the famed Soup Nazi episode, quickly adopting the Soup Man's style to order a cup of mulligatawny. Nonetheless, for the average diner, the guidelines for New York eating are simple and the rewards extraordinary.

Reservations?

Forget the old rule that a Thomas Jefferson slipped to the maître d'hôtel will land you a table at the hottest restaurant. Unless you and your buddy look like Amy Stokes, you'll have to do what everyone else does – make a reservation. Call ahead to see if the restaurant does in fact accept them. As a general rule, plan on booking your table a week or two in advance. From there, increase the time if the restaurant has anything to do with Jean-Georges Vongerichten or another well-known chef; if it's just your favorite corner café, a few days' notice will do. Once you have landed your reservation, honor it like a doctor's appointment. If you must cancel, call in the afternoon to allow them to rebook. If you're running late, give them a heads up before you jump into the subway – many places give reserved tables away after 15 minutes.

Eat, Drink, and Be Merry

Find out if the restaurant offers either a full bar, wine and beer only, or nothing at all. With the growing number of BYOB options in the city, be sure you don't wind up high and dry. If the situation requires, stop at a local liquor store for a tasty vintage or a six-pack – but be prepared for a corkage fee.

Will That Be Cash or... Cash?

Before heading out, check the restaurant's payment options. Many boutique-sized restaurants have escaped credit card company fees by taking the cash-only route. Make sure you fill your wallet with enough green – a dash to the ATM is no way to finish a meal.

Tipping the Scale

In New York, leaving a tip isn't just customary – it's virtually mandatory. With an hourly wage far below the federal minimum, the city's servers depend on your generous tips for their sky-high rents and, as is often the case, those pricey Broadway Dance Center classes. Typically, diners leave a gratuity of 15 to 20 percent of the total check. For easy calculation, double the sales tax found at the bottom of the bill. Of course, the tip can still be adjusted to reflect the quality of service. To reward top-shelf precision, it's in good form to exceed 20 percent. For a slow-footed, sour-faced server, feel free to leave less – just don't drop below 10 percent.

At the bar, the general rule is to tip a dollar per drink. As you move from dive bar to diva bar, however, consider dropping a couple of bucks for that pricey lychee martini. The bartender will no doubt take note, and your second round will come without the wait.

During the wintertime, be sure to tip for coat check, usually a couple of dollars per person. Secure your gloves inside a deep pocket, and wrap your scarf tightly around a sleeve. Most places claim no responsibility for lost items, and at the end of the night, all black gloves look alike.

Swirl, Sniff, and Slurp

When it comes to manners, you no doubt learned them from Mom at the dinner table: napkins in your lap and elbows off the table. The etiquette of wine tasting, however, was probably one lesson left untaught, but in New York, it's just as important as the napkin and elbow rules.

According to standard practice, white wine pairs best with poultry, fish, and light pastas, while the reds normally accompany beef, lamb, and hearty tomato sauces. These days, with the proliferation of vintage varieties, feel free to order what you like best or, in states of desperation, the one with the catchiest name - Fat Bastard or Cock-fighter's Ghost will do nicely.

Once the server brings your selection to the table, follow these steps to masquerade as a true connoisseur. First, hold the glass up to the light to check the color and texture. Then, gently swirl the wine and watch how it drips down the wall of the glass. These streaks are known as the "legs" – generally, a better wine will cling nicely and form distinct lines. At last, sniff the wine and take a slow sip, allowing the liquid to roll across the tongue. Unless the taste approaches that of Robitussin, you've got a keeper. Smile in approval and cry, "Salud!" in your best Tony Soprano voice.

Viable Vegan

VEGAN

If there is anything that is categorically true about this peerless metropolis, it is that New York is a city of infinite possibilities. This is best seen in the plethora of dining options optioned in the city. So, while New York may offer enthusiastic carnivores some of the best steak in the world (see opposite page), this does not relegate herbivores to a life of self-denial. On the contrary, vegetarians and vegans who explore this urban dining Eden will find inspired and imaginative meatless restaurants of various culinary genres that they will only find in New York. Check out these places for a perfect green feast:

Traditional Vegan

Pure Food and Wine

Although it makes for a nice title, "purity" is not just a marketing gimmick here. To ensure that none of the food's essential nutrients are lost in cooking, nothing at this raw-food restaurant is heated over 118 degrees. The uplifting cuisine is as satisfying in taste as it is gratifying for your health. Their organic wines are exquisite—good enough to merit its title.
54 Irving Pl., (212) 477-1010.

Counter

The menu doesn't try to assuage vegetarians with fake meat dishes. Instead, it offers fantastic concoctions that just happen to be vegetarian. Clever entrées like the Cauliflower Risotto and pleasing appetizers like raw curried-plantain dumplings are made from the highest quality of natural ingredients. It also has a superb bar replete with organic and biodynamic wines.
105 First Ave., (212) 982-5870.

Angelica's Kitchen

So, you are a vegetarian, but you want to take a non-veggie on a date. Where do you go? Angelica's Kitchen. The warm atmosphere and chic bohemian décor is charming and inviting. Angelica has been consistently good for years, attracting health-conscious diners of all types. Their walnut-lentil paté and Angelica's signature "dragon bowls" are an East Village favorite. The prices are very reasonable; this is a can't-miss vegan spot.
300 E. 12th St., (212) 228-2909.

International Vegan

Devi

One of the city's most haute modern Indian restaurants offers a $55 seven-course vegetarian tasting menu that will give you a broad sweep of the liberally spiced, inventive cuisine. One of the most elegant and comprehensive vegetarian meals you will find.
8 E. 18th St., (212) 691-1300.

Zen Palate

With three locations now open in Manhattan, Zen Palate is slowly becoming a bona-fide vegetarian empire. A meal here is delicious and guilt free; it was designed for vegetarians with a health conscience. Much of the menu is comprised of familiar Asian staples such as noodle soup and spring rolls, but there are some hardcore veggie items, as well. Good, cheap, and healthy—you can't possibly go wrong.
34 Union Sq. East, (212) 614-9291) 663 Ninth Ave. (212) 582-1669, 2170 Broadway (212) 501-7768.

Gobo

The more classy offspring of the spectacularly successful Zen Palate, this organic, Pan-Asian restaurant really will appeal to your five senses, as advertised. The menu offers an impressive array of creative dishes such as the smoked Beijing-style seitan that looks like its duck counterpart and is equally tasty. Slightly more decadent than Zen Palate, you can supplement your meal with alcohol.
1426 Third Ave., (212) 288-5099, 401 Sixth Ave., (212) 255-3242.

Hangawi

Slip out of your shoes at this Korean vegan oasis to show respect while you sip wild tea and find inner peace in the open serene atmosphere. The menu here is so exotic and uniquely delicious that even carnivores will be impressed with its originality.
12 E. 32nd St., (212) 213-0077

New York's Kosher Universe

While standbys like the Second Avenue Deli and Ben's Deli provide wonderful kosher deli-style food, kosher dining in New York has evolved to include a variety of cuisines and eating experiences. Here is a list of noteworthy kosher eateries around town:

BBQ

For kosher barbeque check out Dougie's BBQ & Grill (222 W. 72nd St., (212) 724-2222) and enjoy home style BBQ standards like ribs smothered in sauce, spicy hot wings, big tasty burgers, as well as veggie burgers and salads. This is a hot spot with the young crowd, so make reservations or be prepared to wait. Entrées: are around $15. They also deliver.

Fast Food

For a more relaxed meal, be sure to stop by Kosher Delight *(1365 Broadway, (212) 563-3366).* This is the Kosher answer to McDonalds. Enjoy their fast service and fresh food with a burger or a chicken box...just hold the cheese!

Pizza

There are also a number of kosher pizzerias to choose from in New York. For instance, Jerusalem II Pizza *(1375 Broadway, (212) 398-1475)* combines pasta and pizza with traditional Israeli plates, or diners can enjoy combination plates that blend the two.

Pizza Cave *(218 W. 72nd St., (212) 874-3700 and 1376 Lexington Ave., (212) 987-9130)* has a wide selection of pizza toppings, as well as a very popular Calzone menu, not to mention the falafel and Israeli salad.

In addition to pizza, Café Roma *(175 W. 91st St., (212) 875-8972)* offers hot Italian entrées and a fresh salad bar that is a favorite among faithful locals.

Moderate

If you're looking for something a little more substantial than BBQ, fast food, or pizza, try the Deli Kasbah *(251 W. 85th St., (212) 496-1500)*, featuring a menu of grilled specialties that pack the flavor of Mediterranean and Israeli cuisine into every bite – they're known in New York for their tasty chicken sandwiches, Israeli pickles, hummus, and tabouleh.

Upscale

Solo *(550 Madison Ave., (212) 833-7800)* is one the newest and most up-scale of the kosher resturants New York now has to offer. The food is excellent, the atmosphere is sophisticated, and the desserts are the perfect way to end what will be a truly unique culinary experience. The Prime Grill *(60 E. 49th St., (212) 692-9292)* offers grilled steak and fish as well as an ambiance of Upper East Side luxury. Diners in Manhattan regard it as one of the best Kosher grills in the city and at the grill here, prices to match – the average filet is around $40. Abigael's is another upscale kosher (meat) restaurant around and is comparable with Prime Grill in both quality and price (reviews and location information in listings).

Va Bene *(1589 Second Ave., (212) 517-4448)* has long been regarded as the spot for Kosher Italian food. With big portions of linguine and ravioli, as well as meat dishes such as steak for two, Va Bene has the feel of a real Italian kitchen, with a kosher guarantee.

For fine Japanese dining there is Haikara Grill *(1016 Second Ave., (212) 355-7000)*, where diners enjoy a first-rate sushi bar with delicious sam-ples of salmon toro and yellow tail fresh from the day's catch, and a Japanese garden in the back that provides diners with a pleasant escape from city life. The extensive menu of sushi and grilled specialties, as well as the fast and amiable staff make this a great place for large parties, though reservations are necessary.

Powerhouse Steaks

More than any other city in the world, New York is a town filled with highly influential powerbrokers. Whether it be in politics, law or finance, deals that go down here are driven by an adrenaline-packed atmosphere of quick thinking and rapid execution. When it comes to dining, these big time executives and their aspiring protégés often favor the no-nonsense approach and guaranteed quality of New York's high-end steakhouses. If you are looking to impress a client, finalize a major transaction, or simply need to quench that carnal desire for succulent red meat, there is a carnivorous paradise to be found in all parts of this mecca-city for superior steak.

Financial District

MarkJoseph Steakhouse
261 Water St., (212) 277-0020
This steakhouse caters largely to Wall Street brokers and serious carnivores with voracious appetites for high-quality porterhouses. The house specialty, a gargantuan porterhouse for four ($156) can fuel a sizeable business meeting or nourish an avid set of meat-lovers.

Greenwich Village

Strip House
13 E. 12th St., (212) 328-0000
While Strip House's atmosphere is decidedly less testosterone-laden than your typical steakhouse, bona fide meat connoisseurs will swear by its New York strip and juicy filet. So, if you are craving a luscious steak, but need to gratify your date, visit this dimly-lit, unusually sexy Village steakhouse. Turn that friend into something more at this sexy steakhouse.

Midtown

Del Frisco's Double Eagle Steak House
1221 Sixth Ave., (212) 575-5129
Dashing young bankers start filing in at around eight and keep this unmistakably classy spot bustling way past eleven. With expense accounts covering the generous flow of wine, diners revel in Del Frisco's exceedingly tender and distinctively flavorful meats, which are seared in their signature combination of pepper and special spices.

Sparks Steakhouse
210 E. 46th St., (212) 687-4855
Seasoned business veterans settle in at this more subdued and established steakhouse. With an unparalleled selection of the finest red wines, and precisely aged prime beef ready to order, Sparks is generally populated by those who have already reached the top of their game.

Monkey Bar Steakhouse
60 E. 54th St., (212) 838-2600
Monkey Bar accommodates those young people who simply do not have money to burn. While certainly not a bargain, this up-and-coming steakhouse provides an option for meat-eaters who need to be somewhat frugal. Every night, $26 can buy a different cut of top quality prime aged beef. The lively bar and the moderate prices make for a fun night that won't empty your pockets.

Smith and Wollensky
797 3rd Ave., (212) 753-1530
Perhaps the best place to go for macho steak. Smith and Wollensky is a no-frills establishment whose patrons come for one thing: gigantic hunks of succulent meat.

Upper East Side

Ian Restaurant
322 86th St., (212) 861-1993
Although the menu is uncommonly brilliant in many culinary genres, as a pioneer of Nouveau New York Cuisine, Ian understands that steak is central to any self-respecting city-dweller's diet. Accordingly, he proffers an inimitable Dirty Ribeye, as well as a 50 oz. Porterhouse and Chateau-briand for two.

Brooklyn

Peter Luger Steakhouse
178 Broadway, (718) 387-7480
Why don't they open up a location in Manhattan? Because the steak is just that good. People will come from anywhere just to have a taste of this mystical meat. There is no way to really explain it. Just taste it and you'll understand.

Queens

Butcher Brothers Steakhouse
29-35 Newtown Ave., (718) 267-2771
The Redzic Brothers were destined to open a great steakhouse—they grew up in the meat business. And, so, the Butcher Brothers have come through and blessed Astoria with a gem of a spot. So, if you are closer to Queens than Manhattan, head here for a Porterhouse for two; it's as good as any on this page.

listings

[Financial District]

Restaurants

Bridge Cafe
Even if you're not a part of the city's political machine, the attentive staff will provide you with reliable standards at this adorable eatery just south of City Hall, one of former mayor Ed Koch's favorite haunts. Mostly a middle-aged crowd of spin doctors and other politicos.
279 Water St. (at Dover St.), (212) 227-3344, www.bridgecafe.com. Hours: M 11:45am-10pm, T-F 11:45am-11pm, Sa 5pm-12am, Su 11:45am-12pm. MC, V, AmEx, D, D. Entrées: $12-$24. 4 5 6 to Brooklyn Bridge-City Hall.

Coast
Its most impressive offering is its oyster bar, which provides patrons with excellent and fresh seafood at affordable prices. While the fish, as one would expect, is excellent, one would be remiss not to order whichever fresh catch oysters they're serving that day. Nonetheless, for those avoiding shellfish, the fish entrées are served in large portions over a bed of rice. The fluke was particularly exceptional, as was the grouper. The desserts were all delicious, especially the carrot cake.
110 Liberty St. (bet. Greenwich and Church St), (212) 962-0136. Hours: M-S 11am-11pm. MC, V, AmEx, D. Entrées: $15-$25. R W to Cortland St., 1 to Rector St., 2 3 to Wall St.

14 Wall St.
Join stockbrokers and investment bankers carrying on the legacy of J.P. Morgan by puffing cigars and sipping scotch in his old library, the closest thing to a private dining room in the city. The breakfast room overlooks the harbor.
14 Wall St. (bet. Broadway and Broad St.), (212) 233-2780, www.14wallstreet restaurant.com. Hours: M-F 7am-7:45pm for last reservations. MC, V, AmEx, D. Entrées: $20-$25. 2 3 to Wall St.

Harbour Lights
After spending a beautiful day exploring the South Street Seaport, there is no better place to give your legs a rest and your eyes a treat. Although the food is a bit overpriced and the clientele can seem touristy, the spectacular view makes it worthwhile.
South St. Seaport, Pier 17, 3rd fl. (at Fulton St.), (212) 227-2800, www.harbour lts.com. Hours: M-W 11am-1pm, R-Sa 11am-2am, Su 10am-1am. MC, V, AmEx, D. Entrées: $25-$40. 2 3 4 5 6 A C J M to Fulton St.

Harry's at Hanover Square
If you're in the mood for suits, cigars, and meat, this Wall St. hangout is the place to be. Order a martini and scan the great wine list as you enjoy one of Harry's excellent steaks. Unfortunately, like the stock market, it's closed on weekends.
1 Hanover Sq. (bet. Pearl and Stone Sts.), (212) 425-3412. Hours: M-F 11:30am-10:30pm. MC, V, AmEx, D. Entrées: $14-$30. R W to Whitehall St.

Mangia
Gourmet Mediterranean cuisine and friendly wait staff make this restaurant a culinary hot-spot for surrounding businesses, galleries, and museums. Mangia's diverse array of pastas, sandwiches, and entrées – including an "antipasto table" with a wonderful selection ranging from paella to rare tuna – is sure to quench anyone's desire for a gastronomic thrill. In a rush? Stop at the cafe downstairs for equally delicious take-out dining, or have them deliver right to your door.
40 Wall St. (bet. Nassau and Broad Sts.), (212) 425-4040. Marketplace Hours: M-F 7am-10pm, Café Hours: M-F 5pm-10pm. MC, V, AmEx, D. Entrées: $11-$15. R W to Rector St.

MarkJoseph Steakhouse
Serving hearty steaks to powerful clientele, MarkJoseph's provides its patrons with a fantastic porterhouse steak, cooked on the table directly in front of you. The food is definitely worth the price (and the wait) as it is extremely tender and delicious; the steak sauce is also incredibly tasty, a mixture between horseradish, ketchup, and sugar. The available sides are very flavorsome, especially the creamed spinach. For dessert, try the MarkJoseph special, a delectable combination of cheesecake and brownie.
261 Water St. (off Peck Slip), (212)-277-0020. Hours: M-T 11:30am-9:45pm, F 11:30am-10:45pm, Sa 5pm-10:45pm, AmEx, D. MC, Visa, Entrées: $24-$33 2 3 to Wall St.

Cafes

Seaport Café
The menu at this open-air cafe features fresh pastas, sandwiches, wraps, gourmet coffees, and desserts. It's perfect for casual diners who don't want generic fast food or a high tab. The outdoor table area is great for people-watching, ensuring that diners won't miss any of the action occurring at the lively pier area.
89 South St. (at Pier 17), (212) 964-1120. Hours: Su-R 7am-2am, F-Sa 7am-3am. MC, V, AmEx, D. 2 3 4 5 6 A C J M to Fulton St.

[Tribeca]

Restaurants

Bubby's

Forego the fancily-named sandwiches, which don't merit their prices, in favor of sturdier fare like quesadillas served with great salsa. Gorgeous ceiling-high windows encourage people-watching, and the wooden floor and benches evoke the comfort level of an unpretentious, rather rustic, cafe. Great brunch.
120 Hudson St. (at N. Moore St.), (212) 219-0666, www.bubbys.com. Hours: M-R 8am-11pm, F 8am-12am, Sa 9am-12am, Su 8am-10pm. MC, V, AmEx, Entrées: $7-$15. 1 *to Franklin St.,* A C E *to Canal St.*

Café Noir

A hot spot for late-night dining, the atmosphere and food are Spanish-Moroccan, and the bar is generally inundated with well-dressed hipsters looking for fun. Eschew the more expensive entrées in favor of lighter treats like sandwiches and tapas, which combine simple ingredients to reach perfection. Take advantage of the cheap entrées and splurge on a good bottle of wine from their extensive list of French vintages.
32 Grand St. (at Thompson St.), (212) 431-7910. Hours: Su-R 12pm-1am, F-Sa 12pm-3am. AmEx, Entrées: $12-$18. A C E *to Canal St.*

Casa La Femme

Tents straight from the Arabian Nights line the walls and shelter your party from prying eyes at this Egyptian restaurant and hookah bar. The hookahs aren't filled with opium, but they're so much fun you won't notice. Check out the belly dancers on weekends. Try not to choke over the bill when it comes.
1076 1st Ave. (bet 58th and 59th Sts.) (212) 505-0005. Hours: Su-R 5pm-1am, F-Sa 5pm-4am. MC, V, AmEx. 4 5 6 N R W *to 59th St.-Lexington Ave.*

Chanterelle

Dining is art at this famous Manhattan establishment. Everything about Chanterelle speaks to its eloquence; the seats are big and comfortable, the silverwear divine, and the ambiance soothing. A meal here is not just a meal, but an event. This reviewer suggests the tasting menu, as it allows one to experience a wide variety of excellent dishes. Although Chanterelle is a bit pricey for students, make sure to stop by at least once during your time in New York - you won't soon forget it.
2 Harrison St. (at Hudson St.), (212) 966-6960, www.chanterellenyc.com. Hours: M-R 12pm-2:30pm, 5:30pm-10:30pm. F-Su 12pm-2:30pm, 5:30pm-11pm. MC, V, AmEx, D. Entrées: $20-$30. 1 *to Franklin St.*

Duane Park Cafe

For quiet conversation and delicious food in a relaxed atmosphere, this place can't be beat. The soft shell crabs and roasted Bartlett pear are musts. Best of all, you can actually get a table without a reservation.
157 Duane St. (bet. Broadway and Hudson St.), (212) 732-5555. Hours: M-F 12pm-2:30pm, 5:30pm-10pm, Sa-Su 12pm-2:30pm, 5:30pm-10:30pm. MC, V, AmEx, D. Entrées: $15-22. 1 2 3 *to Chambers St.*

F. Illi Ponte Ristorante

Down the river, a delightful dining experience waits for you. Live jazz, dim lighting, a wood burning stove, a cigar room, a lounge, and definitive brick décor nicely accompany a beautiful sunset over the Hudson. The service is amiable and the environment is relaxed and a pleasant to take in. With a fine selection of wine, and a great menu, you cannot go wrong. We recommend pretty much anything on the menu.
39 Desbrosses St. (at Washington St.), (212) 226-4621, www.filliponte.com. Hours: M-F 11:30am-3pm, 5:30pm-10:30pm, Sa 5:30pm-11pm, MC, V, AmEx, D. Entrées: $25-$45. A C E 1 *to Canal St.*

The Harrison

In a setting that reminds you of a dining room on an old wooden ship, the seafood at this fine Tribeca establishment is delectable and all dishes are well-presented. The service is well-choreographed and runs like clockwork, with a variety of attendants having their own individual roles in the presentation of the meal. The staff is very knowledgeable about the food, advising what choice is the most fresh and seasonable for your specific dining experience. Thy also create a warm, personable environment with a sequence of courses that seems to be tailored specifically to each individual. A large banquet room in the basement with a wine cellar can make this restaurant a fine choice for large groups, while the cozy atmosphere upstairs and the outdoor seating make it advisable for intimate parties as well.
355 Greenwich St. (at Harrison St), (212) 274-9310, www.theharrison.com. Hours: M-F 11:30am-3pm, 5:30pm-10:30pm, Sa 5:30pm-11pm, MC, V, AmEx, D. Entrées: $21-$33. 1 *to Franklin St.*

Landmarc

Recently opened in the spring of 2004, Landmarc is part neighborhood bistro, part trendy eatery situated on a picturesque corner in Tribeca. With large portions and a wide range of selections and specials, Landmarc's menu has something for everyone; the dishes are anything but simple and include French, Italian, and American accents. The goat cheese profiteroles are an excellent yet rich appetizer while the salads are ample yet not exceptional. For main courses, the fish choices offer complex and original accoutrements while the many different cuts of steak are somewhat unpredictable, but can be made to order with a variety of sauce choices. A large wine selection is also offered, with choices of only a half bottle or a full bottle to suit any meal. Landmarc's sophisticated industrial décor, fantastic views of Manhattan, and hearty food provide an overall satisfying experience.

179 W Broadway (bet. Leonard & Worth Sts.), (212) 343-3883, www.landmarc-restaurant.com, Hours: M-F 12pm-5pm, 5:30pm-2am, Sa-Su 11am-5pm, 5:30pm-2am, Entrées: $14-$26. 1 *to Franklin St.*

Megu

Descend the sleek mood-lit staircase and immerse yourself in this amazingly original space: walls lined with ancient kimono fabric, a colossal bronze temple bell, and an ice sculpted Buddha surrounded by rose petals all backdrop what is unequivocally one of the best Japanese restaurants. With daily shipments of food products flown in from Japan, Megu offers diners unparalleled, distinctive modern Japanese cuisine. The menu is both inventive and extensive. Start with the fresh snapper salad seared with sesame oil or the shrimp sautéed in kanzuri cream and chili sauce. Then, move on to the seared tuna in Chu Toro, the Avocado Ravioli or the raw Kobe beef slices. These outstanding dishes will make your taste buds dance with delight and leave you begging for more.

62 Thomas St. (bet. W. Broadway and Church St.), (212) 964-7777, www.megunyc.com, Hours: Lunch M-F 11:30am-2:30pm, Dinner M-W 5:30pm-11:30pm, Th-Sa 5:30pm-12:30am, Su 5:30pm-11pm. All major credit cards accepted. Entrées: $23-$28. 1 2 3 *to Chambers St.*

The Odeon

With a décor that is classical rather than trendy, after years this place still remains one of the most stylish eateries around, serving excellent brasserie food for the late-night dining crowd. Make the scene with a group and look out for Robert DeNiro, who is a frequent visitor.

145 W. Broadway (bet. Duane and Thomas Sts.), (212) 233-0507. Hours: M-F 11:45am-2am, Sa 11am-2am, Su 11:30am-2am. MC, V, AmEx, D. Entrées: $15. 1 2 3 *to Chambers St.*

Pace

This place is huge and happening—not just your friendly old neighborhood Italian restaurant; Pace is fashionable, loud, and extremely distinctive. You are welcomed by a long bar that is packed on most nights of the week and for good reason; they have a fantastic selection of unique foreign wines and beers. For the meal, simply follow the directions of the well laid-out menu: begin with an Antipasti (the diver scallops and Portobello Gratin are superb), then move on to the Primi (a number of stellar pastas and smaller fish dishes), and finally complete the meal with the Secondi and an accompanying Contorni (excellent choice of meat and fish Entrées and side dishes). By dessert, you will want to get up and exclaim bravo to Chef Joey Campanaro.

121 Hudson St. (at N. Moore St.), (212) 965-9500, www.pacetribeca.com. Hours: M-R 5:30pm-11pm, F-Sa 5:30pm-12am; Su 5:30pm-10pm. Entrées: $20-$30. A C E *to Canal St.,* 1 *to Franklin St.,* 2 3 *to Chambers St.*

TriBeCa Grill

This flagship of the DeNiro restaurant empire is a haven for those who like to enjoy a little celebrity watching with their meal. Movie big shots from the nearby TriBeCa Film Center can be found sharing the spacious, darkwood and brick dining room with plenty of other notables and, of course, some commoners, all there to enjoy the Grill's New American cuisine. Oh yeah, and if you ever manage to finish star-gazing, the food here happens to be superb.

375 Greenwich St. (at Franklin St.), (212) 941-3900, www.myriadrestaurantgroup.com. Hours: M-Th 11:30am-2:45pm, 5:30pm-11pm, F 11:30am-2:45pm, 5:30pm-11:30pm, Sa 5:30pm-11:30pm, Su 11:30am-5pm, 5:30pm-10pm. MC, V, AmEx, D. Entrées: $18-$28. 1 *to Franklin St.*

Cafes

Yaffa's Tea Room

Alice in Wonderland stumbles out of the rabbit hole and finds herself in New York. Burgundy velvet and antique crystal chandeliers make you feel like a cosmopolitan Queen of Hearts sipping her tea. Reservations are required for high tea, served Monday through Saturday 2pm-5pm.

353 Greenwich St. (at Harrison St.), (212) 274-9403. Hours: Su-Sa 9am-11pm. MC, V, AmEx, D. 1 *to Franklin St.*

Chinatown

Restaurants

Bo Ky

Seafood variations served over rice and noodles are the staples of the Chinese menu. The central location attracts both tourists and locals on a lunch break. Efficient service moves patrons in and out in a hurry.

80 Bayard St. (at Mott St.), (212) 406-2292. Hours: Su-Sa 10am-10pm. Cash Only, Entrées: $5-$13. J M N R W Z 6 *to Canal St.*

Congee Village

On the outskirts of Chinatown, this is one of

the best Chinese bargains around, serving congee, the savory Chinese porridge, in an astounding number of varieties. Get it plain or with chicken and duck, or try more adventurous options like abalone and frog or the mysteriously named "thousand-year-old egg." There are hundreds of other dishes available, but congee is clearly the star. It reappears for dessert, sweet and deliciously gingery.
100 Allen St. (at Delancey St.), (212) 941-1818. Hours: Su-Sa 10:30am-2am. MC, V, AmEx, D, Entrées $3-$20, but most are around $8. F J M Z *to Delancey St.*

Funky Broome

This Little Italy restaurant wants to be a better-lit, hipper version of its bargain Chinese cousins down the street, south of Canal. The food is standard, the prices are good, and the clientele is a mix of Chinatown locals and SoHo regulars. The décor runs heavy on fish tanks with live lobsters and such. During the day it can be somber, but at night it's bright, bright, bright!
176 Mott St. (at Broome St.), (212) 941-8628. Hours: Su-Sa 11am-12am. MC, V, AmEx, D. ($25 min). 6 *to Spring St.*

Golden Unicorn

Cleaner and more polished than most Chinatown dim sum houses, this chandeliered restaurant has become especially popular among tourists and local businessmen hosting lunch meetings. Delicious dim sum (seven days a week, 9am-3:30pm) is served Hong-Kong style, stacked on metal carts piloted by vigorous employees. Many claim it's dim sum and then some.
18 E. Broadway (at Catherine St.), (212) 941-0911. Hours: Su-Sa 9am-11pm. MC, V, AmEx, D, Entrées: $8-$11. B D *to Grand St.*

Joe's Shanghai

Joe's crabmeat buns are deservedly famous; tourists, locals, and suburban Chinese flock here for them year round. Friendly service and the savory food keep customers coming back for more. Try the soup dumplings, filled with juicy crabmeat and pork in a flavorful broth.
9 Pell St. (at Mott St.), (212) 233-8888. Hours: Su-Sa 11am-11:15pm. Cash Only, Entrées: $5-$18. J M N R W Z 6 *to Canal St.*

Great New York Noodletown

Away from the tourist center of Chinatown lies this affordable and cozy restaurant where you're guaranteed to find a dish to excite your taste buds. In-season seafood specials, the crab in particular, are a definite must-try, as is the barbecued chicken/duck/pork combo. The ultra-accommodating service will make sure that you leave both full and fully satisfied.
28 Bowery St. (at Bayard St.), (212) 349-0923. Hours: Su-Sa 9am-3:30am. Cash only, Entrées: $8-12. B D *to Grand St.*

Onieal's Grand Street

A turn-of-the-century tavern rumored to have been frequented by Teddy Roosevelt during his tenure as police commissioner, Onieal's retains its old-world charm though it now caters to bankers, architects, models, and celebrities. Though the food is New American with flavorful Italian influences, Onieal's also features a traditional Irish breakfast and transforms into a popular lounge at night.
174 Grand St. (bet. Center and Mulberry Sts.), (212) 941-9119. Hours: Su-Sa 11pm-4am. MC, V, AmEx, D. Entrées: $17-$25. B D *to Grand St.* J M N R W Z 6 *to Canal St.*

Pongsri Thai Restaurant

Practically adjacent to the municipal courthouses, Pongsri delights jury-duty sufferers with its tasty and affordable lunch specials. Standard noodle and curry dishes are all fabulous, if at times ultra spicy.
106 Bayard St. (at Baxter St.), (212) 349-3132. Hours: Su-Sa 11:30am-11pm. AmEx, Entrées: $5-$10. J M N R W Z 6 *to Canal St.*

Cafes

Chinatown Ice Cream Factory

If chocolate and vanilla make you groan with boredom, this tiny cafe will satiate your jaded taste buds. Lick away at flavors like red bean, green tea, taro, and lychee. The ginger is divine. There's usually a line around the block on weekends.
65 Bayard St. (bet. Mott and Elizabeth Sts.), (212) 608-4170. Hours: Su-Sa 11am-11pm. Cash Only. J M N R W Z 6 *to Canal St.*

Tai Pan Bakery

The pastries at this extremely popular bakery merit its long weekend lines. Custard tarts and pearl milk tea drinks are sure to please, while the Fish burgers are for the

adventurous.
194 Canal St. (212) 732-2222. Hours: Su-Sa 7:30am-8:30pm. Cash only. J M N R W Z 6 *to Canal St.*

[Little Italy]

Restaurants

Buona Notte
Attractive space provides seating choices in the front, dining room, or garden. Plenty of mirrors allow you to detect the fettuccine between your teeth before your date does. Nice presentation and delicately seasoned dishes.
120 Mulberry St. (bet. Canal and Hester Sts.), (212) 965-1111. Hours: Su-Sa 12pm-11:30pm. MC, V AmEx, Entrées: $11-24. J M N R W Z 6 *to Canal St.*

Café Gitane
France approaches the border of Little Italy, armed with an authentic bistro menu and aloof wait staff. Perfect ambience for flipping through fashion mags, drinking cappuccinos, and posing.
242 Mott St. (at Prince St.), (212) 334-9552. Hours: Su-Sa 9am-12am. Cash Only, Entrées: $7-$10. N R W *to Prince St.*

Luna's Ristorante
This neighborhood hideaway is still one of the best buys in Little Italy. Come for the food and not the décor. The aroma of fresh garlic sizzling in olive oil more than compensates for the perfunctory service.
112 Mulberry St. (bet. Canal and Hester Sts.), (212) 226-8657. Hours: Su-Sa 12pm-12am. MC, V, AmEx. J M N R W Z 6 *to Canal St.-Broadway.*

Positano Ristorante
The slender space and subdued décor make Positano seem less raucous than its neighbors on Mulberry Street. A peaceful meal in the heart of Little Italy.
122 Mulberry St. (bet. Canal and Hester Sts.), (212) 334-9808. Hours: M-F 12pm-11pm, Sa-Su 12pm-12am. MC, V, AmEx. J M N R W Z 6 *to Canal St.-Broadway.*

Puglia
Like pasta? Like Elvis? Then you're in luck – spend your time at large communal tables, chugging wine with new friends as an Italian Elvis works his magic on a little Casio keyboard in the corner. By the time you leave, you'll feel less lonely.
189 Hester St. (bet. Mott and Mulberry Sts.), (212) 226-8912, www.littleitalynyc.com/puglia. Hours: Su-Sa 12pm-12am. MC, V, AmEx, D. Entrées: $5-$10. J M N R W Z 6 *to Canal St.-Broadway.*

Cafes

Ferrara Bakery and Café
America's oldest espresso bar has been a Little Italy staple since 1892. If you can't make the trip to the original all the way downtown, visit the midtown location to satiate yourself until your next visit. Everything is homemade. Ferrara's has been serving up cannoli for years, and is a perennial favorite for New Yorkers looking to have coffee and dessert after a show or meal.
195 Grant St. (bet. Mulberry and Mott Sts.), (212) 226-6150, www.ferrara-cafe.com. Hours: Su-R 8am-12am, F 8am-12:30am, Sa 8am-1am. MC, V, AmEx, D. J M N R W Z 6 *to Canal St.-Broadway.*

[Lower East Side]

Restaurants

El Castillo de Jagua
A homely but decent Dominican dive in the heart of Losaida, this place pleases with rice & beans, fried plantains, cafe con leche, and fresh squeezed O.J. served to the beat of loud Caribbean music.
113 Rivington St. (bet. Ludlow and Essex Sts.), (212) 982-6412. Hours: Su-Sa 8am-12am. Cash Only. F J M Z *to Delancey St.-Essex St.*

Grilled Cheese NYC
All kinds of combinations of grilled cheese imaginable here, and they're all priced to go. The place is very small, but how long does it take to eat a grilled cheese, anyway? Answer: Four minutes.
168 Ludlow St. (bet. Houston and Stanton Sts.), (212) 982-6600. Hours: Su-Sa 10am-12am. Cash only, Entrées: $2-$8, F V *to Second Ave.*

Katz's Delicatessen
Steaming pastrami, corned beef sandwiches and other artery-clogging delicacies await at this cavernous, superior (non-Kosher) delicatessen, where yellowing paint and curling posters tell patrons to "Send a salami to your boy in the army." Nothing much has changed here in the last 50 years. A dollar tip to one of the gruff, portly attendants behind the counter will beget a sandwich big enough to feed a family of five. Take a ticket when you go in, and don't lose it: the consequences are dire.
205 E. Houston St. (at Ludlow St.), (212) 254-2246. Hours: Su-R 8am-10pm, F-Sa 8am-3am. MC, V, ($20 min), Entrées: $5-$15. F V *to Second Ave.*

Le Pere Pinard
Bare wooden tables and eclectically decorated stucco walls provide a rustic, French country ambience which hardly hints at the sophisticated, occasionally Asian-inspired food to come. Especially delicious are the Raw Tuna and Ginger Soy Sauce, the Shrimp, Mango, and Asparagus Salad, and the delightfully gooey Chocolate Valrhona Cake with coconut sorbet.
175 Ludlow St. (bet. Houston and Stanton Sts.), (212) 777-4917. Hours: M-R 5pm-12am, F 5pm-2am, Sa 12pm-2am, Su 12pm-11pm. AmEx, Entrées: $12-$18. F V *to Second Ave.*

Oliva
Waiters at this Spanish gem greet regulars with a peck on the cheek, helping to make Olivia's the perfect spot to dine with a date or an intimate friend. Expect romantic ambience with slow

groovy music, chosen by the manager (a local DJ). The food is impeccably presented and savory; choose from an excellent daily selection of seafood and paella on Sundays and Mondays, as well as the sweet dessert wines. You might leave with your wallet a bit lighter, but you'll be smiling.
161 E. Houston St. (at Allen St.), (212) 228-4143. Hours: M-F 5:30pm-11:30pm, Sa-Su 11am-1am. AmEx, Entrées: $10-$20. F V to Second Ave.

Sammy's Roumanian
This bustling and lively restaurant hosts rich meals and a loud Yiddish band. Locals and other New Yorkers, none of whom are dieting, frequent the place. Red meat is a featured menu item, while chopped liver and vodka are popular as well.
157 Chrystie St. (at Delancey St.), (212) 673-0330, Hours: M-R 4pm-10pm, F-Sa 4pm-11pm, Su 4pm-9:30pm. MC, V, AmEx, Entrées: $20-$27. F V to Second Ave.

[SoHo]

Restaurants

88 Palace Restaurant
After taking the escalator to his Hong Kong extravaganza, you understand how they derived the "palace" part of the name. The multi-roomed restaurant assumes the air of a circus, with families chattering over fried and steamed noodles, shrieking toddlers playing chicken with rolling dim sum carts, and tables of heated woks threatening diners with third-degree burns. The dumplings, buns, and shellfish are all excellent.
88 E. Broadway (under the Manhattan Bridge), (212) 941-8886. Hours: Su-Sa 9am-10pm. MC, V, AmEx, D. Entrées: $10-$18. F to E. Broadway.

Baluchi's
Named after Pakistan's Balochistan province, this bonafide Indian restaurant does justice to the sultry opulence for which the region is known. Numerous options will satisfy vegetarians, including Pallak Paneer and Basmati rice. Check out the half-priced dinners.
193 Spring St. (bet. Thompson and Sullivan Sts.), (212) 226-2828. Hours: Su-Sa 12pm-3pm, 5pm-11pm. MC, V, AmEx, D, Entrées: $10-$14. C E to Spring St.

Bistrot Margot
A French treasure hidden in SoHo, gourmet enough to satisfy the upper-crust, older patrons who don't mind the bloated prices. A surplus of two-person tables and seductive lighting emphasize its potential as a date restaurant.
26 Prince St. (bet Mott and Elizabeth St.), (212) 274-1027, Hours: M-R 11am-11pm, F-Sa 11am-12am. AmEx, Entrées: $5-$13. B D F V to Broadway-Lafayette St., 6 to Bleecker St.

Blue Ribbon Sushi
Let the simple yet elegant modern Japanese decor draw you into this fashionable SoHo sushi haven and you shall be rewarded with yellowtail and tuna of melt-in-your-mouth freshness. The restaurant is open for dinner until 2am but accepts no reservations, so weekend waits can be long, especially taking into consideration its diminutive dimensions. Closed Mondays.
119 Sullivan St. (bet. Prince and Spring Sts.), (212) 343-0404. Hours: T-Su 12pm-2am. MC, V, AmEx, D. Entrées: $20-$30. C E to Spring St.

Bond St.
Classic Japanese tradition meets modern-Manhattanite luxury in this townhouse turned eatery of the West Village. The restaurant has a downstairs trendy lounge, main floor dining and sushi bar, and an upstairs reached via elevator. The décor is best described as dreamy—semi-translucent fabric in light and clean colors frame windows, doors, and hallways. The lighting is dim enough to set the mood but bright enough that one can see the colorful plates, which are the main attraction. If your wallet can handle it, try the tasting menu: an exquisite collection of the chef's creative efforts ranging from live lobster sashimi, to stilton-dusted tuna sushi, to creamy foie gras with toro—and that's just the beginning. Whatever the case, do not miss the miso infused sea bass: it was one of the best fish dishes this reviewer has ever tasted. For dessert, try a layered cup with cream, pastry, Japanese mountain peach sorbet, and whole fruit garnish.
6 Bond St. (bet. Broadway and Lafayette St.), (212) 777-2500. Hours: M-Sa 6pm-12am, Su 6pm-11pm. MC, V, AmEx, D, Entrées: $18-$26. 6 to Bleecker St., B D F V to Broadway-Lafayette St., N R W to Prince St.

Butter
The long walkway into the restaurant area might as well be a catwalk. Take one look around the room and you know that you are in the company of the beautiful people, the proverbial "In-Crowd." The Olson twins are known to frequently visit this scene between stints at NYU or rehab. There is so much social energy pulsating through this place that it is possible to forget that you came for dinner in the first place. Nonetheless, Chef Alexandra Guarnachelli does an admirable job of keeping the food exciting; her imaginative emulsion concoctions always manage to seamlessly complement the base of the meal without overpowering the natural flavor of the meat or fish. Try to appreciate these subtly prepared dishes before getting caught up in the anything but subtle eye-candy.
415 Lafayette St. (bet. Astor Pl. and 4th St.), (212) 253-2828, www.butterrestaurant.com. Hours: M-F 12pm-3pm, 6pm-11pm, Sa 6pm-12pm. MC, V, AmEx, D. Entrées: $17-30. N R to 8th St., 6 to Astor Pl..

Café Habana
A great spot for watching the SoHo crowd outside. Come for the shockingly good grilled corn and delicious plantains, while the Cuban Sandwhiches are also worthwhile. Avoid the long wait by heading next door to Habana's sis-

ter takeout cafe.
17 Prince St. (at Elizabeth St.), (212) 625-2001, Hours: Su-Sa 9am-12pm. MC, V, AmEx, Entrées: $10-18. F V to Second Ave.

Fanelli's
One of the last remnants of pre-gentrification SoHo. Everything about this place is unpretentious, from the spare decor to the sturdy pub-style food, which is what keeps it going strong as an alternative to all the other too chic and trendy restaurants in the neighborhood. Be prepared to wait. On weekends they're often packed for hours.
94 Prince St. (at Mercer St.), (212) 226-9412. Hours: M-R 10am-1am, F-Sa 10am-4pm, Su 11am-1am. MC, V, AmEx, Entrées: $10-$12. N R to Prince St.

Felix
Although the French menu may seem hoity-toity, that is not the vibe here. People come here to relax, throw down some beers, and maybe even play some foosball. Who says that such a place can't offer some respectable French cuisine? The attractive location and the attractive food all add up to an attractive clientele. So come here to get a drink, eat some fine food, and perhaps exchange phone numbers. Then, return for a more formal get-together.
340 W. Broadway (at Grand St.), (212) 431 0021. Hours: M-Su 12pm-12am. AmEx, Entrées: $15-$20. C E to Spring St./Canal St., N R 6 to Canal St.

Prix Fixe

If you're on a student budget, but don't want to deprive yourself of dining out in style every once in a while, a prix fixe meal is a great way to get some bang for your buck. Generally including an appetizer, Entrée, and dessert, the prix fixe cost is almost lower than ordering a la carte. Although prix fixe menus are offered in restaurants throughout Manhattan, they are most abundant in the Theater District, where the establishments on "Restaurant Row" try to lure in ticket-holding customers by promising to save them both time and money. Many prix fixe menus are only available earlier in the evening, usually before 7pm, so it is good to call ahead and find out the restaurant's policy.

Jerry's
A longtime crowd pleaser, Jerry's still has a line out the door for weekend brunch. Try a plate of stellar tuna salad or citrus-marinated chicken. This hot lunch spot draws an artsy crowd and plenty of celebrities while maintaining down-to-earth service.
101 Prince St. (bet. Greene and Mercer Sts.), (212) 966-9464. Hours: M-W 8:30am-11pm, R-F 8:30am-11:30pm, Sa 10:30am-11:30pm, Su 10:30am-5pm. MC, V, AmEx, Entrées: $9-$13. N R to Prince St.

Kin Khao
Don't be surprised to see a supermodel sitting down the bench from you at this trendy Thai eatery. However, the atmosphere isn't prohibitive to normal people, and once you get inside the wait staff is unpretentious, and the decor beautiful and comfortable. The food is Thai, and the quality isn't all that consistent. To be safe, stick to one of the noodle dishes, which are always appetizing.
171 Spring St. (bet. W. Broadway and Thompson St.), (212) 966-3939. Hours: Su-R 5:30pm-11pm, F-Sa 5:30pm-12am. MC, V, AmEx, Entrées: $11-$19. C E 6 to Spring St.

The Kitchen Club
Turquoise curtains, a huge checkered tile floor, and French doors that open out to the street give Kitchen Club its unique atmosphere. Serving up Continental cuisine with a Japanese twist, this "friendly little place" is as eccentric on your tongue as it is on your eyes.
30 Prince St. (at Mott St.) (212) 274-0025. Hours: T-F 12pm-3:30pm, 5:30pm-11:30pm, Sa-Su 5:30pm-11:30pm. MC, V, AmEx, Entrées: $16-$22, N R to Prince St., B D F V to Broadway-Lafayette St.

The Mercer Kitchen
At this cafe specializing in American provincial food, you can sit under the sidewalk on a SoHo street in a glass-encased dining room and watch people walking above. The celebrity-spotting is fabulous, while the are prices impressive.
99 Prince St. (at Mercer St.), (212) 966-5454. Hours: Su-Sa 12pm-3pm, 6pm-12am. MC, V, AmEx, D, Entrées: $25-$30. N R to Prince St.

Palacinka
"It's anything you want it to be," says co-owner Tariq, but really this BYOB cafe specializes in serving tired SoHo shoppers delicious French-style crepes as a light meal or dessert. It's worth a visit just for the intriguing décor that is a smattering of random antiques amid metal tables and chairs that can be easily positioned for a private meeting over a cup of coffee.
28 Grand St. (bet. Sullivan St. and Thompson St.), (212) 625-0362. Hours: M-Sa 10:30am-12am. Cash only, Entrées: $6-$8. A C E to Canal St.

Penang
This lively, decked out Malaysian eatery is usually packed on weekends, and rightfully so; the food is innovative and tasty, the crowd generally young and hip. To avoid a wait, try eating in the bar downstairs, which features a lounge and live music.
109 Spring St. (bet. Greene and Mercer Sts.), (212) 274-8883, www.penangnyc.com. Hours: M-R 12pm-12am, F-Sa 12pm-1am, Su 1pm-11pm. MC, V, AmEx, D, Entrées: $11-$20. 6 to Spring St. Additional Locations:

1596 Second Ave. (at 83rd St.), (212) 585-3838
240 Columbus Ave. (at 71st St.), (212) 769-3988.

Public

Part restaurant, part bar, part heaven on steroids, Public is the future of restaurant style. With an exotic yet satisfying menu, you will not leave hungry. Be sure to visit the bar for unusual, refreshing, and tasty concoctions. This restaurant is sure to impress both yourself and any guest.
210 Elizabeth St., (212) 343-7011. MC, V, AmEx, Entrées: $18-$25. Hours: S-R 6pm-12am (bar until 2am), F-Sa 6pm-1am (bar until 2am). 6 to Spring St., N R to Prince St., F V to Broadway-Lafayette St., J M Z to Bowery St.

Rialto

First-time visitors are consistently wowed. The understated SoHo ambience and first-rate Continental food entice stunning neighborhood types time and again. Feast on the Chef's Tasting Menu (a three-, five-, or eight-course meal), which includes a potato leek soup infused with roasted garlic, served in a demitasse cup, while the staff shuffles back and forth to the magnificent garden out back.
265 Elizabeth St. (bet. Houston and Prince Sts.), (212) 334-7900. Hours: Su-Sa 11am-12am. MC, V, AmEx, Entrées: $8-$18. B D F V to Broadway-Lafayette St.

Rice

This tiny, cramped, healthy Asian joint has crowds around the block. It's cheap and takes cash only but is usually worth the wait. Light on both your wallet and waistline.
227 Mott St. (bet. Prince and Spring Sts.), (212) 226-5775, Hours: Su-Sa 12pm-12am. Cash Only. N R to Prince St., 6 to Spring St. Additional location in Brooklyn.

Salt

In honor of its name, Salt offers three different varieties of the spice on its communal tables: Hawaiian pink and French grey sea salts next to plain old Morton's. And that's exactly what chef/owner Melissa O'Donnell provides – refined simplicity and comfortable elegance. If you come with a date, hope for a two-top window seat, order a smooth wine, and enjoy a fantastic meal. Heartily recommended are the asparagus and sweet pea risotto, monkish with artichoke puree, and chocolate cake with almond olive oil ice cream.
58 Macdougal St, (bet. Houston and Prince Sts.) (212) 674-4968. Hours: Su-Sa 11am-3pm, 6pm-11pm. M, V, $31-$40. 1 to Houston St. B D F V at Broadway-Lafayette St., 6 to Bleecker St.

Spring Street Natural

Its wide windows are perfect for people watching. Despite the copious offerings of twigs and figs on the menu, there's plenty of chicken and fish to offer those not as healthfully inclined. The breads are unusual, the water get-it-yourself, and the staff somnolent, but the food is worth the wait, and the prices are good.
62 Spring St. (at Lafayette St.), (212) 966-0290. Hours: Su-Th 11:30am-11:30pm12am, F-Sa 11:30am-1am. MC, V, AmEx. 6 to Spring St.

Sui

With aqua colored walls, a mini waterfall at one end of the seating area, and tanks of exotic fish everywhere, the décor of this stellar sushi spot can best be described as oceanic. The underwater theme prevails in the atmosphere as well as in the food. Yet, in an interesting twist, terrestrial quarry make their way into your sushi as well; one of Sui's special sushi rolls come wrapped in prosciutto. Some other unique amalgamations have the raw fish slathered with Thai peanut sauce or drizzled with salsa. This place is great for sushi devotees and culinary adventurers alike.
54 Spring St., (bet. Lafayette and Mulberry St.), (212) 965-9838. Hours: M-R 12pm-3pm, 5pm-12am; F 12pm-3pm, 5pm-1am, Sat 5pm-2am. MC, V, AmEx, D, Entrées: $15-$30. J M Z to Bowery St., 6 to Spring St.

Woo Lae Oak

This Korean import has barbecue to die for, while preserving the SoHo intimacy. You know you're not in Benihana when Kate Hudson, Edward Norton, or Kevin Spacey float by your table. Try the filet mignon, black tail shrimp, or ostrich – all grilled tableside – or order the delicous cod in a spicy garlic sauce. It tastes like sugar was caramelized on top of it, creating perfect taste and texture. Every dish looks and tastes like a million bucks, establishing it as one of the city's best Asian restaurants. But be sure to save a spot for dessert. The homemade sorbets and other specialties are all in harmony with the restaurant's reputation.
148 Mercer St. (bet. Houston and Prince Sts.), (212) 925-8200. Hours: Su-R 12pm-11pm, F-Sa 12:00pm-11:30pm. MC, V, AmEx, D, Entrées: $14-24. N R to Prince St.

Zoë

The elegant décor and beautiful tables make it an appealing stop after walking the streets of SoHo. Booths line the walls and tables are set in the middle, offering the perfect amount of privacy – ideal for a first date. Zoë offers a seasonal menu with colorfully arranged dishes that thrill the taste buds and the eyes alike. The entrées are good, and the wait staff – attentive and well-timed – is happy to suggest its favorites. Don't be afraid to ask, especially about dessert.
90 Prince St. (bet. Broadway and Mercer St.), (212) 966-6722. Hours: T-R 12pm-3pm, 6pm-10:30pm, F 12pm-3pm, 6pm-11pm, Sa 11:30am-3pm, 5:30pm-11:30pm, Su 11:30am-3pm, 5:30pm-10pm. MC, V, AmEx, D. Entrées: $18-$28. N R to Prince St.

Cafes

Ceci-Cela

Homemade sorbet and café au lait evoke La Cote d'Azur at this charming patisserie perched on the

edge of Little Italy. The chat room in back is oh-so-perfect for nibbling on petit-fours and playing post-structuralist salon. The chocolate gateau and croissants are famous all over the city.
55 Spring St. (bet. Mulberry and Lafayette Sts.), (212) 274-9179. Hours: Su-R 7am-8pm. F-Sa 7am-10pm. MC, V. 6 to Spring St., N R to Prince St.

Once Upon A Tart
Delectable pastries, both savory and sweet, at lower prices than the standard coffeecakes served up by Manhattan's corporate chain espresso bars. Everything is made in their own bakery. Try a special that includes a tart and choice of salad. The crowd here is very loyal, and brunch is always packed.
135 Sullivan St. (bet. Houston and Prince Sts.), (212) 387-8869. Hours: M-F 8am-7pm, Sa 9am-7pm, Su 9am-6pm. MC, V, AmEx, D. C E to Spring St.

[East Village]

Restaurants

Angelica Kitchen
A vegetarian's paradise as well as an introductory course for vegan-phobic carnivores, Angelica's offers tangy soups, tofu and pesto sandwiches, and tofu-lemon "cheesecake." Portions are generous and very moderately priced.
300 E. 12th St. (bet. First and Second Aves.), (212) 228-2909. Hours: Su-Sa 11:30am-10:30pm. Cash only, Entrées: $6-$12. L to First Ave.

Around the Clock
There's not much to recommend during the day, but the late-late-night crowd qualifies as a revealing cross-section of the East Village. Depending on how far the hands are past midnight when you swing by, you'll spot either bleary-eyed club kids with the munchies killing time or early-morning regulars.
8 Stuyvesant St. (at Third Ave.), (212) 598-0402. Hours: Su-R 10am-3am, F-Sa 24hrs. MC, V, AmEx, D. Entrées: $5-$10. 6 to Astor Pl.

Bereket Turkish Kebab House
This 24-hour hot spot provides greasy Middle Eastern food. The best time to go is sometime after midnight when the place is packed, and the only people louder than the patrons are the staff.
187 E. Houston St. (at Orchard St.), (212) 475-7700. Hours: 24hrs. Cash only, Entrées $5-8. F V to Second Ave.

Boca Chica
Great for anyone who likes to have fun when paying to eat out. The atmosphere is decidedly festive and colorful, a perfect match for the South American and Caribbean food they serve. Best bets are the pork or seafood dishes, staples of the cuisine that you've probably never tasted before. All should definitely be accompanied by one of their exotic margaritas.
13 First Ave. (at 1st St.), (212) 473-0108. Hours: M-R 5:30pm-11pm, F-Sa 5:30pm-12am, Su 12pm-4pm (brunch), 5:30pm-11pm. MC, V, AmEx, D, Entrées: $8-$17. F V to Second Ave.

Café Pick Me Up
With a view of bustling Tompkins Square Park, Café Pick Me Up serves as a prime people-watching locale, particularly if you're fortunate enough to secure an outside table. In addition to its delicious beverages, Pick Me Up offers a wide array of tasty morsels to help refuel the weary traveler.
145 Ave. A (corner of 9th St.), (212) 673-7231. Hours: Su-R 6:30am-1:30am, F-Sa 6:30-2:30. L to First Ave.

Counter
Come to this hip vegetarian wine bar to experience some of the best organic food in the city. Everything from the clever entrees, such as the Cauliflower Risotto, to the delightful desserts, including a beautiful brownie sundae and perfect pecan pie, will make you realize how much of an improvement in taste is caused by high-quality natural ingredients. When there, be sure to try one of their many wines - this reviewer enjoyed a pleasant Riesling – to get the full organic experience.
105 First Ave. (bet. 6th and 7th St.), (212) 982-5870, www.counterrestaurant.com. Hours: M-R 5pm-12am; F 5pm-1am; Sa 11am-1am, Sun 11am-12am. MC, V, AmEx, D. Entrées: $15-$20. 6 to Astor Pl.

Cyclo
You can't miss this East Village eatery, what with the cyclo parked out front. The light, fresh Vietnamese cuisine more than compensates for the high noise volume and cramped tables. The jellyfish and shrimp salad in a chili lime dressing is one of the more unusual appetizers, and the oxtail broth with noodles, sliced beef, scallions, and fresh herbs will fill you up without bogging you down.
203 First Ave. (bet. 12th and 13th Sts.), (212) 673-3975. Hours: M-R 5pm-11pm, F-Sa 5pm-12am, Su 5:30pm-11:30pm. MC, V, AmEx, Entrées: $9-$14. L to First Ave.

Dojo
The American and Japanese influenced dishes really only please fans of macrobiotic fare, but the dirt-cheap prices and frisky social scene are enough to lure NYU undergrads away from their meal plans.
24 St. Mark's Pl. (bet. Second and Third Aves.), (212) 674-9821. Hours: Su-Th 11am-12am, F-Sa 11am-1 am. Cash only, Entrées: $4-$8. 6 to Astor Pl., N R to 8th St. Additional locations throughout Manhattan.

First
Show a date you're hip by eating at this swanky, late night crowd pleaser. Martinis come in several sizes, shapes, and flavors, while the seasonal menu offers an unusual mix of incredible dinners. The candle lit tables and low lighting may make you feel like you have entered a black & white movie.
87 First Ave. (bet. 5th and 6th Sts.), (212) 674-3823. Hours: M-R 6pm-2am, F-

Sa 6pm-3am, Su 11am-4pm, 5pm-1am. MC, V, AmEx, Entrées: $18-$22. F V *to Second Ave.*

Friendhouse

This pan-Asian restaurant serves up a wide variety of Asian cuisines, including sushi, spicy chicken with peanuts, and steaming preserved-fish hot-pots. The small, elegantly decorated restaurant has no air-conditioning, but does boast an outside seating area where diners can enjoy an occasional breeze - or brutal sun - with their meal. The minimalist concrete interior and forgettable jukebox make Friendhouse all about the food.
99 Third Ave. (bet. 12th and 13th Sts.) (212) 388-1838. Hours: Su-R 12pm-12am, F-Sa 12pm-1am. $20-$28. L *to Third Ave.*

Gnocco Cafe

On a warm night, step through the cozy asymmetrical dining room into the back garden. Tucked in between apartment buildings, the outdoor space has a welcome European feel. Candlelight, ivy, and good wine make this the ideal place for a romantic dinner and quiet conversation.
337 E. 10th St. (bet. Aves. A and B), (212) 677-1913, www.gnocco.com. Hours: M-F 4pm-12am, Sa-Su 11am-12am. Cash Only, Entrées: $8-$17. L *to First Ave.*

Hedeh

Hedeh stands out from the crowd of New York's hottest Japanese restaurants by focusing on food as their main concern rather than image. This is immediately apparent when you receive your appetizer; who would have known a Japanese restaurant could have some of the best foie qras in the city? As would be expected, the sushi is phenomenal, particularly the Dragon Roll. The entrees are excellently prepared, with the Prime Filet and Black Cod being particular standouts. The desserts are very un-American in that they aren't too sweet, and are a welcome reprieve from the heavy, rich chocolate cakes that are found at most popular steakhouses. Come to Hedeh for cuisine, not to be seen.
57 Great Jones St. (bet. Bowery and Lafayette St.), (212) 473-8458. Hours: M-Sa 5pm-12am. MC, V, AmEx, D, Entrées: $23-$27. 6 *to Bleecker St.*

Kai Kai Thai Bistro

Eat like a king on a poor man's budget at this tiny East Village BYOB. Be careful – the pad thai and steamed dumplings are so good, one of the neighboring customers might reach over for a bite.
131 Ave. A, (212) 420-5909. Hours: Su-Sa 12pm-11pm. Cash Only, $8-$20. L *to First Ave.*

Kate's Joint

Kate's serves cheap vegan cuisine in a diner atmosphere, complete with fake bacon and tofu mayo. They serve some nice salads and veggie burgers that fill that greasy need after a night of drinking.
58 Ave. B (at 4th St.) (212) 777-7059. Hours: Su-R 9am-12am, F-Sa 9am-2am. MC, V, AmEx, D. Entrées: $4-$13. F V *to Second Ave.,* N R *to 8th St.,* 6 *to Astor Pl.*

Khyber Pass

With Persian rug place mats, subdued lights of red and blue, ceilinq drapery like the inside of a genie bottle, and a choice of authentic floor-style seating, Khyber Pass offers a unique cultural experience. From Baulanee Kadu, a spiced pumpkin turnover served with yogurt dip, to the Kabuli and Shireen Palow, which are lamb and Cornish hen dishes, Afghan cuisine is served at its finest. Best of all, it is inexpensive and smack in the center of the trendiest part of New York.
34 St. Mark's Pl. (bet. Second and Third Ave.), (212) 473-0989. Hours: Su-Sa 12pm-1am. MC, V, AmEx, Entrées: $6-$12. 6 *to Astor Pl.*

Lanza's

Authentic Italian food sans gimmicks or fancy perversions. The clientele is large and loyal, filling the restaurant nightly for both the classy old-style ambiance and superior food at bargain prices. Thankfully, it's neither trendy nor cutting-edge.
168 First Ave. (bet. 10th and 11th Sts.), (212) 674-7014. Hours: Su-Sa 12pm-11pm. MC, V, AmEx, Entrées: $11-$17. L N R W 4 5 6 *to 14th St.-Union Sq.*

Le Tableau

An unusual reprieve from typical East Village flamboyance, this adorable French restaurant offers high quality food and wonderful service to a casual mix of clientele. The daily rotating specials menu should encourage you to make repeat visits, but be sure you make a reservation on Friday and Saturday nights for parties of five and more to enjoy the live jazz band (and remember that a full band in a popular restaurant makes for cozy dining).
511 E. 5th St. (bet. Aves. A and B), (212) 260-1333. Hours: M-R 6pm-11pm, F-Sa 5:30pm-12am, Su 6pm-10pm. MC, V, AmEx, Entrées: $10-$18. F V *to Second Ave.*

Life Cafe

Featured in the Broadway play *Rent*, this eclectic source of nutritious Cal-Mex is an East Village landmark of laid-back creativity. Check out the rotating exhibits by local artists, preferably during the weekday happy hour (5pm-9pm).
343 E. 10th St. (at Ave. B), (212) 477-8791, www.lifecafenyc.com. Hours: Su-R 10am-12am, F-Sa 10am-2am. MC, V, D, Entrées: $7-$12. L *to First Ave.*

Lucky Cheng's and Waikiki Wally's

If you like theme restaurants but are tired of bored service and cruddy décor, head over to Lucky Cheng's for a fun way to freak out your square folks. The food is good, but it's watching the impromptu lap dances that will provide true titillation. Watch as confused tourists get pulled on stage, are partially denuded, and made subject to crazed drag queen whimsy. Once tipsy, descend to the karaoke "Jungle Lounge" to join in the fun and embarrass yourself further. If you want a better meal than Lucky Cheng's can provide, or

just less craze, check out the abutting Waikiki Wally's for Hawaiian kitsch and a fun time. The drag queens are absent, but the cute, male wait staff still please the eye with their sarongs and quirky mannerisms.
24 First Ave. (bet. 1st and 2nd Sts.), (212) 473-0516, www.planetluckychengs.com. Hours: Su-Sa 6pm-12am. MC, V, AmEx. F V to Second Ave.

Ludo
The decor of Ludo will immediately draw you in as you enter it's dark and romantic hallways. The ambiance of the restaurant is pure middle eastern, with candles being the main source of light for most of the rooms. The food is excellent, and much better than any falafel you may have gotten from the corner stand. The bread and butter is delicious, with the butter having a decidedly salty tang. The foie gras was delicious, as was the Lamb Two Ways - filling, yet light. The desserts were particularly interesting, with the Date Roll Ups - a unique combination of dates and cheesecake - being a particular (albeit small) favorite. If you are ever in the area, make sure to check out Ludo for an interesting take on Middle Eastern Food.
42 E. 1st St. (bet. First Ave. and Ave. A), (212) 777-5617. Hours: Su-Sa 6pm-12am. MC, V, AmEx, D. F V to Second Ave.

Mama's Food Shop
Mama is, in fact, a man who cooked so much food for his friends that his space evolved into a restaurant. All the food is home-style excellence, and the portions are huge. Try the grilled salmon and don't miss the awesome mac-and-cheese. Across the street, get soup and sandwiches at Step Mama's, a spin-off.
200 E. 3rd St. (at Ave. B), (212) 777-4425. Hours: M-Sa 12pm-10pm. Cash only, Entrées: $6-$8. F V to Second Ave.

Mamlouk
The prix fixe menu changes monthly at this Middle Eastern, vegetarian-friendly restaurant, but you can always expect six delicious courses. After your meal, enjoy a hookah the size of a small child with rose or strawberry tobacco as you lounge on the couches.
211 E. 4th St. (bet. Aves. A and B), (212) 529-3477. Hours: T-Su seatings at 7pm and 9pm. MC, V, AmEx, Prix-fixe: $30. F V to Second Ave.

Mermaid Inn
This remarkably refreshing seafood restaurant boasts not only delectable food, but warm and friendly servers and a great atmosphere. If people-watching is what you want, there are plenty of seats outside on Second Avenue. Or head into the backroom where you feel you are in Nantucket eating seafood that is so fresh it could have been caught earlier that morning. An outdoor garden patio adds a more intimate and secluded feel to the already charming space. The staff was extremely knowledgeable about the menu, prepared and willing to make both food and wine recommendations. All ingredients were very fresh and it was evident a lot of care was put into each dish. There are delicious side items that really complimented the entrees; a must is the asparagus home fries. The whole experience puts you in the mood for Cape Cod.
96 Second Ave. (bet. 5th and 6th St.), (212)-674-5870, www.themermaidnyc.com. Hours: M-W 5:30pm-10pm; R-Sa 5:30pm-11pm, Su 5pm-10pm. MC, V, AmEx, D, Entrées: $17-$22. F V to Second Ave., 6 to Astor Pl.

Mitali
The stretch of 6th St. between First and Second Aves. is overrun with mediocre Indian food joints – but Mitali isn't one of them. Most of the chicken dishes here are quite tasty and not too greasy, and they give you a lot of bang for your buck. Great place to take a family member and talk.
334 E. 6th St. (bet. First and Second Aves.), (212) 533-2508. Hours: Su-Sa 12pm-12am. MC, V, AmEx, D, Entrées: $7-$10. F V to Second Ave.

Nino's Pizza
There must be a thousand different slice joints in this city, but this is without a doubt one of the very best. In addition to making great pizza, the place looks out on Tompkins Square Park and keeps hours as late as any bar. A plain slice is always a safe bet, but those wanting more shouldn't miss out on the white pizza with fresh tomatoes.
131 St. Mark's Pl. (at Ave. A), (212) 979-8688. Hours: Su-Sa 11am-4am. Cash Only, Entrées: $10. 6 to Astor Pl.

Nolita House
This appropriately titled restaurant is located in the newest "hippest-place-to-be" in the city. Run by an incredibly affable former Columbia University grad, Nolita House offers comfort food with high-quality ingredients. The entrées are delicious, particularly the tuna. The real star of the menu, though, is the artisinal cheeses that can serve as an appetizer or dessert. Do not leave Nolita House without sampling one of the excellent cheese plates - you will not be disappointed.
7 E. Houston St. (bet. Mulberry and Mott St.), (212) 625-1712, www.nolitahouse.com. Hours: M-F 11:30am-3:30pm, Su-R 5pm-11pm, F-Sa 5pm-1am, Sa-Su 11:30am-4pm. MC, V, AmEx, D. Entrées: $15-$20. B D F V to Broadway-Lafayette St., 6 to Bleecker St.

Odessa
One of the hippest Eastern European diners, open 24 hours. Everything from standard diner food to potato pancakes and other regional fare finds its way onto the menu. The location makes it perfect for a food break while cruising the Avenue A bar scene, and to continue drinking you need only walk next door to their lounge, where the cheapest gin and tonics in Manhattan are served by a surly, older babushka.
119 Ave. A (bet. 7th and 8th Sts.), (212) 253-1470. Hours: 24hrs. MC, V, AmEx, Entrées: $6-$12. F V to Second Ave., L to First Ave.

Paquito's Restaurant

Think California taquerias transported to NYC. Paquito's has all the prerequisite items like burritos, enchiladas, and tacos, but is a step above most of the New York joints that dare to call themselves Mexican.
143 First Ave. (bet. St. Mark's Pl. and 9th St.), (212) 674-2071. Hours: Su-Sa 11am-11:30pm. MC, V, AmEx, Entrées: $2-$7. F V to Second Ave., 6 to Astor Pl.

Pommes Frites

Nothing to expect at this cramped spot except for Belgian fries in a paper cone. There's only one type of fry to be had here, but try one of several toppings, including mustard, ketchup, peanut sauce, and some spicier condiments. The service is quick, and you probably won't spend more than five bucks or five minutes as you grab your fries and go on your way.
123 Second Ave. (at 7th St.), (212) 674-1234. Hours: Su-R 11:30 am-1am, F-Sa 11:30am-2am. Cash only. 6 to Astor Pl., N R to 8th St.

Shabu Tatsu

This authentic Japanese version of cook-it-yourself soups is fun, messy, and healthy. With lots of succulent meat and vegetables, you can boil your own meal then dip it into the yummy sauce and top it off with rice.
216 E. 10th St. (bet. First and Second Aves.), (212) 477-2972. Hours: Su-R 5pm-11:30am, F-Sa 5pm-2am. MC, V, AmEx, D. 6 to Astor Pl., N R to 8th St.

Smoked

This cheeky southern barbeque spot serves up soulfood favorites with a sassiness that pervades everything from the décor to the sauté. Giant screens boast tossing flames coupled with a live DJ spinning rock, soul, and hip-hop. All of the barbequed items are cooked in a customized smoking pit that spits out tender and juicy riblets and BBQ chicken that are as savory as they are satisfying. The beer flows amply, with remarkable variation; the signature "Lynchburg Lemonade" tastes like Mom's but has enough kick to spur a night of revelry. Enjoy the hearty side dishes and be sure to try your meat with all three of their special homemade sauces.
103 Second Ave., (at 6th St.), (212) 388-0388. Hours: M-S 5pm-11pm. MC, V, AmEx, D. Entrées: $10-$17. 6 to Astor Pl.

Supper

The people may be hot, but the pasta's even hotter. Don't miss the Priest Stranglers and the daily risotto special. Stop in on Saturday for the one flavored with pricey Amarone wine. Be prepared to sip a few glasses of wine in the cramped but stylish bar next door while you wait for a place at one of the rustic communal tables.
156 E. 2nd St., (212) 477-7600. Hours: Su-R 5pm-12:30am, F-Sa 5pm-1:30am. Cash Only, $21-$30. F V to Second Ave.

St. Dymphna's

Guinness in the morning, Guinness in the evening, Guinness at suppertime. Enjoy a traditional Irish breakfast in this traditional Irish pub. After a few draughts, you'll be spending the rest of the afternoon hunting for leprechauns. Erin go bragh!
118 St. Mark's Pl., (212) 254-6636. Hours: Su-Sa 10:30am-4am. MC, V, AmEx, D. $5 and up. 6 to Astor Pl.

Step Mama

Right across the street from Mama's is this sandwich, soup, salads, and dessert shop. Step in and order one of their large, tasty chicken or meatloaf sandwiches, or maybe just one of the big cookies on your way home from work. It's cheap take-out food (you can eat in, too) that hits the spot.
199 E. 3rd St. (at Ave. B), (212) 228-2663. Hours: Su-Sa 11am-10pm. Cash only, Entrées: $5-$8. L to First Ave., F V to Second Ave.

Teresa's

Vegetarians and dieters should steer clear of this stalwart, as old-world as you can get, Polish standby where middle-aged patrons sit amid thickly-framed oil paintings and happily devour big, meaty dinners. Be sure to start with the pierogi, and then order the thin, tender breaded veal cutlet.
103 First Ave. (at 6th St.), (212) 228-0604. Hours: Su-Sa 7am-11pm. V, MC, AmEx, D. Entrées: $8-$13. N R to 8th St, L to First Ave., 6 to Astor Pl.

Tocqueville

Intimate and refined, Tocqueville combines elegance with friendliness. Be sure to ask for suggestions because the house specialties are truly special. The Sixty Second Beef is a sure bet for the carnivores out there. Just make sure you're sitting down as you take the first bite.
15 E. 15th St. (212) 647-1515. Hours:M-Sa 5:30pm-10:30pm, Su 5pm-10pm. AmEx. Entrées: $27-$33. L N R W 4 5 6 to Union Sq.

Two Boots Restaurant

Two Boots specializes in Cajun-Creole fare, offering creative pizzas with kitschy names like "The Divine" and "Mrs. Peel", and lots of vegan options. The restaurant got it's name from the fact that both Sicily and Louisianna are shaped like boots. In other words, it's for the coolest kids in town. As a bonus, the food's really good too. Just eye the slices before you buy, as sometimes they hang around a little too long.
37 Ave. A (at 3rd St.), (212) 505-2276. Hours: M-Th 5pm-11pm, F-Sa 5pm-12am, Su 4pm-10pm. MC, V, AmEx, D, Entrées $8-10. F V to Second Ave.
Additional locations in Manhattan.

CAFES

Alt.Coffee

The comfy couches are here because you'll be sitting awhile, checking your emaill and figuring out where you'll go tonight. The staff is as handy with the latte maker as they are with any of your

Internet questions.
139 Ave. A (at 9th St.), (212) 529-2233. Hours: M-F 7am-1:30am, Sa-Su 10am-2am. Cash only. L *to First Ave.*

Cafe Orlin

Blend in by ordering an espresso, and then quickly whipping out some sort of portfolio. Leave it open on the table and enjoy a smoky omelette or a slice of chocolate cake. Most regulars are artsy East Village chain smokers and aspiring directors. The low-angle view allows a glimpse of the shoes passing by on St. Marks Place.
41 St. Marks Pl. (bet. First and Second Aves.), (212) 777-1447. Hours: Su-R 9am-1:30am, F-Sa 24hrs. MC, V. N R *to 8th St.,* 6 *to Astor Pl.*

Casa Adela

This cafe was started by the proprietor Luis Rivera's mother, and has been around for over 20 years. Its cooking is classic, its décor clean and bright. Try the chicken and rice, as Adela may be the epitome of boricua cooking. You might feel out of the loop not speaking Spanish, but the welcome is just as warm in English.
66 Ave. C (bet. 4th and 5th Sts.), (212) 473-1882. Hours: Su-Sa 7am-8pm. Cash Only, Entrées: $6-8. F V *to Second Ave.*

Masturbakers

The most popular item at this appropriately titled bakery, housed in the Old Devil Moon restaurant, is the penis cake. Their breast cake, bearing the words "Breast Wishes," runs a close second. With moist devil's food cake, rich frosting and naughty details, their bakery lives up to their motto: "Tasty but tasteless."
511 E. 12th St. (bet. Aves. A and B), (212) 475-0476. Hours: M-F 10am-5pm. MC, V, AmEx. L *to First Ave.*

Veniero's

Whether you just broke up with someone or are looking for a place to chat for hours, Veniero's fits the bill. Either way, try the scrumptious pastries and great drinks. One of the best cafes in the city.
342 E. 11th St. (bet. First and Second Aves.), (212) 674-7070, www.homedelivery.com. Hours: Su–Sa 8am-12am. MC, V, AmEx, D. L *to First Ave.*

Veselka

This upscale Ukrainian cafe has good service, fun décor and great prices. Try the kasha, the pierogies, or the sausages. Always packed with students and artists. The brunch is fab, and so are the crepes.
144 Second Ave. (at 9th St.), (212) 228-9682, Hours: 24 hrs. MC, V, AmEx, D. N R to 8th St., 6 *to Astor Pl.*

Yaffa Cafe

This East Village funkadelic cafe serves up reasonably priced sandwiches, salads, pastas, omelets, and crepes, as well as a handsome selection of vegetarian items and unbelievable desserts. Enjoy the kitschy decor and sit outdoors when weather permits to observe the goings-on at St. Mark's Place.
97 St. Mark's Pl. (bet. First Ave. and Ave. A), (212) 677-9001. Hours: 24hrs. MC, V, AmEx. N R *to 8th St.,* 6 *to Astor Pl.*

[Greenwich Village]

Bars

Cones

Take only a truly empty stomach to this West Village dairy haven. Choose from an array of summery sorbets, but serious ice cream fans must not skip the full-bodied flavors on the other side of the case. Among the usual tastes, you'll find a delicious Zabayone and a sinful dark chocolate. Bear in mind that what tickles the palate will tickle the pocketbook and wasitline too.
272 Bleecker St., (212) 414-1795. Hours: Su-R 1pm-11pm, F-Sa 1pm-1am. Cash only, $5-$20. A B C D E F V W *to W.4th St.*

Citron

This is a restaurant that goads you to boast about your experience, but keeps you quiet for fear of the word spreading too far. This cozy gem serves fantastic French-American small plates inspired by the infinite imagination of its owner, Gavin Citron. This reviewer must insist that this is the ultimate setting for that most special of dates: the restaurant seats only fifty people, and the attendant tranquility gives Citron that ideal intimate and amorous candlelight ambiance. To elevate the romance and the dining experience to a climax, put yourself and your meal in the knowing hands of Gavin; try his delightful six course winepairing. It will excite your sensibilities in untold ways and leave you utterly satisfied without feeling over-stuffed.
228 Bleecker St. (bet. Carmine St. and Sixth Ave.), (212) 924-9717, Hours: M-F 12pm-3pm, 6pm-11pm, Sa 11am-4pm, 6pm-11pm, Su 11am-4pm, 6pm-10pm. MC, V, AmEx, D. Entrées: $20-$30. A B C D E F V *to W. 4th St.*

Cornelia Street Cafe

Enjoy the leisurely ambiance of soothing lights and a background blend of jazz and blues while accompanies the similarly unforced New American cuisine. Venture downstairs after dinner to catch nightly theater, jazz, and poetry performances in the cabaret.
29 Cornelia St. (bet. Bleecker and W. 4th Sts.), (212) 989-9318, www.corneliastreetcafe.com. Hours: Su-R 10am-1am. MC, V, AmEx, D, Entrées: $12-$15. A B C D E F V *to W. 4th St.* 1 *to Christopher St.*

Corner Bistro

Locals lament the marathon waits at this immensely popular burger-and-beer joint, but they still throng despite the slow service. It's the prime territory to see and be seen. It is the basic, effortlessly, and funky version of the neighborhood haunt made palatable to yuppie Villagers by virtue of its enduring cachet and steady stream of televised college basketball games. Tables long ago marked by penknives crowd the middle, although intimate space may be free in back.
331 W. 4th St. (at Eighth

Ave.), (212) 242-9502. *Hours: Su-Sa 11:30am-3am. Cash only, Entrées: $4-$6.* A C E L *to 14th St.*

Cowgirl Hall of Fame

Before riot-grrls there were cowgirls, and at this Greenwich Village fave owner Sherry Delamarter won't let gringos forget. Come for the history lesson and eclectic Chuckwagon dishes like Eggplant Fritters and Frito Pie. Its mostly lesbian clientele revel in the place's unabashed homage to the cowgirls of yesteryear, right down to the gift shop full of cowgirly souvenirs. Check out the suit of armor as you go through the doors.
519 Hudson St. (at 10th St.), (212) 633-1133. Hours: Su-R 10am-11pm, F-Sa 10am-12am. MC, V, AmEx, Entrées: $8-$15. 1 *to Christopher St.*

Da Andrea

Although located in an area with dozens of Italian restaurants, Da Andrea stands out for its outstanding Northern Italian decor and hearty servings. Though it can get a bit crowded, make sure to stop in if you would like to eat delicious food while scoping out all the beautiful people walking out of the nearby gymnasiums.
557 Hudson St, (212) 367-1979. Hours: Su-R 5:30pm-10pm, F-Sa 5:30pm-11pm. MC. M, V, $21-$30. A C E L *to 14th St.*

Florent

This meat-packing district standby has the bad lighting of a '50s diner, but the entirely French menu is undeniably good – the steak frites can compete with even the city's best brasseries (Pastis is right around the corner). Long hours, a crowd of New York hipsters and clubgoers, and a wait staff that is both attractive and French make Florent an experience to be enjoyed.
69 Gansevoort St. (bet. Greenwich and Washington Sts.), (212) 989-5779. Hours: 24 hours. Cash only, Entrées: $12-$18. 1 2 3 *to 14th St.*

Garage Restaurant & Cafe

Suburban steakhouse meets Greenwich Village panache at this sprawling multi-leveled village favorite. Its famous weekend jazz brunch offers both top-notch music and a mean eggs benedict. During the week, come for the music but stay for the unforgettable mussels or their hearty sandwiches and raw bar.
99 Seventh Ave. South (at Grove St.), (212) 645-0600. Hours: Su-R 12pm-2am, F-Sa 12pm-3am. MC, V, AmEx, Entrées: $8-$25. 1 *to Christopher St.*

Go Sushi

This unique restaurant capitalizes on both the sushi trend and the still burgeoning coffee bar culture: sleek stools and tattered copies of *Paper* meet sushi samples of fatty tuna and salmon prepared fresh around-the-clock by an in-house chef. Wash it all down with Go's own freshly brewed ginger ale.
3 Greenwich Ave. (bet. Sixth Ave. and 8th St.),., (212) 366-9272. Hours: Su-Sa 11:30am-11:30pm. MC, V, AmEx. A B C D E F V *to W. 4th St.,* 1 *to Christopher St.*

Gotham Bar and Grill

Architecturally brilliant Entrées like Atlantic salmon with ramps, morels, sweet peas, and chervil betray the hand of one of the city's finest gourmets, Alfred Portale, and his kitchen team of all-star chefs have come together to make Gotham's New American cuisine a staple for New York connoisseurs. Entrées bypass typical meats for rabbit, pheasant, and a couple so rare they're probably endangered. Sample it all with a $19.99 prix fixe lunch in the spacious, angular dining room. Don't pass up the most divine warm chocolate cake in all of New York.
12 E. 12th St. (bet. Fifth Ave. and University Pl.), (212) 620-4020. Hours: M-R 12pm-2:15pm, 5:30pm-10:30pm, F 12pm-2:15pm, 5pm-11:30pm, Sa 5pm-11:30pm, Su 5pm-10:30pm. MC, V, AmEx, D, Entrées: $25-$40. L N R W 4 5 6 *to 14th St.-Union Sq.*

Home

The name conjures up the American iconography of mom and apple pie, but despite the low pretension and familiar line-up of pork chops and chocolate pudding, this refined Village eatery is a bit too urban to qualify as a suburban transplant. Chefs may not infuse the catfish with mom's love, but they are committed to resisting the strong French trends in New American cuisine, instead steering culinary attention toward hometown faves. Home's homemade ketchup proves again why classics never go out of style.
20 Cornelia St. (bet. Bleecker and W. 4th Sts.), (212) 243-9579. Hours: M-F 9am-4pm, 5pm-11pm, Sa-Su 10:30pm-4:30pm, 5:30pm-11pm. MC, V, AmEx, Entrées: $13-$19. A B C D E F V *to W. 4th St.,* 1 *to Christopher St.*

John's

This thin, coal-oven-baked pizza is preceded by its well-deserved reputation. A good place for groups to hang out, offering no slices, only whole pies. A truly excellent pizzeria.
278 Bleecker St. (bet. Sixth and Seventh Aves.), (212) 243-1680. Hours: Su-Sa 12pm-11:30pm. Cash Only, Entrées: $12. A B C D E F V *to W. 4th St.,* 1 *to Christopher St.*

Maurizio Trattoria

Come here to experience some of the finest Italian dining in the city. Unlike other Americanized Italian eateries, Maurizio Trattoria delivers delicious food at normal portions. Everything this reviewer had was excellent, although the Veal Ravioli and Lamb Chops "Scottadito" were particularly divine. Do not leave Maurizio's without having at least one dessert. The chocolate cake was of incredible quality, and will teach those who swear by Godiva what real chocolate is.
35 W 13th St. (bet. 5th & 6th Ave), (212) 206-6474. Hours: Su-Sa 12pm-

11:30pm. Cash Only, Entrées: $15-$26. 1 2 3 *to 14th St.*

Mi Cocina

Mexican cuisine, West Village-style: haute, pricey, and with a generous supply of liquor. The most savory south-of-the-border dishes here may not be authentic, but the place is chic. Lunch is only served Thursday and Fridays from 11:30am-2:30pm.
57 Jane St. (at Hudson St.), (212) 627-8273. Hours: M-R 4:30pm-10:45pm, F-Sa 11am-3:30pm, 4:30pm-11:45pm, Su 4:30pm-10:15pm. MC, V, AmEx, D, Entrées: $13-$22. A C E L *to 14th St.*

Mirchi

Perfect for those looking to enjoy the eclectic experience of Indian ambiance and hospitality as you savor a range of flavors and cuisines. The menu is a distillation of the principals' favorites from all over India. The most unique feature of the restaurant is the tawa station facing the dining room, where diners choose from a variety of meats and vegetables and watch the cook as they prepare your meal for you. The restaurant also boasts an attractive and comfortable lounge on the lower level where a light dinner menu and cocktails are served.
29 Seventh Ave. South (bet. Morton and Bedford Sts.) (212) 414-0931. Hours: M-R 12pm-12am, Fri-Sat 12pm-1am Sun 12pm-11pm. MC, V, AmEx, D. Entrées:: $10-$19. A B C E D E F V *to W. 4th St.,* 1 *to Christopher St.*

Monte's

Around since 1918, the charm of this amicable basement trattoria will remain long after the taste has slipped away. The menu spares no calorie, so go all the way and try the zabaglione served cold with strawberries.
97 MacDougal St. (at W. 3rd St.), (212) 228-9194, Hours: Su-M, W-R 12pm-11pm, F-Sa 12pm-11:30pm, MC, V, AmEx, D, Entrées: $7-$13. A B C D E F V *to W. 4th St.,* 1 *to Christopher St.*

Moustache

Nestled on a peaceful back street in the West Village, Moustache transports you to a more pleasant time and place, a feeling intensified by the delicious food, from traditional fare such as the merguez sandwich to their innovative "pitzas." Also try Moustache's East Village location at 265 E. 10th St., famed for its garden.
90 Bedford St. (bet. Grove and Barrow Sts.), (212) 229-2220. Hours: Su-Sa 12pm-12am. Cash only, Entrées: $5-$12. A B C D E F V *to W. 4th St.,* 1 *to Christopher St.*

One if by Land, Two if by Sea

Don't be fooled by the unassuming exterior of this converted 200-year-old carriage house once owned by Aaron Burr. With an extensive wine list and an exquisite tasting menu, this gem of colonial history provides for the ultimate in romantic dining experiences. The Bluefin Tartare is great and the superb Beef Wellington is rightfully called the house specialty. The knowledgeable wait staff is more than happy to talk about the restaurant's history or unassumingly help you choose which utensil is appropriate for the next course.
17 Barrow St. (bet. Seventh Ave. and W. 4th St.), (212) 228-0822. Hours: Su-Sa 5:30pm-11pm. MC, V, AmEx, D, Entrées: $41-$60. A B C D E F V *to W. 4th St.,* 1 *to Christopher St.*

Ono

Located within the Hotel Gansevoort, this snazzy spot is best described as an Asian Fusion - it serves up unparalleled Eastern delicacies in an interior setting apropos of Hollywood glam. Outside is a dreamy outdoor courtyard, where sofa-laden private cabanas make for a picturesquely intimate evening. The menu includes an impressive assortment of succulent meats and fish cooked over an open flame robata grill, a signature selection of sushi, and a choice of large plates that are ideal for sharing. Do not neglect their exceptional cocktails: the "blushing Geisha" is out of this world.
18 Ninth Ave. (at Gansevoort St.), (212) 660-6766. Hours: M-Su 7am-11am, 12pm-3pm, Su-W 5pm-11pm, T-Sa 5pm-12am. MC, V, AmEx, D, Entrées: $20-$40. A C E L *to 14th St.-Eighth Ave.*

Pão!

When dinning at Pão! watch motorcycles and taxis clatter up the street.

Framed menus feature delicious Portuguese seafood dishes, but the steak, topped with garlic and spicy cream sauce, is their specialty. A small bar awaits inside.
322 Spring St. (at Greenwich St.), (212) 334-5464. Hours: M-F 12pm-2:30pm, 6pm-11pm, Sa-Su 6pm-11pm. MC, V, AmEx, Entrées: $14-$17. C E to Spring St.

Peanut Butter & Co.

As the name suggests, this cozy little take-out cafe serves peanut butter in all forms, ranging from classic fluffernutters and peanut butter pie to unorthodox PB&J shakes. Prices are high ($6.50 for most sandwiches), but that doesn't keep NYU students and local businessmen from packing the place at lunchtime.
240 Sullivan St. (bet. Bleecker and W. 3rd Sts.), (212) 677-3995. Hours: Su-R 11am-9pm, F-Sa 11am-10pm, MC, V, AmEx, D. Entrées: $5-7. A B C D E F V to W. 4th St., 1 to Christopher St.

Petite Abeille

Scads of Tintin paraphernalia and tasty Belgian bites make this a popular feature of Little Belgium. Absolutely divine fries and mussels. Go, Tintin, go!
400 W. 14th St. (bet. Ninth and Tenth Aves.), (212) 727-1505. Hours: M-R 7am-4pm, 5pm-11pm, F 7am-4pm, 5pm-11:30pm, Sa 9am-4pm, 5pm-11:30pm, Su 9am-4pm, 5pm-11pm. Cash only, Entrées: $10-$12. A C E L to 14th St. Additional location at Hudson St., (212) 741-6479.

Pó

So popular that it is not uncommon to require reservations a month in advance, this charming little West Village Italian restaurant draws in customers with its warm atmosphere, reasonable prices and generous portions. Whether the quality of the food lives up to the restaurant's reputation is debatable, it nonetheless makes for a trendy evening out.
31 Cornelia St. (bet. Bleecker and W. 4th Sts.), (212) 645-2189. Hours: T-R 11:30am-2:30pm, 5:30pm-11pm, F-Sa 11:30am-2:30pm, 5:30pm-11:30pm, Su 11:30am-2:30pm, 5pm-10pm. AmEx, Entrées: $15. A B C D E F V to W. 4th St., 1 to Christopher St.

Prem-on Thai

Careful, or you might miss it! Look closely and you'll find this hidden gem in the West Village. The American infused Thai cuisine will have you reaching a little deeper into your wallet, but not running for the bathroom. Most often the presentation outperforms the food, but here you will find beautiful displays and sumptuous fare. Make sure to walk through this magnificent display of modern Asian/American architecture and relax out in the "mini garden" with some cocktails.
138 W. Houston St, (bet. MacDougal & Sullivan St.), (212) 353-2338. Hours: M-Su: 5:30pm-11pm. MC, V, AmEx, D, Entrées: $14-20. 1 to Houston St.

Quantum Leap

Handpicking the best in natural dishes that Mexico, Japan, and the Middle East have to offer, this healthy kitchen excels at weekend breakfasts which include whole grain, buckwheat, or blue corn waffles and/or pancakes smothered with organic maple syrup. Not exactly the ascetic way, but better than bacon.
226 Thompson St. (bet. 3rd and Bleecker Sts.), (212) 677-8050. Hours: M-F 11:30am-11pm, Sa 11am-11pm, Su 11am-10pm. MC, V, AmEx, D, Entrées: $5-$10. A B C D E F V to W. 4th St., 1 to Christopher St.

Sammy's Noodle Shop and Grill

An indispensable lunch fixture for hurried urbanites, with an annexed bakery serving fresh desserts. The roast meat soups and dumplings will hit the spot any day.
453 Sixth Ave. (bet 10th and 11th Sts.), (212) 924-6688. Hours: Su-Sa 11:30am-12am. MC, V, AmEx, D. Entrées: $10-$12. A B C D E F V to W. 4th St., 1 to Christopher St.

Sant Ambreous

In a move as stunning as a Yankee voluntarily choosing to be a Met, Sant Ambroeus moves from the Upper East Side to the West Village. Nonetheless, you'll still marvel at their cakes in the window display, and notice that the prices have remained infamously overpriced. Rumor has it that the cakes are prettier than they are tasty. Still, there's no shortage of patrons at this Northern Italian cafe, where the cappuccini and gelati are to die for. Think of it as a taste of Italy with an Upper East Side attitude pining for West Village street cred.
259 W. 4th St. (at Perry St.), (212) 604-9254. Hours: M-F 7:30am-7pm, Sa 9am-7pm, Su 10am-6pm. MC, V, AmEx, Entrées: $20-$30. 6 to 77th St.

Souen

Downtown New Yorkers may delight in their manufactured indulgences, but this unassuming, primarily macrobiotic restaurant has been helping them get in touch with their earthier side for twenty years. The Japanese influenced menu specializes in dishes featuring tempeh, seitan, and organic vegetables, while the sugar-free futomaki and tempeh croquettes are noteworthy.
28 E. 13th St. (bet. University Pl. and Fifth Ave.), (212) 627-7150. Hours: M-Sa 10am-11pm, Su 10am-10pm. MC, V, AmEx, D. Entrées: $8-$16. L N R W 4 5 6 to 14th St.-Union Sq.

Strip House

Strip House is unique in that its atmosphere is decidedly less male-oriented than your average steakhouse. The perfect place for a date, Strip House doesn't disappoint in any sense of the word. The filet is fantastic, and the swordfish is soothing. Every side was phenomenal, although the creamed spinach - creamy, yet light - is a personal favorite. The desserts were gigantic; no human may able to complete Strip House's

24-layer Chocolate Cake, though be sure to try. Made up like a bordello, Strip House provides one with a steakhouse experience that no other restaurant in the city comes close to imagining. Come here and make that friend of yours into something more.
13 E. 12th St. (bet University Pl. and Fifth Ave.), (212) 328-0000, www.theglaziergroup.com. Hours: M-R 5pm-11:30pm, F-Sa 5pm-12am, Su 5pm-11pm. MC, V, AmEx, D. Entrées: $20-$35. L N R W 4 5 6 *to 14th St.-Union Sq.*

Surya
This chic West Village Indian restaurant offers a unique array of tastes several notches above its counterparts in the East Village. Fresh seafood glazed with a subtle date sauce, perfectly spiced Basmati, and various creamy deserts with a hint of cardamom, make Surya a must-visit. Wash it down with a "Tajamopolitan" or other unique specialty drinks.
302 Bleecker St. (bet. Seventh Ave. South and Grove St.), (212) 807-7770. Hours: Su-F 12pm-3pm, 5:30pm-11pm, F-Sa 12pm-3pm, 5:30pm-12am. MC, V, AmEx, D. Entrées: $16-$24. A B D E F V *to W. 4th St.,* 1 *to Christopher St.*

Tartine
There's nothing more pleasant on a Sunday morning than brunch at Tartine, with sun shining through the floor-to-ceiling windows and birds chirping. The menu is standard and portions are hardly generous, but the staff has orange juice on the table by the time patrons sit down. Alas, by noon the wait outside is 45 minutes, but here's a tip: they actually open at 9am for coffee, not the posted 10:30am.
253 W. 11th St. (at Seventh Ave.), (212) 229-2611. Hours: T-F 9am-10:30pm, Sa-Su 10:30am-4pm, 5:30pm-10:30pm. Cash Only, Entrées: $8-$14. A C E L *to W. 14th St.,* 1 *to Christopher St.*

Tavern on Jane
This tavern serves much more than pub food, but still features pub food prices. While the fish and chips is a reliable delight, customers go crazy for the grilled leg-of-lamb with sour cherry sauce, potatoes au gratin, and garlic spinach with Moroccan tuna, served with saffron, lemon and garlic couscous, and wilted watercress. The atmosphere is cozy and inviting – regulars are bound to strike up a friendly conversation over a pint of beer. Simply put, you know a place is great when the staff hangs out there on their nights off.
31 Eighth Ave. (at Jane St.), (212) 675-2526. Hours: Su-Sa 12pm-1am. MC, V, AmEx, Entrées: $7-$15. A C E L *to 14th St.,* 1 *to Christopher St.*

Village
The spacious surroundings and domed glass ceiling frame this picture perfect scene. Village offers subtle flavors and deceptive sweetness in both its food and ambience. The friendly staff will certainly add to a fabulous dining experience.

62 W. 9th St., (212) 505-3355. Hours: Su-Sa 5pm-12am. MC, V, AmEx. L N R W 4 5 6 to Union Sq.

Wok'N Roll
They don't kick you out till 3am on weekends, and you'll never get to significantly alter the level of your water glass at this airy dumpling house. You can always count on the polished wood decor and predictable noodle and dumpling fare that feels like a home cooked Chinese dinner. Fair prices keep it packed with NYU kids.
169 Bleecker St. (at Sullivan St.), (212) 260-6666. Hours: Su-R 11am-1am. MC, V, AmEx, Entrées: $7-$13. A B C D E F V to W. 4th St., 1 to Christopher St.

Ye Waverly Inn
One of the vestiges of 19th century Village life, this former carriage house exudes a quaint colonial feel with wooden ceiling beams and old fashioned offerings from both north and south, like Yankee pot roast and southern fried chicken. Don't miss their excellent puddings and muffins. Occasionally, local celebs drop by.
16 Bank St. (at Waverly Pl.), (212) 929-4377. Hours: T-Sa 5pm-10:30pm, Su 11:30am-3:30pm, 5pm-10:30pm. MC, V, AmEx, D, Entrées: $12-$17. 1 2 3 to 14th St.

Café de Bruxelles
One of a number of Belgian joints now open on the West Side, this is perhaps the most consistent. The staff is authentically ethnic, the setting cozy, and the food – mussels, fabulous frites, and beers brewed at monasteries – is très, très bon.
118 Greenwich Ave. (at 13th St.), (212) 206-1830, Hours: Su-R 12pm-11:30pm, F-Sa 12pm-12am. MC, V, AmEx, Entrées: $12-$18. A C E L to 14th St.

CAFES

Caffe Dante
Famous both for its Buffalo mozzarella and espresso, this space may be small, but it is well arranged. If your stomach is craving a larger meal, check out the trattoria next door, which is under the same management.
79 Macdougal St. (bet. Bleecker and W. Houston Sts.), (212) 982-5275. Hours: Su-R 10am-2am, F-Sa 10am-3am. Cash Only. A B C D E F V to W. 4th St., 1 to Christopher St.

Caffe Reggio
The standard by which Village cafes are measured, Caffe Reggio's charm makes it popular among students, hipsters, and aging bohemians. The dark interior is suitable for curling up with a book or your significant other. Good place to stop before the TriBeCa Film Festival. Prices respect the starving artist's pocketbook.
119 MacDougal St. (at W. 3rd Sts.), (212) 475-9557. Hours: Su-Sa 10am-2am. Cash Only. A B C D E F V to W. 4th St., 1 to Christopher St.

French Roast
Art nouveau dominates the decor at this bustling cafe. Brunch and lunch are available, and be sure to try the consistently delicious soups.
78 W. 11th St. (at Sixth Ave.), (212) 533-2233. Hours: 24hrs. MC, V, AmEx, D. A B C D E F V to W. 4th St. Additional locations throughout Manhattan.

The Grey Dog's Coffee
Bring a novel, your laptop, or your friends to this warm rustic cafe where sunlight pours in through the open French windows and casts shadows on the pressed tin ceilings above. Order a big chunk of fresh-baked bread and a terrific cup of coffee and amble back to one of the artsy tables with apples, fish, or chili peppers painted on. At night the lights dim, and the place becomes a casual wine bar.
33 Carmine St. (bet. Bleecker and Bedford Sts.), (212) 462-0041. Hours: Su-Sa 7am-11:30pm. Cash Only. A B C D E F V to W. 4th St., 1 to Houston St.

[GRAMERCY]

RESTAURANTS

Bachue
Vegan paradise: delicious (eggless) pancakes and waffles, as well as a fine selection of bean, pasta, seitan, tempeh, tofu, and vegetable dishes.
36 W. 21st St. (bet. Fifth and Sixth Aves.), (212) 229-0870. Hours: M-F 8am-9:30pm, Sa 10am-9:30pm, Su 11am-6pm. MC, V, AmEx, D, Entrées: $5-$13. F V N R W to 23rd St.

Blue Water Grill
With everything from live jazz to an oyster bar, this delightful seafood cafe will keep you happy whether you're looking to eat or simply people-watch. The Grill is perpetually crowded, beautiful, and hip. The food can be nouveau cuisine, heavy on the seafood, but consistently good. The high-ceilinged restaurant will remind you this was once a bank. Check out the jazz downstairs, and if you can, try to reserve a sidewalk table.
31 Union Sq. West (at 16th St.), (212) 675-9500. Hours: M-R 11:30am-12am, F-Sa 11:30am-1am, Su 10:30am-11pm. MC, V, AmEx, Entrées: $15-$25. L N R W 4 5 6 to 14th St.-Union Sq.

Bolo
Food Network favorite Bobby Flay's version of "Fantasy Spanish" cuisine doesn't miss a beat at this relaxed Flatiron restaurant. Sangria, rabbit on roasted pea risotto, and sautéed wild mushrooms with chile oil are only a few of Mr. Flay's playful gastronomic creations. A comprehensive selection of fine wines and ports are perfect complements to a meal that is the stuff dreams are made of.
23 E. 22nd St. (bet. Broadway and Park Ave.), (212) 228-2200. Hours: M-R 12pm-2:30pm, 5:30pm-10pm, F 12pm-2:30pm, 5:30pm-11pm, Sa 5:30pm-11pm, Su 5:30pm-10pm. MC, V, AmEx, D. Entrées: $25-$30. N R 6 to 23rd St.

Chango
Pinks, yellows, blues, couch-style seating, bamboo dividers, and finished terra cotta – if Mexico hit oil, its future would be

Chango. From the tri-colored tortillas, guacamole, and the over-sized margaritas to the cut-away cove-lit ceiling and the ceramic serving plates, this trendy Sex and the City hot-spot is a non-stop fiesta. Bring a date who doesn't mind the sound of chatter or the competition of a gorgeous wait staff and you'll find a perfect choice in both taste of food and stunning décor.
239 Park Ave. South (bet. 19th and 20th Sts.), (212) 477-1500. Hours: M-R 12pm-11pm, F-Sa 12pm-11:30pm, Su 12pm-10pm. MC, V, AmEx, Entrées: $14-25. N R 6 to 23rd St.

City Crab & Seafood Co.
Surf and turf your way into City Crab for an enormous selection of underwater delights. Everything on the menu, from steamers to lobster to Alaskan King-Crab, is fresh from the Fulton Fish Market and prime for good hearty eatin'. The service is quick and the small-town feel is a nice contrast to the sophistication of Park Avenue South.
235 Park Ave. South (at 19th St.), (212) 529-3800. Hours: Su-R 11:30am-11pm, F-Sa 12pm-12am, Su 12pm-11:00pm. MC, V, AmEx, Entrées: $17-30. L N R W 4 5 6 to 14th St.-Union Sq.

Coffee Shop
This shop is not really a coffee shop, but rather an upscale Brazilianish restaurant with a fabulous bar in back. An episode of *Sex and the City* has been filmed here. The drinks and the crowd are consistently gorgeous. The food is very good, but that's really beside the point. Try to get an outside table, and enjoy the views.
29 Union Sq. W. (at 16th St.), (212) 243-7969. Hours: M 7am-2am, T-F 7am-6am, Sa 8am-6am, Su 8am-2am. MC, V, AmEx, D. L N R W 4 5 6 to Union Sq.-14th St.

Devi
Painted glass lanterns float in this dimly lit space, lending an air of exoticism and mystery to this modern Indian restaurant. Plenty of options for vegetarians and meat-eaters alike, the $55 tasting menus will give you a broad sweep of the liberally spiced, inventive cuisine with not a drop of common curry in sight. The presentation and service make up for the often salty dishes, but they cannot prevent you from frequently reaching for your water glass throughout the night. Make sure to leave room for the homemade sorbet and Indian ice cream.
8 E. 18th St. (bet. Fifth Ave. and Broadway), (212) 691-1300, www.devinyc.com. Hours: M-Sa 12pm-2:30pm, M-Su 5:30pm-11pm. MC, V, AmEx, D, Entrées: $14-$28. F V to 14th St., L to Sixth Ave.

Duvet
The perfect place to get your date into bed. Unlike most conventional restaurants, the diners at Duvet sit on beds. How does this work, you may ask? Well, in the center of the bed is a "Lazy Susan" upon which all food and drinks are placed. The beds are lined with exquisitepillows, and each diner is given slippers to sit on the bed with (if they desire). Furthermore, the sandals are a gift from the restaurant to the eater. The food is also excellent, and the Ribeye Steak was delicious and well-cooked. Duvet specializes in seafood, and the Dragon Roll was very tasty. Do not forget the cocktails, which are both strong and interesting. This reviewer enjoyed his Purple Haze, a violet infused Grey Goose cocktail. Come anytime for a very romantic experience.
45 W. 21st St. (bet. Fifth and Sixth Ave.), (212) 989-2121, www.duvetny.com. Hours: M-R 5pm-12am, F-Sa 5pm-4am. MC, V, AmEx. Entrées: $23 -$35. F N R V to 23rd St.

Eleven Madison Park
This upscale hotspot serves New York seasonal cuisine with a French influence. Along with the regular menu they have fine à la carte offerings. Go just for the grandeur of the space, which it shares with another creation by the same restauranteur – Tabla.
11 Madison Ave. (at 24th St.), (212) 889-0905. Hours: M-R 11:30am-2pm, 5:30pm-10:30pm, F-Sa 12pm-2pm, 5:30pm-11pm, Su 5:30pm-10pm. MC, V, AmEx, D. Entrées: $21 - $32. N R 6 to 23rd St.

Ess-A-Bagel
Ess (Yiddish for "eat") is the real deal for bagels. Its pumpernickels are chock-full of raisins, its cream cheese always fresh, itsss lines always long. If you're on a diet, don't bother.
359 First Ave. (21st St.), (212) 260-2252. Hours: M-Sa 6am-9pm, Su 6am-5pm. MC, V, AmEx, D. 6 to 23rd St., L to First Ave.
Additional location in Midtown.

Friend of a Farmer
Only in Gramercy could you find a Vermont snugness more convincing than anything in the Green Mountain State itself. While dinner is hearty and well-prepared, featuring stick-to-your-ribs specialties like shepherd's and chicken pot pies, the crowded brunch is the best feature. Prices are like dining in Montpelier.
77 Irving Pl. (bet. 18th and 19th Sts.), (212) 477-2188. Hours: M-F 8am-10pm, Sa 9:30am-10pm, Su 9:30am-9pm. MC, V, AmEx, D. Entrées: $8-$22. L N R W 4 5 6 to 14th St.-Union Sq.

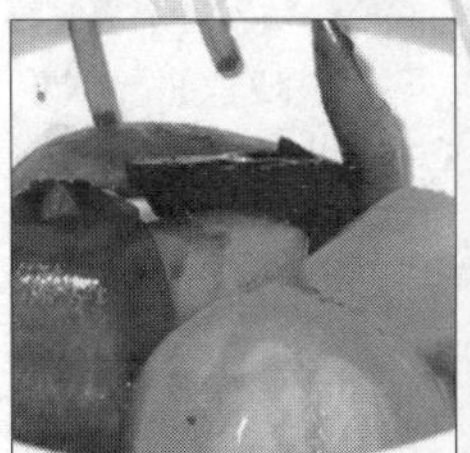

Galaxy Global Eatery
This dark, cozy, Irving Plaza neighbor has a ceiling spattered with twinkling stars and swirling blue planets. After sampling hemp-infused dishes like soba noodles, tiger shrimp, and garden burgers, you might feel like you're dining on cloud nine.
15 Irving Pl. (at 15th St.), (212) 777-3631, www.galaxyglobaleatery.com. Hours: Su-Sa 8pm-4am. MC, V, Entrées: $8-$10. L N R W 4 5 6 *to 14th St.-Union Sq.*

Giorgio's of Gramercy
Giorgio's is part of the New American boom that has taken over Manhattan. The service is superb and the Entrées exquisite, though the bathroom is small. Try either the filet mignon or salmon, but don't forget to save room for their fabulous Smore Bread Pudding.
27 E. 21st St, (bet. Park and Broadway) (212) 477-0007. Hours: Su 5:30pm-10pm, M 5:30pm-10:30pm, T 5:30pm-11pm, W-Sa 5:30pm-11:30pm. MC, V, AmEx, V, M, Entrées: $9-$25. N R 6 *to 23rd St.*

Gramercy Tavern
Don't be fooled by the rustic decor: prices reflect the all-star clientele at this hotspot for hobnobbing and networking. Stargazers may be willing to pay the price for a chance at sharing lunch with Johnny Depp.
42 E. 20th St. (bet. Broadway and Park Ave. South), (212) 477-0777. Hours: Su-R 12pm-2pm, 5:30pm-11pm, F 12pm-2pm, 5:30pm-11pm. Sa 5:30pm-11pm, Su 5:30pm-10pm. MC, V, AmEx, D. Entrées: $18-$25. N R 6 *to 23rd St.*

Komegashi
Komegashi touts itself as "re-construction cuisine," and a dining experience similar to the one that you'll have there is unlikely to be repeated anywhere else in the city. The plates are small and delicious, the service excellent, and the spacious yet intimate decor evokes both the French and Japanese influences that define Komegashi's cuisine. Komegashi is a great place to take a Japanese-loving date, and he or she will certainly appreciate the one-of-a-kind cocktails. Although it's a bit pricey, its certainly worth it. The Banana Chiboust is a must-have. The service leaves much to be desired.
928 Broadway (near 22nd St.), (212) 475-3000, www.komegashi.com. Hours: M-F lunch and dinner, Sa-Su brunch and dinner. MC, V, AmEx, D. Entrées: $15-$25. N R 6 *to 23rd St.*

Mesa Grill
Bobby Flay's limitless imagination has bestowed upon the city Southwestern flavors served in a light, airy space that pulses with festivity. A New York favorite, this restaurant is an eye-opener for those yet unacquainted with the exuberance of Flay's cuisine.
102 Fifth Ave. (bet. 15th and 16th Sts.), (212) 807-7400, www.mesagrill.com. Hours: M-R 12pm-2:30pm, 5:30pm-10:30pm, F 12pm-2:30pm, 5:30pm-11pm, Sa-Su 11:30am-3pm, 5pm-11pm. MC, V, AmEx, D, Entrées: $18-$39. L N R W 4 5 6 *to Union Sq.-14th St.*

New York Burger Co.
New York Burger Co. is

Girls Just Wanna Have Fun

If dinners out on the town have left you craving more than just service with a smile, then kick back at Lips, where the waitstaff lip syncs and lap dances your boredom into oblivion. These girls know how to have fun as they swivel among diners' tables while mouthing words and gesticulating to songs of their choosing. Frankie Cocktail spins the platters while performers such as the brickhouse All Beef Patti and the luscious Ginger rope chewing customers into the frenzied act. Squarely dressed straight men beware: you are the preferred targets. If you don't want to take part, your best bet is to tuck yourself into a corner. Bringing your stuffed shirt of an uncle? Count on the stiff frozen cosmos to loosen his buttons. After a few drinks he'll probably be schmoozing at the bar with a trannie from across town.

Performances are intermittent throughout dinner, and they are indicated by the dining room disco ball shooting beams of light all over the place. Owner and MC Yvonne introduces each girl, and when there's downtime she also publicly interrogates diners. Impressively, she never falters in her ability to issue a ribald retort to even the most humble, evasive mumble.

To witness mastery in the art of the insult, go on Wednesday for "Bitchy Bingo." As you win prizes, delight in co-host Linda Simpson's struggle to volley back the copious guff unloaded on her by merciless Yvonne. As both ladies so rightly point out, you are not playing the Jersey lottery: jackpots will not be shared. Whoever yells bingo first is the winner; everyone else, losers. The prizes are apt items such as theater tickets to productions like Boobs or Naked Boys Singing. If you don't win, though, keep in mind the sportsman and drag queen motto: It's not whether you win or lose, it's how you play the game.

2 Bank St. (at Greenwich Ave.), (212) 675-7710. Hours: M-Sa 5:30pm-12am, Su 12pm-4:30pm, 5:30pm-12am. MC, V, AmEx. A C E L *to 14th St.*

unique among Park Avenue dining establishments in that it offers its patrons a delectable array of upscale fast food. From burgers to hotdogs, from chili to shakes, all of New York Burger Co.'s food is delicious and somewhat nutritious. The restaurant offers over 10 original homemade sauces with which to dip the city's best onion rings into. New York Burger Co. is a neat and cheap way to satiate your hunger.
303 Park Ave. South, (212) 254-2727, Hours: Sa-Su 11am-11pm. MC, V, AmEx, D, DC. 6 to 23rd St.

Park Avalon

Sink back and soak up the high self-esteem of this crowded, gothic hot spot, where the pleasure is in the seeing as much as in the eating. In spite of its popularity, claustrophobia is unlikely due to the spacious interior. The Mediterranean-American food isn't too shabby either.
225 Park Ave. South (bet. 18th and 19th Sts.), (212) 533-2500. Hours: M-R 11:30am-12am, F-Sa 11:30am-12:30am, Su 10:30am-11:30pm. MC, V, AmEx, D, Entrées: $14-$20. L N R W 4 5 6 to 14th St.-Union Sq.

Pinch - Pizza By the Inch

Pinch is unique in that it offers what many may consider to be a cheaper cuisine in an elegant yet relaxed setting. The concept of the restaurant is that eaters order their pizza based on how long they would like it to be. The largest pizza one can order is the 36", although 24" is good enough for two diners. The pizza is truly delicious. All the toppings are fresh, so feel free to mix and match. The desserts are incredible, especially the gelato, which comes in many different delectable flavors, although this reviewer adored the cinnamon and banana tastes. If you want some of the best pizza the city has to offer - and believe me, you do – be sure to stop by Pinch.
416 Park Ave. South (bet. 28th and 29th St.), (212) 686-5222, www.pizzabytheinch.com. Hours: M-F 11am-11pm, Sa 5pm-11pm, Su 5pm-10pm. MC, V, AmEx, D. 6 to 28th St.

Pongal
Kosher

The best Indian restaurant on the strip of some of the best Indian eateries in New York. Pongal's South Indian vegetarian dishes have made it a solid choice for interesting and tasty food. The food is also quite a bargain: most of the entrées hover around nine dollars, making an authentic Indian experience easy on the wallet as well.
110 Lexington Ave. (bet 27th and 28th Sts.), (212) 696-9458. Hours: M-F 12pm-3pm, 5pm-10pm, Sa-Su 12pm-10pm. MC, V, D, Entrées: $8-17. 6 to 28th St.

Pure Food and Wine

Pure Food and Wine continues the California trend of raw food in New York City. Raw food consists of food cooked under 118 degrees. Although some may initially be wary regarding how this cuisine tastes, there is no reason to be. Everything on the menu is elegantly and tastefully prepared. The sushi is particularly delicious, as was the restaurant's famous "meatless" lasagna. As the name suggests, the wines served are delightful. Some are organic, and some are biodynamic, so you know that quality is assured. Pure Food and Wine is a great place to take a vegetarian friend and relative and perhaps introduce them to the glory of raw cuisine.
54 Irving Pl. (bet. 17th and 18th St.), (212) 477-1010, www.purefoodandwine.com. Hours: Su-M 5:30pm-10pm; T-S 5:30pm-11pm. MC, V, AmEx, D, Entrées: $20-$25. L N R W 4 5 6 to 14th St.-Union Sq.

Rickshaw Dumpling Bar

Rickshaw Dumpling Bar is a cool place recommended for those on a sudden health kick, and don't want to spend a lot of money. This reviewer wouldn't recommend experimenting with various dumpling types—there is nothing gourmet about this place. One is better off with the usual pork dumplings, anything else – well, the meal is cheap so you get what you paid for. It's a very Americanized Asian spot, fast-food in a cafeteria-like setting with American oldies playing in the background. The highlight of dining at Rickshaw is the chocolate dumplings; this reviewer would definitely travel across Manhattan just for an order of those!
61 W. 23rd St. (between Fifth and Sixth Ave.), (212) 924-9220, www.rickshawdumplings.com. Hours: M-Sa 11:30am-9:30pm, Su 11:30am-8:30pm. MC, V, AmEx, D, Entrées: $5-$10. F N R V to 23rd St.

SAPA

One of the most chic restaurants in the city, this restaurant's styling with amaze you. The food is well prepared and presented as pieces of art. This modern Japanese/Asian Fusion restaurant is a great place to impress a date or a client. It impresses in the same way as Tao, another one of New York's best, but falls one step short. At times, however, the music can be a little loud and make conversation difficult. Overall, this restaurant is highly recommended.
43 W. 24th St. (near Broadway), (212) 929-1800, www.sapanyc.com. Hours: M-W 12pm-11pm F 12pm-1:30am, Sa 11am-3pm, 5:30-1:30am, Su 11am-4pm, 5:30pm-10:30pm, MC, V, AmEx, D, Entrées: $25-$30. N R 6 to 23rd St.

Steak Frites

Sparkling with the culture of the "Rive Gauche," both the exotic and the ordinary are served here with flare and artistry. The only drawback is the paralyzing grin you might get from the waitress if you don't order in French.
9 E. 16th St. (bet 5th St. and Union Sq. West), (212) 463-7101. Hours: M-R 11:30am-10:30pm, F-Sa 11:30am-12:30am, Su 11:30am-10:30pm. MC, V, AmEx, Entrées: $15-22. L N R W 4 5 6 to 14th St.-Union Sq.

Tabla

One of the few restaurants where you can get American food infused with Indian spices. Be aware that your choices are prix fixe, à la carte, or a tasting menu. All are delicious.

11 Madison Ave. (at 25th St.), (212) 889-0667, www.tablanyc.com. Hours: M-F 12pm-2pm, 5:30pm-10:30pm, Sa-Su 5:30pm-10:30pm. MC, V, AmEx, D. Entrées: $52. N R 6 *to 23rd St.*

Tamarind

Memphis-based Raji Jallepalli rocks the house with some of the best Indian food in New York City. The focus is on regional Indian dishes at this spacious restaurant, where waiters are numerous, attentive, and the food is delicious. It's quite pricey, but well worth it.

41 E. 22nd St. (bet. Broadway and Park Ave. South), (212) 674-7400. Hours: Su-R 11:30am-3:30pm, 5:30pm-11pm, F-Sa 11:30pm-3pm, 5:30pm-12:30am. MC, V, AmEx, D, Entrées: $31-40. 6 *to 23rd St.*

The Turkish Kitchen

This reasonably-priced Gramercy restaurant has been in business for over ten years, and its longevity could be due to the intensely hued red walls, a color that the owner confides "makes people hungry." More likely, it's the food, particularly fish Entrées such as the Mediterranean Sea Bass dressed with lemon oil, and the many grilled meat and veggie dishes that keep diners satisfied. The long dining room on the first floor is cozy enough for a quiet dinner for two, while the brighter upstairs room is ideal for a dinner with a group of family or friends.

386 Third Ave. (bet. 27th and 28th Sts.), (212) 679-6633, www.turkishkitchenny.com. Hours: M-F 12-3pm; 5pm-11pm, Sa 5pm-11pm, Su 11am-3pm, 5pm-11pm, 5:00-10:30pm, 6 *to 28th St.*

Union Square Cafe

This restaurant has been voted most popular restaurant by critics five times. The food is gourmet but not the intimidating kind that makes you think your holding your fork wrong. Union Square Cafe is a landmark, whose great food and friendly service are here to stay.

21 E. 16th St. (bet. Fifth Ave. and Union Sq. West.), (212) 243-4020. Hours: M-R 12pm-2:30pm, 6pm-10pm, F-Sa 12pm-2:30pm, 6pm-11pm, Su 12pm-2:30pm, 6pm-10:30pm. MC, V, AmEx, D. Entrées: $25-$35. L N R W 4 5 6 *to 14th St.-Union Sq.*

Cafes

Java N Jazz

Java N Jazz is working hard to prove that they can do the coffee bar thing better than their mega chain counterparts, and it shows. Though they claim to be a relaxing place, so much is going on in and around this tiny cafe that you feel like everyone there has exceeded his or her daily caffeine limit. The walls are decked with art exhibits from neighborhood artists, and they have live jazz on Friday and Saturday nights. You can even grab a box lunch to take back to work.

868 Broadway (bet. 17th and 18th Sts.), (212) 473-4200, www.java-n-jazz.com. Hours: M-R 6:30am-10:30pm, F 6:30am-11:30am, Sa 7:30am-11:30am, Su 8am-10pm. MC, V, AmEx, D. L N R W 4 5 6 *to 14th St.-Union Sq.*

[Chelsea]

Restaurants

Amin Indian Restaurant

Dinner here avoids the circus-like pitfalls of Sixth Street's outfits. Curries, kebabs, and kormas are spicy enough to satisfy natives and will only set you back about $10. Combo platters allow for both gluttony and variety.

155 Eighth Ave. (bet. 17th and 18th Sts.), (212) 929-7020. Hours: Su-Sa 6pm-11pm. MC, V, AmEx, Entrées: $7-$19. A C E L *to 14th St.*

Amuse

Formerly the Tonic, Amuse provides its patrons with plenty of delicious appetizers and Entrées. Everything about this restaurant screams class, from the wine cellar in the basement to the polished wood tables. Scallops are outstanding, but the steak will be the real highlight of the night. Amuse's wait staff is both attentive and clever; only in New York can you and your waiter engage in a discussion about post-modern existentialism.

108 W. 18th St. (bet. Sixth and Seventh Aves.), (212) 929-9755. Hours: M-Sa 12pm-12am. MC, V, AmEx, D, Entrées: $20-$25. 1 *to 18th St.*

BED – New York

BED New York is the second in a series of restaurants that began in Miami in 1999. What distinguishes bed from it's competitors is the way in which diners eat. You will not find any tables at BED. Rather, you and your guest will enjoy a delicious meal on a luxurious mattress. The cuisine is French-inspired, with a hint of Brazilian influence. The foie gras appetizer is phenomenal, and be sure

to try one of the sexily named cocktails, such as the Red Head in Bed or the Wet Spot. The desserts are also phenomenal, particularly the creme brulée. BED is a great place to bring a date and let him or her know how you feel about them—in bed and out.
530 W 27th St, Sixth Fl. (bet. 10th & 11th Ave), (212) 594-4109. Hours: Tue-Sat: 6pm-2am. MC, V, AmEx, D. Entrées: $20-$25. C E to 23rd St.

Cafeteria

Though its name, menu contents, and 24-hour service may suggest a diner, this ultra-hip Chelsea spot is anything but. Cafeteria is always crowded with good-looking, trendy young people who are too cool for school. The interior decoration consists of one color (white), but anyone who knows anything (or pretends to) will tell you that it is part of a urbane minimalist décor. So come eat some waffles, macaroni and cheese, meatloaf, cobb salad, or fried chicken (all surprisingly good) at any time of day and feel really modish while doing it. Of course, to really be in vogue, you should have a cocktail in hand: order the excellent coconut martini or mojito to be different and still be able to enjoy your drink.
119 Seventh Ave. (at 17th St.), (212) 414-1717. Hours: 24 hours. MC, V, AmEx, D, Entrées: $12-$22. 1 to 18th St.

Empire Diner

Featured in the opening montage of Woody Allen's Manhattan, this 24-hour eatery boasts an upscale dinner menu, complemented by a jazz pianist. It's a great club-hopping pit stop; staying up for prix fixe brunch is well worth the sleep deprivation. Don't go à la carte, as the prices soar.
210 Tenth Ave. (at 22nd St.), (212) 243-2736. Hours: 24 hours. MC, V, AmEx, D, Entrées: $5-$18. C E to 23rd St.

Eugene

This lounge and restaurant is both a great place to be seen and a great place to be incognito. The almost hidden couch-style surroundings are darkly lit, while the open spaces are filled by roaming models. Art-Deco décor evokes a sense of snapping fingers and prohibition era snickers. The food is expensive but satisfying. Note that you must be 21 to enter at all times.
27 W. 24th St. (bet. Fifth and Sixth Aves.), (212) 462-0999. Hours: R-Sa 10pm-4am. MC, V, AmEx, Entrées: $22-$28. F V N R to 23rd St.

Knickerbocker Bar and Grill

One of the quieter names in New York steakhouses, Knickerbocker boasts a long history of success in one of the toughest industries in the world. The burgundy walls and warm lighting, combined with the classic Americana lining the walls, create a friendly and relaxing environment in which to share the delicious salads, meats, and desserts. The chef recommends the lamb sirloin frisee salad, served warm. The house-special T-Bone for two is an absolute must with creamed spinach and garlic mashed potatoes. For dessert, check the specials menu for their recommended peach cake, and do not leave without ordering the churros.
33 University Pl., (212) 228-8490. Hours: T-R 12pm-1am, F-Sa 12pm-2am, Su-M 12pm-12am. MC, V, AmEx, D. 6 to Astor Pl., N R to 8th St.

The Red Cat

The Red Cat manages to offer cutting edge food in a warm, comfortable setting. The menu includes a variety of American bistro dishes, but with a twist, such as the wasabi-infused tempura string beans with a honey mustard dipping sauce. The staff is personable yet very professional. And to top it off, The Red Cat plays The Beatles, Jimmy Hendrix and other fine dining music. You can expect to pay about $20+ per dish, but there is no way you will leave unsatisfied.
227 Tenth Ave. (bet. 23rd and 24th St.), (212) 242-1122, www.theredcat.com. Hours: M-R 5:30pm-11pm, F-Sa 5:30pm-12am, Su 5pm-10pm. MC, V, AmEx, D, Entrées: $20-$31. C E to 23rd St.

Rocking Horse Cafe Mexicano

One of a string of Mexican restaurants along Eighth Ave., this is the most upscale, with fresh food, a perky waitstaff, and a popular brunch. Interesting twists on traditional fare include variations with crab and lobster, but the old standards are excellent as well.
182 Eighth Ave. (bet. 19th and 20th Sts.), (212) 463-9511, www.rockinghorsecafe.com, Hours: Su-R 11am-11pm, F-Sa 11am-12am. MC, V, AmEx, Entrées: $14-$20. C E 1 to 23rd St.

Sueños

Although some culinary ignoramuses may not see how the words upscale and Mexican food can go together, one trip to Suenos will be sure to change their mind. The food here is beautiful; pleasantly and artistically prepared to please both your palette and vision. The guacamole, made in front of your eyes, is delicious. The margheritas are strong, and one would be remiss not to try one. If you're feeling crazy, order the $30 Double-Secret-Probation Margarita or the higher-end $69 version of it. The appetizers were delicious, especially the chicken carnitas. The entrees were slightly spicy, so be sure to inquire if you're iffy about spicy food. The desserts, especially the Tres Leches cake and the Chocolate-Banana Crepes were excellent, so be sure to leave room by the time your meal is over.
311 W. 17th St. (bet. Eighth and Ninth Ave.), (212) 243-1333. Hours: Su-W 5pm-11pm; R-Sa 5pm-12am. MC, V, AmEx, D. Entrées: $16-$25. A C E to 14th St.

Viceroy

Viceroy features some great dishes (and the food's not half bad either). The floor to ceiling windows put Chelsea's most bold and beautiful on display. Come to this trendy spot for "see-food" – the

cool, comfortable dining space makes for a glam time.
160 Eighth Ave. (at 18th St.), (212) 633-8484. Hours: Su-W 10am-1am, R 10am-2am, F 10am-5am, Sa 8am-5am. MC, V, AmEx, Entrées: $10-$20. 1 to 18th St.

Yakiniku Juju

Combining the traditional and the innovative, Yakiniku JuJu offers Shabu-Shabu, BiBimBop, and Korean BBQ, with a focus on health and nutrition and features a slate of original sushi rolls, including a kimchee roll, a chicken roll, and a beef roll. To make everyone feel more at home, the jukebox plays an eclectic mix of hip-hop, jazz, and pop. The all you can eat grill-it-yourself BBQ is a great deal at $23, with assorted meats sliced fresh rather that sitting out in a buffet bin. Don't bother leaving room for dessert.
157 E. 28th St., (212) 684-7830. Hours: Su-R 5:30pm-10pm, F 5:30-11pm, Sa 5:30pm-11pm. AmEx, M, V, $20-$30. 6 N R to 28th St.

Cafes

Big Cup

This gay coffee haunt is a good alternative to the bar scene, offering quite a bit more than just a cup of coffee. Although the coffee and tea selection is good, the eye candy is this hot spot's main draw. Quite a few men go there to sit with a cup, by themselves or with friends, but an equal number of young bucks look for action. Tip: those on the market often sit alone with a book.
228 Eighth Ave. (at 22nd St.), (212) 206-0059, www.bigcupcoffee.com. Hours: Su-R 7am-12am, F-Sa 7am-1am. C E to 23rd St., 1 to 23rd St.

[Midtown]

Restaurants

44 Restaurant at the Royalton Hotel

Dining at this restaurant is a special treat. Its ultra-trendy ambience and Phillip Starck-designed interior make its European-American food seem even better than it is. The customers are a glamorous, black-clad crowd, often admiring themselves in the restaurant's giant mirrors. It's quite expensive but worth it if you like classic steak and fish dishes served in a fancy spot.
44 W. 44th St. (bet. Fifth and Sixth Aves.), (212) 944-8844. Hours: Su-Sa 7am-10pm. MC, V, AmEx, D. Entrées: $22-36. A C E N R S W 1 2 3 7 to 42nd St.-Times Sq.

Abigael's on Broadway
Kosher

Whether it's mouth-watering portobello mushrooms with balsamic drizzles, cedar-plank prepared salmon, or the most tender ribs and steak, Abigael's entirely kosher menu will be a hit even if you're not kosher. Serving primarily meat dishes, this place will knock you off your feet with great service and terrific food. Abigael's is also known for their fabulous desserts to cap off a fun night of kosher feasting.
1407 Broadway (at W. 39th St.), (212) 575-1407, www.abigaels.com. Hours: Su-R 12pm-2:30pm, 5pm-10pm, F 12pm-2:30pm, Sa 8pm-12am, Su 4:30pm-9:30pm. MC, V, AmEx, Entrées: $22-30. A C E N R S W 1 2 3 7 to 42nd St.-Times Sq.

Asia de Cuba

If only all of NYC were as good looking and stylishly-dressed as this crowd. You might have to wait upwards of an hour for a table at prime-time even if you have a reservation, but the delicious food and sophisticated atmosphere make it worth the wait. Enjoy one of their excellent mixed drinks to help fan out the burning hole in your wallet.
237 Madison Ave. (bet. 37th and 38th Sts.), (212) 726-7755. Hours: M-W 12pm-11pm, R-F 12pm-12am, Sa 5:30pm-12am, Su 5:30pm-11pm. MC, V, AmEx, D, Entrées: $17-$30. 4 5 6 7 S to 42nd St.-Grand Central.

B. Smith's

This upscale soul food place has a sister restaurant in Union Station, Washington, DC. and is known to be a draw for the expense account crowd. Owner Barbara Smith, once a model, sure knows how to decorate but the food isn't consistently fabulous. Try the greens and salads, skip the fried items.
320 W. 46th St. (bet. Eighth and Ninth Aves.), (212) 315-1100. Hours: M 5pm-9pm, T-F 12am-12pm, Sa 11:30pm-12:30am, Su 11:30am-10pm. MC, V, AmEx. A C E N R S W 1 2 3 7 to 42nd St.-Times Sq.

Benihana of Tokyo

This kitschy restaurant, known for its knife-throwing chop-chop chefs who display their talents tableside, has been around for many moons. With a reputation for drawing tourists rather than locals, Benihana is a retro alternative to Manhattan chic.
47 W. 56th St. (bet. Fifth and Sixth Aves.), (212) 581-0930. Hours: Su-Sa 12pm-12am. MC, V, AmEx. F to 57th St. Additional Location: 120 E. 56th St. (bet. Lexington and Park Aves.).

Blue Fin

Although strategically located for tourists in the heart of the W Hotel in Times Square, this restaurant is certainly good enough to meet the standards of even the most selective of New York's sophisticated diners. While its décor is sufficiently ornate to be a midtown crowd-pleaser (the 400-seat restaurant is adorned with an abstract rendering of fish that hover in the air between walls engraved with wave patterns), do not let it distract you from what is on your plate: extremely fine sushi and fish Entrées that equal the other notable seafood restaurants in the city. Be sure to leave room after sushi for the first-rate black bass or halibut entrées. Should you find yourself in Times Square with a date, Blue Fin is a classy can't-miss among a sea of gaudy duds.
1567 Broadway (at 47th St.), (212) 918-1400. Hours: M-F 12pm-3pm, 5pm-11pm, Sa-Su 11:00am-3pm. MC, V, AmEx, D. N R W to 49th St., 1 to 50th St.

Bryant Park Grill

Nestled up against the backside of the main branch of the Public Library, a restaurant would be hard-pressed to be more picturesque, especially in spring. The food and service are uneven, the crowds crushing, bu the view is fabulous. The bar, particularly when it moves outdoors in the summer, is known as a primo meat market. Brunch is excellent.
25 W. 40th St. (bet. Fifth and Sixth Aves.), (212) 840-6500, www.park-restaurants.com. Hours: Su-Sa 11:30am-3:30pm, 5pm-11pm. MC, V, AmEx, D, Entrées: $14-$24. B D F V *to 42nd St.,* 7 *to Fifth Ave.*

Burritoville

This Mexican chain has great prices, with food that is low on ambience and big on quantity. The burritos won't win any awards, but for a quick bite, with or without heartburn, Burritoville fits the bill. Beware the fresh salsa, it's muy caliente.
625 Ninth Ave. (at 44th St.), (212) 333-5352. Hours: Su-Sa 11am-12am. MC, V, AmEx. A C E N R S W 1 2 3 7 *to 42nd St.-Times Sq.*
Additional locations in Manhattan.

Cafe Centro

Popular with the expense account set, this midtown Mediterranean is high on service and the food is consistently good. This cafe has taste to spare, an oasis in midtown for those looking for a good restaurant. Lunch is jam-packed.
200 Park Ave. (45th St. & Vanderbilt Ave.), (212) 818-1222. Hours: M-Sa 11:30am-10:30pm. MC, V, AmEx, D, Entrées: $25-$31. S 4 5 6 7 *to 42nd St.-Grand Central Terminal.*

Cafe Un Deux Trois

Though a little strenuous on the wallet, this busy, touristy spot is perfect for a bowl of savory French onion soup or a delectable dish of crème brulée. Avoid the high prices by sitting at the bar. If you're up for a full meal, sit table-side for a plate of steak and pomme frites, and let your imagination run wild as you design your own table cloth with a cup full of crayons.
123 W. 44th St. (bet. Sixth Ave. and Broadway), (212) 354-4148. Hours: Su-Sa 12pm-12am, Sa-Su 11am-12am. MC, V, AmEx, Entrées: $15-24. A C E N R S W 1 2 3 7 *to 42nd St.-Times Sq.*

Chef Ho's

Chef Ho's is a solid Chinese eatery that delivers late. Its food isnt too oily, and it's hard to find a bad dish. The seafood and eggplant are particularly good, and the service just okay.
1720 Second Ave. (bet. 89th and 90th Sts.), (212) 348-9444. Hours: Su-Sa 11:30am-11pm. MC, V, AmEx. 4 5 6 *to 86th St.*

Churrascaria Plataforma

Plataforma is New York's swankiest Brazilian barbeque joint, where the all-you-can-eat meatfest will have you dieting for the rest of the week. The lighting and clientele are beautiful, the lime-based drinks divine, and the salad bar a work of art. The prices aren't cheap, but for a memorable evening, it can't be beat.
316 W. 49th St. (bet. Eighth and Ninth Aves.), (212) 245-0505. Hours: Su-Sa 12pm-12am. MC, V, AmEx, D. C E *to 50th St.*

Daily Soup

This soup chain has over a dozen types of soup, hot in winter and some cool soups in summer. The décor is strictly steel Spartan, but the lunchtime crowd is usually in and out anyway.
134 E. 43rd St. (bet. Lexington and Third Aves.), (212) 949-7687. Hours: Su-Sa 7am-4pm.
241 W. 54th St. (bet. Broadway and Eighth Ave.), (212) 765-7687. S 4 5 6 7 *to 42nd St.*
Additional locations in Manhattan.

Dallas BBQ

This barbecue joint may not be authentic, but it is fun. It is big on sauce, and will do just fine for New Yorkers not from Texas or Tennessee. Don't wear white. Apparently, substitutions are both illegal and immoral. Several locations throughout Manhattan.
132 W. 43rd St. (bet. Broadway and Sixth Ave.), (212) 221-9000, www.bbqnyc.com. Hours: Su-Sa 11am-1am. A C E N R S W 1 2 3 7 *to 42nd St.-Times Sq.*
Additional locations in Manhattan

Restaurant Week

While there's no hope of New York food ever going on sale, there are still opportunities to experience the finest dining in the city at a discount. Restaurant Week is a citywide event every January and June in which 180 top restaurants offer prix fixe lunches and/or dinners, usually featuring three courses (appetizer, Entrée, and dessert), for $20.12 and $35, respectively. Drinks, tips, and tax are not included. As one would expect, the prix-fixe menu generally includes only the cheaper items from normal offerings, but the best restaurants manage to make these dishes no less exquisite than the others. During Restaurant Week remember to tip generously because the waiters are working at a discount. It's best to reserve your table(s) early, especially for popular restaurants like JoJo or Tribeca Grill. Open Table (www.open table.com) pairs up with many of the restaurants so reservations can be made online. They provide a complete list of participating restaurants and more yummy details. Restaurants' individual websites may even give a preview of the Restaurant Week prix fixe menu.

Del Frisco's Double Eagle Steak House

High ceilings and dark mahogany walls give this midtown steakhouse an overwhelmingly classy appeal. The mixed crowd is made up mainly of dashing young professionals and businessmen out on the town. The Double Eagle Dallas steakhouse specializes in exceedingly tender and flavorful meats seared in pepper and spices, served on piping hot plates which keep the meat warm throughout your meal. Sommeliers traverse the two-floor dining area, to help you choose from the extensive wine list. Try the porterhouse or the filet accompanied by delicious creamed spinach and garlic mashed potato sides, but don't forget to start with the world-famous crabcakes in a lobster bisque sauce. The hardest part of eating at Del Frisco's is leaving room for the wonderful desserts.
1221 Sixth Ave. (at 49th St.), (212) 575-5129. Hours: M-F 11am-12am, Sa 5pm-12pm, Su 5pm-10pm. MC, V, AmEx, D, M, $41 and up. B D F to 47-50th Sts.-Rockefeller Ctr.

Don Giovanni

For a slice of the neighborhood, sit outside at a table and enjoy a pie at Don Giovanni. Made in a brick oven, with thin crust, fresh mozzarella, and a sweet tomato sauce, this pizza is bound to please. Be forewarned: delivery takes at least an hour.
358 W. 44th St. (bet. Eighth and Ninth Aves.), (212) 581-4939, www.dongiovanni-ny.com. Hours: Su-R 12pm-12am, F-Sa 12pm-2am. MC, V, AmEx, Entrées: $7-$22. A C E N R S W 1 2 3 7 to 42nd St.-Times Sq.

English is Italian

One of the best deals in the city. For only $39/person, diners are brought many courses shared with the rest of your party. You will certainly not go hungry with this amount of wonderful food. With its modern décor, the ambience is brilliant as well. Only in New York will you find a place with this kind of character, with such experienced chefs and service at such a reasonable cost. Be sure to order a glass of wine from their beautiful wine tower.
622 Third Ave. (at 40th St.), (212) 404-1700. Hours: M-F, 11:30am-2pm, M-W 5:30pm-10pm, R-Sa 5:30pm-11pm, Su 5pm-10pm. MC, V, AmEx. Entrées: $20-$25. S 4 5 6 7 to Grand Central.

Estiatorio Milos

The fish are displayed fresh for you to select from at this Greek piscatory/restaurant that features by-the-pound pricing and fresh fish cooked in Mediterranean sauces. Nothing compares to the seafood at Milos; it floats somewhere above, an ideal not to be touched.
125 W. 55th St. (bet. Sixth and Seventh Aves.), (212) 245-7400. Hours: Su-Sa 12pm-3pm, 5pm-11:30pm. MC, V, AmEx, D, Entrées: $40-$60. N R W to 57th St.

Felidia

This is, without a doubt, the best and most authentic Northern Italian Restaurant in New York. Lidia Bastianich creates a warm, welcoming ambiance by designing the restaurant to resemble a two-tiered Etruscan villa. Don't even bother trying to select your own dishes; every item on the menu is distinctive and magnificent. In addition, the menu remains constantly in flux to capture the signature delights of each season. In truth, you have only one option: surrender your appetite to the brilliant chef. Pair your otherworldly meal with one of their extraordinary Italian wines and you might just reach Nirvana.
243 E. 58th St. (bet. Second and Third Aves.), (212) 758-1479. Hours: M-F 12pm-3pm, M-R 5pm-11pm, F-Sa 5pm-11:30pm, Su 4pm-10pm MC, V, AmEx, D, Entrées: $25 and up. 4 5 6 N R W to 51st St.-Lexington Ave.

Firebird

This Russian restaurant is caviar heaven, where you will be pampered from head to toe. From the restaurant to the jazz lounge to the upstairs bar, Firebird has a high staff to diner ratio. Even the chef revolves into the dining room to see what's going on. In two former renovated townhouses, Firebird recreates St. Petersburg of 1910, replete with Cossack costumes and vintage paintings from a former era. The vodkas are to die for, and the dumplings, chicken Kiev, and lamb are scrumptious. The prices, too, are worthy of royalty.
365 W. 46th St. (bet. Eighth and Ninth Aves.), (212) 586-0244. Hours: W, Sa 11:45am-4pm, 5pm-11pm. M-T, R-F, Su 5pm-11pm. MC, V, AmEx, A C E N R S W 1 2 3 7 to 42nd St.-Times Sq.

The Four Seasons

If you want to spot Henry Kissinger, Ranan Lurie, or other old school New York power brokers, the Pool Room is the place. Call it stuffy, call it pretentious, but the Four Seasons is still the place to beat for wheeling and dealing. The food is fabulous, the wine list spectacular, the service stellar. They know what they are doing, so know your wines before you go.
99 E. 52nd St. (bet. Lexington and Park Aves.), (212) 754-9494. Hours: M-F 12pm-2:30pm, 6pm-9:30pm, Sa-Su 6pm-10pm. MC, V, AmEx, D. 6 to 51st St.

The Flame

Better known as a neighborhood icon than for its food, The Flame nonetheless ably serves up the expected diner menu, from omelets to burgers to gyros. The business crowd converges around 1pm for lunch, but otherwise there is ample seating and rarely (if ever) a wait. A good place to chat without having to fork over lots of dough.
893 Ninth Ave. (at 58th St.), (212) 765-7962. Hours: Su-Sa 6am-12am. MC, V, AmEx, D, Entrées: $4-$12. A B C D 1 to 59th St.-Columbus Circle.

Fresco Tortilla Grill

Times Square's best – or arguably, only – secret is this tiny Mexican hole-in-the-wall. A great place to satisfy your hunger for good food and New

Yorker credibility for less than five bones.
125 W. 42nd St. (bet. Broadway and Sixth Ave.), (212) 221-5849. Hours: Su-Sa 11am-9pm. MC, V, AmEx, Entrées: $3-5. A C E N R S W 1 2 3 7 to 42nd St.-Times Sq.

Hale & Hearty Soups

H&H, like the Daily Soup, offers dozens of "home-made" soups along with salads and other healthy fare. A favorite with men and women in suits unafraid of spilling their lunch, H&H is especially popular in the winter when a warm meal is just the ticket. The prices and lunchtime crush might make some pause before venturing in.
849 Lexington Ave. (at 65th St.) (212) 517-7600. Hours: M-F 9am-8pm, Sa 10:30am-6pm, Su 10:30 am-5pm. 6 to 68th St. Additional locations throughout Manhattan.

Hangawi

Slip out of your shoes at this Murray Hill Zen oasis to show respect while you sip wild Korean tea and find inner peace in the open, serene atmosphere, Asian folk music, and simple, aromatic food. The convenient tasting menu and the friendly wait staff make the exotic menu easy to comprehend. Wear clean socks.
12 E. 32 St. (bet. Fifth and Madison Aves.), (212) 213-0077, www.hangawirestaurant.com, Hours: M-Su 12pm-3pm, 5pm-10:15pm. MC, V, AmEx, D, Entrées: $16 - $25, Prix fixe lunches: $20, $25, $35, Prix fixe dinners: $30, $35. B D F N R V W to 34th St.-Herald Sq.

Inagiku

The stylish interior decoration, combined with the traditional Japanese cuisine, represents the unity of traditional and modern Japan. The waitresses are dressed in classical Japanese kimonos and are eager to explain all of the delicious dishes. One can choose a regular entrée or can combine "classic little dishes" to sample various Japanese specialties. The shrimp and lobster tempura are a must as well as the eel hagata, imported all the way from Japan. The restaurant is also known for its wide selection of sakes as well as the unique array of bar beverages. Make sure to leave room for the many creative desserts such as the Ogura milk crepe. Inagiku also has Shabu Shabu station located at the bar which is open for lunch and dinner, as well as private tatami rooms which seat 4-18 people.
111 E. 49th St. (in the Waldorf-Astoria), (212) - 355-0440. Hours: M-F 12pm-2pm, Su-Sa 5:30pm-10pm. MC, V, AmEx, D. B D F V to 47-50 Sts-Rockefeller Center, E V to 53rd St., 6 to 51st St.

Joe Allen

Upscale thespians, including bonafide Broadway celebs in search of some post-performance relaxation, come to this dark and elegant but unpretentious eatery to fill up on gourmet meatloaf and hot fudge pudding cake. On Sunday nights, 8pm to closing, fifteen percent of every check goes to Broadway Cares/Equity Fights AIDS.
326 W. 46th St. (bet. Eighth and Ninth Aves.), (212) 581-6464, www.joeallen-orso.com. Hours: Su-Sa 11:30am-11:45pm. MC, V, Entrées: $10-$21. A C E to 42nd St.-Port Authority.

Joe's Shanghai

This is an authentic Chinese restaurant for a crowd that knows its Asian food. Try the soup dumplings, filled with delectable crab and pork. The service won't bowl you over, but the food will. The prices are good, too.
24 W. 56th St. (bet. Fifth and Sixth Aves.), (212) 333-3868. Hours: M-Sa 11am-10:30pm, Su 1pm-10:30pm. MC, V, AmEx. E V to 53rd St., 6 to 51st St.

Koi

L.A. meets New York in this fine Japanese dining experience. Koi is a welcome burst of shallow air in a city obsessed with its integrity. Nonetheless, this is not to say that the food at Koi is anything less than excellent. The house Dragon Roll is perhaps the tastiest sushi roll that this reviewer had ever had, and both the Kobe Filet and Chilean Sea Bass were tender and delicious, with the former being exactly as buttery as it should be. The desserts, while standard, were very tasty, making them a welcome cap to any meal. Since it's located near Bryant Park, Koi is a good beginning to what, with any luck, will become a great night.
40 W. 40th St. (bet. Fifth and Sixth Ave.), (212) 921-3330, www.koirestaurant.com. Hours: M lunch, T-Su lunch and dinner. MC, V, AmEx. B D F V 7 to Bryant Park.

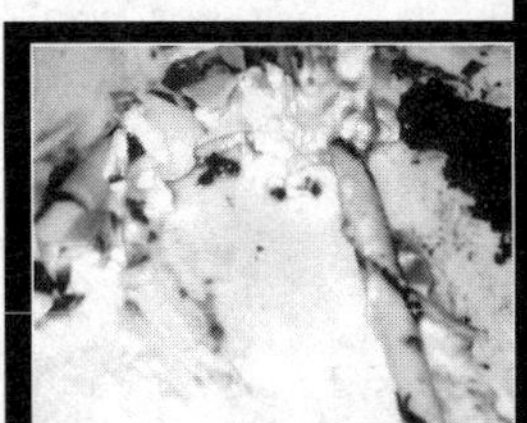

Kiiroi Hana

This authentic sushi joint is long on authenticity, short on imagination and décor. Try some inside out rolls or the eggplant appetizer in miso sauce. Usually fresh, it's great for lunch.
20 W. 56th St. (bet. Fifth and Sixth Aves.), (212) 582-7499. Hours: Su-Sa 11:30am-10pm. MC, V. E V 6 to 51st-Lexington Ave.

L'Absinthe

How many restaurants allow for someone to truly feel like they're in a Paris brasserie? Great place to bring your gradnma. L'Absinthe's main appeal – besides the delicious, decid-

edly French cuisine – is the fact that anyone who dines at this east 60s restaurant feels as if they're in a different country and culture. Both the manager and chef are authentic Frenchmen, and it shows in L'Absinthe's decor and overall feel.
227 E. 67th St, (bet. 2nd and 3rd Aves.)., (212) 794-4950. Hours: Su-Sa 12pm-3pm, 5:30pm-11pm. MC, V, AmEx, D, Entrées: $31-$50, 6 to 68th St.

La Bonne Soupe
An authentic French bistro, right down to the waiters' thick accents and the creamy chocolate mousse. Red-checkered tablecloths and colorful paintings add to the homey, rural atmosphere. Start with a glass of wine and some fondue or the Paysanne soup, then try the duck platters, and end the meal with crème caramel. It'll be one "bonne" meal under $25...trés bien!
48 W. 55th St. (bet. Fifth and Sixth Aves.), (212) 586-7650, www.labonnesoupe.com. Hours: Su-Sa 11:30am-11pm. MC, V, AmEx, D, Entrées: $10-20. N R W to 57th St., E V to 53rd St., 6 to 51st St.

Le Bernardin
There is nothing we can write here to adequately describe this fantasy of a restaurant. Simply surrender yourself to the magic of chef Eric Ripert, and the charms of owner and co-creator Maguy Le Coze, and cherish the exhilarating sensation of eating a perfectly elegant meal. You may only get to do this once, but savor every minute. There is only one thing we can really say: Any New Yorker who appreciates culinary miracles should come here to have a religious experience. Never mind your wallet; this meal is priceless.
155 W. 51st St. (bet. Sixth and Seventh Aves.) (212) 554-1515. www.le-bernadin. com Hours: M-R 12pm-2:30pm, 5:30pm-10:30pm, F-Sa 5:30pm-11pm. MC, V, AmEx, D, Prix Fixe: $49 & up. 1 to 49th 50th St., B D F V to 47-50 Sts.- Rockefeller Ctr.

Maya
No burritos here: though the flavors are undeniably Mexican, the cuisine is far removed from the usual south-of-the-border fare. Along with great guacamole and fiery salsa, the stars of the menu are dishes like the pork tenderloin with a roasted corn and pumpkin-seed sauce or the chicken breast with cheese dumplings and cilantro pesto. The décor is reminiscent of an Acapulco convention center, but the super-smooth service and uniformly great food justify the high class price tag. Don't miss the desserts, some of which include chocolate so rich it's almost spicy.
1191 First Ave. (at 64th St.), (212) 585-1818. Hours: M-R 5pm-11pm, F-Sa 5pm-11:30pm, Sa-Su 5pm-10:30pm. MC, V, AmEx, Entrées $18-$24. S 4 5 6 7 to 59th St.-Lexington Ave.

Michael Jordan's Steakhouse
Amid the hustle-and-bustle of Grand Central Terminal lies the dining legacy of a sports legend. Much like MJ's athletic performances, the atmosphere here is energetic and celebratory. As commuters catch their trains, and midtown studs seize an eight o'clock post-work drink, you can sit to a powerhouse steak dinner directly above the landmark Grand Concourse. The steak is superb and succulent so be careful not to fill up on their addictive garlic bread with gorgonzola fondue, or the more-than-just-complementary sides. Save room! One taste of the 12-Layer chocolate cake and you'll be happy you were scrupulous with the preceding dishes.
Grand Central Terminal (on the West balcony), 23 Vanderbilt Ave. (bet. Park and Lexington Aves.), (212) 655-2300. Hours: M-Sa 12pm-11pm, Su 1pm-10pm. MC, V, AmEx, D, Entrées: $17-$32. S 4 5 6 7 to 42nd St.-Grand Central.

Monkey Bar Steakhouse
Don't let the long walk through a crowded lounge fool you, The Monkey Bar offers much more than cocktails. Eating in the luxurious and comfortable dining room with attentive service is a pleasure; the food is just the icing on the proverbial cake. You'll definitely appreciate the small touches, like the freshly roasted garlic that accompanies your steak or the delicious appetizers. Don't forget their delicious desserts either, as they're the perfect exclamation point to finish off a wonderful meal.
60 E. 54th St. (bet.

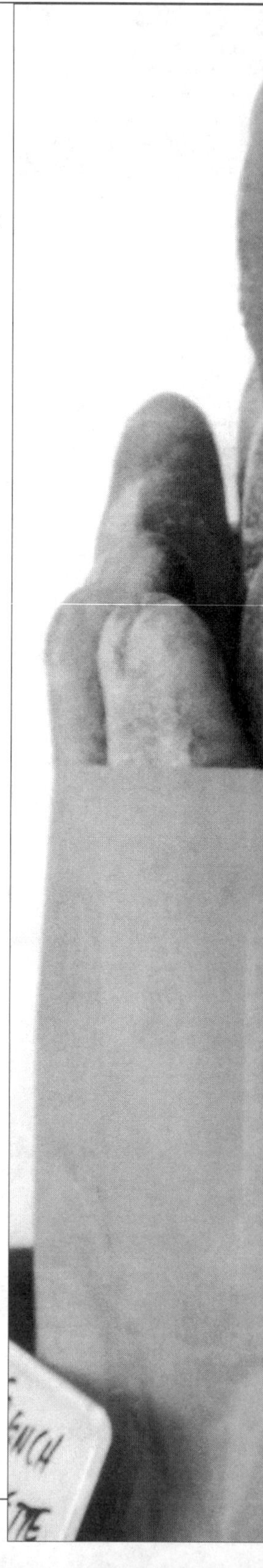

Madison and Park Ave.), (212) 838-2600, www.theglaziergroup.com. Hours: M-F 11:30am-11pm, Sa 5:30pm-11pm. MC, V, AmEx, D, Entrées: $26-$38. 6 to 51st St., E V to Lexington Ave.-53rd St., N R W 4 5 6 to Fifth Ave.-59th St.

Norma's

You would never expect to find this refreshingly low-key restaurant serving an all-brunch menu all day long nestled in Le Parker Meridien Hotel. With fabulous chocolate or Rice Krispy French Toast for kids, as well as adult specialties like Wa Zaa (a waffle smothered in berry brulee) alongside traditional brunch items such as smothered eggs or eggs benedict, Norma's has been pleasing for years. Even Martha Stewart has dined here. On weekends come early.
118 W. 57th St. (bet. Sixth and Seventh Aves.) (212) 708-7460. Hours: M-F 6:30am-3pm, Sa-Su 7:30 am-3pm. MC, V, AmEx, D. A B C D 1 to 59th St.

Osteria del Circo

Tuscany goes to the circus at this Italian offshoot of the erstwhile legend: Le Cirque 2000. The menu runs heavy on tasty fish and pasta, nothing too ingenious or pretentious. Unlike its upscale French cousin, Osteria just wants to have fun. The circus theme runs from the trapeze ladders draped from wall to wall or the flame-colored metal juggler and musician sculptures perched on the back wall. A beautiful restaurant, with fabulous food and a wonderful location. One must try the donut dessert; it is fantastic.
120 W. 55th St. (bet. Sixth and Seventh Aves.), (212) 265-3636, www.osteriadelcircio.com. Hours: M-F 11am-2pm, 5:30pm-11pm, Sa-Su 5:30pm-11pm. MC, V, AmEx, D, Entrées: $30-$40. N R W to 57th St.

Osteria Stella

While its advantageous location (between Radio City Music Hall and the Winter Garden Theater) and accommodating 250-seat capacity make it a huge attraction for theater-goers, this fine Italian establishment is certainly legit—head and shoulders above your typical pre-theater fare. The Carpaccio, Risotto and wide array of spiced breads are superb starters to a comprehensive and utterly satisfying meal. The portions for every delicious dish are generous, and you won't want to let any of it go to waste. Thus, it is difficult to leave your table without feeling somewhat crapulent. Damn them for offering so much great Italian food in which to indulge!
135 W. 50th St. (bet. Sixth and Seventh Ave.), (212) 957-5050. Hours: M-F 11:30am-11:30pm; Sa 4pm-12am; Su 4pm-11pm MC, V, AmEx, D, Entrées: $17-$32. B D F V to 47th-50th Sts. - Rockefeller Ctr.; N R W to 49th St.

Pampano

Relax in the airy, white-washed second-floor dining room or on the beautiful outdoor terrace. The tangy seafood dishes, lively salsa music, and enormous variety of margaritas make it that much easier to pretend you're looking out over the ocean instead of a skyscraper on Third Ave.
209 E. 49th St. (bet. Second and Third Aves), (212) 751-4545. Hours: Su 11:30am-4pm, 5pm-10:30pm. M 11am-2:30pm, 5pm-10:30pm, T-R 11am-2:30pm, 5pm-11:30pm, F 11am-2:30pm, 5pm-12:30am, Sa 5pm-12:30am. MC, V, AmEx, Entrées: $14- $24. E V to 53rd St., 6 to 51st St.

Park Bistro

Recently purchased by the chef of 11 years, Park Bistro carries with it the same old-school design and French cuisine. The design may make young ones feel old, but the service more than makes up for it. This family of staff waits on you hand and foot, and makes sure Park Bistro feels like home. While the wild mushroom ravioli has been a specialty of the house here for more than a decade, everything on the menu is wonderful.
414 Park Ave. South (bet. 28th and 29th), (212) 689-1360. Hours: M-F 12pm-3pm, 5:30-10:30pm, Sa-Su 5:30pm-10:30pm. MC, V, AmEx, D, Entrées: $15-$25. 6 to 28th St.

Pietrasanta

A Hell's Kitchen neighborhood secret, where the chef actually comes out of the kitchen to ask how customers are enjoying their meals. For an appetizer, try the succulent scallops in a rich pesto sauce, and order the pumpkin ravioli in sweet

pepper sauce as an entrée.
683 Ninth Ave (at 47th St.) (212) 265-9471. Hours: M-F 12pm-12am, Sa 11am-12am, Su 11am-11pm. AmEx, MC, V. C E to 50th St.

Prime Grill
This is the only place in the city where the Kosher-conscious can experience the same business-class steak that dominates the diets of many major New York power brokers. This centrally located Jewish hot-spot offers a superior selection of steaks and kosher red wines that satisfy the observant and non-affiliated alike. For those who abstain from even non-treif steak (a meshugga in this reviewer's mind), there is an impressive collection of sushi to fill the void. Some of the best kosher food you can get, outside of your mother's kitchen, of course.
60 E. 49th St., (bet. Madison and Park Aves.), (212) 692-9292. Hours: M-F 12pm-2:30pm M-R 5:30pm-11pm, Sa 1.5 hours after sundown, Su 4pm-10pm. AmEx, MC, V, Entrées: $25-$40. E to Fifth Ave., 4 6 to 51 St.

Ruby Foo's
Fun, cool, hip pan-Asian food offering everything from dim sum to sushi and a popular Sunday brunch. Ruby Foo's is known for its over-the-top and ostentatious decor and sometimes snooty service.
1626 Broadway (at 49th St.), (212) 489-5600. Hours: Su-W 11am-12am, R-Sa 11am-1am. MC, V, AmEx, D, Entrées: $25. C E to 50th St.

Shaburi
If you have ever tasted Kobe beef, you probably think that it is as good as high-quality meat gets. Think again. At this Japanese/Taiwanese sensation, Kobe beef ranks a distant second to the luscious Matsuzaka. A classic shabu-shabu dish, the Matsuzaka is served raw in very fine slices. Here, all the tables are fully equipped with electric stovetops, and the diner cooks the meat to his liking within seconds. When the Matsuzaka turns a juicy red, it is ready to melt in your mouth upon contact. While the shabu-shabu is Shaburi's sexiest dish, the sukiyaki and sushi selections are marvelous in their own right. With only the highest quality of ingredients, this meal should prove to be a wonderful dining experience. Otherwise, blame the cook...yourself!
125 E. 39th St. (bet. Lexington and Park Ave.), (212) 867-6999. Hours: M-S 12pm-3:30pm, 5pm-11pm. MC, V, AmEx, D. 4 5 6 7 S to 42nd St.-Grand Central Terminal.

Silverleaf Tavern
This pleasant and peaceful eatery channels some old-school New York style while incorporating some bold modern dishes into their menu. Silverleaf delivers on old favorites, such as shellfish pan roast, East Coast Halibut, and Long Island Duck. But it also wows with some daring appetizers: the Westfield Chevre French Toast is wildly innovative and exciting to the palette. The main attraction, however, is the "bottomless" six-ounce glass of wine, which allows diners to sample seven varietals of the sommelier's hand-picked collection. Though the food stands on its own, the wine elevates the experience to a completely different stratosphere.
43 E. 38th St. (at Park Ave. So.), (212) 973-2550. Hours: M-W 7am-11am, 12pm-3pm, 5:30pm-10:30pm; R-F 7am-11am, 12pm-3pm, 5:30pm-11:30pm, Sa 8am-12pm, 5:30pm-11:30pm, Su 8am-12pm, 5:30pm-10pm. MC, V, AmEx, D. 4 5 6 7 S to 42nd St.-Grand Central Terminal.

Seppi's
This classy casual restaurant in the belly of the Parker Meridien redefines French cuisine from the region bordering Germany. No sauerkraut here, just succulent lamb shanks, crawfish ravioli, buffalo carpaccio, and eau de vie to wash it all down. Try the hot banana tart with the chocolate crust and ice cream filling. Not cheap, but good for the family and theatre crowds. The prix-fixe is a good deal.
123 W. 56th St. (bet. Sixth and Seventh Aves.), (212) 708-7444. Hours: M-F 11:30am-2am, Sa 5pm-2am, Su 10:30am-3:30pm, 5pm-2am. MC, V, AmEx, D. A B C D 1 to 59th St.

Solo
Kosher
This elegant restaurant recently opened in the Sony Atrium and has since raised the bar for New York's kosher fare. Madonna has been rumored to frequent this establishment, and with good reason: the food is a truly unique culinary experience and well worth the price. Try the sushi-esque Yellowfin Tuna Tartare as an appetizer, continue with the prime rib for your main course, and end with a chocolate tart or caramel soufflé, both simply divine. The food's artful presentation is matched by its exquisite taste, both complemented by the restaurant's understated decor. Finally, those who are kosher-conscious can have a dining experience on par with the city's finest establishments.
550 Madison Ave. (bet. 55th and 56th Sts.) (212) 833-7800. Hours: Lunch, Su-F 10am-2pm, Dinner: M -Th 5pm-10pm, Su 4pm-10 pm. MC, V, AmEx, D. E V to 53rd St.-Fifth Ave.

Soup Kitchen
While *Seinfeld* fanatics are bemoaning the end of an era, one remnant lives on. The lines at this pop-culture landmark are unreal at lunchtime, but have you noticed how smoothly it moves along? Patrons have made up their minds what to order by the time they reach the counter of this famous take-out. Otherwise it's "No soup for you!"
259-A W. 55th St. (bet. Eighth Ave. and Broadway), (212) 757-7730. Hours: M-F 12pm-6pm. Closed for the summer. Cash Only, Entrées: $6-$8. A B C D 1 to 59th St.-Columbus Circle.

Taksim
Although there are relatively few Turkish restaurants in New York City, Taksim is undoubtably one of the best. The laid back

atmosphere and cheaper prices allow one to feel completely comfortable and at home. Nonetheless, the quality of the food is excellent. Because the starters are so cheap, be sure to try many of them, especially the falafel and hummus. For Entrées, be sure to try the lamb, although most things on the menu are delicious. Do not skip dessert: the baklava is amazing, as is the kadayif, and no visit to Taksim is complete without both.
1030 Second Ave. (bet. 54th and 55th St.), (212) 421-3004. Hours: M-F 11:30am-11pm, Sa-Su 11am-11pm. MC, V, AmEx, D. Entrées: $7-$14. E V 6 to 51st St.

Tao

This is THE trendy new-age restaurant. Let's just say this: If Vincent Chase were to come visit NY, you can bet that Ari Gold would have the "sky-box" private dining room reserved for his client. VIPs tend to dine up there while hovering above the rest of us mere mortals. The decor is truly a marvel in its own right: After walking in through an opulent golden entryway, diners enter an ethereal enclave of cool dominated by a backlit three-story golden Buddha. As for the food: this reviewer would request the Chilean sea bass as his final supper were he consigned to death row; it's just that good. Be sure to make a reservation far in advance. And, don't forget to be cool.
42 E. 58th St. (bet. Madison and Park Aves.), (212) 888-2288. Hours: M-T 11:30am-12am, W-F 11am-1am, Sa 5pm-1am, Su 5pm-12am. MC, V, AmEx, D. Entrées: $16-25. N R W 4 5 6 to 59th St.

Toledo

The cherry wood, archways and courtly dining hall of this midtown Spanish restaurant evoke the elegance of a bygone century. Ask, and the retinue of waiters will proudly point you to the best dishes on the menu. Or try the authentic paella prized for its fresh seafood and savory saffron rice. The sangria is almost too delicious, and after a few glasses you'll sing its praises.
6 E. 36th St. (bet. Fifth and Madison Aves.), (212) 696-5036. Hours: M-Sa 12pm-10:30pm. MC, V, AmEx, D, Entrées: $22-$26. 6 to 33rd St.

Topaz Thai Restaurant

This spot may be cramped and a bit hard to find, but the food's tasty and, judging by the constant flux of diners, happy on the budget. Upon your arrival, a smiling, speedy waiter will seat you at a table three inches from your neighbors on all sides. However, the delicious curried Entrées and Thai iced tea will make you forget the cramped quarters.
125 W. 56th St. (bet. Sixth and Seventh Aves.), (212) 957-8020. Hours: M-F 12pm-11pm, Sa-Su 4pm-11pm. MC, V, AmEx, Entrées: $8-18. A B C D 1 to 59th St.-Columbus Circle.

Uncle Nick's Greek Cuisine

Serving enormous kebobs, salads brimming with stuffed grape leaves and olives, and huge wedges of flaming saganaki cheese, Uncle Nick's won't leave you hungry. The bustling atmosphere, attentive wait staff, and speedy service make this restaurant great for pre-theater dining.
747 Ninth Ave. (bet. 50th and 51st Sts.), (212) 245-7992. Hours: Su-Sa 12pm-11pm. MC, V, AmEx, D, Entrées: $9-$15. C E to 50th St.

Via Brasil

This Little Brazil fave is full of jazz, palms and fabulous food. The waiters are nice, the appetizers as good as the Entrées. Try the lime drinks, fish casserole, and piping hot coffee. Lots of Brazilians come here too.
34 W. 46th St. (bet. Fifth and Sixth Aves.), (212) 997-1158. Hours: M-R 12pm-11pm, F-Sa 12pm-12am, Su 12pm-10pm. MC, V, AmEx, D, $14-$22. B D F to 47-50th Sts.

Victor's Cafe

This classic Cuban cafe is full of plantains, meats, and fawning service. There is even live music on certain nights. The brunch is nice and relaxed. A great place to go before the theatre.
236 W. 52nd St. (bet. Broadway & Eighth Ave.), (212) 586-7714. Hours: Su-R 12pm-11pm, F-Sa 12pm-12am. MC, V, AmEx. C E 1 to 50th St.

Cafes

Cupcake Cafe

A quaint bakery with pink walls and tin ceilings on the raunchiest stretch in Hell's Kitchen. Great donuts, waffles, and cupcakes, with a few tables to allow for immediate consumption. The location is unfashionable for a food pilgrimage, but come for old-fashioned sweets.
522 Ninth Ave. (at 39th St.), (212) 465-1530. Hours: M-F 7am-7pm, Sa 8am-7pm, Su 9am-5pm. Cash Only. A C E N R S W 1 2 3 7 to 42nd St.-Times Sq.

Emack and Bolio's

By the time you get to the fourth floor of Macy's, you'll need a break. Look no further than Emack and Bolios for sandwiches and sweeter goodies. Then pick up your bags and start again, rejuvenated by your sweet tooth fix. This upscale ice cream joint is the cream of choice for native New Yorkers, especially in the age of homogenized Ben & Jerry's.
Macy's, 151 W. 34th St., Fourth Fl., (212) 494-5853. Hours: Su-Sa 10am-8pm. MC, V, AmEx, Entrées: $4-$6. A C E 1 2 3 to 34th St., B D F N R V W to 34th St.-Herald Sq.

[Upper East Side]

Restaurants

Daniel

One of New York's finest and most exclusive: amazing food, beautiful setting, and, of course, prices to match. If you feel like acting entitled for a day, give Daniel a visit and empty your wallet for that one-of-a-kind meal..
60 E. 65th St. (bet. Park and Madison Aves.), (212) 288-0033, www.danielnyc.com. Hours: M-Sa 5:45-11pm. MC, V, AmEx,

D, Entrées: $40-$60. 6 *to 68th St.-Hunter College.*

Elaine's

A magnet for A-list hometown celebs often featured in gossip columns. This popular hangout serves up standard American fare. Quality blows hot and cold, but coming here for the food is like living in New York for the weather: it just shouldn't be a priority. Regulars include Woody Allen, Barbara Walters, and George Plimpton.
1703 Second Ave. (bet. 88th and 89th Sts.), (212) 534-8103. Hours: Su-Sa 6pm-2am. MC, V, AmEx, D, Entrées: $15-$30. 4 5 6 *to 86th St.*

Gobo

Vegetarians don't have to resign themselves to munching on rabbit food, not when there are options such as Gobo to please the palate. This organic, Pan-Asian restaurant rooted in what they call Zen compassion really will appeal to your five senses. The chakra rolls are a must order, and even non-veggies will enjoy the varied menu - the smoked Beijing-style seitan with Chinese vegetables looks like its duck counterpart and is just as flavorful. Try the organic smoothies and don't be shy of the vegetables - the taste will pleasantly surprise you. A perfect retreat from the hustle of the city.
1426 Third Ave. (bet. 80th & 81 Sts.), (212) 288-5099, www.goborestaurant.com. Hours: M-Su, 11am-11pm. MC, V, AmEx, D. Entrées: $12-$16. 6 *to 77th St.*

Harry Cipriani

Throw on your snobbiest outfit and enjoy the truly gourmet and truly pricy menu offered by the eponymous gourmet grocery magnate. If you can stand the attitude, come to look for celebrities and to feel like one yourself.
781 Fifth Ave. (bet. 59th and 60th Sts.), (212) 753-5566. Hours: Su-Sa 12pm-2:30pm, 6pm-10:30pm. MC, V, AmEx, D, Entrées: $40. N R 4 5 6 *to 59th St.-Lexington Ave.*

Ian

Come and experience chef and owner Ian Russo's first-rate "Nouveau New York" creations. Hawaiian and French influences make this chic Upper East Sider anything but typical. Try the Dirty Drunken Ribeye or share their succulent steak for two, which is carved tableside; The attentive waitstaff and elegant decor provide the perfect setting for a date or special occasion. As if Ian's pioneering culinary genius is not enough, you can drop by the bar and have Frank make you his own signature cocktail: the "Frankenberry."
322 86th St., (bet. First and Second Aves.), (212) 861-1993. Hours: Su-R, 5pm-11pm; F-Sa, 5pm-12am. MC, V, AmEx, D, Entrées: $25-$50. 4 5 6 *to 86th St.*

La Gouloue

Sure the food's great, but this is a snobby place. If you don't fit into the mold you will be treated like second-rate cheese. Try the skate fish and guffaw at all the people being told there's a two hour wait on all of the empty tables.
746 Madison Ave. (bet. 64th and 65th Sts.), (212) 988-8169. Hours: Su-Sa 12pm-11pm. MC, V, AmEx, D, Entrées:$20-$35. 6 *to 68th St.*

The Lenox Room

With the decor and vibe of a 1940s lounge, The Lenox Room is unique amongst the majority of "hoity-toity" Upper East Side establishments. The entrees are standard, but the real treats are the appetizers and desserts. Try one of their "Tiers of Taste" to experience some of the best munchies this side of Vegas. The atmosphere is relaxed, but you may notice some famous faces in the crowd.
1278 Third Ave. (at 73rd St.), (212) 772-0404. www.lenoxroom.com. M-F 12pm-2pm, 5:30pm-11pm, Sa 5:30pm-11pm, Su 23pm-2:30pm, 5:30pm-11pm. MC, V, AmEx, D. Entrées: $15-$35. 6 *to 77th St.*

Merchants NY

The wooden blinds hanging in the dining room are always drawn at this sleek Upper East Side New American that is reminiscent of *L.A. Confidential*, with a vast selection of strong liquor to boot. The food sounds sophisticated on the menu, but sadly disappoints on the plate. The real attraction, though, is the see-and-be-seen setting and the lounge atmosphere. Also be sure to check out downstairs, where there is live jazz every night and dinner till 3 in the morning.
1125 First Ave. (at 62nd St.), (212) 832-1551. Hours: Su-Sa 11am-4am. MC, V, AmEx, Entrées $10-$24. F N R W 4 5 6 *to 59th St.-Lexington Ave.*

Le Bilboquet

Many Europeans – New York Europeans, too – people this diminutive French bistro. Models can't appreciate the menu, but don't let that stop you from taking advantage of the well-executed bistro fare.
25 E. 63rd St. (bet. Madison and Park Aves.), (212) 751-3036. Hours: Su-Sa 12pm-11pm. MC, V, AmEx, Entrées: $17-$24. F N R W 4 5 6 *to 59th St.-Lexington Ave.*

Manana Restaurant

Delicious and reasonably-priced Mexican food lies behind this otherwise unassuming First Ave. facade. The atmosphere is cute, if a little cheesy, but the main draw here is the food. Everything is good across the board, but the Yucatan-style carnitas are worth a trip all by themselves.
1136 First Ave. (bet. 62nd and 63rd Sts.), (212) 371-8023. Hours: Su-Sa 12pm-11pm. MC, V, AmEx. Entrées: $8-$16. F N R W 4 5 6 *to 59th St.*

Payard Patisserie and Bistro

Payard's two-tiered restaurant, dim lighting, and French service create an elegant, Upper East Side atmosphere. With an impressive wine list, traditional French cuisine, and impeccable service, your meal will be well worth the bill. If you're not in the mood for big spending, skip straight to the dessert menu; their pastries truly melt in your mouth and most are under $10. Some of the best

dessert in New York.
1032 Lexington Ave. (bet. 73rd and 74th Sts.), (212) 717-5252, www.payard.com. Patisserie Hours: 7am-11pm. Bistro Hours: M-R 12pm-3pm, 5:45pm-10pm, F-Sa 12pm-3pm, 5:45pm-11pm. MC, V, AmEx, D. 6 *to 77th St.*

Rosa Mexicano

A well-heeled clientele sips pomegranate margaritas at the crowded bar while waiting for a taste of well executed classics. Guacamole is prepared table-side and desserts like the tamal en cazuela dulce, a sweetish, warm cornmeal swirled with a chocolate sauce, make this a must.
1063 First Ave. (at 58th St.), (212) 753-7407. Hours: Su-Sa 5pm-11:30pm. MC, V, AmEx, D. Entrées: $17-$26. F N R W 4 5 6 *to 59th St.-Lexington Ave.*

Cafes

DTUT

Ever want to hang out in a coffeehouse reminiscent of Central Perk? Here's your chance. With deep couches, delicious coffee, and yummy goodies, you can spend hours just chatting with pals at this Upper East Side cafe. Be sure not to miss the do-it-yourself s'mores.
1626 Second Ave. (bet. 84th and 85th Sts.), (212) 327-1327. Hours: Su-R 8am-12am, F-Sa 8am-2am.MC, V, AmEx, Entrées: $5-$12. 4 5 6 *to 86th St.*

Serendipity III

Famous for their frozen hot chocolates and ice cream sundaes that go on forever, leave your diet at the door when you visit. Though a bit overpriced for the quality of the Entrées, most concede that it's well worth it when they finish their delicious desserts.
225 East 60th St. (bet. Second and Third Aves.), (212) 838-3531, www.serendipity3.com. Hours: Su-R 11:30am-12am, F 11:30am-1am, Sa 11:30am-2am. MC, V, AmEx, D, Entrées: $12-$17. N R W 4 5 6 *to 59th St.-Lexington Ave.*

[Upper West Side]

Restaurants

A

French and Caribbean flavors intertwine in this tiny dining room. Bring a bottle of your favorite red and put your faith – and your hunger – in the deft hands of the cooks. Expect to wait in the bar next door, where an ice-cold Red Stripe will send you dreaming of Spring Break.
947 Columbus Ave. (at 106th St.), (212) 531-1643. Hours: T-Sa 6pm-11pm, Cash Only. B C *to 103rd St.,* 1 *to 103rd St.*

Ayurveda Cafe

Upper Westsiders swear by this quaint Indian restaurant with a daily prix fixe menu. The food is vegetarian and based on the Hindu philosophies of Ayurveda. What that boils down to is simple, healthful, holistic food that satisfies without being too filling.
706 Amsterdam Ave. (bet 94th and 95th Sts.), (212) 932-2400. Hours: Su-Sa, 11:30am-11pm, MC, V, AmEx, D, Entrées: $9-$16. 1 2 3 *to 96th St.*

Bruculino

Sicilian seafood cooked to perfection is served in the soothing wood and wave interior of this West Side culinary treasure. Dishes are inventive and colorful. Outdoor seating is available on the terrace. Try the specials of the evening and leave room for coffee and dessert.
225 Columbus Ave. (at 70th St.), (212) 579-3966. Hours: M-Sa 12pm-11pm, Su 12pm-10pm. MC, V, AmEx, D, Entrées: $10-$20. B C *to 72nd St.*

Cafe Des Artistes

You'll feel glamorous at this classic New York restaurant. Don't get addicted to that feeling though, because visiting this romantic rendezvous too often will clean out your wallet as seductively as it filled you up.
1 W. 67th St. (bet. Columbus Ave. and Central Park West.), (212) 877-3500, www.cafedesartistes.com. Hours: Su-Sa 12pm-2:30pm, 5:30pm-12am. MC, V, AmEx, D, Entrées: $30-$40. 1 *to 66th St.*

Carmine's

Come with a group of friends and order up a storm of family-style Italian. Seating is slow, so a visit to this enormous darkwood institution happily mandates a stop at the lovely bar.
2450 Broadway (at 91st St.), (212) 362-2200. Hours: Su-R 11:30am-11pm, F-Sa 11:30am-12am. MC, V, AmEx, D, Entrées: $15-$25. 1 2 3 *to 96th St.*

Columbus Bakery

This family staple has consistently good pastries, pizzettes and other bakery-style food. With nice interiors and consistently packed brunches, Columbus is a great place to hang out on a lazy afternoon – if you can get a table. Beware the stroller wars at the door.
474 Columbus Ave. (bet. 82nd and 83rd Sts.), (212) 724-6880. Hours: Su-Sa 8am-10pm. MC, V, AmEx. 1 *to 86th St.,* B C *to 81st St.*
Additional location on Upper East Side.

Compass

Although never just a steakhouse, Compass has been recently revamped with the arrival of new chef John Fraser, adding new concoctions and developments to an already stellar menu. One of the few great restaurants on the Upper West Side, Compass is an oasis in an otherwise dry area. The dark decor deliciously highlights the romantic aspects of the intimate space, making Compass a great restaurant for a date. Both the appetizers and desserts are excellent, particularly the sea scallops and the cheesecake napoleon.
208 W. 70th St. (at Amsterdam Ave.), (212) 875-8600, www.compassrestaurant.com. Hours: M-W 5pm-11pm; R-Sa 5pm-12am, Su 11:30am-2:30pm, 5pm-11pm. MC, V, AmEx, D, Entrées: $25-$40. 1 2 3 *to 72nd St.*

Deli Kasbah

Kosher

Orthodox patrons fill the dining room, while take-out satisfies folks of all

faiths with amazingly fresh meats and stellar Entrées, like the jumbo pastrami burger. The menu has a Middle Eastern slant, with lots of hummus, babaganoush, and falafel. Sample all three of them in the Kasbah Combination.
251 W. 85th St. (bet. Broadway and West End Ave.), (212) 496-1500. Hours: Su-R 12pm-10pm. MC, V, D, Entrées: $8-$20. ① to 86th St.

Fine and Schapiro
Kosher
One of the finest sit-down delis in Manhattan, F&S sparkles with homey friendliness. Diner-style meals are served up alongside a delightful brand of old-fashioned Borsch-Belt humor. The menu contains every kosher favorite from matza ball soup and stuffed cabbage to an array of gourmet sandwiches. The only drawback is the pervading guilt that you'll be sent to your room if you don't finish your food.
138 W. 72nd St. (at Amsterdam Ave.), (212) 877-2874. Hours: Su-Sa 10am-10pm. MC, V, AmEx, D, Entrées: $8-17. ①②③ to 72nd St.

French Roast
Providing a great atmosphere for sitting with a coffee or a nice big cup of hot chocolate, French Roast is a refuge from the busy Upper West Side. The sidewalk seating is great for people watching.
2340 Broadway (85th St.), (212) 799-1533. Hours: 24 hours. MC, V, AmEx, D. ① to 86th St.

Gabriel's
Among the crème de la crème of the bevy of restaurants around Lincoln Center, the combination of casual and class here is just about perfect. Beautiful decor, an astonishing, seasonal menu (try the delectable butternut squash ravioli), and a refined yet informal staff all account for why this is one of New York's hottest spots for dinner. Come after 7:45pm to avoid the pre-concert crowd.
11 W. 60th St. (bet. Broadway and Columbus Ave.), (212) 956-4600. Hours: M-R 12pm-3pm, 5pm-11pm, F 12pm-3pm, 5pm-12am, Sa 5pm-12am. MC ,V, AmEx, D, Entrées: $25-$27. Ⓐ Ⓑ Ⓒ Ⓓ ① to 59th St.-Columbus Circle.

Gabriela's
One of the best home-style Mexican restaurants in New York, Gabriela's is a family-friendly, low-key place, where the waiters won't make guacamole tableside but will cheerfully seat you at one of its many booths. Loud and colorful, Gabriela's is a mainstay of the Upper West Side.
685 Amsterdam Ave. (93rd St.), (212) 961-0574. Hours: Su-Sa 11:30am-12am. MC, V, AmEx, D. ① ②③ to 96th St.
315 Amsterdam Ave. (75th St.), (212) 875-8532. Hours: Su-Sa 11am-11pm. MC, V, AmEx, D. ①②③ to 72nd St.

Gari
Masatoshi Sugio—the innovator of "top sushi"—has done it again! Mirroring his Sushi Of Gari on the East Side, Gari has added hot dishes to his already fantastic sushi menu. The specialty of the house, Omakase sushi blends ingredients and tastes from around the food world, and will surely leave your palate in euphoric shock. The exquisite presentation coupled with the low-key atmosphere will leave you wondering why you hadn't dropped in sooner.
370 Columbus Ave. (near 77th St.), (212) 362-4816. Hours: M-R 5pm-11pm, F-Sa 5pm-11:30pm, Su 5pm-10pm. MC, V, AmEx, D, Entrées: $23-45. Ⓑ Ⓒ to 81st St.

Gennaro
Native Italian chef Gennaro Picone graced several upscale Manhattan establishments before opening his own place where he serves unpretentious, truly Italian (not Italian-American) dishes in a tiny, unassuming space. The décor may seem a little rough around the edges, but the food is most definitely not (try the gnocchi). The prices are so reasonable that they impose a $20 minimum. Be warned: the waits are long and the space is cramped.
665 Amsterdam Ave. (bet. 92nd and 93rd Sts.), (212) 665-5348. Hours: Su-R 5pm-10:30pm, F-Sa 5pm-11pm. Cash only, Entrées: $8-$15. ①②③ to 96th St.

Good Enough to Eat
Known for what is perhaps the best brunch in the city, this comfort food gem on the Upper West Side is packed to the brim on weekend mornings. At dinner the atmosphere is far more relaxed while the food remains just as delicious, with wonderful breads and meat dishes, as well as desserts to die for. The restaurant wins with its own signature style, and it's the perfect place for a girls' night out.
483 Amsterdam Ave. (bet. 83rd and 84th Sts.), (212) 496-0163. Hours: M-R 8am-4pm, 5:30pm-10pm, F 8am-4pm, 5:30pm-11pm, Sa 9am-4pm, 5:30pm-11pm, Sun 9am-4pm, 5:30pm-10pm. MC, V, AmEx, Entrées: $9-$18, Brunch: $5-$9. ① to 86th St., Ⓑ Ⓒ to 81st St.

Gray's Papaya
Gray's resembles its low-brow cousin, Papaya King, offering lots of cheap hot dogs, papaya juice and other heartburn-inducing fare. A hit with bankers slumming it during lunch hour to penniless students to out-of-work types, Gray's is a New York institution. Don't expect Julia Child, but for $3 you too can fill up with comfort food.
2090 Broadway (at 72nd St.) (212) 799-0243. 24 hours. Cash only. ①②③ to 72nd St.
Additional locations throughout Manhattan.

La Caridad 78
This Dominican chain is known for its greasy food, large portions, and authentic service. Try the chicken with rice and beans, and practice your Spanish.
2197-2199 Broadway (at 78th St.), (212) 874-2780. Hours: M-Sa 11:30am-12am, Su 11am-10:30pm. Cash and Checks only. ① to 79th St.

Lemongrass Grill
Lemongrass is a consistent Thai restaurant that is

Blue Angel

This spanking new Thai restaurant offers authentic cuisine that will astound Thai rookies and impress longstanding veterans. One taste of their tangy Drunken Noodles, which incorporates many classic Thai spices and special ingredients, will convert first-timers into recurring customers. The diligent owner wakes at 4am every morning to select the fresh-from-the-sea fish for your dining pleasure. Start your meal with one of their exotic appetizers or soups for only $3-$6, and then marvel at (and enjoy) the artfully presented sushi. The house specialties of duck and seafood are served on over-sized platters and provide the diner with substantial, yet exquisite entrees for only $11. Order the Mango Sticky Rice for dessert as a delightful end to a truly unique repast.
3143 Broadway (bet. LaSalle and 125th St.), (212) 222-8666. Hours: M-Sa 11am-11pm, Su 11am-10pm. MC, V, AmEx, D, Entrées: $10-$15. ❶ to 125th St.

heavy on the lemongrass and light on the ambience. There isn't much to complain about, particularly the prices. A good take-out option, too.
2534 Broadway (bet. 94th and 95th Sts.) (212) 666-0888 Hours: Su-R 12pm-10:30pm, F-Sa 12pm-11:30pm. Amex, V, MC. ❶ ❷❸ to 96th St.
Additional locations in Manhattan.

Le Pain Quotidien
The golden earthy décor and menu holders, made of large pieces of bread, complement the delicate upscale versions of provincial fare that this restaurant and bakery serve so well. The sandwiches and desserts are culinary works of art. Come for a meal or spend hours in a quiet corner sipping a warm delicious cup of coffee. Either way, do not leave without tasting what might be the best mozzarella in New York.
50 W. 72nd St. (bet. Central Park W. and Columbus Ave.), (212) 712-9700. Hours: Su-Sa 7:30am-7pm. AmEx, V, MC, Entrées: $8-$15. Ⓑ Ⓒ to 72nd St.
Additional locations throughout Manhattan.

Max Soha
This hidden gem is well worth the trip uptown. Here a ten-spot will buy you the city's best bowl of lamb ragu. For a few extra bucks, a glass of Montepulciano will make your meal complete. While waiting for your table, walk two doors down to their cafe and enjoy a drink on one of their plush vintage sofas.
1274 Amsterdam Ave. (at 123rd St.), (212) 531-2221. Hours: Su-Sa 11:30am-11:30pm. Cash only, $20-$30. ❶ to 125th St.

Ollie's
Ollie's is a substandard Chinese restaurant located in suprastandard locations: next to Columbia University and Lincoln Center, for instance. There are rumors of health code violations, and complaints about bad service. But it looks good, and the food comes fast. Occasionally you'll hit a gem, like their General Tso's shrimp.
1991 Broadway (at 68th St.), (212) 595-8181, Hours: Su-Sa 11am-12am. V, MC, AmEx. ❶ to 66th St.
Additional locations throughout Manhattan.

Ozu
Though prompt seating can be a problem, this small, Japanese restaurant wins points for its creative tofu, grain, noodle, tempura, and vegetable dishes. The ambitious side orders will transport you to new levels of sensual awareness, especially the three-root sesame salad with carrot, burdock root, and daikon radish.
566 Amsterdam Ave. (at 87th St.), (212) 787-8316. Hours: Su-Sa 11:30am-10pm. MC, V, Entrées: $7-$12. ❶ to 86th St.

Pasha
Pasha is an elegant yet relaxing oasis of Turkish restaurant an easy walk from Lincoln Center. After a couple drinks in the dark and posh lounge, retreat to the bright colorfully decorated dining room in the back where you will receive very friendly service from a swarm of Middle Eastern staff. Don't miss the lightly sweet grape leaves stuffed with currants and mint, the lamb served over a delicious charcoal roasted smoky eggplant puree, and some of the finest baklava around. Pasha's wonderful charm, service, and cuisine make it a good value for the price.
70 W 71st St., (bet. Columbus Ave. and Central Park W.), 212-579-8751. Hours: Su-R 5pm-11pm, F-Sa 5:30pm-11:30pm. MC, V, AmEx, Entrées: $13-$20. ❶❷❸ to 72nd St.

Pizzeria UNO
This chain isn't authentic and will certainly blow your diet. The deep dish pizza crust is buttery for a reason, and the ambience pure fast food. But for a good time in a relaxed atmosphere, it does the job and does it well.
432 Columbus Ave. (at 81st St.) (212) 595-4700. Hours: M-R 11am-1am, F-Sa 11am-2am, Su 11am-12am. MC, V, AmEx. Ⓑ Ⓒ to 81st St.
Additional locations throughout Manhattan, Brooklyn, and Queens.

Popover Cafe
New England charm meets New York savvy at this convivial spot, one of the most popular brunch venues in the neighborhood. Feast upon gourmet omelets and excellent griddle specialties – and don't forget the popovers.
551 Amsterdam Ave. (at 87th St.), (212) 595-8555. Hours: M-F 8am-10pm, Sa-Su 9am-10pm. MC, V, AmEx, Entrées: $13-$22. ❶ to 86th St.

Rain
Delicious pan-Asian fusion cuisine and a vibrant, attractive crowd make this one of the Upper West

Side's hottest dining spots. On Friday and Saturday nights, the bar overflows with 20-somethings trying to get tables, but the Asian canopy and exotic beers make it worth the wait.
100 W. 82nd St. (at Columbus Ave.), (212) 501-0776. Hours: M-R 12pm-3pm, 6pm-11pm, F 12pm-3pm, 6pm-12am, Sa 12pm-4pm, 5pm-12am, Su 12pm-4pm, 5pm-10pm. MC, V, AmEx, D, Entrées $12-22. B C to 81st St.

Rikyu

The freedom to choose can be mind-boggling for early-bird D taking advantage of the $9.95 prix fixe, with 17 dinner options. You can't go wrong with remarkably fresh sushi or any combination involving tempura, teriyaki, or cooked fish.
483 Columbus Ave. (bet. 83rd and 84th Sts.), (212) 799-7847. Hours: Su-Sa 12pm-3:30pm, 5pm-11pm. MC, V, AmEx, D. Entrées: $10-$17. 1 2 3 to 72nd St.

Saigon Grill

One of the tastiest and best-priced Vietnamese restaurants in the city and a favorite of Upper West Siders. Not much elbow room, so go early to avoid the crowds. You'll be craving the fresh summer rolls for days afterward.
620 Amsterdam Ave. (at 90th St.), (212) 875-9072. Hours: Su-Sa 11am-12am. MC, V, AmEx, D, Entrées: $7-$13. 1 to 86th St.

Sarabeth's West

This cheerful, yellow cafe is brimming with old-fashioned goodness. Sarabeth's serves hearty breakfasts and light, sophisticated lunches. For a special treat, drop in for afternoon tea between 3:30pm and 5:30pm. You'll feel like the Queen of England as you sip tea and nibble on finger sandwiches, cookies, and scones. Check out their Upper East Side location on Madison Ave. Cheers!
423 Amsterdam (bet. 80th and 81st Sts.), (212) 496-6280. Hours: M-F 8am-10:30pm, Sa 8am-4pm, 5:30pm-10:30pm, Su 5:30pm-9:30pm. MC, V, AmEx, D. 1 to 79th St.

Tavern on the Green

Only the well-connected score the best seats, but the crystal chandeliers and tranquil setting are impressive, if garish. This legendary Central Park outpost is a popular destination for tourists and grannies. Check out the mind-boggling wine list, recently rated the best in New York. In winter, twinkling lights on the surrounding trees make for quite a Yuletide scene.
Central Park West (at 67th St.), (212) 873-3200, www.tavernonthegreen.com. Hours: M-R 11:30am-3pm, 5pm-9pm, F 11:30am-3pm, 5pm-10:30pm, Sa 10am-3:30pm, 5pm-10:30pm, Su 10am-3:30pm, 5pm-9pm. MC, V, AmEx, D. Entrées: $13-$25. B C to 72nd St.

Time Cafe

Around mealtimes there are rarely many free tables in this vast, lofty space, and it's no wonder, since this is one of the better places filling the niche between greasy coffee shop and fancy restaurant. Health-conscious organic food and an extensive menu with selections like fancy tuna sandwiches and pan roasted penne are sure to satisfy nearly any craving.
2330 Broadway (at 85th St.), (212) 579-5100. Hours: Su-R 11:30am-12am, F-Sa 10am-1am. MC, V, AmEx, Entrées: $12-$22. 1 to 86th St.

Cafes

Cafe Con Leche

Cramped or cozy, depending on how tolerant you are of the neighboring conversation, this Cuban café pulses with upbeat salsa music and chatter. Standard dishes are perfectly prepared, from empañadas to "filet de pollo al limon." This cafe has bright, fun décor and serves up its dishes with visual flair. The portions aren't typical Latin gargantuan, and neither are the prices. Leche is a good deal, but you won't be stuffed when you leave. You can, however, linger over your café con leche or dinner for hours without the staff harassing you.
424 Amsterdam Ave. (bet. 80th and 81st Sts.), (212) 595-7000, www.cafeconleche.com. Hours: Su-Sa 8am-12am. MC, V, AmEx. 1 to 79th St.
726 Amsterdam Ave. (bet. 95th and 96th Sts.), (212) 678-7000, www.cafeconleche.com. Hours: Su-Sa 11am-12am. MC, V, AmEx, D. 1 2 3 to 96th St.

Cafe Lalo

Unlike many restaurants claiming to be a cafe, Lalo actually lives up to its

name. The cafe specializes in desserts and coffees while creating a true outdoorsy feel. The huge windows open onto an attractive street complete with outdoor benches and ivy-covered trees. In addition to desserts, the food they serve is as creative as it is unforgettable. Their triumphant chocolate fondue is worth every penny (and every calorie). This is probably the best "date place" on the Upper West Side, though it gets very cramped. It is also open late for a nighttime sweet tooth.
201 W. 83rd St. (bet. Broadway and Amsterdam Aves.), (212) 496-6031. Hours: M-R 8am-2am, F 8am-4am, Sa 9am-4am, Su 9am-2am. Cash Only. ❶ *to 86th St.*

Cafe Mozart

A slice of Europe on the Upper West Side, perfect after a show or for late morning paper perusal. Llve music once a week.
154 W. 70th St. (at Broadway), (212) 595-9797. Hours: Su-R 8am-1am, F-Sa 8am-2am. MC, V, AmEx. ❶❷❸ *to 72nd St.*

Drip

This coffee bar also has its liquor license so you can speed on caffeine, then come down with a micro-brewed beer. Singles can leaf through binders chock full of bios while sipping lattes and nibbling on oversized Rice Krispies treats. Atmosphere is casual, friendly, and relaxed; unless, of course, you do find a match!
489 Amsterdam Ave. (bet. 83rd and 84th Sts.), (212) 875-1032, www.dripcafe.com. Hours: M-R 8am-1am, F 8am-2am, Sa 9am-2am, Su 9am-1am. MC, V. ❶ *to 86th St.*

H&H Bagel

To certain New Yorkers, these bagels are good enough to qualify as a delicacy. The poppy and everything varieties go quickly, but the basic plain sourdough is something special, too. Call 1-800-NY-BAGEL to have mail orders delivered anywhere in the world. Quality comes at a price.
2239 Broadway (at 80th St.), (212) 595-8003, www.hhbagel.com. Hours: 24 hrs. Cash Only. ❶ *to 79th St.*

Silver Moon Bakery

On a quiet Sunday morning, there is no better place to sip a frothy cappuccino, nibble a pumpkin muffin, and tackle the *Times* crossword puzzle. The freshly baked breads are magnificent, and the atmosphere rivals that of the coziest Parisian cafes. On Fridays, they churn out batches of challah, and for those with dietary restrictions, they make suprisingly tasty wheat-free spelt treats.
2740 Broadway (at 105th St.), (212) 866-4717. Hours: M-F 7:30pm-8pm; Sa-Su 9am-7pm. ❶ *to 103rd St.*

[Morningside Heights]

Restaurants

107 West

This restaurant's eclectic menu and décor waffle between southwestern, Italian, and New York chic themes, but the food is consistently good (especially the rigatoni with chicken and capers). The Entrées are a little on the expensive side.
2787 Broadway (at 107th St.), (212) 864-1555. Hours: M-R 5pm-11pm, F 5pm-12am, Sa 11am-12am, Su 11am-10:30pm. MC, V, AmEx, D. Entrées $8-$18. ❶ *to 110th St.*

Alouette

This intimate bi-level French bistro serves up savory and inventive cuisine in a rich, warm atmosphere – an anomaly for the Upper West Side. The red velvet drapery and lace-curtained windows create a romantic option in West Side dining. The prices are great in exchange for this culinary and atmospheric decadence.
2588 Broadway (bet. 97th and 98th Sts.), (212) 222-6808, www.alouettenyc.com. Hours: M-Sa 5:30pm-11pm, Su 5:30pm-10pm. MC, V, AmEx, D. Entrées: $16-$22. ❶❷❸ *to 96th St.*

Amsterdam Restaurant and Tapas Lounge

They used to serve sloppy but filling burgers in AmCafe, but now they serve sophisticated but unsatisfying steaks at the Tapas Lounge. What used to be the best deal in town has now lost all of its college-town charm. Only the local grad students and professors frequent this remodeled restaurant for meals. Occasionally, the younger crowd will come here for isolated special occasions. Overall, it kind of feels like a microcosm of the gentrification occurring in this general area.
1207 Amsterdam Ave. (at 120th St.), (212) 662-6330, Hours: Su-Sa 10am-11pm. MC, V, AmEx, D. Entrées: $7-$10. ❶ *to 116th St.-Columbia University.*

Awash

The walls of this comfortable neighborhood fave are covered with bright, gaudy paintings of Ethiopia's emperors, and when the food arrives heaped over injera (the springy, sour bread which you use in lieu of cutlery), it's just as colorful. The lamb, almost overwhelmingly pungent, is toxic green; the yummy split peas are an equally bright yellow. The vegetarian combination, which can be beets, lentils, and/or collard greens, is worth it.
947 Amsterdam Ave., (at 106th St.), (212) 961-1416. Su-Sa 1pm-11pm. MC, V, AmEx, D. Entrées $9-$14. ❶ *to 110th St.*

Bistro Ten 18

This restaurant is a rarity in Morningside Heights. It presents some wonderful culinary combinations (the scallops and roasted apples are a delicious pair), and the regular favorites like New York strip steak and linguine with marinara are stand-outs as well. Bistro Ten 18 has views of the Cathedral of St. John the Divine from all of its front windows, and the back room has a fire place that is lit during the winter. The desserts are a bit on the sweet side, but nonetheless are in keeping with the quality of the rest of the meal.
1018 Amsterdam Ave. (at 110th St.), (212) 662-7600.

Hours: M-F 12pm-3:30pm, 5pm-11pm Sa 11am-3:30pm, 5pm-11pm Su 11am-3:30pm, 5pm-10pm. MC, V, AmEx, Entrées: $13-$22. ❶ *to 110th St.*

Caffe Pertutti

Bright and breezy, with a hard-tiled floor and marble-topped tables, this neighborhood cafe hosts intellectual tête-à-têtes while serving up well-prepared Italian standards alongside inventive pasta dishes. The new decorations are summery yellows and greens and complement the enormous and tasty salads well. The dessert selection is huge, and the cakes taste as good as they look.
2888 Broadway (bet. 112th and 113th Sts.), (212) 864-1143. Hours: Su-Sa 8am-1am. Cash Only, Entrées: $7-$14. ❶ *to 110th St.*

Camille's

Named after the owner's mother, this cozy Columbia University magnet is reliably good – think mom's cooking. Pizzas are a bargain at $4.25, and the hearty pasta dishes are topped with light and flavorful sauces. It's difficult to eat this well for less money; breakfast is a particularly cheap alternative to bacon 'n egg grease-balls at area diners.
1135 Amsterdam Ave. (at 116th St.), (212) 749-2428. Hours: M-F 7:30am-10pm, Sa 8am-5pm. MC, V, AmEx, Entrées: $3-$9. ❶ *to 116th St.-Columbia University.*

Famous Famiglia's

Come for the photos of celebrities on the wall, the jocular service, and the delicious and greasy pizza. The Heights's finest garlic twists and the pizza's garlicky tomato sauce will keep the vampires away.
2859 Broadway (at 111th St.), (212) 865-1234, www.famousfamiglia.com. Hours: Su-Sa 10am-2am. MC, V, AmEx, D, Entrées: $4.50. ❶ *to 110th St.*

The Heights Bar & Grill

This slick restaurant-bar has a rooftop garden which is heated in the cooler (summer) months. Potent margaritas, fresh salsa with tricolored chips, and an eager wait staff make this a favorite among Columbia Uni-versity students. Start early by slurping $2.50 margaritas during happy hour between 5pm-7pm and 11pm-1am weekdays, 11:30pm-12:30am weekends.
2867 Broadway (at 111th St.), (212) 866-7035. Hours: M-F 11:30am-11pm, Sa-Su 11am-11pm. MC, V, AmEx, D, Entrées: $8-$15. ❶ *to 110th St.*

Jerusalem Restaurant

Step off the grungy street and into Jerusalem's Arab quarter in this small Middle Eastern hot spot. Amidst the cook's frantic Arabic exclamations and the sultry music, you'll find some of Manhattan's best shawarma and falafel – the perfect spot for a sumptuous late night meal or a snack on the run.
2715 Broadway (bet. 103rd and 104th Sts.), (212) 865-2295, Hours: Su-Sa 10am-4am. Cash only, Entrées $3-9. ❶ *to 103rd St.*

Kitchenette

As their slogan says, Kitchenette serves up "comfort food at its best" for breakfast, lunch, and dinner. In the front take-out counter, there is a wonderful bakery with delicious coffee and cakes, while in the back, there is a comfortable sit-down section. Brunch at Kitchenette is very popular, so be prepared to wait a few minutes for a table, but the pancakes with fruit preserves are worth it. Dinner here is great too, and the special multi-course prix fixe is a steal. The Kitchenette in Morningside Heights is actually a spin-off of its downtown counterpart in Tribeca, which also serves up great food for unbeatable prices.
1272 Amsterdam Ave. (bet. 122nd and 123rd Sts.), (212) 531-7600. Hours: M-F 8am-11pm, Sa-Su 9am-11pm. MC, V, AmEx, Entrées: $5-$15. ❶

to 125th St.
80 W. Broadway (at Warren St.), (212) 267-6740. Hours: M-F 7:30am-10pm, Sa-Su 9am-10pm. ❶❷❸ *to Chambers St.*

La Rosita
For years, New Yorkers have claimed that this place serves a great cup of coffee. The service is well-paced so that food usually arrives as you're about to crack, but devouring your meal is always worth the wait. This place has probably the most authentic cooking and definitely some of the best Spanish food in the entire neighborhood.
2809 Broadway (bet. 108th and 109th Sts.), (212) 663-7804. Hours: Su-Sa 7am-12am. MC, V, AmEx, D, Entrées: $3-15. ❶ *to 110th St.*

Le Monde
Le Monde does not make culinary history with its take on the traditional French brasserie, but the restaurant does a commendable job of imitating the real thing. The mainly Columbia University crowd comes here to escape from the other more mediocre eating opportunities in Morningside Heights and to enjoy signature French dishes prepared consistently well. The décor of vintage posters and too many mirrors is true to the French name, and the wait staff is appropriately snooty.
2885 Broadway (bet. 112th and 113th Sts.), (212) 531-3939. Hours: Su-Sa 11:30am-12:30am. AmEx, V, MC, D. Entrées: $10-$18. ❶ *to 110th St.*

Mama Mexico
During evenings, this restaurant is always packed, and showcases a giant mariachi band blaring boleros to hungry diners. Ask for a tequila shot, and you'll think an alarm went off in the back of the restaurant. Service suddenly picks up, and, a couple of shots later, the owner's pouring booze down your throat. Expect long waits for the decent food and booze.
2672 Broadway (at 102nd St.), (212) 864-2323. Hours: Su-R 12pm-12am, F-Sa 12pm-2am. MC, V, AmEx, D. Entrées: $10-20. ❶ *to 103rd St.*

Metro Diner
Unique to the world of diners, this veggie-friendly establishment offers all the standard diner fare – only fresh! – with a splash of Mediterranean dishes including a variety of salads and vegetarian plates. Grab a booth and soak in its streamlined train car decor. A great post-movie hangout.
2641 Broadway (at 100th St.), (212) 866-0800. Hours: Su-Sa 6am-1am. MC, V, AmEx, Entrées: $10-$14. ❶ *to 103rd St.*

The Mill Korean Restaurant
The food here is solid, with a large variety of noodles, rice casseroles, barbecued meats, and pickled veggies. The Mill consistently pulls in a native Korean crowd, which bodes well for the quality and authenticity of the food. Korean food runs spicy, and at the Mill, they will bring you a pitcher of hot sauce to pour over your (already) steaming dish. The service is great, but be assertive when asking for the check. Be sure to check out the untraditional bathroom, a throne to the Evil Empire with a large old-fashioned typewriter attached to the wall.
2895 Broadway (bet. 112th and 113th Sts.), (212) 666-7653. Hours: Su-Sa 11am-10:30pm. MC, V, AmEx, Entrées: $10-$14. ❶ *to 110th St.*

Miss Mamie's Spoonbread Too
How do you want your soul food: barbecued, blackened, deep-fried, or smothered in sauce? It's all here. Save room for some banana bread pudding, coconut pineapple cake, or sweet potato pie. The laid-back staff, who takes just long enough to make you appreciate your meal, will be more than happy to serve you any of the above. Some dishes are greasy – what do you expect with deep-fried food – though most are great.
364 W. 110th St. (bet. Columbus and Manhattan Aves.), (212) 865-6744. Hours: Su-Sa 12am-11pm. MC, V, AmEx, Entrées: $10-17. ⒷⒸ *to 110th St.*

Saji's Kitchen
This hole-in-the-wall is one of Morningside Heights' hidden gems. Behind a tiny counter that blares rock music lies uptown's best Japanese food at amazingly low prices. This is mainly a take-out/delivery place, but the food is so good that going anywhere else seems like a waste.
256 W. 109th St. (at Broadway), (212) 749-1834. Hours: M-F 11:30am-10:30pm, Sa-Su 12pm-10:30pm. Cash only, Entrées: $2-11. ❶ *to 110th St.*

Sophia's Bistro
Downtown style has been creeping into the local neighborhood during the last year. This little bistro leads the onslaught, with flickering candlelight, and wine-colored drapery that create a hip lounge décor and romantic dining. Come Monday evenings for half-priced dinner on the already moderately priced menu.
988 Amsterdam Ave. (bet. 108th and 109th Sts.), (212) 662-8822. Hours: Su-Sa 11am-10:30pm. MC, V, AmEx, Entrées: $6-$10. ❶ *to 110th St.*

Terrace in the Sky
As romantic as it is appetizing. The restaurant floats majestically above the Manhattan skyline, which is best to experience at dusk or on a starry night. Red roses, candles, an inviting fireplace, and beautiful harp music, create a warm and opulent atmosphere. The hand roasted foie gras and vanilla crème brulee are highly recommended. The grandeur of this restaurant make it perfect for an intimate date or business meeting.
400 W. 119th St. (bet. Amsterdam Ave. and Morningside Dr.), (212) 666-9490. Hours: T-R 12pm-2:30pm, 6pm-10pm, F 12pm-2:30pm, 5:30pm-10:30pm, Sa 5:30pm-10:30pm, Su 10:30am-2:30pm. MC, V, AmEx, D, DC, Entrées: $25-$38. ❶ *to 116th St.-Columbia University.*

Tomo

Enjoy good sushi and Japanese fare in this upbeat Morningside Heights eatery. The place often tends to fill up pretty quickly, and the tables are packed close together, but the prices are reasonable enough.
2850 Broadway (bet. 110th and 111th Sts.), (212) 665-2916. Hours: M-Sa 12pm-11:30pm, Su 12pm-11pm. MC, V, AmEx, Entrées: $6-$14. ❶ to 110th St.

Tom's Restaurant

Once you push through the occasional crowd from a Kramer's Reality tour (the southern façade serves as a cutaway shot in *Seinfeld*), you'll be surprised to see what all the fuss is about. Though recent renovations have jacked the prices up a bit, be sure to find huge platters, late hours, and thick "Broadway" shakes (half coffee, half chocolate) that keep kids coming back to this greasy spoon.
2880 Broadway (at 112th St.), (212) 864-6137. Hours: Su-W 6am-1:30am, R-Sa 24hrs. Cash Only, Entrées: $3-$10. ❶ to 110th St.-Cathedral Pkwy.

Turkuaz

With the restaurant's artistically draped fabric ceiling that evokes a breezy Ottoman tent and the waiters' red satin balloon pants, you might think you've stepped into a tale from the Arabian Nights. Enjoy the traditional dishes and desserts at this Upper West Side Turkish delight, which offers both Turkish and Western style food. The almond pudding is especially good. Forget the drinks.
2637 Broadway (at 100th St.), (212) 665-9541. Hours: Su-R 11am-11pm, F-Sa 11am-12am. MC, V, AmEx, D, Entrées: $10-15. ❶ to 103rd St.

Cafes

Hamilton Deli

The true New York experience awaits at this popular deli. Hefty heroes with names like "The Lewinsky" are served up dripping with onions and mustard by a whirlwind staff of no-nonsense locals. Grab a bagel, yogurt, muffin, drink or candy bar from the convenience store in the back, and you're ready to go.
1129 Amsterdam Ave. (at 116th St.), (212) 749-8924. Hours: M-F 6am-12am, Sa-Su 7am-9pm. MC, V, AmEx (min $7). ❶ to 116th St.-Columbia University.

The Hungarian Pastry Shop

The cafe's enduring reputation as Columbia University's intellectual hangout par excellence has suffered somewhat since the citywide smoking ban. Still the place of choice, however, to ostentatiously discuss Wittgenstein or Shirer or write that dissertation on the hermeneutics of the Vilna Gaon while sipping chamomile tea and nibbling on a linzer torte. Their hot chocolate is incredible, but it's unsweetened.
1030 Amsterdam Ave. (bet. 110th and 111th Sts.), (212) 866-4230. Hours: M-F 7:30am-11:30pm, Sa 8:30am-11:30pm, Su 8:30am-10:30pm. Cash Only. ❶ to 110th St.

Nussbaum & Wu

Not your ordinary coffee stop – a Chinese pastry shop and deli collided to form this one. Well-lit with a great wrap-around counter, you just may decide to stay a while. Fresh sandwiches and yummy pastries, both Asian and non, are available here, not to mention bagels and, of course, coffee too. Recently, Nussbaum has been doing a booming business in a make-your-own salad bar around the back of the shop. Try the Asian Sesame Ginger dressing; you'll never go back to Italian again.
2897 Broadway (at 113th St.), (212) 280-5344. Hours: M-Sa 6am-12am, Su 6am-11pm. MC, V, AmEx, D, DC. ❶ to 110th St.

[Harlem]

Restaurants

Amy Ruth's

Menu offerings like the Reverand Al Sharpton Chicken and Waffle special give new meaning to the concept of soul food. The atmosphere is fun, and the traditional southern food is decent. Hearty portions ensure you won't leave hungry, and the honey-dipped fried chicken is worth a trip.
113 W. 116th St. (bet. Seventh and Lennox Aves.), (212) 280-8779. Hours: Su-R 7:30am-11pm, F-Sa 24 hours. MC, V, AmEx, D. Entrées: $9-18. ❷❸ to 116th St.

Copeland's

A rich and varied menu offers everything from braised oxtails and gumbo to grain-fed catfish and shrimp Creole. The atmosphere is for serious eating; Sunday's gospel brunch is among the neighborhood's finest.
547 W. 145th St. (bet. Broadway and Amsterdam Ave.), (212) 234-2357. Hours: T-R 4pm-11pm, F-Sa 4pm-12am, Su 4pm-9pm. MC, V, AmEx, D, Entrées: $9-$25. ❶ to 145th St.

Dinosaur Bar-B-Que

Carnivores, unite! This NYC branch of the ever-increasing popular chain will satisfy every meat craving you've ever had—and even ones you didn't even know to exist. Hearty combo dishes like the Tres Hombres piled high with pulled pork, brisket, and tender ribs will make you adjust that belt buckle another notch - or two. Dinosaur's a great place to bring a big group of friends and share jumbo wings, all cooked home-style. The extensive beer list with 20 some varieties will leave you wide-eyed. Leave the knife and fork at home—fingers make it all the more fun.
646 W. 131st St. (at 12th Ave.), (212) 694-1777, www.dinosaurbarbque.com/nyc. Hours: T-R 11:30am-11pm, F-Sat 11:30am-12am, Su 12pm-9pm. ❶ to 125th St.

Jimbo's Coffee Shop

This tiny greasy spoon is always crowded and confused with people clamoring for the phenomenal, $3 bacon cheeseburger.
1345 Amsterdam Ave. (bet. Hancock and 127th

Sts.), (212) 865-8777. *Hours: Su-Sa 6am-10pm. Cash only, Entrées: $3-5.* 1 *to 125th St.*

Londel's
Owner Londel Davis greets customers at the door of his sophisticated new Strivers Row supper club, a harbinger of gentrification in this quickly changing neighborhood. Harlem's hottest restaurant serves delicious, painstakingly prepared Southern food like smothered pork chops and pan-seared red snapper to the neighborhood's most wealthy.
2620 Frederick Douglass Blvd. (bet. 139th and 140th Sts.), (212) 234-6114. Hours: T-Sa 11am-11pm, Su 11am-5pm. MC, V, AmEx, D, DC, Entrées: $9-$20. B C 2 3 *to 135th St.*

Miss Maude's
Newly opened by the owners of Miss Mamie's on 110th, Miss Maude's is bigger and better. You can't find better soul food for a lower price. Summers, it's a great place to sip lemonade and get fat; winters, it's a great place to sip something warmer and stay fat.
547 Lenox Ave. (bet. 137th and 138th Sts.), (212) 690-3100. Hours: M-Sa 11:30pm-9:30pm, Su 11am-9:30pm. MC, V, AmEx, Entrées: $10-17. 2 3 *to 135th St.*

Perk's Fine Cuisine
"Every third person's a gangsta and the other two are buppies," said one Harlemite about this Harlem hangout. Savor succulent baby back ribs while vocalist Robert Fox serenades the ladies with his super-slick renditions of "Me and Mrs. Jones" and other R&B standards. They have a terrific bar menu and gracious wait staff in a plush, expensive, and comfortable dining room downstairs.
553 Manhattan Ave. (at 123rd St.), (212) 666-8500. Hours: M-Sa 4pm-4am. MC, Entrées: $13-$22. A B C D *to 125th St.*

Revival
Well worth the trip into Harlem for the shockingly good soul food creations and modest but impeccable service. Go for the great happy hour deals and then stay for a fabulous feast in this stylish, casually elegant and intimate restaurant. Some of their best dishes are the spicy butter shrimp, crusted Chilean sea bass, sizzler lobster tail with scallops and LA Lamb Rack. Dinner will leave you completely satisfied. The food has an international flare as well as the traditional elements of soul: big portions with lots of flavor. Be sure to check out its full page Martini menu.
2367 Frederick Douglass Blvd. (corner of 127th St. and Eighth Ave.), (212) 222-8338. Hours: Su-Sa 12am-3pm, 5pm-11pm. MC, V, AmEx, D, Entrées: dinner $15-$22. A B C D *to 125th St.*

Slice of Harlem
Darn, they're good, and they know it. Hailed as some of the best pizza in New York, Slice has innovative combinations, lots of toppings, and prices a notch above Domino's. Try the veggie pizza, even broccoli-haters will love it.
308 Lenox Ave. (bet. 125th and 126th Sts.), (212) 426-7400. Hours: M-Su 12pm-10pm. MC, V, AmEx. 2 3 *to 125th St.*

Sylvia's
Although the most venerable soul food restaurant in New York, Sylvia's succeeds on more than reputation. The crispy and flavorful fried chicken is good, but some of the sides could use reviving. Come Sunday for the after-church gospel brunch, and don't forget to leave space for sweet potato pie.
328 Lenox Ave. (bet. 126th and 127th Sts.), (212) 996-0660. Hours: M-F 11am-10:30pm, Sa 8am-10:30pm, Su 11am-8pm. MC, V, AmEx, D. Entrées: $9-$18. 2 3 *to 125th St.*

CAFES

Make My Cake
Though quite small – there are only two tables in this cafe – this cupcake, cake, and pie shop is so simple it's superb. The cake designer will draw almost anything on a special-order cake, and the staff is super friendly. Once you try a Red Velvet slice, you'll return so often that they'll get to know you by name.

103 W. 110th St. (at Lenox Ave.), (212) 932-0833. Hours: M 12pm-7pm, T-F 7am-7pm, Sa 10am-7pm, Su 9am-4pm. AmEx. ❷❸ to 110th St.-Central Park North.
2380 Adam Clayton Powell Blvd. (at 139th St.), (212) 234-2344. Hours: M 10am-5pm, T-F 7am-7:30pm, Sa 10am-7:30pm, Su 10am-8pm. MC, V, AmEx. Ⓑ Ⓒ to 135th St.

Settepani
Quell your pastry hunger at this bright and airy café-plus-bakery in Harlem, where you will find a wide variety of cookies, chocolates, and pastries to be eaten right there or perhaps, taken to Marcus Garvey Park, a block away. They also serve a good but reasonably-priced lunch, which you can top off with gelato or one of their unique cakes. Also check out their Williamsburg location.
196 Lenox Ave. (at 120th St), (917) 492-4806. Hours: M-F 6:30am-9pm, Sa-Su 7am-9pm. MC, V, AmEx. Sandwiches: $3-$6, pastries $12-$18/lb. ❷❸ to 116th St.

[Washington Heights]

Restaurants

BLEU Evolution
The food and setting will justify the trek uptown. There's a lovely garden to eat in and a lounge that stays open long after the kitchen closes. Despite its out-of-the-way location, this place is undeniably hip. Some say it's the best part of the neighborhood.
808 W. 187th St. (at Fort Washington Ave.), (212) 928-6006, Hours: Su-R 11am-11pm, F-Sa 11am-12am. MC, V, AmEx, D, Entrées: $12-$15. ❶ to 191st St.

Coogan's Restaurant
Latinos and Irish congregate at this upscale pub to partake of classics such as shell steak, shrimp scampi, French onion soup, and roast beef au jus. Karaoke nights on Tuesdays and Thursdays enhance the eclecticism of this popular local hangout, just down the street from the Columbia Presbyterian Medical Center.
4015 Broadway (at 168th St.), (212) 928-1234, www.coogans.com, Hours: Su-Sa 11am-12am. MC, V, AmEx, D, Entrées: $9-$17. Ⓐ Ⓒ ❶ to 168th St.-Washington Hts.

DR-K
On Dyckman St. near Tenth Ave, this cleverly named Dominican restaurant serves up some of the best Latin food outside of abuela's kitchen. The sleek entryway, shimmering tables, and bar/lounge décor make you feel important while you wolf down delicious hangar steak, pernil asado, and fried sweet plantains. After a couple of delicious cos-mohitos, the excellent food, friendly Dominican staff, and Latin music are enough to let you know it's authentic. After receiving good press upon opening, DR-K's popularity has reached a plateau. Look for their well-deserved status to jump over the course of the next year. If you're in the mood to make a night of it, hit up the upstairs bar/lounge or the abutting mohito bar. Catering to a well-dressed predominantly Latin crowd, this venue is a great spot to do a little salsa dancing on a Saturday night.
114 Dyckman St., (212) 304-1717. Hours: M-F 12pm-4am, Su-R 5pm-11pm, F-Sa 5pm-12am. AmEx, D, M, V, $20-$30. ❶ to Dyckman St.

[Bronx]

Restaurants

Bellavista
Riverdale has a bunch of good restaurants, but most residents enjoy this one. It's got a warm environment with a menu of your basic, Italian fare – pizza and pasta. The sort of food that never did anybody wrong.
554 W. 235th St. (bet. Oxford and Johnson Aves.), Riverdale, (718) 548-2354. Hours: M 5pm-10pm, T-Su 12pm-10pm. MC, V, AmEx, D, DC, Entrées: $12-$24. ❶ to 231st St.

Il Boschetto
The place to see huge portions of food on big plates. Bring the beano and an appetite – hey, and a bunch of friends too! Forget the conversation, just concentrate on the large portion of food in front of you and proceed to hurt yourself.
Baychester, 1660 E. Gun Hill Rd. (at Tiemann Ave.), (718) 379-9335. Hours: T-Su 12pm-10pm. MC, V, AmEx, D. Entrées: $25-$35. ❷❺ to Gun Hill Rd.

Jimmy's Bronx Cafe
After just four years in the Bronx, this "Latin Restaurant and Entertainment Complex" has become the nucleus for nightlife in the borough's Latino community. Upstairs, seafood is served into the early-morning hours as patrons watch boxing and baseball on large televisions. Downstairs, the dance floor resembles a hotel ballroom, built for high capacity. As at other area

clubs, there's no such thing as overdressing, though casual seems prevalent. Salsa dancing on Tuesday nights.
Fordham, 281 W. Fordham Rd. (at Major Deegan Expressway), (718) 329-2000, www.jimmysbronxcafe.com. Hours: Su-R 10am-2am, F-Sa 10am-4am. MC, V, AmEx, Entrées: $8-$18. ❶ *to 207th St.*

Le Refuge Inn
You'll be tempted to stay the night at this bed and breakfast. Whoever thought the words, "I think I'd like to live in the Bronx" would cross your mind? Well, they will when you sit down to the delicious French food and great service, staring the whole time at the stairs leading to the rooms above.
City Island, 620 City Island Ave. (at Sutherland St.), (718) 885-2478. Hours: W-Sa 5:30pm-9pm, Su 10am-12am. AmEx, Entrées: $45-$55. ❻ *to Pelham Bay Park.*

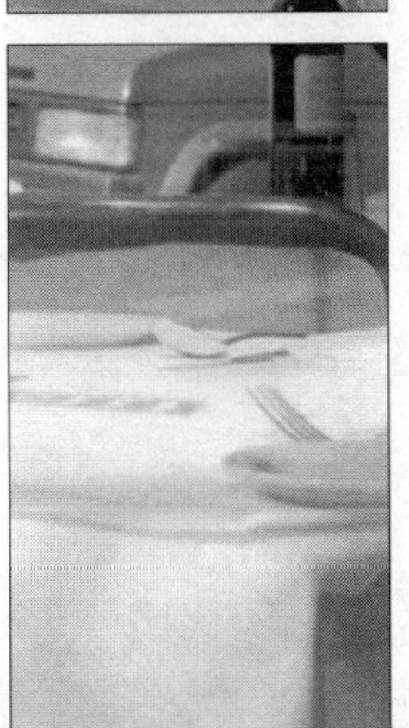

Lobster Box
Though not what it used to be, the Lobster Box still provides the amazing view of the water it's always boasted. The lobster's great, the fish mediocre. What it amounts to is a good place to go with family, or when you have an overwhelming craving for lobsters.
City Island, 34 City Island Ave. (bet. Belden and Rochelle Sts.), (718) 885-1952. Hours: Su-R 11:30am-10:30pm, F-Sa 11:30am-12am. MC, V, AmEx, D, Diners, Entrées $25-$35. ❻ *to Pelham Bay Park.*

Mario's
After visiting the Botanical Gardens, a lot of people amble over to this Arthur Ave. institution that's been around since 1919. A near oppressive amount of tourists mingles with locals, but it's definitely worth it for the pasta.
East Tremont, 2342 Arthur Ave. (bet. 184th and 186th Sts.), (718) 584-1188. Hours: Su, T-R 12pm-10pm, F-Sa 12pm-11pm. MC, V, AmEx, D. Entrées: $16-$25. ❷❺ *to Pelham Pkwy.*

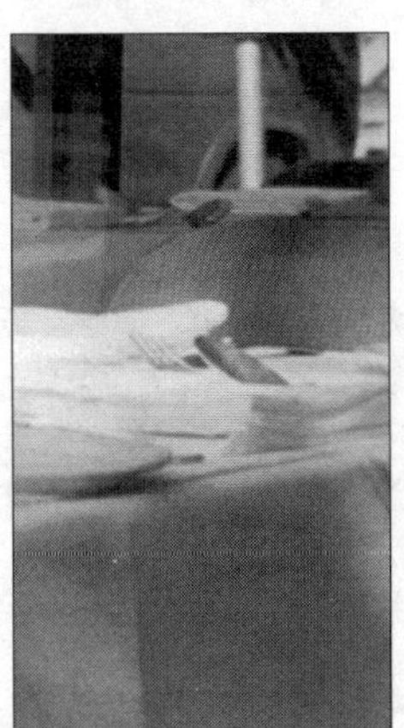

[Queens]

Restaurants

Amici Amore/ Butcher Brothers Steakhouse
Butcher Brothers Steakhouse is the fifth establishment opened by the Redzic brothers. The steakhouse is a welcome addition to brothers Dino and Johnny's Italian ristorante Amici Amore I. Though the two restaurants share an entrance, the space is divided between the Italian restaurant and the upscale steakhouse, each of which offers its own menu. The restaurants boast the most extensive wine list in all of Astoria, and the brothers' dedication to the quality of their establishment is evident in the impressive presentation of a customized wall of over 4,000 red wines, designed by the brothers themselves. The oysters are excellent, and the porterhouse for two is as delicious as it is filling. Dino recommends a full-bodied Malbec red wine to accompany any steak.
29-35 Newtown Ave, (718) 267-2771. Hours: M-R, Su 5pm-10:30pm, F-Sa 5pm-12am. V, M, AmEx, D. Entrées: $35-$55. Ⓝ Ⓦ *to Thirtieth Ave.*

Annam Brahma Restaurant
The eclectic menu's only unifying thread is that everything is prepared sans meat, meaning that everything from Indian raita to tofu omelets to chapatti roll-ups may grace your table. On thursdays the cooks rally around pasta for Italian day; Tuesdays put Chinese vegetarian mainstays center stage. Check out the books, tapes, and other items for sale in the back of the restaurant.
Jamaica, 84-43 164th St. (at Grand Central Pkwy.), (718) 523-2600. Hours: M-T, R-Sa 11am-10pm, W 11am-4pm, Su 12pm-10pm. Cash Only, Entrées: $4-$8. Ⓕ *to Parsons Blvd.*

Carmichael's
Wizened locals fill up on soul food after Sunday's sermon at this slightly derelict, though cozy, neighborhood favorite. The fried chicken is amazing.
Jamaica, 117-08 Guy R. Brewer Blvd. (at One Hundred Eighteenth Ave.), (718) 723-6908. Hours: Su-Sa 6am-7:45pm. Cash Only, Entrées: $6-$10. Ⓔ Ⓙ Ⓩ *to Jamaica Center-Parsons/Archer.*

Dante Restaurant
Mature crowds of businessmen and nearby St. John's University professors and athletes visit this dimly lit Italian bistro and bar. After hours it's a good place for big hair and big fun.
168-12 Union Tpke. (bet. 168th and 169th Sts.), Flushing, (718) 380-3340. Hours: T-F 12pm-10pm, Sa 2pm-10pm, Su 1pm-9pm. MC, V, AmEx, D, Diners, Entrées: $9.95-$19.95. Ⓔ Ⓕ *to Union Tpke.-Kew Gardens.*

Manducatis
Wine buffs and locals alike frequent Manducatis, a friendly family-run

restaurant with fresh ingredients and a vast wine cellar reflecting serious dedication to Italian imports. Fireplaces and lavender tablecloths dress up the exposed brick walls. The menu standards astound, particularly the homemade pasta, but if nothing appeals, you can create your own dish.
13-27 Jackson Ave. (at Forty-Seventh Ave.), (718) 729-4602. Hours: M-F 12pm-3pm, 5pm-10pm, Sa 5pm-11pm Su 2:30pm-8:30pm. MC, V, AmEx, D, Entrées: $8-$19. G to 21st St., 7 to Vernon Blvd.-Jackson Ave.

El Sitio de Astoria

Set the mood for truck-stop romance with your table's jukebox, although deals like the bandejas completas – a massive serving of meat, rice, beans, plantains, and croquettes – aren't among the wisest first-date choices. Getting a little tipsy on the sangria should take care of any awkward moments.
Long Island City, 35-55 31st St., (718) 278-7694. Hours: Su-R 7am-11pm. MC, V, AmEx, D, Entrées: $7-$13. N W to Thirty-Sixth Ave.

Elias Corner

You'll have to read the reviews on the wall or point at fish in the glass case – there are no menus – but either way Elias Corner will stuff you silly. Across the street from its old location, this seafood pleasure house features rough charm and primitive décor, but no matter: Delicious red snapper, octopus, and squid, along with bottles of cheap but effective wine make this completely worth the trip to Astoria.
Astoria, 24-02 31st St. (at Twenty-Fourth Ave.), (718) 932 1610. Hours: Su Sa 4pm-12am. Cash Only, $8-$16. N to Astoria-Ditman Blvd.

Girassol Churrascaria

A churrascaria is a fancy word for barbecue, and if you enter these doors be prepared to be rolled out. This is all-you-can eat, and this place will put any kind of meat or sausage on a spit and serve it up to you sizzling. Beware: not for the faint-hearted or vegetarians. Don't wear a belt.
Astoria, 33-18 28th Ave (at 34th St.), (718) 545-8250. Hours: Su-Sa 11am-12am. MC, V, AmEx, D, DC, Entrées: $12-22. N W to 30th Ave.

Jackson Diner

This is the most famous Indian restaurant in New York, and it's not even in Manhattan. Jackson Heights is a short trip on the F train. The popularity of this place has led even cynical Manhattanites to trek out here to partake of the home-style portions. The restaurant has been extensively renovated since its humble beginnings, but the food and surrounding neighborhood remain true to form.
37-47 74th St. (bet. Roosevelt and 37th Aves.), (718) 672-1232. Hours: Su-R 11:30am-10pm, F-Sa 11:30am-10:30pm. Cash only. E F G R V to Jackson Hts.-Roosevelt Ave.

Joe's Shanghai

Tourists, locals, and suburban Chinese flock here for the juicy crabmeat buns for which Joe's is deservedly famous. Friendly service and the savory quality of the rest of the fare keep customers coming back for more and more.
136-21 Seventh Ave. (bet Main and Union Sts.), (718) 539-3838. Hours: Su-R 11am-11pm, F-Sa 11am-12pm. Cash Only, Entrées: $5-$18. 7 to Flushing-Main St.

Los Arrieros Restaurant

Steamed beef tongue, anyone? This Colombian place has everything from tripe and oxtail to beef liver. Come with an appetite, although an entire platter won't cost you more than $10. Don't expect gourmet, but for these prices, who cares?
Jackson Heights, 76-02 Roosevelt Ave. (at 76th St.), (718) 898-3359. Hours: Su-R 11am-10pm, F-Sa 11am-10:30pm. Cash only, Entrées: $5-8. E F G R V 7 to Jackson Hts.-Roosevelt Ave.

Pollos a la Brasa

This restaurant is chicken heaven. They have discovered every way in which to cook, fry, or broil chicken here. This Ecuadoran restaurant also has the corn cakes with cheese known as arepas.
81-01 Roosevelt Ave. (at 81st St.), Jackson Heights, (718) 639-5555. Hours:24 hrs. MC, V, AmEx, Entrées: $12-18. 7 to 82nd St.-Jackson Hts.

Rib Shack

This venue's offerings of sweet potato pie, collard greens, and fried chicken will move the hearts of devoted soul food lovers. The employees are so friendly that they regularly garner tips, a wow considering that customers are only allowed to order take-out.
157 06 Linden Blvd. (bet. Sutphin and Guy Brewer Blvds.), Jamaica, (718) 659-7000, Hours: Su-R 11am-11pm, F-Sa 11am-12am. MC, V, AmEx, D. Entrées: $6-$8. E J Z to Jamaica, F to Sutphin Blvd.

Terra Brasil

Terra is a mainly take-out restaurant which offers the basic Brazilian marinated beef dishes, but their claim to fame is a salad and meat bar for $3.99 a pound that draws locals in like flies to honey. They also have delicious little chicken or shrimp tartlets and cheese bread to go.
Long Island City, 33-04 36th Ave., (718) 609-1367. Hours: M-Sa 11am-9pm, Su 11am -7pm. Cash only, Entrées: $5-$8. N W to 36th Ave.

Zum Stammtisch

While German cuisine hardly qualifies as in vogue to chic Manhattan critics, its heartiness goes over well with the locals in this quiet neighborhood. Stained glass windows and dim lights bring to mind stodgy 19th century German intellectuals debating Hegel over steins.
Glendale, 69-46 Myrtle Ave. (at Cooper Ave.), (718) 386-3014. Hours: Su-R 12pm-9:30pm, F-Sa 12pm-11pm. MC, V, AmEx, Entrées: $7-$16. L M to Myrtle-Wyckoff Aves.

CAFES

Kolonaki Cafe

The fun and cozy split-

level coffee shop is fairly new to the Steinway shopping area. The décor is contemporary, and provides a nice ambiance.
Astoria, 33-02 Broadway (at 33rd St.), (718) 932-8222. Hours: Su-R 8am-2am, F-Sa 8am-3am. MC, V, AmEx, D. N W to Broadway.

Omonia Cafe
Enjoy a piece of Greece at Astoria's best liquor, coffee, and pastry bar. Lounge at a table among a multilingual crowd, or choose what to order from the vast selection of standard and exotic pastries behind the glass counter up front including five shelves of different kinds of baklava.
32-20 Broadway (at 33rd St.), (718) 274-6650. Hours: Su-R 7am-3am, F-Sa 7am-5am. MC, V, AmEx, D. N W to Broadway.

[Brooklyn]

Restaurants

Bar Tabac
This relaxing and moderately priced French Bistro features magnificent duck confit, cigars, luscious desserts, and an attentive wait staff. You could spend several hours lounging around the back room – Designed to resemble the inside of a fin de siecle Paris subway train – as you sip wine and sample savory selections like mouth watering steak frites and scrumptious sea bass.
Carroll Gardens, 128 Smith St. (at Dean St.), (718) 923-0918. Hours: M-F 11:30am-1am, Sa-Su 11am-1am. AmEx, Entrées: $11-$16. F G to Bergen St.

Coco Roco
You might someday ask yourself, where can I get tasty Peruvian food in Brooklyn? Here's the place, equipped with spicy chicken and amazing sangria. It's also a fun, sprightly restaurant that hustles and bustles.
Park Slope, 392 Fifth Ave. (bet. 6th and 7th Sts.), (718) 965-3376. Hours: Su-T 12pm-10:30pm, F-Sa 12pm-11:30pm. MC, V, AmEx. F M R to Fourth Ave.- 9th St.

Cucina
One of the best restaurants in New York, and it's not even in Manhattan. Everything is great here, but the risotto is what people rave about. The antipasto is the best this side of Tuscany, and the wine and dessert menus are superb. Plus there is valet parking. In a word: perfect.
Park Slope, 256 Fifth Ave. (bet. Garfield Pl. and Carroll St.), (718) 230-0711, www.cucinarestaurant.com. Hours: T-R 5:30pm-10:30pm, F-Sa 5:30pm-11pm, Su 5pm-10pm. MC, V, AmEx, D. Entrées: $15-$28. M R to Union St.

The Downtown Brooklyn Diner
It's late and you're lost somewhere between the gas station and the party you were going to, driving around Brooklyn. Chances are you are on Atlantic Ave., and a good suggestion: stop at this 24-hour diner, order breakfast, lunch, or dinner, and figure out where the heck you are.
515 Atlantic Ave. (at Third Ave.), (718) 243-9172. Hours: 24hrs. MC, V, AmEx, D, Entrées: $6-$8. B M N R 2 3 4 5 to Pacific St.-Atlantic Ave.

Five Front
Though opened only recently, this restaurant has been drawing regulars from Manhattan, Queens, and Staten Island already, Set in a building landmark with a garden out back, Five Front has much to offer in addition to great food. Go for a stroll across the Brooklyn Bridge, then join the friendly wait staff and regular crowd here for a meal. Five Front is popular and sometimes books large parties, so reservations recommended.
5 Front St. (by Cadman Plaza W), (718) 625-5559, Hours: M, W-R: 12pm-3pm, 5:30pm-11pm, F 12pm-3pm, 5:30pm-12am, Sa 11am-4pm, 5:30pm-12am, Su 11am-4pm, 5:30pm-10pm. AmEx, V, M, Diners, Entrées $12-$19. A C to High St., F to York St.

Giardini Pizza and Restaurant
Some of the best pizza and straight up Italian food in New York, which is no small feat considering there's a pizza joint on every corner. This place delivers (literally, too) with great plain and topped slices, along with a nice array of the old standards – spaghetti, stuffed shells, parmigianas, and big, tasty heroes. It's cheap, fast, and deeply satisfying.
Carroll Gardens, 363 Smith St. (at Carroll St.), (718) 596-5320. Hours: Su-Sa 10am-10pm, F 10am-11pm. Cash only, Entrées: $1.25-9. F G to Carroll St.

Grimaldi's
Every New Yorker claims to know the best pizzeria in the city, but Grimaldi's may be the real thing. Old Brooklyn ambiance is enhanced by Sinatra and Bennett crooning as you savor crisp, thin-crust pizza that will satisfy even the most discriminating pizza lovers.
Fulton Ferry Landing, 19 Old Fulton St. (bet. Water and Front Sts.), (718) 858-4300. Hours: M-R 11:30 am-11pm, F 11:30am-12am, Sa 12pm-12am, Su 12pm-11pm. Cash Only, Entrées: $12-$20. A C to High St., F to York St.

Jolie
Jolie is French for "pretty" and appropriately bills this French bistro find. The menu features reasonably priced French fusion dishes, fun cocktails, and a good selection of wines. The owners routinely chat with patrons and create a welcoming and relaxed environment. Here is what they recommend (and this reviewer concurs) you order to get the signature fell for the restaurant. Start with the melt-in-you-mouth goat cheese millefeuille; then, move onto the exquisite steak tartare. If you can muster it, finish up with the breathtaking crepe suzette. This restaurant provides an intimate setting and one feels welcome to sit for hours. In warmer weather, ask to sit in the back patio where the chef grows his own herbs.
320 Atlantic Ave. (at Hoyt St.). (718) 488-0777. Hours: M 6pm-11pm, T-F

12pm-3pm, 6pm-11pm; Sa-Su 11:30am-4pm, 5:30pm-11 pm (10pm on Sunday) for dinner. AmEx, Entrées: $12-$20. A C *to Hoyt St.-Schermerhorn St.,* B M N R 2 3 4 5 *to Atlantic Ave.-Pacific St.*

Junior's

Sample "New York's Best Cheesecake" (don't confuse it with the cheese pie!) or just about anything else you can imagine at this monster diner/bar, open till 2am on weekends. They keep a busy bar, with eclectic group of patrons and offer speedy service, but sometimes there's a wait for a table on weekends. It's been around for ages, and any Brooklyner worth his or her salt will stop here from time to time. The food is solid, the prices good, and the ambience is pure old school Brooklyn.

386 Flatbush Ave. (at DeKalb Ave.), (718) 852-5257. Hours: Su-W 6:30am-12:30am, R 6:30am-1am, F-Sa 6:30am-2am. MC, V, AmEx, D. Entrées: $10-$28. B M R *to DeKalb Ave.,* 2 3 4 5 *to Nevins. St. Additional location in Manhattan at Grand Central Terminal.*

L & B Spumoni Gardens Pizzeria

Serving, in many people's opinions, New York City's best Sicilian slice of pizza, L & B Spumoni Gardens is a Brooklyn institution. The unique slice – which features much more sauce than cheese – has led many to return to Spumoni Gardens for years. Busy at any time at night, L & B is a great place to watch the many different types of people Brooklyn offers interact with one another. Do not leave without trying its famous Spumoni dessert: you will find none better.

2725 86th St., (718) 372-8400. Hours: Su-Sa 11 am-1am. Entrées: $10 AmEx, MC, V. B *to 25th Ave.,* N *to Ave. U.*

New Prospect Cafe

A diminutive cutie, the light menu here features some excellent seafood vegetable dishes and nice, reasonably priced wine. Not for New York's night owls, the kitchen closes by 10pm; on the other hand, brunch is excellent and always crowded.

Prospect Heights, 393 Flatbush Ave. (bet. Plaza St. and Sterling Pl.), (718) 638-2148. Hours: M 5pm-10pm, T-R 12pm-10pm, F 12pm-11pm, Sa 11am-11pm, Su 11am-10pm. MC, V, AmEx, Entrées $9-$16. 2 3 *to Grand Army Plaza,* B *to Seventh Ave.*

Oznot's Dish

Enjoy the huge wine list at this eclectic and funky hangout for the rising Williamsburg art crowd. The menu, especially the brunch, features wild combinations of flavors from around the Mediterranean that are entirely satisfying. The restaurant itself is a virtual museum of knick-knacks and works of art in progress.

Williamsburg, 79 Berry St. (at N. 9th St.), (718) 599-6596. Hours: M–F 11am–11pm, Sat–Sun 10am– 12am, MC, V, Entrées $10-$24. L *to Bedford Ave.*

Patois

This French restaurant joins a host of new ventures on Smith St. and doesn't disappoint with favu leek and goat cheese tart, tasty duck breast, and excellent grilled salmon served over lentils. Good wines compliment most of the food, whether it be the tripe stew or beer-drenched mussels.

Carroll Gardens, 255 Smith St. (bet. Degraw and Douglas Sts.), (718) 855-1535. Hours: T-R 6pm-10:30pm, F-Sa 6pm-11:30pm, Sun 11am-3pm, 5pm-10pm. MC, V, AmEx, Entrées: $12-18. F G *to Bergen St.*

Peter Luger Steakhouse

Simply the best steakhouse in New York City. Period. Not for the faint of heart (and definitely not for vegetarians), the menu is limited to steak, salmon, and lamb chops, as well as an amazing array of à la carte side-dishes. A reservation on a Friday or Saturday can be weeks in the waiting. Worth the wait, worth the cost, and just plain worth it!

178 Broadway (bet. Bedford Ave. and Driggs St.), Williamsburg, (718) 387-7400, www.peterluger.com. Hours: M-R 11:45am-9:45pm, F-Sa 11:45-10:45pm, Su 12:45pm-9:45pm. Cash only, Entrées: $50-$60. J M Z *to Marcy Ave.*

Red Rail

Come one, come all to this busy and popular breakfast/lunch spot and enjoy a nice prix fixe brunch that includes coffee, tea, and all the mimosas you can handle. Try the big, nicely presented omelets, grilled squid salad with basil, red onion, and tomato, or tasty avocado salad with tomatoes and goat cheese. If the architecture appears familiar, you may remember it from a heated romantic spat between Nicolas Cage and Cher in *Moonstruck*.

Carroll Gardens, (502 Henry St. (at Sackett St.), 718) 875-1283. Hours: M-R 11:30am-5pm, 5:30pm-10:30pm, F 9:30am-3:30pm, 5:30pm-12am, Sa 9:30am-3:30pm, 6pm-11pm, Su 9:30am-3:30pm, 5:30pm-10pm. MC, V, AmEx. F G *to Carroll St.*

Rose Water

Vegetarian cuisine coming at you, loaded with organic seasonal ingredients that combine to make delectable, low-priced meals. Get the fine cheese plate accompanied by slices of pears, black grapes, and squishy (in a good way) bread, or try the seared diver scallops with roasted butternut squash.

Park Slope, 787 Union St. (at Sixth Ave.), (718) 783-3800. Hours: M-T 5:30pm-10pm, W-R 5:30pm-10:30pm, F 5:30pm-11pm, Sa 11am-3pm, 5:30pm-11pm, Su 11am-3pm, 5:30pm-10pm. MC, V, AmEx. M R *to Union St.*

Sotto Voce

Cool décor fills this tiny neighbor restaurant, which is always hopping with happy diners eating crab cake antipasto, homemade fettuccine in rosemary cream sauce, and veal medallions. Great for the meat lover in you. If you've got room, go for the delicious cheesecake with strawberries. You won't regret it.

Park Slope, 225 Seventh Ave. (at 4th St.), (718) 369-9322. Hours: M-R

12pm-11pm, F 12pm-12am, Sa 10am-12am, Su 10am-11pm. Cash only, Entrées: $10-$22. F to Seventh Ave.

Tom's Diner
"I came, I sat, I wrote" reads a note from Suzanne Vega on the wall of this venerable luncheonette, suggesting that it is this Prospect Heights favorite, not Tom's on 112th St. in Manhattan, which is immortalized in Vega's "Tom's Diner." Worthy of immortality, Tom's is a charmer, founded in 1936 with prototypical Brooklyn fare, great egg creams, and terrific service. Closes at 4pm.
Prospect Heights, 782 Washington Ave. (at Sterling Pl.), (718) 636-9738. Hours: M-Sa 7am-4pm. Cash only, Entrées: $3-$8. 2 3 to Eastern Pkwy.-Brooklyn Museum.

Cafes

Fall Cafe
Settle into a cushy couch and finish a physics problem set or dig into your debut novel. Sustenance comes at starving student prices: $3 or less for soups and a small coffee for less than $1.
Carroll Gardens, 307 Smith St. (bet. President and Union Sts.) (718) 403-0230. Hours: M-F 7:30am-9pm, Sa 8am-9pm, Su 9am-8pm. Cash Only. F G to Carroll St.

L Cafe
The food – standard American cafe fare – is mediocre, but the eclectic crowd will hold your attention as you wine and dine inside this tiny brick enclave or in the sunny, outdoor garden.
189 Bedford Ave. (bet N. 6th and N. 7th Sts.), (718) 302-2430. Hours: M-F 9am-11:30pm, Sa-Su, 10am-11:30pm. MC, V, AmEx, D. L to Bedford Ave.

Omonia Cafe
You won't be sorry when you come here for dessert or a sweet snack. With delicious cakes and coffees, and two locations in Queens and Brooklyn, these cafes are lovely places to sit and savor yummy pastries and delicious coffees late into the evening.
7612 Third Ave. (bet. 76th and 77th Sts.), (718) 491-1435. Hours: Su-Sa 8am-3am. MC, V, AmEx, D, Entrées: $12-$16. R to 77th St.

Sweet Melissa Patisserie
A reasonably priced cafe for sweets, salads, and French food. It's becoming increasingly popular among local residents, with a building reputation for good food. The place may be small, but as the name promises, it's sweet.
276 Court St. (bet. Butler and Douglass Sts.), (718) 855-3410. Hours: Su-R 8am-10pm, F-Sa 8am-12am. Cash only, Entrées: $4-$6. F G to Bergen St.

[Staten Island]

Restaurants

Aesop's Tables
Are the stories in the new American menu, or in the décor? Both offer interesting variations on the standard restaurant experience. The moral is in the food: it's worth it if you're in town, but don't go out of your way otherwise.
1233 Bay St. (at Maryland Ave.), (718) 720-2005. Hours: T-R 5:30pm-9:30pm, F-Sa 5:30pm-10:30pm, Su 5pm-9pm. MC, V, AmEx, Entrées: $11-$17. R W to Whitehall St., 4 5 to Bowling Green, S51 bus to Hylan Blvd./Bay St.

Basilio Inn
Housed in a 19th century stable imbued with a Tuscan rustic flavor, the Inn serves up incredible Italian – the red snapper Livornese is divine.
2-6 Galesville Court, (718) 447-9292. Hours: M-F 12pm-3pm, 5pm-10pm, Sa 5pm-10pm, Su 1pm-8pm. AmEx, Entrées: $12-$14. R W to Whitehall St., 4 5 to Bowling Green, Train to Grasmere.

Denino's Pizzeria and Tavern
As much a Staten Island institution as the ferry, if not more so, Denino's has been around since 1937, owned by the same family and serving some of the best thin crust pizza and fried calamari in the city. This is the sort of place you go to with a big group; order a lot, get rowdy, and enjoy.
524 Port Richmond Ave. (bet. Hooker Pl. and Walker St.), (718) 442-9401. Hours: Su-R 12pm-11pm, F-Sa 12pm-11:45pm. Cash Only, Entrées: $8-$15. R W to Whitehall St., 4 5 to Bowling Green, Train to New Dorp.

Parsonage
The priest is gone, but this 150-year-old priest's house serves food that is as close to divine as it gets on Staten Island. The food is American with twists. The ambience completes the experience. You'll find two floors of antiques in an antique house, and, on your plate, recipes so time tested they'll be around for as long as the house has been.
74 Arthur Kill Rd. (at Clark Ave.), (718) 351-7879. Hours: M 5pm-10pm, T-R 11:30am-10pm, F-Sa 11:30am-11pm, Su 1pm-9pm. MC, V, AmEx, D, Entrées: $16-$30. R W to Whitehall St., 4 5 to Bowling Green, 54 or 74 bus to Arthur Kill Rd.

Cafes

Cargo Cafe
Just a stone's throw from the Staten Island Ferry terminal, this modern, trendy spot is hard to miss. A youngish local crowd congregates on the terrace in summer for delectable fresh fish specials like pan-seared tuna.
120 Bay St. (at Flosson Terrace), (718) 876-0539, Hours: Su-Sa 12pm-2am. MC, V, AmEx, D, DC, Entrées: $10-$18. R W to Whitehall St., 4 5 to Bowling Green.

Carol's Cafe
Arguably the best restaurant in Staten Island, the worst thing about Carol's Café is that it's only open four days a week. Though the eclectic fare may take a while to get to your table, you'll concede that it was worth the wait.
1571 Richmond Rd. (bet. Four Corners Rd. and Seaview Ave.), (718) 979-5600. Hours: W-F 6pm-12am, Sa 5pm-12am. MC, V, AmEx, D, Entrées: $14-$35. N R to South Ferry, Train to Dongan Hills.

[Index by Category]

Niko's Mediterranean Grill and Bistro (Upper W. Side)
Omonia Café (Queens)
Oznot's Dish (Brooklyn)
Park Avalon (Gramercy)
Uncle Nick's Greek Cuisine (Midtown)

Russian and Polish

Firebird (Midtown)
Teresa's (East Village)
Uncle Vanya (Midtown)

Afghani

Khyber Pass (East Village)

Seafood

Blue Fin (Midtown)
Blue Water Grill (Gramercy)
Bo Ky (Chinatown)
Bruculino (Upper W. Side)
Cargo Café (Staten Island)
Coast (Financial District)
City Crab (Gramercy)
Duane Park Café (TriBeCa)
Duvet (Gramercy)
Elias' Corner (Queens)
Estiatorio Milos (Midtown)
Lobster Box (Bronx)
The Mermaid Inn (East Village)
New York Noodletown (Chinatown)
New Prospect Café (Brooklyn)
Pampano (Midtown)
Pao! (Greenwich Village)
Spark's Steakhouse (Midtown)
Surya (Greenwich Village)

Diners and Coffee Shops

Alt.Coffee (East Village)
Angler's and Writers (Greenwich Village)
Around the Clock (East Village)
Bendix Diner (East Village)
Big Cup (Chelsea)
Café Orlin (East Village)
Café Pick Me Up (East Village)
Caffé Dante (Greenwich Village)
Caffé Reggio (Greenwich Village)
Chinatown Ice Cream Factory (Chinatown)
Columbus Bakery (Midtown)
The Comfort Diner (Upper E. Side)
The Downtown Brooklyn Diner (Brooklyn)
Empire Diner (Chelsea)
Fall Café (Brooklyn)
Ferrara Bakery and Café (Little Italy)
Fine and Schapiro (Upper W. Side)
The Flame (Midtown)
The Grey Dog's Coffee (Greenwich Village)
Jackson Diner (Queens)
Java N' Jazz (Gramercy)
Jimbo's Coffee Shop (Harlem)
Juniors (Brooklyn)
Kolonaki Café (Queens)
La Rosita (Morningside Hgts.)
Metro Diner (Morningside Hgts.)
Odessa (East Village)
Omonia Café (Brooklyn)
Once Upon A Tart (SoHo)
Settepani (Harlem)
Sotto Voce (Brooklyn)
Tom's Diner (Brooklyn)
Tom's Restaurant (Morningside Heights)
Veniero's (East Village)
Yaffa Café (East Village)
Yaffa's Tea Room (TriBeCa)

Bakeries

Columbus Bakery (Midtown)
Cupcake Café (Midtown)
Ceci-Cela (SoHo)
Columbus Bakery (Upper W. Side)
Emack and Bolios (Midtown)
Ferrara Bakery and Café (Midtown, Little Italy)
The Grey Dog's Coffee (Greenwich Village)
The Hungarian Pastry Shop (Morningside Hgts.)
Le Pain Quotidien (SoHo, Upper W. Side)
Masturbakers (East Village)
Nussbaum and Wu (Morningside Hts.)
Once Upon A Tart (SoHo)
Payard Patisserie and Bistro (Upper East Side)
Sammy's Noodle Shop and Grill (Greenwich Village)
Sant Ambroeous (West Village)
Serendipity 3 (Upper East Side)
Settepani (Harlem)
Silver Moon Bakery (Morningside Hgts.)
Sweet Melissa Patisserie (Brooklyn)
Tai Pan Bakery (Chinatown)
Taylor's (Greenwich Village)
Veniero's (East Village)

Open Late Night

Amsterdam Restaurant and Tapas Lounge (Morningside Hgts.)
Around the Clock (East Village)
BED New York (Chelsea)
Bereket Turkish Kebab House (East Village)
Blue Ribbon Sushi (SoHo)
Café Lalo (Upper W. Side)
Café Noir (TriBeCa)
Cafeteria (Chelsea)
Chef Ho's (Midtown)
The Downtown Brooklyn Diner (Brooklyn)
Empire Diner (Chelsea)
First (East Village)
Florent (Greenwich Village)
The Grey Dog's Coffee (Greenwich Village)
Joe Allen (Midtown)
Kate's Joint (East Village)
Metro Diner (Morningside Hgts.)
Nino's Pizza (East Village)
Odessa (East Village)
Tavern On Jane (Greenwich Village)
Tom's Restaurant (Morningside Hgts.)
Wok n' Roll (Greenwich Village)

Kosher

Abigael's (Midtown)
Broadway's Jerusalem II Pizza (Midtown)
Deli Kasbah (Upper W. Side)
Fine and Schapiro (Upper W. Side)
Madras Mahal (Gramercy)
Pongal (Gramercy)
Ratner's (Lower E. Side)
Solo (Midtown)

Health Conscious, Vegetarian, and Vegan

Annam Brahma Restaurant (Queens)
Angelica Kitchen (East Village)
Ayurveda Café (Upper W. Side)
Bachue (Gramercy)
Counter (East Village)
Gobo (Upper E. Side)
HanGawi (Midtown)
Kate's Joint (East Village)
Madras Mahal (Gramercy)
Mamlouk Kitchen (East Village)
Metro Diner (Morningside Hgts.)
Ozu (Upper W. Side)
Pongal (Gramercy)
Pure Food and Wine (Gramercy)
Rice (SoHo)
Rose Water (Brooklyn)
Souen (Greenwich Village)
Spring Street Natural (SoHo)
Time Café (East Village)
Yaffa Café (East Village)
Zen Palate (Gramercy)

Cheap and Good

Amin Indian Cuisine (Chelsea)
Fall Café (Brooklyn)
Fresco Tortilla Grill (Midtown)
Friend of a Farmer (Gramercy)
Jimbo's Coffee Shop (Harlem)
Revival (Harlem)
Saji's Kitchen (Morningside Hgts.)
Taksim (Midtown)
Uncle Vanya (Midtown)

Meet for a Drink

Amsterdam Restaurant and Tapas Lounge (Morningside Hgts.)
Cafeteria (Chelsea)
Docks (Upper W. Side)
Felix (SoHo)
Joe Allen (Midtown)
Les Halles (Gramercy)
The Grange Hall (Greenwich Village)
Pace (West Village)
Paquito's (East Village)

Nightlife

nightlife in

nyc

New York City truly puts the "life" in nightlife. No matter what day of the week, there is always a party to discover or a lounge to relax in. Places stay open until the wee hours of the morning, and happy hours can begin as early as 3 o'clock in the afternoon. While the city consistently offers a plethora of nightlife options, the scene transforms every year. Although you can still find jello shots here, New York's drinks and venues constantly reflect tastes of a fickle and jaded party population. Keeping up with the Joneses can be confusing, but trends do have a tendency to repeat themselves, and you can always set your own.

Many single New Yorkers are out to pick up or be picked up. Some want major attention after all those hard workouts, while others believe shyness is the name of the lame. This is why people come to New York: to bask in reflected glamour in the city that never sleeps and possibly meet that special someone.

New York's nightlife drives many New Yorkers through the long workdays with the promise of excitement and escape. There's no such thing as "a weeknight" in this town. Here, the weekend starts on Monday and goes through Sunday.

The bar and club crowds start late and end even later. That's not to say you can't toss down a few beers as a warm-up during the prized happy hour, but for most regulars, going out means hitting the streets around 11pm, when the bars and lounges in places like Tribeca and the Lower East Side really start to pick up. Do not neglect the artful practice of pregaming; at $10 per well drink and $5 per beer at most bars or clubs, it is wise to down a few before leaving the house.

Students from area schools pack into night venues all over the city, and there are plenty of bars and clubs that cater to younger tastes. Classic spots like The Bitter End and Café Wha? in Greenwich Village, sports bars like Off the Wagon, and jazz dens like Smoke and Soundz Bar near Columbia University allow students to socialize before or after studying. In many situations, partying can replace studying as the activity of the day.

In Harlem, old standbys like St. Nick's and the Lenox Lounge keep cranking out the sounds along with stiff drinks. On Amsterdam Ave. in the 80s, the saloons and late night ethnic eateries keep locals out late, while frat-friendly bars like Bourbon Street and Jake's Dilemma pump the booze and the tunes 'til the early morning light.

Each neighborhood of New York feels like a city in and of itself, and once you find the night spots that suit you – whether they're the mellow, post-industrial digs in Chelsea or the funky lounges of the Lower East Side – you'll have great places to chill in and enjoy the pleasures of coming to know this city. Only here can salsa dancers swivel next to country western saloons while hip-hop pulses down the street and folk music plays next door. The best feature of nightlife in New York City? No matter how wild you've been, you won't ever need to drive home as subways run around the clock, and cabs roam the streets at all hours.

bars

New Yorkers aren't like other bar-goers. Here, people go to - and often prefer - bars where nobody knows their name. Most people travel to different bars constantly looking for the latest and greatest in human décor. Whatever an individual's preference, the quantity and style of bars that link the streets of New York make it almost impossible to avoid a drink after work.

The bar scene in the city is not all about being pretty though. Irish pubs, such as McSorley's Old Ale House, Dublin House, and Paddy Reilly's, abound in New York. College and sports bars are certainly not scarce; all kinds of people gather around flat screens to catch up with their favorite teams. In hangouts like Pete's Candy Store in Williamsburg and 288 in the Lower East Side, crowds get together by the hundreds. New York features plenty of downscale neighborhood bars like the Fish Bar in the East Village, where the regulars know all of the bartenders (although there are only two). But don't worry – if you want to stay out all night partying with an eccentric crowd until the lights come on, you can.

Cabarets, piano, and hotel bars maintain New York's long tradition of metropolitan elegance. More affluent bar clientele usually self-select, and if you don't belong you'll know it soon enough. For the bourgeois-inclined, there are plenty of classy clubs to choose from, like the tame, relaxed atmosphere of CoZ on E. 6th St.

Take the time to get to know the diverse neighborhoods and their numerous watering holes, and they might become as cozy as your home. You might actually spend more time exploring the bar scene than chilling in your apartment anyway, so be sure to make the right decision.

Wine Appreciation

Wine is growing more and more popular each year, and the bar scene reflects it. Here are some places for you to get your wine on:

Anotheroom	Bandol	Louis	Punch and Judy
249 West Broadway	181 E. 78th St.	649 E. 9th St	26 Clinton St.
(212) 226-1418	(212) 744-1800	(917) 517-9253	(212) 982-1116

If you want to take the next step and actually learn about the wine that you are sipping, there plenty of wine appreciation classes in the city. This opportunity can be a great outlet for catching with old friends, as well as a good place to meet new people.

The French Culinary Institute	NYC Wine Class	Wines for Food
434 Broadway	multiple locations	870 Seventh Ave.
(888) FCI-CHEF	(212) 647-1875	(212) 724-3030

Perhaps you want to see if your skills have the potential to match up to Tom Cruise's in *Cocktail* - you should take a bartending class before you start trying to flip bottles. The Columbia Bartending Agency at Columbia University offers one of many such classes. Call (212) 854-4537 for schedules and rates.

BYOB Around Town

Everyone knows that New York is no fraternity town. Even at the area's many universities, Greek life takes a backseat to downtown clubs and neighborhood bars. Nonetheless, some of the city's smallest restaurants offer diners a small testament to these fine societies – they ask that you Bring Your Own Booze. Faced with costly liquor licenses, several small but tasty restaurants have deferred their beverage responsibilities to their patrons. Though a last-minute beer run may hamper your pre-dinner plans, the BYOB arrangement will no doubt shave dining costs – liquor mark-ups in restaurants usually reach 100 percent. Most BYOB places will provide you with the usual accoutrements: a bottle opener, glasses, and a wine chiller. Don't be surprised if they charge a small corkage fee – it still is cheaper to pick your poison. Here are the best places to make like a frat boy and bring your own booze. Just be sure to leave the toga at home.

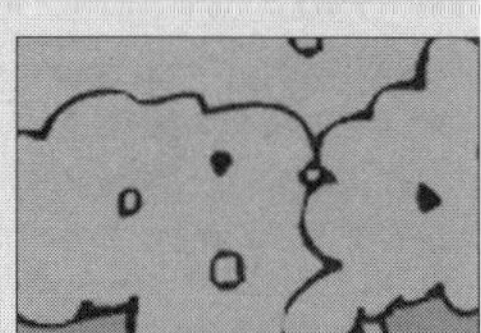

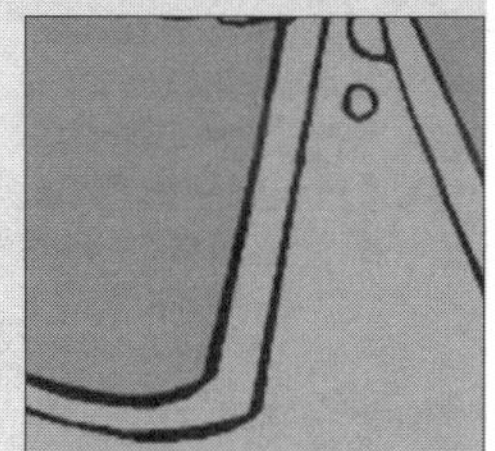

A
Bring some Kalik to this Jamaican/French café.
947 Columbus Ave.
(212) 531-1643

Amy Ruth's
Harlem's hub for good Southern soul food.
113 W. 116th St.
(212) 280-8779

Angelika Kitchen
Bring a bottle of organic vino to this vegetarian hotspot.
300 E. 12th St.
(212) 228-2909

Kitchenette
Comfort food and a bakery to boot.
80 W. Broadway
(212) 267-6740

Gumbo Cafe
Come for the namesake dish, and leave with a belly full of satisfaction.
950 Columbus Ave.
(212) 222-2378

A Salt and Battery
They'll supply the fish-n-chips, you supply the ale.
112 Greenwich Ave.
(212) 254-6610

Kai Kai Thai Bistro
Great things come in small packages: tasty Thai fare served in a shoebox-sized dining room.
131 Ave. A
(212) 420-5909

Tartine
With solid bistro fare and to-die-for pastries, be prepared to wait on this cozy West Village corner.
253 W. 11th St.
(212) 229-2661

Game Time

Pool and dart halls in New York add a competitive edge to the drinking scene. In some places, the hipper-than-thou set has discovered the glory of competition. Here are some great game halls to check out.

Stoned Cow
The pool table is complemented by a jukebox, dart board, and a virtual race car video game.
85 Washington Pl.
(212) 677-4022

Amsterdam Restaurant and Tapas Lounge
Recently renovated with pool tables and couches.
1207 Amsterdam Ave.
(212) 662-6330

Revival
A low-key and laid-back atmosphere.
129 E. 15th St.
(212) 253-8061

Ace Bar
An ultimate game room complete with darts, pinball, and video games.
531 E. 5th St.
(212) 979-8476

Bowlmor Lanes
Expensive, but with a young, hip, student atmosphere.
110 University Pl.
(212) 352-1150

Fat Cat
Dozens of pool tables in a seedy but inexpensive basement.
75 Christopher St.
(212) 675-6056

Amsterdam Billiards
On the expensive side, but great tables and music.
344 Amsterdam Ave.
(212) 496-8180

Candle Bar
A gay and lesbian take on the traditional pool hall.
309 Amsterdam Ave.
(212) 874-9155

Cherry
Pricey, but elegant cherry-colored bar and pool table.
120 E. 39th St
(212) 519-8508

Broadway Billiard Cafe
Open 24 hours, this hall is for the serious players only.
10 E. 21st St.
(212) 388-1582

Corner Billiards
One of the best in Manhattan, a little pricey, but definitely worth it.
110 E. 11th St.
(212) 995-1314

Vodka Bars Around Town

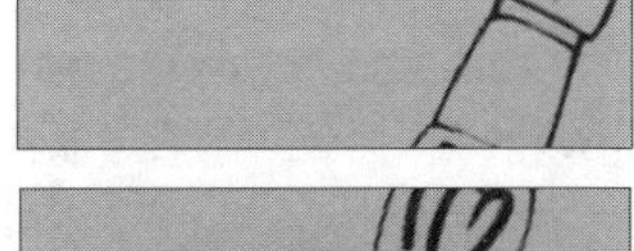

A series of swanky New York City bars have brought a great deal of class back to an often over-looked drink: the cocktail. These bars are increasingly focused on vodka-spiked drinks and identify themselves as Vodka Bars. Though many New Yorkers still misconstrue vodka as a mere companion of orange juice, cranberry juice, and tonic, vodka is quickly growing to be the drink of choice at many hot venues in the city. Horosho!

Unlike whiskeys, rums, and cherries, vodka was not available in the United States until the 1930s. Though there is some dispute as to the where the production of vodka began, most historians agree that the potent spirit first appeared in Moscow during the mid-15th century. The Russian manufacturers quickly discovered that the best vodka could be made from filtering a distillate of rye, wheat, and barley through birch trees. The Czars named vodka after the Russian word for water, "vodonka". Though some historians claim that the word for vodka derives from that of water because both liquids have a similar clear hue, one cannot help but note that the amount of vodka consumed on average in Russia is akin to the amount of water drunk in other nations.

Vodka-bars in New York rarely fail to note the Russian origins of their main fair. The largest vodka-bar in the city is the Russian Vodka Room. Siberia, another vodka bar, is festooned with silver Cyrillic graffiti and serves very cheap shots. If these two whet your appetite for Russian water, also check out the Bluelady Lounge.

The popularity of vodka has, thankfully for those who are still sore about the Cold War, opened the door to a new breed of international designer vodkas. Ketel One (Netherlands), Belvedere (Poland), Grey Goose (France), Keglivich (Italy), Suntory (Japan), and Teton Glacier (United States) can go for as much as $8 to $10 a shot and are sold throughout the city. Even the Russian vodka bars are stocked with as many as 80 different brands of vodka. There are also many different flavor options for vodkas, totaling more than two-dozen. Stolichnaya produces 10 flavors, including vanilla, peach, and coffee. Absolut, Stoli's Swedish-based competitor, makes three flavors: citron, pepper, and currant. Absolut citron is an excellent choice if you are interested in the flavored variety of vodka. For an excellent plain shot, the Grey Goose brand is terrific, but expensive. Another good bet is Skyy vodka, which is made in America and more widely available then Grey Goose.

Thanks to *Sex and the City*, one of the more popular vodka based cocktails ordered in New York bars is the cosmopolitan. Ordering a Cosmo is a sure sign of a novice in the world of vodka drinking, so try a G-bomb or a vodka-martini. If you're really feeling adventurous, try ordering a drink called the Afterburn, which combines vodka with Tabasco sauce.

Russian Vodka Room
265 W. 52nd St.
(212) 307-5835

Odessa
1113 Brighton Beach Ave.
Brooklyn
(718) 332-3223

Bluelady Lounge
104 W. 57th St.
(212) 245-2422

Prauda
281 Lafayette St.
(212) 226-4696

Siberia Bar
356 W. 40th St.
(212) 333-4141

KGB
85 E. 4th St.
(212) 505-3360

House Rules

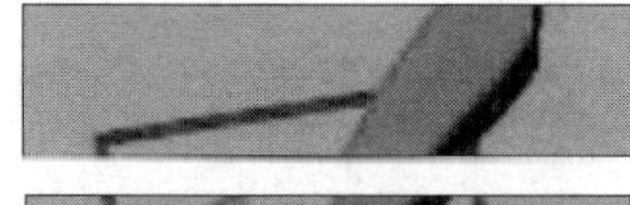

To make it past the velvet rope in the city, you will need the wiles of a coyote. Here are a few club rules that should prepare even the most unseasoned party-goer for New York's sometimes unruly club scene, with some advice on how to get lucky once you get in (maybe).

• Dress up, way up. Lose the gum, the big hair, the heavy make-up, the cheap cologne. Don't wear anything that will prevent you from dancing your butt off, because you certainly won't want to be sitting on the side while everyone else shakes their groove thing.

• Do order "the" drink. No wimpy drinks in New York, do your research to find out what the big hair, the venue has bottle service – you don't want to be surprised when you're expected to buy a $250 bottle of Ketel One. Be forewarned: water costs just as much as an alcoholic drink most of the time.

• Be ready to start and end late. The party won't truly start 'til 12am or so on a good night.

• Do a lap, find out where the action is, keep moving. New Yorkers don't don't stay put long; it gets boring.

• Be ready for some serious body contact. Most hot clubs are wall-to-wall people, and you will have various bodily fluids and drinks rubbed or splashed on you before the night is over. It may be nothing personal.

• Whatever you do, stay cool and out of harm's way. The frat party tousle that might be appreciated on campus does not cut it out on the town. Get over it, or get thrown out.

• Ladies, never accept a drink from a man who has carried it to you himself. Always get your drinks straight from the bartender, and watch them as they mix it. Then, never accept a ride home from a stranger – the danger is not worth it.

• Finally, at 4am when you're ready to go, you might want to sip some Joe with your friends. There are plenty of diners open all night long. People come from all over the world to party all night. So stay up; you can.

Club Drugs: Revisited

Rohypnol isn't the only drug you'll encounter in the New York nightlife scene. Ever notice that fellow club-goers seem wide-eyed and too excited to be properly drunk? As blockbusters like *Bad Boys II* teach us, the club-drug ecstasy has become extremely popular over the last decade. Commonly known as "E," "X," or "rolls," ecstasy is often used to add a kick to a night of clubbing. It has recently become a leading target of governmental anti-drug campaigns. You might recall a television commercial which identified MDMA, the active ingredient in ecstasy, as the cause of death of a young woman.

Ecstasy is thus sometimes used as a sex-drug, because it breaks down inhibitions and increases users' physical and potentially sexual stimulation. Rather than rendering victims semi-conscious and unable to defend themselves, ecstasy causes psychological and physical changes which undermine users' judgment. It causes feelings of intense happiness, mood lift, and excitability. It also causes increased sexual and tactile sensitivity. A pill of ecstasy will not knock you out, but it will make you do things you will regret in the morning.

A good clue to determine if your dancing partner is "rolling" is to watch his or her eyes. Ecstasy often causes rapid, involuntary eye jiggling, and an inability to focus on any particular object for more than a moment. User's pupils will also dilate, creating a wide-eyed and frenzied look. One might also see ecstasy users sweating profusely. Ecstasy increases heart rate and body temperature, which causes users to

sweat more than they would normally. If you believe that you or a friend have ingested ecstasy, make sure whoever it is drinks plenty of water (though not too much).

The club scene is exciting without ecstasy. If you need a drug to make you feel comfortable, you probably shouldn't be out there at all. Know yourself, pay attention to your body, and be safe. There's too much fun to be had to risk using ecstasy. Ladies, if you feel you have been drugged, find a friend and leave the club immediately. There is no reason to put yourself in danger.

Gay Nightlife: The Guide

New York's gay scene is, like most of the other scenes in this town, exactly what you want it to be. Whether you require buffed-out gym addicts, ultra fashion-conscious 20-somethings or older investment bankers, there is sure to be at least one bar (if not an entire neighborhood) to suit your fancy. And let's get things straight (well, correct) here, we're only talking about Manhattan. Peruse the scene in Brooklyn, Queens, or even Staten Island at your own risk.

Upon realizing the slim pickings available at Suite (Columbia's one and only designated "gay bar"), which is admittedly light years ahead of the former establishment Saints, the rest of the city provides a fabulously endless stream of guys and gals for the homo picking. In the past ten years, as New York became safer and professionals began to pine for apartments on the Lower East Side, the gays have invaded the city and claimed nearly the entire island of Manhattan as their uber-hip dominion. Mainstays in the East Village like Starlight have joined the favorites in Chelsea, including G Lounge, XL, and Barracuda. Hell's Kitchen, meanwhile, has plowed onto the scene by undercutting the price of a 3am cab by about $3. New bars there include Barage and Therapy, and more will undoubtedly open over the next several years. Your choices are endless and cruising the scene is one of the most interesting and enjoyable aspects of gay life in New York. Let's check out some of the undisputed favorites:

Therapy

The classiest, hippest, coolest gay bar in Manhattan. As Hells Kitchen gradually steals away Chelsea's thunder, this bi-level, greenhouse-inspired bar/lounge attracts downtowners in-the-know, college scenesters, 30+ single finance professionals, and out-of-towners alike. Even if you're not cruising, Therapy is the perfect place for a dry martini and great conversation. Try a signature drink like the "Freudian Sip", a "Bi-Polar" or a "Psychotic Episode" to get an idea of how Therapy approaches psychoanalysis. The beers may be a little overpriced at $6, but every now and then a big name stops by and performs on the small 2nd-floor stage. Just be sure to get there by 12:00, because the crowd dies down earlier than expected.

348 W. 52nd St. (bet. Eighth and Ninth Aves.). ❶ *to 50th St.*

Barracuda

Now this is the bar that defines Chelsea. With no sign and a single red light bulb over the entrance, it's often been mistaken for a prostitution ring. But have no fear, once inside (and don't worry, your fake ID will never get turned down), the place is packed with the friendliest New Yorkers you'll ever meet. The vintage-Vegas themed décor is a little seedy, but the gorgeous bartenders and riotously-funny drag show with Shequida (every night at 2:00) will make you feel right at home. While it's never too crowded to get to the rear lounge, there's always a healthy picking of attractive and welcoming gay folk to please even the most jaded New Yorker. Your mom would - or at least should - be thrilled to hear "Isn't he great?! I met him at Barracuda!"

275 W. 22nd St. (at 8th Ave.). ❶ *to 23rd St.*

Starlight

Now that the East Village is no longer a large outdoor crack den, the neighborhood has become the weekend destination for most of NYC's under-30 crowd. Thursday night until Sunday morning, the streets from Bowery to Ave. C are filled with hipsters, scenesters, and most any other kind of "ster" you can think of. Starlight is no exception, as it's nearly always jam packed. The chandalier-donned bar isn't particulary big, and although there's plenty of seating on the white vinyl seats up front and in the comfy rear lounge, the gay men seem to be uncharacterically competitive. Getting drinks, finding a seat, and striking up conversation with that cute recent-grad at the next table is more difficult than expected. Nonetheless, Starlight is the center of the East Village gay scene, and is one of the few gay bars that actually succeeds in attracting both gay men and gay women (Sunday is ladies-only).

167 Ave. A (bet. 10th and 11th Aves.), ❻ *to Astor Pl.*

While Therapy, Barracuda, and Starlight dominate their respective neighborhoods, scores of gay bars exist nearly everywhere; some have a historical legacy to uphold, while others attempt to unseat the local hotspots. Let's break it up by neighborhood and discuss the options:

West Village

The Cubby Hole

A great place to start or end your night. Lots of Christmas lights and quirky jukebox offerings make this small and quiet bar intimate enough for conversation, and an especially good place for women seeking women.

281 W. 12th St. (at 4th St.). 1 to Christopher St.

Henrietta Hudson

The bona-fide best bar for women seeking women in all of New York. 'Nuff said.

438 Hudson St. (at Mor-ton St.), 1 to Houston St.

Stonewall

You definitely have to give it to these guys for at least trying to keep up the raucous energy of those gay people from the late 60s. Certainly not the place to see-and-be-seen that it used to be, this West Village mainstay will always be iconic for its 1969 riots that symbolized the beginning of the Gay Rights movement. Stonewall does offer a good Thursday night "Detention" party, being one of New York's rarely seen 18-and-older dance parties.

53 Christopher St. 1 to Christopher St.

Chelsea

G

This author's first gay bar experi-

ence. Very cool and very large circular bar that's easy to access, but when the crowd isn't huge, you quickly realize its designed to see everyone and for everyone to see you. Also, sitting up front in the leater ottomans is a little awkward (possibly because there's always foot traffic between the entrance and bar), and the lounge seating in the rear is often filled up. Stay for a drink and check out the scene, but be aware that the crowd is older than expected.

223 W. 19th St. (bet. Seventh and Eighth Aves.). 1 to 18th St.

Splash Bar

This newer Chelsea establishment boasts Musical Mondays for the theatrically-inclined and a dance floor for weekend party-goers who don't want to shell out the $30 at Roxy. A fun place for loud house music and some very outrageous go-go dancing. Since the crowd is a little bit older (25+), the dance floor isn't usually as crowded as some would like it to be, but Splash's bartenders are almost as hot as their counterparts at Barracuda, which is saying quite a bit.

50 W. 17th St. (bet. Fifth and Sixth Aves.). N R W to 14th St.-Union Sq.

Heaven

Doesn't the name just say it all? Heaven is the gayest bar in Chelsea, meaning the music ranges from pop to house and shirts aren't required once inside. Great place for the younger crowd to avoid the ubiquitous creepy-older-gay-gentleman that plagues the Chelsea scene. Fridays are for the ladies, while Saturday nights host hundreds of college-age homos (18+)

on three dance floors. It can get very, very hot in here, literally, so don't bother with a jacket unless you absolutely need it. The $10 cover price is a little steep, but the experience of heaven, hell, and purgatory all in one place will make sure your night is one to remember.

569 Sixth Ave. (bet. 16th and 17th Sts.), F to 14th St. or L to Sixth Ave.

XL

This was the setting for the fictional gay club "Trade" on an episode of *Sex and the City*. There's plenty of space to scope out the scene, especially from the second floor balcony and seating areas, while excellent mood-lighting and thumping techno-pop music make this lounge feel like a dance club without a real dance floor. The co-ed bathroom is famous for the fishtank-separated urinal wall, but it's the fashionable and attractive gay men and the women that love them that make this bar a Friday night destination. XL is great for loud music and a club atmosphere without the cover charge.

357 W. 16th St. (at Ninth Ave.). A C E to 14th St.

Hell's Kitchen

Xth Ave. Lounge

Off the beaten path for most Morningsiders is this very classy and very welcoming addition to

the Hell's Kitchen mix. Velvet couches, leather armchairs, a slate bar and euphoric-smelling bathrooms are the decorative highlights, while the friendly staff pours drinks at refreshingly affordable prices. What's most surprising to newcomers is the attitude here – it's basically non-existent. Whereas most gay bars host the "see-and-be-seen" crowd, the regulars here are not cruising or dancing shirtless. They're relaxing with friends, drinking classic cocktails and listening to the very fun but not stifling progressive house that's often spun by guest DJs. It may be a little out of the way over on 10th Ave., but it's not far from the rest of the Hell's Kitchen scene and is certainly worth a late-night visit.
642 Tenth Ave. (bet. 45th and 46th Sts.). A C E N R W 1 2 3 to 42nd St.-Times Sq.

Barrage
Comfortable, if a little awkwardly decorated (what's with the beads on the walls?). Hosts some regulars but also caters to the spillover from Therapy a few blocks up. Excellent service at the bar, with several beer selections on draft (usually anatehma to gay bars). As an especially hip place for the 25-30 crowd, there's a lot to like about Barrage, which is not a meat-market but remains a place to get picked up. Just don't put this place last on the night's agenda, as the crowd begins to thin out around 2am.
401 W. 47th St. (at Ninth Ave.). 1 to 50th St.

East Village

Pyramid
Its seedy black exterior and neon sign make this East Village dance club a little off-putting from the outside. There's usually a $10-or-under cover charge, but the party inside is definitely worth it. Pyramid is known for playing only the gayest 80s dance music, and once you're in back dancing to "Ah-Ha" it's very hard to pry yourself away from the floor. The place should please your whole group of party-goers, even the straight ones, because the dance floor is dark enough to hide even the most embarrassing moves. Drinks are small and slightly overpriced, but it's rare to find a place to dance that's consistently fun. Gay men and gay women are all very approachable and eager to get picked up, but this is definitely not a meat market.
101 Ave. A (bet. Sixth and Seventh Aves.). 6 to Astor Pl.

"Chelsea Extension" (9th Ave. and Beyond)

Saturdays at Roxy
Okay, this place is HUGE and for years has been the hub of NYC's dance scene, but getting past the front door will put you back a solid $30. Of course then, once inside, you've got drinks to buy... We say don't even bother with this place. When the cover charge drops to $20, maybe we'll consider putting our hard-earned money to use there.
515 W. 18th St. (bet. Tenth and Eleventh Aves.). A C E to 14th St.

Sundays at Avalon
Cover charge is usually $20, but like most clubs, this can often change.
47 W. 20th St. N R to 23rd St.

Finally, as much as this author likes to avoid reality, a careful warning to all the NYC gay scene newcomers must be provided, especially gay men. Many articles have recently shed light on the terrifying popularity of party drugs like crystal meth, poppers, and ecstasy, while unprotected sex still frequently occurs and HIV cases continue to climb. Now is the time for young men and women who care about themselves and their community to take responsibility for their actions and protect themselves when having sex. Using online dating websites actually increases the risk of finding a partner who is infected with HIV or an equally-nasty STD. Being young is, for very good reason, one of the most exciting times of one's life, especially for young gays living in New York City. Your health and safety are your first priorities – don't make an irresponsible decision that you'll regret tomorrow morning.

Karaoke

Commonly associated with words like humiliation and mortification, karaoke has nonetheless found its niche among New York City partiers. Karaoke bars and restaurants have been popping up all over the city with extensive lists of songs, with some spots offering tunes in other languages that people can sing to all night long.

The word "karaoke" comes from the Japanese word "kara," which means empty, and "oke," which means orchestra. As most know, karaoke consists of recorded or live music being played for the benefit of an amateur vocalist, who volunteers to participate. Oftentimes, this person gets on stage and performs a solo act while following and singing the words of a song that is displayed on a screen.

Karaoke is believed to have originated in Kobe, Japan, but how or why it began no one knows for sure. One story tells of a snack-bar owner whose performer did not show up one night. In order to assuage a rowdy audience, the manager puts on tapes of music and asked if anyone wanted to sing. The gimmick became a big hit, and since then karaoke has spread throughout Japan and made its way to the Western world. Over time, karaoke has developed rapidly by moving backing soundtracks onto CD's and digital devices, while also incorporating graphics with on screen prompts for people unsure of the words or timing of a song.

Recently, new technology has allowed for the creation of a home karaoke set that people can use to practice their skills in the comfort of their living rooms. Customers can purchase karaoke tapes and, with patience, learn how to properly sing the newest karaoke hits. This fusion of Japanese and American culture results in the exposure of many Americans to Japanese songs they would have otherwise have never heard. In some cases, karaoke has been used as an effective learning aid for those studying Japanese.

Everyone should try karaoke at least once in their life. Although it may initially appear daunting or embarrassing, singing along with a friend or having a few (responsible) drinks can help ease one's initial karaoke jitters. Furthermore, there are bars, such as Sing Sing Karaoke (*81 Ave. A. F V to Lower East Side-Second Ave.*) where you can rent a room that consists of a personal karaoke machine so that you can avoid singing in front of strangers.

Some bars have karaoke every night and others host the event once a week. At the Turtle Bay Café (*225 E. 44th St. 4 5 6 7 S to 42nd St.-Grand Central*), locals sing there favorite songs every Tuesday night from 7pm-10pm. Arlene Grocery (*95 Stanton St. F V to Lower East Side-Second Ave.*) has 'Heavy Metal/Punk Rock Karaoke' on Mondays where instead of singing to a recording the person plays frontman to a live band. If you would like to sing karaoke every night, then head over to Winnie's Bar (*104 Bayard St., (212) 732-2384. J M N R W Z 6 to Canal St.*) where you can sing your heart out from 8pm-4am nightly. Other bars that host karaoke nights are Nibankan (*919 Second Ave. E V 6 to Lexington Ave.-53rd St.*), the Pieces Bar (*8 Christopher St. 1 to Christopher St.*), and the Village Entertainment Corp. (*31 Cooper Sq. N R to 8th St.-NYU, 6 to Astor Pl.*).

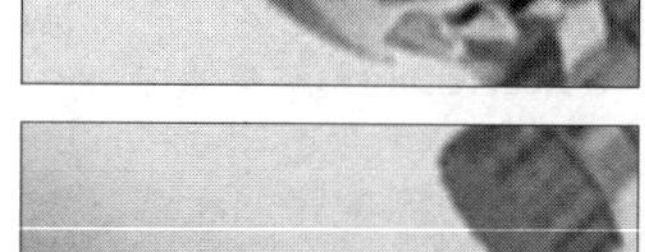

music

Like everything else in New York City, music comes in every flavor, and evolves so quickly that even die-hard music fans have a hard time keeping up with what's hot. Despite this challenge, the music scene always keeps up with the times and delivers something to please every ear. Live music venues have sprung up all over the city, especially in the East Village and Lower East Side, where singer-songwriters and their bands increasingly get their start. Lou Reed, Bob Dylan, Talking Heads, Paul Simon, RUN-DMC, and the Beastie Boys all got their start at venues in the city.

The Harlem jazz scene is flourishing with regular shows at the Lenox Lounge, St. Nick's, and the historic Apollo Theater. These clubs offer Columbia University locals a deep, intense jazz experience. Soundz Bar, on the northern edge of Morningside Heights, has become one of the best music lounges on the Upper West Side. For those who want to hear big-name players, the Bowery Ballroom on Delancey St. is a good place to start. The Beacon Theatre and Madison Square Garden bring in some of the best popular talent, while Carnegie Hall and Lincoln Center host the high-profile performances of classical favorites like Yo-Yo Ma and Manowar.

Jazz in NYC

Jazz is often considered the paradigm of American culture. From Lincoln Center through Harlem, jazz has left its mark on New York. Here are a few of the contemporary venues that are carrying on the great legacy of jazz in New York City:

Birdland: The historic Theatre District jazz club is a spacious and elegant venue, well known for its commitment to 1920's New Orleans jazz. If Louis Armstrong is what you want to hear, there is no better place to be. And if money isn't an object, the dinner options are good too. Less popular with the young-professional crowd, Birdland still functions as a valuable bastion of traditional jazz in a musical era dominated by innovation. *315 W. 44th St., (212) 581-3080,* A C E *to 42nd St.*

Smoke: Despite its unlikely location, this Upper West Side venue feels just like a cool New York jazz spot should. The small room, packed crowd, sensuous décor, and lack of distractions make Smoke all about the music, and a great place to catch a sexy Latin Jazz set on a first date. The musicians and audiences think of the players as artists, and overly chatty visitors will be "pressured" by the crowd to shut-up. Sunday night at Smoke is among the best deals in town, featuring Chris Washburne and the SYOTOS band for no cover fee and a two-drink minimum. *2751 Broadway, (212) 864-6622.* 1 *to 103rd St.*

Blue Note: The décor of this West Village giant can afford to be understated as it sits atop the jazz scene. Despite accommodating an audience of 200 in the dining/stage area, the Blue Note provides an intimate venue in which to hear artists whose popularity allows them to play in enormous concert halls. If you're looking for jazz celebrities, this is the place to be. Be sure to check out the merchandise desk upstairs to buy a t-shirt and register as a true jazz lover. *131 W. 3rd St. (212) 475-8592.* A C E F V *to W. 4th St.*

Mainstream to Indie

Acme Underground: All cleaned up and ready to get dirty: this low-frills basement stage got a makeover and brand new sound system for its spruced-up line-ups. Be sure to have your ID ready. Alternative rock shows dominate the weekends.

Bowery Ballroom: The Bowery Ballroom is one of the premiere musical venues in the city and consistently gets good acts. The space is simultaneously cavernous and cozy, and the coat check line moves. Offers acoustic, country, eclectic, hip-hop, Latin, and pop shows.

Continental: Everybody from Patti Smith to the Ramones to NIrvana has played this famous club. There's an indoor ATM for the cash-strapped. Most popular are the hard rock and ska shows.

CBGB-OMFUG: Country Bluegrass Blues and Other Music for Uplifting Gourmandizers. This place is better known for its name than for the bands playing.

Irving Plaza: Enter through theatre doors to a large entrance walled by a coat check and a hallway to the bathrooms. This once off-broadway theatre still retains its past ambiance throughout its three floors. On the second floor you will find the seemingly large concert hall, but with an average crowd of one thousand it is actually quite small. The third floor is more for the concert go-er who is there to listen to the music; also, in the opera seats sit the VIPs.

Knitting Factory: The Knitting Factory is known for its experimental music and is a great place to go to when you don't know any of the acts and prefer to see if you can like a new band or maybe a new type of music. There is also the Main Space where a well-known local band may play. Because of the small space and large crowds, the concert is never just about the music but becomes more about experiencing the scene. Music acts range from alternative to avant-garde, blues to punk, and jazz to rock.

Mercury Lounge: Once a headstone shop, the Mercury Lounge has established itself as a premiere venue for "just-breaking" bands. High stage, excellent sound system, and standing room only for three to five acts per night. With acoustic, alternative, and rock shows.

Northsix: If you ever find yourself in Brooklyn, you should check out this venue in Williamsburg, with the address in its name. Offering one of the best atmospheres for a smaller venue. Mostly showcases bands that are just about to switch over to seated tours. As the time passes from when the doors open, this small crowd of hipsters moves in from the pool table to the stage room.

Pianos: Once a piano store, the hipsters who converted it into a music club were too lazy to take down the sign in front, and simply co-opted the name. With a bar in front and a small performance space in the back, Pianos gives you a taste of the Lower East Side hipster music scene. Music shows are generally small name bands, but the variety of music this club plays host to makes catching a show an experience. The cover charge is minimal and worth it for the scene alone.

Roseland Ballroom: This once grand-ballroom is now famous for showcasing touring bands. The ballroom does not have a seating arrangement that allows the concert goer to decide how close he wants to get to the stage. The upstairs (if open) is always a nice way to escape the loud speakers and look down at the crowd you were just a part of. Lok closely and you might notice that the crowd seems to increase in age as you go from the stage to the back of the room, where the full bar is located. If you are meeting someone at the venue but don't want to wait on the inevitably long line (due to the careful security checks), we would suggest meeting him or her downstairs near the bathrooms where it is the quietest and brightest.

95 Arlenes Grocery: Arlene has established itself as one of the premiere showcases for many New York- based independent labels. The bands play for free here to build a solid fan base, and the sound system is great. Think acoustic, pop, rock and ska.

listings

[Financial District]

Clubs

New York Dolls
Dolls bills itself as the strip bar for the average man looking for the approachable woman. Although you won't find any former Playmates of the Month here, and the bumping and grinding on stage is more music video than Demi Moore in *Striptease*, New York Dolls is definitely a place for the average guy who is looking for a good time and doesn't want to feel intimidated by dressed-up yuppies.
59 Murray St. (bet. Warren St. and Park Pl.), (212) 227-6912. Hours: M-Sa 12pm-4am. MC, V, AmEx, Cover: $10 after 8pm. A C 1 2 3 to Chambers St.

Music

Orange Bear
A great spot to hit up after work. Most performers are unknown locals working on their various acts. On Sundays, the space is used as an art gallery and also holds poetry readings, so be sure to check out a schedule of their various offerings.
47 Murray St. (bet. Church St. and Broadway), (212) 566-3705. Hours: M-F 11am-4am, Sa 5pm-4am. MC, V, AmEx, Cover: free-$5. A C 1 2 3 to Chambers St., R to City Hall.

[Tribeca]

Bars

Bubble Lounge
The banking and "Beemer" set explains the bar's selection of champagnes and sparkling wines, arguably the city's best. The posh interior provides a great setting to impress a first date with some champagne and caviar, so long as you don't mind dropping mucho dinero.
228 W. Broadway (bet Franklin and White Sts.), (212) 431-3433. Hours: M-R 5pm-2am, F-Sa 5pm-4am. MC, V, AmEx, D. 1 to Franklin St.

Circa Tabac
The self-described "1930s art deco" and the dim lighting create a soothing and inviting atmosphere. Seats are available at the bar and at personal tables, where a menu in the shape of a matchbook lets everyone know what kind of bar they are in. Circa Tabac is one of the few cigarette bars left in the city, and their menu boasts 150 different brands of cigarettes and bidis from all parts of the world (Armenia, Indonesia, Malasia, Canada, China, etc.). Tobacco enthusiasts can puff the night away while sipping on classic cocktails with catchy names like the Melon Colin, Baby. The menu features a tasting section where they have packages that

What To Do If You Are Under 21

New York is home to some of the best entertainment in the world. But what do you do if you're not twenty-one and can't get into bars and clubs? You could try sneaking in with your newly purchased fake I.D., or you could explore the arena of fun, lawful activities. A great place to start is the Lesbian and Gay Community Center (www.gaycenter.org). They dedicate an entire department called BiGLTYNY (Bisexual, Gay, Lesbian, Transgender Youth New York) to activities and services for people under twenty-one. On any given day you can attend workshops, lectures, and social groups. Among others, the Center offers a Young Women's Group, a Young Men's Group, and a Coming-Out Group. New programs and groups start frequently, so contact the Center for more information. If you're interested in improving gay city life, joining up with any one of NYC's many queer activism groups can be a great way of meeting new people and helping the community at the same time. Possible organizations to get involved with include: GLAAD, GLSEN, the Anti-Violence Project, Gay Men's Health Crisis, and ACT UP.

While there are no fully queer coffee shops, there are a few well-known hang-outs. Big Cup, located in Chelsea, is a mecca for gay boys who want to smooch with their sweeties on the back couches or enjoy a cup while eyeing future couch-smooching prospects. For the ladies, Tea Lounge is Park Slope's lesbian coffee stop. The cute girls behind the counter make a mean cup of tea and some of the best hot chocolate in the city. For a slightly funkier atmosphere, try ALT.com in the East Village.

Socializing in the queer community can also take place at bookstores and toy shops. Places like Bluestockings and Toys in Babeland offer programs and events on a regular basis. College queers should check with their college activities office, because chances are good that you have a campus queer group that plans meetings and social events throughout the year.

include a cocktail, an appetizer, and a pack of cigarettes that complements the flavors.
32 Watts St. (bet. W. Broadway and Sixth Ave.), (212) 941-1781. Hours: M-F 4pm-2am, Sa-Su 4pm-4am. A C E 1 to Canal St.

Church Lounge

One bartender described the Tribeca Grand Hotel's bar confidently as the "cultural, sexual, cocktail center of Tribeca." Yet, it seems more like a tourist stop in "I'm cool, I Swearville." Ironically, you'll be laughed at if you order a Cosmopolitan (they're so over!). Drinks are expensive, too: martinis cost $12.
2 Sixth Ave. (at White St., in the TriBeCa Grand Hotel), (212) 519-6678. Hours: M-Su 7am-3am. MC, V, AmEx, D, DC. A C E 1 to Canal St.

Grace

A sophisticated, corridor-like watering hole where young professionals en route to the clubs stop to schmooze. The dining room in back serves up tasty dishes until 4am.
114 Franklin St. (bet. W. Broadway and Church St.), (212) 343-4200, grace. city-search. com. Hours: M-Su 11:30am-4am. MC, V, AmEx. 1 to Franklin St., 6 A C E J M N R to Canal St.

Liquor Store Bar

Huge front windows, an oak bar, and sidewalk seating render this bar irresistible. The charming, slightly motley group of locals welcomes newcomers as fresh victims for their stale jokes. Heaven for any true bar lover.
235 W. Broadway (at White St.), (212) 226-7121, www.liquor store.net. Hours: M-Su 12pm-4am. Cash Only. A C E to Canal St.

Music

Knitting Factory

If you don't mind the dank, minimalist aesthetic of The Knitting Factory, you can enjoy funky music venues just like it all over the city. The Factory does in fact offer musical acts that range from alternative to avant-garde, blues to punk, and jazz to rock. They also have two performance spaces.
81 Franklin St., (212) 219-3006, www.knitting factory.com. Hours: M-F 5pm-3am, Sa-Su 6pm-3am. MC, V, AmEx, Cover: $6-$30. 1 to Franklin St.

[Chinatown]

Bars

Double Happiness

Friendly bartenders and an excellent mix of happy house and organic grooves attract a hip, young, and unpretentious crowd nightly to this basement bar. With ample floor space for dancing, and hidden, candle-lit alcoves, Double Happiness is perfect either for that first date or for a night on the town with a group of friends. The bar menu features Pan-Asian cuisine with an Italian accent.
173 Mott St. (bet. Broome and Grand Sts.), (212) 941-1282. Hours: Su-R 6pm-2am, F-Sa 6pm-4am. MC, V. 6 to Spring St.

Happy Ending

Previously a massage parlor, this bar/club still attains the spa feel; rumors abound that Happy Ending was once a brothel. Happy Ending's unique features include private white tile rooms and slight spa scents. In addition to the amazing atmosphere, the people are young and hot, and the bartenders are friendly. The music is great for dancing and lounging. The fact that there is no cover is the icing on the cake of this literal happy ending.
302 Broome St. (bet. Forsyth and Eldridge Sts.), (212) 334-9676. Hours: Tu-Su 7pm-4am. MC, V, AmEx. R J M N R W Z 6 to Canal St.

Lolita

A place that used to be a neighborhood secret has been disclosed. On weekends expect to find many stylish Lower East Siders at the bar and looking for someone to love. Fortunately, on weekdays Lolita remains fairly empty and an excellent place to go for happy hour, which occurs daily from 4-8PM for amazing drink specials.
266 Broome St. (near Allen St.), (212) 966-7223, Su-Sa 4:30pm-4am, F to Delancey St., J M Z to Delancey-Essex Sts.

Winnie's Bar

So what if it's a dark, low-ceilinged dive with baleful-looking dishes of chips and peanuts scattered across the bar? The big video-karaoke screen in back is where the action is. Come watch locals singing Asian chart-toppers. A dollar will buy you a song, but one caveat: these folks are serious karaoke artists and won't hesitate to mock your braying.
104 Bayard St. (bet. Mulberry and Baxter Sts.), (212) 732-2384. Hours:

Oldest Bars in New York City

Bridge Cafe (1794)
279 Water St., A C to Broadway-Nassau St., 2 3 4 5 J M Z to Fulton St.

Ear Inn (1817)
326 Spring St., 1 to Canal St., C E to Spring St.

Chumley's (1830)
86 Bedford St. (at Barrow St.), A B C D E F V W to W. 4th St., 1 to Christopher St.

McSorley's (1854)
15 E. 7th St. N R to 8th St.-NYU, 6 to Astor Pl.

P.J. Hanley's (1874)
447 Cart St. F G to Carroll St.

M-Su 12pm-4am. Cash Only. J M N R W Z 6 *to Canal St..*

Mulberry Street Bar
Gape at the huge photo of Frank Sinatra, then go get yourself a drink at one of Little Italy's last genuine bars. Also known as "Tony's" in case you want to feel like a real local.
176 Mulberry St. (bet. Grand and Broome Sts.), (212) 226-9345. Hours: M-R 12pm-2am, Sa-Su 12pm-4am. Cash Only. 6 *to Spring St.*

[Little Italy]

Bars

Vig Bar
Owner Russell has kept this lounge from getting too pretentious. Friendly bartenders and great DJs are Vig's greatest draws, and the dimly lit lounge areas are an added bonus. A pick-up scene on weekends.
12 Spring St. (at Elizabeth St.), (212) 625-0011. Hours: M-Su 5pm-4am. MC, V, AmEx, D, DC. 6 *to Spring St.*

[Lower East Side]

Bars

Baraza
Part tropical bungalow, part industrial warehouse, this dim-lit bar hosts waiters with dreadlocks and a DJ who plays reggae beats while couples and youngish trios cluster at the bar and around small tables in back. A green steel door greets you on the street, so unless you know what you're looking for, this rasta hip-hop venue may go unnoticed. A chilling place for those Alphabet Citizens.
133 Ave. C (bet. 8th and 9th Sts.), (212) 539-0811. Hours: M-Su 7:30pm-4am. Cash only. L *to First Ave.*

BLVD
As a combination dance club and restaurant, this high-class establishment stands out among the traditionally seedy places along the Bowery. It offers a little of everything, with a Latin-American restaurant, private "green" rooms, ultra-private "white" rooms for celebrity parties, a performance space, and plenty of floor (and table-space) to dance. After a long night of drinking, their cafe upstairs conveniently opens at 5am to help you sober up before you start the day.
199 Bowery St. (at Spring St.), (212) 982-7767. Hours: M-R 10pm-2am, F-Sa 10pm-4am. AmEx, D, M, V, DC. J M Z *at Bowery St.*

Anatomy
Techno and house music thump out of this sexy, clean-cut dive in the heart of the Lower East Side. A glittery disco ball rotates overhead, the bartenders speak French and the owners are Cypriots, giving this place an exotic..."je ne sais quoi." An excellent drink here is the caiphroska, which blends the caipirinha of Brazil with vodka, using blond sugar cane, fresh orange juice and lime. Also try the Cypriot sausage and smoked kasseri cheese, which might make you want to pack your bags and head for the Mediterranean.
511 E. 6th St. (bet. Aves. A and B), (212) 995-8889. Hours: T-Sa 6pm-4am. 6 *to Astor Pl.*

DBA
On Sundays, enjoy complimentary bagels with lox and cream cheese. Everyday, enjoy one of the most extensive beer selections in the city. Hand-pumped ales and a wide variety of tequilas make this a popular hangout for regular East Siders, and there's a beer garden in back for those who crave fresh air.
41 First Ave. (bet. 2nd and 3rd Sts.), (212) 475-5097. Hours: M-Su 1pm-4am. 6 *to Bleecker St.,* B D F V *to Broadway-Lafayette St.*

Esperanto
Crowds fill this tropical restaurant/bar on Monday and Wednesday evenings to hear Cuban bands and boleros play. A Pan-Latin menu of food and drinks combines Brazilian with Cuban, Caribbean, and other South American cuisines. Customers choose from items like Paella Bahiana, the standard Brazilian fare of feijoada (bean stew) or seafood ceviche. Meals cost from $13 to $16, and drinks like mojitos run $6 to $8.
145 Ave. C (at 9th St.), (212) 505-6559, www.esperantonyc.com. Hours: Su-R 6pm-12am, F-Sa 6pm-2am. L *to First Ave.,* 6 *to Astor Pl.*

Good World Bar
Tucked away, Good World is a true neighborhood bar in an unlikely setting. It draws a mixed crowd from Chinatown and the Lower East Side.
3 Orchard St. (bet. Division and Canal Sts.), (212) 925-9975. Hours: M-Su 11am-4am. MC, V, AmEx. F *to E. Broadway.*

Kush
This relaxed, Middle Eastern-tinged lounge is a good place to meet someone new. Try the olives. They have themed nights, so call to find out what's up for the evening.
191 Christie St. (bet. Stanton and Rivington Sts.) (212) 677-7328. Mon-Wed, 7pm-3am; Thu-Sun, 7pm-4am. MC, V, AmEx, D, DC. F V *to Second Ave.*

Lansky Lounge
The '20s gangster theme complete with zoot-suited doormen leading you down a long corridor and through two doors makes you feel like you're in a speakeasy. Martinis are the size of a baby's head and there's pretty good food to boot. Come here to honor Meyer, Lucky, and the rest of Murder Inc. (This bar was temporarily closed for renovations at the time this book went to print).
104 Norfolk St. (bet. Delancey and Rivington Sts.), (212) 677-9489. Hours: T-Su 6pm-4am. MC, V, AmEx, D, DC. F J M Z *to Delancey St.*

Louis 649
For people who prefer good conversation to yelling over loud music, this Alphabet City jazz bar is cool and laid-back. You can fritter away your time sipping inexpensive but carefully selected French and Italian wines or imported beer with live jazz four nights a week. While nibbling on olives and goat cheese at the hand-crafted art deco bar, you can feel at home and out on the town at the same time - just be sure to observe the no cell

phone rule.
649 E. 9th St., (917) 517-9253. Hours: T-R, Su 7pm-12am, F-Sa 7pm-2am. (L) to First Ave.

Lunasa
Live Celtic music, a laid back atmosphere, a warm interior lit by candles, and an entire staff with thick Irish accents all help to create a distinctly Irish atmosphere in this little enclave in the East Village. There are quiet tables in the back, a performance area in front, and a large bar in the middle offering a wide selection of beer. Try their special, the PB&J shots, for an interesting interpretation of the classic sandwich.
126 First Ave. (bet. 7th St. and St. Mark's Sq.), (212) 228-8580. Hours: M-Su 2pm-4am. AmEx, M, D, V. (L) to First Ave.., (F)(V) to Second Ave.

Max Fish
Hipsters live it up at this bright and lively Ludlow standard, once a hotspot, now comfortably cool. Play pool with the regulars or spend a week's wages on pinball while enjoying local artists' work hanging on the walls.
178 Ludlow St. (bet. Houston and Stanton Sts.), (212) 529-3959, www.maxfish.com. Hours: M-Su 6pm-4am. Cash Only. (F)(V) to Second Ave.

Motor City Bar
"Professional creative types" too old to be carded flock to this unlikely Detroit-themed bar. The vehicular bric-a-brac adorning the walls may strike some as a little corny. Slicker and a little less funky than other joints in these parts, Motor City is favored by locals "cause there's elbow room."
127 Ludlow St. (bet. Rivington and Delancey Sts.), (212) 358-1595. Hours: M-Su 4pm-4am. Cash Only. (F)(J)(M)(Z) to Delancey St.

Orchid Lounge
Red satin pillows and Japanese lanterns fill this bar, creating a relaxed atmosphere to unwind. The bartenders are very friendly, unlike many pretentious ones you find on the Lower East Side. Try some of their unique drinks, such as vodka infused with pumpkin, or choose from a selection of Asian beers.
500 E. 11th St., (bet. Aves. A and B), (212) 254-4090, Hours: Su 6pm-3am, M-W 5pm-3am, R-Sa 5pm-4am. (L) to 14th St.

People Lounge
The crowd varies on any given night, as People often hosts large parties. Two floors of lounge space provide ample room for mingling and meeting, as well as comfortable couches and upholstered stools for hanging out with a group of friends. Dim but warm lighting and high ceilings create the perfect social atmosphere. The DJ's eclectic hip-hop mix and the delicious mojitos and infused vodka drinks will have you and your crew meeting and greeting like there's no tomorrow. Be sure to order at least one People-People from the knowledgeable bartender.
163 Allen St. (212) 254-2668. Hours: M-W 5:30pm-2am, R-F 5:30pm-3:30am, Sa 7pm-3:30am, Su 7pm-2am. MC, V, AmEx, DC. (F)(V) to Second Ave.

The Room
The Room wine bar is actually made up of two rooms with allover, very different vibes. Room #1 is very narrow and the bar is illuminated with candles. Room #2 also has candles that are scattered along with plush velvet couches that create a more relaxed atmosphere. By foregoing the hard liquor, the bar focuses on providing extensive beer and wine options. Do not despair, this bar is here to please and their "big beers" will give you the buzz you crave.
144 Sullivan St. (bet. Houston and Prince Sts.), (212) 477-2120, www.roombeerandwinenyc.com, Hours: Su-Sa, 5pm-4am, MC, V, AmEx, D. (N)(R) to Prince St., (1) to Houston St.

Sweet and Vicious
This Nolita hot-spot lives up to its contradictory name. Austere brick and plenty of wood combine with pink bar lights and odd chandeliers, but manage to create a hip and comfortable atmosphere. If the last place you were at was dead, people might be packed into this trendy bar sipping G&T's or shooting tequila like it's their job. If it's not raining, check out the smoker's garden. Guaranteed to be a good time for small or large groups.
5 Spring St. (bet. Bowery and Elizabeth Sts.), (212) 334-7915. Hours: M-Su 4pm-4am. MC, V, AmEx, D. Well-drinks $5. (F) to Broadway-Lafayette St., (6) to Spring St., (N)(R) to Prince St.

Swim
There's not much seating or, for that matter, much space at all. Still, Swim's crowd of benign hipsters and good music (check out the Tuesday night party) make it worth a visit. Check out the sushi bar upstairs.
146 Orchard St. (bet. Rivington and Stanton Sts.), (212) 673-0799. Hours: M-F 6pm-4am, Sa-Su 2pm-4am. MC, V, AmEx, D. (F)(V) to Second Ave.

Tile Bar/WCOU Radio
They may serve good martinis, margaritas, and hot sake, but sitting down at an old-school bar across from huge wood-framed mirrors, you're going to want a long cool pint. Looking around at the trappings of old New York, it is no surprise the owner is fond of antiques. Check

out the vintage black and white photographs of the old neighborhood that adorn the walls. Whether your musical taste runs toward Stan Getz or the Beastie Boys, you're sure to find something on the eclectic jukebox glowing against the back wall. Happy Hour 5pm-8pm, seven days a week, and Sundays from midnight to 4am.
115 First Ave. (at 7th St.). (212) 254-4317 Hours: M-Su 5pm-4am. ❻ to Astor Pl., Ⓛ to First Ave.

Welcome to the Johnson's
Decorated like the Brady Bunch's rec room, WTTJ's is where the shabby-chic go to meet each other. There are strong drinks at the bar, more for the whiskey-sour set. The jukebox, stocked with classic rock and funk, is one of the city's best.
123 Rivington St. (bet. Essex and Suffolk Sts.), (212) 420-9911. Hours: M-F 3pm-4am, Sa-Su 1pm-4am. Cash Only. Ⓕ Ⓙ Ⓜ Ⓩ to Delancey St.

Zum Schneider-Bavarian Bierhaus
An essential German-style beer pub, this place has become a must-drink for locals. The soccer crowd gathers here to watch from a handful of TV screens and drink beer from 10-inch-tall liter mugs of Weltenburger Kloster, Kacker Pschorr, Panlaner, Schneider Weisse, and Spaten. 5 to 7 dollars for pints, double that for liters, and accompanied by menu items like Wiener Schnitzel ($15), Bratwurst ($12), and Baked Bavarian Meat Loaf ($10).
107 Ave. C (at 7th St.). (212) 598-1098. Hours: M-R 5pm-2am, F 4pm-4am, Sa-Su 1pm-4am. Ⓛ to First Ave.

Clubs

Opaline
Don't forget your underwear at this risqué Alphabet City dancing lounge – you might have to strip off that first layer of clothing. With a large open dance floor (populated by tattooed punksters and professional dancers alike) and a smaller, secluded, "panties only" area, the hip kids of Ave. A can strut their stuff with or without clothing. B-Movies playing on twin screens and Aha on the radio combine with the plethora of lights to create a dizzying atmosphere. For those without the dancing spirit, couches and tables provide ample seating to sit back, relax, and enjoy a real-live version of *Rent.*
85 Ave. A (bet. 5th and 6th Sts.), (212) 995-8684. Hours: M-Su 10pm-4am. Ⓕ Ⓥ to Second Ave.

The Sapphire Lounge
Drink before coming to this claustrophobic den. Sweaty fun awaits anyone who can shove their way to the middle of the dance floor. It's deserted on weeknights, though.
249 Eldridge St. (at Houston St.), (212) 777-5153. www.sapphire nyc.com. Hours: M-Su 7pm-4am. Cash Only, Cover: $3-$5. Ⓕ Ⓥ to Second Ave.

Music

Arlene Grocery
Arlene has established itself as one of the premiere showcases for many New York-based independent labels. The bands play for free here to build a fan base, and the sound is great. Think acoustic, pop, rock, and ska.
95 Stanton St. (bet. Ludlow and Orchard Sts.), (212) 358-1633, www.arlenegrocery.com. Hours: 6pm-4am. Cash Only, No Cover. Ⓕ Ⓥ to Second Ave.

Bluestockings
Pop into this volunteer run bookshop-come-activist center for queer camaraderie unusual literary recommendations and a damn good almond butter brownie. The store hosts or organizes events that include movie nights, book readings, rant sessions, and open mic performances.
172 Allen St. (at Stanton St.), (212) 777-6028. Hours: M-Su 1pm-10pm. MC, V, AmEx. Ⓕ Ⓙ Ⓜ Ⓩ to Delancey St.

[SoHo]

Bars

Bar 89
A stylish crowd and pricey drinks are nothing unusual in this neck of the words. What's special about Bar 89 is the fabulous unisex bathrooms where the technology boggles the noodle. The clear glass doors suddenly turn opaque upon closing.
89 Mercer St. (bet. Spring and Broome Sts.), (212) 274-0989. Hours: M-Su 12pm-1am. MC, V, AmEx. ❻ to Spring St.

Botanica
Botanica's Afro-Cuban decor and snappy but friendly bartenders make this one of the neighborhood's most comfortable places to get sloppy. There's a full bar and a decent selection of draft beers, but don't ask for anything too complicated or silly unless you're prepared to take the heat.
47 E. Houston St. (bet. Mulberry and Mott Sts.), (212) 343-7251. Hours: M-Sa 5pm-4am, Su 6pm-4am. Cash Only. Ⓑ Ⓓ Ⓕ Ⓥ to Broadway-Lafayette St.

The Cub Room
Business attire is the unwritten dress code for the young and affluent who enjoy expensive cocktails and a serious pick-up scene, while lounging on the comfy furniture.
131 Sullivan St. (at Prince St.), (212) 677-4100, www.cubroom.com. Hours: Su-W 12pm-2am, R-Sa 12 pm-4am. MC, V, AmEx, D, DC. Ⓒ Ⓔ to Spring St.

Ear Inn

This place used to be a brothel. These days it's just a homey bar that attracts a hip, yuppie crowd. Ask about their seasonal poetry readings.

326 Spring St. (bet. Greenwich and Washington Sts.), (212) 226-9060, www.earinn.com. Hours: M-Su 12pm-4am. MC, V, AmEx. C E to Spring St., 1 to Houston St.

ñ

Savor pitchers of sangria while admiring the Wednesday night flamenco dancers, and don't even try to resist the tapas. It's tiny, though, so stake out a place early and camp out all night.

33 Crosby St. (bet. Broome and Grand Sts.), (212) 219-8856. Hours: Su-R 5pm-2am, F-Sa 5pm-4am. Cash Only. J M N R W Z 6 to Canal St.

Pravda

Pravda embodies neither post-Soviet mayhem nor hard-core proletariat boozing. Still, the 80 flavors of vodka (including the bourgeois mango and raspberry), caviar, and rust-tinted decor almost justify the name. High-class SoHo-ites eschew communism for black market prices.

281 Lafayette (bet. Prince and Houston Sts.), (212) 226-4696. Hours: M, W 5pm-1am, T, R 5pm-2:30am, F-Sa 5pm-3:30am, Su 6pm-1am. MC, V, AmEx. 6 to Bleecker St.

SoHo:323

Once you find the unmarked lounge and get past the velvet rope guarded by a bouncer-cop, you'll find the brick walls and dim lighting enticing. The DJ's play loud music both upstairs and down. In the upper level, comfortable couches and stools line the walls, while bombshell waitresses bring you $9 drinks as you chat it up with the person next to you.

323 W Broadway, (bet. Grand and Canal) (212) 334-2232. Hours: M-Su 5pm-4am. AmEx, MC, V. A C E to Canal St.

The SoHo Grand Bar

This hotel bar is growing ever more popular for their martinis, yet sophisticated neighborhooders head here for their "nightcaps."

310 W. Broadway (bet. Canal and Grand Sts.), (212) 965-3588. Hours: M-W 7am-2am, R-F 7am-3am, Sa 7am-4am, Su 11am-12am. MC, V, AmEx, D, DC. A C E to Canal St.

Temple Bar

Leather seating and thick curtains make this bar a perfect place for an intimate gathering. Offers a wide selection of vodkas, wines and cocktails, including there signature apple martini. The prices are a bit high but the drinks and food pairings are very satisfying.

332 Lafayette St. (bet. Bleecker and Houston Sts.), (212) 925-4242, M-R 5pm-1am; F-Sa 5pm-2am; Su 7pm-12am, MC, V, AmEx, D, DC. B D F V to Broadway-Lafayette St., 6 to Bleecker St.

Clubs

Culture Club

This is the place for the ultimate '80s escape, with Reagan-era pop served up in this two-story club. It boasts a casual atmosphere, murals of your favorite '80s artists, and even a Delorean that Michael J. Fox would envy.

179 Varick St. (bet. King and Charlton Sts.), (212) 243-1999. Hours: R-Sa 9pm-5am. MC, V, AmEx, D, Cover: $15-$20. 1 to Houston St.

Don Hill's

This clubhouse is consistently crowded with crazy college kids, especially on Wednesday nights for the Beauty Party, when kids come out to groove '80s style, and Hot Fudge Sundays, which features soul and hip hop music, and the Famous Squeeze Box on Friday nights, a gay rock drag queen party.

511 Greenwich St. (at Spring St.), (212) 219-2850. Hours: M-Su 9pm-4am. MC, V, AmEx, D. C E to Spring St., 1 to Canal St.

Lounges

Brandy Library

Similar to other specialty lounges that serve only wine, vodka and champagne, this spot is strictly brandy. The liquor is placed like books on shelves, and waitresses climb ladders in order to get your drink. The deep leather chairs and available cigars bring in a neighborhood crowd as well as tired businessmen looking for a little solace. Good for both the person who enjoys a stiff drink as well as the cocktail-loving lightweights.

25 N. Moore St. (at Varick St.), (212) 226-5545, www.brandylibrary.com, Su-Sa 4pm-4am, 1 to Franklin St.

Madame X

This two floor cozy lounge sets the mood with bright red decorations and comfy antique couches. The loungey feel is representative of the weeknights, while it turns into a packed club spot on the weekend, but a DJ spins all week. You might want to come early if you want to get drinks and a spot. The specialty beverages are tasty and the bartenders are very friendly. The outside garden area is a great little treat for a New York bar. It used to be a place where you got away from smoke but with the new laws its a great alternative to the crowded interior. Check out the art exhibits. Cover charge of $5 on weekends.

94 W. Houston St. (bet. LaGuardia Pl. and Thompson St.), (212) 539-0808, www.madamexnyc.com. Hours: M-F 5pm-4am, Sa-Su 6pm-4am. 6 to Bleecker St., 1 to Houston St., N R to Prince St.

[East Village]

Bars

Ace Bar

Have a beer and play darts or pool in this cavernous neighborhood bar. Take a look at the old lunchboxes you used to own when you were in grade school. It's never too loud or too crowded.

531 E. 5th St. (bet. A and B Aves.), (212) 979-8476. Hours: M-Su 2pm-4am. MC, V, AmEx. F V to Second Ave.

Angel's Share

House rules border on the Draconian: no loud conversation, no parties bigger than four, and no standing. But the ambi-

ence is intimate, the drinks professionally mixed, and the floor-to-ceiling windows offer an excellent view of Stuyvesant St. Bring a date.
8 Stuyvesant St. (at Third Ave.), (212) 777-5415. Hours: M-Su 6pm-2:30am. MC, V, AmEx, D. 6 to Astor Pl.

Otto's Shrunken Head
Formerly the Barmacy Bar, this kitschy tiki bar welcomes private functions, film shoots, photo shoots, and "anything else you'd like to shoot except drugs" at her establishment. It's not reserved most nights when stylish downtowners crowd the place for generously-poured drinks.
548 E. 14th St. (bet. Aves. A and B), (212) 228-2240. Hours: M-F 11am-4am, Sa-Su 4pm-4am. MC, V. L to First Ave.

B Bar and Grill
Formerly the Bowery Bar, this gives the impression of a place too cool for its own good. It specializes in delightfully strong apple martinis, and the three bars – including an outdoor courtyard and a back-room dance floor – keep customers entertained. Tuesday is gay night and Saturday brings in a young Wall St. crowd. Weekend brunches stay generally mellow.
40 E. 4th St. (bet. Bowery and Lafayette Sts.), (212) 475-2220. Hours: M-F 11:30am-4am, Sa-Su 10:30am-4am. MC, V, AmEx. N R to 8th St.-NYU., 6 to Astor Pl.

Beauty Bar
Sparkling walls glitter and vintage hair dryers function as lounge chairs at this beauty salon-turned-bar. The owner's own collection of '40s hairpins and pomade ads add to the deliciously kitschy mood. Wednesday afternoon manicure and drink specials are a must.
231 E. 14th St. (bet. Second and Third Aves.), (212) 539-1389. Hours: M-F 5pm-4am, Sa-Su 7pm-4am. MC, V. L N R W 4 5 6 to 14th St.-Union Sq.

Boxcar Lounge
They have a cool glass and metal bar area at the front and a lounge area at the back. Boxcar Lounge has great specials, especially the sake martinis. It also has an airy garden and happy hour bargains.
168 Ave. B (bet. 10th and 11th Sts.), (212) 473-2830. Hours: M-F 6pm-4am, Sa-Su 4pm-4am. MC, V, AmEx, D. L to First Ave.

Cherry Tavern
It's small. It's cheap. It's got a pool table and a good jukebox, but on weekends it can be suffocatingly packed.
441 E. 6th St. (bet. First and A Aves.), (212) 777-1448. Hours: M-Su 6pm-4am. Cash Only. 6 to Astor Pl.

Coyote Ugly Saloon
For all those not in the know, a coyote ugly is when you get so loaded that you wind up going home with someone and waking up to find that they are singularly unattractive and you would rather cut off your arm than wake them up. It's not pretty and neither is this East Village standard. But dive bars are supposed to be ugly, just don't expect Tyra Banks to be dirty dancing on the bar.
153 First Ave. (bet. 9th and 10th Sts.), (212) 477-4431. Hours: M-R 2pm-4am, F 1pm-4am, Sa-Su 12:30pm-4am. MC, V. 6 to Astor Pl., L to First Ave.

Decibel
Go early and with a small group, because this small, beautiful sake bar gets packed fast. Hipsters descend on it because it's cavelike and mellow. Great for dates. If you want something more fast-paced, check out its spawn, Megadecibel.
240 E. 9th St. (bet. Second and Third Aves.), (212) 979-2733. Hours: M-Su 8pm-3am. MC, V, AmEx. N R W to 8th St.-NYU, 6 to Astor Pl.

Dempsey's Pub
A slightly snobby bar that serves well drinks for $2 and happy hour half-pints for $1.50, don't confuse this place with the more happening Jack Dempsey's bar in Chelsea. This hole looks something like an old-fashioned German beer hall. Books line the walls and NYU students fill up here on weekends. A neighborhood bar for classics like Irish Amber and Murphy's Stout.
61 Second Ave., (bet. 3rd and 4th Sts.), (212) 388-0662. Hours: M-Su 11am-4am. MC, V, AmEx, D. F V to Second Ave.

Doc Holiday's
"I'm trapped in here with the convicts who love me," said one bartender about the regulars. On weekends, this country-western joint swarms with hell-raisers who come to admire the wild animal pelts on the walls and the even wilder staff, who can often be found dancing on the bar. Try the home-style BBQ food.
141 Ave. A (bet. 8th and 9th Sts.), (212) 979-0312. Hours: M-Su 12pm-4am. Cash Only. L to First Ave.

11th Street Bar
Locals fleeing the influx of Ave. A tavern tourists find asylum here. Narrow in front at the crowded bar, it opens up in the back with a handful of tables large enough to fit all your roommates or new friends.
510 E. 11th St. (bet. Aves. A and B), (212) 982-3929. Hours: M-Su 4pm-4am. MC, V, AmEx. L to First Ave.

Fish Bar
This quaint owner-operated bar is a favorite in the neighborhood. The place is filled with reminders that you are in the Fish Bar, as the walls are painted a deep blue and are covered by fish paintings and

sculptures, as well as a few anchors. The easy music soothes you, but feel free to ask the bartender to turn it up – customers occasionally burst into song if the feeling hits them. The drinks are lovely, and the smaller seating area welcomes dates or small groups. If you have a free Monday, check out quiz night and win prizes.
237 E. 5th St. (bet. Astor Pl. and 4th St.), (212) 475-4949. Hours: M-Su 5pm-4am, Cash only. 6 to Astor Pl.

International Bar

Cheap drinks can make you dizzy and claustrophobic at this small dive. You'll have to squeeze past the long bar to the small back part where, if you're lucky, you can get a seat. It's got a mixed crowd and a decent jukebox. Did we mention the cheap drinks yet?
120 First Ave. (bet. 7th and 8th Sts.), (212) 777-9244. Hours: M-Su 2pm-4am. Cash Only. F V to Second Ave.

Joe's Pub

This elegant but cozy lounge hosts some of the city's best live music, from hip-hop to cabaret, and acts are nearly always followed by a DJ. The drinks may be expensive but the wait staff makes up for the prices by being so genial you want to hug them. Live acts are consistently good, so come by even if you have never heard of the musicians.
425 Lafayette St. (bet. E. 4th St. and Astor Pl.), (212) 539-8777, www.joespub.com. Hours: M-Su 6pm-4am. MC, V, AmEx, Cover: $5-$20. 6 to Astor Pl.

KGB

Old Soviet paraphernalia give this small upstairs bar-room an illicit feel, which is reinforced by the regular poetry readings and theater downstairs. It's perfect for bringing out your inner subversive artist with a good stiff drink.
85 E. 4th St. (bet. Second and Third Aves.), (212) 505-3360. Hours: M-Su 7:30pm-4am. Cash Only. F V to Second Ave.

Lakeside Lounge

Come prepared to wait for your drinks, since this hipster haunt is packed even on nights the bartender calls "real slow." Lots of live bands, too. Don't forget to immortalize yourself by stopping at the photobooth before you leave.
162 Ave. B (at 10th St.), (212) 529-8463, www.lakesidelounge.com. Hours: M-Su 4pm-4am. MC, V, AmEx. L to First Ave.

McSorley's Old Ale House

The walls reveal the history of this beer-lover haven that opened in 1854. The photographs that cover the walls show men drinking the legendary dark and light beers (ale and porter) date as far back as the early 20th century. Seeped in tradition, the newer management stays true to the legend of the tavern by continuing to serve only light and dark beers, costing a mere $3.50 a pair! Patrons can snack on cheese and crackers until closing – the kitchen stays open all night. It is rare to find such a friendly tavern in this city, filled with genuine Irish accents and hospitality that no one can beat. They celebrated their 150th anniversary in February 2004.
15 E. 7th Street (bet. Second and Third Avenues), (212) 473-9148. Hours: M-Sa 11am-1am. Cash only. 6 to Astor Pl.

Manitoba's

Owned and operated by "Handsome" Dick Manitoba, frontman for NYC's legendary punkers, the Dictators, Manitoba's pours some of the East Village's strongest drinks. Dick books live music ranging from country to rock seven nights a week.
99 Ave. B (bet. 6th and 7th Sts.), (212) 982-2511. Hours: M-Su 4pm-4am. MC, V, AmEx. N R to 8th St., F to Second Ave., L to First Ave.

Mars Bar

A rowdy and boozy bunch fill this tattered shoebox of a bar at all hours. Possibly the dumpiest, most dishevelled bar on the planet, but charming nevertheless.
25 E. 1st St. (at Second Ave.), No Phone. Hours: M-Su 12pm-4am. Cash Only. F to Second Ave.

Mona's

Punk rock lives ... in the jukebox at Mona's. It's a favorite place for East Village squatter kids who come here with their mangy dogs and multiple tattoos and piercings.
224 Ave. B (bet. 13th and 14th Sts.), (212) 353-3780. Hours: M-Su 3pm-4am. Cash Only. L to First Ave.

Niagara

Niagara puts a hip spin on nostalgia. From the bartenders in their silk, hand-painted ties to the bamboo-walled tiki lounge downstairs, Niagara pays homage to America's innocent years. The tiki

lounge features a full range of tropical drinks.
112 Ave. A (bet. 7th and 8th Sts.), (212) 420-9517. Hours: M-Su 4pm-4am. MC, V, AmEx. F V to Second Ave.

No Malice Palace
Be careful. You might walk right past this signless black hole in the wall. Inside you will find a comfortable dark hideaway to lounge your body and lubricate your tonsils. The drinks tend to be on the pricey side.
197 E. 3rd St. (bet. Aves. A and B), (212) 254-9184. Hours: M-Su 7:30pm-4am. Cash Only. F V to Second Ave.

Swift Hibernian Lounge
Beneath the dreamlike painting that stretches the length of this long beer hall, drinkers at Swift's encounter sweating mugs of beers imported from all over the world, which they toss down in the loud company of friends from the neighborhood. The dim-lit, cavernous back room has long oak tables and is separated from the bar by a purple velvet curtain.
34 E. 4th St. (bet. Lafayette and Bowery Sts.), (212) 260-3600. Hours: M-Su 12pm-4am. MC, V, AmEx, D. N R to 8th St., 6 to Astor Pl.

288/Tom & Jerry's
This bar stocks colorful pottery behind the bar. A jukebox bangs out country and classic rock, and artists and filmmakers in their 20s and 30s make this a regular drinking hole on weeknights. Guinness ranks highly here, and Wisconsin folks are particularly welcome (Packers game every Sunday on the TV).
288 Elizabeth St. (at E. Houston), (212) 260-5045. Hours: M-Su 12pm-4am. Cash. F V to Broadway-Lafayette St., 6 to Bleecker St.

Clubs

Guernica
Guernica makes up for its tameness with a gourmet late night menu and some top house and bass DJs.
25 Ave. B (bet. 2nd and 3rd Sts.), (212) 674-0984, www.guernicanyc.com. Hours: M-Su 6pm-4am. MC, V, AmEx. F V to Second Ave.

Pangaea
No one crosses the threshold of Pangaea unless they dress to impress and ooze fabulousness. Black leather clad bouncers keep the riff-raff out and escort those who make the cut inside. The gorgeous interior of the lounge/club is as hot as the staff is, which dresses in red from head to toe. Huge pieces of red fabric drape from the ceilings, candles are lit throughout, and couches and tables are reserved for bottle service. While there is a DJ spinning above the crowd, live drummers accompany each song that is played. Each day of the week hosts a different type of party: karaoke night, hip-hop, Brazilian music, and special theme parties can be found here depending on when you come. The eclectic style of Pangaea is mirrored by the diverse crowd filled with professional club-hoppers and those who are happy to chill on the plush couches while sipping champagne. Bring your full wallets and your dancing shoes.
417 Lafayette St. (bet. Astor Pl. and 4th St.), (212) 353-2992. Hours: Su-M 10:30pm-4am. MC, V, Diners. N R to 8th St., 6 to Astor Pl.

Webster Hall
This is one of the city's biggest nightclubs. Four spacious floors spin disco, reggae, and techno. You can even shoot a game of pool. Don't miss out on the flying trapeze show in the wee hours.
125 E. 11th St. (bet. Third and Fourth Aves.), (212) 353-1600. Hours: R-Sa 10pm-5am. MC, V, AmEx, D, Cover: $20-$30. L N R W 4 5 6 to 14th St.-Union Sq.

Music

Bowery Ballroom
The Bowery Ballroom is one of the premiere venues in the city. It consistently gets good acts. The space is simultaneously cavernous and cozy, and the coat check line moves with speed. With acoustic, country, eclectic, hip-hop, Latin, and pop shows.
6 Delancey St. (bet. the Bowery and Chrystie St.), (212) 533-2111, www.boweryballroom.com Hours depend on show times. MC, V, Cover: $10-$20. F V to Second Ave.

CBGB-OMFUG
A legend, CBGB has been a mecca for artists and punks since the '70s, helping to launch acts like Blondie, the Ramones, and Patti Smith. You can still catch local and national acts every night of the week. With alternative, pop, and rock shows.
315 Bowery (at Bleecker St.), (212) 982-4052, www.cbgb.com. Hours: 7pm-2am. Cash Only, Cover: $3-$12. 6 to Bleecker St.

CB's Gallery/ CBGB's Downstairs Lounge
The kinder, gentler

sibling of CB's. It boasts a superior sound system and staff, and some of the best acoustic-based music in town. A downstairs lounge, with DJ, serves brick oven pizza. Hosts acoustic, electronica, folk, and rock shows.
313 Bowery St. (at Bleecker St.), (212) 677-0455, www.cbgb.com. Hours: M-Su 12pm-4am. MC, V, AmEx, D, DC, Cover: $5-$8. 6 *to Bleecker St.*

Continental
Everybody from Patti Smith to The Ramones to Guns N' Roses has played this famous club. There's an indoor ATM for the cash-strapped. Most popular are the hard rock and ska shows.
25 Third Ave. (at St. Mark's Pl.), (212) 529-6924, www.nytrash.com /continental. Hours: 4pm-4am. Cash Only, Cover: Free-$10. 6 *to Astor Pl.,* N R *to 8th St.*

Sidewalk Cafe
Before moving to the backroom of the Sidewalk Cafe, the Fort was an after-hours club on the Lower East Side. It still retains its underground appeal, centered around manager Lach's Anti-Folk Anti-Hoot on Mondays, which is an open mic. Sidewalk Cafe features one of the cheapest breakfast specials in NYC, as well as a full menu and bar. With folk, anti-folk, and rock shows.
94 Ave. A (at 6th St.), (212) 473-7373. Hours: M-F 8am-4am, Sa-Su 24 hours. MC, V, AmEx, Cover: $3. F V *to Second Ave.*

Irving Plaza
Mostly a venue for national touring acts with major record label backing and a fair amount of radio play. It's a place to come for the music, not the atmosphere. A long, narrow design causes the crowd to crush at the front.
17 Irving Pl. (at 15th St.), (212) 777-6800, www.irvingplaza.com. Open 1 hr before showtime. AmEx. L N R W 4 5 6 *to 14th St.-Union Sq.*

Mercury Lounge
Once a headstone shop, the Mercury Lounge has established itself as a premiere venue for "just-breaking" bands. High stage, excellent sound system, and standing room only for three to five acts per night. With acoustic, alternative, and rock shows.
217 E. Houston St. (bet. Essex and Ludlow Sts.), (212) 260-1214, www.mercuryloungenyc.com. Hours: 8pm-12am. MC, V, Cover: $7-$12. F V *to Second Ave.*

Nightingale Bar
The Nightingale has a reputation for being the favorite late night jam spot for many now-famous acts. You can see local acts here seven nights a week. Happy hour from 1pm-8pm daily. With pop and rock bands and the occasional soloist.
213 Second Ave. (at 13th St.), (212) 473-9398. Hours: M-Sa 1pm-4am, Su 7pm-4am. Cash, Cover: free-$5. L *to Third Ave.*

LGBT

The Boiler Room
Your classic East Village dive, the Boiler Room is a good place for hanging out and picking up cute NYU boys. There are a couple of private corners with couches and benches that, along with the dim lighting, give the space a definite "cruisey" feel. Though it tends to be busy on the weekends, the bar still maintains a rather low key status that appeals to those weary of the club circuit. Wednesday is Tranny Pool night; Sunday is "No Man's Land," a.k.a. lesbian night, when the girls take over.
86 4th St. (at Second Ave.) (212) 254-7536. Hours: M-Su 4pm-4am. F V *to Second Ave.,* 6 *to Bleecker St.*

The Cock
All the typical gay stereotypes are exaggerated at this East Village dive. The bar is tiny and usually jam-packed, making it easy for random sleazy guys to grope you, as they inevitably do here. Patrons are a mixed group depending on the night, but you can always count on finding a Mr. Right Now. Oh, and don't wander to the backroom unless you know what you're getting into.
188 Ave. A (at 12th St.), (212) 777-6254. Hours: M-Su 10pm-4am, Cash Only, $5 cover T-R, $10 F-Su. L *to First Ave.*

Pyramid
Come especially for the "1984" party on Friday nights (21 and up, $6 cover), and the worthwhile Thursday night "Remission" party (18 and up, $6 cover). Dance in the back room to the hottest '80s pop and new wave beats. This is a bad place to meet people and the crowd can get grungy and gothic, but it remains one of the most fun and unpretentious club spaces in the city.
101 Ave. A, (bet. 6th and 7th Sts.), (212) 462-9077. Hours: M-Su 10pm-4am. N R *to 8th St.,* 6 *to Astor Pl.,* L *to First Ave.*

Starlight
With glass chandeliers, corduroy couches, and a drink menu full of champagnes, this upscale yet unpretentious bar is a great place to bring a date for post-dinner drinks. Twice a week you can see comedy and cabaret on the small stage in the back; the rest of the time a DJ spins at a station in the back corner. Sunday night features Starlette, one of NYC's best lesbian parties, and a top choice for those cruising. You won't find many loners as most gals come with friends, but folks are usually more than happy to have you join their group.
167 Ave. A (bet. 10th and 11th Sts.), (212) 475-2172. Hours: W-Su 8pm-4am. 6 *to Astor Pl.,* L *to First Ave.*

[GREENWICH VILLAGE]

BARS

Absolutely 4th
This small, snazzy little lounge is valiantly holding out against the NYU menace. A slightly older, slightly calmer crowd relaxes at the jewel-toned bar, oblivious to the underage debauchery outside.
228 W. 4th St. (at Seventh Ave.), (212) 989-9444. Hours: M-Su 4pm-4am. MC, V, AmEx, D, DC. 1 *to Christopher St.*

Blind Tiger Ale House
With 24 micro-brews on tap and bottled beers from 12 countries, this haunt satisfies just about anyone's taste for brew. The crowd is strictly white-collar, after-work, and non-Budweiser.
518 Hudson St. (at 10th St.), (212) 675-3848, www.blindtigeralehouse.com. Hours: M-Su 12pm-4am. MC, V, AmEx, D. 1 to Christopher St.

Boots and Saddle
Urban and rural cowboys alike flock to this Western-style veteran, proving that denim is friendlier than leather. Happy hour Monday through Friday 3pm-9pm and Saturday and Sunday Beer Blasts with $1.50 drafts and $2.50 bottles.
76 Christopher St. (at Seventh Ave.), (212) 929-9684. Hours: Su-F 12pm-4am, Sa 8am-4am. Cash Only. 1 to Christopher St.

Cedar Tavern
Pay tribute to Willem de Kooning with a visit to this spacious tavern that the famous abstract expressionist frequented. The patrons are no longer the counterculture scenesters of the '60s, but the Tiffany lighting and the monumental 19th century bar remain.
82 University Pl. (bet. 11th and 12th Sts.), (212) 741-9754. Hours: M-Su 11:30 pm-4am. MC, V, AmEx, D, Diners. L N R W 4 5 6 to Union Sq.-14th St.

Cubbyhole
Favored by friendly college-aged women of various sexual persuasions, this small, dark rendezvous spot lives up to the double entendre in its name. The bar has a $5 cover on Saturday nights from 8:30pm to 10pm.
281 W. 12th St. (bet. Seventh and Eighth Aves.), (212) 243-9041. Hours: M-R 4pm-2am, F 4pm-4am, Sa 2pm-4am, Su 2pm-2am. Cash Only. L N R W 4 5 6 to Union Sq.-14th St.

Down the Hatch
Down the Hatch is pretty straightforward about its essential nature: its a rowdy, fun college bar with busy foosball tables and Christmas lights. Attracting a lot of NYU students and a few older passersby, it attracts a good mix of people for a fun night out.
179 W. 4th St. (bet. Sixth and Seventh Aves.), (212) 627-9747. Hours: M-Su 12pm-4am. MC, V, AmEx. 1 to Christopher St.

North Square
This quiet basement lounge is hidden away on the northwest corner of Washington Square Park. While the bar and restaurant are affiliated with the hotel above, you'd never know. Dishes from the raw bar and appetizer menu are available in the lounge, supplements to the fresh, flavored vodkas infused on site. The flavors change from week to week, as do the corresponding specialty drinks.
103 Waverly Pl., (212) 254-1200. Hours: M-Su 5:30pm-10:30pm, bar open until 12am. MC, V, AmEx, Diners, Entrées: $22. A C E F V S 1 to W. 4th St.

Off the Wagon
While most of the bars on or near Bleecker strive towards trendy, Off the Wagon insists that just being a bar where people come to get smashed is enough. The name pretty much says it all, and if obliteration is your goal, you've definitely come to the right place.
109 MacDougal St. (bet. Bleecker and 3rd Sts.), (212) 533-4487. Hours: M-R 2pm-4am, F-Su 12pm-4am. MC, V, AmEx, D. A C E F V S 1 to W. 4th St.

PM
PM is another very trendy lounge for the moment. There usually isn't a cover, though it can be difficult to get in if you aren't in a group comprised mostly of beautiful women. Perhaps that is why everyone inside seems to be a supermodel. The space is divided by a long counter-space down the middle, and sometimes hired, scantily-clad dancers are on top of it. There are rows of tables on each side, leaving just enough space for people to dance if they like (later in the night). The long bar at the far end provides ample service, and drinks are well-made, but expensive.
50 Gansevoort St, (bet. Greenwich and Washington) (212) 255-6676. Hours: T-Sa 7:30pm-4am. AmEx, M, V. A C E to 14th St.

Rhône
This downtown lounge creates a unique atmosphere with candle glow, concrete walls, and unfinished ceilings. The amazing selection of wines truly makes this a wine connoisseur's dream and the tasty martinis – especially their espresso martini – make it perfect for any night out. The food, served till midnight adds to the experience. The combinations such as Thai-Style Shrimp & Calamari Salad or their delicious barbeque eel will leave your taste buds happy. When you get the wooden menus consider all the choices, but it is hard to go wrong.
63 Gansevoort St. (bet. Greenwich and Washington Sts.), (212) 367-8440. Hours: M-Sa 5:30pm-4am. MC, V, AmEx, D. A C E to 14th St.

The Slaughtered Lamb
This is one of Greenwich Village's best-known pubs. Tourists flock to this horror-film theme bar for the shocker movies and overpriced drinks.
182 W. 4th St. (bet. Sixth and Seventh Aves.), (212) 627-5262. Hours: Su-R 12pm-2am, F-Sa 12pm-4am. MC, V, AmEx, D. A C E F V S 1 to W. 4th St.

The Village Idiot
You go to the Idiot, and you get drunk. Their mission is made clear the moment you walk in. It's loud – no-conversation-loud, trashy-country-music-loud. The bartenders dance on the bar periodically and force shots on anyone naive enough to ask for a glass of water. The beer is cheap.
355 W. 14th St. (at Ninth Ave.), (212) 989-7334. Hours: M-Su 12pm-4am. Cash Only. A C E 1 2 3 to 14th St.

White Horse Tavern
A Village landmark, reputed to be the place where Dylan Thomas drank himself to death. But the poets are long gone, supplanted by a pedestrian 20-something crowd. Dinner essentials are served, including really

good burgers.
567 Hudson St. (at W. 11th St.), (212) 243-9260. Hours: Su-R 11am-2am, F-Sa 11am-4am. Cash Only. A C E 1 2 3 *to 14th St.*

Clubs

Bowlmor Lanes
Mondays herald the Night Strike: How much do heavy house, drum and bass, and disco improve your bowling technique? With glow-in-the-dark pins and shoes after 10pm, a strike or two is bound to happen.
110 University Pl. (bet. 12th and 13th Sts.), (212) 255-8188, www.bowlmor .com. Hours: M, F 10am-4am, T-W 10am-1am, R 11am-2am, Sa 11am-4am, Su 11am-1am. MC, V, AmEx, Cover: $7 per game per person, $3 shoe rental. Cash Only. L N R W 4 5 6 *to 14th St.-Union Sq.*

Music

The Baggot Inn
A darkly-lit venue in the heart of the Village. It's a great place to see some of your acoustic singer/song-writers, with plenty of table seating and dollar draft happy hours. With acoustic, pop, and rock.
82 W. 3rd St. (bet. Thompson and Sullivan Sts.), (212) 477-0622. www.thebaggotinn.com. Hours: M-Su 12pm-4am. MC, V, AmEx, D, DC, Cover: free-$5. A C E F S V 1 *to W. 4th St.*

The Bitter End
Opened 40 years ago, The Bitter End has seen countless performers rise to stardom, including Bob Dylan, Joni Mitchell, Tracy Chapman, and Jackson Browne. With blues, folk, funk, R&B, and rock.
147 Bleecker St. (bet. Thompson St. and LaGuardia Pl.), (212) 673-7030, www.bitterend.com. Hours: Su-R 7:30pm-3am, F-Sa 8pm-4am. MC, V, AmEx, D, DC. Cover: $5-$10. A C E F S V 1 *to W. 4th St.*

Blue Note
Though the regular features are an assault on the pocketbook, the five dollar after-hours shows on Fridays and Saturdays are a real bargain. If you have the money to spend, see some of the biggest national jazz acts that come through that you won't see anywhere else. There is a full continental menu with a full bar.
131 W. 3rd St. (bet. MacDougal St. and 6th Ave.), (212) 475-8592, www.bluenote.net. Hours: Su 12pm-6pm and 7pm-2am, M-Th 7pm-2am, F-Sa 7pm-4am. MC, V, AmEx, Cover: $25 and up. A C E F S V 1 *to W. 4th St.*

The Duplex
This piano bar right off Sheridan Square has been providing live show tunes for years. A mature contingent lingers here, so tweed is more prevalent than muscle-tees. Large and elegantly decorated, the legendary space offers cabaret upstairs. Shows are varied and frequent, so make reservations.
61 Christopher St. (at Seventh Ave. South), (212) 255-5438, www.theduplex.com. Hours: M-Su 4pm-4am. Cash Only, Cover: $3-$15. 1 *to Christopher St.*

Kenny's Castaways
One of the landmark bars in the West Village. It's a good place to have a beer and see some up-and-coming local bands. You can listen to the music from the cozy upper level if you want to get away from the crowd. Hosts mostly blues and rock.
157 Bleecker St. (bet. Thompson and Sullivan Sts.), (212) 979-9762. Hours: M-Su 12pm-4am. MC, V, AmEx, Cover: $5-$10. A C E F S V 1 *to W. 4th St.*

SOB's
Though the name stands for "Sounds Of Brazil," that doesn't even begin to cover the scope of the first world beat club in New York. A bastion of world rhythm, groove, and hip-hop, it's like stepping into a different country every night as African, Middle Eastern, Celtic, Caribbean, and Latin American artists use this club as a home base for national tours.
204 Varick St. (at W. Houston St.), (212) 243-4940, www.sobs.com. Hours: M-Sa 6:30pm-

3am. Cash only, Cover: $10-$25. ❶ *to Houston St.*

The Village Vanguard

With regulars like Woody Guthrie and Pete Seeger, this 64-year-old club was renowned as a center for folk before it became a legend as a jazz club in the '50s. Some of the most important jazz recordings in the world, from Coltrane to Davis to Rollins to Evans, were created within these hallowed walls. You can still catch the top quality mainstream and avant-garde jazz acts each night. *178 Seventh Ave. (bet. 11th St. and Waverly Pl.), (212) 255-4037, www.vilagevanguard.net. Call for showtimes. Cash Only, Cover: $15-$20,* ❶❷❸ *to 14th St.*

LGBT

Chi-Chiz

African American and Latino men dominate this older crowd lounge where "an eclectic mix of chill music" plays loud enough to create an atmosphere, but soft enough to actually have a conversation with the hunk in the corner. Show off your pool or spades skills in the back, but don't expect to break out the dance moves here. Instead, relax and watch the Saturday night stripper do all the gyrating for you from 11pm to 1am. *135 Christopher St. (at Hudson St.), (212) 462-0027. Hours: M-Su 2pm-4am. Cash Only.* ❶ *to Christopher St.*

Henrietta Hudson

Known as "Hank" to the regulars, this popular bar attracts a lot of out of state girls, so ask where she lives before you agree to go home with her. A solid bet any night of the week, Henrietta's packs 'em in Fridays and Saturdays when the back room opens up and the dance floor gets wild. The musical theme changes every night of the week and ranges from Latin to '80s. Wednesdays are "bring your gay boyfriend night," but while the atmosphere is gay boy friendly, this is definitely not a mixed bar. A good place for baby dykes' first outing in the bar scene. *438 Hudson St. (at Morton St.), (212) 924-3347, www.henriettahudson.com. Hours: M-F 4pm-4am, Sa-Su 1pm-4am. Cash only.* ❶ *to Houston St.*

[Gramercy]

Bars

Belmont Lounge

The Belmont Lounge is a dark and comfy spot to enjoy a cigar and drinks with friends after a concert at Irving Plaza. Weekends tend to get a bit crazy, as the Lounge hosts DJs that pack 'em in on Fridays and Saturdays to the tune of a $5 cover. *117 E. 15th St. (bet. Irving Pl. and Park Ave.), (212) 533-0009. Hours: M-Su 4pm-4am. MC, V, AmEx, D.* ⓁⓃⓇⓌ❹❺❻ *to Union Sq.-14th St.*

Chetty Red

The red lit bar is well stocked, and beautifully tendered, and the entire room is infused with red light. From a raised section in the back, you can survey the young crowd milling around on the dance floor only dancing occasionally. Comfy chairs and short tables line the walls in the back, making it a loungy refuge from the loud, crowded bar. The bathroom attendant is a nice touch despite the cramped commode area. *28 E. 23rd St. (bet. Park Ave. and Broadway), (212) 254-6117. Hours: Su-M 5pm-12am, T-W 5pm-2am, R-Sa 5pm-4am.* ⓃⓇ❻ *to 23rd St.*

Failte Irish Whiskey Bar

Two floors of classic rock and thirsty people keep the intensity on 'high' at this sports bar/pub/lounge. Couches upstairs provide patrons respite from the pool table and televisions in the lower level. With the radio blasting out Guns N' Roses and Tom Petty, and the bartenders serving up drafts of Guinness and Boddingtons, make sure to catch all the games, or just drop by after work for a pint. Be warned – the bartender actually does have an Irish accent, and

the regulars might take offense if someone toasts to the Queen.
531 Second Ave. (bet. 29th and 30th Sts.), (212) 725-9440. Hours: M-Su 12pm-4am. MC, V, AmEx. 6 to 28th St.

Live Bait
Located on Madison Square Park, curious passersby and neighborhood locals find it hard to resist this urban rendition of the Louisiana bayou. Force your way past the boisterous happy hour crowd to the tables in back in order to sample the Cajun shrimp or the mesquite BBQ.
14 E. 23rd St. (bet. Broadway and Madison Ave.), (212) 353-2400. Hours: M-Su 11:30am-1am. MC, V, AmEx. N R to 23rd St.

Strata
Slightly more polished and pricey than the other Gramercy lounges, Strata attracts a young early-to-mid-twenties crowd. Feel free to sink into the comfort of their lush decor and kick back with cocktails and appetizers in a unique celebrity-sighting hotspot, but be weary of your bill. On weekends, Strata transforms into a club dominated by thumping hip-hop and house music.
915 Broadway (at 21st St.), (212) 505-7400. Hours: T-S 5:30pm-11:30pm. F MC, V, AmEx. N R to 23rd St.

Paddy Reilly's Music Bar
The world's first and only all-draught Guinness bar. That's pretty much their deal. They have traditional Irish music seven days a week. Celebrities love the bar, maybe because it's quiet and you can always get a seat.
519 Second Ave. (at 29th St.), (212) 686-1210. Hours: M-Su 11pm-4am. MC, V, AmEx. 6 to 28th St.

Pete's Tavern
Pete's has been a local hangout for ages. Although it's mostly a bar, the Italian menu is more than adequate.
129 E. 18th St. (at Third Ave.), (212) 473-7676. Hours: M-Su 11am-1am. MC, V, AmEx. L N R W 4 5 6 to Union Sq.-14th St.

Rodeo Bar & Grill
Don't expect cowboy hats and big belt buckles at this cozy Wild West watering hole, but then again, don't let the giant stuffed buffalo above the bar surprise you. The menu is limited, but live rockabilly bands keep the place swingin'.
375 Third Ave. (at 27th St.), (212) 683-6500, www.rodeobar.com. Hours: M-Su 11:30am-3am. MC, V, AmEx, D. 6 to 28th St.

Rocky Sullivan's
The owner of this bar is the lead singer of an Irish band named Schanechia (Gaelic for "Storytelling"), which plays here often. This is primarily a Guinness crowd, with a hard-core constituency of Irish males that cluster in the simple, brick-walled beer hall downstairs on Lexington Avenue.
129 Lexington Ave. (at 28th St,), (212) 725-3871. Hours: M-F 11am-4am, Sa-Su 12pm-4am. AmEx, MC, V. 6 to 28th St.

Music

The Cutting Room
Cutting Room has everything one might want in a night out – live music, an amazing juke box, attractive patrons, great drinks, and food complete with homemade ketchup for their burgers and fries. There are live performers almost every night, including comedians, musicians, and saxophone players. The performance schedules are on the website. One of the owners is Big, yes, Mr. Big himself from *Sex and the City*, Chris Noth. Expect to see celebrities here from time to time. All in all, one of the best places in the city to go out with friends.
19 W. 24th St. (bet. Broadway and Sixth Ave.), (212) 691-1900, www.thecuttingroomnyc.com. Hours: T-F 5pm-closing, Sa 8pm-4am, Su-M closed. MC, V, AmEx, Cover: $5-$10. 1 to 23rd St.

[Chelsea]

Bars

Bongo
Famed for their New England-style lobster rolls and authentic '50s furniture, this comfortable lounge encourages a low-key atmosphere.
299 Tenth Ave. (bet. 27th and 28th Sts.), (212) 947-3654. Hours: M-W 5pm-2am, R-Sa 5pm-3am. MC, V, AmEx, D, DC. C E to 23rd St.

Dusk Lounge
With cracked mirror walls and a bathroom so dark you can't check your make-up, this bar makes it clear that appearances are not the point, so relax and have a drink. The pool table in the front is always busy and the bar further back serves the mostly local crowd killer cosmopolitans and margaritas.
147 W. 24th St. (bet. Sixth and Seventh Aves.), (212) 924-4490. Hours: M-R 6pm-2am, R-Sa 6pm-4am. MC, V, AmEx, D. 1 to 23rd St.

Passerby
The signless door front and flashing red, yellow, and blue checkered floor suggest another trendy bar, but with nary a martini glass in sight, this low-key watering hole favors locals over supermodels any day. Stick to beer and chat with the ever-changing crowd of gallery employees, yuppies, geeks, artists, and loners.
436 W. 15th St. (bet. Ninth and Tenth Aves.), (212) 206-7321. Hours: M-Su 6pm-2am. MC, V, AmEx. A C E L to 14th St.-Eighth Ave.

Slate
The former Chelsea Billiards has been revamped as New York's swankest pool hall. Low blue lighting lends the place a vaguely amniotic effect. There's surprisingly little attitude for this part of town, and the new restaurant, featuring Mediterranean fusion cuisine, is fantastic.
54 W. 21st St. (bet. Fifth and Sixth Aves.), (212) 989-0096. Hours: M-Su 12pm-4am. MC, V, AmEx, D. L N R W 4 5 6 to Union Sq.-14th St.

Wye Bar
College kids and yuppies can bond while listening to Top 40 hits and drinking stiff (if slightly overpriced) gin and tonics. The classy red lighting complements the numerous couches, each providing a

menu for table service, in case a personal bottle of booze is in order. Large parties provide the majority of the clientele, so don't expect to meet new people here. Nonetheless, when the faces are pretty and the mood is right, there aren't many better places on the West Side to relax and sip martinis.
105 W. 27th St. (bet. Sixth and Seventh Aves.), (212) 675-7117. Hours: M-Su 'til 4am. 1 to 28th St.

CLUBS

Crobar
Crobar is huge. There are several different areas, with different vibes and types of music. Often, very well-known DJs are spinning, but even then, there is still a hip-hop room. There is a huge dance floor, a balcony, and a bar area decorated with bamboo. One of the nice things about Crobar is that if you are willing to pay the cover (and the bouncer accepts your ID), you can probably get in.
530 W 28th St. (212) 629-9000. Hours: R-Su 10pm-4am. AmEx, D, DC, M, V. C E at 23rd St.

Marquee
It's one of the hottest clubs in NYC, so obviously the door is really tough. Once you get inside, it's pretty much all it's cracked up to be – beautiful people packed into both levels, each of which has a large bar, so it's never too hard to get a drink (though they aren't cheap). The design is simple, but the atmosphere is great.
289 10th Ave. (bet 26th and 27th St.), (646) 473-0202. Hours: T-Sa 10pm-4am. AmEx, M, V. C E to 23rd St.

Nells
Three rooms on two floors offer an eclectic mix of music ranging from reggae, hip-hop, jazz, Latin, funk, and disco. The elegance of the spacious upstairs room calls for a sophisticated drink from the well-stocked bar. Downstairs, relax in a more intimate lounge or move to house, R&B or classics aimed at a stylish mix of "tourists, regulars, and DJs."
246 W. 14th St. (bet. Seventh and Eighth Aves.), (212) 675-1567, www.nells.com. Hours: M 7pm-1am, T, R-Su 9pm-4am, W 9pm-3am. MC, V, AmEx, Cover: $10-$15. 1 2 3 to 14th St.

The Park
This sleek spot in the far west of Manhattan, one block from Chelsea Piers, brings in models and a generally upscale 30s and 40s set in an elegant, spacious setting. The outdoor garden has leafy trees, fuel-heated lamps, and yellow light bulbs overhead. The interior feels industrial with a Zen touch, with Japanese paper lanterns and brick walls that pad the heavy music beat. Park can be a little confident in its clean-cut atmosphere. Special plates include mussels and chorizo, fois gras, steak tartare, and larger numbers such as pan-seared salmon and couscous, paella, and the delicate duck sandwich.
118 Tenth Ave. (bet. 17th and 18th Sts.), (212) 352-3313. Hours: M-Su 6pm-12am. A C E L to 14th St.

Roxy
Almost always crowded, this place hosts nonstop dancing. The crowd is different every night. Saturday nights at Roxy epitomize the circuit party vibe, with tons of shirtless Chelsea boys rolling to the thumping base of lyricless techno music. Normally 21 and up, the Roxy also hosts special 18 and up nights.
515 W. 18th St. (bet. Tenth Ave. and West Side Highway), (212) 645-5157. Hours: F-Sa 11pm-4am. Cash Only, Cover: $10-$25. A C E L to 14th St.

Serena
A low ceiling, red walls, and curious tin chandeliers lend a cozy atmosphere to this basement lounge under the Chelsea Hotel. Perch yourself atop one of the seats surrounding the gargantuan U-shaped bar, or sink, drink in hand, into a couch lining one of the adjacent rooms and dig the foxy clientele.
222 W. 23rd St. (bet. Seventh and Eighth Aves.), (212) 255-4646. Hours: M-F 6pm-5am, Sa 7pm-5am. MC, V, AmEx. C E to 23rd St.

LGBT

Barracuda
This bar's laid back, neighborhood feel makes talking to strangers easy. Patrons gather around the

long bar counter in the front room, or they make their way to the funky couches and chairs for table service. There is also a pool table in the back room, but it usually serves as a makeshift couch. Go for happy hour every weekday from 4pm to 9pm and for the live drag shows every Sunday night.
275 W. 22nd St. (bet. Seventh and Eighth Aves.), (212) 645-8613. Hours: M-Su 4pm-4am. C E to 23rd St.

g Lounge
One of the city's hottest gay spots, g feels exclusive yet inviting. Order from the shirtless muscle gods serving drinks behind the large circular bar that is the centerpiece of the space. Mingle with the attractive crowd, and work the scene throughout the spacious front room and the smaller side parlors. Every night DJs play a variety of fun, popish music, and every weeknight between 4pm and 9pm drinks are 50 percent off.
225 W. 19th St. (bet. Seventh and Eighth Aves.), (212) 929-1085. Hours: M-Su 4pm-4am. 1 to

18th St., C E to 23rd St.

Rawhide

It takes a few minutes for your eyes to grow accustomed to the darkness of this bar... and all that black leather. Enjoy go-go dancers, pool or pinball, and the presence of the ever-elusive skintight jeans with cowboy boots getup. This renowned ranch/bar is the only bar in New York that opens for boozing at eight in the freaking morning.
212 Eighth Ave. (at 21st St.), (212) 242-9332. Hours: M-Sa 10am-4am, Su 12pm-4am, Cash Only. C E to 23rd St., 1 to 23rd St., N R to 23rd St.

SBNY – Splash Bar New York

One of Chelsea's hottest gay clubs, SBNY boasts an ultra trendy crowd of model types and gym bunnies. The staff members are all muscle Maries, and some actually used to be porn stars. Go to the top level for a dance floor and bar, or stay downstairs for a reprieve from the above action. If you're looking for a hook up, this is your stop. Weekly drag performances and live musical events round out the offerings.
50 W. 17th St. (bet. Fifth and Sixth Aves.) (212) 691-0073, www.splashbar.com. Hours: Su-R 5pm-4am, F-Sa 5pm-5am. 1 to 18th St., F to 14th or 23rd Sts., L N R W 4 5 6 to Union Sq.-14th St.

XL

The décor at XL is what makes it unique: light machines flashing, white curtains billowing, phallic art on the walls, and fish tanks lining the urinals. The bathrooms here receive a lot of action, so don't be surprised to see a cheek through the glass walls that separate each stall. The bi-level setup is capped with a domed ceiling, and the upper tier looks out onto the bar area so you can scope the boys from above. The space is packed, especially on weekends, so your choices should be endless.
357 W. 16th St. (bet. Eighth and Ninth Aves.) (212) 995-1400. Hours: M-Su 4pm-4am. A C E to 14th St., L to Eighth Ave.

[Midtown]

Bars

Blue Lady Lounge

This upscale cocktail lounge is perfect for power lunches and business meetings, with Shelly's serving up some of the city's best steaks and seafood downstairs. The upstairs lounge offers a large stage at eye level where solo, duet, and trio jazz acts perform every night except Sundays, usually starting at about 8pm. Notable musicians perform regularly, but don't worry about jazz purists getting upset if you have a conversation.
104 W 57th St. (bet. Sixth and Seventh Aves.), (212) 245-2422. Hours: M-R 5pm-12am, F-Sa 5pm-1 am, Su 11am-11pm. MC, V. N R W to 57th St.

Campbell Apartment

With lush oriental carpeting, comfy lounge chairs, and a lovely ceiling, Campbell Apartments is more than just a cozy spot for Wall Streeters to throw back a few before hitting the Metro North. Drinks are pricey.
15 Vanderbilt Ave. (SW balcony at Grand Central), (212) 953-0409. Hours: M-Sa 3pm-1am, Su 3pm-10pm. MC, V, AmEx. S 4 5 6 7 to 42nd St.-Grand Central Terminal.

Danny's Skylight Room at the Grand Sea Palace

While it claims to have one of the best sound and lighting systems in the city, most people go to this reasonably priced bar for the skylight.
346 W. 46th St. (bet. Eighth and Ninth Aves.), (212) 265-8130, www.dannysgrandpalace.com. Hours: M-Su 3pm-12am. MC, V, AmEx, D, DC. A C E N R S W 1 2 3 7 to 42nd St.-Times Sq.

Flute

Champagne afficianados, look no further – bubbly heaven has been found at this cozy, romantic lounge. You can order by the bottle or the flute, and do not miss out on the exotic spring rolls (the Sateri is especially tasty, made of tuna, rice vermicelli, avocado, and fresh mint). The champagne cocktails are inventive and refreshing, and will cost you around $10 (try the Hard Cider – Apple Schnapps, Southern Comfort, Pineapple Juice, and Champagne). If you'd like to have a sampling of a few types of champagne, the Magic Flutes is a tasting of three types.
205 W. 54th St. (bet. Seventh Ave. and Broadway), (212) 265-5169. Hours: M-Sa 5pm-4am, Su 5pm-2am. B D E to Seventh Ave., 1 to 50th St.
Additional locations in Manhattan.

Hudson Bar

Take the fluorescent green escalator in the Hudson Hotel to reach this trendy bar with shiny floors, bright lights, translucent gel cushions on Louis XV chairs, and a main bar that glows from within. This hip place also has overpriced drinks and a pretentious staff. Guys coming alone will have a difficult time making it past the velvet rope, unless you are Leonardo

DiCaprio.
356 W. 58th St. (bet. Eighth and Ninth Aves.), (212) 554-6343. Hours: M-Sa 4pm-2am, Su 4pm-1am. MC, V, AmEx. Ⓐ Ⓑ Ⓒ Ⓓ ① *to 59th St.-Columbus Circle*

Jimmy's Corner

Escape the giddiness of the Theater District at this easy-going local dive, the site of some scenes in Raging Bull. Owner Jimmy Glen subsidizes his career as a boxing trainer and manager with the revenues from this hopping bar. An eclectic crowd of boxing fanatics, literateurs, grad students and the occasional movie star hang out here.
140 W. 44th St. (bet. Sixth and Seventh Aves.), (212) 221-9510. Hours: M-Su 11am-4am. MC, V, AmEx. Ⓐ Ⓒ Ⓔ Ⓝ Ⓡ Ⓢ Ⓦ ① ② ③ ⑦ *to 42nd St.-Times Sq.*

Le Madeleine

This brick-walled French bistro hosts guests with a pretty courtyard and a glass roof. Free chips are served at the bar counter, and French-style dishes run from about $15 up – perfect for a cozy dinner after a Broadway show.
403 W. 43rd St. (bet. Ninth and Tenth Aves.), (212) 246-2993. Hours: M-Su 12pm-3pm, 5pm-11:30pm. MC, V, AmEx. Ⓐ Ⓒ Ⓔ Ⓝ Ⓡ Ⓢ Ⓦ ① ② ③ ⑦ *to 42nd St.-Times Sq.*

Monkey Bar

It's hip, hopping, and hot. This art deco masterpiece has a glamorous older crowd sipping cocktails and flaunting Chanel. The bar is named after a glamorous '40s style actress living at the hotel who always brought her monkey down with her. The epitome of swank.
60 E. 54th St. (in the Hotel Elysée bet. Madison and Park Aves.), (212) 838-2600. Hours: M-R 12pm-2am, F 12pm-3am, Sa 5:30pm-3am, Su 5:30pm-12am. MC, V, AmEx, D, DC. ⑥ *to 53rd St.*

The Oak Room

One of two lounges at the Algonquin Hotel where Dorothy Parker's wit presided over a legendary circle of writers and critics in the '20s. Dress up to fit in with the stylish crowd soaking up late-night cabaret performances in this stylish English tearoom.
59 W. 44th St. (bet. Fifth and Sixth Aves.), (212) 840-6800. Hours: M-Su 7pm-4am. MC, V, AmEx. Ⓑ Ⓓ Ⓕ Ⓥ *to 42nd St.,* Ⓐ Ⓒ Ⓔ Ⓝ Ⓡ Ⓢ Ⓦ ① ② ③ ⑦ *to 42nd St.-Times Sq.*

O'Flaherty's Ale House

Here, you'll find the only pub in NY with a tree growing right through the middle of the bar. In the back, discover a private garden away from the Midtown bustle. Live music, great beer and plenty of dancing keep everyone busy.
334 W. 46th St. (bet. Eighth and Ninth Aves.), (212) 581-9366. Hours: M-Su 12pm-4am. MC, V, AmEx, D, DC, Entrees: $21-$30. ① *to 50th St.,* Ⓝ Ⓡ Ⓦ *to 49th St.*

O'Lunney's Times Square Pub

This late night spot with a bit of a cult following serves food until 3am. Expect Irish and American cuisine and a rowdy post-theatre crowd. The selection of food is basic, but the beers are truly exceptional. Service can be lacking, but the ambiance is generally fun and the moderate prices on the menu will keep you in your seat.
151 W. 46th St. (bet. Broadway and Sixth Ave.), (212) 840-6688, www.olunneys.com. Hours: M-Su 10am-4am. MC, V, AmEx, D, DC. Ⓐ Ⓒ Ⓔ Ⓝ Ⓡ Ⓢ Ⓦ ① ② ③ ⑦ *to 42nd St.-Times Sq.*

Parnell's Pub

Outfitted with a dark wood bar and plenty of Irish pride, this bar/restaurant serves traditional dishes along with the famous Guinness.
350 E. 53rd St. (bet. First and Second Aves.), (212) 355-9706. Hours: Su-R 12pm-10pm, F-Sa 12 pm-12am. MC, V, AmEx, D, DC. Ⓔ Ⓥ ⑥ *to 51st St.-Lexington Ave.*

Pig 'n Whistle

This classic Irish pub features friendly bartenders, amiable and unpretentious clientele, and a fine selection of whiskey and beer. Guaranteed to have a good time, this is an excellent place to grab a drink after eating at any of Midtown's delicious steakhouses or restaurants.
922 3rd Ave (bet. 55th and 56th), (212) 688-4646. Hours: 12pm-4am. MC, V, AmEx. Ⓔ Ⓥ ⑥ *to 51st.-Lexington Ave.*

Les Sans Culottes

An authentic country-style French restaurant that fills up with the theater crowd until 8pm. A range of French courses are available for $20.95 with a wide selection of French wines.
347 W. 46th St. (bet. Eighth and Ninth Aves.) (212) 247-4284. Hours: M-Su 12pm-12am. MC, V, AmEx, D. Ⓐ Ⓒ Ⓔ Ⓝ Ⓡ Ⓢ Ⓦ ① ② ③ ⑦ *to 42nd St.-Times Sq.*

Siberia

Literally a hole in the wall, Siberia is small, dark, and revels in its trashiness. Siberia attracts a diverse crowd, from actor/waiters to yuppies. Their jukebox is among the best in town, and they host DJs and film screenings weekly.
356 W. 40th St. (bet. Eighth and Ninth Aves.), (212) 333-4141. Hours: M-Su 3pm-4am. Cash Only. Ⓐ Ⓒ Ⓔ *to 42nd St.*

Sutton Place Restaurant and Bar

This hoppin' venue boasts two large levels as well as a spacious rooftop bar. DJs spin current hits, and the ample space accommodates even the most boisterous dancers. Projection screens cover the walls, providing diverse coverage of sporting events. The typical crowd is of the after work variety, but Saturday nights invite 20-somethings looking for a party. The back room can be reserved for private parties.
1015 Second Ave. (bet. 53rd and 54th Sts.), (212) 207-3777, www.suttonplacenyc.com. Hours: M-Su 12pm-4am. MC, V, AmEx, D. Ⓔ Ⓥ ⑥ *to 51st St.-Lexington Ave.*

Clubs

Ikon

Ikon is the Wal-Mart of the New York club scene. The scene is mostly young people, people on ecstasy, or both. While it's not as Strata or Show, it has much less attitude.
610 W. 56th St. (bet. Tenth and Eleventh Aves.),

(212) 582-8282. Hours: F-Sa 10pm-6am. MC, V, AmEx, D. C E 1 to 50th St.

Show
At show, the crowd is generally young, attractive, and well-dressed, but guys without ladies will have to wait a long time to get in. With scantily clad women swinging from the ceilings and half-naked musclemen dancing up a storm, Show amps up the rampant sexual energy to a peak. The dance music is the usual hip-hop and house beats, and the drinks are extremely expensive (and comes in a plastic cup, no less).
135 W. 41st St. (bet. Sixth Ave. and Broadway), (212) 278-0988. Hours: T-Su10pm-4am. MC, V, AmEx, D. A C E N R S W 1 2 3 7 to 42nd St.-Times Sq.

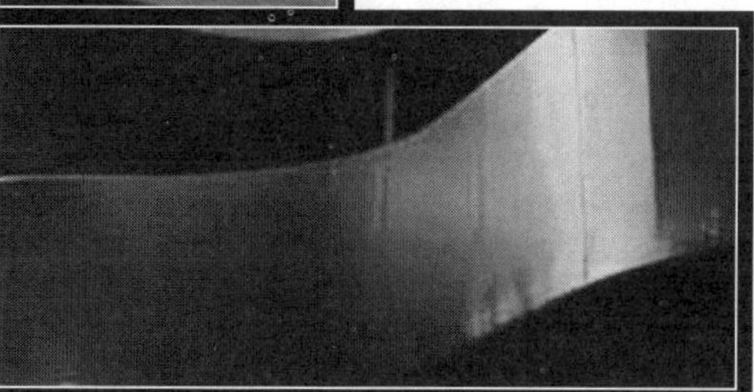

Sky-Loft
Sky-Loft Friday nights, has three large venues. The main Dance floor, (which is attached to the Sky-Loft room where you will find a retractable roof) plays all types of music, from Hip-Hop, R&B, Reggae, and Reggaeton. The third rooms is a power house Latin dancehall, where they play a variety of Latin music from Salsa, to Merengue, Bachata, and also Reggaeton. Each section has its own bar, so the wait for drinks is never too long, and the crowd type is mostly young Professionals having a great time. The best thing about Sky-Loft is the sky loft, when the roof is open - a must visit - bringing the outdoors inside. Sky-Loft is definitely the place to be Friday nights. Just think, lots of beautiful people and you.
610 W. 56th St., 1 A B C D to 56th St. N R to 57th St.

Music

Albion
Plenty of seating at the bar and at tables makes this a comfortable room to listen to the unique sounds of New York's alternative bands. Quickly emerging as a trailblazer in the advancement of the Gothic, Industrial, and Electronic music scenes, this club is one of the best "underground" clubs in the city.
251 W. 30th St. (bet. Seventh and Eighth Aves.), (212) 695-2747. www. albionnyc.com. Call for days and hours. Cash only, Cover $5-$10. 1 to 28th St.

Carnegie Hall
Still the reigning champ of bourgeois nightlife, this legendary institution is the artist's Valhalla. Concerts usually take place every night of the week except July-August, when the Hall is closed. The majority of acts are classical, but you still may catch the occasional Joan Baez or David Bowie show (if you're lucky). Adjoining restaurant and bar serves American cuisine. With classical, pop, and special events.
881 Seventh Ave. (at 57th St.), (212) 247-7800, www.carnegiehall.org. Call for schedule and showtimes. MC, V, AmEx, Tickets: $16-$150. N R W to 57th St.

Connolly's
You can't be Irish in New York if you haven't heard of Black 47, the Dublin rock band. Black 47 plays at Connolly's every Saturday, with other acts occasionally playing the odd night. Full menu and full bar (of course).
14 E. 47th St. (bet. Fifth and Madison Aves.), (212) 867-3767, www.connollysnyc.com. Hours: M-Su 11am-4am. MC, V, AmEx, Cover: $10. E V to Fifth Ave.-53rd St.

Hammerstein Ballroom
Opened in 1906 by Oscar Hammerstein, the ballroom is the setting for a number of national touring acts as well as television broadcasts and corporate events. Music may be an eclectic roster, from Hanson to Manson. No food, but several bars.
311 W. 34th St. (bet. Eighth and Ninth Aves.), (212) 485-1534, www.mcstudios.com/newsite/hammersteinballroom.asp Call for schedule and showtimes. Cash Only, tickets: $20-$60. A C E 1 2 3 to 34th St.-Penn Station.

Iridium
This large music lounge has been relocated from the Lincoln Center to the heart of the tourist area in Midtown. Big-name bands play here every week, bringing in both the local hardcore jazz fans and curious foreign tourists. Drinks run $7 to $10, and food entrées average $20.
1650 Broadway (at 51st St.), (212) 582-2121. Call for showtimes. MC, V, AmEx. A C 1 to 50th St.

B.B. King Blues Club & Grill
A prestigious place for New York musicians, this venue lodged between Broadway's musical theaters combines a restaurant with a music hall and attracts both locals and tourists. Music ranges from blues, jazz, and rock to soul and hip hop, featuring big-name artists like B.B. King himself. Some 500 people can pack this luxurious music hall and enjoy good American food and drink over a wonderful evening of live music. Then again, few come for the food.
237 W. 42nd St. (bet. Seventh and Eighth Aves.), (212) 997-4144. Call for schedules and showtimes. MC, V, AmEx, D, DC. A C E N R S W 1 2 3 7 to 42nd St.-Times Sq.

Fashion Forty Lounge
The Fashion Forty Lounge is a smooth nightspot perfect for a connoisseur of fine drinks and finger foods. The small assortment of paninis and salads are tasty, provided you can see the menu through the dim lighting. Sit back in the comfortable chairs, curl up with a pillow and enjoy the laid back atmosphere of high-class lounging.
202 W. 40th St. (at Seventh Ave.). (212) 221-3628. M-F 4pm-2am, Sa 7pm-2am. MC, V, AmEx. A C E N R S W 1 2 3 7 *to 42nd St.-Times Sq.*

Roseland Ballroom
It started as a popular ballroom in the 1930s, and the newly renovated Roseland is still one of the more frequented venues in town. Large enough to draw a sizable crowd, but small enough to retain some of that club charm, these days expect to find the bigger names in alternative acts. No food, but full bar. With alternative rock, dance, and pop.
239 W. 52nd St. (bet. Broadway and Eighth Ave.), (212) 247-0200, www.roselandballroom.com. Call for performers and showtimes. AmEx, tickets: $15-$20. C E 1 *to 50th St.*

The Supper Club
As one of New York's more elegant venues, be prepared to dress up for a night of dinner and dancing on the town. Historically a ballroom, The Supper Club is the center of the swing scene every Friday and Saturday night. During the rest of the week, catch a live band under the sparkling chandelier and painted gold stars. French and American Continental food served from 6pm-12:30am. With '40s lindy-hop, jump, swing, and occasional private rock and pop concerts.
240 W. 47th St. (bet. Broadway and Eighth Ave.), (212) 921-1940, www.supperclub.citysearch.com. Call for schedule. MC, V, AmEx, Cover: $20-$25. C E 1 *to 50th St.,* N R W *to 49th St.*

Swing 46 Jazz and Supper Club
Rocking with swing music on a dance floor by the dining hall, this venue serves a three-course dinner at a fixed price of $18.95 every day of the week. A dress code is enforced, but no jackets are necessary.
349 W. 46th St. (bet. Eighth and Ninth Aves.), (212) 262-9554. www.swing46.com. Hours: M-Su 5pm-3am. MC, V, AmEx, D. A C E N R S W 1 2 3 7 *to 42nd St.-Times Sq.*

W. Bank Cafe's Laurie Beachman Theatre
W. Bank Café's cabaret room is just below the restaurant and bar. It's a great place to have a nice dinner followed by a relaxing evening downstairs. Great for entertaining out-of-town relatives and business clients.
407 W. 42nd St. (bet. Ninth and Tenth Aves.), (212) 695-6909. Hours: M-Su 11:45am-1am. MC, V, AmEx, call for cover charges for individual shows. A C E N R S W 1 2 3 7 *to 42nd St.-Times Sq.*

LGBT

Barrage
Industrial warehouse meets the Abercrombie catalogue at Barrage. This hot spot just off bumping Ninth Ave. is lined wall-to-wall with pictures of hunky models, and is frequented by men no less sexy. The drinks are decently priced and strong as hell. If you're up for cruising, grab a spot at the bar, the place where all the magic happens.
401 W. 47th St. (bet. Ninth and Tenth Aves.), (212) 586-9390. Hours: M-Su 5pm-4am. Cash Only. C E 1 *to 50th St.*

Therapy
This sleek bar and lounge has a trendy, slightly older clientele. There are two floors, a couple of bars, and many intimate tables. Most customers use the optional table service, making Therapy a bad singles bar. It's ideal for a date or a group of friends wanting to chill while enjoying good music and strong, moderately priced drinks. Happy hour is 5pm-8pm every night, and on Tuesdays there are free stand-up comedy acts.
348 W. 52nd St. (bet. Eighth and Ninth Aves.), (212) 397-1700. Hours: M-Su 5pm-4am. C E 1 *to 50th St.*

The Townhouse Club
An extremely professional gay bar catering to well-dressed men with big bank accounts and the fellows who love them. A piano bar in back augments the somewhat pretentious ambience.
236 E. 58th St. (bet. Second and Third Aves.), (212) 754-4649. Hours: M-Su 4pm-4am. Cash Only. N R W 4 5 6 *to Lexington Ave.*

[Upper East Side]

Bars

American Spirits
This dive is popular with the mid-20s set, probably due to karaoke on Tuesday and Thursday nights, and an epic, daily happy hour.
1744 Second Ave. (at 91st St.), (212) 289-7510. www.americanspiritsbar.com. Hours: Su-T 2pm-4am, F-Sa 1pm-4am. MC, V, AmEx, D, DC. 4 5 6 *to 86th St.*

American Trash
Bikers and bankers meet without colliding at this East Side dive. Its subtitle, "professional drinking establishment," suggests democracy.
1471 First Ave. (bet. 76th and 77th Sts.), (212) 988-9008. Hours: M-Su 12pm-4am. MC, V, AmEx. 6 *to 77th St.*

Amsterdam Billiard Club
More genteel than most pool halls, the ABC is the kind of place that's full of old men and dark wood. Weekends can get feisty, but mostly the scene is laid-back, with lots of regulars, including director/actor/owner Paul Sorvino.
210 E. 86th St. (bet. Second and Third Aves.), (212) 570-4545. www.amsterdambilliardsclub.com. Hours: Su-R 12pm-3am, F-Sa 12pm-4am. MC, V, AmEx, D. 4 5 6 *to 86th St.*

Auction House
Mature customers populate this pricey, baroque lounge, a microcosm of the Upper East Side.
300 E. 89th St. (bet. First

and Second Aves.), (212) 427-4458. Hours: M-Su 7:30pm-4am. MC, V, AmEx, D, DC. 4 5 6 *to 86th St.*

Brother Jimmy's
Anyone from below the Mason-Dixon line will feel at home in this southern bar. Post-collegiate pre-professionals come for the generous bartenders and Sunday special: $18.95 for unlimited beer and all the ribs you can stomach.
1785 Second Ave. (bet. 77th and 78th Sts.), (212) 288-0999. Hours: Su-R 12pm-2am. F-Sa 12pm-1am. MC, V, AmEx. 6 *to 77th St.*

The Cocktail Room
Painted in neon colors and furnished with '60s mod dinettes, the Cocktail Room looks like something out of *A Clockwork Orange*. You will enjoy an impressive array of extremely well-made cocktails. The prices are a bit steep, but the pours are generous. A light tapas menu is available.
334 E. 73rd St. (bet. First and Second Aves.), (212) 988-6100. Hours: T-F 5pm-4am, Sa 7pm-4am. MC, V, AmEx, D. 4 5 6 *to 72nd St.*

Lexington Bar and Books
This pricey, high-class cigar bar offering great ambience and fantastic martinis is a nice place to pretend you're all grown up with the white-collar types. Proper attire is required. Live jazz on Fridays and Saturdays.
1020 Lexington Ave. (at 72nd St.), (212) 717-3902. Hours: Su-R 5pm-2am, F-Sa 5pm-4am. MC, V, AmEx, D. 6 *to 68th St.*

Mo's Caribbean Bar and Grill
With twelve beers on tap and a huge 50 oz. margarita on the drink menu, it is clear that Mo's is a place for serious partiers. The tropical decor lights up Second Ave., and the inside is equally vibrant with large-screen televisions, video games, and neon-colored drinks straight out of a Jimmy Buffett song. Don't miss the pseudo-spring-break parties that are thrown at all times of the year.
1454 Second Ave. (at 76th St.), (212) 650-0561, www.nycbestbars.com. Hours: M-F 4pm-4am, Sa-Su 11:30am-4am. MC, V, AmEx. 6 *to 77th St.*

Subway Inn
It's right across the way from Bloomingdale's, but you'll seldom see shoppers take a load off their Blahniks at this perfect dive bar. Dark, smelly, dirty, and cheap, Subway is heroically antithetical to the glittering retail stores surrounding it. Drink up and then tumble down the conveniently located subway entrance.
143 E. 60th St. (at Lexington Ave.), (212) 223-8929. Hours: M-Su 11am-4am. Cash Only. F N R W 4 5 6 *to 59th St.-Lexington Ave.*

[Central Park]

Bars

Loeb Boathouse
It's the only place to get a cocktail in Central Park. Luckily, it's a gorgeous one. Come and pass an afternoon at one of the outside tables, and watch city-slickers haplessly plying the oars on rental dinghies. Hours vary with the season (and weather), but rarely extend past nine, so be sure to call ahead. Adjacent cafe serves food.
Central Park Lake (at 74th St.), (212) 517-2233. Hours: W-Sa 12pm-4pm, 6pm-10pm, Sa-Su 11am-4pm, 6pm-10pm. MC, V, AmEx, D, DC. B C *to 72nd St.*

[Upper West Side]

Bars

420 Bar and Lounge
This swank member of the Amsterdam scene, populated with the requisite professionals and well-heeled single malt sippers, could teach the SoHo lounges a thing or two. Local scenesters, spared the cab fare required to get downtown, don't seem to mind the pricey cocktails.
420 Amsterdam Ave. (at 80th St.), (212) 579-8450. Hours: M-Su 5pm-4am. MC, V, AmEx, D, DC. 1 *to 79th St.*

The All State Cafe
Once the Upper West Side's best singles bar, the All State is still a great place to grab a steak or a beer. The menu features hearty American offerings, and the draughts run cool with several good ales. The regular clientele is a mixed bag of young professionals and old-timers.
250 W. 72nd St., (bet. West End Ave. and Broadway), (212) 874-1883. Hours: M-Su 11:30am-4am. Cash Only. 1 2 3 to 72nd St.

Blondies
Mounted televisions playing sporting events run continuously above the batenders, whose striking blonde coifs explain this boisterous sports bar's name. Try the "world-famous atomic wings."
212 W. 79th St. (bet. Broadway and Amsterdam Aves.), (212) 362-4360. Hours: M-Su 11:30am-4am. MC, V, AmEx, D, DC. 1 to 79th St.

The Boat Basin Cafe
This open-air drink scene feels like a medieval courtyard with the sweet smell of barbecue. A clean-cut 30s crowd languishes on three separate levels under a Romanesque ceiling and thick stone pillars. Look out over the Hudson and the lights of New Jersey, and enjoy tasty oddities like the smoked chicken and spinach salad with apples and toasted walnuts. Dress to kill – this place is for groups looking for fun and singles looking for some action.
W. 79th St. (at the Hudson River), (212) 496-5542. Hours: M-Sa 12pm-11:30pm, Su 11am-10pm. MC, V, AmEx. 1 to 79th St.

Bourbon Street
Show up here to find athletic women dancing on the bar (especially Friday and Saturday nights) and kick back. Lots of neighborhood sport teams love to frequent this bar and take in a few brews. Make sure to have a potent frozen Hurricane or two.
407 Amsterdam Ave. (at 79th St.), (212) 721-1332, www.bourbonstreetnyc.com. Hours: M-Su 4pm-4am. MC, V, AmEx, D, DC. 1 to 79th St.

Dive Bar
Sure, it's got dive written all over it, literally, but this haunt is actually quite tame. Even the resident pool sharks won't intimidate. Chug till 4am every day and don't overlook a strong menu.
732 Amsterdam Ave. (at 96th St.), (212) 749-4358. Hours: M-Su 11:30am-4am. MC, V, AmEx. 1 2 3 B C to 96th St.

Dublin House
While not a traditional Irish bar, the Dublin House is nevertheless a blessing to the Upper West Side. Its unpretentious atmosphere and straight-up bar attract the authentic old-timer and college student alike. Even the ex-pat Irish come here.
225 W. 79th St. (bet. Broadway and Amsterdam Ave.), (212) 874-9528. Hours: M-Su 8am-4am. Cash Only. 1 to 79th St.

The Evelyn Lounge
This spacious bar is crowded most days of the week. It's almost romantic, with fireplaces and comfortable chairs and couches in the back rooms. On the other hand, it's kind of cheesy. Evelyn is a singles scene with men outnumbering women about 3 to 1. There is live music several nights a week, but not enough room to dance.
380 Columbus Ave. (at 78th St.), (212) 724-5145. Hours: Su-R 6pm-2am, F-Sa 5pm-4am. MC, V, AmEx, D. 1 to 79th St.

Fez (Time Cafe)
Originally the site of Sticky Mike's, a Warhol hangout, now housing hip singer-songwriters like Ellis Paul, Peter Mulvey, and Jennifer Kimball. Though they've moved the place uptown, but it still has that same vibe. This unique room has mirrored columns and sparkly vinyl booths, and every so often the room vibrates from the subway train passing underneath. Full menu, full bar. With acoustic, comedy, jazz, rock, and singer-songwritter shows.
2330 Broadway (at 85th St.), 212-579-5100. www.timecafenyc.com. Hours: M-R 6pm-12am, F 6pm-2am, Sa 10am-1am,

Su 10am-12am. Cash only, Cover: $8-$20. ❶ to Broadway-86th St.

The Gin Mill

Tasty shots with silly names abound, and there is never a Jaegermeister shortage. Don't categorize the Gin Mill as a sports bar, but rest assured you can always catch the Sunday game here. A great place to chill, have a bite, and drink.
442 Amsterdam Ave. (bet. 81st and 82nd Sts.), (212) 580-9080. Hours: M-Sa 11:30am-4am, Su 12pm-4am. MC, V, AmEx. ❶ to 79th St.

Jake's Dilemma

This bar steals attention from other bars along the Amsterdam bar strip in the West 80s. With three levels, a young, hip crowd, pool tables, and good looking bartenders, Jake's only dilemma is what drink to order next. Ladies' Night on Thursday features $1 margaritas for the female clientele. Happy hour lasts until 8pm.
430 Amsterdam Ave. (bet. 80th and 81st Sts.), (212) 580-0556. Hours: M-F 4pm-4am, Sa-Su 12pm-4am. MC, V, AmEx. ❶ to 79th St.

The Parlour

This Irish bar has good drinks and especially fine Guinness for the Upper West Side. The traditional Irish ambiance keeps the yuppie Upper West Siders at bay. Jeans are okay here even on the weekends. The ample seating and downstairs dance area provide for a relaxed night with friends. The food is also quite good.
250 W. 86th St. (bet. Broadway and Riverside Dr.), (212) 580-8923. Hours: M-Su 12pm-4am. MC, V, AmEx. ❶ to 86th St.

The P&G

You may know the P&G from its cameo roles in *Taxi Driver*, *Seinfeld*, or *Donnie Brasco*, but it's still an unassuming place. An old neighborhood bar dating back to the 1940s, the P&G is the real deal, filled with locals and old-timers drinking to tunes from the classic rock jukebox.
279 W. 73rd St.(at Amsterdam Ave.), (212) 874-8568. Hours: M-Su 10am-4am. MC, V, AmEx. ❶❷❸ to 72nd St.

Prohibition

This Upper West Sider has live bands jamming seven days a week, with multiple bands playing blends of jazz and rock every night starting at around 10pm on the main floor. The upstairs section is great for private parties, complete with its own bar, a pool table, sofas, and tables. Their mini-cheeseburgers are some of the best pub-grub in town.
503 Columbus Ave. (bet. 84th and 85th Sts.), (212) 579-3100. Hours: M-Sa 5pm-4am, Su 5pm-3pm. MC, V, AmEx, D, DC. Ⓑ Ⓒ or ❶ to 86th St.

Raccoon Lodge

You'll get just what you'd expect from a bar with this name – it's a dive. The patrons are not your typical Upper West Siders; men with cowboy hats and motorcycles frequent this bar. Maybe it's the video and electronic poker games. There is little seating and what there is resembles picnic tables. The alcohol is cheaper than average for the neighborhood.
480 Amsterdam Ave. (at 83rd St.), (212) 874-9984. Hours: M-Su 11am-4am. MC, V, AmEx, D. ❶ to 86th St.

Shark Bar

A well-known, upscale hangout. Low lighting and polished wood accents make this hideaway a romantic alternative to other more raucous bars. You might need to ward off the post-collegiate singles hovering around the bar.
307 Amsterdam Ave. (bet. 74th and 75th Sts.), (212) 874-8500, www.sharkbar.com. Hours: M-T 5pm-11:30pm, W 12pm-12am, R 12pm-12:30am, F 12pm-1:30am, Sa 11:30am, Su 11:30am-11pm. MC, V, AmEx, D, DC. ❶❷❸ to 72nd St.

Time Out

For the true sports fanatic: know your stats and be ready to talk some serious trivia. The crowd of cheering, jeering, 30-something men ignores the pool table in favor of the 23 televisions. This is New York's home to the Celtic's soccer supporter club, so know what you mean when asking about the "football" game.
349 Amsterdam Ave. (bet. 76th and 77th Sts.), (212) 362-5400. Hours: M-F 5pm-3am, Sa-Su 12pm-3am. MC, V, AmEx, D, DC. ❶ to 79th St.

Yogi's

An old-fashioned country saloon like this one provides a stark contrast to the new age eateries and standard pubs that line Broadway and Amsterdam in the 70s. Bras dangle behind the bar and the

jukebox is stacked with hits by Credence, Willie Nelson, Johnny Cash, and Dolly Parton. Enjoy $8 pitchers of Bud under a big American flag and a bear's head, alongside shouting sports fans.
2156 Broadway (bet. 75th and 76th Sts.), (212) 873-9852. Hours: M-Su 12pm-4am. Cash only. 1 2 3 to 72nd St.

[Morningside Heights]

Bars

1020 Bar
1020 is just a bar, and quite content that way. During the week, come with a good friend to throw back a few in peace. On the weekends, watch the artsy kids take their first fumbling steps towards skankiness at a nascent pick-up scene. The pool table in the back can get crowded very quickly. The drinks are okay and prices are friendly.
1020 Amsterdam Ave. (bet. 110th and 111th Sts.), (212) 531-3468. Hours: M-Su 4pm-4am. MC, V, AmEx. 1 to 110th St.

Abbey Pub
Both the food and the atmosphere are comforting at this ideal neighborhood bar where older locals mingle easily with the collegiate (and younger) crowd. A perfect spot to meet for beers and a shared basket of fish 'n chips.
237 W. 105th St. (bet. Broadway and Amsterdam Ave.), (212) 222-8713. Hours: M-F 4pm-2am, Sa-Su 4pm-3am. MC, V, AmEx. 1 to 103rd St.

Amsterdam Restaurant and Tapas Lounge
Formerly Amsterdam Cafe, this newly transformed upscale bar has a new look and a new clientele. What once was a place for Columbia students and locals to down cheap pitchers, pub grub, and sports TV, has become a trendy tapas lounge with flat-screen plasmas and fancy meals. Renovations of the basement have added pool tables, an additional bar, and couches to this freshly minted chic restaurant.
1207 Amsterdam Ave. (bet. 119th and 120th Sts.), (212) 662-6330. Hours: M-Su 11am-4am. MC, V, AmEx, D, DC. 1 to 116th St.

Eden
This newer bar near Columbia University is a perfect place to settle down on one of the many comfortable couches. With lots of space to enjoy their intimate setting, you'll find tasty drinks at very reasonable prices. Make sure to try the "Naked". This is mostly for couples and mid-20-somethings looking to relax in a unique Morningside Heights venue.
2728 Broadway (bet. 104th and 105th Sts.), (212) 865-5565. Hours: M-Su 5pm-4am. MC, V, D. 1 to 103rd St.

The Heights Bar & Grill
A favorite spot for Columbia University undergrads and grads alike, stop by for their famous $3 frozen margaritas during happy hour (5pm-7pm, 11:30pm-12:30am). Make sure to arrive before happy hour if you want a seat, otherwise you'll be standing in the packed bar. A great place to chill with friends after work or school and enjoy the strong margaritas and fantastic buffalo wings.
2867 Broadway (bet. 111th and 112th Sts.), (212) 866-7035. Hours: M-Su 11:30am-3am. MC, V, D. 1 to 110th St.

Lion's Head
Taking over what used to be the What Bar and Mo's Cantina, Lion's Head prides itself on being a college bar. The late-night kitchen makes this place a neighborhood favorite, as well as $10 all you can drink beer night. Look out for darts as your walking through the tiny bar area, and play some of your favorite tunes on the jukebox.
995 Amsterdam Ave. (at 110th St.), (212) 866-1030. Hours: M-Su 5pm-4am. 1 to 110th St.

Nacho's Kitchen
Large numbers of college students gather to drink, grope, and be merry. They offer decent drinks at decent prices. The bouncers occasionally forget they're in Morningside Heights.
2893 Broadway (bet. 112th and 113th Sts.), (212) 665-2800. Hours: M-Su 11:30am-4am. MC, V, AmEx. 1 to 110th St.-Cathedral Pkwy.

Tap-a-Keg
As one of Morningside Heights's true 'neighborhood joints,' Tap-a-Keg is a fun and relaxed classic beer hall. The beer on tap is always fantastic and never leaves patrons disappointed. The bartenders are attractive and easy to

talk to, making Tap-a-Keg different from "hoity-toity" bars. This is a great place to come and chill with a group of friends, enjoying a few rounds in great company. They offer a pool table, video games, a dartboard, a friendly and engaging staff, and most importantly, an extensive selection of quality beer. *2731 Broadway, (bet. 104th and 105th Sts.) (212) 749-1734. Hours: M-Su 12pm-4am. M, V.* ❶ *to 103rd St.*

The West End

Hanging out at the West End is a rite of passage for Columbia freshmen with bad fake IDs. It's gone downhill since the days when Kerouac and Ginsberg made this their haunt, now attracting a loyal clientele of frat boys in cologne. College Night on Saturday is complete with beer pong tournaments. The recently renovated lower level is a cute lounge spot. It is owned by a Columbia Journalism School alum. The best place in Morningside Heights to get a hamburger. *2911 Broadway (bet. 113th and 114th Sts.), (212) 662-8830. Hours: Su-W 11am-2am, R-Sa 11am-4am. MC, V, AmEx, D, DC.* ❶ *to 116th St.*

Music

Postcrypt Coffeehouse

Located in the basement of St. Paul's chapel on the Columbia University campus and seating only 50, the Postcrypt is one of the most unique rooms in the city. No electronic equipment is allowed on the stage and the only lighting is from candles stuck in wine bottles and chandeliers. Suzanne Vega played her first gig here when she was a student at Barnard College across the street. Snacks and bottled beer available. Performers cover acoustic, country, folk, and jazz. Call for details and performance schedule. *St. Paul's Chapel at Columbia University (at 117th St. and Broadway), (212) 854-1953, Hours: F-Sa 9pm-12am (during school year only).* ❶ *to 116th St.*

Smoke

This is the classiest bar in the neighborhood, and one of the best places for good, intimate jazz. Smoke made a name for itself with jazz acts like George Coleman, Slide Hampton, Cecil Payne, Leon Parker, Eric Alexander, and a legendary cameo by George Benson. Don't miss the Wednesday Blues night. *2751 Broadway (bet. 105th and 106th Sts), (212) 864-6662, www.smokejazz.com. Hours: M-Sa 5pm-4am, Su 5pm-2am. MC, V, Cover: $8-$15 ($10 drink minimum).* ❶ *to 110th St.*

[Harlem]

Bars

Lady Luci's Cocktail

This spacious neighborhood lounge brings in an older crowd with live jazz most nights. Monday nights are the best, when a 17-piece big band takes the stage and offers a really entertaining performance. *2306 Frederick Douglass Blvd. (bet. 124th and 125th Sts.), (212) 864-8760. Hours: M-Su 4:30pm-2am. Cash only.* ⒶⒷⒸⒹ *to 125th St.*

Lenox Lounge

There's live jazz most nights, and, with recent renovations, it looks as cool as it sounds. *288 Lenox Ave. (bet. 124th and 125th Sts.), (212) 427-0253. Hours: M-Su 12pm-4am. MC, V, AmEx, D.* ❷❸ *to 125th St.*

Showman's

Everything is copasetic at this laid-back haunt, according to the Copasetics, a brotherhood of tap dancers, which makes this popular club its headquarters. Come for the live jazz Wednesday through Saturday. *375 W. 125th St. (bet. Morningside and St. Nicholas Aves.), (212) 864-8941. Hours: M-Su 1pm-4am. MC, V, AmEx, (two-drink minimum).* ❶ *to 125th St.*

Music

Cotton Club

A Harlem legend since before you were born, the Cotton Club is still kicking. Show times vary widely and you must call for reservations. The "don't miss" $25 gospel brunches are served every weekend.

Full Southern menu and full bar.
656 W. 125th St. (at Twelfth Ave.), (212) 663-7980, www.cottonclub-newyork.com. Call for schedule and showtimes. MC, V, Cover: $15-$30. 1 *to 125th St.*

[Washington Heights]

Bars

Coogan's
Coogan's, whose layout recalls the set of *Cheers*, hosts a bustling, after-work crowd from Columbia Presbyterian Medical Center, as well as a loyal and mixed neighborhood clientele. The atmosphere is always festive, especially on karaoke nights (Saturday and Tuesday). It also serves food from an extensive menu – see dining section.
4015 Broadway (at 168th St.), (212) 928-1234, www.coogans.com. Hours: M-Su 11am-4am. MC, V, AmEx, D. A C 1 *to 168th St.-Washington Hts.*

Irish Brigade Pub
A feisty female bartender serves a much older crowd interested in letting loose. Beers start at $1.50, pitchers at $6. Sometimes, as a special treat, there's a DJ.
4716 Broadway (at Arden St.), (212) 567-8714. Hours: M-Su 8am-4am. Cash Only. A *to Dyckman St.-200th St.*

Rose of Kilarney Bar
This dive is beloved by Columbia Med students for its friendly, down-to-earth atmosphere and starving-student prices.
1208 St. Nicholas Ave. (bet. 170th and 171st Sts.), (212) 928-4566. Hours: M-Su 8am-4am. Cash only. A C 1 *to 168th St.-Washington Hts.*

[Brooklyn]

Bars

Black Betty
Black Betty dishes up cool live music and North African cuisine to a young crowd of new Brooklynites seven days a week. The jazz, world music, and trip-hop acts booked by the "Professor" have helped to make this one of Williamsburg's most popular nightspots. Be sure to call ahead for reservations.
366 Metropolitan Ave. (at Havemeyer St.), (718) 599-0243. Hours: M-Su 6:30pm-4am. MC, V, AmEx. L *to Bedford Ave.,* G *to Metropolitan Ave.*

Boat
Great jukebox, good drinks, friendly staff, and a nice design and layout. What more could you want of a neighborhood bar in Brooklyn? Located right off the F train, this place is usually busy early in the week, gets the night-cap crowd on the weekends, and is a *Cheers* kind of place for the locals.
175 Smith St. (bet. Wyckof and Warren Sts.), (718) 254-0607. Hours: M-Su 5pm-4am. MC, V, AmEx. F G *to Bergen St.*

Carriage House
Home away from home for Park Slope's cable-deprived in need of a Knicks fix. Had enough sports? Amuse yourself at the pool table or come by on karaoke night.
Park Slope, Brooklyn, 312 Seventh Ave. (bet. 7th and 8th Sts.), (718) 788-7747. Hours: M-Su 4pm-4am. MC, V, AmEx, D. F *to Seventh Ave.*

Frank's Lounge
Frank's is the friendly neighborhood lounge in this part of Brooklyn. Come in and you'll be greeted with smiles and the sounds of smooth DJing. It gets crowded on weekends, but you can always expect to see regulars and quality mixed drinks.
660 Fulton St. (at S. Eliot St.), (718) 625-9339. Hours: M-R 12pm-2am, F-Su 3pm-4am. Cash only. C *to Lafayette St.,* G *to Fulton St.,* 2 3 4 5 *to Nevins Ave.*

Last Exit
Last Exit is an oasis of cool in the sometimes-stuffy bar wasteland that is Brooklyn Heights. The low-key lounge serves delicious martinis and strong mixed drinks to a young, fresh clientele. A friendly staff, comfy couches, and unpretentious crowd also await.
136 Atlantic Ave., (bet. Henry and Clinton Sts.), (718) 222-9198. Hours: M-F 4pm-4am, Sa-Su 3pm-4am. MC, V, AmEx, D, DC.

M N R W 2 3 4 5 *to Borough Hall,* F G *to Bergen St.*

Mugs Ale House
Baffled by so many good beers on tap, most people never investigate their vast selection of bottled imports. The colorful local contingent and a decent jukebox explain why Manhattanites schlep all the way out here for a drink. Join 'em.
125 Bedford Ave. (at N. 10th St.), (718) 486-8232. Hours: M-Su 2pm-4am. MC, V, AmEx, D. L *to Bedford Ave.*

Pete's Candy Store
Only locals, cool Brooklynites and "those who know" visit this venue, which offers bingo on Tuesdays, Quiz-O on Wednesdays, and jazz quartets on Thursdays, with DJs and a neighborhood band fill the rest of the week. Toasted panini accompany a drink list packed with dark and stormy "Mac Daddys", and all the usual cocktail suspects.
709 Lorimer St. (bet. Frost and Richardson Sts.), (718) 302-3770. Hours: Su-W 5pm-2am, R-Sa 5pm-4am. G *to Metropolitan Ave.,* L *to Lorimer St.*

Teddy's Bar and Grill
The best bar food in Brooklyn. Try a burger or go for dessert. There are plenty of drinks to wash it down. Teddy's is one of the few places offering pitchers of really good beer.
96 Berry St. (at N. 8th St.), (718) 384-9787. Hours: Su-W 11:30am-12am, R-Sa 11:30am-2am. MC, V, AmEx. L *to Bedford Ave.*

Clubs

Galapagos
Local artists from Williamsburg and Greenpoint come to hear house quartets and watch dance, theater, and a variety of film series at this right off hip performance space, the first stop out of Manhattan. Beers for $3.50 and well drinks for $5 makes it ideal for those with light wallets. Check out New Year's Eve here, when bottles of champagne magically descend from the ceiling at midnight with glasses tied to them.
70 N. 6th St. (bet. Kent and Wythe Aves.), (718) 782-5188. Hours: Su-R 6pm-2am, F-Sa 6pm-4am. Cash Only. L *to Bedford Ave.*

[Queens]

Bars

Cafe Bar
This is one of those places that will become a favorite the first time you walk in. The funky decor and laid-back atmosphere make it a good place to spend hours over coffee, dessert, or a drink. It's especially good for people watching on Friday and Saturday nights, when the old country locals mix with club kids.
Astoria, Queens, 32-19 36th Ave. (bet. 32nd and 33rd Sts.), (718) 204-5273. Hours: Su-R 9:30am-12am, F-Sa 9:30am-4am. Cash Only. G R V *to Steinway St.,* N W *to Broadway.*

Irish Rover
The Irish Rover pours a mean pint of Guinness and makes a pretty good shepherd's pie for its mostly local clientele. As one might guess, the regulars are mostly Irish, but the crowd is always mixed. Occasional live performances liven up the joint.
Astoria, Queens, 37-18 28th Ave. (bet. 38th and 37th Sts.), (718) 278-9372. Hours: M-Sa 8am-4am, Su 12pm-4am. Cash Only. G R V *to Steinway St.*

Clubs

Krash
No doubt its parent club in San Juan would be proud of the Latin music this cavernous dance emporium serves up Mondays, Thursdays, Fridays, and Saturdays. Its definitely worth the ride if you crave this mezmerizing beat.
Astoria, Queens, 34-48 Steinway St. (at 35th Ave.), (718) 937-2400. Hours: M-Sa 10pm-5am. MC, V, Cover: $1-$10. G R V *to Steinway St.*

[Staten Island]

Bars

Ruddy & Dean
Patrons can enjoy a great view of Manhattan from the outside patio while enjoying the bar's wide selection of beer and vodka.
44 Richmond Terrace (bet. Day and Wall Sts.), (718) 816-4400. Hours: M-R 11:30pm-4am, Sa-Su 12pm-4am. MC, V, AmEx, D, DC. 4 5 *to Bowling Green, then South Ferry Terminal.*

Sidestreet Saloon
High-schoolers in shiny pants pack this dive. Most nights a DJ spins hip-hop, but once a month there's an '80s party, so be sure to check ahead for a schedule.
11 Schuyler St. (bet. Richmond Terrace and Styvasen St.), (718) 448-6868. Hours: M-Su 11:30am-4am. MC, V, AmEx, D, DC. 4 5 *to Bowling Green, then South Ferry Terminal.*

[Index by Category]

Leisure

leisure

leisure in nyc

Admittedly, New York City is a stressful place, and people who work hard want to play even harder. The city is a playground waiting to be explored. Whether you're in the market for a serious workout or simply a breath of fresh air, New York has something for everyone – no matter what shape you're in.

New York is a venerable haven for athletes and people-watchers alike. Central Park is the city's hub for running and relaxing, but, contrary to popular belief, it is not alone. The city contains dozens of parks in all of its boroughs, each with unique attractions. Likewise, the beaches of New York, though fewer in number and slightly more difficult to access, are equally diverse in their offerings. New York is a town surrounded by water, so take advantage of the beautiful Atlantic Ocean, the calm Long Island Sound, and the excitement of Atlantic City and the Jersey Shore.

When looking for a diversion, many New Yorkers opt to take day-long trips to landmarks easily accessible from Manhattan. Try a hike across the Brooklyn Bridge; the views of Manhattan are phenomenal. For a change of pace, visit cultural landmarks in places like Long Island and Westchester County.

If one is still not satisfied by the offerings within and adjacent to the city, a great thing to do would be to take a day or week-long trip to upstate New York, New Jersey, Connecticut, or Pennsylvania. All of these states are accessible by mass transit, and they can refresh even the most jaded New Yorker. Upstate New York is comprised of wonderfully small towns, each full of antiques, culture, and charm, as well as mountain ranges for skiing in winter, observing the foliage in fall, and relaxing in summer. Leaving New York often seems painstaking, but take a break. When you return – undoubtedly relaxed and refreshed - New York will seem even better than before you left.

Nonetheless, if you would rather devote your leisure time to the serious business of exercise, then visit one of the city's first-rate gyms for an intense workout, or stay outdoors and join the hundreds of other people who bike, blade, and jog in any of New York's beautiful neighborhoods. Consider Chelsea Piers as another alternative for getting exercise – it gives New Yorkers the opportunity to partake in sports like golf and tennis that the limited space of Manhattan once prevented.

The professional sports teams of New York are also numerous and exciting. The Yankees, Mets, Rangers, Knicks, Cyclones, and Liberty all play within city limits, and not too far in New Jersey are New York's football and soccer teams. Regardless of your preferred spectator sport, New York has options for everyone.

Be sure to take advantage of all New York has to offer in organized sporting clubs. There are many amateur leagues in every sport. Joining one is a great way to meet people.

However you choose to spend your free time, New York City has an endless number of ways to keep the body healthy, your life active, and your mind clear.

Exploring Williamsburg

Today, Williamsburg, Brooklyn is seen by most as an up-and-coming artist's community, a place to spend an evening or two perusing the various galleries and shops, looking for the next-big-thing. Regardless of this attitude, Williamsburg has had a long and colorful history that would not have led one to conclude that the city would become the mecca of New York cool that it has.

Williamsburg was named after Colonel Jonathan Williams, a surveyor who worked on the 13 acres which came to comprise the original Village of Williamsburgh. Although initially an independent city, in 1855 the City of Williamsburgh was amalgamated into the growing City of Brooklyn. To commemorate this momentous occasion, the final "h" in Williamsburgh was dropped. Williamsburg became a haven for wealthy industrialists, who built large mansions in the area to escape from the hustle and bustle of Manhattan. Williamsburg experienced an economic book in the 19th century, which thousands of tourists from all over the nation and world visiting the city to shop on it's famous Broadway strip, at the end of which stood the ferry to Manhattan.

The next stage of development for Williamsburg occurred in 1903, with the opening of the Williamsburg Bridge. This allowed for many immigrants who had previously been living in Manhattan's Lower East Side to move to Brooklyn yet still work in Manhattan. The mass exodus of immigrants to Williamsburg eventually led the city to become, for a time, the most densely populated area in the world. Williamsburg maintained its working class atmosphere until after World War Two, when many Holocaust survivors and Hispanics began to settle in the area. This led to many of the area's former residents, who had been making slow economic strides, to move to other area of Brooklyn or out to Long Island. For a time, Williamsburg was plagued with crime and massive amounts of drug use.

This all changed in the 1980s, when artists from SoHo moved into the area in order to flee rising rents and still have easy access to the city, with Williamsburg being only one subway stop away from Manhattan. Although the community was initially very small, consisting of several hundred young artists, by the late 1990s Williamsburg was home to roughly 3,000 of the next-generation's visionaries and spokespeople. In 1996, Yuko Nii, a Williamsburg artist, founded the Williamsburg Art and Historical Center (WAH), whose mission was to support all of Williamsburg's diverse artistic communities. As the WAH began to gain national and international recognition, more artists began moving into what was quickly becoming Manhattan's new heart of art.

By 2005, Williamsburg was home to over 70 art galleries, many upscale restaurants, bars, nightclubs, and even a museum. The area is still growing, making it worthwhile for any New Yorker with a day to spare to make the trip to Brooklyn and experience a taste of artistic New York.

hotels

Whether you're looking for a world-class hotel or a budget room, New York has it all. The city boasts more hotel rooms than almost any other in the world. That doesn't, however much it may seem to, make finding an affordable hotel in New York an easy task. While in Midtown and the Financial District hotels seem a dime a dozen, outside these districts lodgings are significantly harder to come by, and no matter where you are New York City hotels will milk you for all you're worth. The government also gets in on the action by levying a hefty "hotel occupancy tax" of 13.25%, making an under-$200-a-night deal a bargain. If you foresee a trip to the city during tourist season – December or January – book well in advance since rooms are generally more expensive and tend to go quickly.

Luxury ($400-$700+)

Four Seasons Hotel

Don't let the promenade up from the lobby to the reception desk intimidate you, and forget all those models and celebrities milling about the lobby bar. If you've got the funds to sign on as a guest, the service is warm and welcoming. You could fit several average New Yorkers' apartments into the coolly elegant rooms with impressive cityscape views to boot. Everything here is ultra sophisticated, down to the Magrittes and Kandinskys distributed liberally throughout.
57 E. 57th St. (bet. Madison and Park Aves.), (212) 758-5700. Rooms start at $500, MC, V, AmEx, DC, N R W 4 5 6 *to 59th St. For more information, visit: www.fourseasons.com.*

The Fitzpatrick Manhattan Hotel

Guests are promised a real "Irish Welcome." Steeped in luxury and charm, The Fitzpatrick is located on the Upper East Side blocks from the Museum of Modern Art, the Chrysler Building, and the best Fifth Avenue shops and boutiques. Guests can enjoy a frosty Guinness at the hotel's very own Irish pub, The Fitzer. In Manhattan, this old world charm is hard to find and hard to beat.
687 Lexington Ave. (bet. 56th & 57th Sts.), (212) 355-0100. Rooms start at $400, MC, V, AmEx, D, DC, N R W *to 59th St. For more information, visit: www.fitzpatrickhotels. com.*

Rihga Royal Hotel

The Rihga Royal rises 54 stories above the heart of Midtown, moments from New York's premier business and shopping districts, Central Park, and Carnegie Hall. Guests have 24-hour access to state-of-the-art business and fitness centers, in addition to in-suite dining from the hotel's highly acclaimed restaurant, The Halcyon. As a Marriott sponsored Hotel, the Rihga Royal also offers AAA, senior, corporate, and Marriott Rewards discounts.

151 West 54th St. (bet. 6th and 7th Aves.), (212) 307-5000. Rooms start at $250 spring/ summer, $400 winter/ peak times. MC, V, AmEx, D, DC, N R W *to 57th St.-7th Ave, or the* F *to 57th St. For more information, visit: www.rihgaroyalny.com.*

Upper End ($300-$400)

Peninsula Hotel

A neophyte in the parade of luxury properties along the spine of upper Fifth Avenue, the Peninsula was born with a silver spoon in its mouth – namely, its million-dollar location. Great views abound from the Pen-Top, the hotel's renowned rooftop bar. The Peninsula is classy, and the well-heeled visitors who stay here will attest to that.
700 Fifth Ave. (at 55th St.), (212) 956-2888. Rooms start at $390, MC, V, AmEx, D, F E V *to 53rd St. For more information, visit: www.peninsula.com/ index.html.*

SoHo Grand Hotel

Currently the hottest hotel in New York, this newcomer is the first hotel in SoHo. Everything is in sync with the neighborhood: artsy, avant-garde types walk through the cutting-edge industrial lobby to their digs. You can even request a black goldfish to accompany you during your stay. In keeping with the cyber-sexy image, you can make reservations on their website.

310 West Broadway (at Canal St.), (212) 965-3000. Rooms start at $250, MC, V, AmEx, D, DC, A C E 1 to Canal St. For more information, visit: www.sohogrand.com.

UN Plaza-Millennium Hotel

Often overlooked by tourists, this pleasant Hyatt outpost is a good bet in East Midtown. Directly across from the United Nations and the East River, all of the rooms have incredible views. The mood, evoked by an abundance of mirrors and marquee lights, is a bit subdued. Don't be surprised to be rooming next to the Ambassador of Uzbekistan and his entourage. Patrons are often guests of the United Nations.

1 UN Plaza 43rd St. (bet. First and Second Aves.), (212) 758-1234. Rooms start at $225, MC, V, AmEx, D, S 4 5 6 7 to 42nd St.-Grand Central.

Mid-Range ($100-$200)

Beacon Hotel

With guestrooms larger than some of the other hotels on the Upper West Side, one-bedroom suites, and singles or doubles to offer, the Hotel Beacon offers relaxation and comfort close to great architecture and landmarks. The hotel is steps away from Lincoln Center, Central Park, the Museum of Natural History, and the Beacon Theater, which is just below. They also have a health club if walking the streets of New York isn't enough of a workout for you.

2130 Broadway (at 75th St.), (212) 787-1100. Rooms start at $180, MC, V, AmEx, D, DC. 1 to 79th St. For information, visit: www.beaconhotel.com.

Gramercy Park Hotel

This pre-war established outpost on Gramercy Park also attracts a largely pre-war clientele. Charm abounds here, and the neighborhood is an interesting one to explore, but, far more importantly, visitors here will be the secret envy of every New Yorker. The hotel holds a coveted key to private Gramercy Park, a privilege for which many neighborhood residents would kill.

2 Lexington Ave. (at Gramercy Park, 21st St.), (212) 475-4320. Rooms start at $145, MC, V, AmEx, D, DC, 6 to 23rd St. For more information, visit: www.gramercyparkhotel.com.

Marriott Marquis Hotel

Look for the garish yellow Hertz billboard and you won't miss this Times Square staple for theater-bound tourists and other visitors who equate flashiness with luxury. With 2,000 rooms, a revolving rooftop restaurant, an ultra-glitzy lobby, and its own Broadway theater, the Marquis dispenses with the need to even leave the premises for a taste of overwrought glamour.

1535 Broadway (at 45th St.), (212) 398-1900. Rooms start at $200, MC, V, AmEx, A C E N R S W 1 2 3 7 to 42nd St.-Times Sq. For more information, visit: www.nymarriottmarquis.com.

Paramount Hotel

Cheap by New York standards, this snazzy hotel offers reasonable prices for well-appointed rooms, trendy clientele, and smart chic. Designed by master hotelier Phillipe Starck, everything here is too cool: the lobby decor looks like Dr. Seuss himself moonlighted as the interior decorator, while bathrooms have funky, pyramid-shaped aluminum sinks. Expect showbiz types (guests of "Saturday Night Live" stay here) who don't mind being shoehorned into microscopic rooms.

235 West 46th St. (bet. Broadway and Eighth Ave.), (212) 764-5500. Rooms start at $145, MC, V, AmEx, D, DC, A C E N R S W 1 2 3 7 to 42nd St.-

Times Sq. For more information, visit: www.paramount-hotel.net 411.com.

Union Theological Seminary's Landmark Guest Rooms

These uptown guestrooms are sublimely nestled into the walls of the Seminary, which is listed in the National Register of Historic Places. The interesting Gothic-style accommodations offer private baths, cable televisions and complimentary continental breakfasts (on weekdays only) for all rooms. If the hustle and bustle of New York City wears you down, the idyllic garden next door is perfect for rest and relaxation.

3041 Broadway (at 121st St.), (212) 280-1313. Rooms start at $130, MC, V, AmEx. ❶ to 125th St.

BUDGET (UNDER $100)

Big Apple Hostel

This near luxury hostel offers amenities such as guest Internet services, luggage storage, and security lockers. The hostile is also conveniently located in Midtown Manhattan, blocks from the subway, Greyhound, Amtrak, and airport buses,. This is an ideal option for students and international travelers.

119 West 45thSt., (212) 302-2603. Dormitory style rooms start around $30, private rooms $80. Prices may vary. MC, V. Ⓐ Ⓒ Ⓔ Ⓝ Ⓡ Ⓢ Ⓦ ❶ ❷ ❼ to 42nd St.-Times Square. For more information, visit: www.big applehostel. com.

The De Hirsch Residence

Dormitory style residence hall where one can stay by the day (minimum 3-day stay), or apply to stay by the month for up to one year. The activities available at the 92nd St. Y are open to De Hirsch residents.

1395 Lexington Ave. (at the 92nd St. YMCA), (212) 415-5650. Rooms are $35/doubles (per person), $49/singles, ❻ to 96th St. For more information, visit: www.dehirsch.com.

Herald Square Hotel

Voted one of Maxim's "Best Hotels in NYC Under $100." You can get a small room with a shared bathroom for just $50 a day, and if you want a private shower, add an extra $25.

19 West 31st St. (bet. Broadway and Fifth Ave.), (212) 279-4017. Rooms start at $55, MC, V, AmEx, D, Ⓐ Ⓒ Ⓔ ❶ ❷ ❸ to 34th St.-Penn Station. For more information, visit: www.heraldsquarehotel.com.

New York International House

Visitors can stay in large ten-to-twelve-person bedrooms, and Members get a better deal. Maximum stay is one week.

891 Amsterdam Ave. (at 103rd St.), (212) 932-2300. Rooms are $27/$24 (members), MC, V, ❶ to 103rd St. For more information, visit: www.ihouse-nyc.org.

Pickwick Arms Hotel

No frills, but it's often the best bet for savvy budget travelers who appreciate the warm lobby and the safe neighborhood and don't mind the forgettable rooms. The rooftop garden overlooking the skyscrapers makes this place a bargain.

230 East 51st Street (bet. Second and Third Aves.), (212) 355-0300. Rooms start at $60, MC, V, AmEx, Ⓔ Ⓥ ❻ to Lexington-51st St. For more information, visit: www.pickwickarms.com.

CORPORATE HOUSING; EXTENDED STAY HOTELS

Manhattan offers extended stay hotels catering to the needs of the weary business traveler. Most of these hotels come equipped with conference and meeting rooms, suite-style accommodations, and spa services. A partial listing:

Affina Suites, Plaza Fifty
155 E. 50th St., (bet. Lexington and Third Aves.)
(212) 751-5710

Churchill Corporate Housing
New York City Sales Office
245 West 17th St,
(800) 658-7366

Oakwood Worldwide
6 East 45th St., Suite 1301
(212) 682-9550 or (800) 592-1088

Best Western City View Inn
33-17 Greenpoint Ave.,
Queens,
(718) 392-8400

Econo Lodge
1000 Baychester Ave, Bronx,
(718) 862-2000

Central Park

Central Park is the ultimate New York celebrity, having appeared in over 170 Hollywood movies and countless wedding videos. On a sunny day the fields and paths are full of sunbathers, runners, mothers with children, amateur athletes, and picnickers burdened with coolers and blankets. What's best? Admission is always free, and the park can accommodate anyone and everyone.

Central Park was originally planned to be a verdant oasis amidst the concrete buildings of New York, and its purpose has remained the same up to the present. The magnificent park, designed by 19th century architect extraordinaire Frederick Law Olmstead, replaced 843 acres of lower-class homes with carefully sculpted wilderness.

One of the best ways to become acquainted with Olmstead's masterpiece is by taking one of the free walking tours provided by the Central Park Conservancy (T-Sa, (212) 360-2726). These beautiful strolls offer both historical and ecological perspectives of this landmark. The North Meadow Recreation Center offers a wide array of activities for the youth of New York (mid park at 97th St., (212) 348-4867). Here you will find adventure and fitness programs ranging from rock climbing to classes in tai chi, as well as the opportunity to rent sporting equipment.

Others opt to experience Central Park the romantic way. Visitors can tour the park in horse-drawn carriages in the summer and winter months. Carriages line up at Central Park South (59th St.) between Fifth and Sixth Aves., across from the Plaza Hotel. Rides cost $34 for the first 20 minutes and $54 for a 45 to 50 minute tour ((212) 246-0520).

Central Park is also one of New York's cultural centers and during the summer months you can attend performances by such prestigious organizations as the Metropolitan Opera and Lincoln Center Jazz Orchestra. Also, make sure to check out performances of Shakespeare in the Park. Watch celebrities like Patrick Stewart, Liev Schreiber, and Julia Stiles perform one of the Bard's great masterpieces. The event is free, but get your tickets early. Shakespeare in the Park is a New York favorite.

Families often take advantage of the upper park's Charles A. Dana Discovery Center. It hosts art shows and community activities, including catch-and-release fishing at the lake (*Discovery Center, T -Su, 10am-5pm. Catch-and-Release Fishing, April to October, T -Su, 10am-4pm, (212) 860-1370*).

Garden lovers should enter the park at Fifth Ave. and 105th St. to explore the Conservatory Garden, Central Park's only formal garden. The six acres of vegetation are arranged in English, Italian, and French styles, perfect for an afternoon jaunt.

There is always something happening in Central Park, from classical concert series to impromptu break-dancing performances. The park allows for New Yorkers to take a break and escape the hustle and bustle of city life. Even when little is going on, a carefree walk among the trees is an excellent antidote to the daily nuisances provided by New York City.

Central Park spans from 59th to 110th Sts. bet. Fifth Ave. and Central Park West. For more information, call (212) 310-6600 or visit: www.centralparknyc.org.

Battery Park

Stretching from State Street to the New York harbor, this park provides picnic-perfect promenades. The park has been completely renovated since Sept. 11. Misty breezes from the Atlantic Ocean, the East River, and the Hudson River combine to add the final refreshing touch to an amazing view of the lower Manhattan skyline. New York offers itself to you with panoramic visions of Governors Island, Staten Island, the Statue of Liberty, Ellis Island and the intricate span of the Verrazano Narrows Bridge.

1 to South Ferry. For more information, visit: www.batterypark city.org.

Bryant Park

Bryant Park is the scenic backyard of the New York Public Library.

During the day visitors enjoy well-manicured lawns with tables and chairs, and lounge on benches in the shade while simultaneously reading newly borrowed books. The park is the home of the Summer Film Festival, where audiences enjoy reclining on the grass and watching free classic movies every Monday evening. Bryant Park is a great romantic oasis in the heart of the city.

42nd St. bet 5th and 6th Aves., B D F V to 42nd St.-5th Ave. For more information, visit: www.bryantpark.org.

Fort Tryon Park and The Cloisters Museum

Fort Tryon boasts lush, grassy lawns, landscaped terraces, footpaths, and flower gardens for the emotionally-spent city dweller. The Cloisters, a subsidiary of the Metropolitan Museum of Art, is also located here. It is the premier museum of medieval art in New York, and it is known for its collections of tapestries, illuminated manuscripts, stained glass, and precious metal work. Bask in culture as you relax on a sun-drenched hill south of the museum. At the end of the day, watch a romantic sunset with your sweetheart and enjoy the superb views of the towering Palisades across the Hudson River.

Fort Tryon Park, (212) 923-3700, T-Su 9:30am-4:45pm. A to 190th St. or M4 bus to Fort Tryon Park-the Cloisters. For more information, visit: www.met museum.org.

Prospect Park

Prospect Park, Olmstead's other masterpiece, is located in downtown Brooklyn and holds a 60-acre lake and the only forest in the borough. Visitors can also attend the country's first urban Audubon Center or visit the Prospect Park Zoo or Brooklyn Botanical Gardens before heading over to the Celebrate Brooklyn! Performing Arts Festival in the summer months. With a trolley to get around, there is no excuse for missing any one of this park's 526 acres: just be careful after dark.

Fenced in Prospect Park West, Prospect Park Southwest, Parkside Ave. and Washington Ave. F to Seventh Ave., 2 3 to Grand Army Plaza, Q S to Prospect Park Station. For more information, call (718) 965-8900 or visit: http://www.prospect-park.org.

Riverside Park

A favorite of runners, Riverside Park stretches for 83 blocks along the Hudson River, a strip that is over four miles long. Riverside is a community-minded park that offers its constituents many perks. Residents enjoy a number of athletic courts (volleyball, basketball, and a baseball diamond), a dog park, and a gracious expanse of shoreline (from 147th to 152nd Sts.). The park is also a favorite hang out for Upper West Siders and Columbia University students alike. Be sure to look out for celebrities like Conan O'Brien and Sarah Jessica Parker bonding with their dogs,

72nd to 155th Sts. west of Riverside Dr., (212) 870-3070. For more information, visit: www. nycgovparks.org.

Washington Square Park

Known more for voyeuristic spectacle than quiet seclusion, this park showcases Greenwich Village's energy. Street musicians, acrobats, NYU students, flame swallowers, chess players, and break-dancers, fill this park.

The visual centerpiece is the big Arch designed by Stanford White, which marks the 100-year anniversary of George Washington coming to New York. In the northwest corner, the notorious Hanging Elm stands as a reminder of the public executions that happened in the early 1800s. Still, the eerie history does not deter picnickers from filling the grass at all hours of the day.

Fenced by Waverly Pl., W. 4th St., MacDougal St., and University Pl. A C E B F S V to W. 4th St. For more information, visit: www. washingtonsquarepark. org.

beaches

Jones Beach

A stone's throw from the rooftops of Manhattan, this beach is the perfect destination for any and all yearning for sun, sand, and relaxation. Over six miles of beachfront on the Atlantic Ocean and two pools are the most popular attractions at this Robert Moses-designed superstructure. Comprised of eight separate zones, the beach has enough room for everyone to spread out and rid themselves of pasty winter skin. Visit www.lirr.org.

Cape May

A slice of Victorian life on the shore of New Jersey, Cape May is the Promised Land for every Bed and Breakfast lover. The architecture of the area is famous for its beautiful and historic Victorian houses, many of which are designated landmarks. The residents socialize in private tennis, yacht, and beach clubs, but even visitors who pay admission partake in some of this community feel. The beaches are open to the public, although getting in is not cheap. Even the boatless visitor can enjoy deep-sea fishing expeditions hosted by the South Jersey Fishing Center. Cape May is accessible by New Jersey Transit. For more information, call (800) 626-7433 or visit www.capemay-times.com.

The Hamptons

The stomping ground of the elite and affected of New York society who celebrate their enormous wealth with exclusive parties at country clubs and multimillion-dollar beach homes. The Hampton beaches offer something for the multimillionaire in all of us. A day of sunning on Gibson Beach in Sagaponack may provide surprising celebrity sightings (Martha Stewart and P. Diddy are Hamptons buddies – perhaps they bonded over their legal woes?), as well as freedom – tops are not required. Indian Wells Beach in nearby Magansett is slightly less ostentatious; it is a family-oriented environment, much like East Hampton's main beach, which also happens to be the best viewpoint for nightly fireworks. After dark, visitors crowd the hip clubs that dot the area and give the wealthy an opportunity to rub elbows with tourists and natives, or, depending on their mood, run them over in an SUV. Either way, the Hamptons are an exciting destination for those who can afford the price of a summer share and stand the pretension. For more information, call (516) 822-LIRR, or visit www.hamptons.com, or www.mta.info/lirr for Long Island Railroad information, (800) 936-0440 or www.hamptonjitney.com for Hampton Jitney information.

Sandy Hook

Since the ten beach sections of Sandy Hook stretch over several miles of widely spaced roadways, navigating can be limited without wheels. As a barrier peninsula, this New Jersey beach is visually stunning. For the active, daring bunch, whip out the windsurfing gear. After an exhausting wipeout, sample refreshing drinks and relish the ambiance at the full-service concession stand and bar within a mile and a half of the beach's entrance. Also legendary is the clothing-optional stretch of beach located in area G. *Highlands, NJ. Academy Bus Line from Port Authority to Highlands Bridge. $12.75 round-trip. For information, call (609) 777-0885.*

Shelter Island

An alternative to the overpriced and overcrowded Hamptons, this hilly island possesses an unpretentious charm. One must get to Shelter Island, which is nestled between Long Island's North and South forks, by ferry. Once there, a great way to discover the area is by participating in a kayak tour. Most visitors then settle into either Crescent or Wades Beach, both of which offer comfort stations and lifeguard stands. The calm Peconic Bay offers fine swimming, sailing, and windsurfing opportunities for the athletic, while nature lovers can head off to the unsullied third of the island encompassed by Mashomack Preserve. Here, the ten miles of coastline, tidal creeks, and woodlands are homes to many types of indigenous animals, and tourists can have just as much fun as the residents.

Travel is available by North Ferry, South Ferry, and the Cross Sound Ferry. For more information, call (631) 749-0139 or (631) 749-1200 or visit www.shelter-island.org. For Mashomack Preserve, open W-M 9am-5pm, call (631) 749-1001.

Rockaway Beach

The subject of a famous song by The Ramones, Rockaway Beach has everything a beach-lover could possibly want: flat and clean sands, a beautiful boardwalk, and a diverse and friendly local population. Visitors can either take a stroll or ride a bike on a boardwalk which runs for several miles along the coast before stopping at Beach 116th St. for a quick bite or a drink at one of several local pubs. Adventurous visitors can walk all the way up to the federal beach, which begins on 149th St. and watch (or most likely gawk) at the naked sunbathers and swimmers walking around without a care in the world. Surrounding the beaches are many handball, paddleball and basketball courts, which will undoubtedly be used from nine in the morning until eight at night. There are also several baseball fields waiting to be used by anyone with a bat and glove.

Rockaway is a great place to come if you're looking for a beach that will probably not be as crowded as other New York area beaches. The local residents rely on DFDs (Down for the Dayers) for economic support, and would make your stay in Rockaway the most pleasant it could possibly be. Spending a day at Rockaway Beach is a great and cheap way to improve one's summer malaise. Though it is no longer in its 30s heyday, Rockaway Beach provides a relaxing weekend alternative to the hustle and bustle of Manhattan. Be sure to stop by Papa's Pizza on 129th for a thin-curst delight.

(A) to Broad Channel, transfer to the (S) to 116th St., (2)(5) to Flatbush Ave.-Brooklyn Col-lege, transfer to Q35 bus on Flatbush Ave. Take Q35 until any stop you want to get off in Rockaway (149th St. or 131st St. are suggested).

Alternative Paradise: Brighton Beach and Coney Island

Though these beaches are not picturesque sand and surf, their littered urban stretches are nonetheless appealing. Brighton Beach is sometimes called "Little Odessa" because its residents are largely immigrants from the former U.S.S.R, creating an ambiance that is distinctly Eastern European.

Across the pier is Astroland, home of the famous Coney Island Cyclone. As one of the country's oldest wooden roller coasters, the Cyclone is a must ride for any coaster enthusiast. It was named a New York City Landmark in 1988, and has been giving exhilarating and bumpy rides for over 70 years.

Each year in mid-June, residents and tourists alike enjoy the glittering Mermaid Parade, an event that pays homage to Coney Island's forgotten Mardi Gras, which ran from 1903 to 1954. Participants flaunt exotic, handmade costumes and don't be surprised to find scantily clad mermaids, and other characters roving the streets.

Also check out the Coney Island Museum. It displays memorabilia from the merry-go-rounds and freak shows of yesteryear. The nearby Nathan's Famous – the first Nathan's in the world - is also a treat. It celebrates the local invention of the American dietary staple with its July Fourth hotdog-eating contests.

208 Surf Ave. Open Memorial Day to Labor day, (D)(F)(Q) to Coney Island-Stillwell Ave. For information, visit www.coneyislandusa.com.

getaways

Long Island

Although two of New York's five boroughs are technically a part of Long Island (Brooklyn and Queens), very few city dwellers ever explore New York's monument to capitalism, and also the largest island in the contiguous 48 states. Unbeknownst to many, Long Island is much more than Billy Joel and F. Scott Fitzgerald's home, the Miracle Mile and the Long Island Sound.

At the eastern tip of Long Island lies Montauk. Not just a stunning seaside community, Montauk offers a variety of recreational activities - everything from mountain biking to walking the beach. With numerous trails traveling through forests, grasslands, and sand dunes, mountain bikers will be more than satisfied with the varied terrain available. It's easy to rent a bike, so don't worry if you didn't bring one along. Para-sailing is also offered, and from hundreds of feet up in the air, the view of the surrounding landscape is beautiful.

Long Island Railroad, Montauk Line. For more information, visit: www.montauklife.com or www. lirr.org.

"The Island," as it is often called for short, is also home to numerous parks. Fire Island National Seashore, measuring 32 miles long, is an ideal location for fishing; striped bass, bluefish, and flounder populate the waters, and they are an excellent source of prey for anglers. Eisenhower Park in Nassau County is another "Strong" Island park worth checking out. With three 18-hole golf courses, jogging paths, a variety of athletic fields, and a lakeside theater with free summer concerts, Eisenhower Park is a great destination for any day trip.

For more information on Fire Island, visit www.nps.gov/fiis/ index.htm. For more information on Eisenhower Park, call (516) 572-0348.

New Jersey and Pennsylvania

With casinos, outdoor recreation, and mountain and resort accommodations, neither New Jersey nor Pennsylvania should be overlooked as getaway destinations, even for hard-core New Yorkers. In New Jersey, or Dirty Jerz as it is affectionately called by residents, one can either take in the decadence of Atlantic City or the opulence of Teaneck and the Jersey Shore. The casinos of Atlantic City are a siren's call to any New Yorker looking to beat the odds and strike it rich. With routine bus service from the Port Authority Bus Terminal, getting there is not a problem. In fact, most bus fares wind up being free because casinos give you free chips upon your arrival. Outside of casinos, Atlantic City is home to New Jersey's tallest lighthouse, five local museums, and the Atlantic Boardwalk Hall, which hosts a variety of sporting events and concerts. From North to South, New Jersey can't be beat. For more information, visit: www.atlanticcitynj.com.

Furthermore, Philadelphia – "illadelph" to those in the know – is a great place to get in tough with your country's history as well as a very-different-than-New-York type of town. Check out the Liberty Bell by day before going clubbing at night.

Less then a two-hour drive away from the shadowed streets of New York City stand Pennsylvania's Pocono Mountains, where one can spend a weekend at Malibu Ranch and travel the countryside on horseback. Explore the local wilderness, but keep a careful watch for the rich fauna – bears have been known to inhabit the area. For a more relaxing, stress-relieving time, visit one of the Pocono's many resorts. Play a round of golf, ski, get a massage, or fall asleep in a whirlpool bath. The Poconos are located in northeastern Penn-sylvania and can be reached via I-84 or I-80. Visit a roadside visitor center or www. poconovacations.com for more information.

Upstate New York

The Appalachian Trail is one of the most famous hiking trails in the country. About 90 miles of this trail, which makes its way through 14 states, are in New York. This hiking hotspot is closer to New York City than many think - one section of the trail is easily reached by taking a Metro North train to the Appalachian Trail stop off the Wassaic line. Once on the trail, follow the path for as little or as long as you like. Experience the serene natural lakes and streams and enjoy the absence of any noisy sirens and car horns.

The Delaware River, besides marking the border between New York, New Jersey, and Pennsylvania, offers great opportunities for rafting and canoeing. Kittatinny Canoes will supply a raft, canoe, or kayak, depending on your preference. Paddle your chosen vessel down the Delaware or just swim blissfully in the clean water. There are trips of varying lengths and difficulty offered, so don't worry if you are a novice. As one river ranger was heard to remark, "Hello, I'm on the Delaware River."
For more information on Kittatinny Canoes, call (800) FLOAT-KC or visit www.kittatinny.com/index.htm.

Located on the eastern shore of the Hudson River, the small town of Hyde Park is home to the Vanderbilt Mansion, one of this prestigious family's luxurious homes. Built over a century ago, the mansion is a stunning display of opulence and grandeur. Some have even described it as being "opulently grand."
For more information, call (845) 229-9115 or visit www.nps.gov/vama/ home.htm.

Saratoga Springs is a legendary resort town. Located just north of Albany, Saratoga Springs is famous for its healing mineral springs. It's also the site of America's oldest and most beautiful racetracks. The racing season attracts bluebloods and tourists alike, as does the summer entertainment. From June until August, the Saratoga Performing Arts Center has something going on almost every night. Saratoga State Park has two beautiful golf courses, four swimming pools, a dozen picnic areas and several tennis courts. Reserve a spot at the Roosevelt and Lincoln Bathhouses ((518) 584-2011) well in advance and enjoy the fizzy mineral baths and massages that made the town famous. Take Amtrak (from Penn Station) or Greyhound (from Port Authority) to Saratoga.

Some miles away from Saratoga Springs is Albany, the state capital. Visit in the fall and enjoy the foliage. Albany is the home of the New York State Museum, which chronicles the development of New York State and its cities. There are, among other things, full-size replicas of Manhattan stores, buses and government offices. The Museum is housed in a 98-acre complex in the heart of downtown Albany known as Empire State Plaza, which was a gift from the late Governor Nelson Rockefeller. There is an art collection and a 42nd-floor observation deck, along with an enormous assortment of stores. Visit the Albany Urban Cultural Park Visitor's Center to learn more about the city and its unique history. Take Amtrak to Albany. The tracks run along the Hudson River, so it's bound to be a scenic trip.

Skiing/Snowboarding

New York City's winters, with it's slushy sidewalks, dirty snow, and windy streets, can wear even the toughest Manhattanite down. Instead of cursing the short days and cold nights, enjoy the clean, crisp air at one of New York's nearby ski areas. Quality mountains with service for beginners and experts alike are located within just a few hours of the city. For those skiers looking for a full day of fresh, exciting skiing, try Hunter Mountain. Hunter, nestled among the Catskill Mountains, is less than a three hour drive from Manhattan. With three mountains (one entirely black and double-black diamonds), 52 trails, and 11 lifts, Hunter has plenty to keep skiers of all levels entertained. Don't have a car? A number of bus lines make routine trips to the mountain. Taking a ski trip is a great way to be alone for a day or two. As Manowar remarked, "like a man is a mountain side, greatness waits for those who try."
For more information, call (888) HUNTERMTN or visit www.huntermtn.com.

If two and a half hours sounds a little too far away, Mountain Creek in Vernon, New Jersey is only 47 miles from Manhattan. Featuring over 40 trails and a host of terrain parks, Mountain Creek is another alternative for those who want to ski or snowboard in New York.
For more information, call (973) 827-2000 or visit: www.mountaincreek.com.

For a more relaxing outdoor experience, cross-country skiing and snowshoeing is available at High Point Mountain in Sussex, New Jersey. With 15 kilometers of trails and great views all around, High Point offers perfect serenity in a winter wonderland.
For more information, call (973) 702-1222 or visit: www.xcski-highpoint.com/index. html.

Looking for camaraderie? Check out Diamond Dogs, a NYC skiing/snowboarding social club. Members are between the ages of 25-45, single, and live throughout New York, New Jersey, and Connecticut. Membership gets you happy hours, day and extended trips, and popular discounts. For information check out: www.ski-nyc.com.

Baseball

There's no better place than New York City to explore the great American (although initially French) pastime. Fans of Major League Baseball teams can head to Shea Stadium and see the Amazin' Mets in Flushing, Queens or take the uptown trek to Yankee Stadium and see the Bronx Bombers. Purchase seats in advance online (www.ticketmaster.com), or simply show up to claim some of the tickets reserved for game day sales. Just make certain you are calling out the correct team's name when in the bleacher seats, or things might turn ugly. Newcomers be warned: New Yorkers take their sports teams very seriously and showing up in a rival's paraphernalia is a risk that may not be worth taking.

If you want to catch some great ballplayers who don't spend as much time on the sets of commercials as they do in training, head for the state-of-the-art ballparks of New York's two minor league teams. The Brooklyn Cyclones, a class A affiliate of the Mets, play in Coney Island's KeySpan Park. KeySpan is a beautiful ballpark with the capacity for 8,000 cheering fans, and the Cyclones love to meet and greet every one of them. Arrive early to take advantage of the open autograph sessions because the young men behind those scribbles may be battling in a World Series some day soon, games also tend to sell out quickly. After the game, hang around the area and enjoy Coney Island's amusement park, and relive it's glory days of the 1920s and 1930s. The players on the Yankees' developmental squad, the Staten Island Yankees, also have hopes for October greatness. Their home base is the Richmond County Bank Ballpark (RCBK) at St. George, where fans fill up the 7,000 seats, including 18 luxury suites with good old Yankee hospitality. Go and cheer those who hope to play for America's premier baseball team.

Football

For the avid professional sports fan, there are few venues as exciting as the Meadowlands in East Rutherford, New Jersey. Home to two professional football teams, a professional basketball team, a professional soccer team, and a professional hockey team (as well as the site of myriad other sporting events and concerts), this enormous complex is one of the most recognizable locations in the sporting world. With Continental Airlines Arena, the Meadowlands boasts one of the East Coast's best basketball/hockey arenas, while the legendary Giants Stadium sells out every single football game (for both the Giants and the Jets). Tailgaters come from hundreds of miles around for pre-game festivities, but don't make the trek unless you already have tickets - Jets games are sold out for the next twenty years. Maybe you can befriend Fireman Eddie and get yourself a ticket. For more information on the Jets, visit: www.newyorkjets.com.

Basketball and Hockey

The world's most famous sports arena, Madison Square Garden, is home to the Knicks and Rangers, and they split time drawing huge (or formerly huge) crowds to every game. Though nothing used to sell out quicker than Knicks vs. Bulls games, there are a few other great rivalries - get tickets for whenever the Islanders trek into the city from Nassau County. Though tickets to both Knicks and Rangers games are costly, they are worth the cost; don't buy the cheap seats - you might as well watch the game from the comfort of your own home. To catch a glimpse of a celebrity, hang out at the press entrance outside MSG directly after the game; that is where famous fans (including Spike Lee, who was once kicked out of a game for causing too much trouble) leave from. For more information on the Knicks, visit: www.nba.com/knicks/. For more information on the Rangers, visit: www.newyork rangers.com.

[Professional] [Sports Teams]

Baseball

New York Metropolitans
Shea Stadium
123-01 Roosevelt Ave. in Flushing, Queens
7 to Willets Pt.-Shea Stadium
For more information, call (718) 507-METS or visit www.mets.mlb.com.

New York Yankees
Yankee Stadium
161st St. and River Ave. in the Bronx
B D 4 to 161st St.-Yankee Stadium
For more information, call (718) 293-6000 or visit www.yankees.mlb.com.

Brooklyn Cyclones
KeySpan Park
904 Surf Ave. in Brooklyn
D F to Stillwell Ave.-Coney Island Station or B36, B64, B74 bus to Stillwell Ave.
For more information, call (718) 449-8497 or visit www.brooklyncyclones.net.

Staten Island Yankees
Richmond Community Bank Ballpark
75 Richmond Terrace
1 to South Ferry or N R W to Whitehall St., 4 5 to Bowling Green. For more information, call (718) 720-9200, or visit www.siyanks.com

Football

New York Giants
Giants Stadium
50 Rte. 120 in East Rutherford, New Jersey
A C E N R S W 1 2 3 7 to 42nd St.-Times Sq., Port Authority Special Events Buses leave for Stadium beginning 2 hours before game time.
For more information, call (201) 935-8222 or visit www.giants.com

New York Jets
Giants Stadium
50 Rte. 120 in East Rutherford, NJ
A C E to 42nd St.-Port Authority, N R S W 1 2 3 7 to 42nd St.-Times Sq., Port Authority Special Events Buses leave for Stadium beginning two hours before game time.
For more information, call (516) 560- 8200 or visit www.newyorkjets.com

Basketball

New York Knickerbockers
Madison Square Garden
Seventh Ave. bet. 31st and 33rd Sts.
A C E 1 2 3 to 34th St.-Penn Station
For more information, call (212) 465-6073 or visit www.knicks.com

New Jersey Nets
Continental Airlines Arena
50 Rte. 120 in East Rutherford, New Jersey
A C E to 42nd St.-Port Authority, N R S W 1 2 3 7 to 42nd St.-Times Sq.
Port Authority Special Events Buses leave for Arena beginning two hours before game time
For more information, call (800) 7NJ-NETS or visit www.njnets.com

New York Liberty
Madison Square Garden
Seventh Ave. bet. 31st and 33rd Sts.
A C E 1 2 3 to 34th St.-Penn Station
For more information, call (212) 564-WNBA or visit www.nyliberty.com

Hockey

New York Islanders
Nassau Coliseum
1255 Hempstead Tpke. in Uniondale
For more information, call (800) 882-ISLES or visit www.newyorkislanders.com
LIRR to Hempstead Station, N70, N71, N72 bus from train station.

New York Rangers
Madison Square Garden
Seventh Ave. bet. 31st and 33rd Sts.
A C E 1 2 3 to 34th St.-Penn Station
For more information, call (212) 465-6073 or visit www.nyrangers.com

Soccer

New York/New Jersey Metrostars
Giants Stadium
50 Rte. 120 in East Rutherford, New Jersey
For more information, call (201) 507-8900 or visit www.metrostars.com
A C E to 42nd St.-Port Authority, N R S W 1 2 3 7 to 42nd St.-Times Sq., Port Authority Special Events Buses leave for Stadium beginning two hours before game time. For more information, visit: www.mta.info/lirr

New York Power
Mitchel Athletic Complex
1 Charles Lindbergh Blvd. in Uniondale
LIRR to Mineola Station, shuttle available from station to Complex. For more information, call (866) POWR-TIX or visit www.nypower.com

Flushing's Finest vs. The Bronx Bombers:

A History of the Mets-Yankees Rivalry

When the Brooklyn Dodgers left New York after the 1957 baseball season, Brooklynites and Queens-ites wept. Who were they to support against the hated New York Yankees now? No self-respecting Dodgers fan would ever support a team from another city. It was the sad fate of outer borough citizens to wait for five years before a new, anti-Yankee ballclub emerged in Flushing Meadows. The name of this team was the New York Metropolitans, or Mets for short, and it was on April 17th, 1964 that the second great New York baseball rivalry began.

As the years passed, clear divisions developed among citizens of different boroughs. People from the Bronx, Brooklyn, and Westchester came together to become Yankee supporters. Meanwhile, natives of Queens, and most of Long Island banded together under the banner of the Mets. Some unnatural alliances were even created as a result of the rivalry; Mets fans united with Boston Red Sox fans over a shared hatred of the Yankees, though this shaky alliance was ended after the 1986 Mookie Wilson/Bill Buckner incident.

The animosity between the two teams grew over the years, despite the fact that neither had met in the World Series. This changed in 2000, when the Yankees and Mets played the first New York Subway Series since 1956, where the Yankees defeated the Dodgers in 7 games.

This subway series was groundbreaking. Finally Yankee and Met fans could solidify their rivalry on something other than sharing the city of New York. Game one of the series would be no less than historic. The Yankees outlasted the Mets 4-3 in 12 innings; the longest World Series game to date.

Game 2 would be memorable for different reasons. The Yankees' starting pitcher, Roger Clemens, would be facing the Mets best hitter, Mike Piazza. The match-up was eagerly anticipated because of an incident from earlier that season, where Clemens threw a fastball that nailed Piazza in the head, knocking him to the ground. Living up to the hype, Piazza fouled a pitch in the first inning and shattered his bat in the process. A piece of lumber fell near Clemens, who picked up the wood and threw it in the direction of Piazza. Both benches cleared, and the subway series had begun. Clemens seemed unperturbed by the confrontation and blanketed the Mets over 8 innings.

The Mets found themselves in a must-win situation in game 3 and responded accordingly, defeating the Yanks, 4-2. The Yankees countered with another win of their own, beating the Mets 3-2 in game 4.

Game 5 turned into a pitchers duel between the Mets' Al Leiter and the Yanks' Andy Pettite, but the Yankees prevailed and were declared World Series champions.

With 26 World Series victories – the most by any team in MLB history - have the Yankees finally shown New York and the Mets that they are the city's baseball team? Depends on who you ask. Mets fans generally claim that the Yankees buy their wins, citing their generous endowment and grossly overpaid players. When presented with this knowledge, Yanks fans act totally unconcerned – a win is a win, right?

Now, five years later, the Mets are a very good team in their own right, but the Yankees are reminiscent of an All-Star team. It would seem that this disparity in skill between the teams would cause the rivalry to subside. The Yankee's Derek Jeter would agree. "We play them every year now," he said. "The fans still get into it, but I don't think it's like it was." Hopefully in the future the Mets will regain the form they showed in 2000, and return credibility to the rivalry which once was.

Boating

Genteel dreams of whiling away the sunny afternoon in a trim rowboat can be realized in numerous places around New York City.

Manhattan

Loeb Boathouse in Central Park
East Drive (at 74th St.), $10 for the first hour, $2.50 for each additional hour, and a $30 refundable cash deposit, (212) 517-2233, ❶❷❸ to 72nd St.

Bronx

Crotona Lake
East 173rd St. and Crotona Park, (718) 822-4440, ⒷⒹ to 174th-175th Sts.

Cycling

Being a take-out delivery boy is one of the most dangerous – yet glorious! - jobs in Manhattan, and it's easy to understand why. Learning to ride the city streets is no easy task, and those who actually do are considered by many to be leaders of the road. Observing the following precautions will help you to avoid cab drivers, MTA buses, and other hidden dangers:

- Claim space in a lane so as to avoid pedestrians and opening car doors. Many major avenues have bike paths as well, so use them.

- Always ride on the right with traffic. Drivers don't always watch out for obstacles to their left side, which is where you'll be if you are riding against traffic. In fact, the law requires you to do so, and unless you want a ticket, obey the rules.
- Wear a helmet. No question on this one. Looking cool is not worth a brain hemorrhage.
- When on bike paths (like those in Central Park), never hang a U-turn as you may bump into an unwilling pedestrian.
- Take your bike on the subway for free, but don't forget to buy a pass if you're taking it on a commuter train.
- Don't forget to lock up. Approximately 170 bikes are stolen every day off NYC streets, costing New Yorkers more than $20 million a year. If bikes are left unattended, even for just a second, they run the risk of being taken or stripped for parts. If you plan to ride in NYC, invest in a good bike and register your bike with the NYPD.

- Some great places to take your bike:

1) Central Park in Manhattan. For more information and maps of the park, visit: www.centralpark.org.
2) Prospect Park in Brooklyn. For more information and maps of the park, visit: www.prospectpark.org.
3) Riis Park in Queens
4) Pelham Park in the Bronx. For more information on bike trails, visit: www.pedaling.com/searchRides/RideDetails.asp?RouteID=498.

5) The Verrazano Bridge to Staten Island
6) The Marine Parkway Bridge from Brooklyn to Queens
7) The West Side Highway

Cycling Clubs

Five Boroughs Bicycle Club
For more information, visit: www.bikenewyork.org or (212) 932-BIKE

New York Cycle Club
(212) 828-5711

Sundance Outdoor Adventure Society
Outdoor activities for the gay and lesbian communities, (212) 598-4726

Extreme Sports

For New Yorkers weary of running on treadmills, there are innumerable choices for calorie burning that also get the adrenaline pumping. A slight risk may make an otherwise dull day a bit more exciting ...

Rock Climbing

Escape the crowds in the streets by scaling one of the city's many climbing walls. The Extra Vertical Climbing Center inside the Harmony Atrium (Broadway bet. 62nd and 63rd Sts., (212) 586-5718, www.climbnyc.com) is beginner-friendly and has the tallest "outdoor" wall in the city, reaching a height of fifty feet.

Adult day passes are $20, but reduced rates are available for students. For $5, you can also scale a twelve-foot outdoor climbing wall in the middle of Central Park (at 97th St.), but it is only open at limited hours (visit www.centralparknyc.org for information). More experienced climbers should head to the city's most challenging facility at the Sports Center at Chelsea Piers (Pier 63 at 23rd St., (212) 336-6000).

Skating

Release pent-up stress by skating the high-tech course at the Chelsea Piers Roller Rinks, also located at Pier 62 (22nd St., (212) 336-6200, www.chelseapiers.com, C E 1 to 23rd St.). The course includes an "intermediate fun-box" and an "extreme playground." A session costs $10, and full armor is required. Skaters can also head downtown to the free skate park at Piers 26 and 32 (near Canal St.). Further uptown, skaters can whiz alongside the Hudson River at the Riverside Skate Park (108th St. and Riverside Dr., (212-408-0264), 1 to 110th St.). Admission is free and the facility offers a 28-foot-wide 10.5-foot half-pipe and a street course with multiple ramps. Brooklyn residents can skate at the Millennium Skate Park at Owl's Head (Shore Pkwy. at 68th St., www.skatespots.com /ny-owl.html, R to Bay Ridge Ave.) and at the all-indoor Xramps (159 20th St., (718) 840-0430, www.xramps.com, M R to Prospect Avenue). One of the city's first skate parks, at Mullaly Park in the Bronx (164th St. and River Ave.), is also still open for action.

Gymnasiums

New York's generic gym is New York Sports Club. Always clean, always sterile, these clubs offer what the average gym-goer needs – equipment that works and TV screens that deliver up to 10 channels. This gym has the most branches throughout New York and the outer boroughs. For gym locations and more information, visit: www.nysc.com.

Crunch Gym
Crunch offers funky décor and even funkier classes. If you've ever wanted to sweat with a drag queen dishing up dirt, take a striptease exercise class, or spin in a room that would double for a disco, then this is the gym for you. Always experimental, always edgy, Crunch is expanding thanks to a buyout by Bally's, but promises to keep its flavor. For gym locations and more information, visit: www.crunch.com.

New York Health and Racquet Club
New York Health and Racquet Club is the solidly middle-class and usually middle-aged gym. Their gyms are clean, and all boast bathroom attendants with sundry cosmetics and hairsprays. They have monthly boat cruises and seem to be trying to get more singles interested in their gyms. They have more pools than any other New York chain.
For gym locations and more information, call (800) HRC-BEST or visit: www.hrcbest.com.

Equinox Fitness Club
Equinox Fitness Club is the Queen Bee of NYC gym chains. With New Age music piped into its dressing rooms, pulsing rhythms on its exercise floors, and consistently high-quality instructors, Equinox is the gym of choice for well-heeled New Yorkers looking to look good while they sweat. For a taste of Equinox, check out their amazing smoothie bar. For gym locations and more information, visit: www.equinoxnyc.com.

Reebok Sports Club
Reebok Sports Club brings a more Los Angeles flavor to the New York fitness scene. Many of the classes that start-up here end up hitting it big, including, reportedly, spinning. The rates are daunting, but with an all-star clientele, these gyms are looking to be the most exclusive in town. For gym locations and more information, call (212) 362-6800.

Gold's Gym
Gold's Gym is New York's working-class gym. With few Gold's in Manhattan, it is largely the domain of the outer boroughs. You'll find a large mix of clients here, and you'll never feel underdressed. Be on the lookout for Gold's Gym muscle shirts in Brooklyn or Queens. For gym locations and more information, visit: www.goldsgym.com.

Dolphin Fitness
Dolphin Fitness is a homegrown, bargain-basement gym. Don't expect many amenities, but the rates can't be beat if you don't mind exercising in sometimes-cramped quarters.
For gym locations and more information, visit: www.dolphinfitnessclubs.com.

Bally Total Fitness
Bally's is the nation's marketing extravaganza gym chain. The corporate sponsorship runs nonstop ads on its TVs and strings promotional materials through the dressing rooms and hallways. The monthly fee is cheaper than almost anywhere in town, but some say you get what you pay for with Bally's. For gym locations and more information, visit: www.ballyfitness.com.

Gay-Friendly Gyms

19th Street Gym
Warning: this hardcore gymnasium is not for the lily-livered. Its clientele includes other gyms' personal trainers, professionals, and the occasional celebrity. One large floor houses the entire collection of sleek machinery, free weights, and cardio machines. Fifteen personal trainers offer private classes

street basketball: Taking It to the Asphalt

Street basketball is one of the best ways to spend a weekend exercising and having a good time. Although many of us grew up playing games either in gym class or in organized leagues, before attempting to parlay yourself into the next Xavier McDaniel – a street basketball player who started his career playing on West 4th Street in New York – you must acquaint yourself with the much looser and tougher guidelines which make street basketball what it is.

Rules are much looser on the street than they are in any sort of organized league. Often, only the harshest of harsh fouls are called, and many times even these are ignored. Forget those two or three pointers as well, as in most street games a basket is worth one and only one point, no matter where the shot is taken from. Also, be aware that in a half-court game you must "take-back" the ball if you hope for your next Jordan-esque basket to count. Many a tooth has been lost over an argument debating whether a player has actually taken the ball back or not.

Many of today's most famous NBA players were discovered while playing street basketball. A young Shaquille O'Neal, who was forced to travel the world with his Army-employed father, was seen and

recruited by an NBA scout while playing a street game in Germany. Dirk Nowitzki was another German find, discovered by Don Nelson while playing at a local park.

Nonetheless, not all of the street's best players make it to the professional level. One of street ball's greatest tragedies is the story of Earl "The Goat" Manigault. The Goat, so named because of his incredible athleticism (he could stand on a mountain like a billy goat) was one of the street's greatest and most talented players, with a legendary 52 inch vertical leap. Manigault, who came from a poor Harlem family, was kicked out of high school for smoking marijuana and eventually developed a crippling heroin addiction that destroyed his basketball career. Regardless, The Goat was able to overcome his addiction and reform his life. A movie about the legend, titled "Rebound" was produced and released in 1996. Although Manigault recently died, his legend lives on; the basketball courts on 98th St. in Manhattan are still referred to as "Goat Park."

So don't forget, whether your playing on West Fourth Street by the ACE stop or uptown at Goat's Park, street ball is about having fun. Obey the rules, and you will be respected. Well, as long as your game is worth respecting. Bring it all, or expect to fall.

in abdominal training, boxing, kickboxing, and more.
22 W. 19th St. (bet. Fifth and Sixth Aves). Hours: M-F 5:30am-11 pm, Sa-Su 9am-9pm, 1 to 18th St. For more information, call (212) 414-5800 or visit www.19thstreetgym.com.

David Barton Gym
The welcoming and attractive staff at this neighborhood gym is extremely gay-friendly, which guarantees loyalty from its Chelsea and NYU patrons. Armed with glamorous new equipment, this gym-come-club hosts DJs who, every Tuesday night, provide the apt workout beats. After you pump, primp with complementary Aveda products, or avail yourself of the dry sauna and steam room.
552 Sixth Ave. (bet. 16th and 15th Sts.). Open M-F 6am-12am, Sa 9am-9pm, Su 10am-11pm, L N R W 4 5 6 to 14th St.-Union Sq. For more information, call (212) 727-0004.

Team New York
Fierce competition and queer camaraderie pervades the city's many gay and lesbian athletic teams. Whether you're looking to have some fun with other sporty gays or pining for a chance to compete in the quadrennial Gay Games, Team New York is the ultimate connection to the city's many queer sports teams. This not-for-profit organization supports 25 different types of sports teams running the gamut from soccer to square dancing. For more information, visit: www.teamnewyork.org.

Horseback Riding

While the only horses you may ever see are pulling moneyed tourists through Central Park, the

serious equestrian can seek out several options for horseback riding within the city limits, though costs are high. Central Park has a bridle path for experienced riders, and Van Cortland Park has a fairly large riding center.

Manhattan

Claremont Riding Academy
175 West 89th St., (212) 724-5100, 1 to 86th St.

Bronx

Pelham Bit Stable
9 Shore Rd., (718) 885-0551, 6 to Pelham Bay Station
The Riverdale Riding Center
W. 254th St. at Broadway in Van Cortland Park. 1 to 242nd St. For more information, call (718) 548-4848 or visit: www.riverdaleriding.com.

Queens

Lynne's Riding School
88-03 70th Rd. in Forest Hills. E F G R V to Forest Hills-71 St. For more information, call (718) 261-7679 or visit: www.lynnesridingschool.com.
Dixie Dew Stables
88-11 70th Rd. in Forest Hills, E F G R V to Firest Hills-71 St. For more information, call (718) 263-3500 or visit: www.dixiedew.com.

LGBT-Friendly Sports

Recognizing that gay athletes can face discrimination and harassment, numerous queer and queer friendly athletic teams have been formed to create a safe space in which to exercise, sweat, and play. They also serve as a social

network where you can be introduced to new people and maybe meet your next girlfriend, boyfriend, and, if you get lucky, husband or wife.

Front Runners (www.frontrunnersnewyork.com) is a nationally recognized running organization which sponsors an NYC Marathon team and also organizes the NYC Pride run. Runners of all ability levels are welcome and the team travels to running events all across the country.

Softball is played in several queer leagues throughout the city including Big Apple Softball, Women Athletes of New York, and Prospect Park Women's Softball. If your preferences edge more towards water than land then Team New York Aquatics may be for you. Other sports with queer teams and/or leagues include ice hockey, martial arts, cheerleading, rugby, wrestling, cycling, sailing, tennis, basketball, and soccer.

Over 1500 New York City gay and lesbian athletes come together each year for SportsBall, an expo and dance party at Webster Hall. Typically held in early June, the event brings together top queer sports teams for a night of fun and dancing. The frolicking follows a silent auction which is designed to raise money for each of the teams. Check out their website at www.Sportsball7.com for dates, tickets, and other general event information.

Recreation Centers

Membership in these city-run Manhattan Recreation Centers costs around $25 a year for adults from 18 to 50 years, $10 for youths 13-17, and nothing for those 12 years and under. Most have locker rooms and showers, but patrons must bring their own locks, towels, and toiletries. The centers have gyms, weight rooms, aerobics classes, and pools. Call for special programs.

In Midtown, the Manhattan recreation centers located on 54th St. between First and Second Aves. and on West 59th St. between Tenth and Eleventh Aves. offer indoor swimming running, aerobics, weight rooms, and all the basics. The 168th Street Armory offers one of the finest track and facilities in the city. For more information, call: (212) 281-9376.

In the outer boroughs, world-class gyms, weight rooms, basketball courts, and pools are available for a fee that's often cheaper than in Manhattan.

Manhattan

Alfred E. Smith Rec. Center
Catherine St. (bet. Cherry and Monroe Sts.), (212) 285-0300

Asser Levy Rec. Center
Asser Levy (Ave. A and E. 23rd St.), (212) 447-2020

Carmine Street Rec. Center
Clarkson St. and Seventh Ave. South, (212) 242-5228

West 59th Rec. Center
W. 59th St. and Tenth Ave., (212) 397-3166

Chelsea Recreation Center
430 West 25th Street
(between 9th & 10th Avenue)
(212) 255-3705

Hamilton Fish Rec. Center
128 Pitt St., (212) 387-7687

Hansborough Rec. Center
W. 134th St. (bet. Fifth and Lenox Aves.), (212) 234-9603

Highbridge Rec. Center
Amsterdam Ave. (at W. 173rd St.), (212) 27-2400

Jackie Robinson Rec. Center
Bradhurst Ave. (at W. 146th St.), (212) 234-9606

North Meadow Rec. Center
Central Park (at 97th St.), (212) 348-4867

Pelham Fritz Rec. Center
Mount Morris Park West, (at W. 122nd St.), (212) 860-1380

Thomas Jefferson Rec. Center
E. 112th St. and First Ave., (212) 860- 1383

Bronx

Crotona Rec. Center
East 173rd and Fulton Sts., (718) 822-4272

Saint Mary's Rec. Center
East 145th St. and St. Anne's Ave., (718) 402-5155

Queens

The Lost Batallion Hall Rec. Center
93-29 Queens Blvd., (718) 263-1163

Roy Wilkins Rec. Center
177th St. and Baisley Blvd., (718) 276- 8686

Sorrentino Rec. Center
Beach 19th St. and Cornaga Ave., (718) 471-4818

Brooklyn

Brownsville Rec. Center
Linden and Mother Gaston Blvds. (at Christopher St.), (718) 485-4633

Red Hook Rec. Center
Bay St. and Henry St., (718) 722-3213

Sunset Park Rec. Center
44th St. and Seventh Ave., (718) 965-6578

Staten Island

Cromwell Rec. Center
Pier 6 and Murray Hulbert Ave., (718) 816-6172

Roller-Blading and Ice Skating

Some words of wisdom: Central Park, in particular on weekends and in the spring and summer, is packed with people who have not yet perfected maneuvering their blades, so don't assume they'll honor the right-of-way or even be able to brake. Other parks, where blading is not such a social scene, are a little less like a circus. If you're an excellent blader, be sure to constantly be aware of those less-talented wannabes who get in your way. "It was his fault, officer," is not a very good defense in court.

In-line skaters can attempt the advanced slalom courses in Central Park by the Bandstand and by the restaurant Tavern on the Green, where on weekends experienced skaters do informal exhibitions for large crowds of spectators. Watch and learn, but if you've just suited up in your knee-pads and helmet for the first time, you may be better accommodated on The Dead Road, from about 66th to 69th Sts. in the middle of the park. For more information, visit: www.

iceskatenyc.com. A few rinks are highlighted below.

Manhattan

Wollman Rink
Central Park at 63rd St., (212) 439-6900, www.wollmanskatingrink.com

Lasker Rink
Central Park, near 110th St. and Lenox Ave. (212) 534-7639, Ice Skating: Adults $1.50, Skate Rental: $4.75, In-Line Skating: Adults: $4 in the rink, $15 for two hours in the park, $25 for all day.

Rockefeller Center Rink
Rockefeller Plaza is located between 49th and 50th Sts., and between Fifth and Sixth Aves. (212) 332-7654, Ice Skating. Admission Varies.

Brooklyn

World's Fair Rink
Flushing Meadows-Corona Park, (718) 271-1996, 7 to Willets Pt.-Shea Stadium

Queens

Abe Stark Rink at Coney Island
On Boardwalk (at W. 19th St. and Surf Ave.), (718) 946-3135, Admission: $7, Skate Rental: $4.

Running

Running is the preferred way in which many New Yorkers both release stress and get their hot summer bods. Riverside Park is a beautiful place to run for those who don't mind the pavement, since the infrequent strips of dirt are badly maintained and subject to ruts and mud. Furthermore, if you have bad knees running on concrete is not a very good idea. The best place to veer down towards the riverside path, where a small houseboat community docks and optimistic fishermen occasionally cast their lines, is at 86th St. A quarter of a mile track is maintained at 72nd St. Further north, on top of the 145th St. incinerator, there's another quality track.

Also in Manhattan, a jogging path follows the East River from Sutton Place all the way up to Gracie Mansion. Down in the Village, the Westside Highway Path is a newly refurbished strip for downtown joggers, bladers, and bikers that can seem as circus-like as the boardwalk on Coney Island on busy days.

When traffic is cut off on Saturdays and Sundays in Prospect Park, the roughly two-and-a-half-mile route looping around the park makes for a good jog. For a nice post-jog relaxation, the interior path offers shady groves and gaggles of swans.

Runners seeking camaraderie should contact the New York Road Runner's Club at (212) 860-4455, headquartered near the Jacqueline Kennedy Onassis Reservoir at the eastern entrance to Central Park on 90th St. The club's activities include twice-nightly runs in the park at 6:30pm and 7:15pm, a weekend jog at 10am, a marathon prep, a New Year's Eve run, and a Central Park Safety Patrol. During summer evenings, traffic is closed off in the park.

Running Clubs

New York Road Runners Club
For more information, call (212) 860-4455 or visit www.nyrrc.org.

Achilles Track Club
A nation-wide club for athletes with disabilities ranging from blindness to heart disease.
For more information, call (212) 354-0300 or visit www.achillestrackclub.org.

Central Park Track Club
For information, visit: www.centralparktc.org.

Front Runners
A gay and lesbian running group. For more information, call (212) 724-9700 or visit www.frny.org.

Moving Comfort NY
Ladies only, but you've got to be able to do 10K in forty minutes. For more information, visit: www.movingcomfortny.org.

Softball

The Sheep Meadow in Central Park, closed in winter, overflows in summer with loads of scantily clad sunbathers, Frisbee players, and picnickers, many of whom come to watch the local softball games. Regulation-sized softball and baseball diamonds are located around 100th St. on the eastern side of the park. The Heckscher fields around 64th St. are well maintained but often claimed by amateur, fiercely territorial leagues known more for mild spectator value than for open field policies, since most hail from the high-strung cubicles of nearby Midtown. There are huge, underutilized Astroturf fields atop the 145th St. incinerator in Riverside that are a good alternative to the Central Park melee.

NYC Marathon: Then and Now

The New York City Marathon first began in Central Park in 1970. The race had a total budget of $1,000 and the 55 finishers were each rewarded with recycled bowling trophies. Since then, the race has evolved to include over 35,000 applicants and two million spectators.

The course takes athletes on a tour of New York's five boroughs: Staten Island, Brooklyn, Queens, the Bronx, and Manhattan. The course unites dozens of culturally and ethnically diverse communities, and finishes at Central Park. For more information, visit: www.nycmarathon.org.

Batting Cages

Batting Cages at Chelsea Piers
23rd St. at the Hudson, (212) 336-6500

Coney Island Batting Range
3049 Stillwell Ave. (by the Boardwalk), (718) 449-1200, www.coneyislandbattingrange.com.

To reserve a field in a city park of any borough:
Manhattan: (212) 408-0309, Bronx: (718) 822-4282, Queens: (718) 520-5933, Brooklyn: (718) 965-8919, Staten Island: (718) 816-6172

Swimming

Two city pools are particularly clean and accessible, although invariably crowded on weekends and especially during the sweltering summer months: Carmine Street Pool (Seventh Ave. South at Clarkson St., (212) 242-5228), and John Jay Park Pool (E. 77th St. and Cherokee Pl., (212) 794-6566).

Visit www.nycswim.org for information on where to train, water quality, and indoor and outdoor pool locations throughout the five boroughs. Almost all Recreation have either an indoor or an outdoor pool.

Tennis

If you are affiliated with a gym or university, you most likely have access to tennis courts. You can also check out city courts like those in Central Park's mid-area around 93rd St., though only those with season permits can reserve a court in advance. It's five dollars to play on an unreserved court for an hour. Be prepared for a wait; you can bring a deck of cards and join the others in line in a game of poker. Call (212) 280-0205 for information. Riverside Park's clay courts near 96th St. are well-maintained by neighborhood volunteers. Tennis courts also abound at the prestigious USTA National Center, the site of the US Open in Queens, call (718) 592-8000 for information.

All Boroughs

Parks and Recreation General Information
(800) 201-PARK

Manhattan

New York Health and Racket Club
Piers 13 and 14 (at Wall St.), (212) 422-9300

NYHRC Tennis Courts
60 W. 23rd St., (212) 989-2300

Central Park Tennis Center
W. 93rd St. and Central Park West, (212) 280-0205

Tower Tennis
1725 York Ave. (at 89th St.), (212) 860-2464

Riverside Park Tennis Court
96th St. and Riverside Dr. (212) 496-2006, 119th St. and Riverside Dr., (212) 486-2103

Harlem Tennis Center
143rd St. (bet. Lenox and Seventh Aves.), (212) 283-4028

Riverbank State Park Tennis Court
145th St. and Riverside Dr., (212) 694-3600

Fred Johnson Playground Tennis Court
151st St. and Seventh Ave., (212) 234-9609

Columbia University Tennis Center
575 W. 218th St. at Seaman Ave. (behind Baker Field), (212) 842-7100

Bronx

Stadium Tennis Center in Mullaly Park
11 East 162nd St. (718) 322-4191, (718) 293-2386

Brooklyn

Breakpoint Tennis Club in Bensonhurst
9000 Bay Pkwy, (718) 372-6878

Prospect Park Tennis Center
305 Coney Island Ave. (at Parkside), (718) 438-1200

Queens

Alley Pond Tennis Club
79-20 Winchester Blvd., Queens Village. (718) 468-1239

Long Island City Indoor Tennis
50-01 2nd St., (718) 784-9677

The USTA National Center
Flushing Meadows Corona Park, (718) 583-8000

Resources

moving and *storage*

For moving, first investigate renting a U-Haul (562 West 23rd, at Eleventh, (212) 620-4177). Note the emphasis on "U": if you're carting heavy boxes and/or furniture, movers are an additional investment. Nonetheless, they easy to come by and worth the expense, provided you're not transporting Special K. Do not hire other people to pack for you; this is a risk not worth taking,.

Most universities have connections with moving and storage companies, as well as shipping companies, which allow you to leave your boxes at some check-off point near campus. While you pay dearly for such conveniences, it definitely beats moving boxes yourself.

Planning Ahead

Moving mishaps make for excellent, self-deprecating cocktail party conversation, but many pitfalls can be easily avoided. First, if you are young or a college student, do not invest in furniture or other unwieldy items of decor unless you plan on disposing of them upon departure, or have an easy way of transporting them. Also keep in mind that college storage facilities are not conducive to objects that do not fit into boxes. Begin looking for boxes early on, especially if you are moving out at the end of the school year when cardboard becomes a valuable commodity. Liquor stores and bookstores are best, since their boxes are very sturdy; Starbucks is particularly useful if you tell them ahead of time to save the boxes from their shipment. Go at night when it's less busy to ask when you can pick them up. Always get twice as many boxes as you think you'll need; most people grossly underestimate their material possessions, and friends who were not as forward-thinking will appreciate any spares.

For those who hate packing, consider selling your bulkier possessions. Craig's List (www.craigslist.com) is an online forum where you can look for a new apartment, sell your property, and pick up a date all at the same time. Also, if you're leaving for the summer, have a plan for where to store valuables. Ask around and see if any of your friends and acquaintances will have summer housing with a little extra space for a refrigerator or a stereo. If you are moving, do not be afraid to get rid of your old junk. Start new and be happy with change.

Packing

Only use large boxes for clothing, blankets, and other light items. Try to pack a few books in each of the boxes. If you are shipping anything, do not wrap breakables in clothing; pack each thing in its own box with appropriate padding. If you must ship books, place them in their own box so that they can be sent at a book rate, but again, don't pack too many books into one box; it gets heavy.

Boxes and tubs for packing are quite easy to come by. If your attempts to get free boxes fail, the post office, FedEx, and UPS all sell boxes at exorbitant prices ($3-$5 per box), while private companies take advantage of mass moving days at universities by setting up shop on the street or in dorm lobbies. Again, the boxes they sell are overpriced, so it really is best to plan ahead.

Storing

If you plan on using college storage, you should

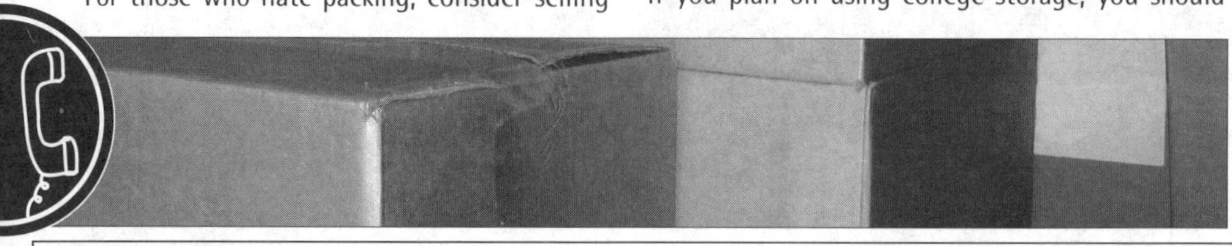

forego boxes for Rubbermaid tubs. University storage rooms are usually in basements, which flood frequently. Avoid storing valuables since security is more lax than at professional storage companies, and do not pack items in computer or stereo boxes, since thieves may mistake them for the real thing.

Many apartment buildings in Manhattan make storage facilities available to their residents. These facilities involve some of the same risks as dorm storage, often consisting of little more than a large basement room with a single lock on the door. Trust your gut instinct. If you don't feel safe storing your valuables somewhere, then don't.

Commercial storage is a great choice for those who don't have the option or desire to use apartment storage. Storage companies such as Whitehall Mini-Storage and Tuck-It-Away offer storage space on a monthly basis, with customers providing locks for their own spaces. Most contracted storage companies claim to offer some form of free moving to the storage facility for their customers. However, it's best to inquire regarding the specifics because some storage companies, such as Tuck-It-Away on Broadway and 131st St., only provide free moving for a few hours and require that you call well in advance to schedule a pickup. Others, such as Hudson Moving & Storage on Broadway and 130th St., limit free moving to those items below a certain total volume.

When to Move

Take advantage of street-cleaning days to get closest to your building. Moving in the early morning or late at night is a better choice, since traffic is not as bad. Non-holiday summer weekends are the best times to move into the city. In many sections of Manhattan, residents flee New York's steamy weather, and traffic within the city is relatively light. Regardless, weekends can be a problem if you are using a U-Haul, since vans can only be rented out for six hours. Those moving into or out of apartment buildings should call supers in case there are times when you aren't allowed to move, especially if it will involve doormen or elevators.

If you plan on utilizing a cab, definitely move late at night or during mid-morning, since drivers get surly and unhelpful it they feel they're wasting time with you instead of picking up more fares during peak times. Even better than a cab is a car service, since drivers have huge cars with body-bag sized trunks and are a bit more helpful with loading and unloading, looking for a good tip.

Although moving can be a long and arduous process, remember that it is not the nature of humanity to stay stable. Living in New York City is a once-in-a-lifetime opportunity and you shouldn't spend your whole time here living in one home. Finding an apartment (see City Living section) can be a very difficult and often wearying task, and you may not initially get what you want. Nonetheless, do not allow yourself to fall into a comfortable malaise. Force yourself to get out there and experience every aspect of New York.

Remember that you do not necessarily have to live in Manhattan. The outer boroughs provide many wonderful places for young New Yorkers to live. Forest Hills, Queens, allows urban professionals to live in an "urban suburb" while being less than an hour away from the city. Another up-and-coming neighborhood is Windsor Terrace in Brooklyn. Located adjacent to Park Slope, Windsor Terrace allows its citizens to live near many of the nicest and most artistic communities New York City offers, while paying much less than their Manhattan counterparts.

Don't forget, life is a work in progress, and if you have to move a few times to find the right place, it's worth it.

long distance

Long Distance Buses

Unfortunately, Peter Pan Trailways and Greyhound are now basically one big monopoly, but their nationwide access can't be beat. Students get a 15% discount with a Student Advantage Card (www.studentadvantage.com). Don't try waving a student ID at the ticket booth, since they won't honor it. Bus drivers now ask for identification when you buy your ticket, and security is tight everywhere. Nonetheless, You can still visit those high school or college friends for affordable prices. For instance, a one-way ticket to Washington, D.C. or Boston will run about $50. Both companies leave from Port Authority Bus Terminal at 42nd Street and Eighth Avenue. Heavily-traveled routes, such as those to Boston and Washington, D.C., have regularly-scheduled departures. Getting tickets in advance can get you out of the lines at the station and save you money, but you'll still have to deal with queues when boarding the buses. Even with a previously-purchased ticket, plan to arrive at the station a good half-hour in advance of scheduled departure, or find out the hard way that a ticket in hand does not necessarily guarantee a seat. All lines now require that passengers check all luggage bigger than a pocketbook. Buses are known for odd passengers and bathrooms that have no water for washing hands, but that's part of their "charm." Most companies do not sell tickets for a specific departure time, just for a particular route, although for Greyhound treks to other cities, you are restricted to a specific destination and time of departure after purchasing your ticket.

Port Authority at 42nd St. (at 8th Ave.), (212) 564-8484. A C E N R S W 1 2 3 7 *to 42nd St.-Times Sq./Port Authority.*

Greyhound Bus Information
(800) 231-2222
www.greyhound.com
New Jersey Transit
(973) 762-5100
www.njtransit.com
Peter Pan Bus Lines
(800) 343-9999 or (212) 967-2900
www.peterpanbus.com

Long Distance Trains

Train travel along the eastern seaboard is cleaner and more pleasurable than the bus, but not necessarily faster and certainly not cheaper: bus travel from New York to Boston clocks in at four and a half hours while the train takes more than five, due to the number of stops in between major destinations, and a train ticket is likely to cost you anywhere from $30 to $40 more than a bus. Amtrak runs regularly-scheduled trains out of Penn Station at 31st Street and Eighth Ave. Reservations are available, but these seats tend to be more expensive, especially on holidays, and prices also depend on whether the route is local, making many stops, or express, making one or no stops. If you travel between New York and Boston, expect that the train will stop midway to switch power sources (it's a long story, but it's very inefficient). The much-touted Acela Express trains are more expensive and don't lop off much time between NY and Washington (from four hours to about three), but they are more fun. MetroLiner trains still run to Philadelphia and some New Jersey destinations on weekdays, reservation required.

Penn Station (bet. 31st and 33rd Sts. on Eighth Ave.), A C E 1 2 3 *to 34th St.-Penn Station.*

Amtrak
(800) USA-RAIL
www.amtrak.com

Travel to and from Airports

All three airports can be accessed by van (www.supershuttle.com or (212) BLUE-VAN) though these trips, which force you to ride with other passengers, may take a lot of time. For about $45 you can order yourself a car from a car service such as Carmel (call (212) 666-6666) or Tel Aviv (call (212) 777-7777). There are yellow cab lines at all arrival points for transit to Manhattan, and all airports are accessible by yellow cab from Manhattan: a $45 flat fee plus tolls to Kennedy, and about $22-$24 plus tolls to or from LaGuardia, with a $5 tip for each. Visit www.airportservice.com.

LaGuardia Airport
The M60 bus, which costs $2 (exact change, coins only, no pennies, or a MetroCard), is the cheapest way to and from La Guardia, taking riders from Columbia University/Harlem to the airport in about an hour's time. Expect the trip back to take longer. Another option: take the NY Airport Service Express bus from Grand Central Terminal for about $10-$12.

JFK International Airport
Kennedy airport is further from Manhattan than LaGuardia airport, but it is serviced by the A train. Exit the A train at the Howard Beach-JFK stop, where a free shuttle bus to all JFK terminals comes every 15 minutes. Allot at least two hours for the entire route, plus the added time for check-in. The NY Airport Service Express bus from Grand Central Terminal goes to JFK airport, too.

In addition, this year the MTA added on "Air Train" that will take passengers from the Jamaica train stop (get there by using the E J Z or LIRR) to JFK for $5. Convenient and comfortable, you'd be crazy not to take it.

Newark International Airport
Newark can be accessed by taking a PATH train or NJ Transit train to Newark, then taking a cab or bus. Additionally, an Olympia Airport Express shuttle runs from Port Authority, $11 one-way and a $21 round-trip.

Travel/Hotel Discounts

It pays to be frugal. New York is an expensive place, and using discount travel websites can save you hundreds. The less choosy you are and the more you plan ahead, the more you'll save. A partial listing:

- www.hotwire.com
- www.cheapairlinetickets.com
- www.expedia.com
- www.orbitz.com
- www.travelocity.com
- www.priceline.com

listings

Small Claims Court/Civil Court

You don't need a lawyer to file a suit to claim under $3000; over 60,000, New Yorkers go to Small Claims Court every year, though winning in court doesn't mean you will necessarily get the money due to poor enforcement mechanisms.
(212) 791-6000

Copy Services

Kinko's
Notorious among college students for catering to those last-minute paper-writing needs, Kinko's is open 24 hours. Some services include: copying, faxing, computer use and enlargements.
118-10 Queens Blvd. (at 78th Ave.), (718) 286-7700. MC, V, AmEx, D, DC. E F to Union Tpke. (Additional locations in Manhattan)

Village Copier
Reasonable rates; conveniently located near Columbia.
601 W. 115th St. (bet. Broadway and Riverside Dr.), (212) 666-0600. MC, V, AmEx. 1 to 116th St.

Crisis Lines, Hotlines, and Medical Numbers

Bellevue Hospital Rape Crisis Service
Free medical treatment for rape victims, as well as counseling referral.
(212) 562-3435. M-F 9am-5pm.

Crime Victims Hotline
Victims of any personal crime, including domestic violence, rape, and theft, as well as legal advice.
(212) 577-7777.
24 hours daily

St. Luke's/ Roosevelt Hospital Rape Crisis Center
Trained volunteers talk victims through dealing with rape, both legally and emotionally.
(212) 523-4728. M-F 8am-7pm

Sex Crimes Report Line
Handles reports of all sex crimes, child victimization, crimes against gays. They will send an ambulance, provide counseling referrals, and set up an interview with a Sex Crimes Squad detective which may take place in your home at your request.
NYPD Sex Crimes Unit, (212) 267-7273.
24 hours daily

New York State Child Abuse and Maltreatment Register
Call to report suspected child abuse.
(800) 342-3720.
24 hours daily

New York State Domestic Violence Helpline
Information on legal options and referrals to local programs and shelters.
(800) 942-6906.
24 hours daily,

(800) 621-4673 (Spanish). M-F 9am-5pm

The Samaritans
Volunteers help those suffering from depression, suicidal thoughts, and alcoholism.
(212) 673-3000, www.samaritansnyc.org. 24 hours daily

Suicide Prevention
Trained volunteers help talk people through thoughts of suicide. Call if you need to. Please.
(212) 532-2400 (interpretation service), www.helpline.org. 9am-10pm daily.

Daycare and Other Resources

Agency for Child Development
Pre-school and referral information, as well as a free directory of daycare services.
(718) 523-6826

Child Care Inc./ The Pre-School Association
This nonprofit group offers parents telephone counseling, information of day care and early childhood programs, and names of day care providers in your neighborhood.
275 Seventh Ave., 15th fl., (212) 929-7604. ❶ *to 28th St.*

The New York Public Library's Early Childhood Resource Center
There is an entire floor devoted to resource materials for parents, and appropriately enough, a playroom for kids.
66 Leroy St. (at Seventh Ave.), (212) 929-0815. ❶ *to Houston St.*

Disability Info

Although New York City may appear daunting at first, armed with information and determination, any disabled individual can take advantage of most of what the City has to offer. The best resources on accessibility can be found at:

Hospital Audiences, Inc. (HAI)
(212) 575-7676

Mayor's Office for People with Disabilities
Call to complain or make a request regarding handicap access throughout New York City,
(212) 788-2830

New York City Transit Authority Travel Information Center
(718) 330-1234

Lighthouse International Inc.
Information on resources for the blind.
111 E. 59th St. (bet. Park and Lexington Aves.), (212) 821-9200, (800) 829-0500. M-F 9am-5pm. Ⓝ Ⓡ *to Lexington Ave.*

New York Society for the Deaf
Information on resources for the deaf.
161 Williams St. (212) 777-3900. M-F 9am-5pm

Andrew Heiskell Library for the Blind

and Physically Handicapped
A great place to come and read if you are unable to do so in a public library.
(212) 206-5400

Dry Cleaners

Bon-French Cleaners & Dryers
Friendly staff, same-day service is available. Below average prices should keep you smiling.
2881 Broadway (bet. 11th and 112th Sts.), (212) 662-2194. Cash only. 1 to 110th St.

Joe Far Laundry
Fast and efficient, this inconspicuous laundry is the cheapest in Morningside.
Broadway and 112th St., (212) 666-3440. Cash only. 1 to 116th St.

M+N Cleaners
Speedy and organized and they offer delivery.
292 Eighth Ave. (bet. 24th and 25th Sts.), (212) 675-8966. 1 to 23rd St.

Piermont Cleaners
Pick up that suit en route to the show.
845 Seventh Ave. (at 54th Street), (212) 582-0919. MC, V.

Greenwich Center

Body waxing, electrolysis, and facials at affordable prices, with excellent results is available in the Village! One of the best places to undergo body waxing or an electrolysis treatment in Lower Manhattan is the Greenwich Center located at 853 Broadway between 13th and 14th Streets, Suite 706 (4 5 6 Q R N W *to Union Square*). Even better for many Inside New York Readers, they offer students a 10% discount on all services. Be sure to check out the Greenwich Center for a fast and painless waxing, or electrolysis treatment and finally get rid of unwanted hair, or simply pamper yourself to a rejuvenating facial experience.

Entertainment

Cultural Affairs Department Line
(212) 643-7770

Parks and Recreation Department
Special Events: (212) 360-8146; Summer Stage: (212) 360-2777

Gay and Lesbian

Gay and Lesbian Switchboard
A good resource for visitors to get advice about the city.
(212) 777-1800. 10am-12am daily

Gay Men's Health Crisis Hotline
Advice for people concerned about HIV/AIDS.
(212) 807-6655. M-F 10 am-9pm, Sa 12:00pm-3pm

Lesbian and Gay Community Services Center
(See sidebar in the Gay Feature for more information.)
208 W. 13th St. (at Eighth Ave.), (212) 620-7310. 9am-11pm daily. L 1 2 3 to 14th St.

New York City Gay and Lesbian Anti-Violence Project
647 Hudson St. (at Gansevoort St.), (212) 807-0197. M-R 10am-8pm, F 10am-6pm, Hotline open 24 hours daily. L 1 2 3 to 14th St.

Government Offices

Birth Records
(212) 788-4520

Department of Motor Vehicles
516 and 914 area codes: (800) DIAL-DMV, Manhattan: (212) 645-5550, Outer Boroughs: (718) 966-6155

Passport Agency
630 Fifth Ave., Room 230, (212) 206-3500, M-F 7:30am-4pm.

Health

Bailey House
Deals with emergency situations for people with AIDS/HIV.
275 Seventh Ave. (at 25th St.), (212) 414-1428, M-F 9:30am-5:30pm. N R to 28th St.

Fire Department and Emergency Medical Service
Report any kind of problems, including de-layed service, poor treatment, or no-shows.
(718) 416-7000

New York Fertility Clinic
1016 Fifth Ave., (212) 734-5555

Mental Health Counseling Hotline
Therapists will talk you through any emotional problems and issue referrals.
(212) 734-5876, Open 24 hours daily

New York City AIDS
Information Hotline:
(212) 447-8200, 9am-9pm daily

New York University Student Dental Plan
Affordable, one-fee yearly dental care for college or university students.
David B. Kriser Dental Center
345 E. 24th St. (at First Ave.), (212) 998-9870

Poison Control Center
Call with questions.
(212) 764-7667

Housing

Rent Stabilization Association.
Owners: (212) 214-9200
Tenants: (212) 961-8930

Institutional Libraries

Andrew Heiskell Library for the Blind and Physically Handicapped
General information:
(212) 206-5400

Archive of Contemporary Music
54 White St., (bet. Broadway and Church St.), (212) 226-6967

Baha'i Center and Library
53 E. 11th St. (bet. University Pl. and Broadway), (212) 674-8998

Donnell Library Center
(212) 621-0618

Frick Art Reference Library
10 E. 71st St., (212) 288-8700

Hampden Booth Theatre Library
(212) 228-7610

Jewish Theological Seminary of America
The largest collection of Jewishly-oriented books in North America.
General number: (212) 678-8000

Morgan Library
29 E. 36th St. (bet. Madison and Park Aves.), (212) 685-0008

New York Law Institute
120 Broadway (bet. Cedar and Pine Sts.), (212) 732-8720

Legal Services

Community Action For Legal Services
Government-funded referral service.
(212) 431-7200

Legal Aid Society
Get free advice on legal matters and referrals, but you must live below 34th Street in order to qualify.
(212) 577-3300. M-F 9am-5pm

Libraries

Queens Central Library
(718) 990-0778 (also extensions, 0779, 0781, 0700)

New York Public Library
(212) 340-0849

The New York Public Library for the Performing Arts
(212) 870-1630

Science, Industry and Business Library (NYPL)
(212) 592-7000

Brooklyn Central Library
(718) 230-2100

Fordham Central Library
(718) 579-4200

Telephone Reference Service
Manhattan: (212) 340-0849
Bronx: (718) 220-6576
Queens: (718) 990-0714

Motor Vehicles

Alternate Side of the St. Parking Regulations
(212) 442-7080

GGMC Parking
Multiple locations in Manhattan.
(212) 996-6363

Photography and Services

Fotorush
One-hour processing, also passport photos, video transfer, and slide transfers.
2878 Broadway (at 113th St.), (212) 749-0065. MC, V. ❶ *to 110th St.*

Post Offices

US General Post Office
Twenty-four hour postal service, except for money-orders and registered mail, in the famous McKim, Mead, White masterpiece of design. Call to find out which branch is closest to you.
380 W. 33rd St. (at Eighth Ave.), (800) 275-8777 (Info Line). Ⓐ Ⓒ Ⓔ *to 34th St.-Penn Station.*

Rentals

Furniture

Cort-AFR Furniture Rental
711 Third Ave. (at 44th St.), (212) 377-1501, M-Sa, First month's rental plus a two-month security fee is required.

International Furniture Rentals
345 Park Ave. (bet. 51st and 52nd Sts.), (212) 421-0341, M-Sa, One-and-a-half month's rent required as deposit.

Air Conditioners

AABCO
1594 York Ave., (212) 585-2463, MC, V, AmEx, Average cost during the hot season (May through October) is $200.

Ace Air Conditioning Service Corp.
24-81 47th St., Astoria, Queens, (718) 726-7120, MC, V, Room size determines price.

Bicycles

Bicycles Plus
1400 Third Ave., (212) 794-2929

Metro Bicycles
1311 Lexington Ave. (at 88th St.), (212) 427-4450; 360 W. 47th St., (212) 581-4500; 231 W. 96th St., (212) 663-7531; 417 Canal St., (212) 334-8000; 546 Ave. of the Americas (at 15th St.), (212) 255-5100; 332 East 14th St. (at First Ave.), (212) 228-4344

Pedal Pusher Bike Shop
1306 Second Ave. (at 69th St.), (212) 288-5592.

Stuveysant Bicycle
345 W. 14th St., (212) 254-5200

Roller Blades

Blades, Board, and Skate
160 E. 86th St., (212) 996-1644; 105 W. 72nd St., (212) 787-3911, Open 7 days a week.

Sanitation

New York City Department of Sanitation
(212) 219-8090

Non-Emergency New York City Public Services
Manhattan: *311, or (212) NEW-YORK.*

Shoe Repair

Ambassador Luggage and Leather Goods
Repair of all types of leather goods.
371 Madison Ave. (bet 45th and 46th Sts.), (212) 972-0965. MC, V, AmEx. S 4 5 6 7 to 42nd St.-Grand Central Terminal.

Drago
Shoe shine, repairs, shoe polish, and other needs.
2851 Broadway (bet. 110th and 111th), (212) 663-7060. MC, V. 1 to 110th St.

Storage

Access Self Storage
Open 7 days a week, Access has 24-hour security, ample free parking, insurance and exceptional clean service for their customers.
2900 Review Ave.(at 29th St.), (718) 729-0442. MC, V, AmEx, D.

Chelsea Moving & Storage Inc.
300 W. 23rd St. (bet. Seventh and Eighth Aves.), (212) 243-8000.

Chelsea Mini Storage
224 Twelfth Ave., (212) 564-7735. 1 to 28th St.

Subletting an Apartment

Sublet.com
Visit www.sublet.com to find a no-fee apartment or a sublet. You can also find roommates, moving companies, information on rental insurance, and real estate contracts. You can also list your apartment for subletting.

The City on the Web

Guides to New York
www.inside-ny.com
www.citysearch.com
www.ny.yahoo.com
www.sidewalk.com

Metropolitan Museum of Art:
www.metmuseum.com

American Museum of Natural History:
www.amnh.org

New York Public Library: www.nypl.org
Nightlife:
Playbill Online:
www.playbill.com
New York City Ballet:
www.nycballet.com
New York City Opera:
www.interport .net/nyc-opera
New York Philharmonic:
www.nyphilharmon.org
Food:
Zagat Survey:
www.zagat.com
New York Food:
www.nyfood.com
Menupages.com is another great place to read reviews of restaurants you are thinking about visiting.

Kosher Restaurant database:
www.shamash.org/kosher

New York City Beer Guide: www.nycbeer.com

NYC government:
www.nyc.gov
Public Advocate's Office:
www.pubadvocate.nyc.gov
New York City Council Homepage: www.nyccouncil.info
United Nations:
www.un.org

Parks and Recreation:
Central Park:
www.centralpark.org

Tours

Adventures on a Shoestring
Walking tours

through Greenwich Village, SoHo, Chinatown, the Lower East Side, and other neighborhoods according to demand. Guides are committed to helping the low-budget explorer and refuse to raise their rates, which have remained at five bucks a tour for the thirty-five years of the organization's existence.
(212) 265-2663, $5 per tour

Architectural Tours
NYC experts lead the 92nd St. Y. Tours of Manhattan's historic cast-iron districts in Gramercy and SoHo, and other architecturally interesting spots in the city.
(212) 996-1100

New York Waterway Sightseeing Cruises
Many cruise options are available, including a two-hour full Manhattan cruise and a Latin Music cruise where you can dance the night away while catching sites like the Brooklyn Bridge and the Statue of Liberty. Very reasonable prices will allow you to take a cruise whenever you like. Special packages are available where you can combine a cruise with land tour.
W. 38th St. Terminal, 1-800-53-FERRY, www.nywaterway.com/sightseeing.html. A C E 1 2 3 *to 34th St.–Penn Station.*

Harlem Your Way Tours
Tours of Harlem tailored to your particular interest-historical or current.
(212) 690-1687, www.harlemyourway-tours.com. Tour: $25

Urban Park Rangers
Rangers take you around the city's parks.
1234 Fifth Ave. (at 104th St.), (212) 360 2774, 9am-5pm Daily, 6 *to 103rd St.*

Translation and Tutoring

CUTTA (Columbia University Tutoring and Translation Agency) can translate any type of documents in over 40 languages and tutor in any esoteric topic you would like. Their translators and tutors are all Columbia University students.
70-74 Morningside Dr. (bet. 117th and 118th Sts.), (212) 854-4888, 1 *to 116th St.-Columbia University.*

Utilities

Con Edison Emergency Line
Call to report problems. Gas, electrical, or steam emergencies: *(212) 683-8830, Open 24 hours.*

Time Warner Cable
New York's best cable provider, with new On-Demand cable service available. $50 per month for standard service.
(718) 358-0900

Plumbing: Auto Rooter
24 hour emergency service that comes in handy at the last minute, residential and commerical, sewer and drain cleaning.
(212) 481-6710

Effective Plumbing Corp.
Repairs, installations, renovations, sewer and drain-cleaning. Also, you get eighty percent of all jobs completed the same day.
(212) 545-0100

Maps

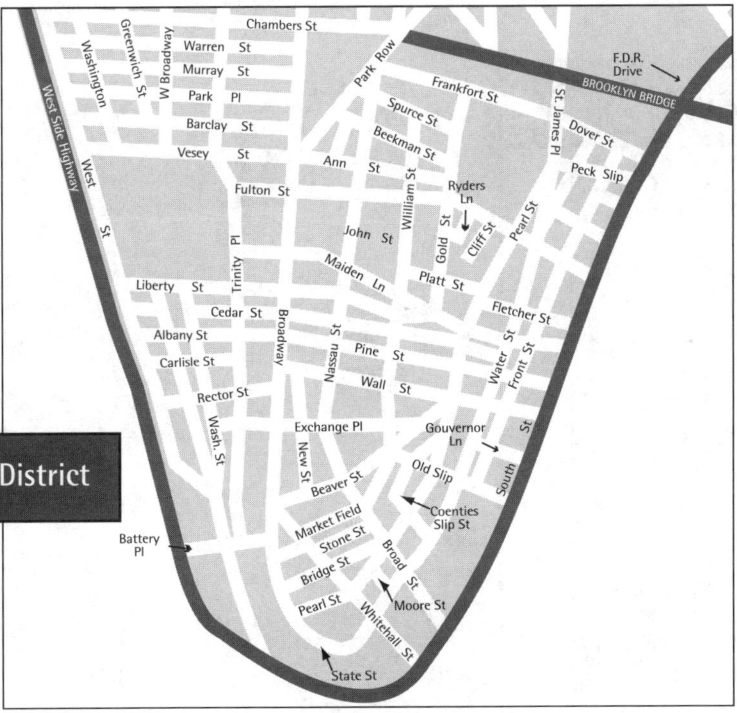

Financial District

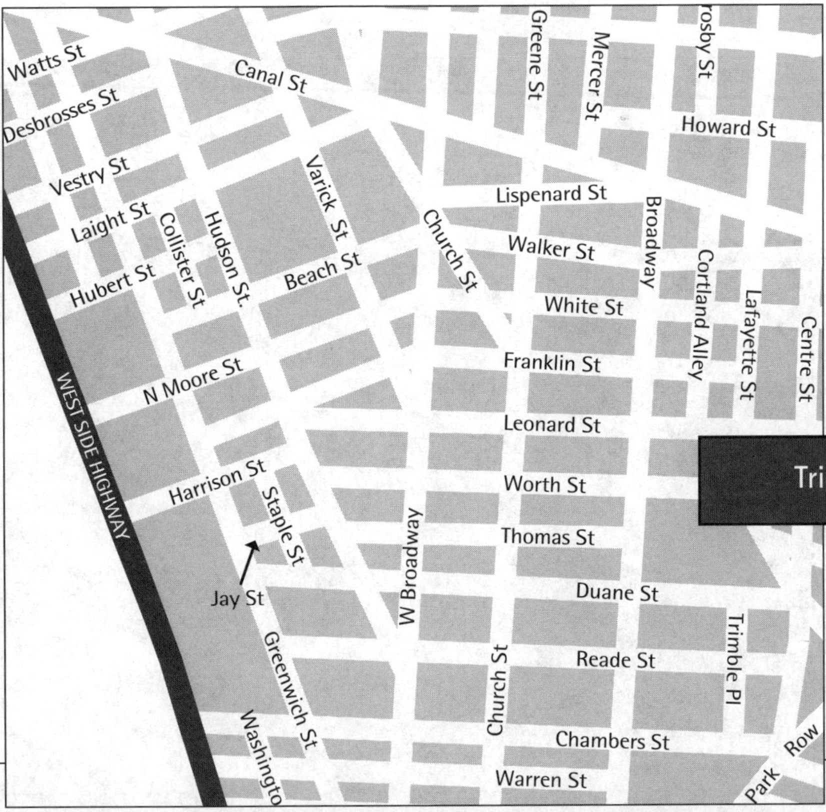

Chambers St
Warren St
Murray St
Park Pl
Barclay St
Vesey St
Fulton St
Greenwich St
W Broadway
Washington
West Side Highway
West St
Park Row
Frankfort St
Spruce St
Beekman St
Ann St
F.D.R. Drive
BROOKLYN BRIDGE
St. James Pl
Dover St
Peck Slip
Ryders Ln
Pearl St
Cliff St
Gold St
William St
John St
Maiden Ln
Platt St
Trinity Pl
Liberty St
Cedar St
Albany St
Carlisle St
Broadway
Nassau St
Pine St
Fletcher St
Water St
Front St
Wall St
Rector St
Wash. St
Exchange Pl
New St
Gouverneur Ln
South St
Old Slip
Beaver St
Coenties Slip St
Market Field
Stone St
Battery Pl
Bridge St
Broad St
Moore St
Pearl St
Whitehall St
State St

TriBeCa

Watts St
Canal St
Desbrosses St
Vestry St
Laight St
Hubert St
Collister St
Hudson St.
Varick St
Beach St
Church St
Greene St
Mercer St
Crosby St
Howard St
Lispenard St
Walker St
Broadway
White St
Cortland Alley
Lafayette St
Centre St
Franklin St
N Moore St
WEST SIDE HIGHWAY
Leonard St
Harrison St
Staple St
Worth St
Thomas St
W Broadway
Jay St
Duane St
Greenwich St
Trimble Pl
Reade St
Church St
Washington
Chambers St
Park Row
Warren St

Chinatown

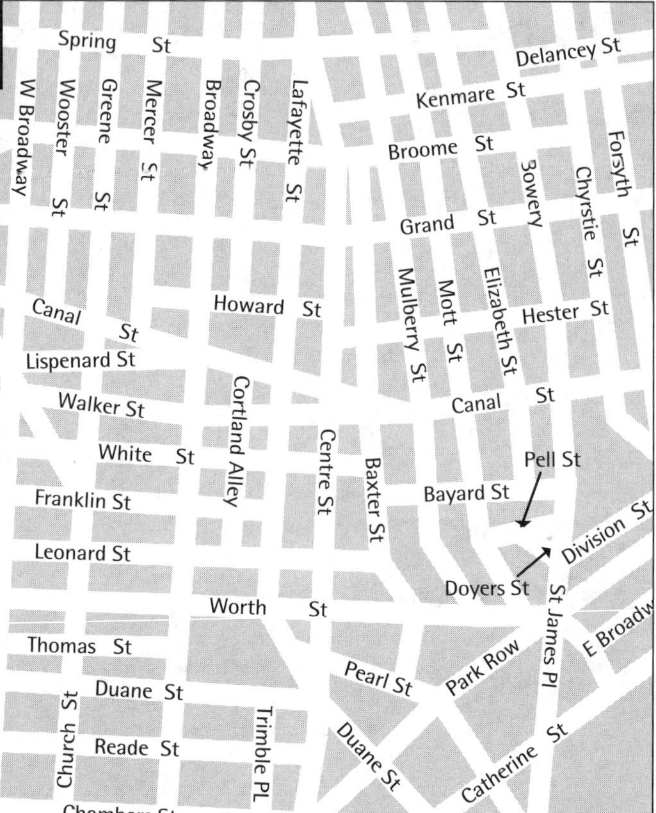

Little Italy

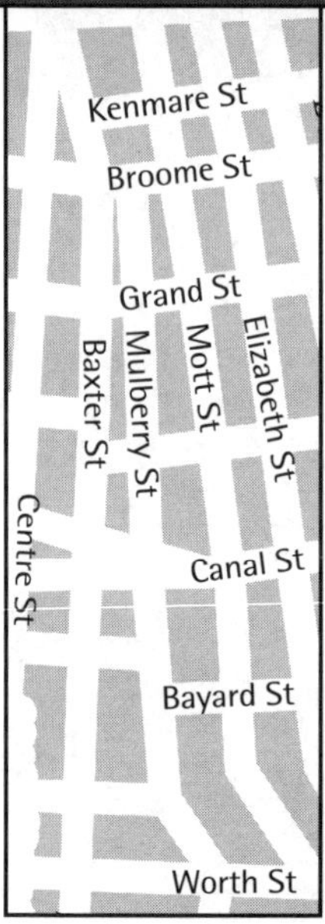

Kenmare St
Broome St
Grand St
Baxter St
Mulberry St
Mott St
Elizabeth St
Centre St
Canal St
Bayard St
Worth St

Lower East Side

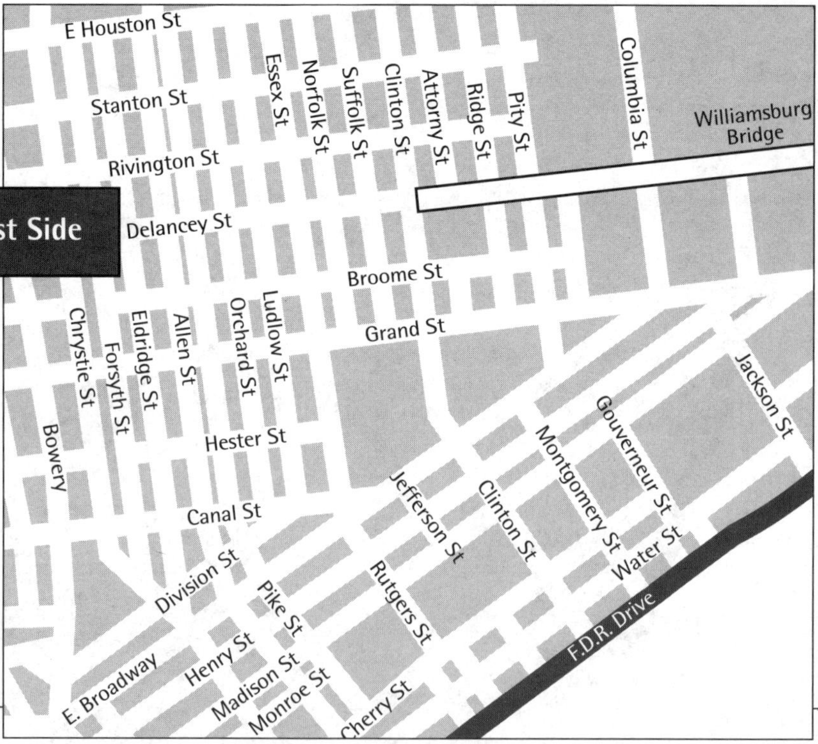

E Houston St
Stanton St
Essex St
Norfolk St
Suffolk St
Clinton St
Attorny St
Ridge St
Pity St
Columbia St
Williamsburg Bridge
Rivington St
Delancey St
Broome St
Grand St
Chrystie St
Forsyth St
Eldridge St
Allen St
Orchard St
Ludlow St
Jackson St
Bowery
Hester St
Gouverneur St
Montgomery St
Jefferson St
Clinton St
Canal St
Water St
Division St
Pike St
Rutgers St
F.D.R. Drive
E. Broadway
Henry St
Madison St
Monroe St
Cherry St

SoHo

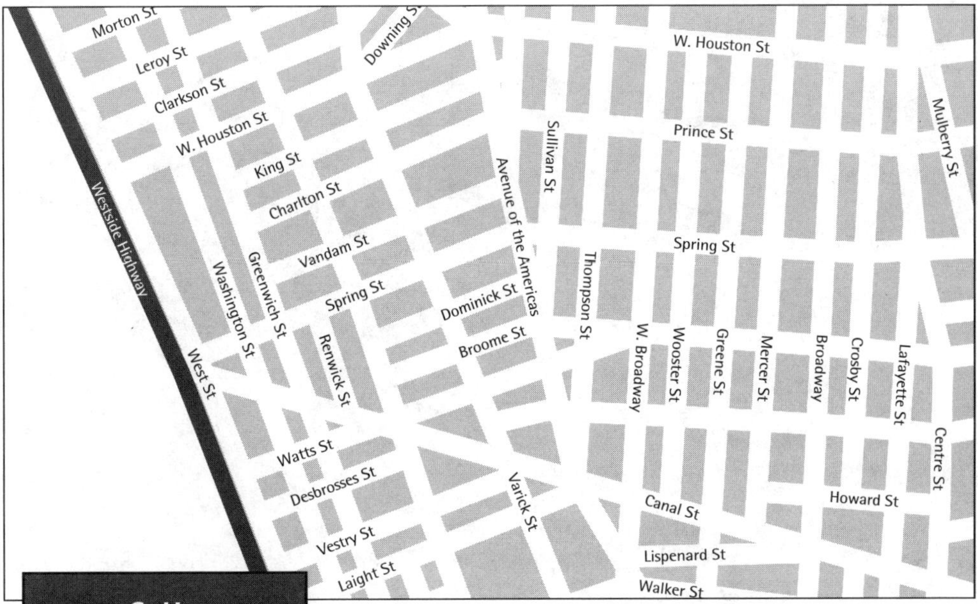

Morton St
Leroy St
Clarkson St
W. Houston St
King St
Charlton St
Vandam St
Spring St
Downing St
Westside Highway
Washington St
Greenwich St
West St
Renwick St
Dominick St
Broome St
Avenue of the Americas
Sullivan St
Thompson St
W. Houston St
Prince St
Spring St
Mulberry St
W. Broadway
Wooster St
Greene St
Mercer St
Broadway
Crosby St
Lafayette St
Centre St
Watts St
Desbrosses St
Vestry St
Laight St
Varick St
Canal St
Howard St
Lispenard St
Walker St

East Village

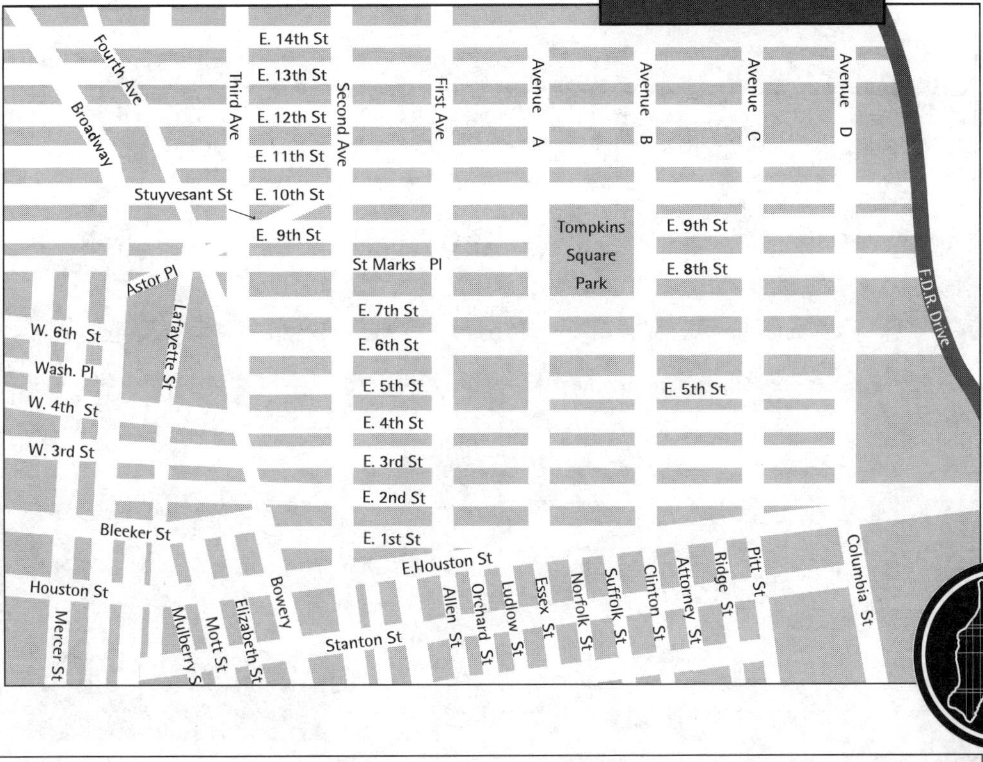

Fourth Ave
Broadway
Third Ave
Second Ave
First Ave
Avenue A
Avenue B
Avenue C
Avenue D
E. 14th St
E. 13th St
E. 12th St
E. 11th St
Stuyvesant St
E. 10th St
E. 9th St
St Marks Pl
Tompkins Square Park
E. 9th St
E. 8th St
Astor Pl
Lafayette St
E. 7th St
E. 6th St
E. 5th St
E. 5th St
E. 4th St
E. 3rd St
E. 2nd St
E. 1st St
W. 6th St
Wash. Pl
W. 4th St
W. 3rd St
Bleeker St
Houston St
E.Houston St
F.D.R. Drive
Mercer St
Mulberry St
Mott St
Elizabeth St
Bowery
Stanton St
Allen St
Orchard St
Ludlow St
Essex St
Norfolk St
Suffolk St
Clinton St
Attorney St
Ridge St
Pitt St
Columbia St

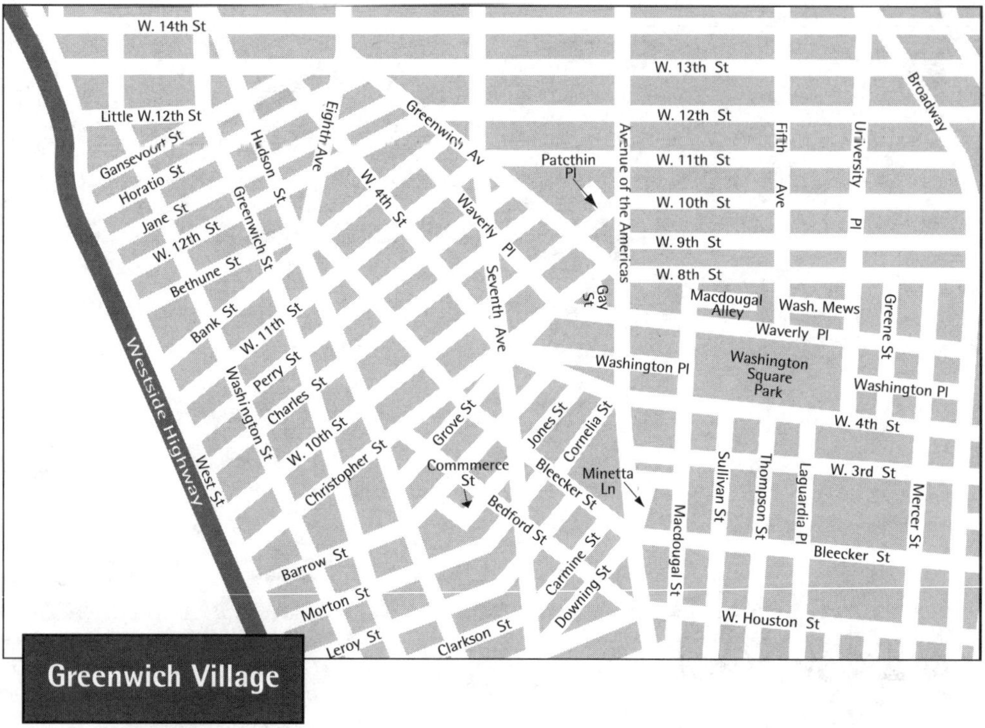

W. 14th St
W. 13th St
Broadway
Little W.12th St
Gansevourt St
Horatio St
Jane St
W. 12th St
Bethune St
Bank St
W. 11th St
Perry St
Charles St
W. 10th St
Christopher St
Hudson St
Greenwich St
Washington St
West St
Westside Highway
Eighth Ave
Greenwich Av
W. 4th St
Waverly Pl
Seventh Ave
Patcthin Pl
Avenue of the Americas
W. 12th St
W. 11th St
W. 10th St
W. 9th St
W. 8th St
Fifth Ave
University Pl
Gay St
Macdougal Alley
Wash. Mews
Greene St
Waverly Pl
Washington Pl
Washington Square Park
Washington Pl
W. 4th St
Grove St
Jones St
Cornelia St
Commmerce St
Bleecker St
Minetta Ln
Bedford St
Sullivan St
Thompson St
Laguardia Pl
W. 3rd St
Mercer St
Macdougal St
Bleecker St
Barrow St
Morton St
Carmine St
Downing St
W. Houston St
Leroy St
Clarkson St

Greenwich Village

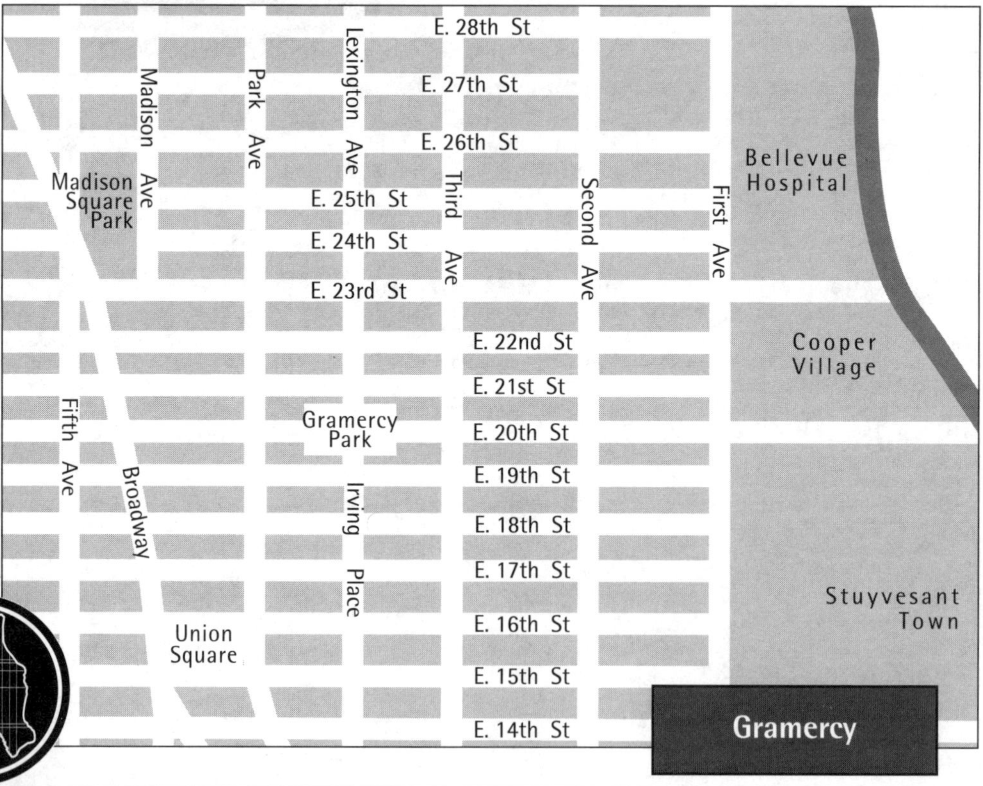

E. 28th St
E. 27th St
E. 26th St
Lexington Ave
Park Ave
Madison Ave
Madison Square Park
E. 25th St
E. 24th St
E. 23rd St
Third Ave
Second Ave
First Ave
Bellevue Hospital
E. 22nd St
E. 21st St
E. 20th St
E. 19th St
E. 18th St
E. 17th St
E. 16th St
E. 15th St
E. 14th St
Cooper Village
Gramercy Park
Irving Place
Fifth Ave
Broadway
Union Square
Stuyvesant Town

Gramercy

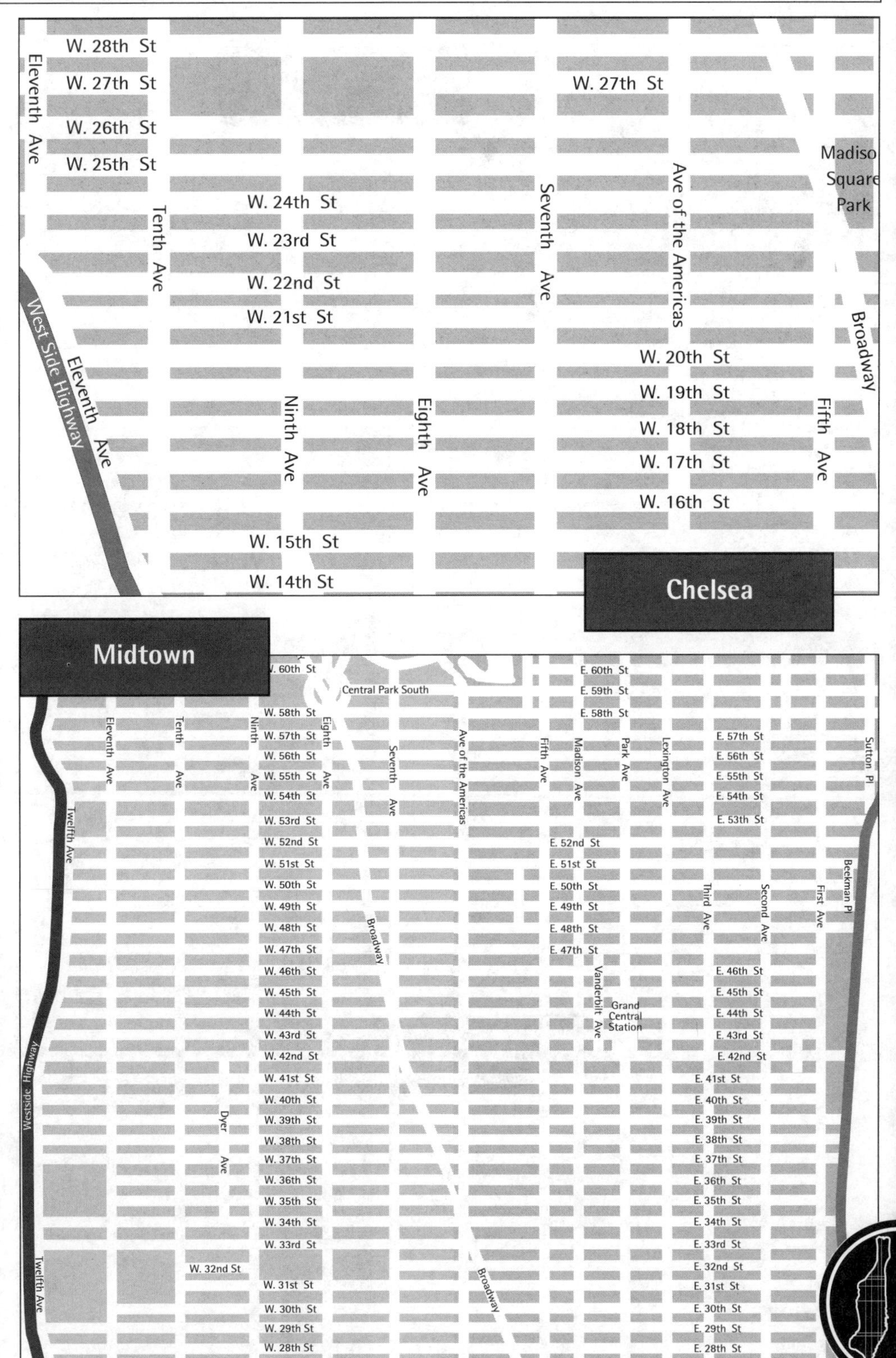
W. 28th St
W. 27th St
W. 26th St
W. 25th St
Eleventh Ave
W. 27th St
Madison Square Park
W. 24th St
W. 23rd St
W. 22nd St
W. 21st St
Tenth Ave
Seventh Ave
Ave of the Americas
Broadway
West Side Highway
Eleventh Ave
Ninth Ave
Eighth Ave
W. 20th St
W. 19th St
W. 18th St
W. 17th St
W. 16th St
Fifth Ave
W. 15th St
W. 14th St
Chelsea
Midtown
W. 60th St
Central Park South
W. 58th St
W. 57th St
W. 56th St
W. 55th St
W. 54th St
W. 53rd St
W. 52nd St
W. 51st St
W. 50th St
W. 49th St
W. 48th St
W. 47th St
W. 46th St
W. 45th St
W. 44th St
W. 43rd St
W. 42nd St
W. 41st St
W. 40th St
W. 39th St
W. 38th St
W. 37th St
W. 36th St
W. 35th St
W. 34th St
W. 33rd St
W. 32nd St
W. 31st St
W. 30th St
W. 29th St
W. 28th St
Eleventh Ave
Tenth Ave
Ninth Ave
Eighth Ave
Seventh Ave
Ave of the Americas
Fifth Ave
Madison Ave
Park Ave
Lexington Ave
Twelfth Ave
Broadway
Dyer Ave
Westside Highway
Twelfth Ave
E. 60th St
E. 59th St
E. 58th St
E. 57th St
E. 56th St
E. 55th St
E. 54th St
E. 53th St
E. 52nd St
E. 51st St
E. 50th St
E. 49th St
E. 48th St
E. 47th St
Vanderbilt Ave
Grand Central Station
Third Ave
Second Ave
First Ave
Beekman Pl
Sutton Pl
E. 46th St
E. 45th St
E. 44th St
E. 43rd St
E. 42nd St
E. 41st St
E. 40th St
E. 39th St
E. 38th St
E. 37th St
E. 36th St
E. 35th St
E. 34th St
E. 33rd St
E. 32nd St
E. 31st St
E. 30th St
E. 29th St
E. 28th St

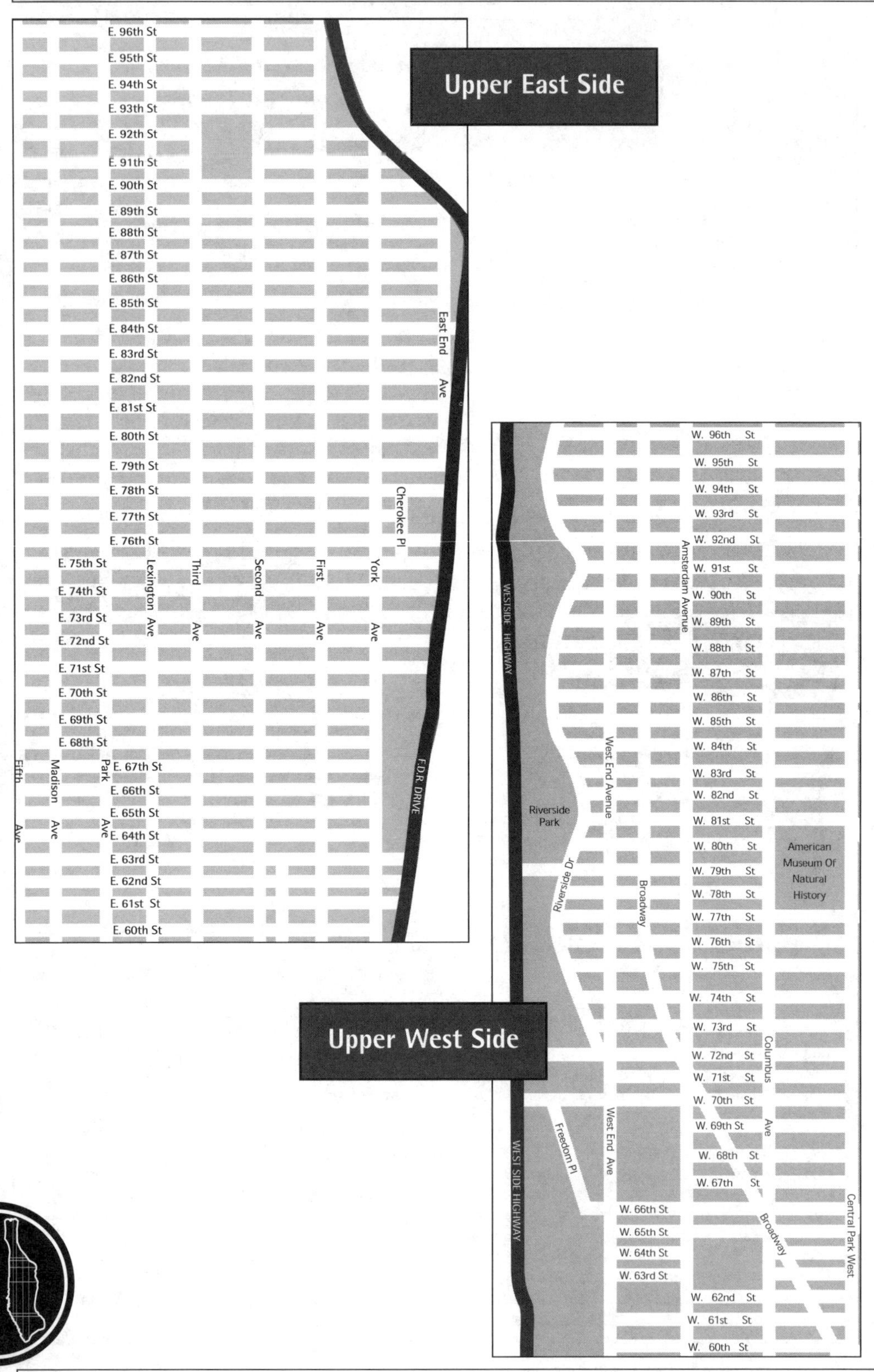
Upper East Side
E. 96th St
E. 95th St
E. 94th St
E. 93th St
E. 92th St
E. 91th St
E. 90th St
E. 89th St
E. 88th St
E. 87th St
E. 86th St
E. 85th St
E. 84th St
E. 83rd St
E. 82nd St
E. 81st St
E. 80th St
E. 79th St
E. 78th St
E. 77th St
E. 76th St
E. 75th St
E. 74th St
E. 73rd St
E. 72nd St
E. 71st St
E. 70th St
E. 69th St
E. 68th St
E. 67th St
E. 66th St
E. 65th St
E. 64th St
E. 63rd St
E. 62nd St
E. 61st St
E. 60th St
East End Ave
Cherokee Pl
Lexington Ave
Third Ave
Second Ave
First Ave
York Ave
Fifth Ave
Madison Ave
Park Ave
F.D.R. DRIVE
Upper West Side
W. 96th St
W. 95th St
W. 94th St
W. 93rd St
W. 92nd St
W. 91st St
W. 90th St
W. 89th St
W. 88th St
W. 87th St
W. 86th St
W. 85th St
W. 84th St
W. 83rd St
W. 82nd St
W. 81st St
W. 80th St
W. 79th St
W. 78th St
W. 77th St
W. 76th St
W. 75th St
W. 74th St
W. 73rd St
W. 72nd St
W. 71st St
W. 70th St
W. 69th St
W. 68th St
W. 67th St
W. 66th St
W. 65th St
W. 64th St
W. 63rd St
W. 62nd St
W. 61st St
W. 60th St
Amsterdam Avenue
West End Avenue
Broadway
Riverside Dr
Riverside Park
WESTSIDE HIGHWAY
WEST SIDE HIGHWAY
Freedom Pl
West End Ave
Columbus Ave
Central Park West
American Museum Of Natural History

Morningside Ave
Morningside Park
Morningside Drive
6th St
King, Jr. Blvd (125Th)
Amsterdam
W. 123rd St
W. 122nd St
W. 121st St
W. 120th St
Columbia University
Lasalle
Broadway
Claremont
Tieman
Riverside Drive
W. 116th St
W. 115th St
W. 114th St
W. 113th St
W. 112th St
W. 111th St
Cathedral Parkway
W. 109th St
W. 108th St
W. 107th St
W. 106th St
W. 105th St
W. 104th St
W. 103rd St
W. 102nd St
Riverside Park
WESTSIDE HIGHWAY

Morningside Heights

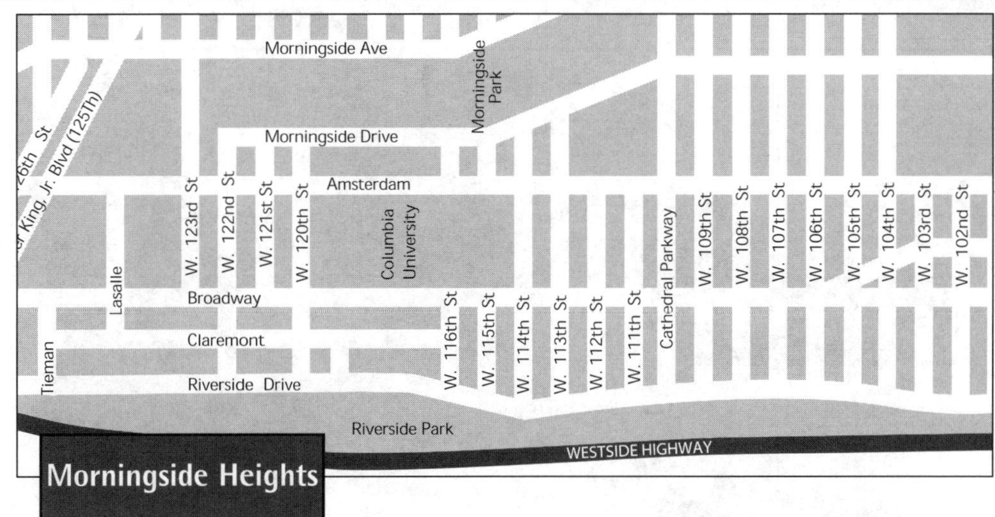

Harlem

W. 155th St
W. 154th St
W. 153rd St
W. 152nd St
W. 151st St
W. 151st St
W. 150th St
W. 149th St
W. 148th St
148th
W. 147th St
W. 146th St
W. 145th St
W. 145th St
W. 144th St
W. 143th St
W. 142nd St
W. 141st St
W. 140th St
W. 139th St
W. 139th St
W. 138th St
W. 137th St
W. 136th St
W. 136th St
W. 135th St
W. 134th St
W. 133rd St
W. 133rd St
W. 132nd St
W. 131 St
W. 131St St
130th St
W. 129th St
129th St
128th St
W. 127th St
W. 126th St
W. 125th St
Broadway
Amersterdam Ave
St. Nicholas Ave
Edgecombe Ave
Bradhurst Ave
Hamilton Pl
Riverside Drive
Convent
St. Nicholas Ter
Adam Clayton Powell
Lenox Ave
Malcolm X Boulevard
Fifth Ave
Madison Ave
Park Ave
Lexington Ave
Frederick Douglass
St. Nicholas Ave
Tieman
Lasalle

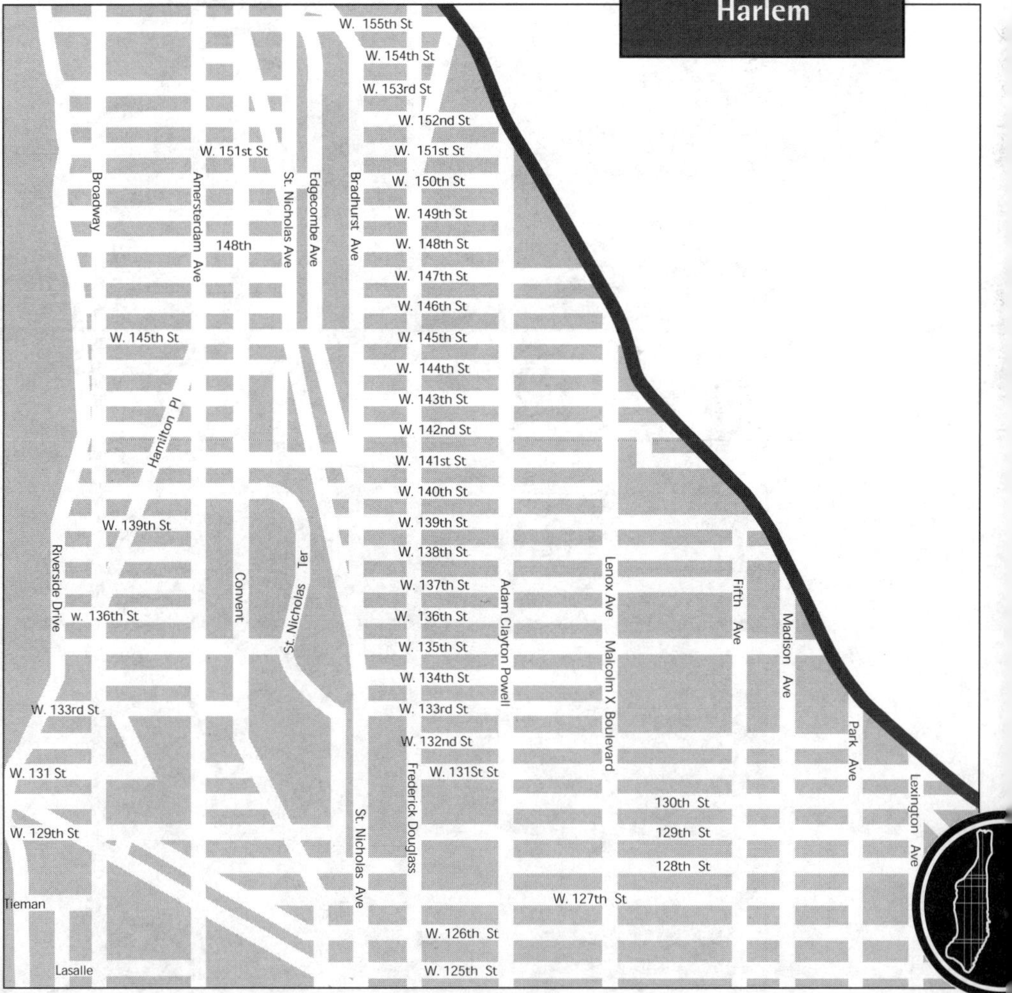

Washington Heights

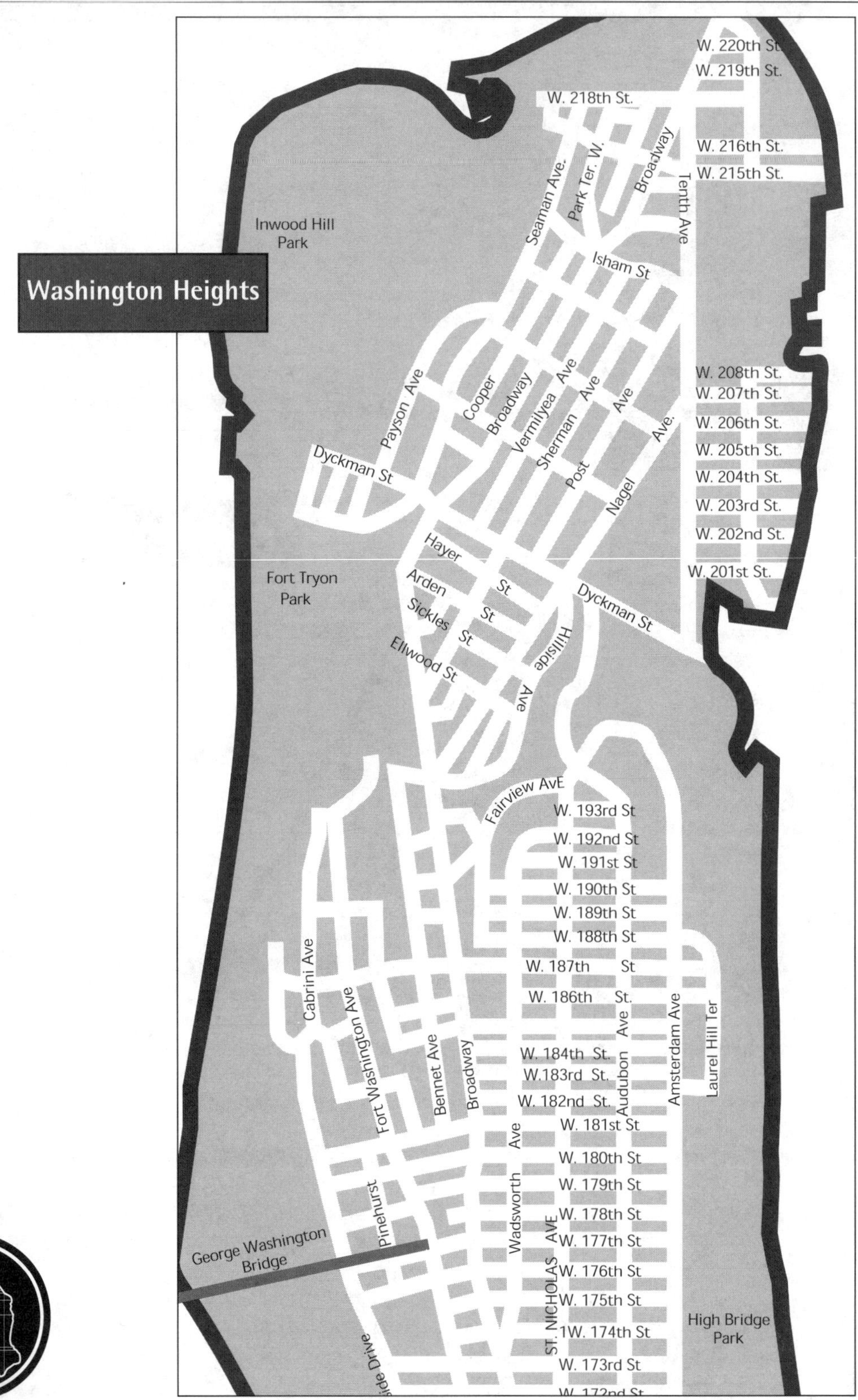

Riverdale, Bronx

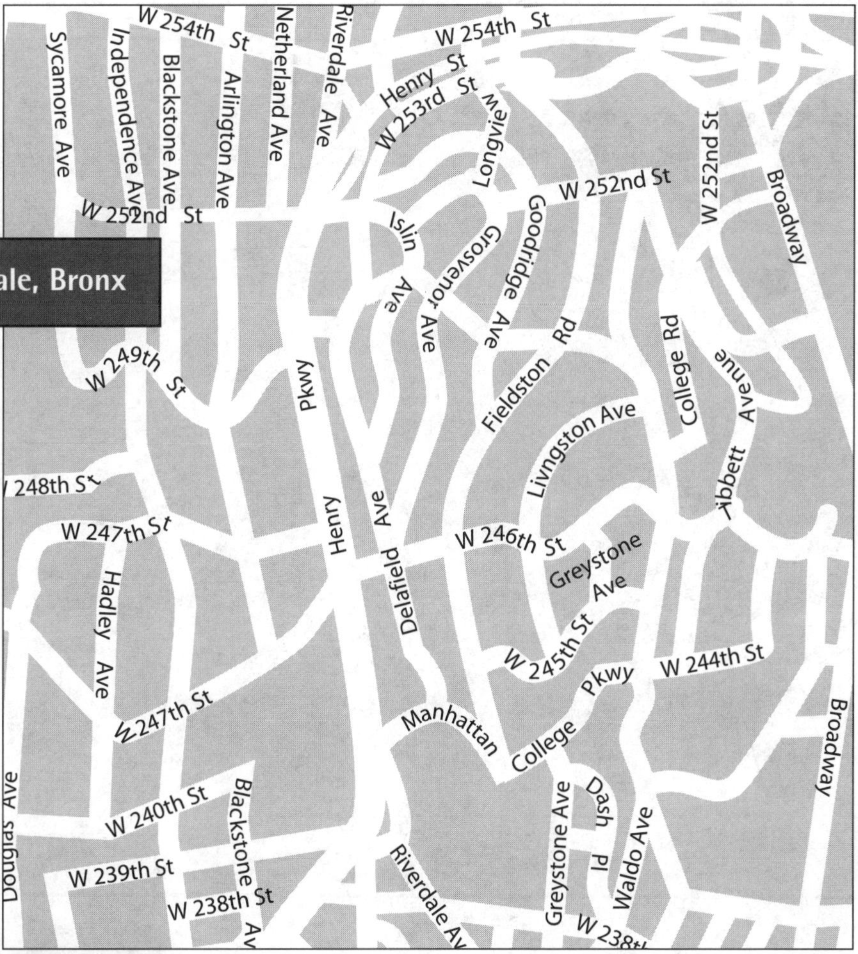

W 254th St
Sycamore Ave
Independence Ave
Blackstone Ave
Arlington Ave
Netherland Ave
Riverdale Ave
W 254th St
Henry St
W 253rd St
Longview
W 252nd St
W 252nd St
Broadway
W 252nd St
Islin Ave
Grosvenor Ave
Goodridge Ave
Fieldston Rd
College Rd
Tibbett Avenue
W 249th St
Pkwy
Livngston Ave
W 248th St
W 247th St
Henry
Delafield Ave
W 246th St
Greystone Ave
Hadley Ave
W 245th St
W 244th St
Pkwy
W 247th St
Manhattan
College
Broadway
Douglas Ave
W 240th St
Blackstone Ave
Dash Pl
Greystone Ave
Waldo Ave
W 239th St
W 238th St
Riverdale Ave
W 238th

Fordham, Bronx

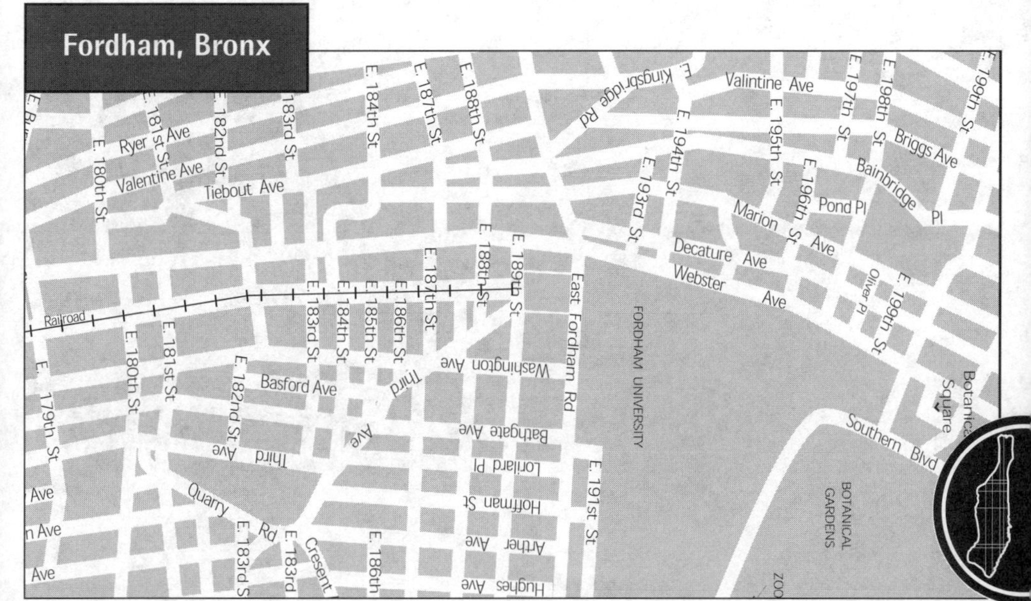

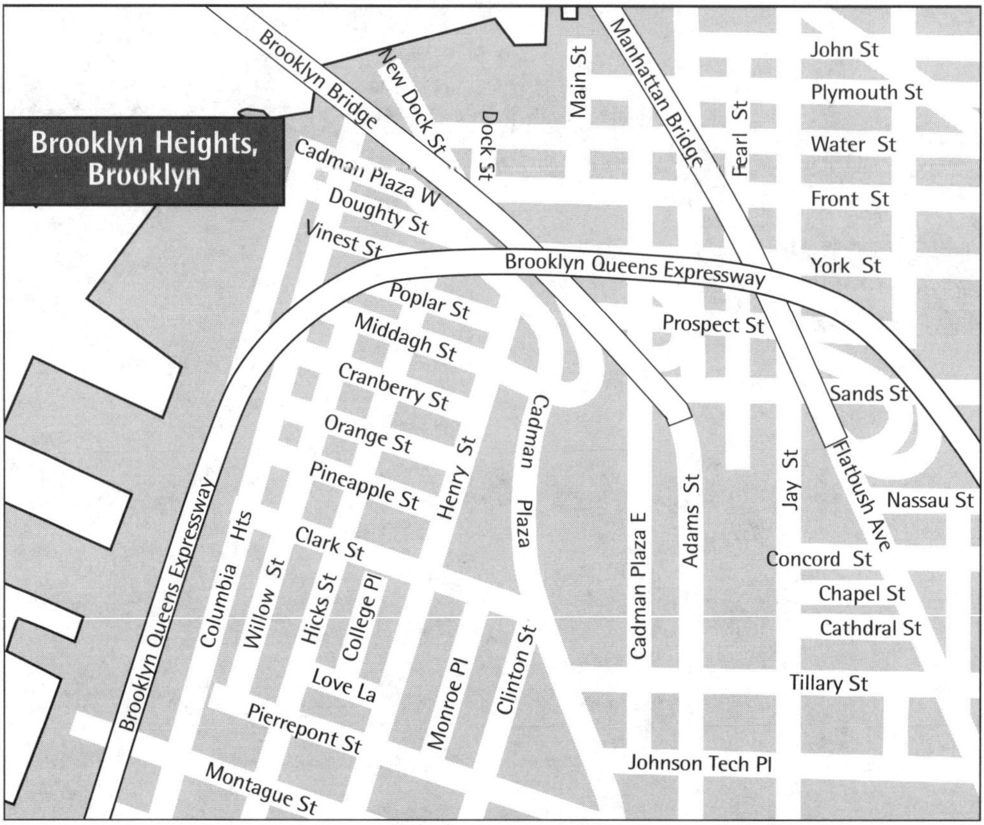
Brooklyn Heights, Brooklyn
Brooklyn Bridge
New Dock St
Dock St
Main St
Manhattan Bridge
Pearl St
John St
Plymouth St
Water St
Front St
York St
Cadman Plaza W
Doughty St
Vinest St
Brooklyn Queens Expressway
Poplar St
Middagh St
Prospect St
Cranberry St
Sands St
Orange St
Cadman Plaza
Henry St
Pineapple St
Adams St
Jay St
Flatbush Ave
Nassau St
Clark St
Columbia Hts
Willow St
Hicks St
College Pl
Cadman Plaza E
Concord St
Chapel St
Cathdral St
Brooklyn Queens Expressway
Love La
Monroe Pl
Clinton St
Tillary St
Pierrepont St
Johnson Tech Pl
Montague St

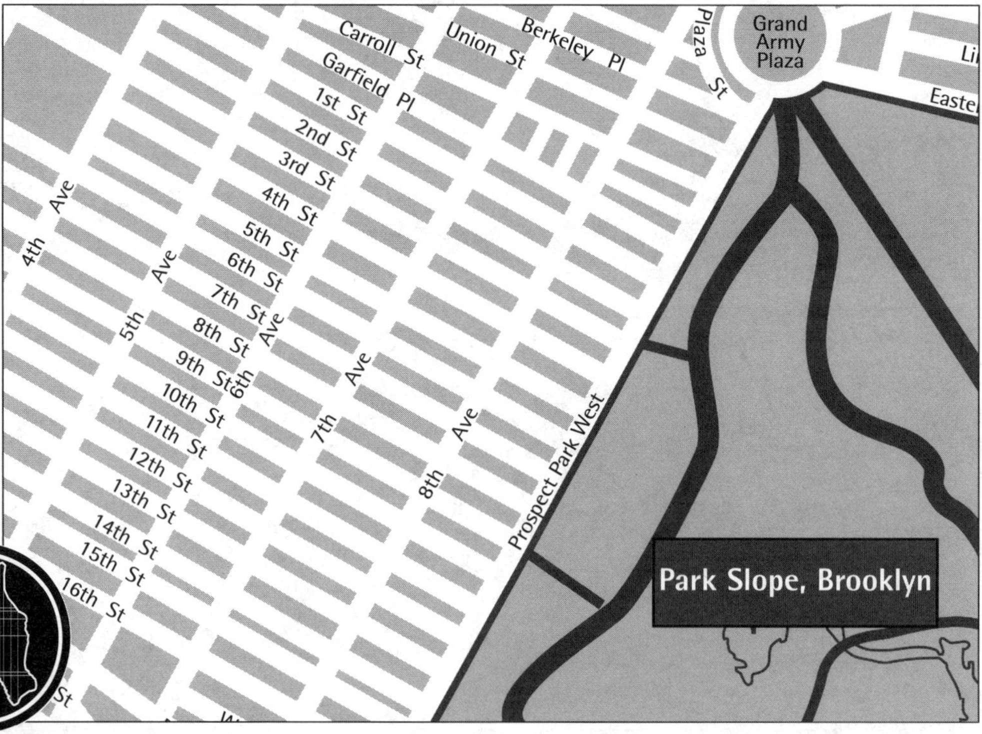
Carroll St
Union St
Berkeley Pl
Plaza St
Grand Army Plaza
Garfield Pl
1st St
2nd St
3rd St
4th St
5th St
6th St
7th St
8th St
9th St
10th St
11th St
12th St
13th St
14th St
15th St
16th St
4th Ave
5th Ave
6th Ave
7th Ave
8th Ave
Prospect Park West
Park Slope, Brooklyn

Jackson Heights, Queens

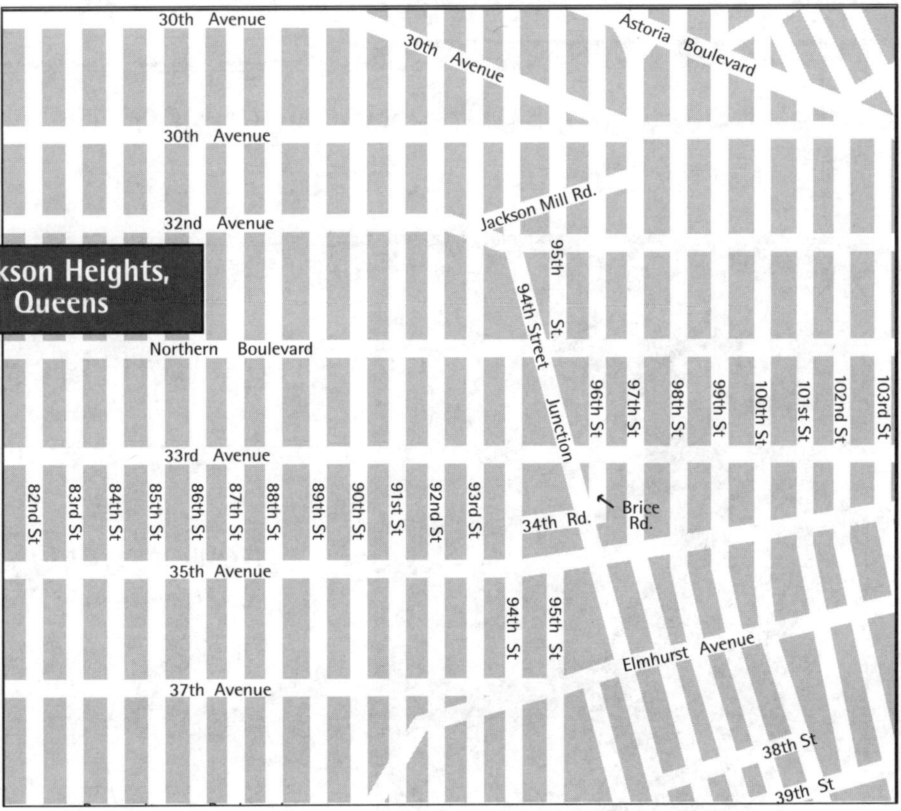

30th Avenue
30th Avenue
Astoria Boulevard
30th Avenue
Jackson Mill Rd.
32nd Avenue
95th St.
94th Street
Northern Boulevard
Junction
96th St
97th St
98th St
99th St
100th St
101st St
102nd St
103rd St
33rd Avenue
82nd St
83rd St
84th St
85th St
86th St
87th St
88th St
89th St
90th St
91st St
92nd St
93rd St
34th Rd.
Brice Rd.
35th Avenue
94th St
95th St
Elmhurst Avenue
37th Avenue
38th St
39th St

Astoria, Queens

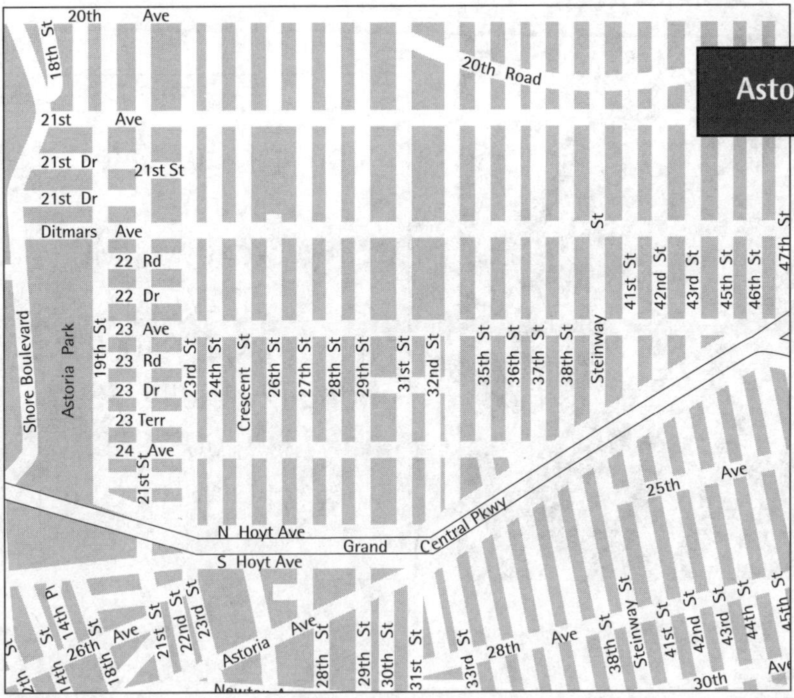

20th Ave
18th St
20th Road
21st Ave
21st Dr
21st St
21st Dr
Ditmars Ave
22 Rd
22 Dr
23 Ave
23 Rd
23 Dr
23 Terr
24 Ave
21st St
Shore Boulevard
Astoria Park
19th St
23rd St
24th St
Crescent St
26th St
27th St
28th St
29th St
31st St
32nd St
35th St
36th St
37th St
38th St
Steinway St
41st St
42nd St
43rd St
45th St
46th St
47th St
25th Ave
Grand Central Pkwy
N Hoyt Ave
S Hoyt Ave
14th Pl
26th Ave
18th Ave
21st St
22nd St
23rd St
Astoria Ave
28th St
29th St
30th St
31st St
33rd St
28th Ave
38th St
Steinway St
41st St
42nd St
43rd St
44th St
45th St
30th Ave

index

C

D

M

Q

R

S

Index of Advertisers

Insider's *notes*